To a sharp
business leader:
Mario

I hope that this
volume adds some value
to your personal business
library.

With my respect
in friendship, David

As clients continue to expand beyond our borders, David Chodikoff once again provides us with a relevant and timely tax manual. Another great addition for any tax practitioner's reference library.

John Doma, Partner and Principal of Bateman MacKay LLP, Chartered Accountants

In the very complex and ever-changing world of international tax, David Chodikoff's Transfer Pricing and Tax Avoidance *is a "must have" resource for the professional advisor. David is a trusted authority who I can rely upon.*

N. Gregory McNally, LLB, MBA, JD, LLM (Int'l Tax), TEP, N. Gregory McNally & Associates Ltd.

Transfer Pricing and Tax Avoidance *is a splendid comprehensive one-of-a-kind reference source for businesses, accountants, lawyers, academics and judges. It provides descriptions of the transfer pricing and tax avoidance regimes operating in 33 countries, based on contributions from experts in each of the countries. Having done some international comparative work myself in the tax avoidance area, I understand that* Transfer Pricing and Tax Avoidance *is the product of an enormous amount of work. A resource of this kind at an earlier time would have substantially shortened the time I've spent researching tax avoidance laws in foreign jurisdictions. On this basis alone I have no hesitation in saying that* Transfer Pricing and Tax Avoidance *represents an outstanding advance in the global literature for these two areas.*

Dr. Robert McMechan, Ph.D., Robert McMechan Professional Corporation

With the boom in M&A activity and worldwide intercompany transactions, this is a valuable one-stop comprehensive resource to identify the legislation, case law, guidelines and methodologies governing transfer pricing in jurisdictions throughout the world. It is interesting to examine which transfer price methodologies have been accepted or rejected in each jurisdiction.

Bruce C. Roher, CPA, CA·IFA, CBV, CFE, Partner, Fuller Landau LLP, Chartered Professional Accountants

Transfer pricing and tax avoidance are the two most vexing topics facing tax practitioners, administrators, and policy makers the world over. This comparative volume provides current, incisive insights on the state of play and details the law and practice in over 33 countries.

Kim Brooks, Dean, Weldon Professor of Law, Schulich School of Law, Dalhousie University

This ambitious volume achieves a deep synthesis of the legislation, case law, and policy surrounding transfer pricing and tax avoidance in numerous jurisdictions. It will soon take a deserved place at the top of the reading list for all students of international transfer pricing.

Benjamin Alarie, Associate Professor & Associate Dean First Year Program, Faculty of Law, University of Toronto

As tax authorities worldwide continue to allocate greater resources to auditing related party transactions, Transfer Pricing and Tax Avoidance *explains clearly the current regulatory environment facing multinationals, the documentary requirements across jurisdictions, and the importance of well-reasoned real time analysis in the allocation of risk/return between non-arm's length entities.*

David Chodikoff has marshalled an impressive group of leading global tax practitioners from 33 countries and assembled a thoroughly comprehensive text explaining the evolving world of transfer pricing and tax avoidance.

Tim Dunham, CBV, CFA, Tax Valuations Partner, Kalex Valuations Inc., Toronto, Ontario

Increasing global trade and the increased complexities and ambiguities in establishing supportable transfer pricing requires careful and precise documentation to support pricing and precise documentation to satisfy the various taxing and regulatory authorities. This work is a wonderful resource for tax professionals and Corporations in international trade. David Chodikoff and associates are to be congratulated for compiling this invaluable work.

Gabriel Nachman FCPA, FCA, Retired Partner, PricewaterhouseCoopers, Chartered Professional Accountants

This comprehensive, all-inclusive, global review of transfer pricing and tax avoidance will save you countless hours of research, time and money. Well-structured and well-written, it is the "go-to resource" when working with clients and counsel in third party jurisdictions.

James E. Ross, B.A., LL.B., President, Stonegate Private Counsel & Senior Vice President, Assante Wealth Management

It is clear that Transfer Pricing and Tax Avoidance *have become two of the most important aspects of current tax laws in virtually all of the world's industrialized countries. Although these issues have become exceedingly complex, David Chodikoff, who is an experienced and highly regarded Canadian tax litigator, has once again managed to put together a template that organizes, compares and simplifies the treatment of* Transfer Pricing and Tax Avoidance *issues in 33 countries.*

David has an outstanding ability as an editor to organize, manage and provide guidelines for contributions to a multi-author book. This book will be of great practical assistance to anyone faced with the complexity of Transfer Pricing and Tax Avoidance *issues.*

Sheldon Silver, Q.C., Counsel, Fogler Rubinoff LLP

Transfer Pricing and Tax Avoidance *is a comprehensive, concisely written study of a wide range of relevant transfer pricing topics including current legislative and regulatory frameworks, issues, methodology and case law, organized by jurisdiction. I have no doubt that it will prove to be a popular resource for income tax executives conducting international business as well as income tax practitioners.*

Steven Hacker, CPA, CA, CBV, Partner, Valuation and Litigation Support, Meyers Norris Penny LLP

Transfer pricing is a quintessential global problem whose solution is primarily local. While purportedly adhering to the "universal" arm's length principle, countries adopt different transfer pricing rules and practices. Obtaining reliable information on various countries' rules and practices is not easy. This collection of papers authored by a large number of country experts should serve as a great resource to those involved in transfer pricing. It is indeed a great service to the community.

Jinyan Li, Professor of Law, Osgoode Hall Law School of York University

This book is a valuable resource for those in the corporate world who currently have business operations throughout the world. Congratulations to David Chodikoff and the many contributors for assembling this timely and well organized information. Transfer Pricing and Tax Avoidance *will be a welcome addition to our corporate tax library.*

James Grundy, CPA, CA, Chief Financial Officer, NRT Technology Group of Companies

Transfer Pricing and Tax Avoidance *is a comprehensive and insightful book for lawyers, administrators and business professionals who seek international perspectives on these topics in an increasingly globalized and connected world. The chapters present key policy issues within sound methodological frameworks, including numerous historical and contemporary case studies providing tremendous breadth and depth. The attention to detail in this book is noteworthy, the given examples are astute and interesting, and the discussions of current trends maintain the relevance of this book in relation to the rapidly changing global economy. While the contributors to this book showcase their topical expertise by critiquing the strengths and weaknesses of various legislative positionalities, the common rhetorical ground across chapters is the push towards sound taxation strategies amidst a collective prioritization of how these positionalities effect and respond to the forces of international relations. Although there are still many problems in the fields of transfer pricing and tax litigation, this book inspires solutions to these problems by bringing to the fore a multitude of issues that, up until now, have not been addressed in sufficient detail.*

Eli Swirsky, President, The Torgan Group

This book is a magnificent resource for anyone responsible for planning, implementing and defending a company's transfer pricing policies.

Brad Rolph, Partner, National Transfer Pricing Leader, Grant Thornton Consulting

Globalization has encouraged increasing cross-border ties among related companies along with a corresponding rise in transfer pricing headaches. This book provides

an essential comparative perspective of national transfer pricing laws and serves as an important contribution given the renewed enthusiasm governments have shown with respect to auditing transfer prices.

Professor Arthur Cockfield, Queen's University Faculty of Law

Once again, David Chodikoff has hit the mark with a comprehensive analysis on Transfer Pricing and Tax Avoidance, *which is both readable and up to date. This book is an excellent resource for any company considering going global.*

Vincent Cosentino, CPA, CA, Johnvince Foods Group of Companies

Transfer Pricing and Tax Avoidance *brings to us straight forward to the point front-line perspectives on the dominant topics of international taxation. Nowhere will you find this level of current, relevant, ready to use insight in one place. Many thanks to David and his extraordinarily distinguished contributors for making this a must have not only for the experienced global tax professional, but for CFOs and Principals demanding a convenient way to become and stay informed.*

Jim Reitan, Chief Financial Officer, Dr. Bernstein Diet & Health Clinics

Globalization will continue to present complex transfer pricing issues for companies and their management team. Minimizing taxes when designing these transfer pricing strategies is one of the best ways of creating shareholder value.

Kin-Man Lee, Chief Financial Officer, St. Joseph Communications

Transfer Pricing and Tax Avoidance *is the latest book effort by David Chodikoff. As the General Editor, David has brought together leading expert contributors from 33 countries to outline and provide fundamental information on the subjects of transfer pricing and tax avoidance. Whether you are a veteran international business player or simply a student of these subjects, this book is an essential resource volume for everyone's tax library.*

Alon Ossip, Chief Executive Officer, The Stronach Group of Companies

With constantly changing tax regulations around the world, the need for corporations to ensure tax efficiency for their businesses this book provides an authoritative and thorough reference guide. It is a must have textbook for anyone dealing with international tax regulations.

Nick Barisheff, CEO Bullion Management Group Inc., Toronto, Ontario

Transfer Pricing & Tax Avoidance

First edition 2014

General Editor:
David W Chodikoff, Miller Thomson LLP

THOMSON REUTERS

General Editor:
David W Chodikoff

Commissioning Editor
Emily Kyriacou

Commercial Director
Katie Burrington

Publishing Assistant
Nicola Pender

Design and Production
Dawn McGovern

Typesetting
Forewords

Published in September 2014 by European Lawyer Reference Series,
Friars House, 160 Blackfriars Road, London SE1 8EZ
part of Thomson Reuters (Professional) UK Limited
(Registered in England & Wales, Company No 1679046.
Registered Office and address for service:
Aldgate House, 33 Aldgate High Street, London EC3N 1DL)

A CIP catalogue record for this book is available from the British Library.

ISBN: 9780414033504

Contents

Foreword

The Honourable Mr Justice Marshall Rothstein, The Supreme Court of Canada

Over the past year, there has been a surge of interest in taxation issues with international aspects. The United States' *Foreign Account Tax Compliance Act*, or FATCA, enacted to address tax non-compliance, affects American citizens residing outside of the US. It subjects financial institutions in those countries to a new set of rules. The enactment of FATCA resulted in an aspect of international taxation unexpectedly becoming the subject of popular media attention and discussion than is usually the case because of its broad effect on individuals.

For those practitioners, taxpayers and financial institutions who deal with cross-border tax issues, familiarity with international and anti-avoidance tax rules in different countries is essential. Each country's tax system is complicated enough in its own right to keep stables of lawyers and accountants busy as they attempt to navigate the inevitable complexities. These complexities are exponentially greater when a tax issue arises that involves more than one tax system. Understanding the ongoing trends of reducing tax avoidance and harmonizing tax rules between jurisdictions is vital for taxpayers, for lawyers and accountants, for governments, and for judges trying to make sense of it all.

Transfer pricing and tax avoidance rules in jurisdictions around the world demonstrate both of these trends. Transfer pricing rules, which affect where profits (and losses) are recognized, target cross-border transactions in which taxpayers seek to minimize their tax liability based on the differences between tax systems and tax rates. Tax avoidance rules, even if they are not designed to specifically address cross-border issues, are often applicable to cross-border transactions. The purpose of both types of rules is to limit tax base erosion made possible by the complexities of, and variations between, tax systems.

However, these rules come at a price: loss of clarity and predictability; being able to know and understand the tax outcome of complicated transactions and situations. International efforts such as the OECD Guidelines and Model Tax Conventions, along with regional efforts such as those effected through the European Union, attempt to achieve some clarification and predictability by establishing common practices and providing for dispute resolution mechanisms. The success of these efforts can be seen in the influence of the OECD Guidelines and Model Tax Conventions on the domestic laws, bilateral agreements, and case law of jurisdictions around the world. But in the end, tax laws are devised and imposed by individual countries (and even subdivisions within countries), meaning there is no end in sight to these issues.

Transfer Pricing and Tax Avoidance is an invaluable resource for assisting readers in understanding these issues and envisioning possible reforms. It brings together the rules, case-law (both current and historical) and trends regarding transfer pricing and tax avoidance of 33 jurisdictions in an accessible and convenient manner. The sections in each chapter regarding the international forums and relations at play in the featured jurisdictions provide valuable insight into the manner in which those jurisdictions may interact.

The cross-jurisdictional analysis made possible by this book will assist practitioners and tax authorities in dealing with specific cases. But I also anticipate that it will permit substantive examination of the principles and long-term trends underlying both domestic and international tax law, allowing interested parties and governments the ability to look ahead to the future of tax law.

This project, which brings together tax experts from around the world, will make an important contribution to this area of the law. It is noteworthy not only for its timeliness, but also for its comprehensive inclusion of numerous jurisdictions. Information regarding the tax rules in foreign jurisdiction can be hard to come by due to both lack of experience and language barriers. *Transfer Pricing and Tax Avoidance* eases those difficulties by setting out the essential concepts and serving as a launching point for more in-depth study.

I want to express my thanks to those who participated in this project. Its General Editor, David Chodikoff, has provided yet another important contribution to the literature of taxation. All contributors should be commended for the expertise and time they have brought to *Transfer Pricing and Tax Avoidance*. I have no doubt that their efforts will prove to have been well worthwhile.

Justice Marshall Rothstein
Ottawa
July 2014

Acknowledgements

David W Chodikoff, Miller Thomson LLP

This was an immense project and there are lots of people to thank for making this book a published reality. As anyone that has worked on an intense project knows, it is always one's family that hears about it or suffers, either directly or indirectly, from the demands of such a project. This explains why so many writers, editors and others in all sorts of fields thank their families first for their tolerance, patience and support. I am no different. This is my sixth edited book and I owe a great deal to my lovely and talented wife, Tanya, and my beautiful and smart son, Daniel. Thank you both!

Once again, I had the great pleasure of working with Katie Burrington. Katie, as the Commercial Director of Sweet & Maxwell's European Lawyer Reference Series, was directly involved in the recruitment of the participating law firms. Katie is also responsible for heading up the UK publishing team. The UK team consists of Emily Kyriacou, Dawn McGovern and Nicola Pender, as well as Chris Myers and Nick Allen (from Forewords). These are exceptional people that worked very hard to bring about the publication of this work in a timely fashion. I would be remiss in not singling out Nicola Pender. Over the course of the last year, Nicola and I became 'e-mail pals'. Nicola was always cheery, helpful and coordinated the proofing and publishing efforts in England. Thank you, Nicola!

In Canada, I had the pleasure of working with Jamie Walker. If the name sounds familiar, it is due to the fact that Jamie was the senior assistant editor for *Tax Litigation*, another book belonging to the family of the European Lawyer Reference Series. At the time of the first book, Jamie was still a law student but now having completed his education he is commencing his legal career by articling at Miller Thomson LLP. We are delighted to have him here. And I could not be more pleased that Jamie agreed to take on the role as senior assistant editor for the second time. Thank you, Jamie! Also returning as an assistant editor is Victoria Rodrigues. Victoria worked as an assistant editor on *Tax Litigation*. Victoria will also be commencing her legal career by articling with Miller Thomson LLP. I should also add that Victoria was a Senior Editor of the *Osgoode Hall Review of Law and Policy* (a publication of Osgoode Hall Law School, York University). Two new members of the Canadian editorial team included: Emma Nicholl (assistant editor) and Kristen Vandenberg (assistant editor). Both Emma and Kristen are second year law school students that are working at Miller Thomson LLP this summer. Both women eagerly accepted the position as assistant editors and I am very happy that they did! Their respective editing efforts have been stellar!

The co-author of the Canadian chapter of this book is Laura Etherington. If that name sounds familiar to some, it is because Laura co-wrote the Canadian chapter in *Tax Litigation*. I can hardly put into words my gratitude for Laura's hard work and gift for writing. It has made my job as co-author of the Canadian chapter exceptionally easy. Laura articled with Miller Thomson LLP last year and she has returned as an associate in the business law group. Watch for her in the years to come, Laura will undoubtedly be a superstar in the practice of law.

In the area of research, my thanks go to Kate Genest who was a student-at-law at Miller Thomson LLP. Kate, a ray of sunshine always, was a diligent worker and made a difference.

At Miller Thomson LLP, we are fortunate to have an absolutely brilliant library staff. I should know as I call upon them often and my office is literally right across from our Toronto library. The staff are always available to assist me and I thank them. They are led by Ines Freeman, the National Director of Library Services, and include: Jennifer Bonomo, Dian-Marie Galita, Julia Luke, Arlene Mazur and Erin Murphy.

It is hard to believe, but my executive assistant, Filomena Mendonca ('Fil'), has now been involved in four of these types of book projects. I cannot say enough good things about Fil. She has been my 'Chief of Staff' since May 2005 and as anyone knows – if you are on Fil's good side, you are likely to be on mine! Fil not only looks after the coordination of special projects like this one, but she is my point person in my private practice. As I have openly admitted, if I am successful in private practice, it is in no small measure a result of Fil's dedication, professionalism and hard work. Thank you, Fil. I am sincerely grateful.

A number of my partners at Miller Thomson LLP were highly supportive of my efforts and I would be remiss in not naming my biggest boosters (or those that listened to my rants and never complained!): James ('Jim') Hutchinson, Martin ('Marty') Rochwerg, Peter Auvinen, Thomas ('Tom') Whitby, Mark Frederick, William ('Bill') Fowlis, Robert Hayhoe, John Campbell, Susan Manwaring, Amanda Stacey, Tamara Farber, Michael Kerr, Emily Cole, Susan Metzler, James ('Jim') Klotz, Greg Shannon, Crystal Taylor, Sandra Gogal, Lyne Gaulin, Hugh Dyer, Kent Davidson, Barbara ('Barb') Doherty, Shashi Malik and last but not least, Andy Chan.

I would also like to thank The Honourable Mr Justice Marshall Rothstein for his wonderful Foreword. Mr Justice Rothstein is an extraordinary jurist and it is truly an honour to have him grace these pages with his words of insight and praise. Thank you, Mr Justice Rothstein!

As readers will note, there are a number of endorsements from business leaders, chief financial officers, chartered accountants, transfer pricing experts and academics. I am sincerely thankful for this incredible and generous support. On behalf of all of the contributors, we thank you!

Finally, my thanks to each and every contributor. This was an extraordinary effort taken on by dozens of people from *33* different countries. Every single contributor truly displayed a great sense of responsibility by meeting tight deadlines and by producing chapters of true value. Thank you, contributors!

David W Chodikoff
General Editor, August 2014

Preface

David W Chodikoff, Miller Thomson LLP

It was in the fall of 2013 that Thomson Reuters, Sweet & Maxwell held a successful launch of the publication of *Tax Litigation* at the annual International Bar Association conference in Boston, Massachusetts; *Tax Litigation* is yet another hardcover volume to be added to the growing stable of titles that make up The European Lawyer Reference Series. I was fortunate to be the General Editor of *Tax Litigation*. I had the very good luck of working with some incredibly talented and devoted people.

As a result of that experience, I thought that two key tax subjects that would benefit from the same type of treatment as *Tax Litigation* were Transfer Pricing and Tax Avoidance. Obviously, the people at The European Lawyer Reference Series, agreed. More to the point, so, too, did the contributors from 32 other participating jurisdictions.

In your hand, you are holding a resource book that has the same template for every chapter. The chapters are broken down into two parts. The first part deals with transfer pricing and covers the following subjects: an overview, the legislative framework, national policy issues, case law, penalties and dispute resolution mechanisms. The second half of each chapter focuses upon tax avoidance. The subjects include: acceptable tax planning areas/subjects, defining abusive tax avoidance, the legislative framework, key areas of interest, penalties and current trends.

On behalf of all of those involved in this project, we hope that you, the reader, find this a useful and stimulating volume of work that will lead you to further reading, thinking and your own writings on the subjects of transfer pricing and tax avoidance.

David W Chodikoff
August 2014

Albania

Wolf Theiss sh.p.k. Sokol Nako & Endri Mykaj

PART ONE: TRANSFER PRICING

1. GENERAL OVERVIEW

The Republic of Albania ('Albania') has recently increased its focus on transfer pricing. In April 2014, Albania amended its income tax legislation and introduced more detailed provisions in respect of transfer pricing. These amendments were prepared by the Ministry of Finance of Albania with the assistance of the International Finance Corporation, and were modeled on the OECD Transfer Pricing Guidelines for Multinational Enterprises and Tax Administrations (the 'OECD TPG 2010'). The 2014 amendments were a response to the difficulties faced by the General Directorate of Taxes and the Regional Tax Branches (the 'Albanian Tax Authorities') in enforcing the previous incomplete and ambiguous transfer pricing regime. Notwithstanding the progress that has been made, it is important to note that the Albanian Tax Authorities and the Albanian judicial system have very limited experience with transfer pricing related matters.

2. IDENTIFICATION OF LEGISLATIVE FRAMEWORK

The transfer pricing legislation in Albania consists of:

- Law No. 8438, dated 28/10/1998 'On income tax' (the 'Income Tax Act'), as amended, including Law No. 42/2014, dated 24/04/2014;
- Law No. 9920, dated 19/05/2008 'On tax procedures in the Republic of Albania' (the 'Tax Procedures Act'), as amended, including Law No. 43/2014, dated 24/04/2014;
- Ministry of Finance Instruction No. 16, dated 18/06/2014 'On transfer pricing' (the 'Guidelines on Transfer Pricing 2014').

2.1 Federal legislation

According to article 36 of the Income Tax Act, if a taxpayer engages in one or more controlled transactions, the taxpayer must determine its taxable income in a manner that is consistent with the market principle. The market principle concept in the Income Tax Act is equivalent to the arm's length principle in the OECD TPG 2010. If the taxpayer engages in a controlled transaction that is not consistent with the market principle, the Albanian Tax Authorities may adjust (ie, increase) the taxpayer's taxable income.[1] As a matter of tax procedure, an adjustment will only be made with the prior approval of the General Directorate of Taxes.

1 Article 36(3) of the Income Tax Act.

Since transfer pricing involves the determination of prices among related parties, article 2(4) of the Income Tax Act provides a detailed definition of 'related parties'. Under article 2(4)(a) of the Act, two persons are considered related parties when (i) one person participates directly or indirectly in the management, control or capital of the other person; and, (ii) the same person or persons participate directly or indirectly in the management, control or capital of both persons. A person participates directly or indirectly in the management, control or capital of another person when (i) the person owns directly or indirectly 50 per cent or more of the share capital of the other person; or, (ii) the person effectively controls the business decisions of the other person. As a matter of procedure, the Albanian Tax Authorities have the burden of proof to establish that a person effectively controls the business decisions of another person.

According to article 2(4)(d) of the Income Tax Act, a 'controlled transaction' is defined as:

(a) Any transaction among related parties where:
   (i) One party is an Albanian resident and the other is a non-resident;
   (ii) One party is a non-resident that has a permanent establishment in Albania to which the transaction is attributable, and the other party is also a non-resident; or,
   (iii) One party is an Albanian resident that has a permanent establishment outside Albania to which the transaction is attributable, and the other party is also an Albanian resident;
(b) Any transaction between a non-resident and its permanent establishment in Albania;
(c) Any transaction between an Albanian resident and its permanent establishment outside Albania; or,
(d) Any transaction between an Albanian resident or a non-resident that has a permanent establishment in Albania to which the transaction is attributable, and a resident of a jurisdiction listed in the Guidelines on Transfer Pricing 2014.[2]

The Albanian Tax Authorities are entitled to review any controlled transaction that may impact the taxable income of a taxpayer, including but not limited to:

- Transactions involving tangible goods such as raw materials, finished goods, etc.;
- Services transactions;
- Transactions involving intangible property such as royalties, licenses, payment for use of patents, trade-marks, know-how, and any other intellectual property;
- Financial transactions including leases, interest, guarantee fees, etc.; and,
- Capital transactions including the purchase or sale of shares or other investments, and the purchase or sale of long-term tangible and intangible assets.

[2] Please refer to Annex 1 of the Guidelines on Transfer Pricing 2014.

In order to determine whether a controlled transaction is consistent with the market principle, the controlled transaction must be compared with the conditions of an uncontrolled transaction. An uncontrolled transaction is comparable to a controlled transaction if:

(a) There are no significant differences between the transactions that could materially affect the financial indicators being examined; or,

(b) Where differences exist, a reasonably accurate comparability adjustment can be made to the relevant financial indicator of the uncontrolled transaction.[3]

Additionally, to determine whether two or more transactions are comparable, the Albanian Tax Authorities consider:

- The characteristics of the transferred property;
- The function of each party in the transactions, taking into account the assets used and the risks assumed;
- The contractual terms of the transactions;
- The economic circumstances in which the transactions took place; and,
- The business strategies pursued by the parties in relation to the transactions.[4]

To determine whether a transaction satisfies the market principle, an appropriate transfer pricing method must be selected. Article 36/2 of the Income Tax Act enumerates five transfer pricing methods, including:

- The comparable uncontrolled price method;
- The resale price method;
- The cost plus method;
- The transactional net margin method; and,
- The profit split method.

A taxpayer may employ a transfer pricing method other than those listed in article 36/2 of the Act if the taxpayer can prove that the traditional methods are unreasonable in the circumstances.[5] Additionally, the taxpayer must provide sufficient documentary evidence to establish that the controlled transaction satisfied the market principle.[6] It is not necessary to apply more than one transfer pricing method to determine whether a controlled transaction conforms to the market principle.[7] Accordingly, an audit of a controlled transaction by the Albanian Tax Authorities should be based on the transfer pricing method employed by the taxpayer.[8]

Article 36/7(1) of the Income Tax Act establishes the framework for entering into an Advance Pricing Agreement ('APA') with the Albanian Tax Authorities. An APA provides the taxpayer with an opportunity to determine the conditions that must be satisfied for the controlled transaction to comply with the market principle. If an APA is reached, and the terms and conditions set out in the agreement are satisfied, the Albanian Tax

3 Article 36/1(1) of the Income Tax Act.
4 Article 36/1(2) of the Income Tax Act.
5 Article 36/2(2) of the Income Tax Act.
6 Article 36/5(1) of the Income Tax Act.
7 Article 36/2(3) of the Income Tax Act.
8 Article 36/2(4) of the Income Tax Act.

Authorities cannot issue a transfer pricing adjustment.[9] The Ministry of Finance of Albania is currently developing rules and procedures relating to APAs.

2.2 State and provincial legislative interplay

Since Albania is a unitary state, legislative powers rest solely with the Parliament of Albania. Further, income tax is within the exclusive jurisdiction of the Parliament of Albania; local authorities are not entitled to levy income taxes under the Constitution of the Republic of Albania.[10]

2.3 International treaties and agreements

In order to prevent double taxation on income and capital, Albania has entered into Double Taxation Avoidance Agreements ('DTAA') with several countries (see table below).[11] Under a DTAA, the income of an entity in one contracting state may be excluded from taxation, or an adjustment may be made to account for taxes levied by the other contracting state. The DTAAs concluded by Albania are based on the OECD model convention, and generally contain provisions regarding:

- Transfer pricing between associated parties (ie, related parties);
- Mutual agreement procedures between the contracting states; and,
- The exchange of information between the tax authorities of the contracting states.

Poland	1 January 1995
Romania	1 January 1995
Malaysia	1 January 1995
Hungary	1 January 1996
Turkey	1 January 1997
Czech Republic	1 January 1997
Russian Federation	1 January 1998
Macedonia (FYROM)	1 January 1999
Croatia	1 January 1999
Italy	1 January 2000
Bulgaria	1 January 2000
Sweden	1 January 2000
Norway	1 January 2000
Greece	1 January 2001
Malta	1 January 2001
Switzerland	1 January 2001

9 Article 36/7(2) of the Income Tax Act.

10 Article 155 of the Constitution of the Republic of Albania (approved by Law No. 8417, dated 21/10/1998, as amended).

11 Please refer to: *http://www.tatime.gov.al/gdt/International_Treaties.aspx.*

France	1 January 2006
Belgium	1 January 2005
Moldavia	1 January 2004
China	1 January 2006
Netherlands	1 January 2006
Egypt	1 January 2006
Kosovo	1 January 2006
Serbia-Montenegro	1 January 2006
Austria	1 January 2009
Slovenia	1 January 2010
Latvia	1 January 2009
South Korea	1 January 2009
Bosnia and Herzegovina	1 January 2009
Luxemburg	1 January 2009
Ireland	1 January 2010
Estonia	1 January 2010
Germany	1 January 2010
Kuwait	1 January 2010
Spain	4 May 2011
Singapore	1 January 2012
Qatar	1 January 2013
India	Not yet effective
Great Britain and Northern Ireland	Not yet effective

3. NATIONAL POLICY ISSUES

Prior to the 2014 amendments, the transfer pricing regime in the Income Tax Act was limited, incomplete and ambiguous. Accordingly, the Albanian Tax Authorities have limited expertise in transfer pricing related matters.

3.1 Overall national policy announcements

Not applicable.

3.2 National revenue authority initiatives

Not applicable.

3.3 Administrative statements

Not applicable.

3.4 Administrative guidelines

To facilitate the implementation of the recent amendments to the Income Tax Act and the Tax Procedures Act, the Ministry of Finance of Albania introduced the Guidelines on Transfer Pricing 2014. The Guidelines on Transfer Pricing 2014 are based on the OECD TPG 2010. However, in the event of a conflict between the OECD TPG 2010 and the Guidelines on Transfer Pricing 2014, the later is binding.

4. CASE LAW

Since Albania is a civil law country, the courts decide cases on a case-by-case basis, and are not bound by previous decisions. Prior to the 2014 amendments, the transfer pricing provisions in the Income Tax Act were limited, incomplete and ambiguous. As a result, there is almost no case law concerning transfer pricing. The former transfer pricing regime provided for the establishment of a Transfer Pricing Committee ('TPC'), which had the authority to challenge any transaction between related parties that did not comply with the market principle. However, in practice, no TPC was ever created, and most transactions between related parties were completed without government oversight. As a result, the very few transfer pricing cases which did go before the Albanian courts were decided in favour of the taxpayers.

4.1 Current cases

Not applicable.

4.2 Historical cases of note

In *Albanian Chrome sh.p.k. v Large Taxpayers Unit and General Directorate of Taxes*, the Albanian Supreme Court held that where the tax authorities suspected that a transaction between related parties did not comply with the market principle, the case was to be referred to the TPC to make adjustments.[12] Furthermore, the Court confirmed that any transfer pricing adjustment imposed without a prior decision from the TPC would be null and void.

5. PENALTIES

The 2014 amendments to the Tax Procedures Act introduced specific provisions regarding the penalties for failing to comply with the transfer pricing provisions in the Income Tax Act.

5.1 Types

If a taxpayer engages in a controlled transaction that, in aggregate, exceeds ALL 50,000,000 (approximately US$481,000) in the reporting period, the taxpayer must file a 'Notice of Annual Controlled Transactions' with the

12 Albanian Chrome sh.p.k. v Large Taxpayers Unit and General Directorate of Taxes (2013), Nr. 83.

appropriate regional tax branch.[13] Failure to file the required notice may result in a monthly fine of ALL 10,000 (approximately US$96).[14]

If the Albanian Tax Authorities impose an adjustment that is not paid by the taxpayer, the taxpayer may be subject to a monthly penalty of 5 per cent or more of the unpaid tax liability, but in any case the penalty shall not exceed 25 per cent of the unpaid tax liability.[15] Where the taxpayer completes and files the relevant transfer pricing documentation in accordance with the Guidelines on Transfer Pricing 2014, the taxpayer will be liable to pay the additional tax liability and accrued interest but will not be subject to any other fines.[16]

5.2 Special or notable cases

Not applicable.

6. DISPUTE RESOLUTION MECHANISMS

If an audit is conducted and it is determined that a transaction concluded between related parties fails to satisfy the market principle, the Albanian Tax Authorities may adjust the taxpayer's taxable profits to bring the financial indicators of the transaction within the median market range. The median market range is the 50th percentile of the profits of the comparable uncontrolled transactions comprising the market range.[17]

The taxpayer may challenge a tax adjustment by filing a claim for an administrative review with the Tax Appeals Directorate (the 'TAD'). Once the taxpayer has exhausted the administrative review procedure, the taxpayer may file a claim with the appropriate administrative court.

6.1 Preferred national options

To appeal an adjustment imposed by the Albanian Tax Authorities, the taxpayer must file a written appeal with the TAD within 30 days of receiving notice of the adjustment.[18] The taxpayer has the burden of proof to establish that the adjustment made by the tax authorities was incorrect. The taxpayer must establish that, as a result of the circumstances surrounding the transaction, an adjustment to a different point in the market range would better reflect the market principle. In deciding the appeal, the TAD may either (i) uphold the decision subject to appeal; (ii) annul or revoke the decision subject to appeal; or (iii) amend the decision subject to appeal.

If the taxpayer is not satisfied with the decision of the TAD, the taxpayer may file a claim with the appropriate Administrative Court of First Instance within 30 days of the decision. Appeals from the Administrative Court of First Instance are heard by the Administrative Court of Appeal. A decision of the Administrative Court of Appeal is final and binding. The taxpayer is entitled to file a complaint with the administrative chamber of the Supreme

13 Article 14(1) of the Guidelines on Transfer Pricing 2014.
14 Article 115/1(1) of the Tax Procedures Act.
15 Article 115/1(2) of the Tax Procedures Act.
16 Article 115/1(3) of the Tax Procedures Act.
17 Article 12 of the Guidelines on Transfer Pricing.
18 Article 116 of the Tax Procedures Act.

Court against the decision of the Administrative Court of Appeal. However, the complaint does not suspend the execution of the decision of the Administrative Court of Appeal.

6.2 International options

Article 36(6) of the Income Tax Act provides that if an adjustment is made by a tax authority in another country that results in the taxation of profits that have been subject to tax in Albania, and the other country has entered into a DTAA with Albania, the taxpayer may request a review by the Albanian Tax Authorities. The taxpayer must submit a written request to the General Directorate of Taxes that includes:

- The name, registered address and trading name(s) of the related party and other registration details;
- The year(s) in which the adjusted transactions took place;
- The amount of the requested corresponding adjustment, and the amount of the adjustment made by the tax administration of the other country;
- Evidence of the tax residence of the related party (eg, a letter or a residency certificate provided by the tax administration of the other country);
- Evidence of the adjustment made by the tax administration of the other country, and the basis for the adjustment;
- Details regarding the comparability factors and the transfer pricing method applied;
- Confirmation that the related party will not, or is unable to, pursue any further recourse under the domestic law of the other country that may result in the adjustment being reduced or reversed; and,
- Any other information that may be relevant to determine the consistency of the adjustment with the market principle.[19]

The Albanian Tax Authorities must determine whether the adjustment is consistent with the market principle. The General Directorate of Taxes must advise the taxpayer if the requested corresponding adjustment will be granted (either partially or in full) within 3 months of receiving the taxpayer's request.[20] If the Albanian Tax Authorities conclude that the adjustment is consistent with the market principle, they must make an appropriate adjustment to the amount of the taxes charged to the taxpayer. If the General Directorate of Taxes rejects the taxpayer's request for a corresponding adjustment, it must provide written reasons for its decision.[21]

PART TWO: TAX AVOIDANCE

Despite the increasing global focus on preventing tax avoidance, Albanian law remains underdeveloped with respect to the issue of tax avoidance. Currently, the only provision that Albanian Tax Authorities may rely upon to prevent tax avoidance is article 71(dh) of the Tax Procedures Act, which

---

19 Article 13(1) of the Guidelines on Transfer Pricing.
20 Article 13(3) of the Guidelines on Transfer Pricing.
21 Article 13(4) of the Guidelines on Transfer Pricing.

gives the Albanian Tax Authorities the power to re-characterize transactions concluded with the sole intention of obtaining a tax advantage. According to article 71(dh) of the Tax Procedures Act, where the taxpayer 'engages in transactions with no substantial economic effect', Albanian Tax Authorities are entitled to use alternative assessment methods in order to establish the taxpayer's tax liability. Once a transaction is re-characterized by the Albanian Tax Authorities, the taxpayer has the burden of proof to establish that the concluded transaction had a substantial economic effect, and was not conducted merely for the purpose of obtaining a tax advantage.

Although article 71(dh) of the Tax Procedures Act has been in force since 2008, it has not been the subject of litigation before the Albanian courts. Further, there are no other provisions in Albania's tax legislation that deal with the issue of tax avoidance. As a result, the Albanian Tax Authorities and the Albanian judicial system have very limited experience with tax avoidance related matters. However, Albania has been in the process of developing its tax legislation to increase consistency with the tax legislation of other European countries. With the increased worldwide focus on tax avoidance, it is expected that Albania will continue to develop its tax legislation by enacting further provisions to prevent aggressive tax planning.

Australia

Corrs Chambers Westgarth Stewart Grieve, Reynah Tang, Kathryn Bertram, Bridie Andriske & Cate Smith

PART ONE: TRANSFER PRICING

1. GENERAL OVERVIEW

In 2012 and 2013, Australia's transfer pricing rules underwent a substantial rewrite. The reforms followed key judicial decisions which were determined under the former transfer pricing regime contained in Division 13 of the Income Tax Assessment Act 1936 (Cth) ('1936 Assessment Act').[1] The reforms were initiated in response to issues identified by those judicial decisions,[2] as well as a broader aim of seeking to modernise Australia's transfer pricing rules and ensure that there is better alignment with guidance established by the Organisation for Economic Cooperation and Development ('OECD').[3]

Subdivision 815-A of the Income Tax Assessment Act 1997 (Cth) ('1997 Assessment Act') was introduced as part of the first stage of the reforms. The subdivision was introduced in September 2012, with retrospective effect from 1 July 2004, and allows the Commissioner of Taxation ('Commissioner') to make transfer pricing adjustments under Australia's tax treaties.

The second stage of reforms introduced Subdivisions 815-B to 815-D of the 1997 Assessment Act which replaced the former regime contained in Division 13 and Subdivision 815-A for tax years commencing on or after 29 June 2013.[4]

Australia's transfer pricing regime may undergo a third stage of reforms in relation to the application of transfer pricing attribution rules to foreign permanent establishments of Australian taxpayers. It is presently unclear when, or if, these proposed reforms will proceed.

2. IDENTIFICATION OF LEGISLATIVE FRAMEWORK

As stated above, Australia's current transfer pricing rules are contained in Subdivisions 815-B to 815-D of the 1997 Assessment Act for tax years commencing on or after 29 June 2013. However, transfer pricing determinations can still be made under Subdivision 815-A of the 1997 Assessment Act and Division 13 of the 1936 Assessment Act for tax years prior to the commencement of the current rules. There is also the potential

1 The key decisions are *Re Roche Products Pty Ltd v Commissioner of Taxation* (2008) 70 ATR 703 (*'Re Roche'*), *SNF (Australia) Pty Ltd v Commissioner of Taxation* (2010) 79 ATR 193 (*'SNF Trial'*) and *Commissioner of Taxation v SNF (Australia) Pty Ltd* (2011) 193 FCR 149 (*'SNF Appeal'*) which are discussed in section 4.2.

2 The Hon Bill Shorten MP, *Robust transfer pricing rules for multinationals* (1 November 2011), Media Release No. 145.

3 Explanatory Memorandum to Tax Laws Amendment (Countering Tax Avoidance and Multinational Profit Shifting) Bill 2013, at paragraph 1.1.

4 The reforms also involved amendments to the Taxation Administration Act 1953 (Cth) ('Administration Act').

for adjustments to be made under the associated enterprises and business profits articles of Australia's international tax treaties.[5]

The interplay between former Division 13, Subdivision 815-A, Subdivisions 815-B to 815-D and Australia's international tax treaties is illustrated in Figure 1.[6]

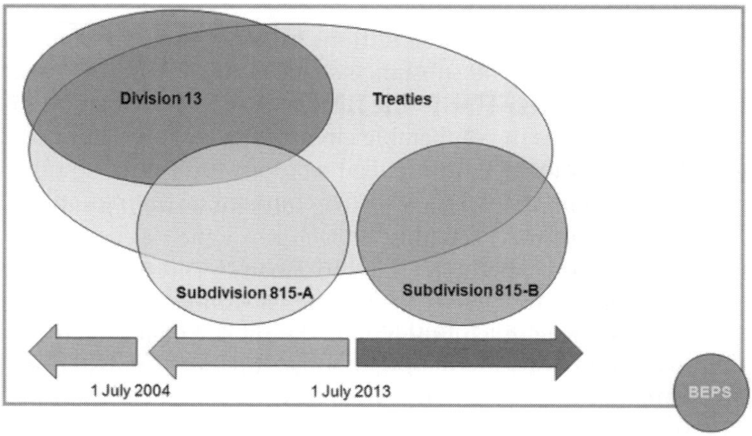

2.1 Federal legislation

Subdivisions 815-B to 815-D

Subdivision 815-B contains the main taxing provisions, and applies where an entity gets a 'transfer pricing benefit'. Essentially, a transfer pricing benefit arises when the cross-border conditions of an entity's commercial or financial relations with another entity differ from the arm's length conditions and produce a beneficial tax outcome.[7] The arm's length conditions are then substituted for the actual conditions.[8] 'Arm's length conditions' include the conditions, such as price, gross margin, net profit, and the division of profit, that might be expected between independent entities dealing wholly independently with one another in comparable circumstances.[9] Circumstances that need to be assessed for comparability include the:

- functions performed, assets used and risks borne by the entities;
- characteristics of any property or services transferred;
- terms of any relevant contracts between the entities;
- economic circumstances; and
- business strategies of the entities.[10]

[5] See for example, Articles 9 and 7 of the Convention between the Government of Australia and the Government of the United Kingdom of Great Britain and Northern Ireland for the Avoidance of Double Taxation and the Prevention of Fiscal Evasion with Respect to Taxes on Income and on Capital Gains.

[6] The reference to BEPS is to the Organisation for Economic Co-operation and Development action plan on base erosion and profit shifting ('BEPS'), *http://www.oecd.org/ctp/BEPSActionPlan.pdf*.

[7] Income Tax Assessment Act 1997 (Cth), s. 815-120.

[8] Income Tax Assessment Act 1997 (Cth), s. 815-115.

[9] Income Tax Assessment Act 1997 (Cth), s. 815-125.

[10] Income Tax Assessment Act 1997 (Cth), s. 815-125(3).

While Subdivision 815-B applies to entities, Subdivision 815-C applies to permanent establishments and Subdivision 815-D to partnerships and trusts.

Other features of Subdivisions 815-B to 815-D include that the rules:

- operate on a self-assessment basis;
- impose a limitation period for the Commissioner to make adjustments under the rules for up to seven years from the original date of assessment;[11]
- require that the arm's length conditions be determined having regard to both the legal form and substance of the arrangements.[12] However, if the form is inconsistent with the substance of the transactions, or if independent entities in comparable circumstances would have entered into different commercial or financial relations (or not have entered into any), then the substance of those other commercial or financial relations will define the arm's length conditions;[13]
- impose penalty consequences for failure to meet transfer pricing documentation requirements. A higher penalty applies where a transfer pricing benefit is found to exist, if the taxpayer does not have contemporaneous documentation to support its taxable income or loss based on the arm's length conditions;[14]
- contain special rules dealing with the pricing of debt and the interaction of the transfer pricing rules with Australia's thin capitalisation regime;[15] and
- are required to be interpreted consistently with relevant guidance, being the OECD Model Tax Convention and Commentaries or the OECD Transfer Pricing Guidelines for Multinational Enterprises ('OECD Guidance').[16]

2.2 State and provincial legislative interplay

Australia's transfer pricing regime is solely contained in federal legislation and is administered at a federal level by the Commissioner and the Australian Taxation Office ('ATO').

2.3 International treaties and agreements

One of the reasons for the recent reforms to Australia's transfer pricing regime was to overcome the uncertainty regarding the ability of the Commissioner to make transfer pricing adjustments under Australia's tax treaties. As a result, Subdivisions 815-B to 815-D apply to all taxpayers irrespective of whether a tax treaty exists.

---

11 Income Tax Assessment Act 1997 (Cth), s. 815-150. For companies, an original assessment is deemed to arise when the company files its tax return disclosing the tax payable by it (Income Tax Assessment Act 1997 (Cth), s. 166A).

12 Income Tax Assessment Act 1997 (Cth), s. 815-130(1).

13 Income Tax Assessment Act 1997 (Cth), s. 815-130(2) to (4).

14 Taxation Administration Act 1953 (Cth), s. 284-250. The penalties for transfer pricing adjustments are discussed at ss. 3.4 and 5 below.

15 Income Tax Assessment Act 1997 (Cth), s. 815-140. See also the thin capitalisation rules contained in Division 820 of the Income Tax Assessment Act 1997 (Cth).

16 Income Tax Assessment Act 1997 (Cth), s. 815-235 and s. 815-135. This is currently based on the 2010 version of those documents.

However, it fails to resolve the question of whether the tax treaties afford the Commissioner a power to make adjustments independently of Australia's domestic transfer pricing laws.[17]

There has been longstanding debate about whether tax treaties provide a taxing power to make transfer pricing adjustments independently of Australia's domestic tax legislation.[18] The ATO is of the view that the tax treaties provide a separate taxing power to the domestic legislation;[19] while taxpayers, commentators and several court decisions have suggested that the tax treaties do no more than allocate taxing rights between treaty parties.[20] However, the Courts have never conclusively determined either position.

To alleviate double taxation resulting from transfer pricing adjustments made by the Commissioner, there is a mutual agreement procedure ('MAP') article in all of Australia's tax treaties. Generally, under a MAP article, an Australian taxpayer can initiate a process of review where the taxpayer considers that the actions of one or more treaty partners have resulted, or potentially will result, in double taxation.[21] The MAP dispute resolution process is described further in section 6.2.

3. NATIONAL POLICY ISSUES

Notwithstanding the considerable reform in recent years, Australia's transfer pricing regime may be subject to further reform in the near future as a result of continued domestic and international focus on BEPS.[22]

3.1 Overall national policy announcements

The OECD released its Action Plan on BEPS ('BEPS Action Plan') on 19 July 2013,[23] and the Australian Government has indicated a commitment to the BEPS Action Plan.[24] In July 2013, the Australian Treasury released a scoping paper titled 'Risk To The Sustainability of Australia's Corporate Tax Base'.[25] This scoping paper considered the broader issues surrounding multinational

---

17 Explanatory Memorandum to Tax Laws Amendment (Countering Tax Avoidance and Multinational Profit Shifting) Bill 2013, at page 37.

18 Australian Taxation Office, Taxation Ruling TR 2001/13, *Income Tax: Interpreting Australia's Double Tax Treaties*; J. Killaly, *Transfer Pricing and Business Restructuring*, presentation to Taxation Institute of Australia Victorian State Convention (9 October 2008).

19 The Australian Taxation Office has placed reliance on the decision of the Taxation Board of Review in *Case N69* (1962) 13 TBRD 270 and a memorandum of advice, see R. Merkel and D. Harding, *Transfer Pricing: Memorandum of Advice* (11 May 2009) and *Transfer Pricing Supplementary Memorandum of Advice* (23 June 2009). The Australian Taxation Office's position was also supported by Middleton J in *SNF (Australia) Pty Ltd v Commissioner of Taxation* (2010) 79 ATR 193.

20 For court decisions, see for example, *Re Roche Products Pty Ltd v Commissioner of Taxation* (2008) 70 ATR 703; *Undershaft (No. 1) Ltd v Commissioner of Taxation* (2009) 175 FCR 150; *Commissioner of Taxation v Lamesa Holdings BV* (1997) 77 FCR 597 and *Chong v Commissioner of Taxation* (2000) 101 FCR 134. For commentary, see for example, D. Preshaw, *The associated enterprises articles in Australia's DTAs and Division 13* (2009) 44 Taxation in Australia 5; P. Korganow and J.P Donga, *Safe Harbour or 'rule of thumb'* (2010) 13 The Tax Specialist 3, at 174; R. Deutsch, *Australia's Double Tax Agreements – An Introduction to Australia's International Taxation System*, presentation to Taxation Institute of Australia, NSW Division, Sydney (15 August 2007).

21 Australian Taxation Office, Taxation Ruling TR 2000/16, *Income tax: international transfer pricing – transfer pricing and profit reallocation adjustments, relief from double taxation and the Mutual Agreement Procedure*, at paragraph 4.1.

22 L. White and M. Butler, *Australia – The Treasury's Scoping Paper on Risks to the Sustainability of the Corporate Tax Base: Precursor to (Tax) Regime Change or Still Simply a Distant Galaxy Many Light Years Away?* (2014) 21 International Transfer Pricing Journal 1; Organisation for Economic Co-operation and Development, *Action Plan on Base Erosion and Profit Shifting* (2013) *http://www.oecd.org/ctp/BEPSActionPlan.pdf.*

23 Organisation for Economic Co-operation and Development, *Action Plan on Base Erosion and Profit Shifting* (2013) *http://www.oecd.org/ctp/BEPSActionPlan.pdf.*

24 David Crowe, *Joe Hockey takes tax crackdown on global giants to G20*, The Australian (10 October 2013).

25 Australian Treasury, *Scoping Paper on Risks to the Sustainability of Australia's Corporate Tax Base* (July 2013) *http://www.treasury.gov.au/PublicationsAndMedia/Publications/2013/Aus-Corporate-Tax-Base-Sustainability.*

profit shifting and made recommendations which aligned with the OECD's BEPS Action Plan.

Australia assumed the G20 chair in December 2013 and Australia's Prime Minister, while addressing the World Economic Forum in Davos in January 2014, stated that he hoped the G20 would continue to 'tackle businesses artificially generating profits' for tax purposes noting that the 'essential principle is that you should normally pay tax in the country where you've earned the revenue'.[26]

The ATO has also introduced a number of initiatives to address challenges it has identified resulting from BEPS.[27]

New legislative measures to increase disclosures and transparency in relation to the tax arrangements of Australian taxpayers were introduced in 2013.[28] Under these transparency laws, the Commissioner is required to publish certain tax information of large corporate taxpayers, including those that have a total income exceeding AUD $100 million.[29] These laws underpin the broader policy objective of discouraging large corporate entities from engaging in aggressive tax avoidance practices as part of the Government's BEPS agenda.

The Commissioner's administration of transfer pricing was recently the subject of a review by the Inspector-General of Taxation.[30] The review was in response to concerns raised by taxpayers, tax professionals and their representative bodies regarding the ATO's management of transfer pricing matters. The review made 18 recommendations, 17 of which the ATO agreed with in whole, part or principle. These 17 include, the recruitment and retention of transfer pricing specialist officers and improving the ATO's identification, assessment and management of risk in transfer pricing matters and their interaction with operational functions.

3.2 National Revenue Authority initiatives

In recent years, the ATO has announced several initiatives relating to transfer pricing and broader cross-border activities.

In July 2012, the ATO introduced the International Dealings Schedule ('IDS')[31] which forms part of the ATO's broader information gathering initiative. The IDS requires taxpayers to provide extensive and detailed information in relation to their cross border activities, including transfer pricing and other international dealings.

---

26 The Hon Tony Abbott MP, *Address to the World Economic Forum, Davos, Switzerland* (23 January 2014) *http://www.pm.gov.au/media/2014-01-23/address-world-economic-forum-davos-switzerland-0*.

27 M Konza, *Base Erosion and Profit Shifting*, presentation given to Macquarie University and Deloitte International Tax Forum (26 November 2013) *http://www.ato.gov.au/Media-centre/Speeches/Other/Base-erosion-and-profit-shifting/*.

28 Tax Laws Amendment (2013 Measures No. 2) Act 2013 (Cth).

29 The Australian Taxation Office is currently consulting with taxpayers and other relevant industry and professional bodies on how limited tax information of certain entities, which the Commissioner must make publicly available under the new transparency rules, is published. See Australian Taxation Office, *List of Consultation Matters, https://www.ato.gov.au/General/About-consultation/In-detail/List-of-consultation-matters/*.

30 Inspector-General of Taxation, *Review into the Australian Taxation Office's management of transfer pricing matters: A report to the Assistant Treasurer* (December 2013) *http://www.igt.gov.au/content/reports/ATO_transfer_pricing_matters/ATO_Transfer_Pricing_Matters.pdf*.

31 Australian Taxation Office, *International Dealings Schedule 2014* (NAT 73345-06.2014) (1 July 2014) *https://www.ato.gov.au/Forms/International-dealings-schedule-2014/*.

In addition, each year the ATO releases its compliance program which outlines the ATO's key compliance activities for the coming year. The most recent compliance program for 2013-14 was released on 16 July 2013. The 2013-14 compliance program states that the ATO would focus on large, and multinational, businesses that engage in offshore profit-shifting and would scrutinize their financial arrangements.[32] In 2013-14, the ATO planned to conduct 125 risk reviews and 26 audits of large and multinational businesses.[33] Further, in July 2013, the ATO stated that it would begin investigating 60 new cases of suspected tax avoidance by multinational companies through profit-shifting, with a particular focus on the energy and resource sector.[34]

In 2013, the ATO also established the 'International Structuring and Profit Shifting' ('ISAPS') program.[35] ISAPS is a four year program which is responsible for reviewing corporate tax and transfer pricing aspects of complex and high value cross border transactions.

As part of the ATO's international engagement strategy, the ATO is currently working with international partner tax agencies to map the global operations of multinational enterprises. The Commissioner recently stated that 'we are committed to working cooperatively to find solutions to the broad challenges faced by the international tax system as a result of globalisation and the increasingly digitalised economy'.[36]

Further detail on the information gathering and audit process is contained in section 6.

3.3 Administrative statements

The following suite of draft transfer pricing rulings and administrative statements was released on 16 April 2014 which, when finalised, will apply to transfer pricing matters in tax years commencing on or after 29 June 2013:

- Draft Taxation Ruling TR 2014/D3 ('TR 2014/D3') which sets out the Commissioner's views about the application of s. 815-130 of the 1997 Assessment Act (referred to below as the reconstruction power);[37]
- Draft Taxation Ruling TR 2014/D4 ('TR 2014/D4') which provides the Commissioner's views on the transfer pricing documentation an entity should prepare and keep to satisfy s. 284-255 of Schedule 1 of the Administration Act;[38]

32 Australian Taxation Office, *Compliance in focus 2013-14* (NAT 74689) (July 2013) *http://www.ato.gov.au/uploadedFiles/Content/CS_C/downloads/CSC35735NAT74689.pdf*, at page 12.

33 Australian Taxation Office, *Compliance in focus 2013-14* (NAT 74689) (July 2013) *http://www.ato.gov.au/uploadedFiles/Content/CS_C/downloads/CSC35735NAT74689.pdf*, at page 28.

34 G Wilkins, *Scrutiny on the bounty: tax probe on global giants*, The Sydney Morning Herald (6 July 2013) *http://www.smh.com.au/national/scrutiny-on-the-bounty-tax-probe-on-global-giants-20130705-2phnr.html*.

35 M Konza, *Base Erosion and Profit Shifting*, presentation given to Macquarie University and Deloitte International Tax Forum (26 November 2013) *http://www.ato.gov.au/Media-centre/Speeches/Other/Base-erosion-and-profit-shifting/*.

36 C Jordan, Australian Taxation Office, *Speech to the Tax Institute of Australia 29th National Convention* (27 March 2014) *https://www.ato.gov.au/Media-centre/Speeches/Commissioner/Commissioner-s-address-to-TIA/*.

37 Australian Taxation Office, Draft Taxation Ruling TR 2014/D3, *Income tax: transfer pricing – the application of section 815-130 of the Income Tax Assessment Act 1997*, *http://law.ato.gov.au/atolaw/view.htm?DocID=DTR/TR2014D3/NAT/ATO/00001*.

38 Australian Taxation Office, Draft Taxation Ruling TR 2014/D4, *Income tax: transfer pricing: documentation requirements*, *http://law.ato.gov.au/atolaw/view.htm?DocID=DTR/TR2014D4/NAT/ATO/00001*.

- Draft Practice Statement Law Administration PS LA 3672 ('PS LA 3672') which provides guidance in respect of the administration of transfer pricing penalties.[39] PS LA 3672 is discussed further in section 3.4 below; and
- Draft Practice Statement Law Administration PS LA 3673 ('PS LA 3673') which provides guidance on the process for documenting transfer pricing.[40] PS LA 3673 is discussed further in section 3.4 below.

TR 2014/D4, PS LA 3673 and PS LA 3672 are intended to be read together.

TR 2014/D3 – reconstruction

The ability for the ATO to reconstruct transactions has been a particularly controversial element of the stage two reforms.[41] Subdivisions 815-B to 815-D allow for the arrangements and dealings that would have occurred if independent entities were dealing at arm's length to be substituted for the actual dealings and arrangements.[42] This contrasts with the OECD Guidance which only allows for reconstruction in 'exceptional circumstances'.[43] Criticism of the new reconstruction power has also highlighted the potential flow-on effects from reconstructing transactions. The potential flow-on effects include the increased potential for double taxation to occur, the increased potential for a reconstructed transaction to have a different tax effect under another area of tax law, and the difficulties faced by taxpayers when undertaking a self-assessment.[44]

TR 2014/D3 states that it is the Commissioner's view that ss. 815-130(2) to (4) must be interpreted consistently with OECD Guidance and contends that they align with the OECD 'exceptional circumstances'.[45] The ruling then provides examples to illustrate situations which the Commissioner deems as satisfying these exceptional circumstances.[46] The examples include:

- the transfer of trademarks and sale of products from an Australian company to a foreign subsidiary. This would be reconstructed under s. 815-130(2) as re-invoicing and reimbursement services, largely because the Australian company continues to undertake all economically

---

39 Australian Taxation Office, Draft Practice Statement Law Administration PS LA 3672, *http://law.ato.gov.au/atolaw/view.htm?docid=%22DPS%2FPSD3672%2FNAT%2FATO%2F00001%22.*

40 Australian Taxation Office, Draft Practice Statement Law Administration PS LA 3673, *http://law.ato.gov.au/atolaw/view.htm?docid=%22DPS%2FPSD3673%2FNAT%2FATO%2F00001%22.*

41 See, for example N Houseman and D Xhemajlaj, *Reconstruction under the new transfer pricing law* (2014) 48 Taxation in Australia 8; G. Gill, *Legislative change to the transfer pricing rules – the state of play*, paper presented to The Tax Institute NSW Division (18 September 2013); P. Balkus and J. Solgaard, *Transfer pricing legislated reform – tranche 2: What does it mean for taxpayers?* (2013) 17 The Tax Specialist 1; J. Sadri, *Responding to Australia's transfer pricing reforms*, paper presented to The Tax Institute International Day (10 May 2013). See also, the criticism of Draft Taxation Ruling TR 2014/D3 in N Khadem, *ATO can reconstruct 'unrealistic' tax transactions*, The Australian Financial Review (17 April 2014).

42 Income Tax Assessment Act 1997 (Cth), s. 815-130.

43 Organisation for Economic Co-operation and Development, *Transfer Pricing Guidelines for Multinational Enterprises* (2008), at paragraph 1.64.

44 R Tang, *Adsidui emptor or taxpayers beware: The implications of new guidance on transfer pricing documentation, reconstruction and penalties* (17 April 2014) *https://www.corrs.com.au/publications/corrs-in-brief/adsidui-emptor-or-taxpayers-beware-the-implications-of-new-guidance-on-transfer-pricing-documentation-reconstruction-and-penalties/*; N Houseman and D Xhemajlaj, *Reconstruction under the new transfer pricing law* (2014) 48 Taxation in Australia 8.

45 Australian Taxation Office, Draft Taxation Ruling TR 2014/D3, *Income tax: transfer pricing – the application of section 815-130 of the Income Tax Assessment Act 1997*, at paragraph 89.

46 Australian Taxation Office, Draft Taxation Ruling TR 2014/D3, *Income tax: transfer pricing – the application of section 815-130 of the Income Tax Assessment Act 1997*, at paragraphs 87-135.

significant tasks and the foreign subsidiary does not have the necessary resources;

- the sale of goods by an Australian manufacturer to a controlled foreign distributor, including payment of a 1% fee to the distributor for taking manufacturing warranty risk. This would be reconstructed under s. 815-130(3) as the manufacturer retaining the warranty risk due to the lack of evidence of other distributors taking on that warranty risk, and because the distributor does not have the financial capacity to take on that risk; and
- the entry into a debt factoring arrangement by an Australian company with its foreign subsidiary for a fee equal to 2% of gross sales. This would be reconstructed under s. 815-130(4) as if no transaction had occurred because the receipt of binding third party guarantees means that there is no possibility of late payment risk.

TR 2014/D4 – documentation

Under the new transfer pricing regime, taxpayers cannot hold a 'reasonably arguable position' in respect of the penalties regime, unless they have appropriate transfer pricing documentation in place. As indicated below, this means higher penalties apply where a transfer pricing benefit exists. TR 2014/D4 reinforces the legislation and provides the following further guidance:

- documentation which does not fully satisfy the requirements of Subdivision 284-E of Schedule 1 to the Administration Act and is not prepared before or at the time of lodgement of the company's tax return, cannot be taken into account to support a reasonably arguable position;[47]
- documentation should demonstrate that the actual conditions that operate are consistent with the arm's length principle;[48]
- records should contain all necessary factual information that allows the ATO to readily ascertain and identify the arm's length conditions and any variance to the actual conditions;[49]
- taxpayers should prepare and maintain documentation in relation to commercial and financial conditions that are relevant and material. In this respect, taxpayers are expected to undertake a risk assessment of their relevant dealings;[50] and
- global documentation must be readily and fully accessible by the Australian entity.[51]

---

[47] Australian Taxation Office, Draft Taxation Ruling TR 2014/D4, *Income tax: transfer pricing: documentation requirements*, at paragraph 26.

[48] Australian Taxation Office, Draft Taxation Ruling TR 2014/D4, *Income tax: transfer pricing: documentation requirements*, at paragraph 27.

[49] Australian Taxation Office, Draft Taxation Ruling TR 2014/D4, *Income tax: transfer pricing: documentation requirements*, at paragraph 46.

[50] Australian Taxation Office, Draft Taxation Ruling TR 2014/D4, *Income tax: transfer pricing: documentation requirements*, at paragraphs 61 and 62.

[51] Australian Taxation Office, Draft Taxation Ruling TR 2014/D4, *Income tax: transfer pricing: documentation requirements*, paragraph 82.

3.4 Administrative guidelines

The ATO's Practice Statements, while not legally binding,[52] provide useful information on the ATO's policy and approach to transfer pricing.

PS LA 3672 – penalties

PS LA 3672 discusses when an entity will be liable for a transfer pricing penalty under subs. 284-145(2B) of Schedule 1 to the Administration Act, including how the ATO will assess any penalty where a transfer pricing adjustment is made. In PS LA 3672, the Commissioner states that the ATO, when assessing remission of penalties, will have regard to whether a taxpayer has made its best efforts to comply with the documentation requirements, and whether a calculation, or mechanical process in the law, results in an unintended or unjust outcome in the entity's particular circumstances.[53]

PS LA 3673 – documentation

PS LA 3673 sets out the ATO's suggested 'five step' process for taxpayers to follow when preparing transfer pricing documentation. The five steps are summarised in the table below.

Step	Action
1	Identify the actual conditions in connection with the commercial or financial relations.
2	Select the most appropriate and reliable method to be used to identify the arm's length conditions.
3	Identify the comparable circumstances relevant to identifying the arm's length conditions.
4	Apply the transfer pricing rules so as best to achieve consistency with the relevant guidance material.
5	Monitor, review and update transfer prices when necessary.

4. CASE LAW

Despite being a high priority issue for the ATO since its introduction in 1982, former Division 13 has been given little judicial consideration. However, the little case law that exists has had a significant impact on the development of the law and was the impetus for the enactment of Subdivisions 815-A to 815-D and associated reforms. While the substantive transfer pricing decisions, *Re Roche, SNF Trial* and *SNF Appeal,* involved interpretations of former Division 13, the discussion of methodologies in these decisions may still provide insight as to the likely future judicial approaches to methodologies under Subdivisions 815-B to 815-D.

52 Australian Taxation Office, Practice Statement Law Administration PS LA 1998/1.
53 Australian Taxation Office, Practice Statement Law Administration PS LA 3672, at paragraph 108.

4.1 Current cases

While there have been no judicial decisions which consider Subdivisions 815-A or Subdivisions 815-B to 815-D, there is at least one current case before the Federal Court in which the Commissioner has been allowed to amend his case to include determinations made under Subdivision 815-A.[54]

4.2 Historical cases of note

Re Roche

Re Roche is an Administrative Appeals Tribunal ('AAT') decision which concerned the pricing of pharmaceuticals supplied by foreign related parties of the Australian taxpayer.

In this case, the ATO relied largely on the transactional net margin method ('TNM Method') for net profit comparisons using independent third party comparables (adjusted to take into account functional differences). The AAT rejected this method and held that a gross profit margin analysis, based on comparable uncontrolled price ('CUP') transactions was appropriate.

In relation to the appropriateness of profit based methodologies under Division 13, the AAT observed:

'One of the problems of profit based methodology is that, when applied to transfer pricing, it inevitably attributes any loss to the pricing. Where operating expenses are higher these may place some of the emphasis of the cause of the loss on the wrong area. After all, it is certainly true that there are companies which make losses for reasons other than the prices for which they acquire their stock. The Australian operations of multinational companies are not necessarily excluded from this.'[55]

In relation to expert evidence, the AAT stated that while such evidence is of assistance in determining the arm's length price, the decision is ultimately for the AAT.[56]

SNF Trial and SNF Appeal

The decisions in *SNF Trial* and *SNF Appeal* considered the application of Division 13 in respect of the purchase of polyacrylamide by an Australian taxpayer from its overseas related parties. The taxpayer successfully argued at trial and on appeal, that appropriate comparables were available and the CUP method demonstrated that the consideration for the purchase of polyacrylamide products was arm's length.

The ATO sought to rely on the TNM Method, arguing that comparable transactions could only be used if the comparable purchasers shared all of the characteristics of the taxpayer. In particular, the ATO argued that the existence of sustained losses by the taxpayer over a 13 year period showed that the transactions were not arm's length. This argument was ultimately rejected by the Full Court.[57]

---

54 R. Tang, S Grieve and B. Andriske, *Are the retrospective transfer pricing measures unconstitutional?* (18 October 2012) *http://www.corrs.com.au/thinking/insights/are-the-retrospective-transfer-pricing-measures-unconstitutional/*.

55 *Re Roche Products Pty Ltd v Commissioner of Taxation* (2008) 70 ATR 703 at [185]. Note that this statement was endorsed by the Court in *SNF (Australia) Pty Ltd v Commissioner of Taxation* (2010) 79 ATR 193.

56 *Re Roche Products Pty Ltd v Commissioner of Taxation* (2008) 70 ATR 703 at [151].

57 *Commissioner of Taxation v SNF (Australia) Pty Ltd* (2011) 193 FCR 149 at [6], [7] and [130].

The following observations were made in relation to the appropriateness and applicability of methodologies for determining arm's length price:

- Middleton J, at first instance, noted that the OECD Guidelines are merely guidelines and Division 13 does not prescribe any particular methodology. As such, it is for the Court to determine which methodology is appropriate.[58] The Full Court found that the OECD Guidelines are not automatically a legitimate aid to the interpretation of Division 13.[59] However, the Full Court did not close-off the possibility for the Guidelines to be used in future cases;[60] and
- the Full Court held that, in circumstances where appropriate comparables are available, it is not necessary to use the TNM Method.[61] Note that the Full Court did not make a finding on the validity of the TNM Method for determining the arm's length price.

5. PENALTIES

5.1 Types

As stated above in sections 3.3 and 3.4, under s. 284-250 of the Administration Act, a taxpayer cannot hold a 'reasonably arguable position' if the taxpayer does not have supporting contemporaneous documentation. Taxpayers may be liable for a 25% base penalty applied to the transfer pricing adjustment amount if they fail to keep the relevant records, although there may be reductions for voluntary disclosure.[62] The following table summarises the base penalties imposed:

	With documentation and reasonably arguable position	Without documentation (or if documentation does not provide reasonably arguable position)
Dominant purpose of getting a transfer pricing benefit	25%	50%
Other cases (with no dominant purpose)	10%	25%

Note that for adjustments made under Subdivision 815-A for tax years prior to 1 July 2012, penalties only apply if a penalty would apply to an adjustment made under Division 13 or a tax treaty.

5.2 Special or notable cases

There is no case law available in relation to the imposition of penalties in transfer pricing disputes.[63]

58 *SNF (Australia) Pty Ltd v Commissioner of Taxation* (2010) 79 ATR 193 at [55] and [58].
59 *Commissioner of Taxation v SNF (Australia) Pty Ltd* (2011) 193 FCR 149 at [116] and [118].
60 *Commissioner of Taxation v SNF (Australia) Pty Ltd* (2011) 193 FCR 149 at [117].
61 *Commissioner of Taxation v SNF (Australia) Pty Ltd* (2011) 193 FCR 149 at [71].
62 Taxation Administration Act 1953 (Cth), s. 284-160.
63 In the preliminary decision of *Re Roche Products Pty Ltd v Commissioner of Taxation* [2008] AATA 261, Downes P set

6. DISPUTE RESOLUTION MECHANISMS

The ATO publishes a large business active compliance manual.[64] The manual provides practical guidance on how the ATO undertakes active compliance activities with large business in relation to post-lodgement risk reviews, and audits for income tax and pre-lodgement compliance review products. Internal ATO work processes provide guidance for ATO officers on how to conduct transfer pricing case reviews.[65]

The ATO conducts general information gathering processes which inform whether the ATO will conduct a risk review and/or audit of a taxpayer. This includes monitoring publically available resources (such as annual reports) and the information provided by taxpayers in the IDS (see section 3.2).

The ATO may then conduct a transfer pricing risk review of a taxpayer which typically involves the ATO requesting detailed information on a taxpayer's business and tax position.

If issues remain unresolved following the risk review stage, then the ATO will proceed to audit and issue formal information requests.[66] At the audit stage, the ATO will review the taxpayer's information with the assistance of economists to determine the appropriate arm's length price, and will issue an audit position paper if this differs from the taxpayer's position.

Large business taxpayers have the opportunity to request an independent review within 10 working days of receipt of the ATO's audit position paper.[67] This involves a reviewer, who has not previously been involved in the audit, considering the technical merits of the audit position paper and the taxpayer's response. As part of the independent review, the reviewer conducts a case conference involving the audit team and the taxpayer to narrow the issues in dispute. Note that the review is limited to the information previously provided during the audit. The reviewer cannot seek additional information in conducting his/her review. Requesting a review does not prevent the taxpayer from objecting to any amended assessments issued by the ATO.

Following finalisation of the audit process, the ATO releases a final position paper and may decide to issue amended assessments to the taxpayer.

6.1 Preferred national options

Litigation process

Following receipt of an amended assessment, the taxpayer has 60 days after service of the notice of amended assessment or four years after the date of

aside the Commissioner's assessments and instead increased the assessable income of the taxpayer by a total of $58,741,000. He also noted at paragraph 194 that 'issues of penalties and interest, which were not fully addressed in argument, may need to be dealt with' once the parties had put further submissions to the Administrative Appeals Tribunal

64 Australian Taxation Office, *Large business active compliance manual – income tax, https://www.ato.gov.au/printfriendly.aspx?url=/Business/Large-business/In-detail/Key-products-and-resources/Large-business-active-compliance-manual---income-tax/.*

65 See Australian Taxation Office, withdrawn Practice Statement Law Administration PS LA 2004/13.

66 The Commissioner has formal access and information gathering powers contained in the Income Tax Assessment Act 1936 (Cth), s. 263 and s. 264.

67 Australian Taxation Office, *Independent review of Large Business and International Statement of Audit Position https://www.ato.gov.au/printfriendly.aspx?url=/Business/Large-business/In-detail/Key-products-and-resources/Independent-review-of-Large-Business-and-International-Statement-of-Audit-Position/.*

the original assessment (or deemed assessment for a company), whichever is the later, within which to lodge an objection to the assessment with the Commissioner.[68] However, taxpayers are generally obliged to make payment of the assessed tax on the due date specified in the assessment.[69]

If the Commissioner does not decide the outcome of the objection within 60 days, a taxpayer may give notice to the Commissioner to make a decision.[70] If, within 60 days of that notice, the Commissioner has still not made a decision, the taxpayer's objection is deemed to be disallowed.[71] If an objection is disallowed, or deemed to be disallowed, the taxpayer can either seek review of the decision by the AAT or appeal the decision to the Federal Court.[72]

Essentially, the difference between a review by the AAT and an appeal to the Federal Court are that reviews by the AAT are designed to be economical, informal and quick.[73] The AAT, in making its decision, conducts the hearing as if it were in the shoes of the original decision-maker. Unlike an appeal to the Federal Court, this allows the AAT to exercise all the powers and discretions that are conferred on the original decision maker.[74] Appeals to the Federal Court are subject to the usual rules of evidence and procedure.[75] A decision of the AAT may be appealed on a question of law to the Federal Court, and a decision of the Federal Court may be appealed on a question of law or fact to the Full Federal Court,[76] and if special leave is granted, to the High Court.[77]

Advance Pricing Arrangements (APA)

The ATO operates an APA program for multinational enterprises. Under the APA program, taxpayers can enter into unilateral, bilateral and multilateral APAs to resolve any uncertainty around the application of the arm's length principle to their international related party dealings on a prospective basis.[78] For bilateral and multilateral APAs, the ATO negotiates with the tax authority in the other foreign jurisdiction(s) under the MAP article of the relevant tax treaty (see s. 6.2 below for further detail on the MAP procedure).

Depending on the circumstances, taxpayers can seek either a Simplified APA, a Standard APA or a Complex APA.[79] The Simplified APA is designed for taxpayers with low value and low risk international related party dealings and is only available for unilateral APAs. The Standard APA deals with less complex international related party dealings that do not qualify for the Simplified APA, for both unilateral and bilateral APAs. The Complex

---

68 Taxation Administration Act 1953 (Cth), s. 14ZW(1).

69 Taxpayers can enter into a '50/50 arrangement', whereby 50% of the disputed tax debt is paid by the taxpayer to the Commissioner of Taxation and, in return, the Commissioner of Taxation agrees to a remission of 50% of the general interest charge, which would normally accrue while an amount of disputed tax debt remains unpaid. See Practice Statement Law Administration PS LA 2011/4, at paragraphs 22-40.

70 Taxation Administration Act 1953 (Cth), s. 14ZYA.

71 Taxation Administration Act 1953 (Cth), s. 14ZYA(3).

72 Taxation Administration Act 1953 (Cth), s. 14ZZC and s. 14ZZN.

73 Administrative Appeals Tribunal Act 1975 (Cth), s. 2A.

74 Administrative Appeals Tribunal Act 1975 (Cth), s. 43(1).

75 See the Federal Court's rules of evidence and procedure in the Federal Court Rules 2011 (Cth).

76 Federal Court of Australia Act 1976 (Cth), s. 27.

77 Federal Court of Australia Act 1976 (Cth), s. 33(3).

78 Australian Taxation Office, Practice Statement Law Administration PS LA 2011/1.

79 Australian Taxation Office, Practice Statement Law Administration PS LA 2011/1, at paragraph 15.

APAs are suitable for high risk international dealings, and are also available for unilateral and bilateral APAs. The process and expected timeline for completing each type of APA is different, with bilateral APAs typically taking longer than unilateral APAs.[80]

6.2 International options

Each of Australia's tax treaties contains a MAP article which allows for a taxpayer to seek a review if that taxpayer considers that they have been subject to, or will be faced with, international double taxation.[81] A MAP article enables the competent authority of each treaty country to consult with each other with a view to resolving the double taxation, although it does not compel agreement.[82] In 2012, 10 new MAP cases were engaged in Australia.[83]

The ATO has adopted the two-stage procedure approach as outlined in the OECD Commentary on Article 25 of the OECD Model Tax Convention on Income and Capital.[84] The first stage involves the taxpayer and the ATO, whereby the ATO considers whether the double taxation can be resolved unilaterally. The second involves the competent authorities of both countries seeking to resolve the case.

At the first stage, to the extent that the foreign competent authority has taxed profits in accordance with the tax treaty, the Commissioner may determine the amount of a taxpayer's taxable income, or loss for an income year, so as to prevent double taxation.[85]

If a solution cannot be reached at the first stage, the ATO will seek to reach agreement with the foreign competent authority through the exchange of position papers setting out their respective views.[86]

Australia's tax treaties with New Zealand and Switzerland also contain an arbitration provision in the MAP article.[87] Under the Australia-New Zealand tax treaty, if the competent authorities of both countries cannot reach agreement, the taxpayer may refer the matter to arbitration once two years have passed since the case was presented to one of the competent authorities. Under the Australia-Switzerland tax treaty, the taxpayer can only refer the matter to arbitration once three years have elapsed.

PART TWO: TAX AVOIDANCE

The following section on tax avoidance focuses on Australia's income tax general anti-avoidance rule ('GAAR').

---

80 Australian Taxation Office, Practice Statement Law Administration PS LA 2011/1, at Chapter 2.

81 ATO, Taxation Ruling TR 2000/16, *Income tax: international transfer pricing – transfer pricing and profit reallocation adjustments, relief from double taxation and the Mutual Agreement Procedure*, at paragraph 1.6.

82 ATO, Taxation Ruling TR 2000/16, *Income tax: international transfer pricing – transfer pricing and profit reallocation adjustments, relief from double taxation and the Mutual Agreement Procedure*, at paragraph 1.6

83 Organisation for Economic Co-operation and Development, *Mutual Agreement Procedure Statistics for 2012, http://www.oecd.org/ctp/dispute/mapstatistics2012.htm.*

84 ATO, Taxation Ruling TR 2000/16, *Income tax: international transfer pricing – transfer pricing and profit reallocation adjustments, relief from double taxation and the Mutual Agreement Procedure*, at paragraph 4.3.

85 International Tax Agreements Act 1953 (Cth), s. 24.

86 ATO, Taxation Ruling TR 2000/16, *Income tax: international transfer pricing – transfer pricing and profit reallocation adjustments, relief from double taxation and the Mutual Agreement Procedure*, at paragraphs 4.17-4.19.

87 International Tax Agreements Act 1953 (Cth), article 25 of schedule 4. The Australia-Switzerland Tax Treaty was signed on 30 July 2013, however it is not yet in force. See *http://www.treasury.gov.au/Policy-Topics/Taxation/Tax-Treaties/HTML/Income-Tax-Treaties/Recently-Revised.*

7. ACCEPTABLE TAX PLANNING AREAS/SUBJECTS

One of the most difficult questions that the Australian legislature and courts face is where to draw the line between acceptable tax planning that ought not attract the operation of the GAAR in Part IVA of the *1936 Assessment Act* and tax planning sufficiently egregious to fall foul of the GAAR. Equally difficult for taxpayers, advisers and tax officials is the assessment of which side of the line a particular tax planning arrangement falls.

Unfortunately, Australia has no bright line test for what is and is not acceptable tax planning. As noted by the High Court of Australia in *Federal Commissioner of Taxation v Spotless Services*[88] ('*Spotless*'):

'A particular course of action may be ... both "tax driven" and bear the character of a rational commercial decision. The presence of the latter characteristic does not determine the answer to the question whether, within the meaning of Part IVA, a person entered into or carried out a "scheme" for the "dominant purpose" of enabling the taxpayer to obtain a "tax benefit".'[89]

In *Commissioner of Taxation v Hart*[90] ('*Hart*') Justices Gummow and Hayne referred to this statement of the High Court in *Spotless* and added that *'[a]lways the question must be whether the terms of the [1936 Assessment Act] apply to the facts and circumstances of the particular case.'*[91]

Ultimately, the best guidance to what is and is not acceptable tax planning is gleaned from observations of the Australian High Court in GAAR cases that have come before it.

Before considering the relevant High Court observations, it is instructive to examine the history of the introduction of the current Australian GAAR. In the second reading speech to the Bill which introduced the GAAR in 1981,[92] the Honourable John Howard, the then Treasurer of Australia, said:

'The proposed [GAAR] ... seek[s] to give effect to a policy that such measures *ought to strike down blatant, artificial or contrived arrangements, but not cast unnecessary inhibitions on normal commercial transactions by which taxpayers legitimately take advantage of opportunities available for the arrangement of their affairs. ...*

...

... It has been decided ... that *the better test of what is blatant, contrived or artificial is the positive one that ... seems to best capture the essence of the views expressed by the Privy Council [in Newton's case] which, in fact, characterised an ordinary family dealing as representing a situation other than one on which it can be predicated that it was implemented in the particular way so as to avoid tax.*'[93] [Emphasis added]

88 (1996) 186 CLR 404.
89 *Federal Commissioner of Taxation v Spotless Services* (1996) 186 CLR 404 at 416.
90 (2004) 217 CLR 216.
91 *Commissioner of Taxation v Hart* (2004) 217 CLR 216 at [52].
92 Income Tax Laws Amendment Bill (No 2) 1981.
93 Income Tax Laws Amendment Bill (No 2) 1981; Second Reading Speech at 4.42.

The Treasurer's reference to 'Newton's case' appears to be a reference to Lord Denning's comments in the Privy Council[94] case of *Newton v Federal Commissioner of Taxation*:[95]

'In order to bring the arrangement within the [GAAR] *you must be able to predicate – by looking at the overt acts by which it was implemented – that it was implemented in that particular way so as to avoid tax. If you cannot so predicate, but have to acknowledge that the transactions are capable of explanation by reference to ordinary business or family dealing, without necessarily being labelled as a means to avoid tax, then the arrangement does not come within the section. ...'* [Emphasis added]

A particular arrangement attracts the operation of the Australian GAAR if two conditions are present: if it generates a 'tax benefit' for a taxpayer and if a person who entered into or carried out the whole, or a part, of the arrangement did so with the main purpose of enabling the taxpayer to obtain the tax benefit. The purpose of the person is assessed by reference to an objective analysis of eight specified matters[96] and not by reference to the person's subjective intention. Because purpose is determined objectively, a tax planning arrangement entered into with the subjective intention of obtaining a tax benefit will not necessarily attract the operation of the GAAR. If, as suggested by Mr. Howard, the test in Part IVA captures the essence of the Privy Council's views in Newton's case, then perhaps Part IVA may only apply to an arrangement containing a tax planning aspect where it is possible to predicate, by looking at the overt acts by which the arrangement was implemented, that it was implemented in that particular way in order to enable the taxpayer to obtain a tax benefit. If the arrangement is capable of being explained as an ordinary commercial or family dealing, then the GAAR ought not to apply.

More recently, the High Court of Australia appears to have implicitly endorsed this line of thinking on what does and does not constitute acceptable tax planning in its decisions in *Spotless*[97] and *Hart*.[98]

Spotless concerned two Australian Spotless Group companies operating in a joint venture to deposit funds on a short term basis in the Cook Islands. Various steps were taken to ensure that the interest on the deposit had its source in the Cook Islands. The interest rate on the Cook Islands investment was 4% lower than the rate that could have been achieved by investing the money in Australia. However, by virtue of the interest having its source in the Cook Islands, a withholding tax of 5% was payable on the interest in the Cook Islands and it was exempt from Australian tax. As such, the joint venture participants enjoyed a higher post tax return on the Cook Islands investment than would have been achieved had the funds been invested in

---

94 The Privy Council was the highest appeals court in Australia until 1986, when the Australia Act 1986 (Cth) and the Australia Act 1986 (UK) resulted in the High Court of Australia assuming that position.

95 (1958) 98 CLR 1 at 8. The Court's comments are in relation to the previous version of the income tax general anti-avoidance rule in the Income Tax Assessment Act 1936 (Cth), former s. 260.

96 The eight matters to be taken into account in the analysis of purpose are set out in s. 177D(2) of the Income Tax Assessment Act 1936 (Cth).

97 *Federal Commissioner of Taxation v Spotless Services* (1996) 186 CLR 404.

98 *Commissioner of Taxation v Hart* (2004) 217 CLR 216.

Australia. The High Court determined that this was a scheme to which Part IVA applied. In the course of his judgment, Justice McHugh commented:

'... Part IVA does not authorise the Commissioner to make a determination [that Part IVA applies] merely because a taxpayer has arranged its business or investments in a way that derives a tax benefit. ... *[A conclusion that Part IVA applies] will seldom, if ever, be drawn if no more appears than that a change of business or investment has produced a tax benefit for the taxpayer. The facts of the present case show much more than a switch of investments resulting in a tax benefit. The elaborate nature of the scheme and its attendant circumstances lead inevitably to the conclusion that the scheme was not merely tax driven but that its dominant purpose was to enable the taxpayer to obtain a tax benefit by participating in the scheme.*'[99] [Emphasis added]

In *Hart*, the taxpayers borrowed money to buy a new house and finance the retention of their former home as an investment property under a 'wealth optimiser structure' offered by a finance provider. Under the 'wealth optimiser structure', the taxpayers borrowed an amount under a single loan facility comprised of two separate loan accounts. One account recorded the loan used to fund the acquisition of the new house, which was to be the taxpayers' principal place of residence. The other account financed the retention of the investment property. The entire loan was secured by both properties. All repayments on the loan were directed to the loan account servicing the principal place of residence. The effect was that the portion of the loan (and hence the quantum of interest expense) attributable to the taxpayers' principal place of residence reduced and the portion of the loan (and hence the quantum of interest expense) attributable to their investment property increased. The interest expense on the portion of the loan attributable to the principal residence was not deductible, whereas the interest referable to the investment property was deductible. The financing arrangement had the effect of increasing the amount of the tax deductions (as compared with the amount of the deductions that would have been available to the taxpayers had two separate loans on standard commercial terms been entered into). The Court found that Part IVA applied in this case. This was because the 'wealth optimiser structure's' efficacy depended entirely on the tax benefits generated and had no explanation other than the fiscal consequences. What 'optimised' the taxpayers' wealth was the additional interest on the loan account servicing the investment property contrived by the particular form of the borrowing.

In the course of their judgment, Gleeson CJ and McHugh J commented:

'... the fact that a particular commercial transaction is chosen from a number of possible alternative courses of action because of tax benefits associated with its adoption does not of itself mean that there must be an affirmative answer to the question posed by s 177D [on dominant purpose]. Taxation is part of the cost of doing business, and business transactions are normally influenced by cost considerations. Furthermore, even if a particular form of transaction carries a tax benefit, it does not follow that obtaining

99 *Federal Commissioner of Taxation v Spotless Services* (1996) 186 CLR 404 at 425.

the tax benefit is the dominant purpose of the taxpayer in entering into the transaction. A taxpayer wishing to obtain the right to occupy premises for the purpose of carrying on a business enterprise might decide to lease real estate rather than to buy it. Depending upon a variety of circumstances, the potential deductibility of the rent may be an important factor in the decision. Yet, if there were nothing more to it than that, it would ordinarily be impossible to conclude, having regard to the factors listed in s 177D, that the dominant purpose of the lessee in leasing the land was to obtain a tax benefit. The dominant purpose would be to gain the right to occupy the premises, not to obtain a tax deduction for the rent, even if the availability of the tax deduction meant that leasing the premises was more cost effective than buying them.'[100]

Given the policy objectives of the Australian GAAR and the guidance provided by the Australian High Court to date on its operation, the following broad, general propositions can be made in relation to the ability of taxpayers to enter into tax planning arrangements:

- the Australian GAAR ought not prevent a taxpayer from entering into an ordinary commercial or family dealing which generates a tax benefit. This is the case even where a person or persons enter into the dealing with the subjective intention of securing the tax benefit;
- a dealing that contains a step or aspect that is 'unusual' and which results in a tax benefit may be defeated by the Australian GAAR if there is an alternative way of pursuing the commercial or family objectives that does not include the unusual step or aspect (and does not give rise to the tax benefit), and the unusual step or aspect is only capable of being explained as a means to obtain the tax benefit; and
- similarly, a dealing may be one to which the Australian GAAR applies if the dealing only makes commercial sense when you take into account the tax benefit that it secures.

In Practice Statement Law Administration 2005/24 ('PS LA 2005/24'), the Commissioner sets out instruction and practical guidance for ATO officers on the application of the GAAR. At paragraph 113 of PS LA 2005/24, the Commissioner lists what he refers to as 'warning signs' that an arrangement may be one entered into for the dominant purpose of enabling a taxpayer to obtain a tax benefit. According to the Commissioner, the warning signs are:

(a) a part, or the whole, of the arrangement is out of step with ordinary family or commercial dealings;
(b) the arrangement is more complex than necessary to achieve the relevant family or commercial objective or includes a step, or steps, that appear to serve no purpose other than gaining a tax advantage;[101]
(c) the tax result of the arrangement appears at odds with the commercial or economic result;[102]

100 *Commissioner of Taxation v Hart* (2004) 217 CLR 216 at [15].
101 Examples cited are transactions interposing an entity to access a tax benefit, intra-group or related party dealings that merely produce a tax result and arrangements involving circular funds flows or no real money.
102 The example cited is of a tax loss claimed for what was a profitable commercial venture or transaction.

(d) the arrangement results in little or no risk in circumstances where significant risks would normally be expected;[103]
(e) the parties to the arrangement are operating on non-commercial terms or in a non-arm's length manner;[104] and
(f) there is a gap between the substance and legal form of the arrangement.[105]

8. DEFINING ABUSIVE TAX AVOIDANCE

In Australia, there is no concept of 'Abusive Tax Avoidance'. Either an arrangement satisfies the statutory elements set out in Part IVA of the 1936 Assessment Act necessary to be treated as a scheme to which Part IVA applies or it does not. Arrangements to which Part IVA applies are not graded as more or less 'abusive'.

Further, the existence of the GAAR in Part IVA means that the doctrine of fiscal nullity developed by the United Kingdom courts to defeat abusive tax avoidance arrangements[106] does not find expression in Australian tax law.[107]

9. THE LEGISLATIVE FRAMEWORK

Australia's income tax assessment and collection laws are set out largely in the 1936 Assessment Act, the 1997 Assessment Act and the Administration Act, as well as being informed by common law. As mentioned above, the Australian GAAR is contained in Part IVA of the 1936 Assessment Act.

Whilst the focus of this chapter is Part IVA of the 1936 Assessment Act, there are numerous specific income tax anti-avoidance rules in the 1936 Assessment Act and the 1997 Assessment Act, designed to address particular income tax avoidance schemes.[108] In addition, there are general and specific anti-avoidance rules in the legislative regimes for other Australian federal[109] and state[110] taxes and imposts.

Part IVA

In order for Part IVA to apply:

---

103 Examples cited are the use of non-recourse or limited recourse loans and put options.

104 Examples cited are financial arrangements made on unusual terms such as interest rates above or below market rates, insufficient security or deferment of repayment of the loan for a lengthy period and transactions that do not occur at market rates or value.

105 The example cited is a series of transactions that together produce no economic gain or loss such that the whole scheme is self-cancelling.

106 See the decisions of the House of Lords in *W.T.Ramsay Ltd. v I.R. Commrs* (1982) A.C. 300; *I.R. Commrs v Burmah Oil Co. Ltd.* (1981) (1982) S.T.C. 30 and *Furniss v Dawson* (1984) A.C. 474.

107 See the High Court's comments in *John v Federal Commissioner of Taxation* (1989) 166 CLR 417 at 434-435.

108 For example, the recently enacted 'dividend washing' rules contained in Subdivision 207-F of the Income Tax Assessment Act (1997) (Cth).

109 For example, the Fringe Benefits Tax Assessment Act 1986 (Cth), which imposes fringe benefits tax on employers in relation to the benefits provided to employees or their associates, contains a GAAR provision in s. 67 and the A New Tax System (Goods and Services Tax) Act 1999 (Cth), which imposes the goods and services tax on 'taxable supplies' of certain goods and services, contains a GAAR provision in Division 165. For a recent High Court decision on this GAAR provision, see *Federal Commissioner of Taxation v Unit Trend Services Pty Ltd* (2013) 297 ALR 190.

110 Stamp duty is a state-based tax imposed in every jurisdiction in Australia. All duty acts contain specific anti-avoidance rules, such as landholder rules and land rich rules: (See Chapter 4, Part 4, s. 145-163 of the Duties Act 1997 (NSW); Chapter 3, s. 70-89 of the Duties Act 2000 (Vic); Chapter 3, s. 157-197 of the Duties Act 2001 (Qld); Part 4, s. 91-102G of the Stamp Duties Act 1923 (SA); Chapter 3, s. 148-204 of the Duties Act 2008 (WA); Chapter 3, s. 58-77 of the Duties Act 2001 (Tas); Part 3, Division 8A, s. 56C-56W of the Stamp Duty Act 1978 (NT) and Part 3.2, s. 78-95 of the Duties Act 1999 (ACT). In addition, certain Acts also contain a GAAR (See Chapter 11A of the Duties Act 1997 (NSW); Chapter 2, Part 6 (s. 69A-69D) of the Duties Act 2000 (Vic); Chapter 11 of the Duties Act 2001 (Qld); ss. 70 and 71E Stamp Duties Act 1923 (SA); Division 3A of the Taxation Administration Act 1997 (Tas); Chapter 7, s. 267-271 of the Duties Act 2008 (WA); s. 4B of the Stamp Duty Act 1978 (NT).

(a) a taxpayer must obtain a *tax benefit*[111] in connection with a *scheme*[112]; and
(b) a person who entered into or carried out the whole or a part of the scheme must have done so for the *dominant purpose*[113] of enabling a taxpayer to obtain a tax benefit in connection with the scheme.[114]

Scheme

The concept of a 'scheme' is broad.[115] A scheme within the meaning of s. 177A(1) of the 1936 Assessment Act is not limited to the step which produces the tax benefit,[116] although the tax benefit in question must be related to the scheme identified, as must any conclusion of dominant purpose.[117] Generally, for any transaction or arrangement, it is a relatively easy matter to identify one or more schemes.

Tax benefit

Broadly, a tax benefit is a 'tax advantage' that arises for a taxpayer which would not have arisen, or which might reasonably be expected would not have arisen, but for the scheme. The different types of tax advantages that can constitute tax benefits are set out in s. 177C of the 1936 Assessment Act and include the non-inclusion of amounts in assessable income[118] and taxation deductions being allowable.[119]

In determining whether a taxpayer has obtained a tax benefit, it is necessary to identify and consider an 'alternative postulate' to the scheme – that is, what would have occurred, or might reasonably be expected to have occurred, if the scheme had not been entered into or carried out.[120]

The tax benefit test in Part IVA was amended on 29 June 2013.[121] New s. 177CB of the 1936 Assessment Act sets out two bases for identifying tax benefits by reference to alternative postulates to the scheme:

(a) the 'Annihilation Approach' involves consideration of an alternative postulate to the scheme that consists solely of the events or circumstances that happened or existed other than those that formed part of the scheme.[122] If the result of annihilating the events or circumstances that formed part of the scheme is that the remaining

---

111 Section 177C of the Income Tax Assessment Act 1936 (Cth) outlines the types of tax benefits which a taxpayer may obtain.
112 Defined in s. 177A(1) of the Income Tax Assessment Act 1936 (Cth).
113 Section 177A(5) of the Income Tax Assessment Act 1936 (Cth) states that a reference in this Part to a scheme or a part of a scheme being entered into or carried out by a person for a particular purpose shall be read as including a reference to the scheme or part of the scheme being entered into or carried out by the person for 2 or more purposes of which that particular purpose is the dominant purpose. 'Dominant' purpose is the 'prevailing, ruling or most influential purpose': *Federal Commissioner of Taxation v Spotless Services Ltd* (1996) 186 CLR 404 at 416.
114 Income Tax Assessment Act 1936 (Cth), s. 177D(1).
115 Income Tax Assessment Act 1936 (Cth), s. 177A(1). A 'scheme' means any agreement, arrangement, understanding, promise or undertaking, whether express or implied and whether or not enforceable, or intended to be enforceable, by legal proceedings, or course of conduct. See also *Commissioner of Taxation v Hart* (2004) 217 CLR 216 at [43], [47]-[50] and [55].
116 *British American Tobacco Australia Services Ltd v Commissioner of Taxation* (2010) 189 FCR 151 at [31].
117 *Commissioner of Taxation v Hart* (2004) 217 CLR 216 at [5].
118 Income Tax Assessment Act 1936 (Cth), s. 177C(1)(a).
119 Income Tax Assessment Act 1936 (Cth), s. 177C(1)(b).
120 Income Tax Assessment Act 1936 (Cth), s. 177CB(1).
121 With retrospective affect from 16 November 2012. At the time of publication, there have been no court decisions on the operation of the new provisions.
122 Income Tax Assessment Act 1936 (Cth), s. 177CB(2).

steps in the arrangement do not enable the taxpayer to obtain the relevant 'tax advantage', then there is a tax benefit in connection with the scheme; and

(b) the 'Reconstruction Approach' involves considering an alternative postulate to the scheme which is based on a reasonable reconstruction of what might have occurred had the scheme not been entered into.[123] In determining whether a postulate is a reasonable alternative to the scheme, you need to have particular regard to the substance of the scheme and any result or consequence for the taxpayer that is or would be achieved by the scheme other than an Australian income tax result. Further, you must disregard Australian income tax consequences for any person that would be achieved by the postulate.[124]

A relevant question is when it would be appropriate to use each approach to identify whether there is a tax benefit. Based on comments in the Explanatory Memorandum to Tax Laws Amendment (Countering Tax Avoidance and Multinational Profit Shifting) Act 2013 (Cth),[125] it would seem that it may be appropriate to take the Annihilation Approach where the scheme in question does not produce any material non-tax results for the taxpayers or the scheme shelters economic gains already in existence.[126] The Reconstruction Approach is likely to be appropriate where the scheme achieves substantial non-tax results – typically where the scheme both produces and shelters economic gains.[127]

The challenge for taxpayers in identifying an alternative postulate that is reasonable is that the alternative may not necessarily be the most reasonable or realistic postulate as a matter of commercial reality. This is because the legislation prescribes that, in determining whether a particular postulate is reasonable, you must disregard, or not have particular regard to, each of certain factors that would inevitably impact upon what would or would not occur, as a matter of fact, but for the scheme (ie, Australian income tax results of alternative postulates to the scheme for any person, any result or consequence of the scheme for any person other than the taxpayer and Australian income tax results of the scheme for the taxpayer).[128]

Dominant purpose

When determining the dominant purpose of a person who entered into or carried out a part or the whole of the scheme, regard must be had to eight matters outlined in the legislation.[129] Further, it is necessary to determine a person's purpose by reference to an objective assessment of the eight matters.

The eight matters in s. 177D(2) are:

---

123 Income Tax Assessment Act 1936 (Cth), s. 177CB(3).
124 Income Tax Assessment Act 1936 (Cth), s. 177CB(4).
125 The Act that introduced s. 177CB into the Income Tax Assessment Act 1936 (Cth).
126 Explanatory Memorandum to the Tax Laws Amendment (Countering Tax Avoidance and Multinational Profit Shifting) Act 2013 (Cth), paragraphs 1.82 and 1.84.
127 Explanatory Memorandum to the Tax Laws Amendment (Countering Tax Avoidance and Multinational Profit Shifting) Act 2013 (Cth), paragraphs 1.89 and 1.90.
128 Income Tax Assessment Act 1936 (Cth), s. 177CB(4).
129 The 8 matters are listed in the Income Tax Assessment Act 1936 (Cth), s. 177D(2).

(a) the manner in which the scheme was entered into or carried out;[130]
(b) the form and substance of the scheme;[131]
(c) the time at which the scheme was entered into and the length of the period during which the scheme was carried out;[132]
(d) the result in relation to the operation of the 1936 Assessment Act and the 1997 Assessment Act that, but for Part IVA, would be achieved by the scheme;[133]
(e) any change in the financial position of the relevant taxpayer that has resulted, will result, or may reasonably be expected to result, from the scheme;[134]
(f) any change in the financial position of any person who has, or has had, any connection (whether of a business, family or other nature) with the relevant taxpayer, being a change that has resulted, will result or may reasonably be expected to result, from the scheme;[135]
(g) any other consequence for the relevant taxpayer, or for any person referred to in paragraph (f), of the scheme having been entered into or carried out;[136] and
(h) the nature of any connection (whether of a business, family or other nature) between the relevant taxpayer and any person referred to in paragraph (f).[137]

There is naturally some overlap between the eight matters.[138] In PS LA 2005/24, the Commissioner suggests that the matters can be broadly grouped into the following three sets:

(a) the first set (comprising the matters in ss. 177D(2)(a), (b) and (c)), which considers how the scheme was implemented and how its results were obtained;
(b) the second set (comprising the matters in ss. 177D(2)(d), (e), (f) and (g)), which deals with the effect and consequences of the scheme; and
(c) the third set (comprising the matters in s. 177D(2)(h)), which considers the nature of the connection between the taxpayer and any other parties.[139]

In practice, it is the first set of factors which will often be the focus of the s. 177D(2) analysis and shed most light on the question of whether a person entered into or carried out a part or the whole of the scheme to enable the taxpayer to obtain a tax benefit.[140]

---

130 Income Tax Assessment Act 1936 (Cth), s. 177D(2)(a).
131 Income Tax Assessment Act 1936 (Cth), s. 177D(2)(b).
132 Income Tax Assessment Act 1936 (Cth), s. 177D(2)(c).
133 Income Tax Assessment Act 1936 (Cth), s. 177D(2)(d).
134 Income Tax Assessment Act 1936 (Cth), s. 177D(2)(e).
135 Income Tax Assessment Act 1936 (Cth), s. 177D(2)(f).
136 Income Tax Assessment Act 1936 (Cth), s. 177D(2)(g).
137 Income Tax Assessment Act 1936 (Cth), s. 177D(2)(h).
138 For instance, in *Commissioner of Taxation v Spotless Services Ltd* (1996) 186 CLR 404 at 420, the High Court noted that consideration of the time and duration of the scheme would throw further light upon the form and substance of the scheme and the manner in which it was carried out.
139 Australian Taxation Office, Practice Statement Law Administration PS LA 2005/24, *Application of General Anti-Avoidance Rules*, at paragraph 91.
140 At paragraph 93 of ATO Practice Statement Law Administration PS LA 2005/24, *Application of General Anti-Avoidance Rules*, the Commissioner states that '[t]hese three factors are very important because they examine exactly how a scheme achieves its effects.'

10. KEY CASES OF INTEREST

In this section, we consider some of the key Part IVA cases of interest decided over the last five years. These cases fall into two broad categories being where:

(a) the Commissioner has been successful in applying Part IVA to the scheme in question and the focus of the analysis has been on whether it is possible to identify a person who entered into or carried out the scheme with the dominant purpose of enabling the taxpayer to obtain the tax benefit (the 'dominant purpose cases'); and

(b) the taxpayer has been successful in showing that the scheme in question did not give rise to a tax benefit (the 'tax benefit cases').

In each of the 'dominant purpose cases', the Court concluded that the manner in which the scheme was formulated and/or carried out, when compared with the alternative postulate, was explicable only by taxation consequences. That is, the Commissioner was successful because a step (or steps) or aspect of the relevant transaction/arrangement made no sense without the tax benefit produced.

In contrast, in each of the 'tax benefit cases', the taxpayer was successful in showing that the scheme did not produce a tax benefit when compared to the most reasonable alternative postulate. Prior to the decisions in the tax benefit cases, the Commissioner had viewed the need for the existence of a tax benefit as a 'gateway' requirement readily satisfied where any 'tax advantage' was identified as arising in relation to the scheme.[141] Losses by the Commissioner in the 'tax benefit cases' led the Australian Government to introduce legislative changes in 2013 which, amongst other things, make it easier for the tax benefit criteria in Part IVA to be satisfied. [142]

The 'dominant purpose cases'

The main 'dominant purpose cases' in the last five years were *British American Tobacco Australia Services Ltd v Commissioner of Taxation*[143] ('BAT') and *Commissioner of Taxation v Citigroup Pty Ltd*[144] ('Citigroup'). In both cases, the Courts held that, having regard to the eight matters in s. 177D of the 1936 Assessment Act, a person or persons entered into the scheme with the main purpose of enabling the taxpayer to obtain a tax benefit.

In *BAT*, the Court identified a transfer of brands between wholly owned group companies, prior to a third party sale of the brands, as only capable of explanation by reference to a purpose of obtaining certain capital gains tax ('CGT') relief. The fact that the sale of the brands was part of a broader transaction, a global merger of the BAT and Rothmans groups, that was undoubtedly commercial, did not prevent Part IVA from applying to a scheme involving or including the internal transfer step. Essentially, the

141 See, for example, the Commissioner of Taxation's application for special leave to appeal to the High Court of Australia from the decision in *Federal Commissioner of Taxation v AXA Asia Pacific Holdings Ltd* [2010] 189 FCR 204, at *Commissioner of Taxation v AXA Asia Pacific Holdings Ltd* [2011] HCATrans 63 at 2.

142 The amendments were contained in Tax Laws Amendment (Countering Tax Avoidance and Multinational Profit Shifting) Act 2013 (Cth).

143 (2010) 189 FCR 151.

144 (2011) 193 FCR 380.

reason that the Court was prepared to conclude that a person entered into the scheme with the dominant purpose of enabling a taxpayer to obtain a tax benefit, was that the taxpayer was unable to show that there was a commercial or legal reason for the internal transfer of the brands. The commercial objective of achieving a sale of the brands to the third party could have been achieved on the same terms without first undertaking the internal transfer.

In *Citigroup*, the Court determined that Part IVA applied to a scheme involving a number of transactions in Hong Kong which resulted in the taxpayer becoming entitled to a foreign tax credit in Australia. The Court found that the transaction only made sense from a commercial perspective if the foreign tax credit was obtained. The gains that arose from the transactions were generated not from any commercial return but only from the foreign tax credit. In this sense, obtaining the foreign tax credit was the 'commercial engine that drove the scheme'.[145]

The 'tax benefit cases'

The 'tax benefit cases' are *Federal Commissioner of Taxation v AXA Asia Pacific Holdings Ltd*[146] (*'AXA'*), *RCI Pty Ltd v Commissioner of Taxation*[147] (*'RCI'*) and *Commissioner of Taxation v Futuris Corporation Ltd*[148] (*'Futuris'*). In each of these cases, the taxpayer was able to demonstrate that there was no tax benefit in relation to the scheme identified. This was because the most reasonable alternative course of action to the scheme ('the alternative postulate') would not have resulted in a lesser tax advantage to the relevant taxpayer than the tax advantage obtained under the scheme.

AXA involved certain pre-sale structuring activity which resulted in the taxpayer achieving CGT relief. The structuring activity was devised by an investment bank which was paid substantial fees in relation to its structuring of the sale. The Commissioner identified as alternative postulates to the scheme two different sale scenarios that would not have achieved the CGT relief for the taxpayer. The Court rejected these alternative postulates as reasonable because, in each case, the particular sale structure would not have resulted in the investment bank securing its fees. As such, the bank would not have allowed either sale structure to proceed and neither postulate could constitute a reasonable alternative to the scheme.

RCI involved a global restructure of a multinational group including the payment of a dividend by a company resident in the United States ('US') to its Australian parent company followed by a transfer of the US company to another group company resident in Malta. The dividend payment was not assessable income of the parent company in Australia and, as a result of the value of the US company being reduced by the dividend, there was no CGT on the internal transfer of the shares. The Commissioner identified, as an alternative postulate to the scheme, a transfer of the US company without

145 *Commissioner of Taxation v Citigroup Pty* Ltd (2011) 193 FCR 380 at [68].
146 [2010] 189 FCR 204.
147 (2011) 84 ATR 785. The Court also found that, even if there was a tax benefit, there was no person who entered into or carried out the scheme with the main purpose of enabling the taxpayer to obtain the tax benefit.
148 (2012) 205 FCR 274.

the payment of the dividend. The tax outcome of this alternative postulate was a large taxable capital gain to the Australian parent company. The Court was unwilling to accept that the Commissioner's alternative postulate was reasonable. The Court concluded that it would be unacceptable for a large multinational group to undertake an internal restructure that resulted in substantial tax cost. The most reasonable alternative postulate to the scheme was that the taxpayer would have abandoned the restructure, deferred it or altered it, but it would not have proceeded with a transfer of the shares in the US company at substantial tax cost.

Futuris involved the sale of a division of the taxpayer's business by initial public offering of the shares in a subsidiary company ('IPO'). There was various restructure activity undertaken prior to the IPO which resulted in an uplift in the cost base of the taxpayer's shares in the subsidiary and, consequently, a lower taxable capital gain on the IPO. Of three possible alternative postulates to the scheme, the Court concluded that:

(a) one of the postulates would have given rise to a substantial taxable capital gain to the taxpayer and, on that basis, was not a reasonable alternative to the scheme because, had this been the only option, the taxpayer would not have entered into the sale transaction at all;
(b) a second postulate would have given rise to a large taxable capital gain to a member of the taxpayer's group, other than the taxpayer, but a capital gain to the taxpayer of the same amount as the gain under the scheme; and
(c) a third postulate, which the Court concluded was the most reasonable alternative to the scheme, would have given rise to taxable capital gains for two members of the taxpayer's group, but not the taxpayer itself.

On the basis that the taxable capital gain for the taxpayer under the most reasonable alternative postulate to the scheme was lower than the taxable capital gain under the scheme, the Court concluded that there could not be a tax benefit in relation to the scheme.

The main legislative response to the 'tax benefit cases' is s. 177CB(4) of the 1936 Assessment Act which says, amongst other things, that in determining whether a postulate is a reasonable alternative to entering into or carrying out the scheme in question:

(a) particular regard must be had to any result or consequence for the taxpayer (and no other person) that would be achieved by the scheme (if *AXA* was decided under the current law then, in determining whether the Commissioner's alternative postulates were reasonable, presumably particular regard could not be had to the investment bank not obtaining its fee under those postulates);
(b) particular regard cannot be had to any Australian income tax result of the scheme for the taxpayer (if *RCI* was decided under the current law then, in determining whether the postulate of transferring the US company but not paying the dividend was reasonable, particular regard could not be had to the fact that the scheme did not result in an Australian CGT liability); and

(c) disregard any Australian income tax result that would be achieved by the postulate for any person (if *RCI* was decided under the current law then, in determining whether the postulate of transferring the US company but not paying the dividend was reasonable, regard could not be had to the fact that this postulate would generate a large CGT liability for the taxpayer; and if *Futuris* was decided under the current law then, in assessing the reasonableness of the potential alternative postulates, regard could not be had to the tax consequences for the various Futuris companies, including the taxpayer).

As such, it appears that each of the successful taxpayer arguments in the 'tax benefit cases' as to why it was not possible to identify a reasonable alternative course of action to the scheme which resulted in a tax benefit to the taxpayer is no longer available. Assuming a tax benefit is found to exist, the dominant purpose test still needs to be satisfied for Part IVA to apply.

10.1 Key historical cases

As mentioned above, the current Australian GAAR, contained in Part IVA of the 1936 Assessment Act, was enacted with effect from 1981. Prior to Part IVA, the GAAR was contained in s. 260 of the 1936 Assessment Act. Over a number of years, there were various cases decided by Australia's High Court which highlighted the deficiencies in s. 260 as an effective GAAR. Eventually these cases led to s. 260 being replaced by Part IVA. In that sense, the relevant High Court cases were of key historical significance.

However, the focus of this chapter is the current GAAR in Part IVA. An understanding of how Part IVA operates has developed over time as cases have come before the Courts. Apart from the 'tax benefit cases', referred to in section 10 above, that led to changes to the provisions in Part IVA, the most important Part IVA cases have been those heard by Australia's High Court. In Australia there is no automatic right of appeal to the High Court from the decision of a lower court including the Federal Court of Australia which is Australia's main tax court. The prospective appellant from a decision of the Full Federal Court of Australia must seek special leave from the High Court for it to hear the matter.[149]

To date, there have been four Part IVA cases that the High Court has decided to hear. In each case, the decision of the High Court has been seminal in providing guidance on the scope and application of Part IVA and/or in correcting apparent misconceptions of taxpayers, tax officials and/or lower courts on how the Part operates. Each of the High Court cases is considered below.

[149] Generally, the High Court will only hear a matter if:
- it is in the interests of the administration of justice that it does so;
- the matter involves a question of law that is of public importance; or
- a High Court ruling is necessary to resolve differences of opinion between the courts of one State or between the courts of different States, (per s. 35A of the Judiciary Act 1903 (Cth)), and
- the case is an appropriate vehicle for an appeal to the High Court where the matter can be heard.

Federal Commissioner of Taxation v Peabody[150] ('Peabody')
Peabody was the first Part IVA case to come before the High Court. The case was instructive in the guidance that the High Court provided on:
(a) the Commissioner's ability to advance alternative schemes in support of a Part IVA determination; and
(b) the difficulties the Commissioner may face at times in identifying the taxpayer that has received the tax benefit.

The case involved pre-transaction structuring in relation to the public float of 50% of the Pozzolanic Group of companies. It was proposed that prior to the float one of the two principals in the business (Mr. Peabody) would acquire the shares owned by the other principal (Mr. Kleinschmidt). It was anticipated that the ensuing public float would be capitalised at a figure well in excess of the amount that was the basis of the price agreed for the Kleinschmidt shares. At that time, there was a rule that any gain on disposal of property (including shares) held for less than 12 months would be subject to Australian tax. To overcome the application of this rule to the contribution of the Kleinschmidt shares into the float, the shares were acquired by a company called Loftway Pty Ltd ('Loftway') and converted into 'Z' class preference shares carrying restricted rights, thereby reducing their value to a nominal amount. The trustee of the Peabody Family Trust, TEP Holdings Pty Ltd ('TEP'), transferred all of the ordinary shares in the Pozzolanic Group to a float company in consideration for a mixture of cash and 50% of the shares in the float company. The remaining 50% of the shares in the float company were then offered to the public.

The Commissioner claimed that the pre-float structuring represented a scheme to which Part IVA applied and assessed Mrs Peabody to an additional amount of tax on the basis of her being presently entitled (as a beneficiary of the Peabody Family Trust) to one third of the taxable profit that TEP would have realised had it, rather than Loftway, bought the Kleinschmidt shares and sold them within 12 months of their acquisition.

The Commissioner had identified as the scheme to which Part IVA applied, 10 steps, one of which was the conversion of the shares in the Pozzolanic Group into the 'Z' class shares. The High Court rejected the earlier Full Federal Court view that the Commissioner was confined to the scheme identified in the particulars. Rather, the Commissioner was entitled to put his Part IVA case in alternative ways. If within the broader 10 step scheme identified, the Commissioner also wished to rely upon a narrower scheme involving the devaluation of the Kleinschmidt shares (by their conversion into 'Z' class shares) and their subsequent disposal, as meeting the Part IVA requirements, then he was entitled to do so.

However, the High Court was unwilling to find that Mrs. Peabody had received a tax benefit in this case because it was not reasonable to expect that, but for the scheme, she would have derived the gain on the sale of the Kleinschmidt shares. In order for this to have occurred, it would have been necessary for TEP rather than Loftway to have acquired the Kleinschmidt

---

150 (1994) 181 CLR 359.

shares. This was not a reasonable expectation as it was uncertain that TEP would have been entitled to a tax rebate on the dividends on those shares (a necessary pre-requisite of it acquiring the shares). As such, had the devaluation not occurred, any profit on the sale of the Kleinschmidt shares would have been obtained by Loftway so that it was the party that obtained the tax benefit in connection with the scheme.

As such, *Peabody* was an early demonstration of one of the difficulties that can arise for the Commissioner at times in seeking to apply Part IVA by identifying the taxpayer that received the tax benefit. The difficulty lies in showing that it is a reasonable expectation that, but for the scheme, that particular taxpayer would have received the unfavourable tax outcome obviated by the scheme. *Peabody* may also be viewed as a precursor to the 'tax benefit cases', referred to in section 10 above, which led to the recent amendments to Part IVA.

Spotless

The facts and decision in *Spotless* are set out in section 7 above.

As mentioned in section 7, *Spotless* provided guidance on what constitutes acceptable tax planning to which Part IVA ought not to apply, and what constitutes unacceptable tax planning that attracts the operation of the Part.

In addition, *Spotless* was instructive in the guidance that the High Court provided that:

(a) a person may enter into a scheme to which Part IVA applies where the person's dominant purpose is consistent with the pursuit of commercial gain in the course of carrying on a business.[151] A particular course of action may be both 'tax driven' and bear the character of a rational commercial decision by virtue of being directed to achieving the highest net (after-tax) return for the taxpayer. The presence of the 'rational commercial decision' in undertaking the scheme does not necessarily mean that it is not a scheme to which Part IVA applies.[152]

(b) the 'dominant' purpose of a person in entering into or carrying out a scheme is the 'ruling, prevailing, or most influential purpose',[153] rather than the purpose that is more dominant than all other purposes combined.

Commissioner of Taxation v Consolidated Press Holdings Ltd & Anor[154] ('CPH')

CPH involved a proposal that the Consolidated Press group of companies ('CP group') would participate in a takeover bid for a United Kingdom ('UK') company, BAT Industries plc ('BATI'). The Part IVA issue related to interest on money borrowed for the purpose of the takeover. The funding of the CP group's involvement in the takeover bid involved three Australian CP group companies. The first company ('CP 1') loaned funds to a second company

151 *Federal Commissioner of Taxation v Spotless Services Ltd* (1996) 186 CLR 404 at 415.
152 *Federal Commissioner of Taxation v Spotless Services Ltd* (1996) 186 CLR 404 at 415-416.
153 *Federal Commissioner of Taxation v Spotless Services Ltd* (1996) 186 CLR 404 at 416.
154 (2001) 207 CLR 235.

('CP 2') which then used the funds to subscribe for preference shares in a third company ('CP 3'). Through further share subscriptions, the funds flowed down a chain of offshore companies, with the ultimate recipient of the funds announcing its takeover bid for BATI. Subject to the potential application of Part IVA, interest paid by CP 2 on the funds borrowed from CP 1 for the immediate purposes of taking up shares in CP 3 and the broader purpose of allowing the CP group to participate in the takeover of BATI would have been tax deductible to CP 2. The Commissioner claimed that, but for tax considerations, it would be reasonable to expect that the Australian funding flows for the takeover bid would have taken the form of a loan from CP 1 to CP 2 and an acquisition by CP 2 of shares in the first company in the offshore chain of companies. The Commissioner argued that the interposition of CP 3 in the funding structure was critical to securing the deductibility of the interest paid by CP 2. But for this step, s. 79D of the 1936 Assessment Act would have operated to quarantine tax deductions for the interest to offset against dividends flowing from the offshore investments as a result of the BATI takeover. The impact of this would have been a significant denial of deductions in the early years.

The High Court determined that the interposition of CP 3 in the funding structure was a scheme to which Part IVA applied.

In so concluding, the High Court advised that:

(a) when assessing the purpose of a person who entered into or carried out the scheme, the Court may form a global assessment of purpose, provided that in doing so it takes all eight of the matters in s. 177D(2) into account;[155]

(b) the Court may attribute the purpose of a professional advisor to one or more parties to a scheme, particularly where, given the scope and complexity of the scheme, it would be expected that the parties would seek expert advice. One of the reasons for s. 177D turning upon an objective view of the matters listed in the section is to avoid the operation of Part IVA depending upon the fiscal awareness of the taxpayer; and[156]

(c) as held by the High Court in *Spotless*, a person may enter into or carry out a scheme for the dominant purpose of enabling a taxpayer to obtain a tax benefit where that dominant purpose is consistent with the pursuit of commercial gain in the course of carrying on a business. Part of the structure of a transaction pursued for commercial gain may be explained by reference to a s. 177D purpose. Further, it is a valid approach to look to the wider transaction in order to understand and explain the scheme and the eight matters listed in s. 177D(2).[157]

Hart

The facts and decision in *Hart* are set out in section 7 above.

155 *Commissioner of Taxation v Consolidated Press Holdings Ltd & Anor* (2001) 207 CLR 235 at [94].
156 *Commissioner of Taxation v Consolidated Press Holdings Ltd & Anor* (2001) 207 CLR 235 at [95].
157 *Commissioner of Taxation v Consolidated Press Holdings Ltd & Anor* (2001) 207 CLR 235 at [96].

Again, as mentioned in section 7, *Hart* provided guidance on how to draw the distinction between acceptable tax planning and unacceptable tax avoidance.

In addition, *Hart* was instructive in the guidance that the High Court provided on:

(a) the importance in the Part IVA analysis of the composition of the scheme. The Court stated that any tax benefit identified must be related to the scheme as must any conclusion as to dominant purpose. In *Hart*, the special, or non-standard, features of the financing arrangements were critical to the scheme in connection with which the tax benefit (the additional interest on the borrowing referable to the investment property) was obtained. These features involved applying all payments to the home loan portion of the borrowing, leaving interest on the balance of the loan referable to the investment property to accrue and be capitalised and compounded;[158]

(b) whether the scheme is defined broadly or narrowly ought not to impact upon the ultimate question of whether Part IVA applies. The reason for this is that the central question in the Part IVA analysis is whether it would be concluded, having regard to the eight matters listed in s. 177D(2), that a person entered into the broader scheme, the narrower scheme or any part of either scheme with the dominant purpose of enabling the taxpayer to obtain a tax benefit in connection with the scheme;[159] and

(c) to draw a conclusion about the purpose of a person who entered into or carried out the whole or a part of a scheme, it is necessary to consider what other possibilities existed to achieve the non-tax objectives of the scheme.[160] The existence of other ways of achieving those objectives may inform the objective assessment and conclusions as to purpose reached on an application of the eight matters in s. 177D(2).[161]

11. PENALTIES

The Administration Act imposes specific administrative penalties in respect of schemes entered into to which Part IVA or other anti-avoidance provisions apply.[162]

In addition, entities that engage in the promotion or implementation of tax exploitation schemes may be subject to civil penalties under what is known as the promoter penalty regime.[163]

158 *Commissioner of Taxation v Hart* (2004) 217 CLR 216 per Gleeson and McHugh JJ at [5]-[6].

159 *Commissioner of Taxation v Hart* (2004) 217 CLR 216 per Gummow and Hayne JJ at [54]-[56]. In the Full Federal Court decision of *Hart v Commissioner of Taxation* (2002) 121 FCR 206 at 231, Justice Hely had determined that '[t]he more the scheme can be confined to the essential elements by which the tax benefit is obtained, the more likely it will be that the conclusion will be drawn that the dominant purpose for a person entering into a scheme so defined was to obtain the tax benefit.'

160 *Commissioner of Taxation v Hart* (2004) 217 CLR 216 per Gummow and Hayne JJ at [66].

161 In *Commissioner of Taxation v Hart* (2004) 217 CLR 216 per Gummow and Hayne JJ at [66], in the context of the first matter in s 177D(2)(a) (the manner in which the scheme was entered into), the existence of other ways of achieving those objectives which have less advantageous tax consequences may mean that the manner in which the scheme was entered into or carried out points towards a conclusion that it was directed to obtaining the tax benefit.

162 Taxation Administration Act 1953 (Cth), Schedule 1, Subdivision 284-C.

163 Taxation Administration Act 1953 (Cth), Schedule 1, Subdivision 290-B.

11.1 Legislative provisions

Scheme penalties

Broadly, a taxpayer is liable to a penalty where:

(a) the taxpayer would, apart from a provision in a taxation law, receive a 'scheme benefit' from a 'scheme'; and

(b) it is reasonable to conclude that a person entered into the whole or a part of the scheme for the 'sole or dominant purpose' of the taxpayer receiving a scheme benefit from the scheme.[164]

Scheme has the same broad meaning as in Part IVA (discussed at section 9). An entity receives a 'scheme benefit' if its tax-related liability 'is, or could reasonably be expected to be, less than it would be apart from the scheme', or an amount the Commissioner must pay or credit the entity 'is, or could reasonably be expected to be, more than it would be apart from the scheme or a part of the scheme'.[165]

Under the penalties regime, a base penalty amount applies which may then be adjusted up or down, depending on various factors. For Part IVA schemes, generally the base penalty amount is either 25% or 50% of the 'scheme shortfall amount'.[166] The 'scheme shortfall amount' is the amount of the scheme benefit the taxpayer would have received but for the application of the anti-avoidance rule.[167]

The 25% rate applies where the taxpayer has a "reasonably arguable position" that the anti-avoidance rule does not apply. A matter will be reasonably arguable where, taking account of relevant authorities 'what is argued for is about as likely to be correct as incorrect, or is more likely to be correct than incorrect.'[168] 'Relevant authorities' is defined to include the law itself, certain material which assists in interpreting the law, decisions of a court or tribunal and public rulings.[169]

The base penalty amount can be a lesser amount to the extent that it was caused by the taxpayer applying the law in a way which is consistent with general administrative practice or advice given to the taxpayer by the Commissioner.[170]

The base penalty amount can then be increased or reduced depending upon the circumstances. The base penalty amount may be increased by 20% in certain circumstances where the taxpayer prevents or obstructs the

164 Taxation Administration Act 1953 (Cth), Schedule 1, s. 284-145. For schemes within the ambit of Division 165 of the A New Tax System (Goods and Services Tax) Act 1999 (Cth) or Division 75 of the Fuel Tax Act 2006 (Cth), the test is whether a person entered into the whole, or a part, of the scheme for the 'sole or dominant purpose' of the taxpayer receiving a scheme benefit from the scheme or 'the principal effect of the scheme, or of part of the scheme, is that you would, apart from the adjustment provision, get the scheme benefit from the scheme directly or indirectly': s. 284-145(1)(b)(ii) of Schedule 1 of the Taxation Administration Act 1953 (Cth).
Part IVA includes specific provisions, ss. 177EA and 177EB of the Income Tax Assessment Act 1936 (Cth), directed at countering franking credit schemes. For these sections to apply, it is enough if a person entered into the whole, or a part, of the scheme 'for a purpose (whether or not the dominant purpose but not including an incidental purpose)' of the taxpayer obtaining imputation benefits. This is a lower threshold than the test for the imposition of penalties in s. 285-145 of Schedule 1 of the Taxation Administration Act 1953 (Cth) and raises the possibility that a franking credit scheme might be found to exist but penalties found not to apply because, although a person had a non-incidental purpose of enabling the taxpayer to obtain the imputation benefits, it was not the person's 'dominant' purpose.

165 Taxation Administration Act 1953 (Cth), Schedule 1, s. 284-150(1).

166 Taxation Administration Act 1953 (Cth), Schedule 1, s. 284-160(1).

167 Taxation Administration Act 1953 (Cth), Schedule 1, s. 284-150(2).

168 Taxation Administration Act 1953 (Cth), Schedule 1, s. 284-15(1).

169 Taxation Administration Act 1953 (Cth), Schedule 1, s. 284-15(3).

170 Taxation Administration Act 1953 (Cth), Schedule 1, s. 284-224.

Commissioner from finding out about a scheme shortfall amount or where a similar penalty was imposed for a previous accounting period.[171] Conversely, the base penalty amount may be reduced by 20% where the taxpayer voluntarily discloses the scheme shortfall to the Commissioner after the Commissioner has told the taxpayer that an examination of its tax affairs is to be made or by 80% where the taxpayer's disclosure occurs prior to the Commissioner telling the taxpayer of the examination.[172]

Promoter penalty regime

The promoter penalty regime is intended to deter the promotion and implementation of 'tax exploitation schemes' and applies in addition to any action that may be taken against a taxpayer under Part IVA. Broadly, it applies where an entity:

(a) is a promoter of a tax exploitation scheme; or

(b) engages in conduct that results in a scheme that has been promoted on the basis of conformity with a taxation product ruling being implemented in a way that is materially different to that described in the ruling.[173]

If the Federal Court considers that the promoter penalty regime applies then it may, on application from the Commissioner, impose civil penalties or grant injunctions.[174] The Commissioner may also accept a written undertaking from an entity for the purposes of furthering the objects of the promoter penalty regime.[175] In the event that the entity breaches the undertaking, the Commissioner may apply to the Court for an order directing that the entity comply with the undertaking, or any other order the Court considers appropriate.[176]

11.2 Examples of penalties imposed

In the event that Part IVA applies, the level of penalties imposed will depend largely upon whether the taxpayer has a reasonably arguable position that the Part does not apply.[177]

Case law provides guidance on what makes a position 'reasonably arguable' in the context of a GAAR.[178] The Commissioner has also published guidance on his view.[179] The test has been described as whether 'on balance, the taxpayer's argument can objectively be said to be one that, while wrong, could be argued on rational grounds to be right.'[180]

171 Taxation Admininstration Act 1953 (Cth), Schedule 1, s. 284-220(2).

172 Taxation Administration Act 1953 (Cth), Schedule 1, s. 284-225.

173 Taxation Administration Act 1953 (Cth), Schedule 1, s. 290-50.

174 Taxation Administration Act 1953 (Cth), Schedule 1, s. 290-50(3) and Subdivision 290-C.

175 Taxation Administration Act 1953 (Cth), Schedule 1, s. 290-200(1).

176 Taxation Administration Act 1953 (Cth), Schedule 1, ss. 290-200(3) and (4).

177 Penalties may be higher in the circumstances referred to in Taxation Administration Act 1953 (Cth), Schedule 1, s. 284-220(2) and lower in the circumstances referred to in Taxation Administration Act 1953 (Cth), Schedule 1, ss. 284-224 and 284-225.

178 See, for example, *Walstern v Commissioner of Taxation* (2003) 138 FCR 1 at [108].

179 Australian Taxation Office, Miscellaneous Tax Ruling MT 2008/2, *Shortfall Penalties: Administrative penalty for taking a position that is not reasonably arguable.*

180 *Spotlight Stores Pty Ltd v Commissioner of Taxation* (2004) 55 ATR 745 at [118].

12. CURRENT TRENDS

Over many years, successive Australian governments have attempted to implement measures to combat abusive tax avoidance practices. In that regard, Australia has had a form of GAAR since the introduction of Federal income tax in 1915.[181] In addition, Australia has enacted numerous specific anti-avoidance provisions over the years in attempts to curb particular arrangements viewed as taking advantage, inappropriately, of particular concessions in the tax law.

There is no indication that the policy settings of the current Australian government will lead to any change in this focus. In addition, Australia will continue to be a strong proponent of international efforts to eradicate tax avoidance including BEPS.

12.1 National policy and law

As mentioned, the current GAAR contained in Part IVA of the 1936 Assessment Act was introduced in 1981. The general efficacy and scope of application of Part IVA have been tested in the Courts on numerous occasions. This has identified weaknesses in the operation of the provisions, in particular, in relation to how you identify a 'tax benefit', which the legislature has sought to address.[182] Following the changes, we anticipate a further period of uncertainty in Australia regarding the scope of operation of the new GAAR until the Courts hear and decide some additional Part IVA cases.

12.1.1 The impact and role of the OECD and other international relations

From an international perspective, it is highly likely that Australia will seek to co-operate closely with other OECD members to combat BEPS by multinational companies. It seems to us that efforts in this area will include possible co-operation between countries in amending and harmonising, as necessary, taxation treaties and specific anti-avoidance rules including transfer pricing. Additional areas of focus may include base taxation principles (eg, the efficacy of source and residency rules in the digital global economy) and information sharing.

The operation of the Australian GAAR is unlikely to be a particular focus of the international efforts. Its scope of application is broader than dealing with international tax avoidance arrangements (although there may be some such arrangements that come within its terms)[183] and there are specific anti-avoidance measures such as transfer pricing rules which are more effective in addressing international tax avoidance practices.

---

181 Part IVA was introduced in 1981 to replace s. 260 of the Income Tax Assessment Act 1936 (Cth). The origins of s. 260 can in turn be traced to s. 53 of the Income Tax Assessment Act 1915 (Cth).

182 Refer to Tax Laws Amendment (Countering Tax Avoidance and Multinational Profit Shifting) Act 2013 (Cth) and the commentary at section 10 above.

183 Note that an objective of double tax treaties is to counter fiscal evasion. Generally, where a term of a treaty and a provision in the Income Tax Assessment Act 1936 (Cth) or the Income Tax Assessment Act 1997 (Cth) conflict, the treaty prevails. However, a treaty does not prevail over the provisions in Part IVA. As discussed in section 2.3, the Australian Taxation Office is of the view that the tax treaties provide a separate taxing power to the domestic transfer pricing legislation.

Austria

BMA Brandstätter Rechtsanwälte GmbH
Dr Jürgen Brandstätter & Victoria Rosengren, LLM

PART ONE: TRANSFER PRICING

1. GENERAL OVERVIEW

Based on the assumption that budgetary needs require an increase in tax, the Austrian government has taken several measures to ensure, in its own words, fair and efficient taxation. When multi-national corporations are taxed in Austria according to double taxation treaties which are based on the OECD Double Taxation Model Treaty, authorities want to make sure that this does not lead to effective double non-taxation. To achieve this, Austria, one of the founding members of the Organisation for Economic Co-operation and Development (OECD), has adopted the OECD Transfer Pricing Guidelines (TPG).[1] In addition, the Austrian Ministry of Finance has published the Transfer Pricing Directive 2010 (*Verrechnungspreisrichtlinie*[2] or *VPR 2010*).[3] It is currently working on the automatic exchange of information with as many foreign tax authorities as possible.[4]

2. IDENTIFICATION OF LEGISLATIVE FRAMEWORK

According to Article 9 para. 1 of the OECD Double Taxation Model Treaty, a state may adjust profits if '*conditions are made or imposed between the two enterprises in their commercial or financial relations which differ from those which would be made between independent enterprises, then any profits which would, but for those conditions, have accrued to one of the enterprises, but, by reason of those conditions, have not so accrued, may be included in the profits of that enterprise and taxed accordingly*'. In other words, the Austrian Revenue Service may make an adjustment if a corporation has disregarded the arm's length principle. The primary adjustment to the Austrian tax base is done under Austrian tax law since this is an Austrian tax matter. The main statutory provision enabling the Austrian authorities to make these adjustments is Section 6 EStG 1988 (*Einkommensteuergesetz 1988*; the Austrian Income Tax Code 1988 abbreviated as EStG 1988).[5] However, since the provision is merely the national codification of the international 'arms-length-

1 The German version for Austria, Switzerland and Germany is published under AÖF Numbers 114/1996, 122/1997, 155/1998 and 171/2000.

2 To be found under *https://findok.bmf.gv.at/findok?execution=e100000s1&dokumentId=2416ddaa-05dd-457d-a3cf-26c113f9e197*.

3 The transfer pricing guidelines may be used in the version in which they were available at the time the double taxation treaty was concluded, unless the later transfer pricing guidelines had a mere explanatory function and were not in contradiction with the applicable version at the time that the double taxation agreement was concluded (UFS July 30, 2012, RV/2515-W/09).

4 To be found under *http://www.oecd.org/ctp/exchange-of-tax-information/automaticexchange.htm*.

5 VPR marginal note 14.

principle', it needs to be interpreted in consistence with the double taxation treaties, the TPG[6] and the VPR 2010,[7] which are considered 'leges speciales'. A secondary adjustment (ie, another state has made the adjustment and Austria needs to make the corresponding adjustment to avoid double taxation) is made according to the OECD Double Taxation Model Treaty.

2.1 Federal legislation

The main provision with regard to transfer price adjustments is Section 6 ciff. 6 EStG 1988 in its current version. There are also provisions in the *Körperschaftsteuergesetz 1988* in its current version (the Corporate Income tax Code 1988, abbreviate as KStG) and the *Bundesabgabenordnung* (The Austrian Federal Fiscal Code abbreviated as BAO). There are also general provisions such as 'substance over form', fictitious transactions, hidden capital contributions and constructive dividends, which are assessed under prevailing (case) law. Since double taxation is part of international law, the court may also look at case law from other countries with similar statutory provisions.[8]

2.2 State and provincial legislative interplay

Although there are state and local taxes, such as tourist taxes, these do not play a role when determining a potential adjustment to transfer prices.

2.3 International treaties and agreements

The transfer pricing guidelines have the status of administrative decrees. Nevertheless, since they are used to determine the scope of double taxation treaties, they have legal relevance and are considered by the courts to be an important tool for interpretation.[9] These double taxation treaties exist with numerous countries.[10] Some agreements like the double taxation agreement with Liechtenstein (1901) date back to the first half of the twentieth century and are therefore well established. Most of the Agreements are based on the OECD Model Convention which has evolved into an Austrian Model since 1998. Nevertheless, there have been problems when profit adjustments, based on transfer pricing considerations by foreign revenue services, have led to a heavier tax burden for the Austrian taxpayer and effective double taxation. However, if presented with proper documentation, the Austrian Revenue Service may make the correlative adjustment retrospectively

6 The TPG were published in Austria as administrative decrees. Although they do not have the force of law, they are an important indication on the approach the authorities are likely to take with regard to transfer pricing.

7 The guidelines provide help when interpreting the arm's-length principle and, according to the introduction, do not create rights in themselves.

8 See the reference to German case law in the VPR and in particular, marginal note 12 and 13.

9 UFS 14.3.2005, RV/2154-L/02.

10 Albania, Algeria, Argentina, Armenia, Azerbaijan, Australia, Bahrain, Barbados, Belarus, Belgium, Belize, Bosnia Herzegovina, Brazil, Bulgaria, Canada, China, (former) CSSR, Croatia, Cuba, Cyprus, Czech Republic, Denmark, Egypt, Estonia, Finland, France, Georgia, Germany, Great Britain, Greece, Hong Kong, Hungary, India, Indonesia, Iran, Israel, Italy, Japan, Kazakhstan, Kuwait, Kyrgyzstan, Latvia, Liechtenstein, Lithuania, Luxembourg, Macedonia, Malaysia, Malta, Morocco, Mexico, Moldavia, Mongolia, Nepal, Netherlands, New Zealand, Norway, Pakistan Philippines, Poland, Portugal, Qatar, Republic of Ireland, Romania, Russia, San Marino, Saudi Arabia, Serbia, Singapore, Slovakia, Slovenia, South Africa, South Korea, Spain, Sweden, Switzerland, Tadzhikistan, Thailand, Tunisia, Turkey, Turkmenistan, (former) USSR (Soviet Union), Ukraine, United Arab Emirates, United States of America, Uzbekistan, Venezuela, Vietnam.

and has done so in the past.[11] So far, the application has not given rise to concerns and the number of audits performed by the Austrian Revenue Service is more or less stable.[12]

3. NATIONAL POLICY ISSUES

The main policy is to combat tax avoidance and transfer of profits through aggressive tax planning and legal offshore structures.[13] This includes, but is not limited to, the battle against shell corporations and tax havens.[14] Financing interests, patent rights and licencing fees are no longer deductible if transferred to a country with low taxation. However, recognizing that such legislative effort might not be enough, a new department in the Ministry of Finance shall be set up.[15] As a measure to increase revenues, the financial transaction tax seems to be one of the main priorities of the Austrian government [16] even though it raises legal and economic concerns.

3.1 Overall national policy announcements

So far, the Ministry of Finance has taken note of the OECD's action plan on base erosion and profit shifting but has not indicated any concrete changes to the Austrian tax codes. It has also not taken any initiatives with regard to documentation requirements for transfer pricing purposes. However, the Ministry of Finance has taken action to avoid double-non-taxation by modifying Section 12 para. 1 ciff. 10 KStG which now states that interests or license fees are not deductible as expenses if the receiving entity only pays taxes at a level lower than what would have been due in Austria, or if it pays no taxes at all. Nevertheless, the new regulation leaves many questions for the courts to answer and even the Revenue Service is dissatisfied with it.

3.2 National revenue authority initiatives

The Austrian Revenue Service has started the new pilot project of 'Horizontal Monitoring' where, rather than evaluating tax statements afterwards, the authorities continuously evaluate the tax situation with a company. Some companies have volunteered to participate and have signed a participation agreement with rights and duties. The aim is to establish a culture of tax compliance and use existing information in the company (eg, information gathered for filing under the Sarbanes-Oxley Act) to facilitate, in time, the determination of a fair tax base. Participating companies are not only scrutinized but have also received training and support by the fiscal authorities. Further assistance to the taxpayer is provided by the possibility to request an Advanced Ruling in transfer pricing matters since January 1, 2011.

---

11 EAS 2493, 19.7.2004.

12 As published by the Ministry of Finance for the years 2013, 2011 and 2010: *https://www.bmf.gv.at/services/publikationen/berichte-bilanzen.html*.

13 Summarized by the OECD as „base erosion'.

14 Characterized by the OECD in 1998 by the following elements: No or very little tax on capital gains, no or very little disclosure or supervision, rules for shell corporations without the need for commercial activity and no exchange of information with other jurisdictions.

15 *'Arbeitsprogramm der österreichischen Bundesregierung 2013–2018'* (Working Paper by the Austrian Government, 2013-2018), page 107.

16 Statement by Austrian Federal Chancellor Faymann on August 21, 2013.

3.3 Administrative statements

Since issuing the VPR in 2010 the Ministry of Finance has not issued any further statements, guidelines or decrees. However, if a question of transfer pricing arises in a particular context, there is the possibility to request an EAS (abbreviation for 'Express-Answering-Service' or the German translation 'Express-Antwort-Service). Nevertheless, the EAS was, and is, only able to answer simple transfer pricing questions and they are neither binding nor coordinated with other governments. Interested parties may also separately or in addition request an 'Auskunftsbescheid' which translates as an administrative statement for information purposes (Section 118 BAO). This can be done if the taxpayer can prove that due to significant fiscal consequences there is a legal interest in a decision before actions are taken. With regard to transfer prices, these decisions are binding. The question underlining such a request must be very precise since only the facts presented to the Federal Ministry of Finance are covered by the statement. Unsatisfactory statements may be appealed and subsequently changed (compare Section 108 para. 9 BAO).[17] With regard to transfer pricing, the past has shown that it makes sense to request a statement with regard to the choice of the proper transfer pricing method, its application (eg, actual or planned costs) and the necessary documentation.

3.4 Administrative Guidelines

The Ministry of Finance has published the Transfer Pricing Directive 2010 (*Verrechnungspreisrichtlinie* or VPR 2010). No additional guidelines are currently planned.

4. CASE LAW

There are very few cases, past and present, dealing with transfer pricing. What can be said is that the courts look very carefully at the facts and the evidence and so far have taken a very balanced approach.

4.1 Current cases

The most recent decision by the Federal Court for Finance of May 7, 2014[18] dealt with a case where the prices charged to the Austrian subsidiary were underpinned with documentation evidencing an arms-length transaction. However, the subsidiary had such a number of outstanding receivables that it had to make value adjustments in the annual accounts. The Revenue Service argued that this clearly was a sign of intra-company dealing in violation of the arm's length principle because independent entities would work for profit. Nevertheless, the court concluded that it was not uncommon to make adjustments with large clients and that depreciation in itself does not mean that the companies would not demand settlement at some point in the future. Thus, the court rejected an adjustment of the Austrian tax base.

17 Details are provided in the Advanced Ruling Directive *https://findok.bmf.gv.at/findok?execution=e100000s1&segmentId=bc51ee4e-7a28-4a9d-9487-2a8def41955c.*

18 RV/7100052/2012.

In a ruling passed December 6, 2013,[19] the court of appeal rejected a decision by the Revenue Service to reopen the tax files of an Austrian subsidiary for the years 2006, 2007 and 2008 with regard to corporate income tax. Revenue Services was of the opinion that it was imperative for a dependant subsidiary (sales company) to make a profit. Hence the resale price method, as used by the company was to be rejected and prices were to be set at the level of cost plus 10 per cent. The court rejected the argument that the company had presented insufficient documentation and in particular, that it had failed its duties by not submitting annual accounts of the parent company. It also rejected the argument that the fact that the company generated losses for three years was in itself an indicator that transfer pricing was wrong.[20] The court determined that due to the fact that the same prices had produced profit in other years they should have let Revenue Services look at other reasons to justify the losses. Since prices were determined according to the prevailing resale method and the documentation supported the calculation according to this method, this should have been recognized by Revenue Services. Since the annual accounts of the parent company were not needed to support the calculation, there was no obligation to submit it and Revenue Services had exceeded its powers by requesting it. The court's conclusion was that if a standard method is used to calculate transfer prices and if such method is supported by proper documentation, if the Revenue Service wants to assume a different tax base in calculating prices, they have the burden of proof. The court was very explicit in stating that the Revenue Service may not willfully set a desired tax base without legal justification.

4.2 Historical cases of note

In an appeal July 30, 2012,[21] the court had to decide with regard to prices charged by the parent company to the Austrian subsidiary (sales company). The court found that transfer prices had to be determined from evidence gathered before the prices were set. The court urged a careful application of data base studies when determining appropriate prices. The court rejected the determination according to quantitative data but determined that such data could be used to cross reference the plausibility of qualitative data base studies. In the decision of April 28, 2010,[22] the court overturned a decision by Revenue Services to adjust prices 15 per cent based on the sole argument that when dealing with services, a profit margin of 5 per cent to 15 per cent are common. The court found that Revenue Services had failed to satisfy the burden of proof in the individual case.[23] The Federal Administrative Court, in its decision of October 20, 2009,[24] ruled that if Revenue Services wants to

[19] RV/0514–F/10.

[20] The Federal Ministry for Finance already decided, in 1993, that losses in three consecutive years were to be recognized and were not per se an argument against the arm's length principle (published in ecolex 1993, 125).

[21] RV/2515-W/09.

[22] RV/3837-W/09.

[23] The Administrative Supreme Court has ruled in other cases that the burden of proving that the arm's length principle was observed shifts to the company if it did not observe the 'close relatives rule' (*'Angehörigenjudikatur'*). Close relatives need to provide (written) proof of an agreement and its content must be definite, clear and beyond questioning (VwGH November 22, 2012, 2008/15/0265).

[24] VwGH 2006/13/0116.

adjust the tax base and increase prices, it has to be done in a way that third parties may understand the reasoning behind such a price increase. At the same time, the court must first examine the methods and results of transfer pricing as chosen by the taxpayer.

The very limited jurisdiction shows that so far, Austrian case law is hard to predict. What can be said is that courts seem to look very carefully at attempts made by the Revenue Service to increase profits randomly. If the company can show that prices are calculated according to the prevailing method, based on the proper documentation, Revenue Service has to present counter evidence to warrant a price adjustment.

5. PENALTIES

There is no specific penalty regime regarding the non-compliance with transfer pricing obligations in Austria. However, incomplete transfer pricing documentation increases the risk that the responsible tax auditor at the Revenue Service will regard a transaction as non-compliant with the arm's length principle and apply a tax base adjustment. In cases where the taxpayer is involved in cross border transactions, the general duty of cooperation according to Section 115 BAO is increased and the taxpayer has to provide Revenue Service with full documentation of the cross border dealings.[25] In cases where the tax payer is unable to provide documentation, Revenue Service may even be allowed to estimate the tax base pursuant to Section 184 para. 3 BAO. Additionally, the company runs the risk that such intra company payments will be deemed hidden dividends and thus, subject to dividend tax.[26] The company and its officers may also face criminal liability under the *Finanzstrafgesetz* (Criminal Fiscal Code abbreviated as FinStrG). Transfer prices in violation of the arm's-length principle may constitute intentional or negligent tax fraud (Sections 33, 34 FinStrG). Even though the taxpayer does not have to incriminate himself in the criminal proceeding (Section 84 FinStrG), the provision is unlikely to help in criminal proceedings since the evidence was, in all likelihood, gathered in the prior administrative proceedings under the taxpayers duty to cooperate (Section 115 BAO).[27]

5.1 Types

Although there are no statutory penalties for violating transfer pricing provisions, the consequences as shown above are no less severe.

5.2 Special or notable cases

Although there do not seem to have been cases with regard to transfer pricing violations, there have been criminal charges for the payment

25 VwGH October 28, 2010, 2006/15/0326.
26 UFS April 1, 2008, RV/0099-I/07.
27 In the Supreme Court decision of April 23, 2014 (13 Os 40/13a), the court confirmed its opinion that there is an assumption that the facts gathered in the administrative decision were professionally scrutinized and can therefore be used as facts for the criminal proceedings. Hence, these facts only need to be verified by an expert if they are still unclear.

of (hidden) dividends without filing the proper tax returns.[28] If this jurisprudence were applied to transfer pricing cases where Revenue Service could very well classify intra-company payments, or lack thereof, as hidden dividends, criminal charges would be possible and should be kept in mind.

6. DISPUTE RESOLUTION MECHANISMS

If the Austrian Revenue Service or a foreign revenue service has taken action which would lead to an adjustment of transfer prices, a party may, under Article 25 para. 1 and 2 OECD Double Taxation Model Treaty, initiate a Mutual Agreement Procedure. The procedure has to be started in the country of residence of the taxpayer ie, the seat of the corporation whose pricing is subject to primary adjustment under the OECD Double Taxation Model Treaty. The Austrian procedure is conducted by the Ministry of Finance. It may use administrative discretion to decide whether to open proceedings. Proceedings are conducted under the general provisions of the BAO.

Mutual Agreement Procedures may also be started on a European Union level under Article 6 of the 'Agreement to eliminate double taxation in connection with the adjustment of profits of associated enterprises'.[29] In these cases, the agency involved has to present the case to an arbitration committee if the responsible administrative bodies are unable to reach an agreement within two years with regard to the question of double taxation.

Parties may file a request for Mutual Agreement Procedures under both treaties. In the case of a national court decision, the decision is binding for the administrative bodies.

6.1 Preferred national options

Apart from initiating a Mutual Agreement Procedure, the taxpayer may also challenge a tax assessment notice under national law. However, since such a decision will only bind the Austrian authorities, the taxpayer will usually have to start the Mutual Agreement Procedure as well, to avoid double taxation. If the Mutual Agreement Procedure does not produce the desired results and the party is left with double taxation, there are national options. The decision may be challenged in court.[30] The Revenue Service may use their discretion to waive its tax claim in cases not covered by a double taxation agreement (Section 48 BAO). The other measure is called *Nachsicht* ('leniency') and is also solely in the Revenue Service's discretion (Section 236 BAO).

6.2 International options

So far the European Union Arbitral Procedure has not played a significant role which is due to the fact that nobody seems to be sure how it is properly applied. [31] Disputes are therefore resolved under the Mutual Agreement Procedure.

28 The latest case: OGH April 23, 2014, 13 Os 102/13v.

29 EU Arbitration Convention on the elimination of double taxation in connection with the adjustment of profits of associated enterprises (Official Journal L 225, 20/08/1990 P. 0010–0024).

30 Compare VPR marginal note 357.

31 The EU has passed a code of conduct (IP/04/542) where it freely admitted that the effectiveness of the convention

PART TWO: TAX AVOIDANCE

7. ACCEPTABLE TAX PLANNING AREAS/SUBJECTS

One has to keep in mind that tax avoidance of today maybe tax evasion of tomorrow. Hence, any kind of corporate planning needs to be based on sound and well documented business reasons to fall under the definition of tax planning rather than tax avoidance (see next section). One of the areas where tax planning, with regard to transfer pricing, is still acceptable are Cost Contribution Arrangements (CCA).[32] If the arrangement is in the interest of all parties and is equally used by all parties, contributions do not have to be calculated with profit.[33] The advantage is that development of certain products and services can be done in countries with high taxation. The Revenue Service accepted such an arrangement where the parent company bought Software for its subsidiaries and transferred ownership rights against payment of costs to them.[34] The Revenue Service ruled that subsidiaries did not have to pay additional licence fees. Hence, there are areas where careful tax planning is still acceptable.

8. DEFINING ABUSIVE TAX AVOIDANCE

In order to determine instances of tax avoidance, the Austrian Revenue Service and the courts will look at whether a structure is exceptional and unreasonable and whether there are no other reasons for the structure other than tax motives. [35]

9. THE LEGISLATIVE FRAMEWORK

The legislative framework against tax avoidance can be summarized as follows: Section 22 BAO contains the general rule 'substance over form' which allows the Revenue Service to tax the intended transaction regardless of the form. For income tax purposes, transfer prices may be adjusted according to Section 6 ciff. 6 EStG to reflect the true value of a transaction. If this leads to something being classified as dividend, Section 94 para. 2 EStG has to be kept in mind as well as Section 10 para. 4, 5 and 7 KStG for parent-subsidiary tax issues.

10. KEY CASES OF INTEREST

In the Dublin Docks decision where Austrian limited liability companies had set up companies in Ireland and these Irish companies invested the money back in Austrian banks, the Supreme Administrative Court stated that a business structure violates the anti-avoidance rule if it is exceptional and unreasonable and there are no other reasons for the structure other than tax motives.[36] Such a tax motivated scheme is assumed by the Austrian tax

lags behind expectations since application has proved more difficult.

32 Compare VPR marginal notes 112ff.

33 EAS 3196.

34 EAS 3055.

35 VwGH December 10, 1997, 93,13/0185; VwGH October 8, 2005, 2001/13/0018.

36 VwGH October 8, 2005, 2001/13/0018.

authorities in cases of dividend or bond stripping[37] and where the company uses an intermediate corporation in a jurisdiction with low taxation.[38] However, the courts have also stated that if the taxpayer can show important reasons for a transaction even if the transaction itself is unusual, this must rule out a misuse of form and thus needs to be recognized by the Revenue Service.[39]

There are also four noteworthy cases from the European Court of Justice, ECJ (Lankhorst-Hohorst,[40] Test Claimants,[41] Lammers & Van Cleef[42] and SGI[43]). The EJC affirms a Member State's rights not to recognize certain business structures if they are wholly artificial arrangements and not in compliance with the arms-length-principle (Article 9 OECD) as long as the national rules and regulations are applied discriminatorily to nationals and EU member states alike. The court also held that the tax payer must be allowed to present evidence that there is an economic reason for the transaction.

10.1 Current cases

A former Minister for Finance is currently being investigated for his use of shell corporations and lack of disclosure thereof.[44]

10.2 Key historical cases

The Austrian tax authorities have taken a very balanced approach. All in all, there were only 2294 convictions between 1999 and 2010 with only 226 defendants receiving prison sentences.[45] Most cases deal with outright value added tax fraud and simple non-payment. In one of the more interesting decisions, the Supreme Court in 2009 rejected the defence that a tax avoidance scheme was used by many taxpayers and recommended by experts.[46]

11. PENALTIES

There are specific statutory provisions with regard to fiscal crimes and misdemeanours regulated in the *Finanzstrafgesetz*. Tax fraud may be punished by up to ten years in prison (Section 39 FinStrG). However, at the same time, tax avoidance also raises the question of additional criminal liability for embezzlement (according to Section 153 Criminal Code), as well as falsification of balance sheets (Section 255 Stock Corporation Act, AktG, and Section 122 Limited Liability Corporation Act, GmbHG).

37 EAS GZ 3020/76/1-IV/4/98.
38 VwGH April 26, 2012, 2009/15/0220.
39 VwGH October 18, 2012, 2010/15/0010.
40 Case C-324/00 Lankhorst-Hohorst GmbH v. Finanzamt Steinfurt.
41 Case C-524/00 Test Claimants in the thin Cap Group Litigation v. Commissioners of Inland Revenue.
42 Case C-105/07 NV Lammers & Van Cleef v. Belgischer Staat.
43 Case C-311/08 Société de Gestion Industrielle SA (SGI) v. Belgischer Staat.
44 *http://www.ots.at/presseaussendung/OTS_20130816_OTS0131/kurier-in-der-causa-grasser-liegt-der-abschlussbericht-der-finanzstrafbehoerde-vor-495-millionen-euro-nicht-versteuert.*
45 Published in 2012, 242.
46 OGH 19.3.2009, 13 Os 105/08b.

11.1 Legislative Provisions

If a violation of the arms-length principle is found, it might have the following consequences: liability for tax evasion (Section 33 FinStrG), negligent non-payment of taxes (Section 34 FinStrG), tax fraud (Section 39 FinStrG), as well as tax declaration misdemeanours (Section 49 FinStrG). The preparation stages may be sufficient to incur criminal liability (Section 13 FinStrG). Taxes do not have to be permanently lost to the IRS, a temporary tax benefit is sufficient.[47] However, there is a possibility to avoid liability by voluntary declaration in time (Section 29 FinStrG).

There can also be general criminal liability which would carry an additional sentence on top of a sentence under the Finanzstrafgesetz[48], such as embezzlement (Section 153 Criminal Code) and falsification of a balance sheet (Section 255 Stock Corporation Act, AktG and Section 122 Limited Liability Corporation Act, GmbHG). The latter provision is also applied to the auditor who compiled the annual accounts.

11.2 Examples of penalties imposed

The Supreme Court in the decision of February 17, 2011, imposed a fine of EUR 272.657 which was ten percent of the taxes the defendant had failed to pay.[49] The defendant was found guilty under Section 33 FinStrG of filing false tax statements since 1996. Due to length of time during which the offence was committed, the court could have imposed the maximum prison sentence of two years. However, the decision followed the trend that Austrian courts were very reluctant to impose prison sentences and opted for fines instead.

12. CURRENT TRENDS

The current trend is towards closer scrutiny of business models and in particular, shell corporations. The government wants it to be known that tax evasion is not a trivial offense and will be pursued.[50] This has led, despite constitutional concerns, to changes in the *Amtshilfegesetz* (Law on Mutual Administrative Assistance) to allow for group requests from foreign governments and to introduce prohibitions against banks informing their clients of such requests. Although 'fishing expeditions' are technically still illegal, it is hard to imagine that they shall be detected under the new regime.

12.1 National policy and law

As mentioned above, the Ministry of Finance has introduced 'horizontal monitoring'. This project is based on the assumption that traditional tax auditing is costly and time consuming. Rather than a contradictory approach, the Ministry of Finance aims at tackling tax issues proactively. At

---

47 OGH, March 15, 2000,13 Os 172/99.

48 Section 22 FinStrG.

49 13 Os 12/10d.

50 Compare the announcement by the Ministry of Finance on May 29, 2013 *https://www.bmf.gv.at/ministerium/presse/archiv-2013/mai/multilaterales-amtshilfeabkommen.html.*

the same time, one will probably encounter less tolerant judges in coming years if caught in tax avoidance schemes.

12.1.1 The impact and role of the OECD and other international relations

Recommendations by the OECD are usually adopted, if not exceeded, in the case of the prohibition of deductions of interests and licence fees (Section 12 para. 1 ciff. 10 KStG). However, what seems to be missing from the debate is the question whether the OECD's interests are actually the same as national interests. The OECD is a political organization and the debate is dominated by exporting countries, such as the United States and Germany, who have a strong interest in the current system. There seems to be no willingness to actually consider the appropriateness of corporate tax rates and the influence on the economy. The debate about supposed tax havens has sometimes obscured the fact that countries such as Austria have invested heavily in a 'user-friendly' environment in corporate and fiscal matters to create an attractive environment for companies to invest (most filings may be done online). Even if (commercial) cases arise, Austrian courts are amongst the fastest to decide in Europe.[51] Together with the Ministry of Finance's efforts to create predictability when it comes to tax matters, companies are not lured to Austria by the supposed promise of lower taxes.

[51] *http://ec.europa.eu/justice/effective-justice/files/com_2013_160_de.pdf.*

Belgium

Loyens & Loeff Natalie Reypens & Aldo Engels

PART ONE: TRANSFER PRICING

1. GENERAL OVERVIEW

Belgian tax law currently contains two different notions of the arm's-length standard: the internationally accepted arm's-length principle through Article 185 §2 of the Belgian Income Tax Code ('ITC') and the so-called 'abnormal or benevolent advantage' as prescribed by Articles 26, 79 and 207 of the ITC. Compared to the analytic and objective arm's-length standard of Article 185 §2 ITC, the interpretation and assessment of the abnormal or benevolent advantage traditionally occurs through a more empirical, pragmatic and subjective approach.

Neither Belgian legislation nor the administrative guidelines issued by the Belgian tax authorities ('BTA') ('BTA Guidelines') provide specific guidelines or recommendations regarding the methods to be used in determining the arm's length price of a transaction. Absent Belgian regulations, the selection of the most appropriate transfer pricing method should take into account the nature of the functions performed, risks assumed and assets used in accordance with the OECD Transfer Pricing Guidelines for Multinational Enterprises and Tax Administrations ('OECD Guidelines'). The latter are officially accepted by the BTA and generally followed in Belgian tax practice.

With regard to the search for comparables and the performance of benchmark studies, the BTA accept the use of both pan-European databases and, under conditions, non-European databases. In keeping with the OECD Guidelines, the BTA generally accept that a price is arm's length if it falls within the inter-quartile range of results.

2. IDENTIFICATION OF LEGISLATIVE FRAMEWORK

2.1 Federal legislation

(i) Upward adjustment

- Article 26 ITC allows the BTA to add to a Belgian taxpayer's taxable basis the abnormal or benevolent advantages granted by the taxpayer to a beneficiary. No profit adjustment is made if these advantages are taken into account to determine the taxable basis of the beneficiary (escape clause). Irrespective of whether the advantage has been taken into account to determine the beneficiary's taxable basis, a profit adjustment will be made if the beneficiary is: (i) a non-resident company with which the Belgian taxpayer has any direct or indirect relationship of interdependence; (ii) a non-resident company or a non-resident establishment which is established in a tax haven; or (iii) a non-resident company that shares common interests with the company or establishment mentioned in (i) or (ii).

According to the Belgian Minister of Finance, an abnormal or benevolent advantage is always taken into account in the determination of the taxable basis of a beneficiary if the beneficiary is a Belgian company.[1] While the profit of the Belgian taxpayer granting the advantage will not be adjusted based on Article 26 ITC in such case, the Belgian beneficiary of the advantage might face adverse Belgian tax consequences on the basis of Articles 79 and 207 ITC (see below).

Belgian law does not define the concept of 'abnormal or benevolent advantage'. The BTA Guidelines state that an abnormal or benevolent advantage includes any enrichment of the recipient of an advantage without accurate and actual consideration. Pursuant to the BTA Guidelines, an 'advantage' is an enrichment of the recipient without equivalent real compensation to the grantor for the benefit provided. 'Abnormal' is that which is not consistent with common practice. A 'benevolent advantage' is an advantage that is granted without a contractual obligation or that is granted without sufficient consideration.[2] An intentional element is not required.[3] The identity of the beneficiary is also irrelevant.[4]

Whether an abnormal or benevolent advantage is granted is a question of fact. The economic circumstances of the moment, the situation in which parties are involved and the factual circumstances of the case should be taken into consideration.[5]

- Article 185 §2 a) ITC governs the recognition of profits on cross-border commercial and financial transactions for Belgian taxpayers[6] that are members of multinational groups. Here, any profits that were not recognized from an arms-length cross-border transaction are added to the taxpayer's taxable profit.

  In theory, an upward adjustment of a Belgian taxpayer's taxable basis under Article 185 §2 a) ITC can only occur by entering into an individual agreement ('Ruling') with the Belgian Service for Advance Decisions ('Ruling Commission'). This applies notwithstanding the application of the Arbitration Convention or the international conventions on the avoidance of double taxation. Strictly speaking, this means that the BTA cannot apply Article 185 §2 a) ITC and proceed with an upward adjustment where the Arbitration Convention is not

1 Parl. Q. No. 174 of Mr Cooreman dated 26 Apr. 1990, *Q. and A.*, Senate, 12 Jun. 1990, 1640; Parl. Q. No. 302 of Mr Cooreman dated 9 Mar. 1993, *Q. and A.*, Senate, 13 Apr. 1993, 2457; Parl. Q. No. 866 of Mrs Pieters dated 29 Jun. 2005, *Q. and A.*, Chamber, 27 Mar. 2006, 21901; Parl. Q. No. 916 of Mr de Seny dated 9 Dec. 1994, *Q. and A.*, Senate, 14 Feb. 1995, 7692.

2 Administrative Guidelines to ITC, No. 26/16 and 26/17.

3 Court of First Instance Mons 18 Jan. 2006, *Fiscoloog* No. 1019, 10: a Belgian company has received an invoice from an Irish company to be paid in German currency. By mistake, the company paid the amount in USD which exceeded the amount due in German currency. The Court held that the excess part constitutes an abnormal or benevolent advantage.

4 Contra: Court of First Instance Namur 25 Sep. 2002, *FJF* 2003, No. 1, 50.

5 Brussels 29 Jun. 2007, *TFR* 2008, 329; Antwerp 4 Apr. 2006, *FJF* 2007, No. 2, 143; Court of First Instance Antwerp 4 Jun. 2003, *FJF* 2004, No. 5, 421; Liège 20 Mar. 2002, *FJF* 2006, No. 3, 277; Court of First Instance Antwerp 25 Oct. 2002, *Fisc.Koer.* 2003, No. 4, 250 and *FJF* 2004, No. 2, 122. Reference is also made to ss. 2.4. and 7.2.

6 This applies to both companies and establishments.

requested. However, in those situations, the BTA could still invoke Article 26 of the ITC to make an upward adjustment.

There are two major differences between Article 26 ITC and Article 185 §2 a) ITC. The first is the interpretation of the internationally accepted arm's-length principle versus the notion of abnormal or benevolent advantage. The second difference is the scope of application.

(i) Where the arm's length principle under Article 185 §2 a) ITC is consistent with the internationally accepted objective arm's length standard, more subjective arguments should be taken into account to assess the presence of an abnormal or benevolent advantage.

(ii) In theory, Article 185 §2 ITC only applies by Ruling. This applies notwithstanding the application of the Arbitration Convention or the international conventions on the avoidance of double taxation. Moreover, Article 185 §2 ITC does not apply in domestic transactions, cross-border transactions between a company and an individual or transactions between two individuals. Additionally, Article 185 §2 ITC does not apply in uncontrolled transactions. For uncontrolled transactions or situations where no Ruling is requested or obtained, Article 26 ITC applies. In that case, the taxpayer may invoke the escape clause to avoid an upward profit adjustment. According to the traditional interpretation, Article 26 ITC does not apply to transactions between establishments of the same legal entity or between an establishment and the head office of the same legal entity.[7]

(ii) Downward adjustment

Under certain circumstances, Article 185 §2 b) ITC allows a Belgian taxpayer[8] to make a downward profit adjustment for corporate income tax purposes. This provision offers the legal basis to reduce the taxable basis to prevent the occurrence of double taxation. If it can be shown that a Belgian taxpayer's accounting result exceeds the arms-length result, the difference between the two amounts is exempt from tax. A downward adjustment under Article 185 §2 ITC is only available by way of a Ruling. This applies notwithstanding the application of the Arbitration Convention or the international conventions on the avoidance of double taxation.

(iii) Abnormal or benevolent advantage received

Articles 79 and 207 ITC exclude deductions from profits derived from an abnormal or benevolent advantage received by a taxpayer where there is a relationship of direct or indirect interdependence between the parties. The deductions that are excluded are: the deduction of a current year's losses and losses carried forward from prior years, tax-deductible gifts, dividends under the dividend-received deduction, the investment deduction and the notional interest deduction.

7 *Parl. Doc.* Chamber, 2003/2004, No. 1079/001, 10; Administrative Guidelines to ITC, No. 26/12.

8 This applies to both companies and establishments.

The purpose of these provisions is to prevent a Belgian or non-Belgian entity from shifting profits to a Belgian related company where the amount is not subject to tax because of the availability of certain tax deductions.

As mentioned above under Article 26 ITC, whether or not an abnormal or benevolent advantage has been received is a question of fact. In the context of Article 207 ITC, the Belgian Supreme Court has extended the definition of an 'abnormal or benevolent advantage' to include the results from transactions that take place in economically abnormal circumstances.[9][10]

2.2 State and provincial legislative interplay

No.

2.3 International treaties and agreements

The OECD Guidelines and other OECD reports (eg, OECD Report on the Attribution of Profits to Permanent Establishments of 22 July 2010) play a central role within Belgian transfer pricing. The fact that the OECD initiatives are followed and applied to the letter by the BTA and that no deviating rules exist in the Belgian legal framework gives significant legal certainty to multinationals investing in Belgium.

In addition to this, Belgium has concluded over 90 double tax treaties. These often contain a 'related persons / associated enterprises' article setting out the arm's length principle; an 'exchange of information' article; as well as a 'Mutual Agreement Procedure' ('MAP') article. Double tax treaties concluded by Belgium have a direct impact in the domestic legal order and take precedence over domestic law.

3. NATIONAL POLICY ISSUES

Since the early nineties, the BTA have become increasingly aware of the risk of base erosion. This is largely due to the active role adopted by the US and other countries in the field of transfer pricing and the fact that the adoption of the EU Arbitration Convention forced the BTA to accept the concept of correlative adjustments. Owing to this increased awareness, Belgian tax authorities have significantly increased their focus on transfer pricing and have become more skilled in the field over the last couple of years.[11]

In 2004, Article 185 §2 ITC introduced the internationally accepted arm's-length standard into Belgian tax law. This was intended to align Belgian tax law as much as possible with the international rules, provide clarity and transparency and to avoid interpretation differences. A new general tax ruling system was also introduced to reduce the volume of tax litigation and make Belgium more attractive for investors.

---

9 See below, under 4.2.

10 Supreme Court 26 Apr. 1966, *Pas* 1966, I, 1081 (the 'Craft' case); Supreme Court 22 Sep. 1972, *JPDF* 1972, 292; Supreme Court 28 Sep. 1984, *AFT* 1985, 18; Supreme Court 22 Mar. 1990, *FJF* No. 90/95 (the 'Au Vieux Saint Martin' case); Supreme Court 23 Feb. 1995, *FJF* 1995, 63; Brussels 22 Dec. 1987, *FJF* 1988, 80; Brussels, 31 Mar. 1987, *AFT* 1987, 285; Antwerp 2 Feb. 1993, *AFT* 1993, 225, annotation B. Nibelleand *TRV* 1993, 240, annotation S. Van Crombrugge.

11 P. Vanhaute, Belgium in international tax planning, Amsterdam, IBFD, 2008, 190.

Following to the increased international attention regarding abuse of transfer pricing rules, Belgian transfer pricing has also been subject to increased scrutiny. The 2008 economic crisis has also led to transfer pricing becoming an increasingly important tool to fund the treasury without having to change legislation. In recent years, Belgium has witnessed a significant increase in the amount of transfer pricing audits by the BTA.

3.1 Overall national policy announcements

None.

3.2 National revenue authority initiatives

On 28 June 1999, the BTA issued their first transfer pricing Circular Letter. This was intended to assist tax inspectors to investigate transfer pricing and to assess whether or not a more in depth investigation should be performed.[12] The Circular Letter was also designed to increase the awareness of the BTA; provide a general overview of the domestic legal and conventional framework of Belgian transfer pricing; and provide a discussion on some of the practical aspects of transfer pricing. The Circular Letter includes a summary of the Chapters I to V of the OECD Guidelines.

On 1 July 2006, a Transfer Pricing Unit ('TP Unit') was officially established as a special department of the BTA.[13] The TP Unit is an autonomous team that operates as a knowledge-center, giving technical and operational assistance in transfer pricing audits and transfer pricing disputes. The TP Unit is also authorized to perform transfer pricing audits of Belgian enterprise members of multinational groups.

Another Circular Letter followed on 14 November 2006. This Circular Letter contained general guidance to tax inspectors and taxpayers on how a transfer pricing audit should be performed in addition to transfer pricing documentation.[14] According to the BTA, the following situations could give rise to a transfer pricing audit:

- the use of tax havens in which little or no economic value is added (eg, re-invoicing activities) and direct or indirect payments to establishments in tax havens (eg, commissions, royalties and management fees);
- the use of back-to-back arrangements to hide the true nature of the transaction;
- complex arrangements and circular structures that add little or no economic value;
- Belgian group entities in a structural loss position;
- business reorganizations and relocation of establishments, particularly with respect to the valuation and compensation of intellectual property[15] as well as with respect to the location of the legal and economical ownership of intellectual property;
- invoicing service/management fees at the end of the financial year.

---

12 Circular No. AFZ/98-0003 dated 28 Jun. 1999.
13 Circular No. Cp.221.4/A/601.321 (AOIF 26/2006) dated 4 Jul. 2006.
14 Circular No. Ci.RH. 421/580.456 dated 14 Nov. 2006.
15 Such property includes patents, know-how and goodwill.

The Circular Letter includes a general list of useful information and documentation that can be used in a transfer pricing audit. It also advises tax inspectors to hold a pre-audit meeting. The purpose of the meeting is to determine, in a consultation with the taxpayer, the scope of investigation and the documentation that is relevant and useful in the case at hand. The 2006 Circular Letter is aligned with the provisions of the OECD Guidelines and the European Code of Conduct on Transfer Pricing Documentation.

In recent years, the TP Unit has been expanded substantially. This has resulted in a significant increase in the amount of transfer pricing audits. Currently, the BTA apply a data mining system for selecting companies to be subject to audit and send out extensive standard questionnaires. This practice applies equally to multinationals as to SME's.

3.3 Administrative statements

None.

3.4 Administrative guidelines

In addition to the Circular Letters of 1999 and 2006 mentioned under 3.2., a Circular Letter was issued by the Belgian tax authorities on the application of the EU Arbitration Convention of 23 July 1990. The Belgian government adopted this Convention in 2000.[16]

4. CASE LAW

Case law in the Belgian transfer pricing field is limited. Since the number of transfer pricing audits is substantially increasing in Belgium, more case law might be expected in the years to come.

4.1 Current cases

None.

4.2 Historical cases of note

There is extensive case law on the interpretation of the notion of abnormal or benevolent advantage. These cases confirm that whether or not such an advantage exists is a question of fact and that the economic circumstances of the moment, the situation in which parties are involved and the factual circumstances of the case should be taken into account.[17] In the application of Article 26, 79 and 207 ITC, Belgian courts have advocated for an empirical and pragmatic approach. As such, courts have accepted more subjective arguments to determine the arm's-length character of transactions. These include the global balance at group level, the specific characteristics of the group relationship and financial difficulties of group companies.

For example, no abnormal or benevolent advantaged is deemed to be present in cases where companies have provided financial support to related

16 Circular No. AFZ/INTERN. IB/98-0170 dated 7 Jul. 2000.

17 Brussels 29 Jun. 2007, *TFR* 2008, No. 338, 329; Antwerp 4 Apr. 2006, *FJF* 2007, No. 2, 143; Court of First Instance Antwerp 4 Jun. 2003, *FJF* 2004, No. 5, 421; Liège 20 Mar. 2002, *FJF* 2006, No. 3, 277; Court of First Instance Antwerp 25 Oct. 2002, *Fisc.Koer.* 2003, No. 4, 250 and *FJF* 2004, No. 2, 122.

entities experiencing financial difficulties. This is because taxpayers have demonstrated that without special pricing arrangements, the related entity would fail and disadvantage the group as a whole.[18]

Belgian case law has generally accepted that financial support to group companies in financial difficulty does not constitute an abnormal or benevolent advantage. The specific circumstances of the group relationships must be taken into account in each case.

The argument for economic solidarity has also been accepted in cases involving the waiver of debt and the granting of interest free loans. Courts have accepted that a waiver of debt by a resident parent company to its non-resident subsidiary is not an abnormal or benevolent advantage if the parent company can establish that it intended to preserve the subsidiary from bankruptcy and reduce its own losses from its participation in the subsidiary.[19]

Additionally, interest free loans to non-resident group companies will not constitute an abnormal or benevolent advantage under certain circumstances. For example, a loan may be issued where it is necessitated by financial difficulties of the foreign enterprises and preserve taxable income. A loan aimed at preserving the commercial and financial reputation of the resident company granting the advantage is also permissible.[20]

The same logic has been applied in cases involving the granting of discounts.[21]

Courts have also accepted set-offs based on the economic reality in a group context. In 1997, a Belgian Court allowed the indirect set-off in a case involving a Belgian company transferring the distribution rights of its manufactured products to a Swiss group company. The price charged by the Belgian company to the Swiss company was lower than the price the Belgian company charged to third parties. Upon commercial reorganization of the group, the Belgian company received distribution rights to international brands from another group company. The Court confirmed that, based on the economic reality in a group context, no abnormal or benevolent advantage was granted by the Belgian company. In reaching its decision, the court held that the agreed upon conditions between the parties, the transaction as a whole, and the group relationship between the companies are relevant considerations. The evaluation of whether a transaction is abnormal or benevolent should not be limited to the fact that the consideration for the advantage is granted by another group entity.[22] Case law also exists in which direct set-offs are accepted.[23]

---

18 Liège 26 Nov. 1980, *AFT* 1981, 223; Mons 1 Mar. 1978, *JDF* 1978, 258; Antwerp 9 Jan. 1990, *Fisc.Koer.* 1990, 258; Mons 19 Mar. 2004; Ghent 20 May 2003, *RABG* 2003, No. 18, 1032, annotation R. Rabaey, R. Van Hecke; Court of First Instance Antwerp, 16 Oct. 2006, *Fisc.Koer.* 2007, No. 9, 455 and *FJF* 2008, No. 2, 137; Mons 13 Oct. 2006, *FJF* 2007, No. 7, 607 and *Fiscoloog* 2006, No. 1049, 12 and *TFR* 2007, No. 321, 394; Court of First Instance Liège 17 Mar. 2005, *Fisc.Koer.* 2005, No. 18, 646.

19 Liège 26 Nov. 1980, *AFT* 1981, 223; Mons 1 Mar. 1978, *JDF* 1978, 258; Brussels 11 Feb. 1977, *JDF* 187, annotation J. Nemmery de Bellevaux.

20 Antwerp 9 Jan. 1990, *Fisc.Koer.* 1990, 258; Mons 19 Mar. 2004; Ghent 20 May 2003, *RABG* 2003, No. 18, 1032, annotation R. Rabaey, R. Van Hecke.

21 Ghent 29 Apr. 1999, *AFT* 1999, 315–318, annotation P. Cauwenbergh.

22 Liege 21 May 1997, *Fisc.Koer.* 1997, annotation P. Cauwenbergh.

23 Brussels 17 Feb. 1999, *FJF* 2000, 545.

The Belgian Supreme Court has applied Article 207 ITC to business reorganizations whereby assets of a profitable business were contributed to a loss making entity. Here, the Supreme Court extended the notion of 'abnormal or benevolent advantage received' to transactions that take place in economically abnormal circumstances. The Supreme Court has confirmed that it is insufficient to investigate whether an equivalent consideration for the advantage was granted. Instead, it is necessary to investigate whether the advantages have been received directly or indirectly in economically justified circumstances.[24] In this respect, the Supreme Court has ruled that an abnormal or benevolent advantage can result from shifting profitable activity into a dormant company with substantial carried forward tax losses. This reasoning also applies to the merger of a profitable company into a moribund company with carried forward tax losses under abnormal circumstances. Such a transaction is designed to offset the carried forward tax losses against the profits realized after the merger.

The most notable cases concern the 'Au Vieux Saint Martin' cases.[25] A Belgian Company A with no activities, no personnel and substantial tax losses merged with Belgian Company B with the sole intention of shifting Company B's profits to the newly merged enterprise to offset the latter's losses. The Supreme Court has denied loss deductions in these circumstances on the basis that such mergers are entered into for the sole purpose of using tax losses.[26]

5. PENALTIES

Belgian tax law does not contain specific penalties related to transfer pricing. However, the general penalties of the ITC are applicable :

- On the basis of Article 444 ITC, a tax increase can be applied when a tax audit leads to an increase in declared taxable income.
- On the basis of Article 445 ITC, an administrative fine can be imposed for each violation of the provisions of the ITC.
- On the basis of Article 351 ITC, the tax authorities can establish an 'ex officio assessment' in case a taxpayer does not provide the tax inspector with sufficient information and documentation upon a tax audit.

5.1 Types

As mentioned above, the general penalties of the ITC are applicable.

The first type of penalty is a tax increase under Article 444 ITC. This would generally be the case if a transfer pricing audit results in a profit adjustment. Depending on the nature and frequency of the infringement, the tax increase ranges between 10 per cent and 200 per cent of the tax due

---

[24] Supreme Court 26 Apr. 1966, *Pas* 1966, I, 1081 (the 'Craft' case); Supreme Court 22 Sep. 1972, *JPDF* 1972, 292; Supreme Court 28 Sep. 1984, *AFT* 1985, 18; Supreme Court 22 Mar. 1990, *FJF* 1990, 95 (the 'Au Vieux Saint Martin' case); Supreme Court 23 Feb. 1995, *FJF* 1995, 63; Brussels 22 Dec. 1987, *FJF* 1988, 80; Brussels 31 Mar. 1987, *AFT* 1987, 285; Antwerp 2 Feb. 1993, *AFT* 1993, 225, annotation B. Nibelle and *TRV* 1993, 240, annotation S. Van Crombrugge.

[25] Supreme Court 22 Mar. 1990, *FJF* 1990, 95 (the 'Au Vieux Saint Martin' case); Supreme Court 23 Feb. 1995, *FJF* 1995, 131 (the 'Au Vieux Saint Martin II' case).

[26] Liège 17 Feb. 1993, *FJF* 1993, 141 and Supreme Court 23 Feb. 1995, *FJF* 1995, 63, 131 (the 'Au Vieux Saint Martin II' case); Liège 8 Feb. 1963, confirmed by Supreme Court 26 Apr. 1966, *JPDF* 1966, 245 (the 'Craft' case).

on the undeclared part of the income. No tax increase is due if the income has not been declared correctly due to circumstances that are beyond the taxpayer's control.

In addition to the tax increase, an administrative fine ranging from EUR 50 to EUR 1,250 can be imposed for each violation of the provisions of the ITC on the basis of Article 445 ITC. This fine can be imposed if the taxpayer refuses to cooperate during a transfer pricing audit.

The third type of penalty is the establishment by the BTA of an 'ex officio assessment' on the basis of Article 351 ITC. This triggers a reversal of the burden of proof such that the taxpayer must demonstrate the correct amount of its taxable income.

Criminal penalties may also be imposed if a taxpayer acts with fraudulent intent or with the intention of causing harm.

5.2 Special or notable cases

None.

6. DISPUTE RESOLUTION MECHANISMS

Belgian domestic law does not provide for dispute resolution processes that are specifically designed to resolve transfer pricing issues. It is possible to call upon the Belgian Tax Mediation Service ('BTMS') when being involved in an ongoing dispute with the BTA regarding the levy/assessment or collection of tax due. Advance Pricing Arrangements ('APA') also play an important role in the prevention of transfer pricing disputes. International mechanisms such as the MAP under Article 25 of the OECD Model Tax Convention and the mechanisms provided by the Arbitration Convention are also available.

6.1 Preferred national options

If a dispute with the BTA regarding the assessment or collection of tax has not been brought before the courts, taxpayers have the option of filing a request for mediation with the BTMS. The BTMS is an independent service that assesses requests for mediation with objectivity, independence and impartiality. The BTMS attempts to reconcile the different points of view of the taxpayer and the BTA and proposes solutions in accordance with the law.

Taxpayers that wish to obtain certainty in advance and avoid potential transfer pricing disputes may obtain APAs. Unilateral APAs can be obtained from the Ruling Commission. Bilateral or multilateral APAs can be obtained with the Department of International Conventions within the BTA. APAs are generally valid for a maximum period of 5 years.

6.2 International options

Where double taxation arises, the MAP under Article 25 of the OECD Model Convention is available. The BTA have adopted the OECD Commentary to Article 25 of the OECD Model Convention, which provides that transfer pricing adjustments fall within the scope of the MAP under the treaties.

Under the MAP, however, competent authorities are not required to reach an agreement.

Belgian taxpayers are also entitled to use the Arbitration Convention, which provides for a mandatory relief from double taxation. This occurs in situations where the tax authorities of a Contracting State unilaterally adjust the profit of a domestic taxpayer regarding a transaction the taxpayer entered into with a related taxpayer situated in another Contracting State.

PART TWO: TAX AVOIDANCE

7. ACCEPTABLE TAX PLANNING AREAS/SUBJECTS

In the landmark 'Brepols' case of 1961, the Supreme Court acknowledged the fundamental right of taxpayers to freely choose the route of least taxation.[27] In the years that followed, Belgian legislative authorities have nevertheless taken certain measures to restrict this fundamental right. In this respect, a series of specific anti-avoidance rules were issued as a reaction to aggressive base eroding structures that were set up by taxpayers. However, these provisions were often considered insufficient. If a specific provision did not apply, the BTA could only disregard an agreement or transaction between parties on the basis of the simulation or sham doctrine or on the basis of the general anti-abuse rule ('GAAR').

Under the GAAR of Belgian tax law (Article 344 §1 ITC), the BTA were allowed to reclassify legal act(s) provided that they could demonstrate that the transaction was predominantly tax driven and it was ultimately intended to avoid tax. According to the Supreme Court, a requalification by the BTA to a legal act should have the same non-fiscal legal consequences as the original legal act(s). Nevertheless, it is practically impossible to achieve similar legal consequences upon requalification when a transaction was established by one deed. For this reason, the GAAR was often proven to be ineffective to combat abusive tax avoidance.

Therefore, a new GAAR was introduced in 2012 and adopted a *fraus legis* approach. With the revised Article 344 §1 ITC, the fundamental right of taxpayers to freely choose the route of least taxation continues to exists but has been further restricted. This was done in order to resolve the application problems of the previous version of the GAAR and allow the BTA to efficiently counter abuse without fundamentally impacting legal certainty. Because this new rule was recently introduced, there is currently no case law on point. As such, aggressive tax planning schemes that the old version of the GAAR could not successfully challenge remain to be assessed under the new GAAR. See further sections 8 and 9.

The following is a non-exhaustive list of legal tax planning structures to which the new GAAR should not apply, assuming the taxpayer has non-fiscal motives:

[27] Cass. 6 Jun. 1961, *Pas* 1961, 1082. Also, the Courts have traditionally upheld legal constructions and transactions entered into by taxpayers, even when such transactions were clearly entirely tax-driven.

(a) Structures involving the use of notional interest deduction

Notional interest deduction ('NID') is a deemed interest deduction equal to a certain percentage of the adjusted net equity of a Belgian taxpayer. The regime was introduced to preserve Belgian industrial groups and related financing and service activities and to restore Belgium's tax competitiveness.[28] As a result of the introduction of the NID regime, Belgium has become a popular location for finance and treasury companies. Belgian authorities have observed that the NID regime has led to aggressive tax planning schemes exceeding the regime's intended purpose. In response, the BTA have issued Circular Letters that identify permissible tax structures involving the NID as well as arrangements that should be considered as purely abusive tax avoidance. The latter will not receive the benefit of the NID.

The BTA's Circular Letters make reference to Belgian financing and treasury companies of MNEs.[29] Finance companies are capitalized by way of capital contributions and subsequently use these funds to issue loans to group members. Under this structure, lenders enjoy tax-deductible interest expenses while the interest income is not taxed (or subject to a low effective tax rate) in the hands of the Belgian finance companies by virtue of the NID. Such an arrangement is only permissible if: (i) it is not solely artificial; (ii) it corresponds to the economic reality; (iii) it is not set up with the sole purpose of avoiding tax in Belgium; and (iv) the group uses the Belgian entity as a finance company on a consistent basis.

(b) Patent income deduction ('PID')

Belgian law provides for an 80 per cent deduction of the income derived from patents or complementary certificates of protection from a taxpayer's taxable basis. This deduction applies to income derived from patents that are licensed by the Belgian taxpayer or used in the manufacturing process of patented products. These patents should be developed or acquired/licensed and further improved by the taxpayer at its own R&D center located in Belgium or abroad.

Because of the PID and other R&D incentives, Belgium is an attractive location for intangible property centers and joint developers of IP.

Assuming that a structure matching the requirements of the PID is established and that income derived from patents is received at arm's length, it is unlikely that the BTA would be able to successfully challenge such an arrangement.

(c) Profit participation loans ('PPL') and other derivative financial instruments

One advantage of Belgium's legal and tax system lies in the area of hybrid financial instruments. Because Belgium has traditionally been a 'form-over-

---

28 Circular No. Ci.RH. 840/592.613 (AOIF 14/2008) dated 3 April 2008.

29 2nd Addendum dated 20 June 2011 to Circular No. Ci.RH. 840/592.613 (AOIF 14/2008) dated 3 April 2008.

substance' jurisdiction, foreign qualifications and tax treatment of financial instruments may be considered irrelevant under Belgian law.[30]

Generally, the distinction between debt and equity under the civil law criteria is valid for tax purposes. The civil standard also applies to the tax treatment and qualification of assets, liabilities, income and expenses. An exception to this general rule is where Belgian tax law explicitly provides for a deviation.

Because Belgian tax law does not define 'interest', taxpayers should look into the civil law definition. According to Belgian civil law, the concept of a loan is not incompatible with the fact that the interest is wholly or partly determined as a portion of the debtor's profits or in relation to its level of profitability.

As a result, arm's length payments under a well-structured PPL are deductible so long as a taxpayer can demonstrate proper economic and financial motives.

8. DEFINING ABUSIVE TAX AVOIDANCE

As a result of the new GAAR of Article 344 §1 ITC, the concept of 'abuse of tax law' was recently incorporated into the Belgian legislative framework. This concept was further developed in a Circular Letter issued by the BTA.[31]

The concept of 'abuse of tax law' has two aspects: an objective and a subjective component.

The objective component is present if the taxpayer:

- avoids the application of a provision of the ITC or its Decree of execution in a way that is incompatible with the provision's objectives;
- claims the application of a provision of the ITC or its Decree of execution conferring a tax benefit in a way that is incompatible with the provision's objectives.

These imply a conflict with the objectives of the involved legal provision. In other words, the purpose and scope of the legal provision must be frustrated as a result of a certain legal act not being taxed or leading to a specific tax benefit.[32] According to the Preparatory Works to the law introducing the new GAAR, the conflict with the objectives of the fiscal legislation should also be understood in the light of the concept of 'artificial construction'. An 'artificial construction' is defined as a transaction that does not pursue the underlying economic objectives of the fiscal legislation, does not have any connection with the economic reality, or does not take place under commercial or financial market conditions. In other words, it refers to legal acts that are solely performed to avoid taxes.[33]

The subjective component refers to the fact that the essential objective behind the taxpayer's choice of legal act(s) was to avoid tax or to secure a tax benefit.

---

30 P. Vanhaute, Belgium in international tax planning, Amsterdam, IBFD, 2008, 380.
31 Circular No. Ci.RH. 81/616.207 (AFZ 3/2012) dated 4 May 2012, 6.
32 Circular No. Ci.RH. 81/616.207 (AFZ 3/2012) dated 4 May 2012, 6.
33 *Parl. Doc.*, Chamber, 2011/2012, No. 53-2081/001, 114.

9. THE LEGISLATIVE FRAMEWORK

Under Article 344 §1 ITC, the BTA can disregard a legal act or a series of legal acts if they demonstrate that tax abuse has been committed. Under the GAAR, the BTA are only required to establish the existence of the objective aspect of an abuse of tax law. To do so, the BTA may use all means of evidence, with the exception of testimony or oath. If such abuse of tax law has been established, the taxpayer must then argue the existence of underlying reasons for his act(s) other than avoiding Belgian income tax. In the event that the taxpayer cannot provide this counterproof, the BTA shall 'repair' the taxpayer's taxable base. In doing so, the transaction will be subject to tax in accordance with the objectives of the law as if the abuse would not have taken place.[34] In this respect, the BTA are not required to substitute the abusive legal act by another legal act.[35]

The BTA will only apply the GAAR if:

- the only objective of the series of transactions was to avoid tax;
- the non-fiscal objectives are not specifically connected with the legal act(s) but are so general that they are present for any similar legal act;
- the non-fiscal objectives are so immaterial that no reasonable person would perform the legal act for such objectives.[36]

Next to the GAAR, Belgian tax law contains other anti-abuse provisions targeting specific forms of abusive tax avoidance:

- Under Article 18 4° ITC, deductible interest is reclassified into non-deductible dividends if paid to certain beneficiaries and certain thresholds are exceeded;
- Under Article 32 ITC, rental income is reclassified into professional income if paid to certain beneficiaries and certain thresholds are exceeded;
- Under Article 54 ITC, interest and royalty payments to offshore entities are not tax deductible under certain circumstances;
- Under Article 183bis ITC, corporate reorganizations (mergers, demergers, transfers of business units) in Belgium can only benefit from an exemption from corporate income tax if tax evasion or tax avoidance is not the principal objective or one of the principal objectives;
- Under 198 §1 10° ITC, payments exceeding EUR100,000.00 per year should be reported if they are directly or indirectly made to a recipient established in a tax haven. If not reported, such payments are not tax deductible. Where the reporting obligation is fulfilled, the payments will be tax deductible if it can be proven that the payments relate to 'actual and true transactions' involving 'persons other than artificial constructions';
- Under 198 §1 11° ITC, a 5:1 debt to equity ratio applies for the deduction of interest payments directly or indirectly made to (i) related beneficiaries or (ii) beneficiaries located in tax havens;

34 Circular No. Ci.RH. 81/616.207 (AFZ 3/2012) dated 4 May 2012.
35 *Parl. Doc.*, Chamber, 2011/2012, No. 53-2081/016, 37.
36 Circular No. Ci.RH. 81/616.207 (AFZ 3/2012) dated 4 May 2012, 8.

- Under 203 ITC, 'subject-to-tax requirements' should be met in order to benefit from the participation exemption for received dividends;
- Under 344 §2 ITC, certain transfers of certain well-defined income-producing assets to offshore entities are deemed non-opposable to the BTA.

10. KEY CASES OF INTEREST

Because the new GAAR has only been introduced in 2012, no cases have yet been published dealing with its application. We refer to section 4.2. above for interesting cases regarding tax avoidance in the area of transfer pricing and profit shifting.

10.1 Current cases

There are no current cases of interest dealing with tax avoidance. The most recent published cases deal with the application of the previous version of the GAAR and are therefore of limited relevance.

10.2 Key historical cases

(a) Brepols case[37]

In this 1961 landmark case, the Supreme Court affirmed the fundamental right of taxpayers to freely choose the route of least taxation. The case dealt with (deductible) interest payments made by a subsidiary to its parent company with the sole purpose of reducing the subsidiary's taxable base. The lower Tax Court held that the underlying loan arrangements were not concluded for the purpose of obtaining or preserving profit in the hands of the subsidiary but for the sole benefit of the parent. The arrangements were not considered to be genuine loans but equity contributions. Subsequently, the Tax Court reclassified the interest payments in (non-deductible) dividend distributions.

The Supreme Court upheld taxpayers' freedom of contract to structure transactions in order to benefit from a more favorable tax regime. Assuming that taxpayers do not infringe any legal obligations, there will be no tax fraud notwithstanding that the legal form of the transaction is abnormal. This is the case so long as the taxpayers are willing to accept the legal consequences and ramifications resulting from their choice of transaction.

(b) Au Vieux Saint Martin case[38]

The Supreme Court again followed the Brepols doctrine in the Aux Vieux Saint Martin case. The Supreme Court affirmed that legal arrangements can be upheld against the BTA, even if it appeared from the facts and circumstances that the legal form chosen by the parties was purely motivated by tax reasons and the pursuit of an economic or commercial purpose is lacking. In the case at hand, the BTA tried to apply an 'economic reality' doctrine to disallow deduction of carried forward tax losses when

37 Cass. 6 Jun. 1961, *Pas* 1961, 1082.
38 Supreme Court 22 Mar. 1990, *FJF* 1990, 95.

the motive for the merger was to obtain the benefit of such deduction. The Supreme Court officially confirmed the fundamental right of the 'free choice of the least taxed route' based on two fundamental principles. The first principle is the 'legality of tax' and the second is that tax law is governed by private law.[39]

11. PENALTIES

11.1 Legislative provisions

The general provisions of the ITC regarding penalties are applicable where the BTA successfully apply the GAAR to a legal act set by a taxpayer. For more information regarding these general penalties, we refer to Sections 5 and 5.1.

Because Article 344 §1 is a provision that forms part of the means of proof of the BTA, it can technically not be violated. Therefore, the application of this provision does not entail the existence of a material violation of the fiscal legislation. Additionally, the Circular Letter providing guidance on the application of the GAAR confirms that the application of the provision does not raise a presumption that the taxpayer has committed tax fraud.[40] It follows that the provision needs to be applied within the normal period of assessment of three years. It also follows that a tax increase may be applied by the BTA but the rate of the increase cannot exceed the rate that applies to cases without the intent to evade taxes.

11.2 Examples of penalties imposed

None.

12. CURRENT TRENDS

Belgium takes on an active role in international developments and participates in international discussions. It is clear that the international developments, especially initiatives from the OECD, will directly shape Belgium's attitude towards tax avoidance.

12.1 National policy and law

Over the years, Belgian legislators have taken on an active role in combating abusive tax avoidance. In the past years, multiple provisions have been adopted to curb general or specific forms of tax avoidance. These include laws restricting the application of the NID, the law introducing a new version of the thin capitalization rule and the new version of the GAAR. Because the latter has only recently been introduced, it remains to be seen what the impact will be on Belgian tax practice and tax planning structures in particular.

A minimum tax for MNEs has also been recently been introduced in Belgian tax law. This so-called 'Fairness Tax' will apply where a Belgian taxpayer distributes profits to its shareholders that have not been subject to

---

39 The taxpayer ultimately lost the discussion and the case, but based on the application of Article 207 ITC (see above under 4.2.).

40 Circular No. Ci.RH. 81/616.207 (AFZ 3/2012) dated 4 May 2012.

tax due to deduction of NID and/or carried forward tax losses. The Fairness Tax has been introduced in light of the BEPS discussions.

12.1.1 The impact and role of the OECD and other international relations

The impact of international trends and initiatives such as BEPS on the Belgian tax landscape cannot be underestimated. As a general rule, the OECD initiatives are closely followed by the BTA.

As a result of the increased international attention regarding abuse of transfer pricing rules, transfer pricing is the subject of increasing scrutiny in Belgium. The new approaches of the OECD will continue to impact the attitude and interpretation of the BTA. Going forward, it is expected that the OECD's general focus on 'significant people functions' and substance in tax planning structures and transfer pricing will determine the future of Belgian tax practices.

Brazil

KLA–Koury Lopes Advogados Henrique Lopes

PART ONE: TRANSFER PRICING

1. GENERAL OVERVIEW

Transfer pricing rules are designed to prevent Brazilian legal entities from avoiding taxes by means of underpaying or overpaying (as the case may be) related parties, parties domiciled in low tax jurisdictions or entities subject to a privileged tax regime.

Brazilian transfer pricing rules apply to:

- costs/expenses with acquisitions and imports of assets, goods, services or rights (pursuant to the tax authorities, the application of the transfer pricing rules does not depend on the actual entry of the assets, goods, services or rights into Brazilian territory);
- revenues deriving from export of goods, services or rights (the tax authorities understand that the transfer pricing rules apply irrespectively of the actual exit of the assets, goods, services or rights from Brazil); and
- interest expenses and revenues.

Brazilian transfer pricing rules do not apply to:

- domestic transactions, which fall under the scope of the disguised distribution of profit rules, the general deductibility rules (necessary and ordinary expenses), or the rules on arbitration of profits, as the case may be; and
- royalties and remuneration for the transfer of technology (the law expressly excludes only acquisitions/imports by Brazilian companies from the transfer pricing rules, but the Brazilian Revenue understands the exclusion to be extensive to exports).[1]

1.1 Related parties

Transactions carried out between related parties include those carried out between the Brazilian legal entity and (i) its branches; (ii) its headquarters; (iii) its controlled companies; (iv) its controlling shareholders (individuals or legal entities); (v) companies under common corporate or common management control; and (vi) its managers; and/or (vii) spouses and relatives by blood or marriage, up to the third degree, of the managers or of the controlling shareholders, as well as those involving:

- the Brazilian legal entity's foreign affiliated companies as defined by article 243, paragraphs 1 and 2 of Law 6404/76 – Brazilian Corporation Law;

[1] IN RFB 1312/12.

- companies that participate with the Brazilian legal entity in a joint enterprise, under a 'consortium' or 'condominium', as defined by Brazilian law;
- foreign legal entities that grant exclusive rights to buy or sell assets/goods/services/rights to its Brazilian agent, distributor or dealer;
- foreign individuals or legal entities who, together with the Brazilian legal entity, hold an equity stake in a third legal entity that qualifies them as controlling shareholders or affiliated in relation to this third legal entity;
- foreign agents, distributors or dealers of the Brazilian legal entity, to whom the latter has granted exclusive rights to buy or sell assets/goods/services/rights; and
- foreign companies, when the same individual or legal entity holds an equity stake of at least 10 per cent in both the foreign company and the Brazilian legal entity.

The transfer pricing rules also apply to transactions between a Brazilian company and a related foreign party by means of an interposed person.

1.2 Low taxation jurisdictions and privileged tax regimes

Low taxation jurisdictions[2] are defined as those countries or jurisdictions whose legislation:

- does not allow access to information about the shareholding structure of legal entities, their ownership, or the identification of the beneficial owner of income earned by non-residents; and/or
- does not tax the income or taxes the income at maximum rates which are lower than 20 per cent, considering: (i) the tax legislation applicable to individuals or legal entities, according to the qualification of the person with whom the relevant transaction is performed; and (ii) separately, the taxation on the work and capital.

Privileged tax regimes[3] are those that meet one or more of the following requirements:

- do not tax income, or tax income at maximum rates lower than 20 per cent;
- provide tax advantages to non-residents (individuals or legal entities) conditioned upon the non-performance of substantial economic activities in the relevant jurisdiction, or without requiring the performance of substantial economic activities in the relevant jurisdiction;
- do not tax income earned outside the relevant territory, or taxes such income at maximum rates lower than 20 per cent; and/or
- do not allow access to information about the shareholding structure of legal entities, ownership of assets and rights or economic transactions performed.

---

2 Article 24 of Law 9430 – as amended.
3 Article 24-A of Law 9430 – as amended.

The Brazilian Federal Revenue Normative Instruction 1037/2010 ('IN RFB 1037'), as amended, described cases that address the concept of low taxation jurisdictions[4] and privileged tax regimes.[5] Despite the prevailing practice of considering these lists as all-inclusive, disputes may arise regarding this matter. It is also important to note that the lists of low taxation jurisdictions and privileged tax regimes may be reviewed at the request of the interested government in accordance with a procedure described under the Federal Revenue Normative Instruction 1045/2010.

1.3 Import methods

In Brazil, only methods specifically provided for in the law may be employed by both the taxpayers and the tax authorities. With respect to imports, four methods may be used to calculate the benchmark:

- Comparable Independent Prices ('PIC');
- Resale Price Less Profit ('PRL');
- Production Cost Plus Profit ('CPL');
- Imported Quoted Price ('PCI').

If the benchmark reached by the application of one of these methods (methods may be freely chosen by product and by period, without preference, except for commodities, for which the method is exclusive and mandatory) is greater than the import prices subject to transfer pricing control, no adjustments are required when calculating the Corporate Income Tax (IRPJ) and the Social Contribution on Profits (CSLL).

If the benchmark is lower than said import prices, and this difference exceeds the variations accepted by the legislation, such difference must be added to the IRPJ and CSLL tax bases.

Below is a brief description of each of the transfer pricing methods listed above.

PIC. The benchmark corresponds to the weighted arithmetic average of purchases and sales between unrelated parties in Brazil or in other countries, of the same or similar assets, goods, services, or rights, under similar payment conditions.

---

4 According to IN RFB 1037 the following jurisdictions fall under the concept of low taxation jurisdictions: Andorra; Anguilla; Antigua and Barbuda; Netherlands Antilles; Aruba; Ascension Island; Bahamas; Bahrain; Barbados; Belize; Bermuda Islands; Brunei; Campione D'Italia; Channel Islands (Alderney, Guernsey, Jersey and Sark); Cayman Islands; Cyprus; Singapore; Cook Islands, Costa Rica; Djibouti; Dominica; United Arab Emirates; Gibraltar; Granada; Hong Kong; Kiribati; Labuan; Lebanon; Liberia; Liechtenstein; Macao; Madeira Island; Maldives; Isle of Man; Marshall Islands; Mauritius; Monaco; Montserrat Islands; Nauru; Niue Island; Norfolk Island; Panama; Pitcairn Islands; French Polynesia; Qeshm Island; American Samoa; West Samoa; San Marino; Saint Helena Islands; Saint Lucia; Saint Kitts and Nevis Federation; Saint Peter and Saint Miguel Islands; Saint Vincent and Grenadines; Seychelles; Solomon Islands; Swaziland; Sultanate of Oman; Tonga; Tristan da Cunha Islands; Turks and Caicos; Vanuatu; British Virgin Islands; and US Virgin Islands.

5 [5]The following regimes qualify as privileged tax regimes: (i) of the Sociedad Anonima Financiera de Inversion (SAFI) set out in the legislation of Uruguay until December 31, 2010; (ii) of holding companies set out in the legislation of Denmark and the Netherlands, if they do not carry significant economic activities; (iii) of International Trading Company (ITC) set out in the legislation of Iceland; (iv) of Limited Liability Companies (LLCs) applicable in American States, formed of non-residents and not subject to federal income tax, set out in the legislation of United States of America; (v) of Entidad de Tenencia de Valores Extranjeros (ETVE) set out in the legislation of Spain; (vi) of International Trading Company (ITC) and International Holding Company (IHC) set out in the legislation of Malta; and (vii) with respect to Switzerland, of holding company, domiciliary company, auxiliary company, mixed company and administrative company, as well as companies favored by rulings, which tax regime results in an income tax rate of less than 20 per cent. The inclusion of the regimes applicable to the Dutch holding companies and the ETVEs in the list above was challenged by the respective governments and the cases have been temporarily excluded from the list by ADEs 10/10 and, 22/10 until a final decision is granted about the matter.

The following transactions can be used for calculating the aforementioned benchmark:

- same or similar assets, goods, services, or rights sold by the same foreign related party to unrelated legal entities, domiciled in Brazil or not;
- same or similar assets, goods, services, or rights purchased by the same Brazilian company from unrelated legal entities, domiciled in Brazil or not; and
- same or similar assets, goods, services, or rights purchased or sold between unrelated legal entities, domiciled in Brazil or not.

Comparable prices must be adjusted to equalize different commercial conditions as described in IN RFB 1312/12.

PRL. As of January 1, 2013[6] the benchmark is calculated according to the steps below:

(i) net sales price: weighted arithmetic average of sales prices in Brazil of the asset, goods, services or rights traded/produced less unconditional discounts shown on the relevant invoices, which are those that do not depend on future events/conditions, taxes included in the sales price (eg, ICMS, ISS, PIS and COFINS), brokerage fees and commissions paid;

(ii) the share of the imported assets, goods, services or rights in the total cost of the asset, goods, services or rights sold: percentage ratio between the weighted average cost of the imported asset, goods, rights or services and the total weighted average cost of the assets, goods, services or rights sold, calculated according to the taxpayer's cost spreadsheet;

(iii) the share of the imported assets, goods, services or rights in the sales price of the assets, goods, services or rights sold: percentage resulting from item (ii), multiplied by the net sales price resulting from item (i);

(iv) profit margin: a percentage that varies according to the economic activity developed by the taxpayer multiplied by the share of the imported assets, goods, services or rights in the sales price of the assets, goods, services or rights traded, calculated according to item (iii); and

(v) benchmark: difference between the share of the imported assets, goods, services or rights in the sales price of the assets, goods, services or rights sold, calculated according to item (iii), and the profit margin calculated as per item (iv).

The profit margin in item (iv) above is provided by law 12715/12 as follows:

- 40 per cent for pharmaceutical and pharmachemical industry, tobacco products, optical, phonographic and cinematographic equipment, medical and dental hospital equipment and machines, extraction of oil and natural gas and products derived from oil;
- 30 per cent for chemical products, glass and products derived from glass, cellulose and products derived from cellulose and metallurgy; and
- 20 per cent for the remaining sectors.

6 Law 12715/12. Until December 31, 2012, the PRL margins were 20 per cent for products not subject to manufacture in the country and 60 per cent for products manufactured in the country.

Until December 31, 2012 companies were allowed to opt for the new PRL method provided by Law 12715/12 or the PRL 20 (profit margin of 20 per cent) or PRL 60 (profit margin of 60 per cent) method provided for in the previous legislation (Law 9430/96 and IN SRF 243).

CPL. The benchmark shall be calculated by taking the weighted average of the production costs of the imported assets, goods, services, or rights (in the country where they were originally manufactured) and adding a profit margin of 20 per cent, plus the taxes levied upon exportation (charged by that same country).

In addition to direct costs, costs of any goods, services or rights used or consumed in the manufacturing process, reasonable process losses, depreciation, and lease and maintenance expenses related to the production process may be considered for the purpose of such calculations, as determined by IN RFB 1312 (controversies arise as to whether costs not mentioned in IN RFB 1312 can be considered in the calculation of the benchmark according to this method).

The calculation of the benchmark can also be performed based on production costs of similar assets, goods, services, or rights, adjusted as provided by the legislation.

PCI. The benchmark shall result from the daily average price of goods and rights listed in internationally recognized future and commodities exchanges (commodities) adjusted by the average market premium. This method is mandatory for the importation of commodities. IN RFB 1312 nominates the products that are classified as 'commodities' and the 'future and commodities exchanges' considered as internationally recognized for purposes of transfer pricing controls.

In case a specific commodity is not listed in one of the recognized exchanges, the price of the imported good may be compared with the information provided by internationally recognized research institutions of the relevant sector.

The commodities, the recognized future and commodities exchanges and the recognized research institutions are listed in exhibits I, II and III of IN RFB 1312/2012.

The quoted price may be adjusted for the market premium paid in relation to the quality, characteristics and concentration of the relevant good. Other admissible adjustments are:

- payment terms;
- quantities negotiated;
- climate influences on the characteristics of the goods;
- commissions paid to unrelated parties;
- storage; and
- freight and insurance.

1.4 Export methods

Transfer pricing rules will only apply to exports if the average export price is lower than 90 per cent of the average price of the same or similar goods, services, or rights sold in the Brazilian market, during the same period and under similar payment conditions.

For purposes of such safe harbor, only transactions involving independent parties can be used for comparison. Brazilian sales prices may be deducted from ICMS, ISS, PIS and COFINS and unconditional discounts. Export prices shall be free of freight and insurance costs borne by the seller.

In addition to the foregoing, IN RFB 1312 releases Brazilian legal entities from calculating transfer pricing adjustments based on the methods described in the legislation, if they demonstrate that:

- their net export revenues (including exports to parties domiciled in low taxation jurisdictions) in the calendar year do not exceed 5 per cent of the total net revenues for the period; or
- their net profits from exports to related parties, before the CSLL and the IRPJ provision, are equivalent to at least 10 per cent of the total revenues from such exports, considering the annual average for the current tax base period and for the two preceding years[7], and exports to related parties do not exceed 20 per cent of the total exportations for the period.

These two safe harbors provided by IN RFB 1312 do not apply to transactions with residents in low taxation jurisdictions (disputes may arise regarding their application to transactions carried out under privileged tax regimes), do not prevent the Brazilian tax authorities from investigating the relevant prices and issuing tax assessments whenever the applicability of those exceptions is deemed inadequate, and are not applicable to the export of commodities.

There are five methods to calculate the benchmark for exports:

- Export Sales Price ('PVEX');
- Wholesale Price in Country of Destination Less Profit ('PVA');
- Retail Price in Country of Destination Less Profit ('PVV'); and
- Purchasing or Production Cost Plus Taxes and Profit ('CAP').
- Export Quoted Price ('PECEX')

Comparable prices must be adjusted to balance different conditions as described in IN RFB 1312.

If the benchmark obtained by one method (most favorable at the option of the taxpayer except for the export of commodities, where the PECEX method is mandatory) is lower than actual export prices subject to transfer pricing controls, no adjustment shall be made to the IRPJ and CSLL bases. If the benchmark is higher than said export prices and this difference exceeds the variations deemed acceptable by the legislation, such difference must be added to IRPJ and CSLL bases.

PVEX. The benchmark is the weighted arithmetic average of export prices of the Brazilian company to non-related parties, or export prices of the same or similar assets, goods, services or rights performed by any other Brazilian company to non-related parties. The transactions considered in the

[7] Tax authorities usually issue an act allowing the calculation of this safe harbor to be made exclusively with data from the previous year.

benchmark calculation shall relate to the same reference period and must be carried out under similar payment conditions.

PVA. The benchmark is the weighted arithmetic average of wholesale prices of the same or similar assets or goods in the country of destination, subject to similar payment conditions, reduced by:

- taxes charged by that country on the sales price (similar to PIS/COFINS, ICMS and ISS); and
- a 15 per cent profit margin on the gross wholesale price.

PVV. The benchmark is the weighted arithmetic average of retail prices of the same or similar asset/goods in the importer country, subject to similar payment conditions, less:

- taxes charged by that country on the sale price (similar to PIS/COFINS, ICMS and ISS); and
- the 30 per cent profit margin on the gross retail price.

CAP. The benchmark is the arithmetic weighted average of purchase or production costs of the exported assets, goods, services, or rights plus Brazilian taxes and a 15 per cent profit margin over the total amount.

PECEX. The benchmark is the daily average price of goods and rights (commodities) subject to public prices, adjusted by the average market premium. This method is mandatory for the export of commodities and is not covered by the safe harbor of 90 per cent of the domestic price of the same goods.

In the event a specific commodity is not listed in the internationally recognized futures and commodities exchanges, the price of the exported good may be compared with (i) the information provided by the internationally recognized sector research institutions indicated by IN RFB 1312, or (ii) prices determined by regulatory agencies or organizations and published in the Official Federal Gazette.

The quoted price may be adjusted for the market premium paid in relation to the quality, characteristics and concentration of the good. Other admissible adjustments are:

- payment terms;
- quantities negotiated;
- climate influences on the characteristics of the goods;
- commissions paid to unrelated parties;
- storage;
- freight and insurance; and
- unloading, internal transportation, storage and clearance costs incurred at the commodity's destination.

To mitigate the effects of the appreciation of the Real, taxpayers were authorized to multiply the following by 1.00 in 2012,[8] 1.11 in 2011,[9] 1.09 in

[8] IN RFB 1321/2013.
[9] IN RFB 1233/12.

2010,[10] 1.00 in 2009,[11] 1.20 in 2008,[12] 1.28 in 2007,[13] 1.29 in 2006,[14] and 1.35 in 2005:[15] (i) their export revenues for comparison with sales of the same assets, goods, services and rights in the domestic market, when confirming the application of the 90 per cent export safe harbor; (ii) their export revenues to related parties in the calculation of the 5 per cent net profit safe harbor; and (iii) the price in exports to related parties to be compared with the corresponding benchmark based on CAP.

1.5 Common rules on imports and exports

Similar products. Similar products are those that concurrently: (i) have the same characteristics and application; (ii) have equivalent specifications; and (iii) can be mutually exchanged, in view of their intended purpose.

Variation margins. No transfer pricing adjustments are required for variations of up to 5 per cent between the benchmark and the prices practiced by the taxpayer. In case of import and export of commodities, variations of up to 3 per cent are acceptable.

Prices excluded for comparison purposes. Specially reduced prices (during sales season) or other unusual prices cannot be used for purposes of calculating benchmarks.

Taxpayers are allowed to choose the method which best suits their particular case and leads to the lowest tax adjustment, except in the case of commodities, for which a specific method shall be used. The chosen method shall be used consistently per type of asset, goods, right and service and there are disputes about the so-called 'basket approach' (which consists in bundling different types of items for transfer pricing purposes), which is normally not admissible.

Only the methods provided for expressly by law are allowed. No other method can be used, even if based on arm´s length principles and OECD guidelines.

2. IDENTIFICATION OF LEGISLATIVE FRAMEWORK

Transfer pricing is strictly a federal matter in Brazil. The main Brazilian transfer pricing rules are Law 9430/96, Normative Instruction (IN) SRF 243/02 (until it was revoked in 2012), Laws 12715/12 and 12766/12, which promoted substantial amendments to the Brazilian transfer pricing rules (in the calculation of the benchmark through the resale less profit method, the benchmark for commodities and imposing controls on back to back transaction, among other changes), and IN RFB 1312/12 (which revoked IN SRF 243/02).

10 Finance Minister Ordinance 4/11 and IN RFB 1124/11.
11 IN RFB 1010/10.
12 Finance Minister Ordinance 310/08 and IN RFB 898/08.
13 Finance Minister Ordinance 329/07 and IN RFB 801/07.
14 Finance Minister Ordinance 425/06 and IN SRF 703/06.
15 Finance Minister Ordinance 436/05 and IN SRF 602/05.

2.1 Federal legislation

Transfer pricing controls are a tax issue, and are thus under the competence of the Brazilian Federal Revenue. Even though all inspectors are, in theory, competent to address any issues of federal tax, for purposes of internal organization, the Brazilian Federal Revenue has created a special division (*Delegacia de Assuntos Internacionais*) to handle international matters, including transfer pricing. This division was subsequently renamed *Delegacia de Maiores Contribuintes*, and has offices in São Paulo and Rio de Janeiro.

In addition to the transfer pricing rules, taxpayers shall meet the general requirements for the deductibility of costs and expenses, as well as the specific thin capitalization rules.

2.2 State and provincial legislative Interplay

In Brazil there is no interaction between the Federal tax authorities and the State and Municipal tax authorities on transfer pricing matters. The only other auditing activity which may trigger a transfer pricing review is a customs audit, which is also federal, and under the competence of a specific division of the Brazilian Federal Revenue.

2.3 International treaties and agreements

Though the tax treaties signed by Brazil generally contain a provision equal or similar to article 9 of the OECD Model Tax Convention, there is no internal legislation expressly incorporating the arm's length principle or providing for correlative adjustments, which are not applied.

All Brazilian treaties contain exchange of information clauses and it is expected that Brazil will greatly increase the use of such tools in the future. Brazil also has various instruments designed to gather information internally. Brazilian companies are required to provide a great deal of information regarding their activities in general, and regarding their international transactions specifically. All transactions involving goods are registered in a system called Siscomex, and all transactions involving services and intangibles are registered in a system called Siscoserv, managed by the Brazilian Federal Revenue, together with the Ministry of Development, Industry and Commerce.

3. NATIONAL POLICY ISSUES

3.1 Overall national policy announcements

One general policy statement the Brazilian Federal Revenue has made in the past, though not officially, is that traditional transfer pricing rules based on OECD parameters are too complex and expensive to comply with. The Brazilian rules are consequently designed for easier compliance and less complexity.

While the Brazilian rules do accomplish such goals to a certain extent, this simplification causes certain distortions. These distortions should be corrected by direct interaction between the tax authorities and the taxpayers, though in practice this is rare.

3.2 National revenue authority initiatives

Brazilian legal entities must inform the tax authorities of the method chosen for transfer pricing purposes in their annual income tax returns, and provide them with all supporting documents required for the transfer pricing calculations upon request. Transfer pricing may be the subject of a random audit, but it is generally a specific review conducted by a specialized division of the Brazilian Federal Revenue in charge of international transactions.

3.3 Administrative statements

Since transfer pricing controls were introduced in Brazil, the Brazilian Federal Revenue has issued many rulings at the request of taxpayers on various matters of interpretation of transfer pricing legislation. Among these are rulings asserting that the Brazilian transfer pricing legislation does not conflict with the tax treaties to which Brazil is a party because Brazilian rules do not violate the arm's length principle (despite the formulaic approach of most methods). Other important recent rulings are those stating that back to back transactions (a transaction where a Brazilian company buys goods from a foreign supplier and has them delivered to a foreign customer, without physical transit through Brazil). In those transactions, two benchmarks shall be calculated: one for the acquisitions transaction, and another for the sale transaction. In both cases, the legal parameters of the method elected shall be observed.

3.4 Administrative guidelines

The Brazilian tax authorities do not normally issue guidelines. They either issue rulings at the request of taxpayers, or Normative Instructions, which set forth their understandings of any given laws.

4. CASE LAW

4.1 Current cases

From 2002 to 2012, Normative Instruction 243 specified the formula for calculating the parameter for the PRL method. However, this formula was disputed by taxpayers in numerous cases because it caused much greater adjustments than the formula taken directly from the wording of Law 9430. In decision 1201-00.658, the calculation of PRL pursuant to Normative Instruction 243 was overturned for exceeding the boundaries of the Law. However, recent decisions, such as Decision 1402-001.327 have rejected this argument, stating that the formula in the Normative Instruction was simply providing greater detail to the general provision of the Law, with which it did not conflict.

Another relevant subject of litigation is the possibility of taxpayers electing the resale less profit method in the period when this method was not expressly designed for the importation of goods to be used in the importer´s productive process. Taxpayers argue that they should be able to use this method in the absence of prohibition. The tax authorities argue that the method was only available for pure resale transactions, without any addition of value in the country. In decision 9101-001.349, the superior administrative appellate body found that the taxpayers were entitled to apply the resale method even if there had been some manufacturing in the country.

Another dispute refers to the choice of method. Tax inspectors are bound to apply the method chosen by the taxpayer. However, if that given method cannot be applied (or if no method at all was employed), the tax inspector is free to calculate adjustments under any remaining method available. This was the holding of the administrative court in Decision 1401-000.800. This is relevant because taxpayers often try to overturn assessments by arguing that the tax authority must apply all the methods and charge taxes according to the method that offers the least adjustment.

4.2 Historical cases of note

Tax litigation may occur in Brazil at the administrative level or in the courts. There are several cases on transfer pricing already judged at the highest administrative level. The most relevant cases discuss the conflicts between normative instructions issued by the Federal Revenue Service and transfer pricing legislation regarding the application of the PRL method, as discussed above.[16]

Other relevant cases address issues involving the PIC method, such as the requirements for eligible samples,[17] the use of CIF prices as benchmark[18] and the adoption of the basket approach,[19] as well as the compliance of transfer pricing controls with the arm's length principle embodied in tax treaties signed by Brazil.[20]

5. PENALTIES

5.1 Types

Violations of transfer pricing legislation are subject to the regular penalties applicable to any lack of payment of federal taxes in Brazil. The basic penalty is of 75 per cent of the amount of the tax unpaid. If there are indicia of fraud, the penalty is doubled to 150 per cent. If there is lack of collaboration, these penalties are increased by 50 per cent (to 112.5 per cent and 225 per cent respectively). If the taxpayer does not challenge the assessment and makes payment within 30 days, the penalty is reduced by 50 per cent.

All Brazilian legal entities must add the amount in excess to the tax bases of IRPJ and CSLL, regardless of being taxed on the Actual, Deemed or Arbitrated Profit, which are different forms of assessment of corporate taxes.

Brazilian taxpayers should recognize interest revenues arising from transactions subject to transfer pricing control when calculating their IRPJ and CSLL (irrespective of the method chosen to calculate both taxes), in an amount not lower than that obtained by calculating the interest rate provided in the transfer pricing legislation (as defined above).

16 Decisions 9101-001.349, 1302-00.915 and 1402-001.028, issued by the Taxpayer's Council of the Federal Revenue Service.
17 Decisions 105-16.718 and 1201-00.453.
18 Decision 1402-001.403.
19 Decisions 101-96.678 and 1103-00.104.
20 Decision 1401-000.801.

5.2 Special or notable cases

Transfer pricing rules are essentially a tax matter in Brazil. If there are no taxes due, penalties tend to be irrelevant (a fixed amount in Reais for inaccurate information in the returns).

6. DISPUTE RESOLUTION MECHANISMS

6.1 Preferred national options

A transfer pricing assessment may be challenged in two (in exceptional cases, three) administrative levels. In the first level the case is judged by tax inspectors with the specific function of serving as first level judges. The second level is judged by a court comprised of half representatives of the taxpayers and half representatives of the Revenue. If the decision diverges from precedents of the administrative court, an appeal to a Special Chamber is available. If the decision at the administrative level is favorable to the taxpayer, it is definitive. If unfavorable, the taxpayer may resort to the courts of law, where the case will be judged in three levels (two ordinary levels and one special appeal based on violation of federal law). Virtually all transfer pricing disputes in Brazil follow this path.

Brazilian legislation does not provide for Advance Pricing Agreements.

6.2 International options

Brazil has no experience with mutual agreement procedures, even though they are theoretically possible.

PART TWO: TAX AVOIDANCE

7. ACCEPTABLE TAX PLANNING AREAS/SUBJECTS

Brazil does not have clear legislation dealing with the limits of tax planning. Traditionally, Brazilian doctrines and jurisprudence have adopted a concept of strict legality, meaning any actions not considered illegal may be used as tax planning tools. That view has changed in the past few years, starting with the decisions of the administrative tax court, and ultimately leading to the issuance of Article 116, sole paragraph of the National Tax Code, intended to be a general anti-avoidance rule. According to that rule, *the administrative authority may disregard acts or legal transactions carried on with the intent to mask the taxable events occurred or the nature of the elements of the taxable event, subject to the procedures to be established by ordinary law.*

As the rule expressly states, it is still subject to regulation by subsequent legislation (and its constitutionality is being questioned before the Brazilian Supreme Court), but its principle is being adopted by the courts (in particular the administrative tax court) without much method; sometimes based on the concept of abuse of law, other times the doctrine of substance over form and lack of business purpose of the transactions, and still other times invoking the concept of fraud in the Brazilian Civil Code (a transaction that appears to confer or transfer rights to persons other than those who actually receive them).

Given the lack of clarity in the law, it is not surprising that the administrative tax court has ruled in different directions on this matter, but a review of the decisions, both domestic and international, show concern with artificial structures, put together for the exclusive purpose of saving taxes[21]. It is too early to identify any trends in the judicial courts, but the general view among practitioners is that abusive tax planning will become a highly litigated matter in the courts, at least until the guidelines on the limits of legitimate tax planning are better defined.

8. DEFINING ABUSIVE TAX AVOIDANCE

The only definition of tax avoidance there is in Brazil is that of article 116, sole paragraph of the National Tax Code, which deals with the concept of dissimulation of the taxable event.

9. THE LEGISLATIVE FRAMEWORK

The relevant rules for purposes of tax avoidance analysis are article 5 of the Brazilian Constitution, which sets forth the principle of legality (nobody is obliged to do or not do anything, except by virtue of law); article 116, sole paragraph, of the National Tax Code, referred to above; and article 118 of the same National Tax Code, according to which the occurrence of the taxable event shall be interpreted irrespective of the legality of the act and of the effects it produces.

10. KEY CASES OF INTEREST

10.1 Current cases

There are several cases under trial addressing abusive tax planning. Some of the most relevant cases involve billions of Reais. One notorious example is the assessment of Banco Santander for the amortization of goodwill in the acquisition of the Brazilian bank Banespa, which the tax authorities argue could not amortize because the goodwill was artificially created in Brazil (it should have been booked in Spain). Another notorious case is that of cosmetics company Natura, which organized its operations in two separate legal entities. The tax authorities argue that the effects of this segregation should be disregarded.

10.2 Key historical cases

Specifically in relation to transactions involving international structures, the CARF issued two different rulings about the same transaction, which give a good idea of the different lines of thinking of that court. The case in question involved two individual quota holders (residents of Brazil when the transaction took place) who carried on multiple transactions overseas (distribution of dividends – sales of participations – capital increase – capital decrease), each of which was tried separately.

[21] Decisions No. 103-07.260, 106-14.720, 101-95.208, 107-08.326 – 1st Council of Taxpayers.

In one of the cases,[22] the CARF accepted the structure adopted by the taxpayer and ruled that transactions carried on with the intent of tax savings are lawful when: (**i**) they are structured before the occurrence of the taxable event; (**ii**) the actions taken are lawful; and (**iii**) the actions taken are real (not simulated).

Additionally, the CARF understood that the use of companies in other jurisdictions is lawful and it may have other purposes than tax savings, for example: (**i**) separation of assets; (**ii**) succession planning; and (**iii**) hedging.

In the second case,[23] the CARF did not accept the structure adopted by the taxpayer and ruled that transactions structured in sequence with their only intent being to save taxes were to be disregarded.

The substance of legal entities or contractual arrangements is often the subject of litigation.

In a well known case called *Grendene*,[24] a shoe manufacturer, its shareholders created eight new commercial companies, which operated under a more favorable tax regime, and sold the product to such companies for a price close to cost, well below market value. The eight commercial companies sold the products to third parties at market price. The tax authorities assessed the company disregarding the eight commercial companies and combining their sales with those of the manufacturing company for purposes of calculating the applicable taxes, under the regular regime, applicable to the manufacturing company. The tax court upheld the assessment based on the following facts: (i) the structure's only purpose was to avoid taxes[25]; (ii) there was no true exercise of the mercantile activity by the eight companies; and (iii) the eight companies did not have physical premises and everything else a company needs to fully undertake its activities, four of them had no employees and the other four had one employee each.

In another case[26] the tax court understood that there was simulation in a situation where a company split itself into two in order to qualify for a beneficial tax treatment only available to small companies (Simples). The court understood that the split was ineffective for tax purposes because: (i) the new company was a dismemberment of the original company; (ii) they operated at the same address; (iii) the partners of the new company were closely related to the partners of the original company (sons); (iv) the water, electricity and phone bills were all paid by the original company, since the new company had no machinery, equipment, assets or real estate; (v) the activities of the new company were almost entirely directed to supply the needs of the original company and (vi) the partners of one company received remuneration from the other company.

The court reached a different conclusion in the case of a boat manufacturer, which split its activities into two companies, one dedicated

22 Decision No. 104-21.729 – 4th Chamber of the 1st Council of Taxpayers.

23 Decision No. 104-20.749 – 4th Chamber of the 1st Council of Taxpayers

24 Decision 103-07260, judged February 25, 1986.

25 According to the court *'One thing is to set up a company with the end purpose of evading taxes, another thing, very distinct, it to set up a company in which, incidentally, one happens to pay less taxes.'*

26 Decision 303-32460.

to selling the hull and the other dedicated to assembling, finishing and maintaining boats,[27] The court understood that the tax authorities had not presented sufficient evidence or indicia of simulation, because it was possible that the split was motivated by corporate reasons (the partners were not the same, because the partner of the original company retired from the new company) or with the intent of rationalizing operations. The court stated that result would have been different if the tax authorities had produced evidence that the new company did not keep proper books and records, did not have employees, did not enter into contracts and did not issue documents related to its business activities. The split in itself was not sufficient reason to disregard the structure.

At the State level there are cases dealing with the split of activities between companies subject to ICMS and to ISS (a municipal tax charged at the rates of 2 per cent to 5 per cent). In the case of *G5 Blindagens Especiais Ltda.*,[28] the tax authorities wanted to include the service revenues of one of the companies (specialized in installation of armored in cars) in the basis of the sales of goods of the other company (the armor kits). The companies had the same partners and one of them collected orders and received payments on behalf of the other. They were, however, located in different municipalities and effectively conducted different activities. The court found for the defendant, upholding the two-entity structure.

As with the notion of substance, the concept of business purpose is still evolving in Brazil. Some guiding elements, however, may be found in cases already tried, as in the following examples:

In the case of a company that sold kitchens,[29] the company was assessed to include in its revenues the sales of a related company, with which it operated as one single company. The operation was structured with two legal entities, one selling the kitchens and the other providing project and assembly services. Most of the price of the kitchens was attributed to the project and assembly activity, which is subject to lower taxes than the sale of the kitchens. The court found that the revenues of the project and assembly services company should be added to the revenues of the manufacturing company in order to determine the applicable taxes because in practice they worked as one single enterprise.

In a case of bus manufacturer Marcopolo,[30] the tax authorities wanted to disregard two foreign subsidiaries operating in privileged jurisdictions (BVI and Uruguay), which bought buses from Marcopolo and sold them in the international markets for a mark-up of around 15 per cent. The tax authorities argued that such companies were not truly operational and that the parent company Marcopolo was the one who ultimately sold the buses to the end customers. The defendant brought to the proceeding evidence that the companies in question had employees (a few, but sufficient to coordinate the commercial representatives operating in various companies),

---

27 Decision 103-23357, 3rd Chamber of the 1st Taxpayers Council, judged January 23, 2008.
28 Process DRT-14-300883/2006, 5th Temporary Chamber TIT/SP, judged June 24, 2009.
29 Decision 107-08326, judged November 9, 2005.
30 Decision 1402-00.753, 4th Chamber of the 2nd Group of CARF, judged September 30, 2011.

offices, phone bills, correspondence and agreements with the commercial representatives and end customers. The tax authorities were not able to support their assertion that it was Marcopolo who in reality performed the sales. The court found in favor of Marcopolo.

In the absence of comprehensive anti-avoidance legislation, jurisprudence has become the main source of guidance on the limits of tax planning in Brazil. It will be a few years, however, until such limits are established with some clarity.

11. PENALTIES

11.1 Legislative provisions

The system of tax penalties is fairly simple in Brazil, though very harsh. The regular applicable penalty is 75 per cent of the amount of the unpaid tax. If there are indicia of fraud, the penalty is doubled to 150 per cent. If there is lack of collaboration, these penalties are increased by 50 per cent (to 112.5 per cent and 225 per cent respectively). If the taxpayer does not challenge the assessment and makes payment within 30 days, the penalty is reduced by 50 per cent.

The imposition of the 150 per cent penalty is quite common in tax avoidance cases, but it only prevails when the elements of fraud are very clear.

11.2 Examples of penalties imposed

All cases of tax avoidance are subject to the imposition of penalties. It is very common that the tax authorities identify elements of fraud or abuse and try to impose the 150 per cent penalty, rather than the usual 75 per cent penalty. The 150 per cent penalty is usually upheld only in cases where fraudulent intent is very clear.

12. CURRENT TRENDS

The current trend in Brazil is that the tax system will become even more complex, in terms of both legislation and compliance, despite the clamor of taxpayers for simplification and consciousness on the part of the Government that the Brazilian tax system overall is inefficient. Rather than an overall reform, what has occurred and will probably continue to occur in Brazil is a very large number of exceptions to the general rules to accommodate the needs of various industries or economic sectors, without any integration or consistency, making the exception the rule. The requirements of electronic filings are enormous, reaching all areas of operations of the taxpayers (accounting, purchases, sales, human resources, services, payments abroad, several specific tax filings, etc.). In the next few years, Brazil will likely structure itself to begin intensive exchange of information with other jurisdictions, based on international treaties. The Government will probably continue to aggressively assess taxpayers while a clearer line is drawn by the jurisprudence between legitimate and illegitimate tax planning. The very frequent tax amnesty programs should continue to be issued from time to time.

12.1 National policy and law

There are no stated policies aimed at curbing abusive tax avoidance, but recent history shows a great effort on the part of the Government to do so. There are legislative initiatives, such as the creation of an intended general anti-avoidance rule, not yet regulated, and the creation of several specific anti-avoidance rules and administrative initiatives, such as the aggressive assessment of taxpayers, large investments in tax intelligence and the reorganization of the administrative tax court, making it less taxpayer-friendly. This is in addition to judicial initiatives, with very active litigation, close contact with the judges, and the presentation of arguments of economic consequences to the country of certain key tax matters subject to the appreciation of the courts.

12.1.1 The Impact and role of the OECD and other International relations

Brazil is not a party to the OECD, but it follows the discussions very closely, as well as the developments and recommendations of the various OECD *fora*, including BEPS – Base Erosion and Profit Sharing Actions Plan.

Brazilian tax authorities are in constant exchange with other tax administrations on best practices, though in many matters they prefer to forge their own path. Some of these initiatives are very positive (for example, the wide use of internet for filing income tax returns of individuals, which come partially filled in), while some are less so (for example, the peculiar views the Brazilian tax authorities had on treaty interpretation until recently).

Given the competitive view of taxation in today's world of global trade, the tendency is that tax systems become more and more uniform. This is no different for Brazil, whose system should become more consistent with international practices over time, despite the internal political challenges of changing the current tax system of the country.

Canada

Miller Thomson LLP
David W Chodikoff & Laura Etherington

PART ONE: TRANSFER PRICING

1. GENERAL OVERVIEW

The Canada Revenue Agency (the 'CRA'), the federal agency responsible for collecting and administering tax laws for the Canadian government and most Canadian provinces/territories, defines transfer prices as 'the prices at which services, tangible property, and intangible property are traded across international borders between related parties'.[1] As such, transfer pricing relates to transactions and arrangements as between a taxpayer and a non-resident person, who is not at arm's length. In such cases, penalties may arise where the transfer prices charged differ from those that would have been charged between persons dealing at arm's length. Canadian tax law establishes that the correct transfer price is that which parties dealing at arm's length would have agreed upon for a particular transaction.

The origin of transfer pricing regulation is tied to the concern that certain enterprise's may transfer profits to lower tax jurisdictions, with the aim of reducing taxes that would otherwise be payable by them. In Canada, legislation has been enacted which governs transfer pricing, and the CRA has promulgated administrative policies/guidelines aimed at providing additional guidance with respect to transfer pricing. In recent years, there has been increased focus on transfer pricing.

2. IDENTIFICATION OF LEGISLATIVE FRAMEWORK

(a) Federal

The key piece of federal tax legislation in Canada is the Income Tax Act[2] (the 'Act'). In particular, s. 247 of the Act governs transfer pricing. Section 247 of the Act mandates arm's length transfer prices for transactions with non-arm's length non-residents (*discussed in more detail below in section 2.1 – Federal Legislation*).

(b) Provincial

In Canada, the provinces/territories legislate their own corporate income tax rules, however the CRA administers corporate income taxes for all provinces/ territories (with the exception of Alberta and Quebec). A discussion of the implications of this are discussed further below (*see section 2.2 – State and*

1 CRA, Information Circular IC87-2R, *International Transfer Pricing* (September 27, 1999) at page 1, s. 2, online: *http://www.cra-arc.gc.ca/tx/nnrsdnts/cmmn/trns/menu-eng.html*.

2 [2]Income Tax Act, RSC 1985, c 1 (5th Supp).

provincial legislative interplay) – but essentially, the federal *Act* encompasses the rules applicable to transfer pricing in Canada.

2.1 Federal legislation

Section 247 of the Act encompasses transfer pricing provisions.[3] The following is a summary of some of the major subsections contained within s. 247.

Subsection 247(2) sets out the heart of s. 247 – the 'arm's length principle'. Section 274(2) establishes that it applies in two scenarios: (i) a transaction between a taxpayer and a non-resident person, where the parties are not dealing at arm's length; and (ii) a transaction between a partnership/member of a partnership and a non-resident person, where the parties are not dealing at arm's length.[4] Section 247(2) also states that where the terms/conditions of the applicable transaction differ from those that would have been made between persons dealing at arm's length, the following will apply:

- Any amounts determined under the Act for a taxpayer will be adjusted, so as to reflect those amounts that would have been determined if the terms/conditions of the transaction were those that would have been made between arm's length parties; and
- A re-characterization of the transaction will be permitted to determine the amounts that would have been determined if the transaction had been one that would have been entered into between arm's length parties, where the following conditions are present: (i) the parties entered a transaction that would not have been entered into between arm's length parties; and (ii) it is reasonable to consider the transaction was not entered into primarily for *bona fide* purposes other than to obtain a tax benefit.[5]

The arm's length principle treats parties not dealing at arm's length as if they operate as separate entities (and not as inseparable parts of a single business) and compares prices/margins between non-arm's length parties on cross-border transaction as against prices/margins on similar transactions between arm's length parties. [6]

Subsection 247(3) establishes the penalty that arises where the net result of transfer pricing adjustments made under s. 247(2) for a taxpayer in a tax year exceed the lesser of: (i) 10 per cent of the taxpayer's gross revenue for the year; and (ii) $5,000,000.[7]

Subsection 247(4) requires taxpayers to make or obtain, on or before the tax year filing date, certain records/documents and provide those records/

3 It is important to note that s. 247 applies to tax years beginning after 1997 (replacing the previously applicable ss. 69(2) and 69(3) under the *Act*), but that ss. 247(3) and (4), pertaining to penalties, generally apply to adjustments under s. 247(2) for tax years beginning after 1998.

4 Including where a partnership is dealing with a non-resident that is a member of that partnership.

5 CRA, Information Circular IC87-2R, *International Transfer Pricing* (September 27, 1999) at page 2, ss. 8 & 9, online: *http://www.cra-arc.gc.ca/tx/nnrsdnts/cmmn/trns/menu-eng.html.*

6 CRA, Information Circular IC87-2R, *International Transfer Pricing* (September 27, 1999) at page 2, ss. 12 & 13, online: *http://www.cra-arc.gc.ca/tx/nnrsdnts/cmmn/trns/menu-eng.html.*

7 Further details pertaining to transfer pricing penalties are set out in section 5 – Penalties below.

documents to the Minister of National Revenue ('MNR') within 3 months of a written request to do so.[8]

Subsection 247(10) provides the MNR with the discretion to make downward transfer pricing adjustments (ie, adjustments resulting in decreased taxpayer's income, increased taxpayer's loss or increased taxpayer's capital expenditures for the year) in favour of the taxpayer, where the 'circumstances are such that it would be appropriate that the adjustment be made'.

Reference should be made to s. 247 of the Act for further details with respect to the subsections not addressed here.[9]

2.2 State and provincial legislative interplay

The transfer pricing rules set out in the various provincial/territorial corporate income tax statutes are harmonized with the transfer pricing rules set out in the federal Act. While the federal CRA does not administer corporate income taxes in Alberta and Quebec, neither of these provinces have a separate levy for transfer pricing penalties.[10]

2.3 International treaties and agreements

(a) Paramountcy

When considering transfer pricing issues, it is important to assess whether any international tax treaties apply to override the domestic rules. Bilateral income tax conventions often contain 'a related persons'/'associated enterprises' article setting out the arm's length principle applicable in transfer pricing matters.

For example, Canada entered the Canada-United States Convention with Respect to Taxes on Income and on Capital[11] ('CRTIC'). Article IX of the CRTIC deals with 'related persons' and s. 1 therein establishes that each country may adjust the amount of income, loss or tax payable to reflect the income, deductions, credits or allowances which would – but for arrangements made between related parties differing form those that would be made between unrelated persons – have been taken into account in computing such income, loss or tax. Notably, where the CRTIC applies, and

---

8 The records/documents must contain a description with respect to such things as: the property/services to which the transaction relates, the terms/conditions of the transaction their relationship to the terms/conditions of each other transaction entered into between the parties to the transaction, the identity of the parties and their relationship to each other, the functions performed/property used/risks assumed by the parties in the transactions, the data/methods considered and analysis performed to determine the transfer prices/allocations of profits and losses/contributions to costs, and the assumptions/strategies/policies influencing the determination of transfer prices/allocations of profits or losses/contributions to costs.

9 Subsections 247(5) and (6) deem certain matters relating to a member of a partnership for purposes of s. 247. Subsections 247(7) and (7.1) establish two scenarios in which an adjustment in subs. 247(2) will not apply (ie, loans to enumerated controlled foreign affiliates and enumerated guarantees). Subsection 247(8) deals with paramountcy of provisions and subs. 247(9) sets out a penalty anti-avoidance provision. Subsections 427(11) and (15) deal with applicability and non-applicability of other provisions of the Act. Finally subss. 427(12), (13) and (14) deal with deemed dividends to non-residents and repatriation associated with same.

10 In Alberta, s. 8.4 of the Alberta Corporate Tax Act, R.S. A. 2000, c. A-15, sets out that all of s. 247 of the Act applies -with the exception of subss. (3) and (11) – ensuring that no separate levy exists for transfer pricing penalties. In Québec, s. 1082.3 – 1082.13 were added to the Taxation Act, R.S. Q. c I-3, in 2001 in order to harmonize the legislation with s. 247 of the Act. This resulted in the doubling of transfer pricing penalties imposed. As a result, the transfer pricing penalty imposed under the Québec legislation was retroactively abolished, so as to remove the separate levy for transfer pricing penalties in Québec.

11 *Canada-United States Convention with Respect to Taxes on Income and on Capital*, S.C. 1984, c. 20, Schedule I.

where there is an inconsistency between the provisions of the Act and the provisions of the CRTIC, the CRTIC will prevail over the Act.[12]

(b) Mutual agreement procedure and competent authority

Furthermore, issues may arise where the CRA applies transfer pricing rules under the Act in a way that differs from the assessment of a foreign revenue authority (ie, double taxation issues). In such instances, the income tax conventions entered into by Canada with various countries, often provide for a mutual agreement procedure.[13] The CRA has a mutual agreement procedure program which may be used by taxpayers to request assistance from a competent authority of the CRA to resolve tax disputes.

(c) Exchange of information

Tax treaties may also provide for the exchange of information among the participant countries. For example, Article XXVII of the CRTIC allows the CRA to gather information through exchange of information with the United States, as long as the information is relevant to carrying out the provisions of the convention or the provisions of the domestic laws. This is highly relevant for audits – as countries may exchange information during audits to gather information on both countries affiliate entities.

3. NATIONAL POLICY ISSUES

In the past few years, the CRA has placed increased emphasis on transfer pricing examinations. The CRA continues to issue guidance to supplement the transfer pricing rules contained in the Act. Most recently, emphasis has been placed on increased documentation requirements, and increased auditing/penalization for transfer pricing.

3.1 Overall national policy announcements

The CRA has explicitly stated that the *Transfer Pricing Guidelines for Multinational Enterprises and Tax Administrations* ('OECD Guidelines') should be consulted in ensuring compliance with transfer pricing rules. The OECD has recently proposed reforms[14] to the OECD Guidelines in order to increase the documentation and reporting obligations applicable to multinational enterprises. [15]

The reforms would require disclosure of taxes paid in all jurisdictions in which a business operates. Multinational enterprises would be required to submit each year a 'master file' for all countries it does business in.

---

12 See s. 3(2) of An Act to Implement a Convention between Canada and the United States with respect to Taxes on Income and on Capital, S.C. 1984, c. 20.

13 The Organisation for Economic Co-operation and Development (the 'OECD') model convention recommends that bilateral tax conventions include a mutual agreement procedure to establish a dispute resolution mechanism in order to resolve the double taxation issue (*discussed further below, see section 6.2 – Dispute resolution mechanisms: international options*).

14 The reforms are aimed at complying with the 19 July 2013 Base Erosion and Profit Shifting Action Plan, which directed the OECD to develop rules regarding transfer pricing documentation to enhance transparency for tax administration, including a requirement that multinational enterprises provide all relevant governments with needed information on global allocation of income, economic activity and taxes paid among countries according to a common template.

15 OECD, *Revised Discussion Draft on Transfer Pricing Documentation and CbC Reporting*, (January 30, 2014) at 1, online: *http://www.oecd.org/tax/discussion-draft-transfer-pricing-documentation.htm*.

This file would contain details of the enterprise's organisational structure, descriptions of its businesses, intangibles, intercompany financial activities, as well as its financial/tax position (broken down for each country). Multinational enterprises would also be required to submit separate 'local files' for each jurisdiction, limited to only those details pertaining to the local entities and material transactions within those jurisdictions.

This would allow the revenue authorities to better identify high-risk situations for transfer pricing, as well as allow more thorough audits. The flip side is that businesses may be unduly burdened with increased compliance costs associated with the reforms.[16]

3.2 National revenue authority initiatives

(a) Advance Pricing Arrangements

With respect to initiatives, the CRA is a participant in advance pricing arrangements ('APAs'). An APA is an arrangement between the tax authority and a taxpayer with a cross-border related party transaction, which sets out the arm's length transfer pricing methodology that all parties agree to and which is to be used by the taxpayer.

The CRA developed the APA program to avoid high cost audits and to increase certainty with respect to international transaction pricing. The use of an APA allows taxpayers to avoid transfer pricing audits through a process which instead involves due diligence, development of transfer pricing analysis and a position paper by the CRA. Given that Canada is among one of the top countries in pursuing transfer pricing, involving audits and adjustments, the use of an APA can provide considerable advantages in some circumstances. An APA has the potential of providing taxpayers certainty in transfer pricing for a period of up to five years, in addition to avoiding transfer pricing penalties.

(b) Pacific Association of Tax Administrators ('PATA') transfer pricing documentation package

Currently, Canada is a PATA member[17] which entails involvement in an initiative to provide principles under which taxpayers will be able to create uniform transfer pricing documentation ('PATA Documentation Package'). This allows for one set of documentation to meet the various members' transfer pricing documentation provisions. The PATA Documentation Package is not mandated under law, and its use will be entirely voluntary on the part of the taxpayer. Its use will avoid the imposition of transfer pricing penalties associated with documented transactions in PATA member jurisdictions. However, taxpayers may still be subject to transfer pricing adjustments and related interest on adjustments by the CRA. The aim of this initiative is to reduce the burden and costs associated with

[16] The discussion draft setting out these reforms is still in the consultation phase. Should it be implemented the CRA would likely issue a transfer pricing memorandum to provide an overview of the implications. The CRA previously circulated a transfer pricing memorandum providing an overview of the updates to the OECD Guidelines in 2010 – see CRA, TPM-14, *2010 Update of the OECD Transfer Pricing Guidelines*, (October 31, 2012), online: *http://www.cra-arc.gc.ca/tx/nnrsdnts/cmmn/trns/menu-eng.html*.

[17] Along with Australia, Japan and the United States.

duplicative administrative requirements and assist in efficient preparation of documentation requirements, while avoiding related penalties.[18]

3.3 Administrative statements

The administrative rules of the CRA are contained within information circulars. Of particular relevance to transfer pricing is Information Circular 87-2R: International Transfer Pricing[19] ('IC87-2R').

IC87-2R provides in depth explanation as to the transfer pricing rules in Canada. To begin, IC87-2R provides an overview of s. 247 of the Act and breaks down the various subsections. It then goes on to explain the arm's length principle and methods of applying the arm's length principle. IC87-2R defines and discusses qualifying cost contribution arrangements[20], and specific considerations relating to intangible property and intra-group services. Next, IC87-2R explains how transfer pricing penalties are calculated, explains what 'reasonable efforts' are required to be made to determine arm's length prices/allocations and discusses other matters pertaining to penalties. It then discusses the confidentiality of third party information used for comparables by the CRA in determining the proper arm's length prices/allocations, and the implications of transfer pricing adjustments for tax withholdings under Part XIII of the Act. IC87-2R sets out information pertaining to the competent authority procedures pertaining to double taxation, and introduces the CRA's APA program. Finally, it states that the CRA is not obliged to accept values reported for duty when considering income tax implications of non-arm's length importation.

Three other information circulars of relevance to transfer pricing, and which discuss in more detail items addressed in IC87-2R, are Information Circular 94-4R: International Transfer Pricing: Advanced Pricing Arrangements;[21] Information Circular 71-17R4: Request for Competent Authority Consideration Under Mutual Agreement Procedures in Income Tax Conventions;[22] and Information Circular IC06-1:Income Tax Transfer Pricing and Customs Valuation.[23]

3.4 Administrative guidelines

(a) Transfer pricing memoranda

The CRA periodically issues transfer pricing memoranda, which supplement information circulars and provide additional guidance as to particular

[18] CRA, *Pacific Association of Tax Administrators (PATA) Transfer Pricing Documentation Package*, online: *http://www.cra-arc.gc.ca/tx/nnrsdnts/cmmn/trns/pt-eng.html.*

[19] CRA, Information Circular IC87-2R, *International Transfer Pricing* (September 27, 1999), online: *http://www.cra-arc.gc.ca/tx/nnrsdnts/cmmn/trns/menu-eng.html.*

[20] Qualifying cost contribution arrangements are defined as arrangements where two or more parties share costs and risks of producing, developing or acquiring any property, or acquiring or performing any services, in proportion to the benefits which each participant is reasonably expected to derive from the property or services as a result of the arrangement.

[21] CRA, Information Circular 94-4R: *International Transfer Pricing: Advance Pricing Arrangements (APAs)* (March 16, 2001), online: *http://www.cra-arc.gc.ca/menu/ICSC-e.html.*

[22] CRA, Information Circular 71-17R4: *Request for Competent Authority Consideration Under Mutual Agreement Procedures in Income Tax Conventions* (May 12, 1995), online: *http://www.cra-arc.gc.ca/menu/ICSC-e.html.*

[23] CRA, Information Circular IC06-1: *Income Tax Transfer Pricing and Customs Valuation* (October 5, 2006), online: *http://www.cra-arc.gc.ca/menu/ICSC-e.html.*

aspects of transfer pricing rules. For example, there are transfer pricing memoranda which explain:

- Repatriation policy application to international transfer pricing;[24]
- Downward transfer pricing adjustments;[25]
- Use of confidential third-party information in the context of transfer pricing audits;[26]
- Requests for contemporaneous documentation;[27]
- Bundling of transactions in relation to transfer pricing and non-resident tax;[28]
- Cases under audit concerning fixed base or permanent establishment determinations under Canadian income tax conventions;[29]
- Definition of 'reasonable efforts' to determine/use arm's length transfer prices/allocations;[30]
- APA requests to cover prior taxation years;[31]
- Accelerated competent authority procedure requests;[32]
- Referrals to Transfer Pricing Review Committee regarding possible assessments, penalties;[33] and
- Changes made in the 2010 version of the OECD Guidelines and of CRA's position regarding these changes.[34]

(b) OECD Guidelines

The OECD Guidelines serve as a very important transfer pricing resource in Canada.[35] In Canada, transfer pricing rules are heavily interpreted based upon the OECD Guidelines – which are incorporated by references throughout IC87-2R and IC94-4R. The OECD Guidelines should be referenced when dealing with transfer pricing matters, despite the fact that they are not binding law.

4. CASE LAW

In Canada, there are only a handful of federal tax decisions, which serve as precedents for taxpayers as to the substantive requirements of s. 247 of the

24 CRA, TPM-02: *Repatriation of funds by Non-residents – Part XIII Assessments* (March 27, 2003), online: *http://www.cra-arc.gc.ca/tx/nnrsdnts/cmmn/trns/menu-eng.html.*

25 CRA, TPM-03: *Downward Transfer Pricing Adjustments Under Subsection 247(2)* (October 20, 2003), online: *http://www.cra-arc.gc.ca/tx/nnrsdnts/cmmn/trns/menu-eng.html.*

26 CRA, TPM-04: *Third Party Information* (October 27, 2003), online: *http://www.cra-arc.gc.ca/tx/nnrsdnts/cmmn/trns/menu-eng.html.*

27 CRA, TPM-05: *Contemporaneous Documentation* (October 13, 2004), online: *http://www.cra-arc.gc.ca/tx/nnrsdnts/cmmn/trns/menu-eng.html.*

28 CRA, TPM-06: *Bundled Transactions* (May 16, 2005), online: *http://www.cra-arc.gc.ca/tx/nnrsdnts/cmmn/trns/menu-eng.html.*

29 CRA, TPM-08: *The Dudney Decision: Effects on Fixed Base or Permanent Establishment Audits and Regulation 105 Treaty-Based Waiver Guidelines* (December 5, 2005), online: *http://www.cra-arc.gc.ca/tx/nnrsdnts/cmmn/trns/menu-eng.html.*

30 CRA, TPM-09: *Reasonable Efforts Under Section 247 of the Income Tax Act* (September 18, 2006), online: *http://www.cra-arc.gc.ca/tx/nnrsdnts/cmmn/trns/menu-eng.html.*

31 CRA, TPM-11: *Advance Pricing Arrangements (APA) Rollback* (October 28, 2008), online: *http://www.cra-arc.gc.ca/tx/nnrsdnts/cmmn/trns/menu-eng.html.*

32 CRA, TPM-12: *Accelerated Competent Authority Procedure (ACAP)* (December 12, 2008), online: *http://www.cra-arc.gc.ca/tx/nnrsdnts/cmmn/trns/menu-eng.html.*

33 CRA, TPM-13: *Referrals to the Transfer Pricing Review Committee* (October 20, 2012), online: *http://www.cra-arc.gc.ca/tx/nnrsdnts/cmmn/trns/menu-eng.html.*

34 CRA, TPM -14: *2010 Update of the OECD Transfer Pricing Guidelines* (October 31, 2012), online: *http://www.cra-arc.gc.ca/tx/nnrsdnts/cmmn/trns/menu-eng.html.*

35 The OECD Guidelines were put into place to provide guidance to member countries, who signed the convention of the OECD, as to the application of the 'arm's length principle' for valuation.

Act. A large percentage of these transfer pricing cases are decisions occurring fairly recently, since 2000. The CRA has placed an emphasis on certain sectors, including the oil and gas, pharmaceutical, automotive and financial services industries – and this is reflected in the jurisprudence.[36] Much of transfer pricing jurisprudence has historically demonstrated a greater success rate for taxpayer appellants, as compared to tax authority success rates.

4.1 Current cases

(a) Canada v GlaxoSmithKline Inc

A recent decision, *Canada v GlaxoSmithKline Inc*,[37] dealing with the pricing of the active ingredient in an anti-ulcer drug called Zantac, was the first transfer pricing decision to be heard by the Supreme Court of Canada ('SCC'). While the Court remitted the case back to the Tax Court of Canada for a determination of the arm's length price, the decision provides useful guidance as to the Canadian judiciary's approach to be applied in determining an arm's length price.

In particular, the Court held that the totality of the 'economic and business realities' must be considered.[38] In applying the arm's length principle, courts must have regard to the 'economically relevant characteristics' of both the arm's length and non-arm's length corporations' circumstances in order to ensure they are sufficiently comparable.[39] The Court stated that such characteristics may include 'other transactions that impact the transfer price under consideration'.[40] Based on this consideration, a transaction-by-transaction approach may or may not be appropriate.[41]

(b) Burlington Resources Finance Co v Canada

The Tax Court of Canada, in *Burlington Resources Finance Co v Canada*,[42] looked at whether a Nova Scotia unlimited liability company that borrowed $3 billion by issuing seven bonds guaranteed by its parent corporation is correct in challenging the CRA for disallowing deductions for the guarantee fees ($83 million was paid in guarantee fees in taxation years 2002–2005), on the basis of s. 247(2) of the Act. The taxpayer argued that the CRA had no reasonable chance of success based on the arguments as pleaded, as the CRA was erroneously challenging the terms and conditions of the guarantee fees as opposed to the guarantee itself.

The Court agreed with the taxpayer, stating that the CRA's framing of the issue – as whether the terms or conditions made with respect to the guarantee fees payable by the taxpayer to the parent company differed from those that would have been made by persons dealing at arm's length – was manifestly incorrect and a fatal deficiency. The Court stated the correct

36 Historically, the courts also placed emphasis on the forestry sector, but no recent decisions have dealt with the forestry sector.
37 *Canada v GlaxoSmithKline Inc*, [2012] 3 SCR 3, 2012 SCC 52 (SCC).
38 *Canada v GlaxoSmithKline Inc*, [2012] 3 SCR 3, 2012 SCC 52 at para. 53 (SCC).
39 *Canada v GlaxoSmithKline Inc*, [2012] 3 SCR 3, 2012 SCC 52 at para. 41 (SCC).
40 *Canada v GlaxoSmithKline Inc*, [2012] 3 SCR 3, 2012 SCC 52 at para. 42 (SCC).
41 Notably, the Court also made it clear that the OECD Guidelines are not to be considered controlling as if they were a Canadian statute, and the Act must be referenced with respect to the assessment of transactions or prices, rather than any methodology or commentary included in the OECD Guidelines.
42 *Burlington Resources Finance Co v Canada*, [2013] TCJ No 199, 2013 TCC 231 (TCC).

question to ask under s. 247(2)(a) and (c) of the *Act* is whether the terms or conditions imposed in respect of the guarantee itself, not the terms or conditions of the guarantee fees, differed from those that would have been set between persons dealing at arm's length.[43] As such, the Court allowed the CRA leave to file a further amended reply.

(c) McKesson Canada Corp v Canada

Most recently, in *McKesson Canada Corp v Canada*,[44] the Tax Court of Canada looked at a case in which the taxpayer was the principal Canadian operating company of a US health care multinational. The taxpayer was appealing the CRA's transfer pricing adjustment made to its income, pursuant to s. 247(2)(a) and (c), with respect to transactions between the taxpayer and related non-Canadian affiliates pertaining to the sale of accounts receivable. The taxpayer was also liable for failure to withhold and remit non-resident withholding tax from the disallowed amounts paid to it by the non-resident parent company. The CRA argued that the amounts paid to the non-Canadian entity differed from what would have been paid between arm's length entities.

The Court dismissed the taxpayer's appeal stating that it failed to establish that the discount rate used for its receivables transaction was computed based on arm's length terms and conditions. The taxpayer also failed to disprove the key assumptions of fact made by the CRA. In making its holding, the Court stated 'this appears to have been much more of a tax avoidance plan than a structured finance product.'[45]

4.2 Historical cases of note

(a) Indalex Ltd v Canada

The Federal Court of Appeal ('FCA') decided *Indalex Ltd v Canada*[46] in 1987. This case involved a taxpayer corporation in the business of moulding of aluminum billet, which was indirectly controlled by a company in England. The British company had a wholly-owned subsidiary in Bermuda. When purchasing aluminum, the taxpayer sent a copy of the purchase order to both the Bermuda subsidiary and a Canadian supplier of aluminum billet. The Canadian supplier would then receive an official purchase order from the Bermuda subsidiary, but would act prior to receipt of the formal purchase order, on the basis of the purchase order received from the taxpayer. The Canadian supplier would then ship the aluminum billet directly to the taxpayer and send its invoice to the Bermuda subsidiary, who would then invoice the taxpayer for the same amount. Afterwards, the taxpayer would credit the Bermuda subsidiary's bank account the invoice price, the Bermuda subsidiary would credit the Canadian supplier's account the same amount, and lastly, the Canadian supplier's parent company would credit the Bermuda subsidiary bank account in US dollars an amount

43 *Burlington Resources Finance Co v Canada*, [2013] TCJ No 199, 2013 TCC 231 at para. 29 (TCC).
44 *McKesson Canada Corp v Canada*, [2013] T CJ No 349, 2013 TCC 404 (TCC).
45 *McKesson Canada Corp v Canada*, [2013] T CJ No 349, 2013 TCC 404 at para. 274 (TCC).
46 *Indalex Ltd v Canada*, [1987] FCJ No 1150, 16 FTR 240 (FCA).

for 'discounts' attributable to the purchase price. Discounts in Canadian dollars were also paid to the taxpayer. The MNR included in the taxpayer's income the amounts paid as discounts to the Bermuda subsidiary.

At the Federal Court, Trial Division level, the court rejected the taxpayer's argument that the price would be the same with an arm's length transaction. However, it held that a portion of the discounts paid to the Bermuda subsidiary did not amount to artificial reduction of income on the basis that the Bermuda subsidiary's increased purchasing power resulted in lower prices being paid to the Canadian supplier. As such, the taxpayer's appeal was allowed in part. The taxpayer appealed to the FCA and the Crown cross-appealed.

The FCA dismissed the taxpayer's appeal and allowed the Crown's cross-appeal. The Court found that the trial judge erred in finding that any part of the discount could be sustained as a result of the Bermuda subsidiaries purchasing power. This was because the increased purchasing power was solely due to the pooling of purchasing power of members of the Bermuda subsidiaries group – to which the taxpayer was an important contributor – and there was no evidence to show that the Bermuda subsidiary contributed anything to the pooled purchasing power.

(b) Safety Boss Ltd v Canada

In 2000, the Tax Court of Canada decided *Safety Boss Ltd v Canada*.[47] The company was in the business of oilfield firefighting and paid a bonus of $3 million to an individual ('Miller') who was the president and 99 per cent shareholder of the taxpayer. The bonus was paid in recognition of Miller having obtained key work for the taxpayer, and having done high quality work, as a result of his expertise in the area. The work involved oil fields in Kuwait, as a result of the Gulf War. The bonus was paid on a pro-rata basis. Miller became a non-resident of Canada during the period of payment, and declared the pro-rata amount of his bonus that was earned while he was resident in Canada as income earned in Canada. An additional fee was paid to Miller's non-resident company at a later time. The MNR disallowed a portion of the bonus and fee paid to Miller's company on the grounds that they would not have been paid between parties dealing at arm's length. Additionally, the MNR treated the disallowed amounts as benefits conferred on Miller so as to impose a non-resident withholding tax and penalty.

The Court allowed the taxpayer's appeal, stating that it was not unreasonable for the taxpayer to pay Miller or his company the amounts paid in bonus or fee. In reaching this conclusion, the Court stated that the government of Kuwait, clearly at arm's length, had paid exceptionally more than the amounts in question to the taxpayer, in exchange for Miller's expertise and services. It was important to consider that Miller's experience and contacts made the contract with Kuwait possible to begin with.[48] In

[47] *Safety Boss Ltd v Canada*, [2000] TCJ N. 18, 3 CTC 2497(TCC [General Procedure]).
[48] *Safety Boss Ltd v Canada*, [2000] TCJ N. 18, 3 CTC 2497 at paras. 51 & 53 (TCC [General Procedure]).

reaching its decision, the Court also considered the fact that Miller had taken very little remuneration in past years when business was lean.

(c) General Electric Capital Canada Inc v Canada

In 2010, the FCA decided *General Electric Capital Canada Inc v Canada.*[49] This case dealt with an assessment by the MNR denying the taxpayer the full amount of deductions claimed in computing income with respect to fees paid to its US parent company, for guaranteeing its capital borrowings, on the grounds that the fees would not what would have been paid by an arm's length party for the guarantee. The MNR also assessed with respect to consequential adjustments that arose from the fees deemed to be dividends held by the US parent.

The Tax Court of Canada ruled in favour of the taxpayer, assessing the arm's length price of the guarantee based on the value of the benefit provided using the yield approach, and held that the 1 per cent fee charged was less than the interests the taxpayer would have paid on the guaranteed portion of its debt given its assumed credit rating without the guarantee. The FCA dismissed the appeal of the Tax Court's decision, holding that the Tax Court judge did not err in considering the parent company's implicit support as a factor in calculating the value of the guarantee under the yield method.

(d) Alberta Printed Circuits Ltd v The Queen

The Tax Court of Canada decided *Alberta Printed Circuits Ltd v Canada*[50] in 2011. The facts of the decision involved a taxpayer who was reassessed on the basis of having overpaid a non-resident Barbados corporation for services. The overpaid amount was then added back into the taxpayer's income for the applicable tax years. An individual who owned 25 per cent of the taxpayer entity's shares was also the sole director, president and chief executive officer of the Barbados corporation.

The Court found that the two entities were not dealing at arm's length, as they acted in concert and without separate interests, and that the interests of both entities were to move money off-shore for their mutual benefit.[51] The Court did, however, reduce the amounts added to the taxpayers income based on the prices paid for services, after a detailed analysis of the transfer pricing adjustment provisions. [52]

5. PENALTIES

There are a variety of penalties applicable to transfer pricing. Section 247(3) of the Act sets out the penalty associated with adjustments to taxpayer's revenue for transfer pricing. Additionally, s. 227(8) of the Act sets out penalties for failure to withhold, and s. 163.1 sets out penalties for

49 *General Electric Capital Canada Inc v Canada*, [2010] FCJ No 1603, 2010 FCA 344 (FCA).

50 *Alberta Printed Circuits Ltd v Canada*, [2011] TCJ No 184, 2011 TCC 232 (TCC [General Procedure]).

51 The Court also clarified that the reassessments were not statute-barred, as they fell within the six year limitation period within s. 152(4)(b)(iii) of the *Act*, which took precedence over the five year limitation period within the Tax Agreement between Canada and Barbados.

52 *Alberta Printed Circuits Ltd v Canada*, [2011] TCJ No 184, 2011 TCC 232 at para. 246 (TCC [General Procedure]).

underestimation of an instalment of tax. The *Act* also contains penalties for failure to file T106 forms,[53] as well as for false statements or omissions made pertaining to T106 forms. Penalties for failure to comply with requests for information are set out in s. 231 and s. 234 of the Act. Lastly, the Act establishes that tax preparers may be liable for civil penalties in connection with transfer pricing.

5.1 Types

(a) Transfer pricing adjustment penalties

Section 247(3) of the Act establishes that a taxpayer will be liable to a penalty, where the net result of certain adjustments made under s. 247(2) (ie, adjusting for what arm's length parties would have agreed to) for the taxpayer in a tax year are greater than the lesser of: (i) 10 per cent of the taxpayer's gross revenue for the year; and (ii) $5,000,000. With respect to the net calculation, adjustments will be made as follows:

(i) **upward adjustments** (ie, adjustments resulting in increased taxpayer's income, decreased taxpayer's loss, or decreased taxpayer's capital expenditures for the year) will be made where the taxpayer failed to make reasonable efforts to determine and use arm's length transfer prices or allocations; and

(ii) **downward adjustments** (ie, adjustments resulting in decreased taxpayer's income, increased taxpayer's loss or increased taxpayer's capital expenditures for the year) will be made where the taxpayer has made reasonable efforts to determine and use arm's length prices/allocations.[54] Downward adjustments are, however, subject to the MNR's discretion pursuant to s. 247(10) of the Act.

Where a transfer pricing adjustment is made pursuant to s. 247(3), it should result in a secondary adjustment pertaining to withholding tax on the over/under payment under Part XIII of the Act. Where there is a failure to withhold taxes, s. 227(8) imposes a penalty of: (i) 10 per cent of the amount that should have been deducted or withheld; or (ii) where the failure was made knowingly, or under circumstances amounting to gross negligence, 20 per cent of that amount.[55]

Another penalty which may arise where a transfer pricing adjustment is made pursuant to s. 247(3) is set out under s. 163.1 of the Act pertaining to late or deficient instalments. Section 163.1 of the *Act* states that where a taxpayer fails to pay part of an instalment of tax, they will be liable to a penalty equal to 50 per cent of the amount by which the interest payable under s. 161 of the Act exceeds the greater of: (i) $1,000; and (ii) 25 per cent of the interest that would have been payable under s. 161 of the *Act* in respect of all instalments for the year if no instalment had been made for that year.

---

53 T106 Forms are Information Returns of Non-Arm's Length Transactions with Non-Residents.

54 CRA, Information Circular IC87-2R, *International Transfer Pricing* (September 27, 1999) at page 2, online: *http://www.cra-arc.gc.ca/tx/nnrsdnts/cmmn/trns/menu-eng.html*.

55 Section 247(12) of the Act deems a dividend paid, in levying the secondary adjustment, and s. 227(8) references s. 215 of the Act which requires tax to be withheld on such amounts paid or deemed to be paid.

(b) T106 penalties

Pursuant to s. 233.1 of the Act, the T106 form must be filed annually by reporting persons[56] involved in transactions with non-resident, non-arm's length persons. Where there is a failure to file the T106 form, s. 162(10) of the Act establishes a penalty equal to the amount determined by the formula '($500 × A × B) – C'. The formula elements are defined as follows:

A = (i) **where the person knowingly or under circumstances amounting to gross negligence fails to file T106**, the lesser of 24 and the number of months, beginning with the month in which the return was required to be filed, during any part of which the return has not been filed; or alternatively,
(ii) **where the person knowingly or under circumstances amounting to gross negligence fails to comply with a demand made by the MNR to file or re-file the T106,**[57] the lesser of 24 and the number of months, beginning with the month in which the demand was served, during any part of which the return has not been filed;

B = 1 in all cases, other than where the person fails to comply with a demand by the MNR to file or re-file the T106, in which case B = 2;

C = penalty to which person is liable under s. 162(7) of the Act.[58]

Furthermore, s. 163(2.4)(a) states that where false statements or omissions are made in the T106 form, knowingly or under circumstances amounting to gross negligence, the person will be liable for $24,000 for each false statement or omission. More general penalty provisions are also applicable to the T106 forms. Section 162(5) of the Act establishes a $100 fine for failure to provide information required per prescribed form. Section 163(2) states that a person may be liable to a penalty in the amount of the greater of: (i) $100; and (ii) 50 per cent of the difference between the tax payable as declared in the original return and tax payable after reassessment, where the person knowingly or under circumstances amounting to gross negligence makes a false statement or omissions in a form. Section 239(1) provides that every person who made, participated in, assented to/acquiesced in the making of false or deceptive statements in any return required by the Act (including the T106) is guilty of an offence and is liable on summary conviction to: (i) a fine of not less than 50 per cent and not more than 200 per cent of the amount of tax sought to be evaded; or (ii) both the fine and imprisonment for up to 2 years. [59]

---

56 'Reporting persons' is defined to include taxpayers resident in Canada or non-residents carrying on business in Canada under s. 233.1(1) of the Act.

57 See: s. 233 of the Act.

58 Section 162(7) states: 'Every person (other than a registered charity) or partnership who fails: (*a*) to file an information return as and when required by this Act or the regulations, or (*b*) to comply with a duty or obligation imposed by this Act or the regulations – is liable in respect of each such failure, except where another provision of this Act (other than subsection 162(10) or 162(10.1) or 163(2.22)) sets out a penalty for the failure, to a penalty equal to the greater of $100 and the product obtained when $25 is multiplied by the number of days, not exceeding 100, during which the failure continues.'

59 Section 239(2) states that persons guilty under s. 239(1) may on election of the Attorney General of Canada be prosecuted on indictment, and be liable to a fine of not less than 100 per cent and not more than 200 per cent of the tax sought to be evaded and imprisonment for a term not exceeding 5 years.

(c) Request for information penalties

There are also penalties for failure to provide the CRA with information requested. Section 231.1(1)(d) provides CRA auditors with the right to require that owners/managers of property/businesses and other persons on the premises answer all proper questions relating to the administration and enforcement of the Act.[60] In addition, s. 231.2(1) of the Act provides the CRA with the right to require that any person provide any information or any document. Section 238(1) of the Act establishes that failure to comply with such requests can lead to fines of not less than $1,000 and not more than $25,000, or both a fine and imprisonment for up to 12 months.[61]

Furthermore, s. 231.6(2) of the Act allows the CRA to require that a person resident in Canada or a non-resident person carrying on business in Canada provide any foreign-based information/document.[62] Section 231.6(8) states that the penalty for failing to provide such information/document, is the risk that a court, upon motion of the MNR, may prohibit the introduction by the taxpayer of any foreign-based information/document.[63]

Requests for contemporaneous documentation under s. 247(4)(c) of the Act may also result in a penalty to the taxpayer to the extent that there are adjustments resulting in a transfer pricing penalty pursuant to s. 247(3).

(d) Tax preparer civil penalties

Tax preparers should also be aware of s. 163.2(2) of the Act. This section establishes that a person who makes or furnishes, participates in the making of or causes another person to make or furnish a statement that the person knows, or would reasonably be expected to know but for circumstances amounting to culpable conduct, is a false statement that could be used by another person for a purpose of this Act is liable to a penalty. Section 163.2(3) sets out the amount of the penalty as $1,000 in all cases, other than where the statement is made in the course of a planning/valuation activity, in which case it will be the greater of: (i) $1,000; and (ii) the total of the person's gross entitlements, at the time the notice of assessment of the penalty is sent to the person, in respect of the planning/valuation activity.

5.2 Special or notable cases

Notwithstanding that the case was later withdrawn by the taxpayer, the *HSBC Bank Canada v The Queen*[64] case specifically addressed the topic of penalties. Here, the taxpayer argued that the MNR's past behaviour should be taken into account in reaching a decision as to the application of a transfer pricing penalty. Arguably, the taxpayer would be seen to have made 'reasonable efforts', for the purpose of ss. 247(3) and (4) of the Act, because

---

60 Judges also have the power to order a person to provide any access, assistance, information or document sought under s. 231.1 of the *Act* (assuming solicitor-client privilege does not protect against disclosure).

61 Section 238(2) also states that a court may make such order as it deems proper in order to enforce compliance with the provision where a person is convicted of an offence pursuant to s. 238(1).

62 Section 231.6(1) of the Act defines 'foreign-based information or document' as any information or document that is available or located outside Canada and that may be relevant to the administration or enforcement of this Act, including the collection of any amount payable under this Act by any person.

63 See: *Glaxo Smithkline Inc v Canada*, [2012] 3 SCR 3, 2012 SCC 52 (SCC), for further discussion on the preclusion of documents requested pursuant to s. 231.6(2).

64 *HSBC Bank Canada v The Queen*, 2007 DTC 1109, 2007 TCC 307 (TCC [General Procedure]).

its transfer pricing practices were reviewed in the past, and not challenged, by the CRA. In response to this proposition, the Court stated that it was not in a position to second guess the trial judge in determining such a matter, but stated that 'He or she may decide that one element of reasonableness of the taxpayers' efforts is a consideration of a long standing and unchallenged practice of the taxpayer. I am not saying I would, if I were the trial judge, regard that factor as determinative or even persuasive, but another judge might.'[65] As such, it is unclear as to whether this past behaviour would be taken into account.

6. DISPUTE RESOLUTION MECHANISMS

Where disputes arise with respect to transfer pricing in Canada, there is a typical process that is followed, which is discussed in more detail directly below. The CRA also has an APA program, which is implemented in order to prevent future transfer pricing disputes (further discussed below). With respect to international options, the section below will discuss the mutual agreement procedure, as it relates to competent authority negotiations.

6.1 Preferred national options

Transfer pricing disputes in Canada begin with a CRA audit and are followed by reassessments by the CRA. Where the taxpayer disagrees with the CRA's reassessment, the taxpayer would then be required to file a Notice of Objection in order to commence the appeal process with the appeals division of the CRA (alternatively, the taxpayer could commence the competent authority process, as described further in the section directly below). Should the appeals division of the CRA rule against the taxpayer, the taxpayer's next step would be to file a Notice of Appeal to the Tax Court of Canada. Once in the courts, the taxpayer would then have the ability to appeal the decision to the FCA, and subsequently, the SCC.

In order to avoid the entire process set out above, the taxpayer has the option of entering an APA with the CRA. An APA, as defined earlier, is an advance pricing arrangement between the CRA and taxpayer that is aimed at determining the appropriate transfer pricing methodologies for transactions or arrangements that the taxpayer participates in with non-arm length non-residents. The APA program is open to all taxpayers, and while there is no requirement to enter an APA, the benefits of doing so may be exponential in terms of savings in time through efficient resolution and increased certainty with respect to transfer pricing issues.[66]

6.2 International options

Where transfer pricing disputes arise between tax authorities in different jurisdictions (ie, double taxation matters), the taxpayer may use the competent authority mutual agreement procedures contained in international tax conventions entered into by Canada with foreign

---

65 *HSBC Bank Canada v The Queen*, 2007 DTC 1109, 2007 TCC 307 (TCC [General Procedure]), para. 8.

66 CRA, Information Circular 94-4R: *International Transfer Pricing: Advance Pricing Arrangements (APAs)* (March 16, 2001), online: *http://www.cra-arc.gc.ca/menu/ICSC-e.html.*

governments. The mutual agreement procedure allows Canadian taxpayers to request competent authority assistance where double taxation issues arise. In such instances, the competent authorities of both jurisdictions involved will then attempt to reach a resolution with respect to which jurisdiction will be entitled to tax certain portions of the income in question.[67]

PART TWO: TAX AVOIDANCE

7. ACCEPTABLE TAX PLANNING AREAS/SUBJECTS

In Canada, taxpayers are entitled to select courses of action or enter into transactions that will minimize tax liability as long as they are consistent with the Act and the overall spirit of the law.[68] Tax evasion typically occurs when a taxpayer ignores a specific part of the law. In comparison, tax avoidance occurs when a taxpayer takes actions, that are within the letter of the law, to minimize tax, but which contravene the object and spirit of the law.

Tax avoidance is regulated by the Act's general anti-avoidance rule ('GAAR'). The GAAR is designed to prevent actions undertaken primarily to obtain a tax benefit (referred to as an 'avoidance transaction') involving a *misuse* of a provision of the Act or an *abuse* having regard to the Act as a whole.

However, certain aggressive tax plans/options may be acceptable. In CRA Information Circular 88-2 ('IC88-2'), the CRA provides examples of transactions that may or may not be prevented by the application of the GAAR (some of which are discussed below). These examples demonstrate that the GAAR will not normally be applied where:

(a) A specific anti-avoidance provision already applies to the transaction – the GAAR is a provision of last resort after the application of specific anti-avoidance rules;

(b) A specific anti-avoidance provision makes an exception for the transaction at issue;

(c) A specific provision permits the transaction, and the transaction was not entered into for the purpose of circumventing a specific anti-avoidance rule; or

(d) There is no specific provision addressing the tax effects of the transaction, but the transaction is consistent with the object and spirit of the Act as a whole.[69]

The following is a non-inclusive list of some aggressive tax planning strategies, which may or may not be legitimate (and which GAAR may or may not apply to), depending on the circumstances at hand:

---

67 CRA, Information Circular 71-17R4: *Request for Competent Authority Consideration Under Mutual Agreement Procedures in Income Tax Conventions* (May 12, 1995), online: *http://www.cra-arc.gc.ca/menu/ICSC-e.html.*

68 *Copthorne Holdings Ltd v Canada*, [2011] SCJ No 63, 2011 SCC 63 (SCC).

69 William I. Innes, Patrick J. Boyle, & Joel A. Nitikman, *The Essential GAAR Manual: Policies, Principles and Procedures* (Toronto, CCH Canadian Limited) at pages 183–184.

(a) Divisive (or butterfly) reorganizations

According to IC88-2, the GAAR only applies to divisive/butterfly reorganizations that involve a distribution of property which fails to comply with the object and spirit of s. 55(3)(b) of the Act.[70] Otherwise, such tax planning will be acceptable.

(b) Consolidation of profits and losses in a corporate group

Generally speaking, the Act allows the transfer of property, as well as the payment of income/transfer of losses, between related corporations. However, if a transfer of property or other transaction is undertaken to avoid a specific rule,[71] the GAAR would apply.

For example, the CRA states in IC88-2 that the GAAR would not prevent a corporation, which owns property with an unrealized capital gain that it wishes to sell to a third party, from first transferring the property to a related corporation with a net capital loss. Instead of selling the property directly to the third party and realizing a capital gain, the corporation transfers the property to the related corporation and elects under s. 85(1) to defer the recognition of the gain. The related corporation sells the property to the third party and reduces the resulting taxable capital gain by the amount of its net capital loss.

GAAR does not apply because the transfer to the related corporation is permitted, by implication, under s. 69(11). This section only prohibits a transfer to an unrelated corporation on a tax deferred basis where it is intended that the unrelated corporation will sell the property and reduce the amount of the gain by amounts of losses or similar deductions which it may claim.

(c) Disposition of property

Generally, if a taxpayer disposes of property for cash, it must account for the income and/or a capital gain at the time of receipt, otherwise the GAAR may apply. Examples of differing circumstances in which the disposition of property would be acceptable/not acceptable (ie, GAAR would/would not apply) are set out in IC88-2.[72]

---

70 This might occur, for example, if a transferee does not receive its proportionate share of each type of property of the particular corporation.

71 Such as a rule to preclude the deduction of losses after the acquisition of control of a corporation by an arm's length person.

72 The CRA provides the following two examples:

- GAAR would apply: A taxpayer (the seller) and another taxpayer that wants to buy certain property (the purchaser) form a partnership and the seller transfers the property into the partnership and elects under s. 97(2) to defer the recognition of the gain which would otherwise arise. The purchaser contributes cash to the partnership in an amount equal to the fair market value of the property. The seller withdraws all the cash from the partnership and, because of the withdrawal, the seller's share of the income and loss of the partnership is reduced. The partnership continues to carry on business. In this case, a partnership is used to circumvent the provisions that provide that proceeds of disposition of property are to be accounted for at the time of receipt and would be contrary to the scheme of the Act read as a whole.
- GAAR would not apply (unless): A corporation (the seller) sells property (with an unrealized capital gain) to an arm's length Canadian corporation (the purchaser) in consideration for redeemable shares having a redemption amount equal to the fair market value of the property sold. The seller and purchaser elect to defer the recognition of the capital gain that would be realized on a straightforward sale of the property under s. 85(1). The shares have paid-up equal to the amount elected so that on the redemption of the shares the seller receives the profit on the sale as a taxable dividend deductible under s. 112(1) of the Act. If the property transferred is non-depreciable capital property, s. 55(2) applies and the taxpayer would realize a capital gain equal to the difference between the redemption amount and the adjusted cost base of the redeemable preferred shares. The

(d) Deductibility of interest

According to IC88-2, the GAAR would not apply to the following situation. A profitable taxable Canadian corporation owns a wholly-owned taxable Canadian corporation that is sustaining losses and needs additional capital to carry on its business. The subsidiary could borrow the monies from its bank but the subsidiary could not obtain any tax saving in the current year by deducting the interest expense. Therefore, the parent corporation borrows the money from its bank and subscribes for additional common shares of the subsidiary and reduces its net income by deducting the interest expense. The subsidiary uses the money to gain/produce income from its business. Since the borrowing by the parent corporation is for the purpose of gaining/producing income as required by s. 20(1)(c) of the *Act*, the GAAR does not apply.

(e) Capital gains exemption

Under the Act, qualified small business corporation ('QSBC') shares are eligible for a capital gains exemption upon disposition. In order to claim the exemption, the corporation must use substantially all of its assets in an active business carried on primarily in Canada. According to IC88-2, if the corporation's assets are not used in an active business in Canada, the GAAR does not prevent shareholders from 'purifying' the corporation so they can take advantage of the QSBC capital gains exemption.

For example, the shareholders could incorporate a corporation and transfer to this corporation shares of the operating corporation that have a fair market value equal to the fair market value of the assets that are not used in the active business of the operating corporation. The operating corporation purchases these common shares from the new corporation and pays the purchase price of the shares by transferring the non-business assets to the new corporation. The operating corporation may have a tax liability arising from the disposition of the non-business assets. The new corporation may be subject to s. 55(2) of the Act if the gain on the purchased shares is attributable to something other than income earned or realized by the operating corporation.

According to the CRA, the formation of the new corporation and the transfer of the shares to the new corporation is not an abuse of the Act. The transfer of the non-business assets is governed by s. 55(2) of the Act. Since the definition of a QSBC share does not require that all or substantially all of the assets be used in carrying on an active business in Canada for a particular period of time prior to the sale of the shares, the distribution of the non-business assets prior to the sale is acceptable. Therefore, in this case, the transactions undertaken to 'purify' the corporation are in accordance with the scheme of the Act.

GAAR would, therefore, not apply. On the other hand, if the property transferred is depreciable property or property the proceeds of disposition of which would result in the realization of income, the GAAR would apply on the basis that the issue of the preferred shares is undertaken to avoid the consequences of a straightforward disposition of the property.

8. DEFINING ABUSIVE TAX AVOIDANCE

The Act's GAAR provides that tax avoidance (or an 'avoidance transaction') involves a transaction or series of transactions undertaken primarily to obtain a tax benefit, and that is not undertaken primarily for *bona fide* purposes other than to obtain the tax benefit. A bona fide purpose might include transactions undertaken for business or commercial purposes, regulatory compliance, corporate reorganizations, and so on.

According to the SCC in *Canada Trustco Mortgage Co v Canada*[73] ('*Canada Trustco*') abusive tax avoidance occurs when:

(a) a taxpayer relies on specific provisions of the Act in order to achieve an outcome that those provisions seek to prevent;
(b) a transaction defeats the underlying rationale of the provisions that are relied upon; or
(c) an arrangement circumvents the application of certain provisions, such as specific anti-avoidance rules, in a manner that frustrates or defeats the object, spirit or purpose of those provisions.[74]

9. THE LEGISLATIVE FRAMEWORK

(a) Overview – government policy on curbing abusive tax avoidance

When the GAAR was first proposed, the government issued a white paper on tax reform.[75] This paper highlighted the government's concern that tax avoidance erodes the tax base and undermines the fairness of the Canadian tax system, which is essential to the integrity of Canada's self-assessment system. By introducing the GAAR, the government's goal was to reduce the use of transactions carried out primarily for tax advantage with no genuine business purpose.

(b) Statutory provisions

Subsection 245(2) of the Act contains the GAAR, stating: 'where a transaction is an avoidance transaction, the tax consequences to a person shall be determined as is reasonable in the circumstances in order to deny a tax benefit that, but for this section, would result, directly or indirectly, from that transaction or from a series of transactions that includes that transaction.'

In *Canada Trustco*, the SCC set out the framework for determining whether the GAAR applies. The first step is to determine whether there is a 'tax benefit'[76] arising from a transaction or series of transactions.

The second step is to determine whether the transaction giving rise to the tax benefit is an 'avoidance transaction.' Subsection 245(3) of the Act defines an 'avoidance transaction' as any single transaction or one that is part of a series of transactions where the single transaction or series of transaction

[73] *Canada Trustco Mortgage Co v Canada*, [2005] SCJ No 56, 2005 SCC 54 (SCC).
[74] *Canada Trustco Mortgage Co v Canada*, [2005] SCJ No 56, 2005 SCC 54 at para. 45 (SCC).
[75] Canada, Department of Finance, *The White Paper: Tax Form 1987* (Ottawa: Department of Finance, June 18, 1987).
[76] Subsection 245(1) defines a 'tax benefit' very broadly as 'a reduction, avoidance or deferral of tax or other amount payable under this Act or an increase in a refund of tax or other amount under this Act, and includes a reduction, avoidance or deferral of tax or other amount that would be payable under this *Act* but for a tax treaty or an increase in a refund of tax or other amount under this Act as a result of a tax treaty.'

results directly or indirectly in a tax benefit, unless the transaction may reasonably be considered to have been undertaken or arranged primarily for bona fide purposes other than to obtain the tax benefit. This provision prevents the GAAR from applying to transactions done primarily for non-tax purposes.

The third step is to determine whether the avoidance transaction giving rise to the tax benefit is abusive. Subsection 245(4) provides that the GAAR applies to a transaction only if it may reasonably be considered that the transaction:

(a) would result directly or indirectly in a *misuse* of the provisions of the Act, Regulations and Rules, as well as a tax treaty or any other enactment relevant in computing tax or any other amount payable by or refundable to a person under the Act or in determining any amount that is relevant for the purposes of that computation; or
(b) would result directly or indirectly in an *abuse* having regarding to those provisions read as a whole.

10. KEY CASES OF INTEREST

10.1 Current cases

(a) Copthorne Holdings Ltd v Canada[77]

In *Copthorne*, a parent and subsidiary corporation reorganized to become sister corporations owned directly by the same non-resident shareholder. These sister corporations then amalgamated (known as a horizontal amalgamation) and the paid-up capital ('PUC') of their respective shares was aggregated to form the PUC of the amalgamated corporation. The amalgamated corporation then redeemed a large portion of its shares and paid out the PUC attributable to the redeemed shares to its non-resident shareholder. The payment was treated as a return of capital by the non-resident shareholder, not income.[78]

Although no provision required the return of the PUC to be treated as taxable, the MNR applied the GAAR to the transaction by which the parent and subsidiary became sister corporations. As a result, the MNR cancelled the PUC of the shares of the former subsidiary upon amalgamation with its former parent corporation. The effect was that the amount paid to the non-resident shareholder in excess of the reduced PUC would have constituted a deemed dividend subject to tax.

The SCC upheld the MNR's application of the GAAR. The Court approached the three part test in *Canada Trustco* (*discussed in section 10.2 – Key historical cases below*) as follows:

1. **There was a tax benefit:** According to the Court, the existence of a tax benefit can be established by comparing the taxpayer's situation with an alternative arrangement that could reasonably have been carried out but for the existence of the tax benefit. The taxpayer could

---

77 *Copthorne Holdings Ltd v Canada*, [2011] SCJ No 63, 2011 SCC 63 (SCC).
78 It is important to note that if the parent and subsidiary were not reorganized prior to the amalgamation and had engaged in a vertical amalgamation, the PUC of the shares of the subsidiary would have been cancelled on amalgamation.

have amalgamated the parent and subsidiary (a vertical amalgamation) instead of using a horizontal amalgamation, which was more complicated. The only difference between the two options was how PUC was treated.[79]

2. **The transaction giving rise to the tax benefit was an 'avoidance transactions':** The Court determined that the transaction was not primarily undertaken for a *bona fide* non-tax purpose. Reorganizing the parent and subsidiary corporations to be sister corporations introduced an additional step into the taxpayer's process of simplification and consolidation. A vertical amalgamation would have resulted in the same simplification and consolidation.[80]
3. **The avoidance transaction was abusive:** Finally, the Court concluded that the object, spirit and purpose of the PUC provisions was to preclude preservation of the PUC of the shares of a subsidiary corporation upon amalgamation of the parent and subsidiary where such preservation would permit shareholders, on a redemption of shares by the amalgamated corporation, to be paid amounts as a return of capital without liability for tax, in excess of the amounts invested in the amalgamating corporations with tax-paid funds. [81]

(b) The Federal Court of Appeal Trilogy

In 2012, the FCA released its decision in a trilogy of 'value shift'/'paper loss' cases. The theme in these cases involved taxpayers shifting value from one class of shares to another, which triggered a (paper) loss.

In the first case, **Triad Gestco Ltd v Canada,**[82] the taxpayer corporation realized a capital gain of $7,799,545 by disposing of a building in an arm's length sale. Afterwards, a new corporation was incorporated ('Newco'). The taxpayer transferred assets with a fair market value of $8 million to Newco in exchange for 8,000 common shares. Newco then declared a stock dividend and issued 80,000 preferred shares redeemable for $8 million. The effect of this dividend was to reduce the value of the common shares to zero. The taxpayer then sold its 8,000 common shares in Newco to a newly created trust (the beneficiary of which was the controlling shareholder of the taxpayer) for $65 thereby resulting in a capital loss of $7,999,935. This capital loss was applied by the taxpayer to offset the $7,799,545 capital gain, as well as another capital gain.

The taxpayer conceded that the claimed loss resulted in a tax benefit under s. 245(1) and did not challenge the Tax Court judge's conclusion that the transactions were avoidance transactions under s. 245(3).[83]

The FCA upheld the application of the GAAR on the grounds that there was a misuse/abuse of the Act. There was no economic loss because the value of the common shares was moved to the preferred shares (using the dividend) resulting in the common shares having a high tax cost, but

[79] *Copthorne Holdings Ltd v Canada*, [2011] SCJ No 63, 2011 SCC 63 at paras 35–37 (SCC).
[80] *Copthorne Holdings Ltd v Canada*, [2011] SCJ No 63, 2011 SCC 63 at paras 62–63 (SCC).
[81] *Copthorne Holdings Ltd v Canada*, [2011] SCJ No 63, 2011 SCC 63 at para. 126 (SCC).
[82] *Triad Gestco Ltd v Canada*, [2012] FCJ No 1274, 2012 FCA 258 (FCA).
[83] *Triad Gestco Ltd v Canada*, [2012] FCJ No 1274, 2012 FCA 258 at para. 37 (FCA).

nominal value. This loss was realized on the disposition of the common shares to the trust. Allowing the loss was inconsistent with the purpose of Canada's capital gains system which is aimed at taxing increases in economic power and economic power is unaffected by paper losses[84]

In the second case, **1207192 Ontario Limited v Canada**,[85] the facts were similar. The taxpayer corporation transferred property to a subsidiary in exchange for shares of similar value. The taxpayer then sold the shares to a family trust for less than cost and used the capital loss to offset a capital gain. The taxpayer was able to sell the shares for less than cost because immediately before the sale of shares to the trust, the subsidiary issued a stock dividend on a separate class of shares. The effect of the dividend was to shift value from the shares that were later sold to the trust to the shares for which the dividend was paid, and which the taxpayer retained.

The taxpayer conceded that the transactions gave rise to a tax benefit for purposes of GAAR, but maintained that each of the transactions was undertaken primarily for a *bona fide* non-tax purpose and that the GAAR did not apply since there was neither an avoidance transaction nor any abuse.

The FCA held that the tax benefit (ie, the capital loss) was the result of an 'avoidance transaction.' Although the principal objective of the transactions was to achieve protection from potential future creditors (and not to get a capital loss), the transactions could have been structured differently to achieve creditor protection without generating the tax benefit/capital loss. Since there was no evidence that the transactions were required for creditor protection, it was open to the trial judge to conclude the principal purpose was to achieve the tax benefit.[86]

The Court also held that there was an abuse/misuse of the relevant provisions based on its reasoning in the *Triad Gestco Ltd* decision.[87]

Canada v Global Equity Fund Ltd[88] was the third case in the trilogy of cases, and featured similar facts to the other two cases. The main difference, however, was that the taxpayer was involved in the securities trading business and reported the sale of the common shares to the family trust as a business loss, instead of a capital loss. As such, the Court's analysis on whether the transactions were an abuse/misuse of the Act was different than in *Triad Gestco Ltd* and *1207192 Ontario Limited.*

According to the Court, while there is some flexibility with the concept of a business loss, the relevant provisions of the *Act* provide that if a business loss is to be used for taxation purposes, there must, at the very least, be an air of economic/business reality associated with that loss.[89]

In this case, the loss generated by the taxpayer resulted from a value shift between one class of shares (the common shares) to another class (the

84 *Triad Gestco Ltd v Canada*, [2012] FCJ No 1274, 2012 FCA 258 at paras 41–42 (FCA).

85 *1207192 Ontario Limited v Canada*, [2012] FCJ No 1294, 2012 FCA 259 (FCA), leave to appeal to SCC refused.

86 *1207192 Ontario Limited v Canada*, [2012] FCJ No 1294, 2012 FCA 259 at paras. 16–20 (FCA), leave to appeal to SCC refused.

87 *1207192 Ontario Limited v Canada*, [2012] FCJ No 1294, 2012 FCA 259 at para. 21 (FCA), leave to appeal to SCC refused.

88 *Canada v Global Equity Fund Ltd*, [2012] FCJ No 1363, 2012 FCA 272 (FCA), leave to appeal to SCC refused.

89 *Canada v Global Equity Fund Ltd*, [2012] FCJ No 1363, 2012 FCA 272 at para. 63 (FCA), leave to appeal to SCC refused.

preferred shares) that were issued as a dividend. It was simply a paper loss. [90] As such, there was no air of economic/business reality associated with the loss – the transactions creating this artificial loss defeated the underlying rationale of the relevant provisions allowing for the use of business losses for income tax purposes.[91]

10.2 Key historical cases

(a) Canada Trustco Mortgage Co v Canada, 2005 SCC 54

In the landmark SCC case of *Canada Trustco*, the Court set out three requirements for GAAR:

1. There must be a *tax benefit* resulting from a transaction or series of transactions;
2. The transaction must be an *avoidance transaction* in the sense of not being arranged primarily for *bona fide* purposes other than to obtain the tax benefit; and
3. There must be abusive tax avoidance in the sense that it cannot be reasonably concluded that a tax benefit would be consistent with the object, spirit or purpose of the provisions relied upon by the taxpayer.[92]

The Court also set out the following important principles[93]:

- The burden is on the taxpayer to refute requirements (1) and (2), and on the MNR to establish point (3).
- If the existence of abusive tax avoidance is unclear, the benefit of the doubt goes to the taxpayer.
- The courts proceed by conducting a unified textual, contextual and purposive analysis of the provisions giving rise to the tax benefit in order to determine why they were put in place and why the benefit was conferred. The goal is to arrive at a purposive interpretation that is harmonious with the provisions of the Act that confer the tax benefit, read in the context of the whole Act.
- Whether the transactions were motivated by any economic, commercial, family or other non-tax purpose may form part of the factual context that the courts consider. However, any finding in this respect would form only one part of the underlying facts of a case, and would be insufficient by itself to establish abusive tax avoidance. The central issue is the proper interpretation of the relevant provisions in light of their context/purpose.
- Abusive tax avoidance may be found where the relationships/ transactions as expressed in the relevant documentation lack a proper basis relative to the object, spirit or purpose of the provisions that are purported to confer the tax benefit, or where they are wholly

---

[90] *Canada v Global Equity Fund Ltd*, [2012] FCJ No 1363, 2012 FCA 272 at para 66. (FCA), leave to appeal to SCC refused.

[91] *Canada v Global Equity Fund Ltd*, [2012] FCJ No 1363, 2012 FCA 272 at para. 68 (FCA), leave to appeal to SCC refused.

[92] *Canada v Global Equity Fund Ltd*, [2012] FCJ No 1363, 2012 FCA 272 at para. 66 (FCA), leave to appeal to SCC refused.

[93] *Canada v Global Equity Fund Ltd*, [2012] FCJ No 1363, 2012 FCA 272 at para. 66 (FCA), leave to appeal to SCC refused.

dissimilar to the relationships/transactions that are contemplated by the provisions.

In *Canada Trustco*, a taxpayer ('T') used mostly loan funds to purchase trailers from a vendor ('V'), which it leased back to the vendor through a third party ('C'). As a result, T was able to claim capital cost allowance ('CCA') on the trailers and defer the payment of taxes on the amounts of profits reduced by the CCA deductions, which would be subject to recapture into income when the trailers were disposed of in the future.

CRA disallowed the CCA claim arguing that T's 'cost' of the trailer's was zero under the GAAR since there was no economic risk to the taxpayer. This was because V had prepaid the full amount of the lease to C, who then placed a deposit sufficient to cover T's loan.

The Court disagreed with CRA and refused to apply the GAAR because this was not abusive tax avoidance. According to the Court, there was nothing in the object of the CCA provisions that would allow 'cost' to be interpreted to mean 'amount economically at risk' as argued by CRA. To do so would be to invite inconsistent results, as the result would vary with the degree of risk in each case. This would offend the goal of the *Act* to provide sufficient certainty and predictability to permit taxpayers to intelligently order their affairs.

(b) Matthew v Canada (sub Kaulius v the Queen), 2005 SCC55

In *Matthew*, which was released by the SCC at the same time as *Canada Trustco*, the Court reached the opposite conclusion and applied GAAR. In this case, Standard Trust Company ('STC') transferred a portfolio of mortgages with unrealized losses to a non-arm's length partnership ('Partnership A'), thereby acquiring a 99 per cent interest in it. STC then transferred the unrealized losses to Partnership A using s. 18(13) of the Act and sold its 99 per cent interest in it to an arm length's party. Finally, Partnership B was formed to acquire a 99 per cent interest in Partnership A. The taxpayers then joined Partnership B to offset the losses against their own income, while STC recorded a portion of those losses associated with the defaulted mortgages.

The Court held that GAAR applied. The Court found that to allow the taxpayers to claim the losses would defeat the purpose of s. 18(13) and certain partnership provisions. Interpreted textually, contextually and purposively, these provisions do not permit arm's length parties to purchase tax losses preserved by s. 18(13) and claim them as their own. The purpose of s. 18(13) is to transfer a loss to a non-arm's length party in order to prevent a taxpayer who carries on a business of lending money from realizing a superficial loss. [94] A purposive interpretation of the interplay between s. 18(13) and the partnership provisions indicates that they allow the preservation and sharing of losses on the basis of shared control of the assets in a common business activity. In this case, the absence of such a basis

[94] *Canada v Global Equity Fund Ltd*, [2012] FCJ No 1363, 2012 FCA 272 at para. 58 (FCA), leave to appeal to SCC refused.

leads to an inference of abuse. Neither Partnership A nor B ever dealt with the property.[95] Essentially, the taxpayers had taken an anti-avoidance rule and used it to achieve a tax benefit.

11. PENALTIES

11.1 Legislative provisions

As discussed above, there are no penalties associated with the GAAR. A penalty cannot be imposed as a consequence of the successful application of GAAR by CRA when the Act allows a taxpayer to self-assess its taxes on the basis of compliance with the technical provisions of the Act.

If a transaction/series of transactions violates the GAAR the remedy specified in s. 245(2) is that the 'tax consequences'[96] will be reassessed in a manner 'as is reasonable in the circumstances' in order to deny a tax benefit that would otherwise result from the transaction.

In terms of what 'is reasonable in the circumstances', the Act states that:

Without restricting the generality of subsection (2), and notwithstanding any other enactment,

(a) any deduction, exemption or exclusion in computing income, taxable income, taxable income earned in Canada or tax payable or any part thereof may be allowed or disallowed in whole or in part,

(b) any such deduction, exemption or exclusion, any income, loss or other amount or part thereof may be allocated to any person,

(c) the nature of any payment or other amount may be recharacterized, and

(d) the tax effects that would otherwise result from the application of other provisions of this Act may be ignored,

in determining the tax consequences to a person as is reasonable in the circumstances in order to deny a tax benefit that would, but for this section, result, directly or indirectly, from an avoidance transaction.[97]

If GAAR applies, then there will also be a compensatory interest charge under s. 161 of the Act, unless the funds are paid pending the appeal.

11.2 Examples of penalties imposed

In *Copthorne Holdings Ltd v The Queen*,[98] the CRA applied the GAAR to a series of transactions in a corporate reorganization. The effect of the transactions was to avoid a withholding tax. After the CRA applied GAAR, the taxpayer was required to pay the withholding tax. In addition, the CRA assessed penalties against the taxpayer for failure to withhold tax. The Tax Court of Canada held that GAAR applied and the taxpayer was required to pay the withholding tax. Nevertheless, the Court disallowed the penalties imposed by CRA based on two grounds. First, the Court reasoned that the taxpayer was not technically required to withhold the tax – it was only required to

---

95 *Canada v Global Equity Fund Ltd*, [2012] FCJ No 1363, 2012 FCA 272 at para. 62 (FCA), leave to appeal to SCC refused.

96 Section 245(1) defines 'tax consequences' very broadly as 'the amount of income, taxable income, or taxable income earned in Canada of, tax or other amount payable by or refundable to the person under this *Act*, or any other amount that is relevant for the purposes of computing that amount'.

97 Income Tax Act, RSC 1985, c 1 (5th Supp), s. 245(5).

98 *Copthorne Holdings Ltd v The Queen*, 2007 DTC 1230, 2007 TCC 481 (TCC [General Procedure]); affirmed [2009] FCJ No 625, 2009 FCA 163 (FCA); affirmed [2011] SCJ No 63, 2011 SCC 63 (SCC).

withhold the tax *after* the application of the GAAR by CRA. Second, based on s. 245(7), there is nothing in the GAAR provisions that would allow a taxpayer to self-assess on the basis that GAAR applies.

12. CURRENT TRENDS

In November 2012, CRA released a breakdown of GAAR cases considered by the CRA. Since GAAR's introduced in 1988 – common issues appear to be surplus strips, kiddie tax, loss creations via stock dividends, capital and non-capital losses, and Part I.3 Tax.[99]

12.1 National policy and law

In 2013, the government enacted s. 237.3 of the Act requiring the disclosure of 'reportable transactions' to the CRA. The purpose of this requirement was to address concerns about aggressive tax avoidance by imposing penalties on tax advisors, rather than the taxpayers.

A 'reportable transaction' is an 'avoidance transaction' with at least two of the following three features/hallmarks:

1. The promoter or advisor, including any non-arm's-length party (referred to collectively as '**promoter or advisor**'), is entitled to a fee that is:
    a. based on the amount of the tax benefit from the transaction;
    b. contingent upon obtaining a tax benefit that results from the transaction; or
    c. attributable to the number of persons participating in the transaction (or similar transaction) or who have been provided access to advice from the promoter or advisor about the tax consequences of the transaction (or similar transaction).
2. The promoter or advisor of the transaction obtains 'confidential protection'[100] for the transaction.
3. The taxpayer, the person who entered into the transaction on behalf of the taxpayer (including any non-arm's-length party), or the promoter or advisor has or had 'contractual protection'[101] for the transaction (other than as a result of a fee described in the first hallmark).

Absent an exception, if an information form for a reportable transaction is not filed when required, each person who must file this form will be liable

---

99 See chart excerpted from the GAAR statistics provided by the CRA at the Canadian Tax Foundation's 2012 Annual Conference in Alan M. Schwartz, Q.C., *GAAR Interpreted: The General Anti- Avoidance Rule*, loose-leaf (consulted on May 15, 2014) (Toronto: Carswell) at page 2-6; Also see: Jinyan Li and Thaddeus Hwong, 'GAAR in Action: An Empirical Exploration of Tax Court of Canada Cases (1997–2009) and Judicial Decision Making', (2013) vol 61 Canadian Tax Journal, 321–366.

100 'Confidential protection,' in respect of a transaction or series of transactions, means anything that prohibits the disclosure, to any person or to the Minister, the details or structure of the transaction or series under which a tax benefit results (not the same as client-solicitor privilege).

101 'Contractual protection' refers to any form of insurance (other than standard professional liability insurance) or other protection, including, without limiting the generality of the foregoing, an indemnity, compensation, or a guarantee that, either immediately or in the future and either absolutely or contingently:

(i) protects a person against a failure of the transaction or series to achieve any tax benefit from the transaction or series; or

(ii) pays for or reimburses any expense, fee, tax, interest, penalty, or similar amount that may be incurred by a person in the course of a dispute about a tax benefit from the transaction or series; and

any form of undertaking provided by a promoter, or by any person who does not deal at arm's length with a promoter that provides, either immediately or in the future and either absolutely or contingently, assistance, directly or indirectly in any way, to a person in the course of a dispute about a tax benefit from the transaction or series.

to pay a penalty, notwithstanding any agreement between the parties as to who will file the return. The amount of the penalty is equal to the total of all the fees for the transaction that the promoter or advisor is entitled to receive (these fees are described in the first and third hallmarks). A promoter or advisor is liable to pay a penalty only to the extent of the fees to which he/she is entitled.[102] In addition, the tax benefit is denied until the obligation to file the information form has been satisfied and the penalty and interest have been paid.[103]

Notwithstanding the above, a person required to file an information return in respect of a reportable transaction is not liable for a penalty if the person has exercised the degree of care, diligence and skill to prevent the failure to file that a reasonably prudent person would have exercised in comparable circumstances. [104]

Finally, it should be noted that filing an information return in respect of a reportable transaction is not an admission that the GAAR applies. [105] Practically, however, since a 'reportable transaction' must be an 'avoidance transaction' and the GAAR applies to 'avoidance transactions', one has to wonder if the CRA or a Court for that matter would have difficulty concluding that a reportable transaction is not an avoidance transaction for the purposes of the GAAR.

12.1.1 The impact and role of the OECD and other international relations

In 2013, the OECD released their Base Erosion and Profit Shifting Action Plan. The Action Plan identifies 15 specific actions needed to allow governments to prevent companies from avoiding taxation in their home countries by pushing activities abroad to low or no tax jurisdictions.

The Federal Government's 2014 budget proposes to address more of the OECD's concerns regarding international aggressive tax avoidance by:

- Ensuring that financial institutions do not avoid paying Canadian tax on income associated with the insurance of Canadian risks through the use of derivative 'insurance swap' arrangements between foreign affiliates of Canadian taxpayers and third parties.
- Ensuring that the offshore regulated bank provisions are not inappropriately used to circumvent the foreign accrual property income rules through foreign affiliates that are not part of a Canadian financial institution group.
- Ensuring that non-residents cannot avoid Canadian withholding tax or thin capitalization rules by entering into back-to-back loan arrangements with third party financial intermediaries to effectively make indirect loans to their Canadian subsidiaries.
- Inviting comments from stakeholders on a proposed rule to prevent treaty shopping.

102 Income Tax Act, RSC 1985, c 1 (5th Supp), s. 237.3(8).
103 Income Tax Act, RSC 1985, c 1 (5th Supp), s. 237.3(6).
104 Income Tax Act, RSC 1985, c 1 (5th Supp), s. 237.3(11).
105 Income Tax Act, RSC 1985, c 1 (5th Supp), s. 237.3(12).

Inviting input from the public on issues related to international tax planning by multinational enterprises and other cross-border tax integrity issues, such as ensuring the effective collection of sales tax on e-commerce sales to Canadians by foreign-based vendors.[106]

[106] See the 2014 Budget tabled in the House of Commons by the Honourable James M. Flaherty, Minister of Finance (February 11, 2014) at page 247.

China

King & Wood Mallesons
Tony Dong, Daisy Duan & Alice Zhang

PART ONE: TRANSFER PRICING

1. GENERAL OVERVIEW

The transfer pricing regime in the People's Republic of China (the 'PRC' or 'China') made significant progress in 2009 with the issuance of Circular Guo Shui Fa [2009] No. 2 ('Circular 2'), which established guidelines for the enforcement of the special tax adjustment and documentation requirements.[1] The rules under Circular 2 are largely consistent with the OECD Transfer Pricing Guidelines (the 'OECD Guidelines'). However, because China is not an OECD member, the OECD Guidelines have not been formally adopted in China and are not legally binding. Nevertheless, in practice, the Chinese tax authorities often make reference to the OECD Guidelines when outlining transfer pricing rules and assessing transfer pricing audit cases.

It should be noted that the OECD Guidelines are not necessarily the 'gold standard' to be employed by the Chinese tax administration in applying the 'arm's length principle'. In recent years, the State Administration of Taxation (the 'SAT') has been exploring other transfer pricing theories suitable for the unique and challenging issues faced by China as a developing country.[2] Notably, the SAT has shared its insights in the United Nations Practical Manual on Transfer Pricing (the 'UN TP Manual').[3] Some of the unique challenges faced by developing countries include the lack of appropriate comparables, the quantification and allocation of location-specific advantages ('LSAs'),[4] and the valuation of intangibles.

Recently, the Chinese tax authority has strengthened its efforts in investigating transfer pricing. In addition to traditional cross-border transactions involving tangible goods, greater attention has been directed towards more sophisticated and complicated transactions involving services and intangibles.

---

1 On January 8, 2009, the PRC State Administration of Taxation ('SAT') issued Circular 2, the Implementation Measures for Special Tax Adjustments (Provisional), which took effect retrospectively from January 1, 2008.

2 The SAT is the highest-level tax authority in the PRC and is in charge of tax administration. The SAT may also issue detailed implementation or clarification rules with regards to the enforcement of the tax laws and administrative regulations in China.

3 Refer to *http://www.un.org/esa/ffd/tax/documents/bgrd_tp.htm* for the full text of the UN Practical Transfer Pricing Manual for Developing Countries.

4 LSAs are preferences for production arising from assets, resource endowments, governmental industry policies and incentives that exist in specific localities. The SAT provides that certain additional profits arising from LSAs shall be allocated to China.

2. IDENTIFICATION OF LEGISLATIVE FRAMEWORK

2.1 Federal legislation

The transfer pricing legislation in China consists mainly of the:

- Enterprise Income Tax Law ('EIT Law'); and
- Implementing Rules of the EIT Law

The current EIT Law was enacted by the National People's Congress (ie, the legislative body in China) on March 16, 2007, and came into force on January 1, 2008. The EIT Law contains a specific chapter, titled 'Special Tax Adjustments', which sets out the basic transfer pricing and anti-avoidance principles.

The Implementing Rules are the more detailed rules accompanying the EIT Law.[5] While the EIT Law prescribes the basic and general rules, the Implementing Rules provide more specific guidelines regarding interpretation and enforcement.

2.2 State and provincial legislative interplay

The local tax authority may issue more detailed guidelines and administrative rules under the framework of the existing laws, administrative regulations and the SAT rules.

A transfer pricing audit may be initiated in one of two ways. First, the local tax authority may commence a transfer pricing audit. In such cases, the local tax authority generally conducts the transfer pricing audit on its own, unless the case is high profile, complicated or involves a significant volume of assets. The local tax authority then reports the case to the SAT, and the SAT organizes an expert panel to review the case. Second, a transfer pricing audit may be initiated by the SAT. This usually occurs in the case of an enterprise group that has a number of enterprises across the country. Generally, the SAT works with the relevant local tax authority to conduct the investigation.

In China, transfer pricing investigations focus primarily on the following types of enterprises:

- Enterprises with a large volume of related party transactions or several types of related party transactions;
- Enterprises with continuous losses, low profitability or fluctuating profitability;
- Enterprises with profit levels lower than that of other enterprises in the same industry;
- Enterprises with profits not matching their performed functions and assumed risks;
- Enterprises engaging in related party transactions with enterprises incorporated in a tax haven;
- Enterprises that fail to file their related party transaction reports or to prepare contemporaneous documentation; and,
- Enterprises that expressly violate the arm's length principle.

[5] The current Implementing Rules of the EIT Law were passed by the State Council on November 28, 2011, and came into force January 1, 2008.

2.3 International treaties and agreements

China has entered into more than 100 bilateral income tax treaties with other countries and regions. Where there is a conflict between the tax treaty and the domestic tax rules, the tax treaty prevails. However, the taxpayer must complete the relevant application and comply with the filing rules in order to enjoy the benefits available under a tax treaty. In general, there are no provisions in the income tax treaties that China has concluded which would limit or expand the scope of transfer pricing audits. However, some treaties contain a Mutual Agreement Procedure ('MAP') clause, which provides a mechanism to resolve transfer pricing issues through consultation between the countries (see section 6.2 below).

3. NATIONAL POLICY ISSUES

3.1 Overall national policy announcements

In the past year, China has been working with the United Nations (the 'UN') and the Organisation for Economic Co-operation and Development (the 'OECD') on several initiatives involving transfer pricing, including the transfer pricing study on base erosion and profit shifting ('BEPS')[6], as well as intra-group services and management fees. China has also been active in the OECD's efforts to combat BEPS. In January 2014, the Administrator of the SAT attended the FTA Steering Committee Meeting held by the OECD on the topic of BEPS. At the meeting, the Administrator made several recommendations, including that proactive cooperation be used to tackle the challenges in international taxation; that decisions regarding the subjects of international tax cooperation be made in a scientific manner; and that the status and influence of international tax cooperation be enhanced. This indicates that Chinese tax authorities will pay closer attention to the BEPS issue in tax administration in the future.

At the request of the UN, the SAT delivered a report in April 2014 to share its views on intra-group services and management fees.[7] In its report, the SAT generally agreed with the framework discussed in the OECD TP Guidelines. Additionally, the SAT emphasized the use of the 'benefit test' for the purpose of determining whether intra-group services had actually taken place. The SAT also proposed several suggestions with regards to properly differentiating between royalties and the technical service fee. On the basis of these developments, key areas for transfer pricing investigations in the coming years may include:

- Cross-border service fee payments (eg, profit repatriation by means of service fees from Chinese subsidiaries to offshore headquarters);
- Cross-border financing arrangements (eg, related-party loans with unreasonable interest expenses);

---

6 BEPS results from the interaction of different national tax systems. Multinational companies take advantage of the tax rules of different countries and use the treaty benefits under double taxation treaties in order to reduce their overall tax burden. In order to create a more effective mechanism to deal with BEPS, the OECD issued a BEPS report in February 2013 and an Action Plan in July 2013.

7 Refer to *http://www.un.org/esa/ffd/tax/TransferPricing/CommentsPRC.pdf* for the full text of the UN Practical Transfer Pricing Manual for Developing Countries.

- Intangibles transactions (eg, profit shifting by means of trademark and/or patent licensing among members of multi-national companies);
- LSAs (as indicated in the UN TP Manual 2012, the SAT suggests that more profits should be allocated to China because of savings derived from the large pool of well-educated low cost labour, market capacity, consumers' general preference for foreign brands, preferential government policies, etc.); and
- Abuse of tax treaties and tax havens (eg, profit shifting by taking advantage of shell companies established in tax havens).

3.2 National revenue authority initiatives

Each year, the SAT selects specific industries that will be the primary targets for tax audits. For 2014, the selected industries include real estate and construction enterprises, medical distribution enterprises, and transportation enterprises. The tax audit may include a review of transfer pricing activities, as well as other tax areas. The local tax authorities (usually the provincial tax authorities) select the key transfer pricing investigation sectors within their jurisdiction.

3.3 Administrative statements

The SAT may issue implementing rules to clarify and/or address specific issues relating to transfer pricing. Some transfer pricing rules issued by the SAT have been summarized below.

(a) Circular 2

Circular 2 came into effect on January 1, 2008, with the current EIT Law. It sets out comprehensive rules on transfer pricing in China, including:

- Basic transfer pricing concepts and rules;
- Contemporaneous transfer pricing documentation;[8]
- Transfer pricing methods;
- Transfer pricing investigation and adjustment rules;
- Certain transfer pricing mechanisms such as advance pricing arrangements ('APAs') and cost sharing agreements ('CSAs'); and
- The legal consequences of failure to comply with Circular 2.

It is expected that the SAT may make amendments to Circular 2 in the near future.

(b) Circular 363

Circular 363 provides that enterprises with limited functions and risks (eg, import processing, contract processing, etc.) must maintain reasonable

[8] According to Circular 2, enterprises must prepare documentation annually unless they meet one of the following exceptions: (a) the annual total amount of related party purchases and sales is less than RMB 200 million (with the amount of contractual processing calculated based on the annual declared value of imports and exports) and other related party transactions amount to less than RMB 40 million (with the amount of related party financing calculated based on the interest paid or received); (b) related party transactions are covered under APAs; or (c) foreign owned shares account for less than 50 per cent of the entity, and related party transactions are conducted only with domestic related parties.

profits in accordance with the principle that profits shall be commensurate with the functions and risks of an enterprise.[9]

(c) Circular 13

Circular 13 sets out the working manuals for the implementation of the transfer pricing regime by the local tax authorities.[10]It also encourages taxpayers to make voluntary adjustments to their taxable income and taxes payable, and to report adjustments to the SAT through the transfer pricing case management system.

(d) Circular 16

Circular 16 clarifies the joint review system for significant transfer pricing cases.[11]In particular, cases shall be subject to review by a joint committee. The joint committee is to be an ad hoc committee formed for the purpose of reviewing the case (ie, not a standing committee). The members of the joint committee are selected by the SAT from a pool of transfer pricing specialists who work at local tax authorities.

A transfer pricing audit may be categorized as a significant transfer pricing case if one of the following conditions is met:

- The main business revenue of the enterprise is more than RMB 1 billion in the relevant period, and the registered capital of the enterprise exceeds RMB 100 million;
- The case is being investigated under the nationwide industrial inspection or group inspection;
- The case is considered to be complicated by the provincial tax authorities; or
- Other cases as determined by the SAT.

(e) Circular 41

Circular 41 provides that the transfer pricing administration shall adopt the 'administration, service and investigation' approach.[12]

3.4 Administrative guidelines

Not applicable.

4. CASE LAW

4.1 Current cases

Since China is a civil law country, decisions in previous cases do not have a legally binding effect on future judicial practice. Additionally, most tax cases are resolved through administrative procedures before the tax authorities,

[9] Circular 363 refers to the Circular of Enhancing the Monitoring and Investigation of Cross-Border Related Transactions as issued by the SAT, GuoShui Han [2009] No. 363.

[10] Circular 13 refers to the Internal Working Manuals on the Special Tax Adjustment as issued by the SAT, GuoShuiFa [2012] No. 13.

[11] Circular 16 refers to the Working Manuals of the Joint Review for the Significant Special Tax Adjustment Cases as issued by the SAT, GuoShuiFa [2012] No. 16.

[12] Circular 41 refers to the Circular of the Opinion on Strengthening the Establishment of the International Tax Management System as issued by the SAT, GuoShuiFa [2012] No. 41.

and are rarely heard by the courts. As such, this section focuses on recent transfer pricing cases handled by the Chinese tax authorities.

(a) Xiamen case

Many multinational companies have subsidiaries in China that shift their profits to an offshore parent company through the payment of management service fees. However, as evidenced by the Xiamen case, the remittance of management service fees has become one of the key areas targeted by the Chinese tax authorities.

In this case, the Xiamen tax authority discovered that the profits of a Chinese subsidiary under investigation had declined sharply since 2008, despite an increase in sales during the same time period.[13] The tax authority initiated an investigation and found that the costs and expenses sharing arrangement used by the Chinese subsidiary was not consistent with the method used by the multinational company. As a result, the tax authority imposed a tax adjustment plan on the cross-border service fees, including the business consulting fees, the information system supporting fees, the research and development fees and the market supporting fees. The taxpayer eventually accepted the adjustment plan. The investigation in the case lasted approximately 4 years and the final adjusted tax and interest totaled more than RMB 800 million, making it the largest tax adjustment of cross-border service fees in China.

(b) Chengdu case

In 2013, the Chengdu tax authority discovered that a Chinese subsidiary had paid a significant amount of trademark fees to a related company registered in the British Virgin Islands (the 'BVI Company'). Upon investigation, the Chengdu tax authority found that the Chinese subsidiary had paid royalties of RMB 100 million between 2008 and 2012, and its profit margin was lower than the median profit margin of selected comparable entities.

Despite the fact that the trademark was registered under the name of the BVI Company, the Chengdu tax authority concluded that the Chinese subsidiary had made significant contributions to the value of the trademark by conducting advertising and promotional activities. As a result, the profits derived from marketing the trademark were attributed to the Chinese subsidiary as opposed to the BVI Company. After negotiations with the tax authority, the Chinese subsidiary eventually agreed to the adjusted enterprise income tax amount of RMB 23 million.

(c) Beijing case

The Beijing case involved a manufacturing company that produced electronic products (the 'Electronic Company'). The Beijing tax authority had conducted a functional analysis of the Electronic Company and determined that the company had undertaken certain R&D activities in

[13] Refer to the news article published on the Xiamen State Tax Bureau's website: *http://www.xm-n-tax.gov.cn/ssbd/gshyw/sjyw/324846.htm*.

addition to its manufacturing activities, which could result in increased profits for an independent company. As a result, the Beijing tax authority re-characterized the Electronic Company as a contract manufacturer with a limited R&D function. Based on this re-characterization, a new set of comparable entities were selected, and it was determined that the profit margin of the Electronic Company was lower than that of the selected comparables.

The Beijing tax authority also re-characterized an external transaction wherein the Electronic Company sold semi-products to an unrelated company, which then sold the semi-products to the parent company of the Electronic Company. The Beijing tax authority concluded that the transaction was a related-party transaction because the selling price of the semi-products was actually controlled by the foreign parent company of the Electronic Company, and was lower than the arm's length price. The tax authority adjusted the selling price of the semi-products so that the profit margin of the Electronic Company would fall within the reasonable benchmark range.

The case was the Beijing tax authority's largest transfer pricing case. The investigation took more than 5 years, and the tax authority conducted more than 20 negotiation sessions with the enterprise. The case was concluded in 2013, with a total adjusted enterprise income tax of approximately RMB 425 million, and an additional RMB 70 million in interest.

4.2 Historical cases of note

(a) Dalian case

The Dalian case involved the acquisition of a multinational company by a US multinational company, which included the equity transfer of several subsidiaries in Dalian, China.[14]After the acquisition, the Dalian subsidiaries undertook a series of group re-structuring transactions. The transactions attracted the attention of the Dalian tax authority, which initiated a transfer pricing investigation of the restructuring transactions and the value of the equity transfer price. The equity transfer price had been set using the cost approach. However, the Dalian tax authority concluded that the cost approach did not reflect the fair market value of the transferred shares, and used the income approach to re-assess the equity transfer price. By applying the income method, the Dalian tax authority came to an adjusted tax payment of approximately RMB 11 million.

(b) Shaanxi case

The Shaanxi case was the first thin capitalization case in China.[15] In 2011, the Shaanxi tax authority was conducting a regular review of related-party transactions and discovered a company that had a large amount of related-party loans with high debt-to-equity ratios. The company has also incurred

---

14 Refer to the news article published at the SAT's website: *http://www.chinatax.gov.cn/n480462/n503673/n543124/n543229/10006054.html.*

15 Refer to the news article published on the China Tax News Website: *http://www.ctaxnews.com.cn/syxw/csjd/201111/t20111107_1583279.htm.*

continuous losses in the past several years. The tax authority initiated an investigation of the company. After the investigation was concluded, the tax authority entered into negotiations with the company. The case was eventually settled for a total adjusted tax payment of over RMB 30 million.

5. PENALTIES

5.1 Types

Where an enterprise fails to submit or maintain the required documentation, the tax authority may impose a fine of RMB 2,000 to 10,000. Where an enterprise refuses to provide information about a related-party transaction or provides false or incomplete information, the tax authority may impose a fine of up to RMB 50,000. Further, if the tax authority makes a tax adjustment, the taxpayer must pay the adjusted tax amount and the corresponding interest. Regular interest is calculated in accordance with the relevant RMB loan interest rate published by the People's Bank of China. However, where an enterprise fails to submit required documentation or submits false or incomplete information, the tax authority may impose interest at an annual rate of 5 per cent in addition to the regular interest rate. Taxpayers who are unable to pay a transfer pricing adjustment by the due date must apply for an extension. Otherwise, a daily late payment surcharge of 0.05 per cent will be imposed.

5.2 Special or notable cases

Not applicable.

6. DISPUTE RESOLUTION MECHANISMS

6.1 Preferred national options

If the taxpayer disagrees with the decision of the tax authority, the taxpayer can initiate an administrative appeal with the higher-level tax authority within 60 days of the notice issuance date. However, the taxpayer must pay the taxes as determined by the tax authority prior to commencing an appeal. If the taxpayer is not satisfied with the result of the administrative appeal, the taxpayer may commence legal proceedings within 15 days of receiving the written decision.

China does not have a specialized tax court, and taxpayers rarely apply for administrative appeals or to the court for resolution. Instead, most tax disputes are resolved by the tax authorities through negotiations. Given the technical nature of transfer pricing, the tax authorities have substantial discretion in investigating and deciding cases. Therefore, the taxpayer's efforts to cooperate and negotiate with the tax authority during the investigation process have a significant impact on the outcome of the case.

APAs provide a mechanism to reduce the administrative costs and to manage the unpredictability of potential transfer pricing adjustments for the taxpayer.[16] Circular 2 sets out detailed guidelines for the implementation of

16 According to Circular 2, APAs will be applicable to taxpayers that meet the following conditions: (1) the annual amount of related party transactions exceeds RMB 40 million; (2) the taxpayer complies with the related party disclosure requirements; and (3) the taxpayer prepares, maintains and provides contemporaneous documentation.

an APA in China. More than half of the APAs concluded by the Chinese tax authorities are unilateral APAs.[17]

6.2 International options

In general, most of the tax treaties concluded by the Chinese government have an MAP clause, which allows the tax authorities of the contracting states to settle cross-border tax disputes by agreement. Circular 2 provides that where the SAT accepts an application for a bilateral or multilateral APA, the SAT will enter into a negotiation with the competent authority of the contracting state in accordance with the relevant MAP clause.

At this time, MAPs are not commonly applied in China. However, with the further expansion of the Chinese tax authority in cooperation with other countries, it is anticipated that more MAPs will be utilized in the future.

PART TWO: TAX AVOIDANCE

7. ACCEPTABLE TAX PLANNING AREAS/SUBJECTS

Tax planning is different from tax avoidance or tax evasion because it achieves both tax efficiency and tax compliance. Proper tax planning must take into account both the substance of the taxpayer's business and the planning strategies permitted under the relevant tax rules. The tax planning mechanisms commonly used in China are outlined below.

(a) The use of offshore holding structures

In a typical foreign direct investment project in China, the foreign investor establishes its subsidiary in China through one or more offshore holding companies. Since many tax treaties provide a reduction or exemption from withholding tax, the use of an offshore holding company as the direct shareholder in a Chinese subsidiary may reduce the tax costs incurred when transferring profits out of China. However, since China has intensified its efforts in preventing treaty-shopping and other tax avoidance schemes, the investor should conduct a thorough tax assessment when devising the investment structure. The tax authority will apply the 'beneficial owner' test before approving preferential treatment under a tax treaty, and offshore holding companies that are merely conduit or shell companies will be denied eligibility for tax treaty benefits.

Over the past few years, outbound investments by Chinese investors have increased rapidly. For these investments, the location of the offshore holding company is one of the most important considerations in tax planning.

(b) Selection of the proper business structure

In China, common business structures include legal entities, such as wholly foreign-owned enterprises ('WFOEs') and equity joint ventures ('EJVs'), and non-legal entities such as limited liability partnerships ('LLPs').WFOEs and

[17] Refer to *http://www.chinatax.gov.cn/n8136506/n8136608/n9947993/n9948014/12360820.html* for the full text of the China Advance Pricing Arrangement Annual Report (2012).

EJVs are independent taxable entities that are subject to enterprise income tax, while LLPs are flow-through entities where income is flowed through to the partners and taxed at the partners' level. In general, private equity or venture capital investment funds are more likely to adopt an LLP structure, while entities engaged in active business operations favour a WFOE or EJV structure. However, since there is no universal rule applicable to every business, a case-by-case assessment is recommended.

In addition to the above-mentioned business structures, there are also other forms that may be considered, including representative office and branch (for certain industries such as banks, insurance, etc.). When making an investment in China, investors are advised to take into account commercial considerations, regulatory rules and tax implications in selecting the most viable and efficient investment vehicle.

(c) Selection of the proper financing method

In a typical investment in China, the foreign investor may make an investment using equity financing, debt financing or a hybrid of the two. From a tax perspective, a loan investment may be more tax beneficial than an equity investment, since the interest would be deductible from taxable income. Therefore, the investor may be able to maximize their investment through a shareholder loan. However, China has a set of debt-equity ratio rules which require shareholder loans in foreign currency to be registered with the foreign exchange administration in China. The rules prescribe a maximum percentage for permitted shareholder loans.

In addition, the thin capitalization rule should be taken into consideration. Under the thin capitalization rule, the prescribed debt-to-equity ratios are 5:1 for financial institutions and 2:1 for all other enterprises. If the related-party interest payments exceed the aforementioned ratio, such interest payments may not be deducted from taxable income unless the enterprise can produce the relevant supporting documents to demonstrate the financing is at arm's-length, or that the effective tax rate of the borrowing entity is not higher than the tax rate of the domestic related party that receives the interest.

(d) Utilization of tax incentive policies

Chinese tax authorities have offered a variety of tax incentives that may be utilized by investors. Most of the tax incentives are industry-specific, with a few incentives issued to promote the development of local regions and districts. Industry-specific incentives include the agriculture, forestry, animal husbandry, fishery, public infrastructure, environmental protection, energy, water conservation, and new technology industries. The regions and districts that are currently entitled to tax incentive policies include the central and western regions of China, Hengqin (Guangdong province), Qianhai (Shenzhen), Pingtan (Fujian province), and the Shanghai Free Trade Zone.

8. DEFINING ABUSIVE TAX AVOIDANCE

The distinction between tax evasion and tax avoidance is not always clear. Chinese literature and official publications often conflate the two into a single category of 'tax evasion/avoidance.' The concept of abusive tax avoidance was virtually non-existent until the introduction of the General Anti-Avoidance Rule ('GAAR') under the current EIT Law, which came into effect on January 1, 2008. According to current PRC regulations, the term 'tax avoidance arrangement' refers to an arrangement that results in an 'abuse of tax incentives, tax treaties, or a company's legal form; avoidance of tax through the use of a tax haven; and other arrangements lacking a bona fide commercial purpose.'

9. THE LEGISLATIVE FRAMEWORK

Article 47 of the EIT Law sets out the basic principle of GAAR, which provides that the tax authority is empowered to make adjustments where a transaction is structured without a reasonable business purpose and results in a reduction of taxable income. Article 120 of the Implementing Rules defines a transaction without a reasonable business purpose as one structured 'to reduce, avoid or defer tax payments'.

Article 92 of Circular 2 provides that GAAR investigations should target arrangements involving the abuse of tax incentives, tax treaties or corporate organizational forms; avoidance of tax through a tax haven; and any other arrangement without a reasonable business purpose. Article 93 of Circular 2 establishes the principle of substance over form, and provides that the following matters should be considered:

- The form and substance of an arrangement;
- The time of conclusion and the term of execution of an arrangement;
- The methods for completing an arrangement;
- The connections between the different steps or components of an arrangement;
- Changes in the financial status of each party involved in an arrangement; and
- The tax results of an arrangement.

Circular 2 also sets out the procedures that the tax authority should follow in GAAR investigations. It empowers the tax authority, based on the economic substance doctrine, to re-characterize the nature of tax-avoidance transactions and deny taxpayers the right to retain benefits derived from these transactions. Specifically, the tax authority can deny the existence of an enterprise that lacks economic substance, particularly an enterprise that is established in a tax haven. This gives the tax authority a legal basis to challenge the substance of offshore transactions once these transactions are detected.

In addition to the above rules, the SAT may issue other specific rules with regard to the administration of tax avoidance schemes. Some well-known rules include the following:

- Circular Guo Shui Fa[2009] No. 82, which sets out the factors for the determination of PRC tax residency status, and the tax treatment of enterprises incorporated offshore but controlled by PRC enterprises.
- Circular Guo Shui Han [2009] No. 601, which clarifies the test for 'beneficial owner' status and entitlement to preferential tax treaty benefits.
- Circular Guo Shui Han [2009] No. 698, which stipulates the tax reporting obligations for eligible offshore indirect equity transfers.
- Circular Guo Shui Han [2009] No. 124, which provides procedural rules for the application of tax treaty benefits.

10. KEY CASES OF INTEREST

10.1 Current cases

Since 2008, Chinese tax authorities have increased their efforts in preventing tax avoidance schemes. Some recent landmark cases have been summarized below.

(a) Wal-Mart case

The Wal-Mart acquisition case was the first case published by the SAT dealing with indirect equity transfer deals. In 2007, the foreign buyer acquired a 35 per cent equity interest in the target entity, a British Virgin Island intermediary holding company, from a foreign seller (the 'First Transaction'). Before the First Transaction, the seller was the sole owner of the target company, which in turn held a 100 per cent equity interest in a chain of 65 subsidiaries in China. On June 15, 2012, the foreign buyer acquired the remaining 65 per cent equity interest in the target entity from the seller for consideration of US$476.5 million (the 'Second Transaction'). The consideration included US$100.5 million in cash and a discharged loan valued at US$376 million (see Figure 1 below).

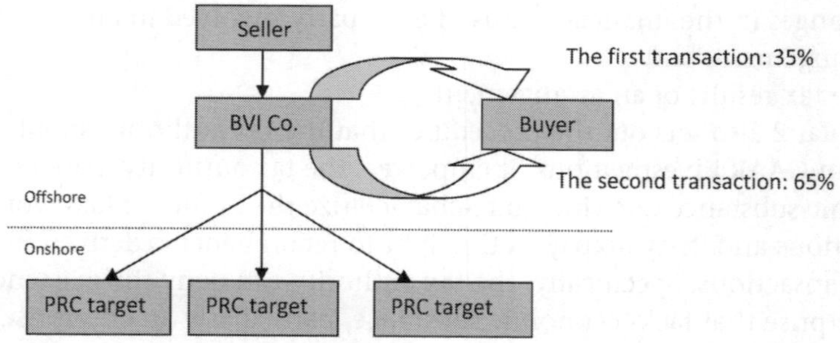

The Chinese tax authorities disregarded the intermediate holding company and treated the transaction as if the seller was disposing of the Chinese targets directly. The Second Transaction was assessed as falling under Circular 698, and the relevant capital gains associated with the disposal were treated as China-sourced income and therefore subject to withholding tax in China.

Since this case was published in the SAT's reply to the local tax authority, it is technically not binding in regards to other cases. However, local tax authorities may follow the SAT's approach in conducting tax assessments on similar indirect transfer transactions, including the method used to allocate equity transfer proceeds among the group of PRC companies being indirectly transferred, and the method used to determine the foreign exchange rate for the computation of capital gains.

(b) Shaanxi case

The Shaanxi case was initiated when the tax authority was conducting a routine review of the use of tax treaty benefits by the taxpayer. During the review, the tax authority discovered that the offshore holding company, a company incorporated in Hong Kong (the 'HK Company'), might be a treaty-shopping vehicle. As a result, the provincial and municipal tax authorities formed a taskforce to conduct a formal investigation. Upon the completion of the investigation, the tax authorities concluded that the HK Company was a shell company lacking an adequate business purpose, and therefore was not eligible for the benefits under the China-Hong Kong Double Taxation Arrangement. The tax authorities also suspected that the HK Company had been involved in other tax avoidance schemes, and decided to conduct further investigations. Thereafter, it was determined that the HK Company constituted a permanent establishment in China between October 2006 and June 2012. Accordingly, the tax authorities imposed enterprise income tax for the income attributable to the HK Company's permanent establishment in China.

10.2 Key historical cases

(a) Xinjiang case

In 2008, the SAT issued the Circular of Correct Treatment by the Xinjiang State Tax Bureau regarding an Abusive Use of Treaty Application (GuoShui Han [2008] No. 1076), which published the Xinjiang case and the tax adjustment made by the tax authority. It was the first major anti-avoidance case after the introduction of the current EIT Law on January 1, 2008. The case involved two Chinese companies ('Company B' and 'Company C') that established a joint venture ('Company A') in Xinjiang in 2003. In July 2006, Company B transferred part of its shares of Company A to a Barbados Company for US$33.8 million. Shortly thereafter, Company B increased the registered capital of Company A by the amount of US$33.8 million. In June 2007, the Barbados Company sold its shares of Company A back to Company B for approximately US$46 million, and claimed an exemption from the applicable Chinese tax under the provisions of the China-Barbados tax treaty (see Figure 2 below).

The issue in the case was whether the Barbados Company should be considered a resident of Barbados, thereby entitling it to benefits under the China-Barbados tax treaty. The Xinjiang tax bureau determined that the Barbados Company did not qualify as a resident of Barbados because (1) the company was registered in Barbados but had no place of management there;

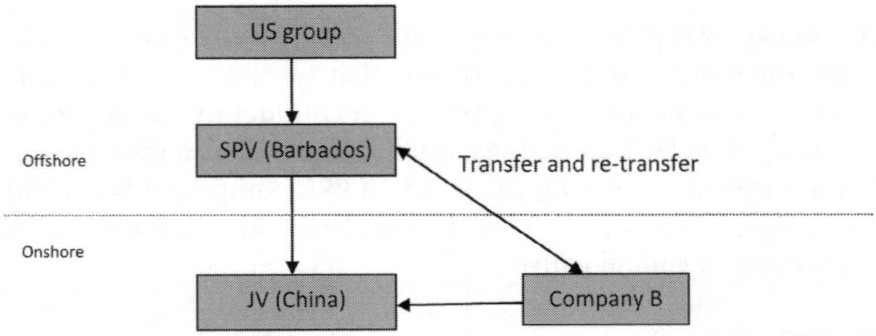

(2) all three of the company's registered directors were US nationals; and (3) the company had no directors resident in Barbados. The Xinjiang tax bureau also concluded that the transaction amounted to tax treaty abuse for several reasons, including:

- the entire transaction appeared to be 'pre-determined' as a result of a prior agreement which provided the Barbados Company with a 'locked-in' gain;
- the Barbados Company had been established only two months prior to acquiring its interest in the joint venture, and there was no apparent commercial purpose for its establishment; and
- there was only a short time period between the acquisition and disposition of the interest in the Chinese joint venture, which further suggested that the Barbados Company had no interest in participating in the management of the joint venture.

As a result, the Xinjiang tax bureau concluded that the Barbados Company could not be regarded as a Barbados tax resident and imposed a Chinese withholding tax of 10 per cent on the capital gain realized on the share sale.

The Chinese authorities are now focusing on the purpose or motive for a commercial transaction in order to prevent tax treaty abuse. Therefore, foreign investors should pay close attention to commercial arrangements that might be considered a mere attempt to avoid, reduce, or delay taxes. In order to prove a valid business purpose, foreign investors should be prepared to demonstrate, with appropriate documentation, the economic substance of companies located in jurisdictions covered by Chinese tax treaties.

11 PENALTIES

11.1 Legislative provisions

Where an adjustment has been made by the tax authority under the GAAR provisions, the taxpayer must pay the adjusted tax amount and the corresponding interest surcharge to the tax authority.

11.2 Examples of penalties imposed

While the existing rules are not clear as to whether the tax authority may impose a penalty on the adjustment, no such penalty has been imposed in published GAAR cases.

12. CURRENT TRENDS

12.1 National policy and law

Trends for 2014 include the increasing focus on transfer pricing administration, and the continued prevention of tax-avoidance schemes. Over the past few years, Chinese tax authorities have shifted their attention from transfer pricing on multinational companies to Chinese group companies. Quite frequently, adjustments are being made to the tax returns of Chinese companies resulting in increased tax revenue in China. China is also keen to collect its fair share of multinational company profits in China through mechanisms such as levying taxes on advantages related to operating in China. Since it is expected that China's focus on transfer pricing will continue in the years to come, multinational companies should be cautious when devising transfer pricing policies for business transactions in China.

As discussed in section 3.1 above, China has been working with the UN and the OECD on a number of transfer pricing initiatives including BEPS and intra-group management and services fees. In addition, China has signed the Multilateral Convention on Mutual Administrative Assistance, which establishes a multilateral framework of cooperation in tax assessment and revenue collection with the objective of preventing offshore tax evasion. As a result, it is expected that in 2014 or the coming few years, China will amend the relevant domestic tax regulations and increase the number of tax avoidance investigations, particularly in the area of cross-border trading and e-commerce activities.

Finally, Chinese tax authorities are expected to increase investigations of outbound investments made by Chinese companies. In recent years, outbound investments by Chinese companies have increased as a result of the 'going out policy' and the attractive underpricing of overseas assets. As a result, the enforcement activities of Chinese tax authorities may begin targeting the tax issues arising from these outbound investments, such as the application of tax credits on foreign-sourced income and controlled foreign corporation legislation.

12.1.1 The impact and role of the OECD and other international relations

On August 27, 2013, China became the 56th signatory to the Multilateral Convention on Mutual Administrative Assistance in Tax Matters (the 'Convention'). The signing of the Convention reflects China's intention to increase its efforts in preventing international tax evasion. The Convention allows China to automatically exchange information with other signatories and conduct simultaneous tax investigations of multinational companies, both within and outside China. This increased access to a multinational company's tax-related information from other foreign jurisdictions introduces a new deterrent for tax arrangements whose feasibility depends on not being detected by Chinese tax authorities. Moreover, China has been actively involved in the development of the OECD's BEPS rules and action plans, and is expected to enter into an intergovernmental agreement with the US in a joint effort to prevent offshore tax avoidance.

In light of the ongoing developments in the transfer pricing and anti-avoidance regime in China, multinational enterprises with sizable investments in China and Chinese enterprises making outbound investments are likely to be under closer scrutiny by the Chinese tax authorities. As a result, investors should take a more prudent approach in respect of tax planning by making certain that transactions are commercially reasonable, and ensuring consistency and stability of transfer pricing policies among intra-group entities in different jurisdictions.

Cyprus

Law Chambers Nicos Papacleovoulou LLC
Evi N Papacleovoulou & Chrysthia N Papacleovoulou

PART ONE: TRANSFER PRICING

1. GENERAL OVERVIEW

Cyprus has been a member of the European Union since 2004 and a member of the Eurozone since 2008. The Cyprus tax legislation is fully compliant with the EU Acquis Communautaire and EU Directives. The legislation is also in full compliance with the code of Conduct for Business Taxation and is against harmful tax competition. As of April 2009, Cyprus is proudly featured on the White list of the OECD. Cyprus offers one of the most favourable tax regulated jurisdictions, making it an ideal location for the creation of Cyprus holding companies, financing and royalty structures. Moreover, Cyprus offers very attractive, transparent and efficient tax-planning opportunities which are supported by the stability of the legal system and the efficiency of service professionals.

Transfer pricing aims to regulate the price at which goods and services are sold between associated enterprises, and is acknowledged as the most important international tax issue facing multinational businesses. In uncertain economic times, such as the one that the world economy is currently facing, transfer pricing becomes a double-edged sword, as a balance between risks undertaken, seized opportunities and functionality, must be reached.

Most territories with developed tax systems have adopted transfer pricing rules in their Tax Laws that require transactions between related parties to be treated as arm's length, and require transparency for tax purposes. Therefore any Group Company, which is essentially a cost centre because it provides service to another Group Company, should be assumed to be subject to a requirement to earn an adequate reward for the service it provides. Considering that transfer pricing audits are becoming more common and more aggressive by tax authorities worldwide, Cyprus transfer pricing regime offers important incentives for tax and corporate planning of groups that use Cyprus corporate vehicles.

2. IDENTIFICATION OF LEGISLATIVE FRAMEWORK

There is no specific transfer pricing legislation in Cyprus, other than a provision in the Income Tax Law which requires transactions between 'related parties' to follow the 'arm's length principle'. Cyprus tax legislation applies the OECD model and guidelines to determine whether a transaction is at arm's length.

The arm's length principle is the cornerstone of transfer pricing rules and regulations in Cyprus, and it is codified in article 33 of the Income Tax Law of 2002 No. 118(I) (hereinafter the 'Income Tax Law'). Section 33 of the Income Tax Law provides that, where:

(a) a business in the Republic participates directly or indirectly in the management, control or capital of a business of another person; or
(b) the same persons participate directly or indirectly in the management, control or capital of two or more businesses;

and in either case conditions are made or imposed between the two businesses in their commercial or financial relations which differ from those which would be made between independent businesses, then any profits, which would, but for those conditions, have accrued to one of the businesses, but, by reason of those conditions, have not so accrued, may be included in the profits of that business and taxed accordingly.

On this basis, the Revenue may adjust the profits of a resident company or other person for income tax purposes where it is of the opinion that, because of the special relationship between the Cyprus resident and the other party to a transaction, the Cyprus profits are understated. The usual relationship between two companies encompassed by these provisions is that of holding and subsidiary, whether direct or indirect. The rules apply to all types of transactions, including loans. Cyprus, however, has no specific anti-avoidance legislation on thin capitalisation.

Section 33 of the Income Tax Law contains definitions of related or connected parties for the purpose of applying the arm's length principle. Moreover, the Income Tax Law includes general documentation requirements. Although the Cyprus Tax legislation does not provide for specific transfer pricing documentation requirements, it is necessary for transactions between related/connected parties to be supported by appropriate agreements and other supporting legal documentation. It is advisable that such agreements be legalized at the tax office by the payment of the relevant and applicable stamp duty. There are no deadlines to produce transfer pricing documentation, and no changes have been made to the legislative transfer pricing provisions since the introduction of s. 33 of the Income Tax Law. However, it is advisable that documentation be maintained by companies in case of an audit.

It is highly recommended to keep written agreements to cover intercompany transactions. Tax returns in Cyprus need to be signed by the auditor tax consultant of the company who re-confirms to the tax authorities that specific tax returns are compliant with the laws, rules and circulars issued by the Revenue, hence, all transactions and Agreements between related parties are usually examined during an audit of a Cyprus company.

Cyprus does not publish documentation of methods of Advance Pricing Agreements. Therefore, there is no requirement for return disclosure, though advanced rulings are highly advisable.

The arm's length principle is monitored by the Inland Revenue Department. Following the directions for the tax reform by TROIKA, as of June 5, 2014, the House of Representatives passed a new law whereby the Inland Revenue and VAT departments are unified under the Taxation Department.

This is illustrated by the fact that the Company tax return form, Form IR4 2012, requires a company to specify in different sections its balances with group companies, its balances with other related subsidiaries and other undertakings, its other non-trading debtors and creditors, and the balances of directors and shareholders. At the end of each section, the company must confirm that all sales, purchases and other charges were at market price by ticking the relevant 'yes' or 'no' box.

It must be noted that no guidance is provided by the Cyprus Inland Revenue on how the company taxpayer can prove market prices have been applied to sales, purchases and other charges with related/connected parties, but advanced ruling can be obtained.

2.1 State and provincial legislative interplay

In Cyprus there are no state or provincial laws that come into play, as s. 33 covers all transactions.

2.2 International treaties and agreements

In terms of international agreements that have the greatest impact on transfer pricing provisions, Cyprus follows the OECD Transfer Pricing Guidelines. In fact, the arm's length principles contained in s. 33, are based on the international standard that member countries of the OECD have agreed should be used for determining transfer prices for tax purposes. These principles are set forth in article 9 of the OECD Model Tax Convention. Any method described in the Guidelines can be used, provided it is considered the most reliable method for the particular case. As per the Transfer Pricing guidelines, where traditional transaction methods are equally as reliable as transactional profit methods, then they must be preferred.

(a) Traditional transaction methods

(a) The Comparable Uncontrolled Price ('CUP') method: comparison of selling price/fee of the seller under question with similar transactions between unrelated parties

(b) The resale price method: comparison of the gross margins of party purchasing goods/ services from related parties with similar businesses where the supplier/provider is unrelated.

(c) The cost plus method: comparison of the mark up over costs of a supplier of goods/services to related parties with similar businesses selling to unrelated parties.

(b) Transactional profit methods

(a) Profit split method: split of the combined profits of the related parties on the basis of an arm's length agreement.

(b) Transactional net margin method: comparison of net profit indicators.

By seeking to adjust profits by reference to the conditions which would have been obtained between independent enterprises in comparable circumstances, the arm's length principle follows the approach of treating the members of an international group as separate entities rather than separate parts of a unified business. The ultimate result of such treatment is to avoid the tax advantages or disadvantages that would otherwise distort the relative competitive positions of either type of entity. In removing these tax considerations from economic decisions, the arm's length principle promotes the growth of international trade and investment.

3. NATIONAL POLICY ISSUES

Cyprus is by no means a tax haven. It is a highly regulated full member of the European Union State that offers great tax benefits and advantages through its attractive pro-investor tax regime. Succeeding the trend of last November's *OECD Global Forum Report on Transparency and Exchange of Information for Tax Purposes*, Cyprus' Fiscal authorities – applying the more efficient fiscal administration approach – seem to act in a manner that ensures companies registered on the Island, or tax registered on the Island, comply with their statutory filing obligations. This is done in an effort to protect the status of Cyprus as a reputable, reliable and efficient International Business Centre.

3.1 Overall national policy announcements

On April 7, 2011, the Taxation Department confirmed in a letter to the Institute of Certified Public Accountants of Cyprus, that when a Cyprus tax resident company is engaged in group financing transactions (for example, obtains a loan and, using the amount of that loan, provides a related party with a loan) the following interest profit margins (the net of all directly related expenses) will be accepted by the Taxation Department for the purpose of applying s. 33 of the Income Tax Law.

In the case of interest bearing loans:

The amount of loan receivable (EUR)	Net interest profit margin (per cent)
Less than 50,000,000	0.35
Between 50.000.000 and 200,000,000	0.25
Over 200,000,000	0.125

In the case of interest free loans:

The minimum net interest profit margin that the Taxation Department is prepared to accept, irrespective of the amount of the loan, is 0.35 per cent of the principal amount of the interest free loan receivable.

The aforementioned margins shall be accepted by the Taxation Department on the following conditions:

- the ultimate shareholder of the Cyprus taxpayer company is not a Cyprus tax resident;
- the financing arrangements are back-to-back, that is, a Cyprus tax resident company receives a specific amount from a related company through a loan, and using the amount of the relevant loan, provides loans to another related company;
- the time period between the date on which the company receives the loan and the date on which it provides a loan does not exceed 6 months;
- the above margins are the net of all directly related expenses; and
- foreign exchange differences arising on principal amounts of such loans whether realized or not, do not constitute tax allowance expenses in case of a loss and are not taxable in case of a profit.

Additionally, the above margins will apply under the following circumstances:

- when a company receives a loan and uses the relevant amount received to provide more than one loan, or where a company receives more than one loan and provides only one loan;
- when a company borrows from a third person such as a bank, and lends to a related company, provided that the bank has guarantees from other related companies;
- when, instead of a loan, other debt instruments are used, and the advanced ruling and approval of the Cyprus Taxation Department is advisable and required for the application of the aforementioned interest margins.

It must be noted that this policy, as contained in the letter direction of the Taxation Department, does not contain any transfer pricing documentation requirements. Moreover, the above direction is to be considered a general direction and therefore it is highly advisable in each specific case to confirm the application of the abovementioned margins with the Taxation Department in advance and in writing through the so-called unilateral advance pricing agreement (APA). Indeed, the group financing arrangements described above are currently the only possible area where an APA can be obtained under the Cyprus tax policy applied by the Taxation Department.

3.2 National revenue authority initiatives

From a tax perspective, transfer pricing is a powerful legal tool that can directly affect multinational enterprises' effective tax rate. Consequently, like most tax administrators, the Cyprus Taxation Department is focused on audits on the pricing between related entities.[1] Despite the fact that Cyprus has not issued transfer pricing regulations as yet, considering its place as the headquarters of many multinational enterprises, it is important for auditors and tax managers to rely on transfer pricing planning to minimize the

[1] 'Related' with respect to companies means: (a) one company in the Republic participates directly or indirectly in the management or control or capital of another company, or (b) the same persons participating directly or indirectly in the management, control or capital of two or more companies.

effective tax rate and transfer pricing audit risk. Cyprus' tax provisions offer substantial incentives that encourage the use of corporate vehicles in Cyprus to take the benefit of transfer pricing planning through Cyprus.

3.3 Administrative statements

Often, the Cyprus Taxation Department will issue directions for guidance regarding a policy that will impact how the authorities will carry out transfer pricing audits.

3.4 Administrative Guidelines

For the security of an international investor, a tax lawyer or an accountant can obtain an anonymous advanced ruling for the anticipated transaction. It is advisable to take advantage of the tax rulings that can be obtained from the Revenue Office, albeit they may not provide specific guidance in terms of the amounts and/or rates to be changed. It is, however, an essential practice as there is no specific requirement for the maintenance of documentation for companies for all transactions undertaken, and the preparation of such documentation within 30 days of the transaction. The great advantage of Cyprus is that although Greek is the official language of the Tax office, they also accept documentation in English. It is vital to point out that from January 1st, 2013, documentation supporting tax returns, books and records shall be kept for a period of six years from the end of the tax year to which it relates.

4. CASE LAW

Most cases only reach the Tax Tribunal and these are not reported cases.

4.1 Current cases

No current cases reported.

4.2 Historical cases of note

No history of transfer pricing jurisprudence.

5. PENALTIES

The penalties imposed by the Taxation Department may be a reassessment of the tax, imposition of penalties, and interest for late payment. Taxpayers are selected for review on the basis of risk. Indicators of high risk cases are specified above, and usually involve transactions with:

(a) tax heavens;
(b) related entities that have high tax losses;
(c) companies that have tax losses for utilization in a Group Structure

In accordance with the Cyprus tax legislation, the burden of proof is on the taxpayer, to provide evidence to satisfy the assessor that prices used are at arm's length and that these prices have been decided in accordance with the OECD Transfer Pricing Guidelines. Additionally, companies are obligated by law to file audited accounts, meaning that a company's accounting books are inspected by independent auditors before they are submitted to the taxation department.

Transfer pricing adjustments fall within the scope of tax avoidance, unless the Taxation Department proves there has been fraud or wilful default (tax evasion). Therefore, provisions of the law relating to tax avoidance will be applied (interest since the tax year in which the avoidance took place and penalties not exceeding 10 per cent of the additional tax imposed). In cases of fraud or wilful default, additional penalties will be imposed, provided the case is in agreement with the Taxation Department (to avoid further legal action).

5.1 Types

Not applicable.

5.2 Special or notable cases

No cases have been reported in relation to transfer pricing. This is mainly because (a) an advanced ruling is usually obtained, and (b) most cases are settled before the Tax Tribunal, and therefore litigation with the Taxation Department is avoided.

6. DISPUTE RESOLUTION MECHANISMS

In case of a disagreement with a ruling of the Taxation Department, taxpayers can object the decision of the Taxation Department in the following bodies:

(a) Tax Tribunal[2]

(b) Cyprus District Courts (to appeal the decision of the Tax Tribunal)

(c) High Court of Justice (to appeal the decision of the District Court)

Note that Tax Tribunal decisions are binding on the Taxation Department.

6.1 Preferred national options

The favoured method for settling or resolving transfer pricing disputes is the Tax tribunal.

6.2 International options

Non-resident taxpayers and foreign tax authorities who wish for a corresponding adjustment in a Cyprus company's/individual's taxable profits as a result of a primary adjustment made abroad due to transfer pricing, must apply for a Mutual Agreement Procedure ('MAP') to the Taxation Department. The MAP will follow the European Union's Arbitration Convention or the Double Taxation Treaty ('DTT') provisions to resolve the case, depending on the origin of the claim. If the MAP is successful, the Taxation Department will give a tax credit to the taxpayer. Cyprus tax legislation does not provide for the application of secondary

---

2 Established under articles 4A and 20A of the Confirmation and Tax Collection Law, Law 4/78 as amended, and under the Confirmation and Tax Collection (establishment of the Tax Tribunal) Regulations of 1999-2006 (Κ.Δ.Π. 139/99, Κ.Δ.Π. 95/01, Κ.Δ.Π. 915/03, Κ.Δ.Π. 314/2006).

adjustments. A secondary adjustment is an adjustment made in addition to the primary adjustment to deal with excess cash in the hands of an enterprise after a primary adjustment takes place. For example, if a purchase price of a specific invoice is adjusted downward to meet the arm's length standard, then the adjustment value (invoice price vs. arm's length price) is treated as a constructive dividend, a constructive loan or a constructive equity contribution and taxed accordingly.

PART TWO: TAX AVOIDANCE

Cyprus is by no means a tax haven. It is a highly regulated full member of the European Union that offers great tax benefits and advantages through its attractive pro-investor tax regime. Succeeding the trend of last November's *OECD Global Forum Report on Transparency and Exchange of Information for Tax Purposes*, Cyprus' Fiscal authorities, applying the more efficient fiscal administration approach, seem to act in a manner that ensures companies registered on the Island or tax registered on the Island comply with their statutory filing obligations. This is done in an effort to protect the status of Cyprus as a reputable, reliable and efficient International Business Centre. Tax evasion is illegal under Cyprus law.[3] Tax avoidance is permitted under certain circumstances and therefore the distinction between the two is of considerable importance.

Since the Cyprus banking crisis in March 2013, Germany's allegations against Cyprus of money laundering of the Russian oligarch's moneys, and the ensuing TROIKA reforms, the challenges for Cyprus as a jurisdiction of international tax planning have increased substantially. Faced with declining tax revenues and increased attention from the public, non-governmental organizations and the media on where the burden of austerity measures falls, governments from the major economic powers are showing increased hostility towards legitimate tax avoidance, and the international organizations they control have taken initiatives for global cooperation on worldwide action against what they see as excessively aggressive tax planning. Furthermore, in recent years, the tax authorities in Russia and other former members of the USSR have become more familiar with, and confident in challenging, complex tax concepts and elaborate tax schemes. These two factors make it essential that no detail is overlooked and nothing is left to chance when designing and implementing an international tax mitigation structure, so as to minimize the risk of a successful challenge by following acceptable tax planning strategies.

7. ACCEPTABLE TAX PLANNING AREAS/SUBJECTS

Cyprus generally follows the common law dictum that a taxpayer is entitled to legitimately minimize the payment of tax by acceptable legislative provisions. Cyprus has adopted a foreign direct investment policy that offers advantages and incentives to international investors who transact and use Cyprus corporate vehicles with a view to reducing tax obligations

3 See, for example, article 53 of the Value Added Tax Law 1990 (. 246/90) defining deceitful vat evasion.

and sheltering income. In the following paragraphs, the plans and options available and attractive to the 'aggressive' taxpayer for minimizing tax are discussed.

(a) The Cyprus holding company

A multitude of tax and non-tax factors are taken into consideration to allow a jurisdiction to be regarded as an attractive location in which to set up a holding company, always taking into account the particular circumstances of the investor. The underlying goal, however, remains the same – to minimize the tax charged on income and gains.

Cyprus currently provides one of the most beneficial and versatile 'Holding Company Regimes' available in the world. Available tax advantages are as follows: There is no withholding tax on dividends received by a Cyprus Holding Company from an EU subsidiary as a result of the EU Parent Subsidiary Directive; there is nil or minimal withholding tax on dividends received by a Cyprus Holding Company from a non-EU subsidiary as a result of Double Tax Avoidance Agreements (DTAA) in place; and the incoming dividends received by a Cyprus Holding Company from an overseas subsidiary are tax-exempt. They may also be exempt from SCDF (Special Contribution for the Defence Tax) subject to easily met conditions; dividends paid from one Cyprus tax resident company to another are exempt from corporation tax in Cyprus; there is no withholding tax on dividends paid by the Cyprus Holding company to non-resident shareholders and on payments of interest and royalties outside Cyprus; there is no tax on the disposal of shares, unless it relates to immovable property situated in Cyprus, allowing for the tax free disposal of any kind of property; there are no participation requirements; a tax credit will be afforded for any taxes paid abroad according to the DTAAs concluded by Cyprus; in the absence of a DTAA , Cyprus unilaterally affords a credit for the foreign tax paid on the same income; losses can be carried forward indefinitely; mergers and acquisitions can be effected without tax cost; the trading income of a Cyprus holding company is taxed at a flat rate of 12.5 per cent; under Cyprus law all expenses incurred for the production of income are deducted before arriving at the taxable income; and there are no thin capitalisation rules. A Cyprus company can be capitalised entirely with loans and any interest paid to a parent company will be fully deductible.

(b) Double tax treaties

Cyprus combines a low-tax regime of 12.5 per cent corporate tax with a network of double tax treaties. It has concluded the highest number of double tax treaties compared to any other offshore jurisdiction, particularly Central and Eastern European Countries and a number of Middle Eastern countries. Most of the Treaties follow the OECD model, and all of them have the impact of reducing or eliminating the normal withholding taxes imposed by the Contracting states on dividends, interest and royalty payments. This is beneficial for trade with certain Eastern European Countries and Russia because foreign investors investing in Eastern Europe have the opportunity to channel their investments through a country, such as Cyprus, which has a treaty with the investment recipient country, allowing for the reduction, and in some cases elimination, of withholding taxes.

(c) The IP box

In May 2012, Cyprus introduced changes to Income Tax law, which portray Cyprus as the ultimate royalty jurisdiction, enabling it to compete successfully with other established jurisdictions like Luxemburg, Netherlands etc. The main features of the Cyprus IP box are outlined below:

(a) The amendment to the Income Tax Law is effective from January 1st 2012 and applies to all categories of intellectual property, including the rights set out in the Patent Law of 1998 as amended, the Intellectual Property Rights Law of 1976, as amended, and the Trademarks Law cap, as amended, covering all IP assets, including patents, trademarks, copyrights, formulas, designs, know-how and processes.

(b) The new tax regime provides for favorable tax treatment in relation to income generated from IP rights, by exempting 80 per cent of royalty profit from corporation tax, ie, only 20 per cent of the IP income after deducting all costs relating to the generation of the income is subject to 12.5 per cent corporate tax.

(c) Thus, the effective tax rate of a Cyprus royalty company is 2.5 per cent or less, taking into consideration the capital allowances and expenses being the lowest in Europe, compared to the Netherlands where it is 5 per cent and Luxembourg where it is 5.75 per cent.

(d) In the event that IP related costs and deductions exceed revenue earned from IP assets, the loss may be offset against other income for the year or future profits.

(e) The 80 per cent exemption also applies for capital gains arising from the disposal of the IP. But in this case, a full tax exemption from capital gains tax applies if the shares of the IP Company are sold.

(f) The cost of acquisition or development of an IP right acquired by a Cyprus company may be capitalized and written off on a straight line basis over 5 years, giving an annual writing-down allowance of 20 per cent.

These advantages are complimented by the additional benefits of Cyprus companies: (a) there are no withholding taxes upon distribution of dividends to non-Cyprus tax residents; (b) since Cyprus is member of the European Union, the EU royalty directive applies, under which royalty paid by other EU countries to a Cyprus royalty company has zero withholding tax; (c) In case of non EU countries, with which Cyprus has favorable double tax treaties, lower or zero withholding taxes on royalties apply and tax credits are issued against Cyprus taxation, for example, under the double tax treaty with Russia there is 0 per cent withholding tax on royalties. In the case of the Double Tax Treaty with Ukraine, 2 per cent withholding tax on royalties apply, but tax credit is issued, reducing tax paid in Cyprus at the effective rate of 2,5 per cent. As noted, Cyprus's IP box regime provides a maximum tax rate of 2.5 percent on income earned from IP assets. The comparable rate of its nearest competitor, the Netherlands, is twice that amount at 5 percent. Luxembourg (5.76 per cent) and Belgium (6.8 per cent) are close to the Netherlands but far behind Cyprus.

The Cyprus IP box regime applies to a wider range of income than any other European scheme, most of which restrict benefits to income from patents and supplementary patent certificates. There is no cap on benefits, no requirement regarding self-development of the IP and no restrictions on where the expenditure of the acquisition or development of the IP is incurred. While the Luxembourg, Netherlands and UK schemes offer partial exemption of gains on disposal, the exemptions are less attractive than those provided by Cyprus, due to limitations on qualifying assets and generous deduction rates. Furthermore, full exemptions can be relatively easily obtained in Cyprus by holding the IP assets in a separate company and disposing of the shares in the company, as described above.

Therefore, Cyprus offers the most flexible and favorable tax regime for 'IP box'. In most cases, immediate economic and tax savings can be accomplished by transferring intellectual rights currently held by entities located in low or no-tax jurisdictions to Cyprus resident companies in order to take advantage of the new exemptions. The transfer of IP rights into a Cyprus company will not attract any form of taxation in Cyprus, and the benefits and substantial exemptions will become available as soon as the asset is transferred.

(d) The shipping company box

Cyprus' simplified registration procedures, favorable taxation regime, well-developed infrastructure and advanced safety policies have established the Cyprus flag as one of the most prominent in the world. Therefore, it is no wonder Cyprus is one of the most highly sought-after registration jurisdictions for ship owners, charterers, ship managers and other shipping-related companies.

Moreover, the Merchant Shipping Legislation of 2010 was a turning point for the country, as it placed Cyprus in a very competitive position. Cyprus became the only European country with a tonnage tax system that is approved by the EU and covers the three main shipping categories of ship-owning, ship-management and the chartering of vessels. The new taxation system provides for the imposition of a tonnage tax on the net tonnage of ships, rather than a corporate tax on the profits derived from their activities. It is important to note that the tonnage tax legislation is regulated by the Department of Merchant Shipping and not by the tax authorities.

Under the tonnage tax system, shipping companies which possess or charter vessels are exempted from income tax on their profits and are automatically taxed based on the tonnage of the Cypriot flag ships they own or charter. Moreover, they are not liable to capital gains taxation upon selling a vessel, or selling and transferring shares. In addition, these companies are not subject to stamp duty on ship mortgage deeds or other documentation, or to estate duty imposed on inheritance of shares. Officers and crew of vessels registered in Cyprus are fully exempted from income tax.

Ship-management companies are entitled either to pay tax at a rate of 25 per cent, calculated on the tonnage of the international ships they manage, or based on their profits at a rate of 4.25 per cent. If they undertake the full management of Cyprus flag vessels, ship-management companies are fully exempted from tonnage tax. Moreover, no tax is withheld from dividends paid out of profits derived from ship management activities, and no tax is levied on the recipient shareholder with regard to these dividends. Ship-management companies are also exempt from defense contribution imposed on paid dividends.

Non-shipping income from ship-owning, chartering and ship-management companies invested in other activities is subject to corporate tax at the normal rate of 12.5 per cent which is one of the lowest corporate tax rate in the EU. The taxation legislation provides for several exemptions that may decrease the payable tax rate on non-shipping income.

(e) Cyprus international trusts

The long-awaited reform of the Cyprus International Trusts Law effected by the enactment of Law 20(I)/2012 on March 9, 2012, introduced important changes to the tax law provisions for the taxation of Cyprus International Trusts. A major change in the new 2012 law was the redefinition of the concept of the beneficiary under the new Cyprus International Trust law. This, in combination with the new Income Tax Law s. 31, changed the taxation of Cyprus International Trusts and Cyprus 'non-international trusts' substantially. Let us consider how these two provisions interplay and set the tax provisions for Cyprus trusts.

The Law No. 20(I) of 2012 amendments to the Cyprus International Trusts, addressed and clarified issues relating to taxation by introducing flexibility and allowing a beneficiary to become a Cyprus tax resident following the formation of the Trust. Arguably, while trusts have historically been used to plan and preserve family wealth, the tax regime applicable to trusts has transformed them into tax planning vehicles.

Whether the trust will be taxed in Cyprus depends on the residency of the beneficiary. The test is as follows: (a) Where the **beneficiary is resident in Cyprus**, the income and profits of a Cyprus International Trust which are earned or deemed to be earned from **sources within and outside of** Cyprus, are subject to every form of taxation imposed in Cyprus. (b) Where the **beneficiary is not a resident** of Cyprus, the income and profits of a Cyprus International Trust which are earned or deemed to be earned from **sources within Cyprus**, are subject to every form or taxation imposed in Cyprus.

In effect, Cyprus International Trusts will remain exempt from taxation in Cyprus and the beneficiaries will still be taxable via the trustees. Where a beneficiary is a resident, income and profits of an international trust earned from sources within and outside Cyprus are subject to every form of taxation imposed in Cyprus. Where the beneficiary is a non-resident, only Cyprus-sourced income and profits are subject to Cyprus tax.

8. DEFINING ABUSIVE TAX AVOIDANCE

There is no single definition of abusive tax avoidance, and Cyprus does not have a specific provision that defines abusive tax avoidance. It is instead assessed on an *ad hoc* basis by the Taxation Department.

In accordance with their mission statement, the Taxation Department is responsible for the application and enforcement of direct tax legislation and Double Tax Agreements concluded between Cyprus and other countries, as well as the collection of public revenue. To this end, it ensures the consistent, fair and impartial application and enforcement of the law and the relevant Agreements, and secures prompt revenue collection in a cost effective and professional manner. As a result, it is consistent with Government policy which aims to ensure sound public finances, combat tax evasion and avoidance and provide appropriate quality service to taxpayers, thus contributing to the overall well-being of society. Under the general anti-avoidance provision, any artificial or fictitious transaction may be disregarded, and the commissioner of income tax may assess tax on the person concerned.

9. THE LEGISLATIVE FRAMEWORK

Cyprus follows the '*substance over form*' and '*business purpose test*' doctrines, which allow the tax authorities to disregard any artificial transactions and structures they consider to be in place solely for the reason of obtaining a tax benefit. The Assessment and Collection of Taxes Law, which was amended to transpose the Mutual Assistance Directive (77/799/EEC) into domestic legislation, contains general anti-abuse rules, under which the tax authorities may disregard artificial or fictitious transactions and assess the taxpayer on the proper object of tax. The provisions apply for both local and international transactions, and for residents and non-residents.

A company may enjoy the benefits of the business-friendly tax framework of Cyprus and its extensive treaty network, if it is 'managed and controlled' in Cyprus. The determination of the locus of management and control of a company is crucial for the company's tax residency, as it is a determining factor on both the issue of Cyprus tax residence and residence in relation to the tie-breaker rules included in the double tax agreements entered into by Cyprus.

As no domestic precedent on the matter exists, Cyprus courts follow English case law in relation to the concept of management and control. UK courts have concluded that the 'management and control' test is met if key strategic decisions are taken in the location concerned. There is no requirement that the day-to-day management of the company should be undertaken from there. The UK courts have made clear that the test is not satisfied if no 'intellectual activity' is performed at board meetings where decisions are made – that is, if the board merely gives formal approval to decisions that have already been made elsewhere. In the same case, it was also decided that at least some information capable of giving guidance to the board in making a decision must be proven to have been at the disposal of the board, even if it is less comprehensive than what would normally be expected of a board of directors.

Even if Cyprus tax residence is established, foreign anti-avoidance rules, the interpretation of the notion of 'management and control' and the facts of each case as perceived by foreign tax authorities make it prudent to ensure that there is real substance in each tax structure.

10. KEY CASES OF INTEREST

Substance requirements – international perspective

(a) International

The OECD recently announced its Base Erosion and Profit Shifting initiative ('BEPS'), which is in many ways a continuation of the Harmful Tax Practices initiative of the 1990s. The OECD has published an action plan and has set ambitious deadlines to achieve its goals. One of the key components of the action plan is the strengthening of Controlled Foreign Corporation rules, with a target date of September, 2015 for recommendations on how this subject is to be developed, and the prevention of treaty abuse (for example by measures such as denial of treaty benefits in cases of double non-taxation). The publication of the action plan has been followed by the release from Working Party 6 of the OECD on the discussion draft on the Transfer Pricing Aspects of intangibles.

(b) European Union

In 2012 the European Commission began a similar initiative, adopting an Action Plan which included more than 30 measures to combat tax fraud and tax evasion. These measures included a proposal to close loopholes in the Parent-Subsidiary Directive (2011/96/ EU) (the 'Directive'). According to the European Commission, these loopholes had been used by some companies to escape taxation, particularly by exploiting differences in the way intra-group payments are taxed.

In November 2013, the European Commission adopted a proposal to amend the Directive, introducing a uniform general anti-avoidance rule which will deny the benefits of the Directive to tax structures that are deemed to be 'wholly artificial', and a provision to ensure that a specific form of tax planning arrangement, namely hybrid loan arrangements, cannot benefit from tax exemptions.

(c) Russia

Russia has been increasingly active in implementing rules to eliminate what the authorities consider aggressive tax planning. The Russian Tax Code has recently been amended to oblige Russian companies to disclose the ultimate beneficial owners of securities registered by means of depository accounts of nominee shareholders. Additionally, taxpayers are obliged to report transactions carried out during previous years to the Russian tax authorities which meet the definition of 'controlled transactions' under the Tax Code (for example, transactions with tax residents of a jurisdiction which is included in the list of offshore jurisdictions issued by the Russian Ministry of Finance where the parties are related or where the transactions amount to more than RUR 60 million).

(d) USA

The importance of substance and valid business reasons behind each structure was reiterated by the office of the Associate Chief Counsel of the US Internal Revenue Service ('IRS') in its Memorandum issued in relation to the granting of treaty benefits to Cyprus companies owned by US and non US residents.

In order for the Cyprus-US treaty to apply, the recipient of the income must be a resident of one of the two contracting states, and no other provision in the treaty providing for the denial of such benefits must apply. In the case in respect of which the Memorandum was issued, the IRS concluded that the Limitation of Benefits clause of the treaty did not apply, and benefits were not to be denied, since the structure was put in place for reasons other than merely to obtain a tax advantage through the application of the treaty.

It therefore follows that US authorities will be inclined to deny such benefits to structures which they consider to be artificial (eg, structures with no business rationale or insufficient substance).

(e) Other countries

More and more countries are introducing anti-avoidance rules and CFC rules where no such rules previously existed. In addition to the examples above, in the past year, Greece has put in place CFC rules, Belgium has introduced anti-avoidance rules (including a new thin capitalization rule), the United Kingdom has introduced a General Anti-Avoidance rule and Germany has introduced a rule denying hybrid instruments in German outbound structures the benefit of the German participation exemption.

Meeting the substance requirements in practice

The importance of substance and valid business reasons behind each corporate structure is cardinal for its efficacy and compatibility with the new emerging era of tax planning. Substance is now an absolute necessity. While the existence of adequate substance required to achieve tax residency and not fall foul of anti-avoidance rules is a question of fact, there are some best practice standards that can be followed to increase the chances of success, such as exercising management and control of the company in Cyprus, with the board of directors meeting in Cyprus as frequently as required in order to adequately direct the company's activities, and establishing a real physical presence in Cyprus by setting up a fully resourced and independent office in Cyprus.

Economic substance can be further enhanced by employing suitably qualified people to administer management activities and carry out the day-to-day management of the company in Cyprus and complying with the relevant legal and regulatory requirements. These requirements include tax and social insurance obligations, opening local bank accounts to settle expenses incurred by the company, including employment costs, maintaining accounting records in Cyprus and ensuring that the company discharges all its statutory corporate and fiscal obligations on time, and by using the Cyprus office as the principal address for notices, letters and other correspondence.

10.1 Current cases

No current cases to be discussed. None reported at Supreme Court level.

10.2 Key historical cases

No historical cases.

11. PENALTIES

Penalties are targeted at failure to pay tax and increased powers are, as of June 20, 2014, given to the Taxation department to collect taxes, and confiscate moneys in bank accounts to settle outstanding tax liabilities. Hefty penalties are placed on any director, officer or employee of a banking institution that 'tips-off' a company or individual about which/whom the Taxation Department has requested information, and as a result, the company/individual has withdrawn or transferred funds. In this case, the penalty on such directors, officers or employees is up to 1 year of imprisonment or a fine up to EUR 5.000, or both. Penalties for abusive tax avoidance or non-payment of due tax include, depending on the facts of each case, a fine or imprisonment. The severity of the penalty depends on whether there was deceit or intent to defraud the Republic of Cyprus.

11.1 Legislative provisions

Cyprus is in full conformity with all European legislation including the Directive 2011/16/EC of the Council dated 15.2.11 on the administrative cooperation in the area of taxation, which is ratified by the Law on the Administrative Cooperation in the area of taxation Law 205(I)/2012.

Following considerable criticism that Cyprus was complicit to money laundering practices, on December 21, 2012 the House of Representatives discussed and passed a Law which regulates the provision of administration services, called 'The Law Regulating Companies Providing Administration Services and Related Matters of 2012' (the Law). In accordance with the provisions of the Law, companies that provide such services and are not exempted by the Law, should apply and obtain the relevant license from the Cyprus Securities and Exchange Commission (CySEC), in order to continue to provide these services. Since 2012 three registries have been created for Trusts, one regulated by CySEC, one regulated by the Cyprus Bar Association and one regulated by the Association of Certified and Chartered Accountants.

On the matter of serious tax offices, on February 2, 2014, CySEC issued a direction to Cyprus Investment Firms, Management Companies and

Administrative Service Providers ('the Regulated Entities') informing them that the Financial Action Task Force, the international body responsible for setting standards and promoting the effective implementation of measures for combating money laundering and terrorist financing, amended its recommendations, according to which the definition of 'predicate offense' includes serious tax offenses related to direct or indirect taxes. It must be noted that similar provisions apply to lawyers and accountants who are regulated by their own professional bodies.

According to Article 3(4) of the European Commission's Proposal on the prevention of use of the financial system for the purpose of money laundering and terrorist financing, which is still pending adoption:

'"criminal activity" means any kind of criminal involvement in the commission of the following serious crimes: ...

(f) all offences, including tax crimes, as defined in national law of the Member States, related to direct taxes and indirect taxes, which are punishable by deprivation of liberty or a detention order for a maximum of more than one year or, as regards those States which have a minimum threshold for offences in their legal system, all offences punishable by deprivation of liberty or a detention order for a minimum of more than six months.'

According to s. 51A of the Assessment and Collection of Taxes Law, as amended in December 2012, a person who is found to have fraudulently omitted or delayed payment of the amount of tax which required under this law, is guilty of a criminal offence, punishable, if convicted, by imprisonment of at least one year.

Additionally, according to s. 5 of the Prevention and Suppression of Money Laundering and Terrorist Financing Laws of 2007–2013 ('the Law'), predicate offences are, amongst other things, criminal offences punishable by imprisonment over one year, if proceeds have been acquired that may qualify as a money laundering offence.

Based on the foregoing, fraudulent tax evasion falls under the scope of the Law. Therefore, the regulated entities of the CySEC are required to follow a risk based approach:

(i) To implement adequate and appropriate systems and processes to detect, prevent and deter money laundering arising from serious tax offences.
(ii) To not knowingly aid or abet clients of prospects in committing tax offences.
(iii) When performing due diligence measures, to screen clients against databases or third party checks for adverse tax-related news.
(iv) To conduct ongoing monitoring of the business relationship with their clients and to ensure that the actual amount of funds deposited by clients are consistent with the amount of funds indicated at account opening, as well as with the economic profile of the client.

While the regulated Entities are not expected to determine if their clients are fully compliant with all their tax obligations globally, they are expected to determine whether there are reasonable grounds to suspect that client accounts contain proceeds derived from serious tax offences, and when this is the case, they should proceed with the appropriate reporting obligations.

11.2 Examples of penalties imposed

The penalties imposed are fines and interest for each day of delayed tax payment. Following TROIKA's reforms, substantial amendments have been effected to the Tax Collection Law 31(I)/1962 until 80(I)/2014. In accordance with the amendment effected by Law 80(I)/2014 as of 20.6.14, the Taxation Department has the right, under certain conditions, to confiscate moneys in any bank accounts in order to collect taxes due over the amount of EUR 3,000. Moreover, under Law 66(I)/2014, which introduced new s. 9B(4)(a), any director, officer, employee or representative of a credit institution where a bank account is located, who reveals or, through any action or omission, hinders the collection of overdue taxes, commits a criminal offence punishable with up to one year of imprisonment or a fine of up to EUR 5,000, or both. These amendments have caused concern to lawyers, accountants and other fiduciaries, as the Taxation Department may confiscate any amount from any account, and therefore clarifications have been requested in relation to, for example, moneys in clients' accounts or trust accounts.

12. CURRENT TRENDS

The long-awaited removal of Cyprus from the 'List of the States and Territories providing preferential tax treatment and (or) not requiring disclosure and furnishing of the information upon conducting of financial transactions (offshore zones)' appended to Order 108n of the Ministry of Finance of the Russian Federation dated 13 November 2007 took effect from the beginning of 2013. Order 115n of the Ministry of Finance of the Russian Federation dated 21 August 2012 provides that the Republic of Cyprus will be removed from the list with effect from 1 January 2013. Companies incorporated in Cyprus will now be able to benefit from the Russian participation exemption, under which dividends received by Russian companies from qualifying participations will be exempt from tax, provided that:

- The recipient holds at least half the equity of the distributing entity and the participation confers the right to receive at least half of the dividend distributed;
- The recipient has held the investment for at least one year at the time the decision is made to distribute the dividend; and
- The cost of the investment is RUR 500 million (approximately EUR 13.6 million) or more.

Furthermore, transactions between unrelated Russian and Cyprus companies will no longer be subject to the automatic transfer pricing control scrutiny in Russia that applies to locations on the 'blacklist'. This is important for Cyprus as it has always kept close links with Russian companies that use the Cyprus holding structure. It is anticipated this will generate greater inflow of transactions through Cyprus.

Since March 2013, Cyprus has experienced what can be described as the catastrophic consequences of a financial 'warfare'. The bail-in, the stagnation of the Cyprus economy, the collapse of the banking system and the negative reports in relation to Cyprus banks, the uncertainty caused by the Central Bank restrictions on banking transactions, the instability of the systemic shock and its aftermath on the banking, financial and legal system, the unprecedented unemployment rates and the deficit have caused serious problems to the economy and business in general. Service providers such as lawyers, accountants and fiduciaries have been negatively affected, as there is a substantial slowdown of business and transactions. Nevertheless, the Ukraine–Russia crisis over Crimea and the EU's search for alternative energy supplies has placed Cyprus back in the spotlight as an alternative for fuelling the EU with natural gas. It is anticipated that as of 2015, the negativity will give way to development. By 2015–16, it is anticipated that the TROIKA reforms to the Cyprus legislation will be in place, with provisions against abusive tax practices as well as more efficient and effective reporting and transmission of information to the EU counterparties that request it.

12.1 National policy and law

Following TROIKA's recommendations and reforms, it is anticipated that Cyprus will adopt stricter rules aimed towards curbing abusive tax avoidance and penalizing abusive tax avoidance behavior. Already, the law that allows the confiscation of moneys from bank account as a means of tax collection indicates a trend towards a stricter approach to companies or individuals who avoid their tax obligations. Cyprus is also expected to implement and ratify the European Directives, such as the 4th Anti-Money Laundering Directive, once adopted.

12.1.1 The impact and role of the OECD and other international relations

The re-negotiation of the Cyprus–India Double Tax Treaty is an example of the impact of the OECD and international efforts in Cyprus at combating abusive tax avoidance and encouraging exchange of information.

India and Cyprus concluded the current double tax avoidance agreement in 1994. The agreement includes particularly favourable provisions regarding the taxation of interest income and capital gains on disposals of investments. As a result, and due to its other attractions as a holding company jurisdiction, Cyprus has become one of the most attractive locations through which to route investment into India. However, since November 11, 2013, following the Indian government's decision to declare Cyprus a 'notified jurisdiction' for allegedly failing to exchange information effectively with Indian tax authorities, there is much concern. Notified jurisdiction status has meant that transactions carried out by Indian taxpayers with entities based in Cyprus could potentially come under increased scrutiny from Indian tax authorities, and that a withholding tax might be imposed on payments by Indian taxpayers to recipients in Cyprus, which would subsequently have to be reclaimed. While the difficulties appear close to resolution, it is unfortunate that there was not more consultation by the Indian authorities before Cyprus was classified as a notified jurisdiction, as it caused considerable uncertainty for taxpayers and their advisers.

Following a renegotiation of the double tax-avoidance agreement, India withdrew the notification suspending tax benefits for investments from Cyprus, on the condition that the new agreement adopted Article 26 of the OECD Model Tax Convention relating to exchange of information. Cyprus also agreed to establish efficient channels of communication with India to deal with requests for information efficiently and promptly. On this basis, it was agreed that the declaration of Cyprus as a notified jurisdictional area under s. 94A of the Indian Income Tax Act 1961 would be withdrawn retroactive from January 11, 2013. To facilitate information exchange, the Indian government also decided to establish an income tax overseas unit, similar to those already operating in Mauritius and Singapore, as part of its multi-pronged strategy to combat money laundering and tax evasion. The units in Mauritius and Singapore have generally been viewed as successful in facilitating cooperation and consultation between the respective tax authorities, and it is expected that similar benefits will result for Cyprus.

Since December 2013 the Cyprus Government and the Government of India have agreed to re-negotiate the existing treaty, looking to sign a new double tax treaty in 2014, but this has caused considerable uncertainty for Indian investors that contemplate using Cyprus corporate and tax vehicles. It is anticipated that a new agreement can be reached and that a mutually beneficial relationship can be established that recognises the tax authorities' legitimate rights to obtain information, while at the same time protecting taxpayers against abuse of the authorities' powers.

Another example is the signing on February 25, 2014 of the Agreement on the Avoidance of Double Taxation and the Prevention of Tax Evasion, concerning Income Taxes, as well as a relevant Protocol between Cyprus and Norway, which is based on the OECD Model Convention for the Avoidance of Double Taxation on Income and on Capital, and provides for the exchange of information.

Finland

Alder & Sound
Henri Becker, Tero Ahonen, Petteri Rapo & Irina Lindberg

PART ONE: TRANSFER PRICING

1. GENERAL OVERVIEW

Transfer pricing is one of the key areas of a tax auditing and applies to Finnish multinationals as well as Finnish subsidiaries of foreign multinationals. Finnish transfer pricing and related regulations entered the spotlight in 2007 when specific legislative provisions were added to the Act on Assessment Procedure.[1]

In 2012, the Tax Administration adopted a more structured approach to the supervision and monitoring of transfer pricing compliance. Transfer pricing audit work was administratively centralized to the Large Taxpayers' Office in Helsinki under a separate project, with 37 specialized tax auditors working on the topic. It is anticipated that the centralized transfer pricing project will increase the number of tax audits.

During the first year of the project in 2012, 27 tax audits were carried out and resulted in tax assessments and total added taxable income of nearly EUR 300 million. In addition to the administrative interest in the topic, transfer pricing has recently been a frequent topic in the local news headlines. This increased scrutiny increase has led to criticism from both the business community and academic circles.

2. IDENTIFICATION OF LEGISLATIVE FRAMEWORK

The key national legislative provisions regarding transfer pricing are included in the Finnish Act on Assessment Procedure. This Act contains information regarding the arm's length principle, provisions on the definition of associated enterprises, transfer pricing documentation and adjustments and penalties.

The Act on Assessment Procedure includes the following transfer pricing provisions:

- Section 14 a–c regarding documentation requirements;
- Section 31 regarding transfer pricing adjustments and the definition of related companies; and
- Section 32 regarding penalties, including penalties for failure to comply with documentation requirements.

In addition to the specific provisions, Section 28 of the Act contains the General Anti-Avoidance Rule (GAAR). The GAAR, which was already

[1] Laki verotusmenettelystä 18.12.1995/1558.

enforced prior to the provisions listed above, may also apply in certain transfer pricing cases.

The OECD Transfer Pricing Guidelines[2] (OECD Guidelines) are not legally binding under Finnish legislation. However, the government bill behind the specific transfer pricing legislation implemented in 2007 makes a clear reference to the OECD Guidelines. As a result, the Guidelines have a significant practical importance in the interpretation of the national transfer pricing provision and are referred to in most transfer pricing reassessments made by the tax authorities as well as in recent court cases.

2.1 Federal legislation

Section 14 of the Act on Assessment Procedure contains the requirements regarding transfer pricing documentation. Under the provision, the following information should be included:

- Description of the business and relationships of the related parties;
- Details of controlled transactions;
- Functional analysis;
- Comparability analysis and information on comparables, if available; and
- Description of the pricing method and its application.

According to the Section 31 of the Act on Assessment Procedure, the tax authorities are authorized to adjust a price in transactions between associated enterprises if the price is not in accordance with the arm's length principle. Under the provision, the adjustment may be applied to the profits of a taxpayer, in relation to both domestic and cross-border transactions, in cases where the associated enterprises have agreed on conditions of the transaction that differ from those that would have been agreed upon between independent parties. Therefore, any profits that would have accrued to the taxpayer under the non-arm's length terms are subject to tax and must be included in the company's profits. It should be noted that the Section in question does not mention the arm's length principle but merely describes it. In practice, however, it is understood to refer to the arm's length principle as described in the OECD Guidelines.

Section 31 also includes the definition of associated parties. Parties are deemed to be associated if one party controls the other party, or if a third party, alone or together with an associated party, has control over both parties to the transaction. A party is deemed to have control over the other party if the party directly or indirectly owns more than 50 per cent of the capital or voting rights of the other party; is directly or indirectly entitled to appoint more than half the members of the board of directors or a similar body that has this right; or is otherwise capable of being in control of the other party.

Section 32 of the Act on Assessment Procedure contains provisions on documentation requirements as well as penalties for non-compliance

[2] OECD Transfer Pricing Guidelines for Multinational Enterprises and Tax Administration, 22.7.2010.

with the arm's length principle.[3] For more specific details on the available penalties, please refer to section 5 (Penalties) below.

2.2 State and provincial legislative interplay

State or provincial laws are not applicable in Finland, as no specific state or provincial laws exist regarding transfer pricing. At the federal level, transfer pricing audit work has been centralized to the Large Taxpayers' Office. At the same time, regional tax offices focus on carrying out general direct and indirect audits. Some interplay may occur, ie, regional tax auditors raising flags for the Large Taxpayers' Office to continue from; however, there is no official link between the regional and federal level audits when it comes to transfer pricing.

2.3 International treaties and agreements

Traditionally, and in relation to transfer pricing, the key international treaties having an impact are the double tax treaties, which follow the principles of the OECD Model Tax Convention. These treaties are all equally important and mainly stem from the mutual agreement procedure (MAP) provisions. Their efficiency is, however, often overshadowed by the lack of sufficient resources in the Tax Administration.

Within the European Union, the EU Arbitration Convention[4] is the most influential agreement affecting international relationships, mainly acting as an alternative mediation route. Recently, the Finnish authorities have also been active in negotiating and signing tax information exchange agreements (TIEAs). To date, it remains to be seen what the impact that these agreements will be on audits and other inspections.

3. NATIONAL POLICY ISSUES

In Finland, recent key developments pertaining to transfer pricing have related to the recharacterization of business models. This has enabled the Large Taxpayers' Office to perform large assessments through the utilization of primarily the profit split method.

Additionally, intra-group financing transactions and the commonplace use of foreign financing companies has drawn much attention from the local tax authorities. Intra-group charges related to IT investment projects, such as enterprise resource planning (or ERP), are also being increasingly targeted.

3.1 Overall national policy announcements

The most recent policy announcements have related to the central role of the OECD Guidelines in the interpretation of the arm's length principle. A recent case by the Supreme Administrative Court also addressed the use of different valuation methods in the case of transferring intra-group shares.[5]

In addition, tax auditors working for the transfer pricing division of the Large Taxpayers' Office have published articles regarding transfer pricing

3 Non-compliance with the arm's length principle typically takes the form of a false tax return.
4 Convention 90/436/EEC.
5 KHO:2014:33. For further discussion of the case, see section 4.1 (Current cases) below.

issues concerning to intra-group financing transactions. These articles signal, at least indirectly and unofficially, the increased interest and approach towards the topic among the tax authorities.

3.2 National revenue authority initiatives

As mentioned above, the Tax Administration adopted a more structured approach to the supervision and monitoring of transfer pricing compliance in 2012. During this time, the transfer pricing audit work was centralized to the Large Taxpayers' Office in Helsinki under a special project with 37 specialized tax auditors.

In addition, the Ministry of Finance is currently preparing a legislative proposal for an APA program to be published in the near future. Nevertheless, the schedule of the expected timeline for the introduction of the proposal or launch of the program has not been published.

3.3 Administrative statements

Currently, there are no recent statements from the tax authorities regarding the monitoring of transfer pricing compliance and the carrying out of related audits. That said, recent experience has show that transfer pricing audits carried out by the Large Taxpayers' Office will focus primarily on large multinational companies. There have also been initiatives towards enhanced cooperation between large taxpayers and the Tax Administration in general tax matters. These initiatives have suggested an increased emphasis on risk management as it relates to transfer pricing.

3.4 Administrative guidelines

The Finnish tax authorities have published detailed transfer pricing guidelines[6] regarding the documentary requirements outlined in the Sections 14 a–c, as well as the related proposal of the Act on Assessment Procedure.

4. CASE LAW

Due to the relatively late introduction of national transfer pricing legislation and the long processing times, relatively little case law has been decided under the legislation. In addition, some of the existing cases have resulted in inclusive and inconsistent rulings. Because most of the existing cases have dealt with fact-specific issues, it does not appear that Finnish courts have adopted a clear general approach and attitude to transfer pricing. As a result, the future implications and developments of Finnish case law remain unclear.

4.1 Current cases

There are several recent transfer pricing cases that are of interest with respect to setting future precedents and describing the approach adopted by the Finnish Supreme Administrative Court:

[6] Verohallitus, Siirtohinnoittelun dokumentointi, 19.10.2007.

KHO:2014:33

The Supreme Administrative Court issued a ruling on February 18, 2014 in a case where a Finnish company, which was owned by a Norwegian group, sold its fully owned Finnish subsidiary to a Norwegian company. The latter company subsequently sold the shares on the same day by exchanging its shares to another Norwegian company that was listed on the Oslo stock exchange.

In the tax audit of the original Finnish seller, the tax authorities argued that the sales price of the Finnish subsidiary's shares[7] was not in compliance with the arm's length principle and adjusted the price according to the book value of the shares. As a result, the taxable income of the Finnish seller was adjusted and a tax penalty was imposed.

In its ruling, the Supreme Administrative Court approved the use of the cash flow calculation as a basis for setting the transfer price. The Court also noted that such calculations are highly dependent on the assumptions taken and factors chosen. As a result of several insufficiently justified factors included in the original cash flow calculation, the Court held that it was permissible to adjust the transfer price according to the book value of the shares (at the moment of the sale). This amounted to a rejection of the use of the share value at the stock exchange, even though the eventual buyer of the shares was listed in the Oslo stock exchange shortly after the sale.

Although the Court ruled in favour of the tax authorities, the decision regarding the tax penalty was ultimately overruled. According to the Court, if the taxpayer has made a bona fide attempt and tried to arrive at an arm's length price within reason, there is no gross negligence involved and no tax penalty can be imposed. This was especially the case given the Finnish seller's efforts, as well as the fact that the issue was unclear and open to interpretation.

The Court also cited the OECD transfer pricing guidelines as a significant source of interpretation regarding the arm's length price in intra-group transactions.

KHO:2013:36

The Supreme Administrative Court released another important decision on March 25, 2013. The case concerned the allocation of "location savings" and the arm's length price of service fees pertaining to contract manufacturing services. In this case, the Finnish group parent company (Company A) had a subsidiary (Company B) in Estonia. The Estonian subsidiary manufactured goods solely for Company A. Based on the contractual arrangement, Company B could be regarded as a contract manufacturer.

Company A had previously manufactured goods in Finland, but relocated the production to Company B in 2004. Company B then further developed the manufacturing process by introducing new manufacturing technologies and automating certain production steps that were previously performed by hand in Finland and, in some instances, in workers' homes. As a result, most

[7] The sales price was calculated based on future cash flow estimates.

of the manufacturing methods used by Company B in Estonia were never used by Company A in Finland.

In issuing its decision, the Court considered that notional location savings may be relevant when functions previously located in a high-cost country are transferred to a low-cost country. Nevertheless, the Court found that the nature of the functions performed by the low-cost country subsidiary were separate from those previously conducted by the taxpayer (Company A) in Finland.

The Court also upheld the decision by Finland's Large Taxpayers' Office to retroactively apply the 2010 amendments to the OECD Transfer Pricing Guidelines in making its tax assessments. Despite the fact the OECD Transfer Pricing Guidelines are not legally binding in Finland, the Finnish Supreme Administrative Court nevertheless recognized the Guidelines as an international standard for interpreting the arm's length principle. Although Chapter X of the Guidelines was added in 2010, the Court explained that this addition did not include any new interpretations relating to the transfer pricing aspects of business restructurings. As a result, the Court held the guidance provided by Chapter IX could be retrospectively (and retroactively) applied to the facts of the case.

The Court then turned to consider the issue of notional 'location savings'. According to its interpretation, location savings are relevant if certain activities located in a high-cost country were transferred to a low-cost country. Here, the Court held that the nature of the functions performed by the Estonian subsidiary was separate from those previously conducted by Company A in Finland. As a result, the facts in this case did not correspond to the location savings example presented in Chapter IX of the OECD Transfer Pricing Guidelines. Lastly, the Court held that locations savings could not be determined by comparing the actual costs in a low-cost country with the notional costs in a high-cost country.

Although the amount of location savings claimed by the Finnish taxpayer was unacceptable, there was no rule against finding an acceptable margin favourable to the Finnish company. The Court reasoned that companies operating in low-cost jurisdictions might have higher margins than companies operating in high-cost jurisdictions.

Ultimately, the Court accepted the location savings by applying a higher arm's length mark-up on the operating expenses. The Court compared two Estonian companies that were included in the initial pan-European benchmark study provided by the taxpayer. In the end, the Estonian companies had higher profit margins than the Western European comparables.

KHO 2010:73

The Supreme Administrative Court considered another significant case in 2010. The case pertained to the determination of the arm's length interest level in intra-group financing structures.

In this case, a Finnish company (Company A) had settled its external debts in connection with the reorganization of the group's financing, in which the company refinanced its business activities with an internal debt from a Swedish group (Company B). The interest rate of the external debts was at a level of 3.125 to 3.25 per cent. In comparison, the interest rate of the new intra-group debt was at a level of 9.5 per cent based on the interest rates of the group's external loans, bonds and shareholder loans.

The Supreme Administrative Court ruled that the arm's length interest rate of Company A's debts to Company B was 3.25 per cent. This was due to that fact that the financial position of Company A had not changed in the refinancing and had not received any financial services from Company B which could have been taken into account when determining the arm's length interest rate. It should also be noted that the overall financing need or capital structure of the Company A had not changed either. Consequently, neither the average interest rate of external group financing (7.04 per cent) nor the interest rate of the company-specific financing conditions of Company A (9.5 per cent) was accepted in taxation.

It is noteworthy that the Court held the financial position and credit rating of a separate group company might differ from the overall financial standing and credit rating of the group. Where a company's circumstances and credit rating enable it to be substantially more profitable, the arm's length interest cannot be determined based on the terms of external loans of the whole group.

Based on this case, it seems that the financial terms of external loans of the whole group do not dictate the arm's length loan terms[8] between group companies. Internal rates must be determined separately for each relation and in consideration of the arm's length principle.

It should be noted that the Swedish Supreme Administrative Court (Högsta förvaltningsdomstolen) came to an opposite conclusion in an identical case.

KHO:2009:70

In this case, a Finnish subsidiary of a multinational group sold shares of a foreign company owned by the group to another group company below market price. The Finnish subsidiary applied for an advance ruling regarding to the taxation of the sale of the shares. Because the sale of the shares was not considered taxable income to a legal person, the Court held that the capital losses from the transaction did not affect the taxable income of the seller. There was therefore was no need to adjust the sales price, even though it was below the market price of the shares.

4.2 Historical cases of note

Historically, and prior to the implementation of the specific legislation, there are only a few cases discussing transfer pricing. A brief description of those cases are presented below:[9]

8 This is especially true for interest rates.

9 In addition to the cases decided by the Supreme Administrative Court, there is a historical case from the Helsinki Administrative Court (HAO 06/1258/4 10.11.2006). However, as the cases decided by the regional Administrative Courts do not constitute a precedent, the case is not further discussed at this occasion.

KHO 1990/483

In this case, a Finnish company paid an interest penalty to its Swedish parent company for payments made after the agreed upon due date. The parent company had not paid an interest penalty on similar late payments to the Finnish subsidiary. In these particular circumstances, the Supreme Administrative Court held that the interest penalty was not a hidden distribution of profit as defined in Section 73 of the Act on Assessment Procedure.

KHO:1986-B-II-578

In the case, a Finnish company manufactured and marketed lures, 90 per cent of which were exported to North America. In 1981, the company established an Irish subsidiary. Two models in the product range were exported incomplete to Ireland, where they were finished and sold to the North American market. The Irish company benefited from favourable tax rates in the first 10 years of its activities.

In the following tax year, the parent company sold incomplete lures to Ireland for FIM 916,488. With production costs of FIM 724,856, the Finnish company earned a profit of FIM 191,632 with a gross profit margin of 20.9 per cent. The Irish company finished these lures and sold them in the North American market for FIM 4.3 million. Including associated costs of FIM 1.9 million, the Irish company made a profit of FIM 2.4 million with a gross profit margin of 55.8 per cent.

The Court held that the transfer price was different from what would have been agreed between two parties acting on an arm's length basis. As a result, the Finnish parent company's taxable profit was increased by FIM 291,605 to account for the hidden profit distribution to the subsidiary.

KHO 1986/2772

In this case, a Finnish company made service fee payments to its Dutch parent company. Based on a prior agreement, this included costs derived from research, product development and other service payments maintained by the parent company. All of the group companies incurred this service fee. The group had also agreed to a CCA between subsidiaries based on the sale to third parties. The Court held that because the company did not make a declaration and was not engaged in manufacturing the product, it was unable to deduct the service fee as an expense incurred in gaining income.

Ultimately, the Supreme Administrative Court held that the terms and conditions between a parent company and its subsidiary ought to be treated differently from the terms and conditions reached between independent parties.

5. PENALTIES

General legislative penalties are typically imposed in transfer pricing matters for failure to file, late filing or filing a fraudulent return. These penalties also apply to abusive tax avoidance. In addition to the additional taxes due to the added income, an increase in tax is often ordered as an administrative penalty. Criminal penalties may also apply, although there are currently no cases involving the use of criminal penalties in transfer pricing disputes.[10]

5.1 Types

As mentioned above, the general legislative penalties in transfer pricing matters also apply to abusive tax avoidance. These penalties are typically imposed for failure to file, late filing or filing a fraudulent return. According to the Section 32 of the Act on Assessment Procedure, minor non-compliance (such as late filing) is subject to a maximum tax increase of EUR 150. In more severe cases, however, the maximum tax increase is EUR 800. In the case of intentional or gross negligence,[11] a maximum tax increase of 30 per cent of adjusted income (or maximum of 1 per cent of the adjusted assets) is applicable. Where there are alternative interpretations involving a dispute or potential case of abuse, the penalties may be reduced or removed altogether.

Section 32 also contains a specific provision for failure to comply with the transfer pricing documentation requirements set out in the Section 14 c of the Act. The maximum penalty for non-compliance with the documentation requirements is EUR 25,000.

In addition to taxes and penalties, the taxpayer is also obliged to pay an interest penalty. This penalty is assessed on debited taxes and any tax increases not paid by their due date.

In cases involving tax fraud, criminal penalties may also apply. According to Chapter 29, Section 1 of the Criminal Code, a person who:

(1) gives a taxation authority false information on a fact that influences the assessment of tax,
(2) files a tax return concealing a fact that influences the assessment of tax,
(3) for the purpose of avoiding tax, fails to observe a statutory duty pertaining to taxation that is of significance in the assessment of tax, or
(4) otherwise acts fraudulently,

and thereby causes or attempts to cause a tax not to be assessed, a tax to be assessed too low or a tax to be unduly refunded, shall be sentenced for *tax fraud* to a fine or to imprisonment for a maximum of two years.

According to the Section 2 of the same Chapter and Act, if a tax fraud takes place where:

(1) considerable financial benefit is sought, or
(2) the offence is committed in a particularly methodical manner,

and the tax fraud is aggravated when assessed as a whole, the offender shall be sentenced for *aggravated tax fraud* to imprisonment for at least four months and at most four years.

However, according to Section 3 of the same Chapter and Act:

(1) If the tax fraud, when assessed as a whole, with due consideration to the amount of financial benefit sought and the other circumstances

[10] It should also be noted that the *ne bis in idem* rule, ie, the right not to be tried or punished twice for the same matter, restricts the simultaneous application of administrative and criminal penalties.

[11] This category is typically where high-profile transfer pricing cases most often occur.

connected with the offence, is deemed to be petty, the offender shall be sentenced for *petty tax fraud* and subject to a fine.

(2) If a punitive tax increase is deemed to be a sufficient sanction, the report, prosecution, or punishment involving the petty tax fraud may be waived.

Section 4 of the same Chapter and Act also sets out the framework for tax violations.[12]

Although it is possible to impose criminal penalties in transfer pricing cases, there are currently no instances involving in the use of criminal penalties in transfer pricing disputes.

5.2 Special or notable cases

In general, the determination and imposition of penalties is assessed and decided on a case-by-case basis. This determination follows the above-mentioned guidelines for different levels of non-compliance.

On the topic of penalties, a Supreme Administrative Court ruling from 2005[13] is particularly important because it discusses the applicability of the penalty provisions to varying degrees of non-compliance. The Court held that every case of non-compliance and the related assessment of taxable income must be evaluated separately. The potential penalties are also to be imposed on a case-by-case basis.

A recent decision by the Supreme Administrative Court on the use of a percentage-based tax increase is also worth noting.[14] Here, the Court held there is no gross negligence where a taxpayer can be shown to have acted in a bona fide manner and attempted to arrive at a reasonable arm's length price. As a result, no tax penalty can be imposed. This is especially the case if the steps taken by the taxpayer are considerable and the issue is unclear and open to interpretation.

6. DISPUTE RESOLUTION MECHANISMS

Finnish legislation and common practice contains both national (appeal) and international options (MAP and arbitration) with regard to dispute resolution mechanisms. These options are discussed in more detail in the following sections.

6.1 Preferred national options

An appeal may be made against any adjustment in the same way as against an ordinary assessment. According to Section 34 of the Act on Assessment

---

12 A person who, in order to gain financial benefit for himself or herself or another, fails to pay in time one of the following for a reason other than insolvency or a stay on payments imposed by a court:
(1) a withholding tax, a tax-at-source or a conveyance tax,
(2) a turnover tax calculated per calendar month or a comparable tax payable on certain insurance premiums,
(3) a value-added tax, or
(4) an employer's social security contribution,
shall be sentenced, unless the act is punishable as tax fraud, for a tax violation to a fine or to imprisonment for at most six months. (934/1996)
However, a slight failure which has been rectified without delay is not deemed a tax violation.
If a punitive tax increase is deemed a sufficient sanction, the report of, prosecution for or punishment for a tax violation may be waived.

13 KHO:2005:61.

14 KHO:2014:33.

Procedure, the taxpayer has the right of appeal to the Tax Reassessment Board. The appeal must be made within 60 days of receiving notification of the assessment and no later than the end of the fifth year following the year of assessment.

Where taxpayers disagree with the reviewed decision by the Tax Reassessment Board, the next level of appeal is to the Administrative Court. An appeal against a decision of the Tax Reassessment Board must be made within the same time limits mentioned above.

The next appellate level is the Supreme Administrative Court, in which appeals against the decision of the Administrative Court must be made within 60 days of the decision. However, the taxpayer can only appeal to Supreme Administrate Court if the Court grants its permission for the appeal. In general, leave to the Supreme Administrative Court will be granted on the basis of the following criteria:

- The appeal has an important bearing on similar cases or would otherwise secure the uniformity of legal practice;
- An error in procedure or other error has taken place in the case, which by virtue of law requires the decision to be reversed; and
- There are other weighty grounds for granting permission to appeal.

6.2 International options

The double tax treaties signed by Finland contain a provision concerning the mutual agreement procedure (MAP). Although the Finnish Tax Administration is generally responsible for handling MAPs, there is some existing case law to suggest that the Finnish Ministry of Finance is in fact the competent authority. According to current statistics,[15] the number of appealed MAP cases is becoming increasing common, along with the process duration.

Another alternative dispute resolution mechanism is the procedure contained in the EU Arbitration Convention (specifically, what is this process called & how does it work?). This procedure has yet to gain priority among taxpayers,[16] mainly due to similar efficiency concerns as the OECD's MAP process. Unlike the MAP process, however, it contains provisions for mandatory arbitration within a fixed time period.

PART TWO: TAX AVOIDANCE

7. ACCEPTABLE TAX PLANNING AREAS/SUBJECTS

In general, taxpayers' attitudes towards aggressive tax planning and tax avoidance are rather negative. As a result, there are only a limited number of existing methods to shelter income or reduce tax. In addition to this generally negative attitude, periodically renewing tax legislation plays an important role in curbing taxpayers' aggressive arrangements.

---

[15] *http://www.oecd.org/ctp/dispute/mapstatistics2012.htm.*

[16] *http://ec.europa.eu/taxation_customs/resources/documents/taxation/company_tax/transfer_pricing/forum/jtpf/2013/jtpf_012_2013_en.pdf.*

Despite these unfavorable attitudes, there are some arrangements available that may appear attractive to the more aggressive taxpayers. With regard to corporate taxation, these options relate to the use of branch structures; excessive (internal) leverage; separate IP or financing companies in beneficial locations; corporate migration; and cross-border hybrid mismatching.[17] There are two common methods used in personal taxation planning. The first method involves the conversion of earned income (taxed at progressive rates) into capital income (taxed at a flat rate). The second method is personal migration in cases involving expatriate employees.

With Finnish authorities increasingly interested in securing the national tax base (discussed below), most of the traditional options for tax avoidance have been or will shortly be subject to increased scrutiny and targeted legislation. This legislation is likely to involve both administrative and, in the severe cases, criminal penalties.

8. DEFINING ABUSIVE TAX AVOIDANCE

Until 1995, Section 56 of the Taxation Act contained the general anti-avoidance rule. Since January 1, 1996, Section 28 of the Finnish Act on Assessment Procedure has contained a similar provision and has effectively taken the role in defining the general anti-avoidance rule. In addition, Section 52h of the Act on Taxation of Business Income contains regulations on tax evasion in business restructuring situations.

With regard to administrative statements and policies, the Finnish government published its action program to combat the international tax avoidance in May 2014. Drawing inspiration from the OECD BEPS Action Plan and similar EU initiatives, the government has set a goal to act in the forefront of ending international tax avoidance, in which the action program is an essential part.

The action program includes measures both on the domestic and international level and focuses on developing cross-border cooperation and appropriate legislative measures. More specifically, the work to be conducted under the action programme shall focus on the following areas:

- Securing the national tax base and combating harmful tax competition;
- Developing tax supervision and control of information exchange;
- Increasing the transparency of tax-related information;
- Preventing the use of tax havens in public procurements; and
- Providing assistance to developing countries in the development of tax legislation and retention of taxing rights.

The first focus area deals with measures aiming to secure the national tax base while combating harmful tax competition. Effectively, it means actively participating in the implementation work of the OECD BEPS Action Plan and corresponding EU initiatives, enforcing existing transfer pricing legislation with increased scrutiny, assessing the needs for changes in the existing General Anti-Avoidance Rule (GAAR) and signed double tax

[17] This is especially in relation to financing and leasing.

conventions, and contributing to the EU-level project aiming tocreate a common black list of non-cooperative countries.

The second focus area is entirelyabout measuresaiding the development of tax supervision and information exchange. The practical implications include active participation in the work of the OECD Global Forum on Transparency and Exchange of Information for Tax Purposes, expanding the network of information exchange agreements (TIEAs) and Competent Authority Agreements (CAAs), assessing the current level of tax supervision on foreign companies and employees, and forming a view on the necessity and possible efficiency of a tax amnesty program for reporting undisclosed foreign funds.

The third focus area aims at finding measures to increase transparency of tax-related information, including country-specific reporting, information on beneficial owners and the use of tax havens in investment structures, whereas the fourth focus area emphasizes the importance of preventing the use of tax havens in public procurements.

The fifth and final focus area deals with providing assistance to developing countries in thedevelopment of local tax legislation and the retention ofappropriate taxing rights over natural resources and industrial activities taking place in the country in question.

9. THE LEGISLATIVE FRAMEWORK

Until 1995, Section 56 of the Taxation Act contained the General Anti-Avoidance Rule (GAAR). Since January 1, 1996, Section 28 of the Finnish Act on Assessment Procedure has contained a similar provision and has effectively become the key provision in defining the GAAR. Under Section 28, if a transaction is given a legal form that does not correspond to its actual character or purpose, the original transaction is considered void for tax purposes and the taxation is to be carried out as if the real form had been used.

In certain circumstances, the Act allows for the taxable income and assets to be estimated. This occurs where the price, other compensation or execution time set in an agreement has been taken with the objective of avoiding the payment of taxes due. If allegations of tax avoidance are made, the burden of proof lies with the taxpayer to demonstrate that there was no inconsistency between the legal form and the actual character or purpose of the transaction. The taxpayer may also demonstrate that other measures were taken without the objective of avoiding the payment of taxes due.

In addition, Section 52 of the Act on Taxation of Business Income contains regulations on tax evasion in business restructuring situations. This Act effectively prevents the taxpayer from benefiting from certain demerger and merger provisions where an arrangement has been motivated solely or primarily by tax evasion or tax avoidance. The source and interpretation of this specific provision originates from the EU Merger directive.[18]

[18] 90/434/EEC, amended with 2005/19/EC.

Alongside the international community, the Finnish government and Tax Administration have spent the past year have been stepping up their efforts to curb abusive tax avoidance. Specifically, the government has focused on developing measures to aid in protecting the national tax base and increasing the transparency of tax information. In May 2014, the Finnish government also initiated an action programme to curb abusive tax avoidance. It is anticipated that this programme will eventually lead to the introduction of additional legislation on abusive tax avoidance and tax evasion.

10. KEY CASES OF INTEREST

There has been a recent increase in the importance of Finnish cases pertaining to the interpretation of the General Anti-Avoidance Rule (GAAR) and other regulations aimed at curbing abusive tax avoidance. This is largely because published cases, especially decisions from the Supreme Administrative Court, have become more detailed in terms of their background information and reasoning. It should be noted, however, that most of these cases deal with one-of-a-kind situations in relation to tax evasion. This complicates the analysis of general trends with regard to the local anti-avoidance regulation.

10.1 Current cases

The Supreme Administrative Court of Finland decided the most recent GAAR case on May 2, 2014.[19] The main question presented to the Court was whether the benefits received by the top management of a publicly traded Finnish company through a separate holding company should be treated as earned income for the recipients due to the GAAR.

The process was initiated when a member of the top management and a shareholder of the holding company applied for a preliminary ruling from the Central Tax Board of Finland (*Keskusverolautakunta*). The preliminary ruling considered the correct tax treatment of the income that the applicant would be entitled to, received either in the form of dividends or profits on the sale of the holding company's shares.

The Tax Recipients' Legal Services Unit appealed the Central Tax Board's ruling to the Supreme Administrative Court. The Supreme Administrative Court ultimately overturned the ruling and decided that the income received by the shareholders of the holding company[20] was earned income. This was because the holding company structure constituted a management incentive scheme aimed at enabling the shareholders of the holding company to benefit from the increase in the value of underlying shares of the operating company without being subject to income tax. As there were no credible business reasons to justify the arrangement, the Court disregarded the arrangement under the GAAR and decided that the benefits received by the

19 KHO:2014:66.

20 According to the Court, it was irrelevant whether the income was received in the form of dividends or as a capital gain.

shareholders of the holding company should be treated as earned income for the recipients.

Another case[21] decided by the Supreme Administrative court in 2014 dealt with personal taxation and the classification of income in a generational change situation.[22]

10.2 Key historical cases

Historically, the most interesting cases to the broader tax community dealing with anti-avoidance and tax evasion involve the so-called balance sheet company cases in the 1980s and 1990's.[23] In addition to these are cases involving the imposition of penalties for abusive tax avoidance and tax evasion.[24]

As mentioned above, it should be noted that most of the cases deal with one-of-a-kind situations in relation to tax evasion. This complicates the analysis of general trends with regard to the local anti-avoidance regulation.

11. PENALTIES

The general administrative penalties also apply to abusive tax avoidance. These are typically imposed for failure to file, late filing or filing a fraudulent return. In cases of tax fraud, criminal penalties may also apply.

11.1 Legislative provisions

As mentioned above, the general legislative penalties in tax matters also apply to abusive tax avoidance. A tax increase is often ordered in addition to the additional taxes from the added income.

According to Section 32 of the Act on Assessment Procedure, minor non-compliance (such as late filing) is subject to maximum tax increase of EUR 15. In more severe cases, the maximum tax increase is EUR 800. In the case of intentional or gross negligence,[25] a tax increase of 1–30 per cent of adjusted income (or of 0–1 per cent of the adjusted assets) applies. Where the situation or dispute is open to various alternative interpretations, these penalties may be reduced or removed altogether.

Besides additional taxes and penalties, the taxpayer is also required to pay penalty interest. Penalty interest is assessed on debited taxes and any tax increases that have not paid by their due date.

Criminal penalties may also apply in cases of tax fraud. According to Chapter 29, Section 1 of the Criminal Code, a person who:

(1) gives a taxation authority false information on a fact that influences the assessment of tax,
(2) files a tax return concealing a fact that influences the assessment of tax,

---

21 KHO:2014:4.

22 In addition to the rulings issued by the Supreme Administrative Court, the Helsinki Administrative Court issued a ruling in 2014 in a case (HAO 07.03.2014) that concerned a transfer of shares between group companies in an international group. As the intra-group arrangement related to the transfer lacked credible business reasons, the Court viewed it as being carried out with an aim to avoid taxes and, thus, rejected the tax deductibility of the interest charges related to the arrangement and the resulting situation.

23 Eg, KHO:1996-B-534, KHO 3.10.1997/2461, KHO 3.10.1997/2458.

24 Eg, KHO:2005:61 where the Court insisted the tax increase be assessed and calculated separately for each type and tranche of added income.

25 This is the category where abusive tax avoidance most often occurs.

(3) for the purpose of avoiding tax, fails to observe a statutory duty pertaining to taxation that is of significance in the assessment of tax, or
(4) otherwise acts fraudulently,
and thereby causes or attempts to cause a tax not to be assessed, a tax to be assessed too low or a tax to be unduly refunded, shall be sentenced for *tax fraud* to a fine or to imprisonment for a maximum of two years.

According to the Section 2 of the same Chapter and Act, if a tax fraud takes place where:
(1) considerable financial benefit is sought, or
(2) the offence is committed in a particularly methodical manner,
and the tax fraud is aggravated when assessed as a whole, the offender shall be sentenced for *aggravated tax fraud* to imprisonment for at least four months and at most four years.

However, according to Section 3 of the same Chapter and Act:
(1) If the tax fraud, when assessed as a whole, with due consideration to the amount of financial benefit sought and the other circumstances connected with the offence, is deemed to be petty, the offender shall be sentenced for *petty tax fraud* and subject to a fine.
(2) If a punitive tax increase is deemed to be a sufficient sanction, the report, prosecution, or punishment involving the petty tax fraud may be waived.

Section 4 of the same Chapter and Act also sets out the framework for tax violations.[26]

In recent years, there has been an increased interest regarding possible violations[27] of the *ne bis in idem* rule.[28] This interest resulted in a new Act[29] being drafted and implemented at the end of 2013. According to the Act, the Tax Administration may issue a tax assessment decision but cannot impose a tax increase in order to report the offence to the police for charging the taxpayer with an offence.

In addition to the possible violation of the *ne bis in idem* rule, the interrelation between Sections 28 and 31 of the Act on Assessment Procedure has been questioned in some transfer pricing cases. This is especially true for cases relating to the re-characterizations performed by the tax authorities.

---

26 A person who, in order to gain financial benefit for himself or herself or another, fails to pay in time one of the following for a reason other than insolvency or a stay on payments imposed by a court:
(1) a withholding tax, a tax-at-source or a conveyance tax,
(2) a turnover tax calculated per calendar month or a comparable tax payable on certain insurance premiums,
(3) a value-added tax, or
(4) an employer's social security contribution
shall be sentenced, unless the act is punishable as tax fraud, for a tax violation to a fine or to imprisonment for at most six months. (934/1996)
However, a slight failure which has been rectified without delay is not deemed a tax violation.
If a punitive tax increase is deemed a sufficient sanction, the report of, prosecution for or punishment for a tax violation may be waived.

27 In 2014, The European Court of Human Rights (ECHR) issued two decisions – Glantz v. Finland (no. 37394/11) and Nykänen v. Finland (no. 11828/11) – finding Finland in violation of the *ne bis in idem* rule. The two applications were brought by Finnish nationals, and concerned complaints of having been punished twice for the same offense after tax surcharges had been imposed on them and had also been convicted of tax fraud or aggravated tax fraud.

28 The *ne bis in idem* rule is the right not to be tried or punished twice for the same matter.

29 *Laki erillisellä päätöksellä määrättävästä veron- tai tullinkorotuksesta* (781/2013).

11.2 Examples of penalties imposed

In general, the determination and imposition of penalties is assessed and decided on a case-by-case basis. This process follows the above-presented guidelines for different levels of non-compliance.

With regard to cases pertaining to imposed penalties, a Supreme Administrative Court ruling from 2005[30] is of particular interest. This case discusses the applicability of penalty provisions to a series of actions with varying levels of non-compliance. According to the decision, each act of non-compliance and related assessment of taxable income are to be evaluated separately. This also applies to the imposition of penalties.

12. CURRENT TRENDS

Alongside the international community, the Finnish government and Tax Administration have spent the past year have been stepping up their efforts to curb abusive tax avoidance. Specifically, the government has focused on developing measures to aid in protecting the national tax base and increasing the transparency of tax information. With regard to the third focus area of the OECD's BEPS Action Plan (ie, combating harmful tax competition), the proposed actions have remained scarce. This is potentially due to the recent cut in the general corporate income tax rate that effectively brought Finland into the middle of the discussion.

Due to the recent nature of the actions and initiatives, the implications and future developments for this legislative framework will be better assessed after more concrete actions have taken place. What is clear is that increasing transparency and combating aggressive tax planning will continue to be key trends in the near future, both nationally and internationally.

12.1 National Policy and Law

As mentioned above, the Finnish government initiated an action programme to curb abusive tax avoidance in May 2014. In the future, it is likely that Finland will focus on five key areas in curbing abusive tax avoidance:

- Securing the national tax base and combating harmful tax competition;
- Developing tax supervision and control of information exchange;
- Increasing the transparency of tax-related information;
- Preventing the use of tax havens in public procurements; and
- Providing assistance to developing countries in the development of tax legislation and retention of taxing rights.

It is anticipated that these measures will take advantage of state-owned companies introducing new transparency and self-regulatory measures, with publicly listed companies likely to follow this trend. Combined with the stricter enforcement of existing transfer pricing legislation, it is likely that multinational enterprises[31] will be pressured to adopt a centralized operating model to maximize the taxable income in Finland. At the same time, the

[30] KHO:2005:61.

[31] This applies to multinational enterprises with value-adding functions whose profits are located abroad.

absence of efficient dispute resolution measures has increased the risk of international economic double taxation.

In addition, the chancing relationship between administrative and criminal penalties is likely to impact the practical aspects of disputes. This is especially the case in assessing the fine line between tax avoidance and abusive tax avoidance.

12.1.1 The impact and role of the OECD and other international relations

As mentioned above, the Finnish government's recent action programme to curb abusive tax avoidance has drawn upon the OECD BEPS Action Plan and corresponding EU initiatives. As a result, any changes in the international agenda are likely to have at least an indirect effect on national efforts.

France

Tirard, Naudin Jean-Marc Tirard

PART ONE: TRANSFER PRICING

1. GENERAL OVERVIEW

Like many other countries, France has developed legislation which provides that the correct transfer price is that which parties dealing at arm's length would have agreed upon for a particular transaction. Although France adopted the generic statutory provision dealing with transfer pricing in 1933, the French tax authorities (the 'FTA') have become much more aggressive in the transfer pricing arena over the last few years, mainly vis-à-vis foreign corporations dealing with their French affiliates, but also vis-à-vis French corporations dealing with foreign affiliates. They have also become more sophisticated in their approach. Very recently, the FTA implemented or tried to implement new and very severe statutory provisions which will inevitably lead to a significant increase in transfer pricing adjustments and subsequent litigation. When there is a transfer pricing adjustment, in addition to an increase of the taxable income of the French taxpayer, a correlative constructive dividend is deemed to have been paid which generally gives rise to withholding tax.

2. IDENTIFICATION OF LEGISLATIVE FRAMEWORK

There are a number of statutory provisions impacting transfer pricing in France. The key provision is codified under article 57 of the French Tax Code (FTC) which requires arm's length transfer prices for transactions with non-arm's length non residents. On 1st January 2016, transfer pricing documentation requirements will be introduced. Articles L 13 AA, L 13 AB and L 13 B of the French Tax Procedures Code (FTPC) set out the formal documentation requirements in France.

Article 57 FTC, which may apply only in respect of cross border transfer pricing issues[1], provides more specifically that to determine the income tax owed by companies that either depend on or control enterprises outside France, any profits transferred to those enterprises indirectly via increases or decreases in purchase or selling prices, or by any other means, shall be added back into the taxable income shown in the companies' accounts. The same procedure shall apply to companies that depend on an enterprise or a group

---

1 The doctrine of *acte anormal de gestion*, which was developed by case law, is used for domestic transfer pricing issues and to a lesser extent to cross border transfer pricing issues. As a general rule, expenses are tax deductible only to the extent that they are incurred for the benefit of the business. To invoke an *acte anormal de gestion*, the FTA should prove that a transfer of profits has taken place and that there was a deliberate intention to move profits or losses from one taxpayer to another. It may be applied to domestic as well as international transfer prices. Under this concept, a tax deduction may be refused for charges not incurred for the benefit of the business, or for not being what is considered by the FTA and tax courts as arising from normal business operations.

that also controls enterprises outside France. As a general rule, enforcement of Article 57 requires the tax authorities to prove that a dependent relationship existed between the parties involved in the transaction under review and that a transfer of profits occurred.

There are a number of other statutory provisions which are relevant in addition to the legislation specific to transfer pricing.

Article 238A FTC limits the deductibility in France of commissions and other payments paid to entities located in tax havens. A company is deemed to benefit from a privileged tax regime when the difference between the foreign corporate tax and the tax that would have been paid in France exceeds 50 per cent.

Article 188A FTPC provides for an extension of the statute of limitations and is open to the authorities when they request information from foreign tax administrations. This new specific statute of limitations expires at the end of the year following the year when the information is requested or, in the absence of a response, at the end of the fifth year following the year that is audited.

Dependency can be legal or *de facto*. Legal dependency is relatively easy for the tax authorities to prove. It is defined as direct control by a foreign entity of the share capital or voting rights of the French entity under review. It can also mean dependency through indirect control, such as through common management. *De facto* control may result from the commercial relationship that exists between two or more enterprises. For example, where A and B use the same trade names or produce the same product, they are considered to be dependent even in the absence of any direct common ownership.

Article L13 AA, since 1st January 2010, has imposed contemporaneous transfer pricing requirements on legal entities established in France which meet the following legal criteria:

(a) Their turnover or their gross assets exceed EUR 400 million.
(b) They hold directly or indirectly more than 50 per cent of capital or voting rights of a legal entity that meets the test mentioned in (a).
(c) More than 50 per cent of their capital or voting rights is held directly or indirectly by a legal entity that meets the same above-mentioned test.
(d) They are part of a French tax group and at least one legal entity of the group meets one of the above-mentioned requirements.

Article L13AB FTC provides that operations that are conducted by French companies with an associated entity situated in a non-cooperative state or territory[2] are subject to an additional documentation obligation. The French company must notably provide the financial statements of the associated entity.

Article L13B which is, in practice, applied mainly to small and medium businesses (SMBs), gives the FTA the right to request information on the taxpayers' transfer pricing policy in the course of a tax examination when

[2] A non-cooperative state is a state which does not satisfy the exchange of information standards.

it has evidence to presume that an indirect transfer of profits abroad, as defined by Article 57 FTC, has occurred.

Four types of information may be requested under this procedure:

- The nature of the intercompany transactions;
- The method for determining prices for transactions;
- The activities of the foreign enterprises, companies, or joint ventures; and
- The tax treatment of the intercompany transactions.

A new Article 223 quinquies B FTC, which was recently introduced by the Law against tax fraud and economic and financial crime on 6th December 2013, added new transfer pricing documentation requirements to the FTA's arsenal.

Furthermore, the Finance Bill for 2014 contains provisions in relation to transfer pricing that strengthen the powers of the FTA in case of a tax audit.

Companies already subject to the French contemporaneous transfer pricing documentation requirement pursuant to Article L13AA of the French Tax Procedure Code, ie, mainly companies whose gross annual turnover or gross assets equal or exceed EUR 400 million, or which hold or are held by, directly or indirectly, a legal entity exceeding the above-mentioned thresholds, will have to file documentation with the FTA within six months following the deadline for filing their annual income tax return. This documentation should contain some of the elements included in the transfer pricing documentation which they also have to prepare in the event of a tax audit pursuant to that same article. Before Article 223 quinquies B of the FTC came into force, such documentation was only required to be made available at the beginning of a tax audit. Part of it (with notable exceptions such as a legal chart, a detailed functional analysis or benchmarks), will therefore now have to be filed in a simplified format at the end of every tax period.

The Finance Bill for 2014 also expands contemporaneous transfer pricing documentation requirements as set forth in Article L13AA of the FTPC. Transfer pricing documentation should include a copy of the rulings obtained from foreign tax authorities by associated enterprises. These rulings may concern the tax rate or calculation of the tax base for any income that would be paid by the French company under a tax audit.

The Finance Bill for 2014 also introduces a new requirement to disclose management accounting and/or consolidated accounts (new paragraphs II and III of Article L13 of the FTPC in case of a tax audit).

The disclosure requirement regarding management accounts applies to companies to the extent they keep such accounts and meet one of the following criteria:

- For companies providing goods or supplying houses, a turnover exceeding EUR 152.4 million;
- For any other business, a turnover exceeding EUR 76.2 million;
- For all companies, a gross amount of assets equal to or greater than EUR 400 million.

The Finance Bill for 2014 also intended to modify Article 57 FTC. If adopted it would have shifted the burden of proof to the taxpayer where functions or risks are transferred by a French entity to a related party in case the EBIT of the transferring company decreases by at least 20 per cent, compared to the average EBIT over the three financial years preceding the transfer. In such cases, the company should demonstrate that it received compensation equivalent to the compensation non-related parties would have agreed to. However, this provision was censured by the Constitutional Court, which ruled that the concepts used by the legislator were insufficiently defined, and would likely make the law difficult to understand.

2.1 International treaties and agreements

In France, international treaties override domestic rules.[3] In practice, however, this is not an issue since the statutory provisions of Article 57 CGI are very similar to the transfer pricing provisions of the numerous tax treaties concluded by France. As a general rule, they follow the provisions of Article 9 of the OECD Model Treaty and should receive the same interpretation. Though unlikely, in practice, if there was a discrepancy between the provisions of Article 57 CGI and the tax treaty, the relevant provision of the tax treaty would prevail.

(a) Mutual agreement procedure

Where the French tax authorities make a transfer pricing adjustment which is different from the assessment made by the tax authorities of a tax treaty partner, consideration should be given to apply to the mutual agreement procedure (MAP) in order to resolve the tax dispute[4]. The difficulty is that under the MAP, the obligation of the contracting state is only to try to eliminate double taxation; there is no obligation to reach a result.

(b) Exchange of Information

As a general rule, the tax treaties concluded by France provide for the exchange of information between the contracting countries. For example, Article 27 of the tax treaty between France and the USA allows the French tax authorities to gather information through exchange of information with both countries' affiliate entities.

3. NATIONAL POLICY ISSUES

In the past few years, French tax authorities have significantly increased the number of transfer pricing investigations. More recently, emphasis has been placed on increased documentation requirements, increased auditing, and increased penalisation in respect of transfer pricing adjustment.

[3] Article 55 of the Constitution.
[4] See below 6.2.

3.1 Overall national policy announcements

The French tax authorities, as opposed to some other countries (eg, the USA), did not issue developed guidelines dealing with transfer pricing, other than a guide to the SME in 2006[5]. Instead, they generally apply the OECD guidelines.[6]

3.2 National tax authorities initiatives

The French tax authorities adopted an advance pricing agreements (APA) program in 1999. This was the first administrative instruction,[7] which was subsequently codified under Article L80 B, 7° of the LPE.

(a) Bilateral advance pricing agreements

In a regulation issued on 7th September 1999, the FTA defined the conditions under which they were willing to grant a bilateral APA. It may be initiated only with states that have signed a treaty with France containing a section equivalent to provision 25.3 of the OECD model treaty. This regulation is a fundamental change from the prior opinion expressed by the FTA, where they saw an APA procedure as a breach of the principle of equality between taxpayers. Under this regulation, the application process can be initiated either in France or in the other state. The application may cover all transactions or only certain transactions, as well as all or part of the companies' operations (product, function, type of transaction or line of business). The scope of the information (tax, financial, legal, industrial, commercial, etc.) to be provided is defined through preliminary meetings with the FTA. A formal request may then be addressed to the FTA, and within two months of this application, the same application must be submitted to the other tax administration. An indicative list of information to be provided is included in the regulation, but the basic idea behind this list is to establish constant debate and exchange of information with the FTA as part of the review of the application. Once the review is completed, a draft agreement is issued for final approval by the taxpayer.

The agreement defines the parties, transactions, transfer pricing method(s) elected, assumptions used, revision formula, date of application of the ruling and its duration (three to five years), and contents of the annual report to be issued by the taxpayer. The APA may not have a retroactive effect, except within the limit of the financial year during which the application is made.[8]

(b) Unilateral advance pricing agreements

Unilateral APAs, which until the rectifying finance Bill of 2004 were not authorised in France, may now be accepted by the French administration. However, in an instruction issued on 24th June 2005[9], the FTA made it clear that it would still favour the conclusion of bilateral APAs. As a general rule, unilateral APAs could only be granted if the bilateral tax treaty does not

5 *Les prix de transfert, guide à l'usage des PME*, Direction Générale des Impôts.
6 See Section 3.1 of the Canada chapter.
7 Administrative Instruction 7th Sep 1999, BOI 4-A.8.99.
8 Multilateral agreement are also possible but are rare in practice.
9 Administrative Instruction 24th June 2005, BOI 4.A.11.05.

provide for a MAP, or if, despite the MAP provided in the bilateral tax treaty, the foreign competent authority refuses to conclude an APA. A unilateral APA might also be granted for simple issues such as management fees or allocation of key issues.

(c) simplified APA procedure for small and medium-sized businesses (SMBs)

As the FTA recognise that the standard APA procedure can be burdensome, a simplified APA procedure for SMBs has been available as from 28th November 2006.[10] Under this simplified procedure:

- Less transfer pricing documentation is required for the APA request. The documentation is limited to a legal chart of the group, a list of transactions and prices between related parties, a functional analysis, and the description and justification of the transfer pricing method. The financial statements of the foreign companies involved in the transactions should also be provided.
- The FTA assist in the preparation of the functional analysis and in the choice of the appropriate transfer pricing method.
- Although an economic analysis is also requested, during an experimental period the FTA may perform the benchmarking analysis at the request of the SMB. The annual compliance report requested in the follow-up years of the APA (eg, details of the computation of remuneration and a statement on the substantial changes to the conditions described in the APA request, such as activities, functions performed, risks borne, legal/de facto dependence, assets used, and accounting methods) is also simplified.

Only SMBs that meet the following two criteria are eligible for the simplified APA procedure: They should (1) have fewer than 250 employees, (2) a net turnover of less than EUR 50 million or assets that do not exceed EUR 43 million, and (3) 25 per cent or more of the capital or voting rights are not owned by one enterprise, or jointly by several enterprises that do not meet the previous conditions.

To determine whether the criteria are met, reference should be made to the financial year preceding that in which the request to initiate the procedure is submitted.

3.3 Administrative statements

The administrative rules of the French tax authorities are contained in administrative instructions. The first instruction of particular relevance to transfer pricing is a note of 4th May 1973, which provides the FTA's interpretation of the transfer pricing legislation.[11] This regulation is the main element of the FTA doctrine, and in April 1983, the tax authorities finalised and published this commentary on their interpretation of the transfer

10 BOI 4-A.II.05.
11 BOI 4-A.13.06.

pricing legislation once Article 57 was amended to cover transactions with tax havens.

Other administrative regulations of relevance to transfer pricing were subsequently published[12].

4. CASE LAW

Over the years, a number of tax decisions have been rendered by the tax courts in respect of transfer pricing. With the increasing number of tax reassessments, it is not surprising that the number of cases and decisions has also increased. The administrative jurisdictions have developed strong control of the use of Article 57 (FTC) by the FTA, particularly on the key issue of burden of proof. The following is a short selection of cases of particular interest.

4.1 Current cases

(a) Sté SOUTIRAN[13]

The Supreme Court recently examined a case where the taxpayer argued that Article 57 was unconstitutional due to a 'presumption' of profit shifting in case of a mere dependency relationship with a foreign entity, and that the FTA established that an advantage was granted to the latter. According to the taxpayer, Article 57 violates the principle of equality of taxpayers in front of public expenses. Putting the burden of proof on the taxpayer arguably leads to different treatment of taxpayers who deal with foreign entities in relation to others.

For the Supreme Administrative Court (SAC), the presumption of profit shifting set by Article 57 is a rebuttable presumption which can be fought by the taxpayer. Moreover, the difference of treatment is due to a difference of situation between taxpayers who have relations with foreign entities and those who do not, which is to be considered as based on objective and rational criteria. Furthermore, the fight against tax evasion is a constitutional objective. As a consequence, the SAC refused to refer to the Constitutional Court a preliminary ruling on constitutionality in relation to the question of whether the presumption of profit shifting set by the Article 57 is constitutional. Based on this case, it is reasonable to consider Article 57 to be constitutional.

(b) Sté CAP GEMINI[14]

This case involved the holding company of a corporate group which did not charge royalties for the exploitation of its trademark and logo to its American and European subsidiaries, as opposed to the French one which had to pay a royalty equal to 4 per cent of its annual profits. According to the FTA, the absence of royalties was to be treated as profit shifting. Pursuant to Article 57, the FTA re-added the royalties to the profits of the French

12 A new instruction was published on 23rd February 2006, on bilateral and EU mutual agreement procedures. An instruction was published on 7th September 1999 on bilateral advance pricing agreements, and on 24th June 2005 on unilateral advance pricing agreements (BOI 4-A.II.05).

13 CE, 2nd Mar 2011, no 342099.

14 CE, 3è et 8è s.-s., 7th Nov 2005, no. 266436 and no. 266438.

holding company that, according to the FTA, should have been paid by the other subsidiaries.

The SAC judged that the FTA could not demonstrate an advantage was granted to the foreign subsidiaries only by comparing the royalties due by the French subsidiary with those due by the foreign subsidiaries. For the SAC, the value of the right to use a trademark may be different according to the market where it is exploited. Different situations and markets can explain different royalty rates from one country to another. To demonstrate that there was profit shifting, the FTA should have compared the royalties due by the French subsidiary with the royalties paid by another French company to demonstrate a non-arm's length price. In this decision, the SAC reaffirmed that transfer pricing adjustments must be based on solid evidence.

(c) Sté NESTLE FINANCE INTERNATIONAL LTD[15]

This decision illustrates the application of Article 57 in case of a cross-border business restructuring. In this case a French company transferred its cash pooling activity to a related Swiss entity without any compensation. The FTA considered that this transfer entailed profit shifting on the basis of Article 57, due to the absence of a payment equal to the value of the transferred activity.

The Administrative Court first agreed with the FTA considering that the transfer of any activity, even if it is a mere internal administrative function, requires the payment of an arm's length compensation. But the Administrative Court of Appeal (ACA) overturned this decision, finding that the FTA did not satisfy the burden of proof due to a lack of precision regarding the identity of the other groups used for the comparison and the similarity of the operating conditions of their own cash pooling activities.

This case stressed that the FTA still have to support the burden of proof even in respect of cross-border restructuring plans which may appear aggressive.

(d) SA GUERLAIN[16]

This case deals with the articulation between transfer pricing and waiver of receivables toward foreign branches. In France, economic assistances granted by a parent company to its subsidiaries are deductible from its taxable amount if they are justified by normal business operations. In this case, a parent company deducted the economic assistance granted to two branches of a subsidiary owned at 99.99 per cent to ensure its development in Asia. The subsidiary had created branches in Australia and in Singapore to distribute the products of the parent company in these countries. The branches accumulated losses to such an extent that the parent company decided to waive its receivables towards the two branches. The FTA added back the waived receivables on the basis of Article 57.

15 CAA Paris, 5th Feb 2013, n° 11PA02914
16 CE, 11th Apr 2008, n°281033

For the SAC, the waiver of receivables in favor of the branches was to be treated as profit shifting. Indeed, despite the fact that the branches were losing money, the subsidiary was profitable. Moreover, it had distributed an important amount of dividend to its parent company. As a consequence the waiver of receivables in favor of the branches cannot be justified by the commercial development of the parent company because of the profitable situation of its subsidiary.

This decision shows that the provisions of Article 57 are similar to the concept of abnormal business operations.[17] To examine whether the waiver of the receivables was to be treated as profit shifting, the SAC examined the normality of the operations, namely, whether the advantage granted by the corporation that gave the advantage had an interest other than tax avoidance.

4.2 Historical cases

(a) SARL Boutique 2M[18]

After auditing a corporation, the FTA considered that the payment of a 6 per cent and 7 per cent commission to its single supplier established in Sweden disguised profit shifting. The FTA added back the commission paid in the taxable profit of the audited corporation on the basis of Article 57.

This case deals with the important question of who should bear the burden of proof when Article 57 is applied. For the SAC it is a two-step process. First, the FTA has to demonstrate both the existence of a dependent relationship between the parties and the existence of an advantage granted by the French entity to a foreign entity. It is only if the FTA manage to prove that these two conditions are met that the taxpayer has to demonstrate that the granted advantage resulted in a matching compensation. If the taxpayer fails to do so, the advantage will be added back to its profit. In this case, the FTA managed to prove the existence of a dependent relationship and the payment of the commission. The taxpayer was then able to demonstrate the commission was justified by the supplier's support of the development of sales in France.

(b) SA ANDRITZ[19]

In this case, a French subsidiary paid interest on loans granted by its Austrian parent company. The FTA considered that the loan aimed to offset the deficiency of equity and reduce the taxable profit of the French subsidiary through a deduction of interest. The FTA added back the interest on the basis of Article 57.

The SAC judged that article 57 did not allow the FTA to evaluate the 'normality' of the choice made by a foreign company to finance the activity of its foreign subsidiary through a loan contract rather than equity. This case placed an emphasis on the general privilege of freedom of management.

17 See footnote 1
18 CE, Plén, 27th Jul 1988, no 50020.
19 CE, 30th Dec 2003, no 233894.

Under French Law, the FTA cannot interfere in the management of a company.

(c) BANCO DI ROMA[20]

In this case, the Court of Appeal reiterated that the FTA are not allowed to decide whether a business is to be financed through debt or equity.

5. PENALTIES

As a general rule, a reassessment made in respect of transfer pricing adjustments does not give rise to specific penalties. All reassessments give rise to interest for late payment at the rate of 0.40 per cent per month[21] and a penalty which varies between 10 per cent and 80 per cent.[22] The penalty amounts to 40 per cent when good faith is challenged, which has almost become the general rule in case of transfer pricing adjustments. It is raised to 80 per cent when the taxpayer is considered guilty of tax fraud.

On the other hand, specific penalties are due by companies subject to TP documentation if they do not comply with their requirements. The penalty for each audited year is to up to 5 per cent of the transfer pricing reassessment basis, with a minimum of 10,000 EUR in case of failure to provide information on time or providing only partial information.

6. DISPUTE RESOLUTION MECHANISMS

In order to resolve transfer pricing disputes, French law and international treaties provide both national and international options.

6.1 National options

Unless the taxpayer has entered an APA with the FTA as explained above (see Section 3.2), the national options are either an internal appeal to the tax authorities or litigation.

When transfer pricing adjustments have been made, the taxpayer is entitled to take the case to a special body (the 'Commission départementale'), consisting of representatives of both the tax authorities and the taxpayer. The role of the Commission départementale is to review technical as opposed to legal issues. Although its decision is not binding on the FTA, they are not allowed to issue an assessment before the Commission has reached its final decision. If they do not follow the Commission's decision and the taxpayer decides to appeal, the burden of proof then shifts to the administration.

The most common dispute resolution process is to file an administrative claim against the assessment with the tax authorities. If they reject the taxpayers' claim or if they do not respond within six months of the claim, the taxpayer may then appeal to the lower administrative courts (Tribunal Administratif). At this stage, the taxpayer may still require that payment of tax and penalties be postponed, but he must provide guarantees. Either party

20 CAA Paris, 16th Dec 2010.
21 Article 1727 FTC.
22 Article 1737 bis FTC.

may appeal the lower court's decision to the Administrative Court of Appeal, but this does not postpone the tax due. In limited circumstances, either party may file a final appeal with the administrative Supreme Court (Conseil d'Etat).

As a general rule, when a tax treaty applies, the taxpayer may decide to file a complaint authority claim instead of resorting to litigation. However, it is generally recommended that the taxpayer pursue both routes simultaneously.

6.2 International options

Less common methods for resolving transfer pricing disputes are available through international options. These are (a) the mutual agreement procedure, and (b) arbitration.

(a) Mutual agreement procedure (MAP)

When a dispute arising from double taxation involves a country with which France has signed a tax treaty, a mutual agreement procedure is generally provided for, which generally follows the OECD model tax convention.

In February 2006, the French revenue issued new detailed instructions regarding the MAP, which provides guidance pertaining to the scope, conditions and implementation of the MAP in France. The instructions also aim to apply the recommendations of the code of conduct expanded by the EU Joint Transfer Pricing Forum with respect to the implementation on the EU Arbitration Convention.

Until recently, the taxpayer was particularly encouraged to enter into such procedures, since according to French law[23], any tax assessment made by the French tax authorities which gives rise to an application for recourse for elimination of double taxation might not be claimed for payment until a signed agreement exists between the authorities (or a notice of disagreement). Unfortunately, this very favourable provision was repealed by the Finance Law for 2014 in respect of all national agreement procedures initiated as of 1st January 2014.

The drawback of the MAP is that the contracting states are not bound to reach an agreement. Although a significant number of transfer pricing cases are resolved under the MAP, there are difficult cases where the competent authorities cannot agree.

(b) Arbitration

Some bilateral tax treaties (eg, between France and the USA) contain a tax arbitration clause which provides that when the competent authorities are unable to reach an agreement, any unresolved issues arising from the case may be submitted to mandatory arbitration.

The EU Arbitration Convention establishes a procedure to resolve disputes where double taxation occurs between enterprises of different Member States as a result of an upward adjustment of profits of an enterprise of

[23] Article L 189 A Livre des Procédures Fiscales.

one Member State. Whilst most bilateral double taxation treaties include a provision for a corresponding downward adjustment of profits of the associated enterprise concerned, they do not generally impose a binding obligation on the Contract States to eliminate the double taxation.

The Convention provides for the elimination of double taxation by agreement between the contracting states including, if necessary, by reference to the opinion of an independent advisory body.

If no common agreement has been reached between the relevant tax authorities within two years, to benefit from an arbitration procedure, the decision must be handed down within six months following the expiration date of the above-mentioned two-year period.

(c) Advance pricing agreements

Article L80 B.7° has provided a legal basis for the administrative regulations implemented by the guidelines of 7th September 1999 and also enlarged their scope. Initially reserved for bilateral agreements with states that have a tax treaty with France, this procedure now extends to unilateral agreements under certain conditions.

PART TWO: TAX AVOIDANCE

7. ACCEPTABLE TAX PLANNING AREAS/SUBJECTS

In France there is a thin line between legitimate tax planning and abusive tax avoidance, known as 'abuse of law'. The abuse of law principle stems from the general rule on civil liability contained in Article 1382 of the French Civil Code. Although this statutory provision does not contain any explicit reference to such a doctrine, its broad statement of principle was used by the French courts to develop the doctrine of abuse of rights. French law imposes sanctions of the use of a right if the use exceeds the limits of reasonable use and enforcement. Over the years, the French courts have found that the abuse of law encompasses both deliberate actions that are carried out to divert the intended operation of a law in order to achieve a result the legislature would not have intended, or with the sole intention of harming a third party.

As a consequence of the above, although the taxpayer is entitled to choose the legal framework most favourable to his transactions, the French tax courts have developed case law recognising a right for the French tax authorities to examine the same transactions to discover the true substantive nature of contractual agreements. This right arose from instances of fraud, which, in this context, includes evasion as well as what a Common Law court would call avoidance.

Contrary to other jurisdictions, the FTA do not provide a list of transactions immune to challenge under the abuse of law doctrine. Their policy is, instead, to create sufficient uncertainty for the taxpayers to refrain from entering into aggressive tax planning strategies due to fear that they might be attacked by the FTA. Fortunately, over the years, tax courts have ruled that certain transactions challenged by the tax authorities are legitimate.

For example, in France, the sale of shares of a limited liability company is subject to a higher rate of transfer tax than the sale of the shares of a public company. A common tax planning technique is to transform a limited liability company into a public company before selling the shares. Not surprisingly, the FTA considers that such a transformation, especially when made immediately before a sale, is purely tax motivated and consequently qualifies as an abuse of law. The 'Cour de Cassation'[24] ruled, however, that the transformation of the legal form of the company was independent from the subsequent sale of its shares and thus is not an abuse of law. The only qualification is that the new public company is not to be transformed back into a limited liability company shortly after the sale.

Another example is the merger of an unprofitable company with a profit-making one. The Cour de Cassation ruled that it is not an abuse of law to merge a big profit-making company with a small loss-making company as long as the merger is not artificial and is motivated by economic reasons.[25]

8. DEFINING ABUSIVE TAX AVOIDANCE

The French abuse of law doctrine enables the FTA to disregard any legal agreement and to tax the corresponding transaction on the basis of its actual substance in two types of situations.

The first situation is where the relevant transaction is fictitious. This test is rarely used by the French tax authorities – a typical example is when a gift subject to very high gift tax duties is disguised as a sale with no intention on the part of either the seller or the buyer that the price will ever be paid.

The second situation is where a given transaction is purely tax motivated and the parties have obtained the tax benefit by a literal application of the relevant rules while disregarding the spirit of such rules.

9. THE LEGISLATIVE FRAMEWORK

The abuse of law doctrine initially developed by case law was first enacted as a statutory provision in 1925 in relation to transfer taxes, and then in 1941 in relation to income tax. It was codified in Article L64 of the LPF (*Livre des procedures fiscales*).

For a long time, the French courts have denied legal effect to transactions on the grounds of abuse of law that were artificial or 'fictitious' (ie, a sham). In 1981 the Supreme Administrative Court (Conseil d'Etat) ruled that a transaction is abusive not only when the arrangement under review is fictitious, but also when it cannot be justified by any reason other than the exclusive and intentional purpose of reducing or avoiding tax.[26]

Until the *Janfin* case (see 10.2), it was generally thought that only transactions that fell under the statutory definition of abuse of law (Article

[24] Cass Com, 10th Dec 1996, no 20848 Sté RMC France.

[25] Under French law, when a loss-making company is absorbed its losses cannot be carried forward against the profits of the absorbing company, hence the planning strategy (a so-called reverse merger).

[26] 12th June 1981 no 19079, RYF 9/80 no 787.

L64 of the French Tax Procedure Code) could be reclassified by the tax authorities. The problem is that Article L64 does not cover all tax matters (eg, tax credits which was the issue of the *Janfin* case). The Supreme Court held that in situations where the specific statutory provisions of Article L64 cannot be applied, the tax authorities can disregard a transaction on the basis of the general abuse of law principle. The Supreme Court also ruled in the same case that it is not sufficient to find a transaction abusive only on the basis that it is solely motivated by a tax purpose. The purpose of the transaction must also be to benefit from the literal application of a rule that is in contradiction with its author's objectives. In other words, a transaction should not be considered abusive if, even though it is tax motivated, it only seeks a tax benefit which results from a legitimate application of French tax law.

This new definition of abuse of law was codified, and Article L64 of the LPF now provides that: 'In order to restore their true character, the Administration has the right to ignore, as not binding, acts that constitute an abuse of law, either because these acts are fictitious, or because, by seeking the benefit of a literal application of the law or decisions contrary to the objectives pursued by their author, they cannot have been inspired by any other motivation than avoiding or reducing the tax burden that the person would have normally borne in view of his/her situation or his/her real activities.'

10 KEY CASES OF INTEREST

10.1 Current cases

(a) Min c/ SA AXA[27]

This case involved a French bank which realized a significant number of transfers of French share operations with the option to repurchase or acquire stock loans over the dividend date. These transactions allowed the bank to become the owner of the shares and to benefit from the '*avoir fiscal*' attached to the dividends, which was shared by the bank with the seller/ lender. The bank used the *avoir fiscal* and resold the shares immediately after. For the FTA, these transactions were purely tax motivated and the parties had obtained the tax benefit through a literal application of the relevant rules while disregarding the spirit of such rules. The Supreme Administrative Court (SAC) analysed the legislative preparatory works of the statute providing for the *avoir fiscal*. The SAC's conclusion was that the law was designed to eliminate the double taxation on dividend and that no minimum period of ownership of the shares was required. Thus the SAC concluded that the FTA had not proved that the parties obtained the tax benefit by a literal application of the relevant rules while disregarding the spirit of such rules.

This case emphasized the burden of proof required to demonstrate an abuse of law. It strengthened the conditions under which a transaction would be found abusive. In addition to being solely motivated by a tax

[27] CE, 7th Sep 2009, no 305586, *Min c/ SA AXA*.

purpose, the tax benefit sought must result from a literal application of the relevant rules that is in contradiction with its author's objectives.

(b) Min c/ Sté BANK OF SCOTLAND[28]

In *Sté BANK OF SCOTLAND*, the SAC looked at a financial arrangement between a British bank and a US company in November, 1992. The bank bought the usufruct for three years of shares without voting rights of the French subsidiary of the US parent company. In September, 1993 the French subsidiary of the US company distributed dividends to the bank. In December, 1993 the bank requested a refund of the French withholding tax as well as the transfer of the *avoir fiscal* tax credit under the France–US tax treaty.

The FTA rejected the bank's claim on the ground that the beneficial owner of the shares was not the bank but the US parent company. The SAC agreed with the FTA to disregard this financial arrangement on the basis of the general abuse of law principle, and to characterize the transaction as granted by the bank to the US company. The SAC ruled that the usufruct arrangement was motivated solely by tax reasons with the aim of benefiting from the transfer of the *avoir fiscal* tax credit, which was available under the France-United Kingdom treaty but not under the France–US tax treaty.

This case shows that the general abuse of law concept can apply to international issues (eg, treaty shopping).

(c) BOURDON[29]

This case is the first decision about the tax validity of an operation of an LBO's transaction. The two shareholders of a company sold their shares to the holding company they created. The holding financed the acquisition of the shares for 50 per cent by the dividend income and 50 per cent through a loan. The FTA considered the operation an abuse of law, because it allowed the two shareholders to benefit from the capital gain tax treatment, which is more favourable than the tax treatment of dividend income.

The SAC held that the operation was not purely tax motivated, since it allowed the increase of the shareholders' financing capacity, and made the acquisition of other companies easier, as the holding company could use its equity to serve as a guarantee for loan financing. According to the SAC, the FTA was consequently not able to prove that the creation of the holding company was purely tax motivated.

10.2 Historical cases

(a) CE. Plén 10th june 1981, no 19079

This landmark case extended the concept of abuse of law to all transactions which cannot be justified by any reason other than the exclusive and intentional purpose of reducing or avoiding tax. Before this decision, it was generally accepted that the only transactions that fell under the statutory

[28] CE, 29th Dec 2006, no 283314, *Min c/ Sté BANK OF SCOTLAND*.

[29] CE, 27th Jan 2011 no 3203, Bourdon.

definition of abuse of law were artificial or 'simulated', and could be reclassified by the FTA.

In this decision the SAC ruled against the FTA that the estate planning arrangement designed to keep the cohesion of a family after the parent's death is a valid motivation and is not indicative of an arrangement which is purely tax motivated.

(b) Sté JANFIN[30]

This other landmark case involved a taxpayer corporation which purchased the shares of another company. Once the stock was purchased, the buyer distributed the dividend and sold the shares, making a capital loss equal to the amount of the distributed dividend less tax credits. The tax credits allowed the buyer to pay the entire amount of the corporate tax, but were not covered by article L64.

The SAC allowed the FTA to disregard a transaction using the general abuse of law under the general abuse of law principle when the specific statutory provisions of Article L64 cannot be applied. (ie, the transactions are purely tax motivated where the parties have obtained the tax benefit by a literal application of the relevant rules while disregarding the spirit of such rules).

This landmark case led Parliament to approve the new Article L64 in 2008[31] which now gathers two alternative definitions of abuse of law: (1) abuse of law by fictitious transactions, and (2) abuse of law by general abuse of law principle (transactions are purely tax motivated where the parties have obtained the tax benefit by a literal application of the relevant rules while disregarding the spirit of such rules).

(c) Min. c/ Sté SAGAL[32]

This case deals with a widespread tax planning strategy in the late 1990s. Various French companies jointly invested in an exempt Luxembourg 1929 holding company. The holding company wound up several years later, distributing dividends to the French companies which were also tax exempt under the affiliation privilege. The FTA determined that the operation was purely tax motivated and applied Article L64. The taxpayers argued that the structure had an economic and financial interest, and that Article L64 infringed on the freedom of establishment of the EU.

The SAC confirmed the abuse of law considering that the Luxembourg holding company had no substance and that the structure was purely tax motivated. Moreover, SAC Article L64 does not infringe on freedom of establishment, as it is only applicable to transactions which are fictitious or purely tax motivated.

---

30 CE, 27th Sep 2006, no 260050, *Sté JANFIN*.

31 See above 9.

32 CE, 18th May 2005 no 267087.

11. PENALTIES

In addition to income subject to reassessment being added back to the taxable income, additional tax is increased by a specific penalty of 80 per cent. Interest for late payment is calculated at a rate of 0.4 per cent per month. The penalty is reduced to 40 per cent when there is no proof that the taxpayer was primarily responsible for initiating the abusive transaction or was its main beneficiary. The FTA has the burden of proving that the 80 per cent penalty is applicable. Apart from the tax penalties, the FTA can also decide to prosecute the taxpayer for a criminal offense.

12. CURRENT TRENDS

At the end of 2013, the French Parliament sought to redefine what constitutes an abuse of law by replacing the test of sole purpose with the test of main purpose. Fortunately, the Constitutional Council[33] found that this modification of the definition of abuse of law had the effect of giving the FTA considerable discretionary power, which goes against the constitutional objective of accessibility and intelligibility of the law. The Constitutional Council struck down another provision of the same Finance Act, which was the requirement to report to the FTA tax optimization on the ground that this would have restricted the freedom to do business derived from Article 4 of the 1789 Declaration of the Rights of Man and of the Citizens.

---

[33] Decision no 2013-65 DC, 29 Dec 2013.

Germany

Oppenhoff & Partner Axel Bödefeld & Gunnar Knorr

PART ONE: TRANSFER PRICING

1. GENERAL OVERVIEW

For many years, transfer pricing was not a major area of interest for the German tax authorities; tax adjustments were rare, and occurred only in extreme cases. However, after the issuance of the US White Paper on Section 482 of the Internal Revenue Code in 1988, the German tax authorities began taking a closer look at the profitability of international group companies.[1] Since that time, Germany has incorporated the OECD principles into its tax legislation, and has enacted a detailed system of rules on transfer pricing.

2. IDENTIFICATION OF LEGISLATIVE FRAMEWORK

2.1 Federal legislation

The main provisions in Germany's tax legislation dealing with transfer pricing are s. 8(3) of the Corporate Income Tax Act (the 'CITA'), and s. 1(1) of the Foreign Tax Act (the 'FTA'). Section 8(3) of the CITA deals with hidden distributions. A hidden distribution will be subject to tax if a business transaction between affiliates results in a loss or forgone increase in net assets, which would not have been accepted by a prudent managing director in a transaction between unrelated parties. This is commonly referred to as the arm's length principle. The arm's length principle applies to any unjustified benefit that a subsidiary provides to its shareholders. It also applies to benefits provided to sister companies, as these are assumed to be a hidden distribution to the joint shareholder and a subsequent hidden contribution of the shareholder to the sister company. While any kind of benefit might be a hidden distribution, a hidden contribution can only be assumed if a tangible or intangible asset is transferred. Therefore, interest free loans to a subsidiary are not covered by these rules. Section 1(1) of the FTA establishes the basis for an adjustment if a taxpayer's taxable income is reduced as a result of a violation of the arm's length principle. Although s. 1(1) is similar to s. 8(3) of the CITA, it only applies to cross-border transactions where no other provision is applicable.

In 2003, the German General Tax Code (the 'GTC') was amended to include s. 90(3), and the accompanying Ordinance on Transfer Pricing Documentation.[2] These rules establish the general documentation

1 'White Paper' of the IRS and the Treasury Department, Notice 88-123 (1988-2 C.B. 458), dated Oct. 18, 1988.
2 Section 90(3) of the GTC, introduced by Section 9 No. 3 of the law of May 16, 2003, BGBl. I 2003, 660, which came into force on May 21, 2003; Ordinance on the Documentation for the Allocation of Profit, effective Nov. 13, 2003, BGBl. I 2003, 2296.

requirements for compliance with the arm's length principle. The required documentation may be requested during a tax audit, and must be provided to the auditor within 60 days of a request. In the case of an extraordinary transaction (eg, a reorganization, the sale of a business, the introduction of a new supply chain, etc.), the required documentation must be prepared within 6 months of the end of the fiscal year, and submitted within 30 days of a request. If the taxpayer does not submit the required documentation by the deadline, a penalty of EUR 2,500 to EUR 250,000 may be imposed.

In practice, the tax authorities do not frequently impose late penalties. However, if the taxpayer fails to submit the required documentation, or if the documentation is of no use to a 'reasonable expert', the taxpayer has the burden of proof to establish that the transaction satisfies the arm's length principle. A tax auditor may impose adjustments to a transaction to bring it within the range of arm's length results. Where the taxpayer fails to submit the required documentation or the documentation is insufficient, a penalty of 5 to 10 per cent of the adjustment may be charged. Further, where documentation is submitted late, a penalty of up to EUR 1,000,000 may be imposed, with a minimum charge of EUR 100 per day.

2.2 State and provincial interplay

In Germany, tax legislation is federal. However, tax administration is the responsibility of the German states. As a result, tax returns must be filed with the local tax offices. The local authorities are also responsible for conducting tax audits. In recent years, the local authorities have acquired trained experts on transfer pricing. These experts are typically included in the audit team whenever the transaction involves a significant business relationship with a non-German affiliate. Additionally, a group of transfer pricing specialists exist at the federal level. These experts may elect to partake in any audit, and are entitled to determine the direction and intensity of any audit in which they participate. The involvement of both local and federal authorities imposes a substantial burden on the taxpayer, and tends to make the audit procedure lengthier. Where both the local and federal authorities are involved, a period of 3 years for a tax audit is not uncommon.

2.3 International treaties and agreements

Germany has entered into tax treaties with most of the key economic countries. German tax treaties typically follow the OECD model, and include rules on corresponding adjustments. Additionally, most treaties include provisions on the mutual authority procedure (the 'MAP'), as well as the exchange of information between the contracting states.

3. NATIONAL POLICY ISSUES

3.1 Overall national policy announcements

German tax authorities support the OECD's Base Erosion and Profit Shifting ('BEPS') initiative. However, this initiative does not involve concrete actions in the short-term. As a result, Germany has managed the predominant issues relating to BEPS through effective CFC legislation and detailed transfer pricing rules. Additionally, in 2008, Germany introduced special rules on the transfer of risks and functions. These rules have been incorporated in s. 1(3) of the FTA, together with an accompanying ordinance.[3]

In a cross-border transaction involving the transfer of business functions, it is desirable that the value of the transferred assets be determined as a whole (known as the 'transfer package'). Before the implementation of the special rules, a cross-border transaction was a taxable event only if assets (tangibles and/or intangibles, including goodwill) were involved. The special rules in s. 1(3) of the FTA impose a four-part valuation process on the transfer package. First, the transferring entity must be evaluated before and after the transfer. The difference between the valuations is deemed to be the minimum selling price of the business functions. Second, the receiving entity must be evaluated before and after the transfer. The difference between the valuations is deemed to be the maximum price a buyer would pay for the business functions.

Since the valuation process is based on the assumption of perfect knowledge between the buyer and the seller, the average price as determined must be paid by the receiving entity. If the average price is not paid, the profit of the transferring entity will be adjusted accordingly. Further, the rules provide that where profits are different from the original valuations, the deemed purchase price may be retroactively adjusted for a period of ten years. It has been argued that these rules violate both EU law and constitutional law. However, this issue has not yet been determined by the courts.

Germany has also incorporated the Authorized OECD Approach (the 'AOA') for permanent establishments.[4] Once the AOA is incorporated into German treaties, it will apply to the taxation of a permanent establishment. But even if not, the AOA applies on the basis of domestic law, unless the taxpayer can prove that he or she calculated the German tax on the basis of the old rules, and that the foreign tax of the other permanent establishment has been calculated accordingly. Therefore, permanent establishments should begin to consider the application of the AOA.

In regard to transfer pricing methodologies, the German tax authorities have displayed a clear preference for the standard methodologies. However, s. 1(3) of the FTA provides that the transactional net margin method (the 'TNMM') and the profit split method (the 'PSM') are acceptable if no comparables are available. In Germany, disputes frequently arise because the TNMM is only accepted for routine functions, and limited risk distributors are often not accepted as routine entities. Further, auditors typically focus on the qualification of functions exercised in Germany, and lengthy questionnaires are used to identify any intangibles that should be allocated to the distribution entity using the PSM rather than the TNMM.

---

3 Section 1(3) of the FTA introduced by Section 7 No. 1 Letter b of the law of Aug. 14, 2007, BGBl. I 2007, 1921; Ordinance on the Application of the Arms-Length-Principle in Cases of Relocation of Functions effective Aug. 12, 2008, BGBl. I 2008, 1680.

4 *http://www.oecd.org/tax/transfer-pricing/41031455.pdf.*

With respect to dispute resolution mechanisms, German tax authorities tend to favor arbitration. The recent German tax treaties concluded with the US and Liechtenstein include a clause providing for last-best-offer arbitration. Additionally, although the recent German tax treaty with Switzerland did not explicitly provide for last-best-offer arbitration, official announcements from both Germany and Switzerland have confirmed that arbitration under the treaty shall follow the same principles established in the Germany–US treaty.

3.2 National revenue authority initiatives

Advance Pricing Agreements ('APAs') are available in Germany. The Federal Ministry of Finance has issued a detailed circular describing the APA process.[5] Although the Federal Tax Office is responsible for negotiating an agreement with the other country, it must include both the federal and state auditors in the fact-finding process. As a result, the procedure is lengthy, and the APA period often expires before an agreement is reached.[6] Thus, APAs should only be considered in very important cases. APAs are frequently used in combination with MAPs. Additionally, a 'roll-back' may be used to extend the period during which a binding result can be negotiated.

3.3 Administrative statements

Not applicable.

4. CASE LAW

There are relatively few cases on transfer pricing in Germany. However, the cases summarized below have played a major role in the development of the German transfer pricing rules.

4.1 Current cases

(a) Federal Tax Court I R 75/11 as of October 11, 2012

In this case, the tax authority took the position that a hidden distribution could be assumed if no written agreement was concluded between the affiliated companies prior to the transaction, notwithstanding the fact that the terms and conditions of the transaction might be at arm's length.[7] This position was consistent with court decisions in domestic cases. However, the Court held that the respective treaty (Article 9 in the OECD model) did not permit such a formalistic approach; rather, it was necessary to identify the arm's length price.

(b) Federal Tax Court I R 45/11 as of April 10, 2013

In this case, the taxpayer argued that the transfer pricing documentation requirements in the GTC were a violation of EU law because they only applied to cross-border transactions, while domestic transactions between

5 German Federal Ministry of Finance, Letter dated Oct. 5, 2006, IV B 4-S 1341-38/06, BStBl. I 2006, 594.

6 Kevin Bell, 'Germany Entering into More Bilateral APA's' in Bloomberg BNA, Tax Management, Transfer Pricing Report, May 29, 2014.

7 German Federal Tax Court, Decision of Oct. 11, 2012, Case Number: I R 75/11, BStBl. II 2013, 1046.

affiliates were not subject to any documentation requirements.[8] The Federal Tax Court held that existing options for the tax authorities to obtain information from other EU member states under the Directive of Mutual Assistance were insufficient. As a result, the transfer pricing documentation requirements were justified given the objective of maintaining equitable tax collection, and did not violate EU law.

4.2 Historical cases of note

(a) Federal Tax Court I R 3/92 as of February 17, 1993

The first major transfer pricing case in Germany was decided in 1993.[9] This case involved the German subsidiary of a Danish group that acted as a distributor for its parent company. The German subsidiary had incurred losses for a number of years. On the basis of general principles, the Court held that an unrelated distributor would not have accepted ongoing losses for more than three years.

(b) Federal Tax Court I R 103/00 as of October 17, 2001

In this case, the Federal Tax Court settled a number of transfer pricing issues that had been in dispute at the time.[10] The decision resulted in the introduction of the transfer pricing documentation rules in 2003. Among other things, the Court held that:

- According to s. 8(3) of the CITA, the arm's length principle is relevant to determine the amount of a hidden distribution;
- An estimate made by a tax authority can be replaced by the tax court even if the estimate is within the reasonable range;
- Although the right to inspect files extends to third party files where the third party is used as a comparable, this rule does not apply if it would violate a tax secret;
- Although anonymous evidence may be used by the court, such evidence must comply with legal requirements, and any remaining doubts should be taken into account in determining the weight to be given to the evidence;
- If a German entity has not provided information on how transfer prices have been determined, it is assumed that transfer prices have been influenced by the affiliation;
- The tax authorities have the burden of proof to establish inappropriate transfer pricing;
- External comparables are not relevant if they have not been in place in all disputed fiscal years, or if they represent 5 per cent or less of the total turnover; and
- If an estimate is required, the range of reasonable prices (as opposed to the average) is relevant because it is still an arm's length price.

8 German Federal Tax Court, Decision of Apr. 10, 2013, Case Number: I R 45/11, BStBl. II 2013, 771.
9 German Federal Tax Court, Decision of Feb. 17, 1993, Case Number: I R 3/92, BStBl. II 1993, 457.
10 German Federal Tax Court, Decision of Oct. 17, 2001, Case Number: I R 103/00, BStBl. II 2004, 171.

5. PENALTIES

5.1 Types

If taxes are increased retroactively after an audit, German tax law generally does not provide for the imposition of penalties. However, interest is charged at a rate of 6 per cent per annum for any adjustment made, starting 15 months after the end of the relevant fiscal year. While this interest charge has some characteristics of a penalty, interest may also be paid in favor of the taxpayer in the event of a downward adjustment.

(a) Penalties on the adjustment

Section 162(4) of the GTC provides that if a taxpayer fails to submit the required documentation, or if the documentation provided by the taxpayer is of no use to a 'reasonable expert', the tax authorities have the discretion to impose a penalty. The penalty must be between 5 and 10 per cent of the adjustment, with a minimum of EUR 5,000. However, this section is used infrequently, as cases where the taxpayer fails to provide documentation are rare, and the issue of usefulness to a 'reasonable expert' may be disputed. Additionally, where documentation is submitted late, a penalty may be imposed. However, in practice, the taxpayer may seek an extension of the deadline if more time is required. In the case of an extraordinary transaction, documentation that is submitted late is subject to a penalty of up to EUR 1,000,000, with a minimum charge of EUR 100 per day.

(b) Penalty for not responding on information request

During an audit, auditors have a broad discretion to make necessary inquiries. The only limit imposed on the auditors' discretion is that questions must not be inappropriate or disproportionate. If a taxpayer fails to respond to a reasonable inquiry, s. 146(2)(b) of the GTC provides for a penalty of EUR 2,500 to EUR 250,000.[11] Although this provision is occasionally used as a threat to put pressure on the taxpayer, it is rarely applied, as it would prevent co-operative discussions between the taxpayer and the auditors.

(b) Criminal fines

In transfer pricing cases, criminal investigations are rare. However, if documentation is purposely misleading or incorrect with regard to obvious facts, criminal fines or a term of imprisonment may be imposed. For example, in a recent case, the owner of a medium-sized family company was arrested for tax fraud because of transfer pricing.

5.2 Special or notable cases

Not applicable.

---

11 Section 146(2)(b) of the GTC introduced by Section 10 No. 8 of the law of Dec. 19, 2008, BStBl. I 2008, 2794, which came into force on Dec. 25, 2008.

6. DISPUTE RESOLUTION MECHANISM

When a transfer pricing dispute arises that cannot be settled by way of a compromise, the taxpayer has two options. First, the taxpayer may commence litigation in the domestic tax courts. Second, the taxpayer may proceed under the MAP in accordance with the applicable tax treaty. Where there is no benefit to be gained under the MAP, the taxpayer may decide to commence litigation. This might be the case where the affiliate in the other country is in a loss position, and there would be no cash benefit from increasing losses carried forward. This might also be the case where, for various reasons, the entity in the other country has a much lower tax burden. On the other hand, where litigation is not feasible, the taxpayer may elect to proceed under the MAP. This might be the case where existing precedents do not support the taxpayer's position, or where evidence is not available in the form required by the courts. Each decision should be evaluated on a case-by-case basis, and should involve consultation with an experienced litigator.

In theory, the taxpayer may proceed under the MAP, and if the desired result is not achieved, subsequently commence litigation to obtain a more favorable result. For this purpose, a protest must be filed against the amended tax assessment notice, which is stayed for the duration of the MAP. At the end of the MAP, the taxpayer is asked if he or she accepts the result agreed upon by the two countries. If the taxpayer refuses to accept the agreement, the stay is lifted and the taxpayer may proceed with litigation. However, it is possible that the result of the litigation may be the same or less favorable than the MAP. Further, in rendering its decision, the court may be influenced by the agreement reached between the countries.

(a) The MAP

If the MAP is selected, the taxpayer should still file an administrative protest against the amended tax assessment notice in order to suspend the requirement for payment. If the taxpayer fails to file a protest, the additional tax becomes due immediately. Although the additional tax is refundable if the MAP is resolved successfully, such payment might considerably reduce the cash position of the group. Additionally, the filing of an administrative protest is necessary to preserve the taxpayer's right to commence litigation in the event that the MAP does not achieve the desired result.

During the MAP, the taxpayer is not formally involved as a party to the procedure. However, the taxpayer receives additional information requests which may be coordinated between the two countries. Additionally, the taxpayer typically has informal contact with at least one competent authority. Where more than one country is involved in a potential corresponding adjustment, a strategic decision must be made as to which procedure should be initiated first. This might depend on procedural considerations, such as the availability of arbitration. It might also depend on context, such as the economic position of the other country.

(b) Litigation

In Germany, tax audits tend to be very lengthy. As a result, it is common for litigation to commence several years after the end of the fiscal year under dispute. Although memoranda may be used as the factual basis for an audit or MAP, a taxpayer who elects to proceed with litigation must provide sufficient evidence to satisfy the burden of proof. To be used in the course of litigation, documents such as contracts, invoices and expert valuations must comply with the requirements of the court. Since new evidence is not permissible on an appeal, any relevant fact must be submitted to the court of first instance. To ensure compliance with the formal requirements, a taxpayer should consult with an experienced tax litigator prior to commencing litigation.

PART TWO: TAX AVOIDANCE

7. ACCEPTABLE TAX PLANNING AREAS/SUBJECTS

In Germany, taxpayers have the discretion to structure their businesses as they see fit. However, artificial structures chosen solely or primarily to circumvent otherwise applicable tax provisions, or to obtain a tax benefit that otherwise would not be available, are disregarded for tax purposes. This rule applies to abusive business structures designed to avoid the payment of taxes, as well as those aimed at obtaining unwarranted tax advantages. Additionally, this rule does not distinguish between different areas of tax law, and generally disallows an abuse of legal means for all potential tax law provisions. However, this rule does not affect the legal validity of a chosen business structure. Thus, contracts that are re-classified into another transaction under the anti-avoidance rules remain effective for civil law purposes.

8. DEFENDING ABUSIVE TAX AVOIDANCE

Where the tax authorities allege that a business structure is abusive, the taxpayer has two principal lines of defense. First, the taxpayer may challenge the allegations that the selected business structure abuses legal means. Where a business structure does not abuse legal means, it does not constitute tax avoidance that would give rise to the anti-avoidance rules. Second, the taxpayer could adduce evidence of legitimate tax structuring. In order to prove a legitimate structuring objective, the taxpayer must demonstrate that there are valid business reasons underlying the selected business structure.

9. THE LEGISLATIVE FRAMEWORK

The general anti-avoidance rule ('GAAR') is set out in s. 42 of the GTC. The core passage of the provision, para 2, reads:

'An abuse shall be deemed to exist where an inappropriate legal option is selected which, in comparison with an appropriate option, leads to tax advantages unintended by law for the taxpayer or a third party. This shall not apply where

the taxpayer provides evidence of non-tax reasons for the selected option which are relevant when viewed from an overall perspective.'[12]

Thus, a structuring decision is not acceptable if it is aimed at circumventing German taxes. As a general rule, structures that are artificial, complex or cumbersome are more likely to be deemed to be abusive. Likewise, structures that are simple, straightforward, and economically efficient are generally not deemed to be abusive. Further, German tax law accepts structuring decisions that are made on the basis of valid business reasons. As such, tax savings do not necessarily render a business structure abusive. For example, the reduction of foreign taxes is usually deemed to be a legitimate business reason for selecting a particular business structure. Other business reasons that have been accepted in the past include limiting personal liability or effecting other non-tax savings. Additionally, the allocation of assets to individuals may serve as a justification for certain gifts to be made and to be accepted for tax purposes.

The tax authorities have the burden of proof to establish that a chosen business structure is abusive. While complex structures are not per se abusive, the tax courts have imposed a rebuttable presumption that objectively inappropriate structures constitute abusive structures aimed at circumventing tax laws. The onus to prove the existence of a valid business reason rests with the taxpayer. Therefore, it is the taxpayer's duty to establish the non-tax reasons underlying the structuring decision.

The purpose of GAAR is not to impose penalties, but rather, to achieve consistent and uniform taxation. Therefore, the application of GAAR should not give rise to double taxation. Where a business structure is deemed to be abusive, the application of GAAR will ensure that the overall transaction is taxed in the same manner as an economically suitable transaction with the same result. However, in practice, this creates uncertainty as it is usually not clear what the alternative, non-abusive structure would have been.

Apart from GAAR, there are several other anti-avoidance provisions targeting particular forms of perceived abuse. Most of these provisions were enacted after the emergence of specific model transactions, in order to prevent the wider use of such structures. Examples of specific anti-avoidance rules include the limitation of losses carried forward upon a change of ownership[13]; the holding requirements for tax neutral contributions[14]; and the indirect change of control rules in the Real Estate Transfer Tax Act.[15] The applicability of the special anti-avoidance rules does not affect the application of GAAR. Thus, any structure must be measured against GAAR as well as the specific anti-avoidance rules.

---

12 Translation provided by language service of the Federal Ministry of Finance: *http://www.gesetze-im-internet.de/englisch_ao/englisch_ao.html#p0239*.

13 Under the current version of the law (s. 8(c) of the CITA), a loss carried forward will generally be lost if a shareholder acquires more than 50 per cent in a corporation within a 5-year period. Additionally, part of a loss carried forward will be lost on a pro rata basis if more than 25 per cent up to 50 per cent are acquired by one shareholder within a 5-year period.

14 Under s. 22 of the Merger Tax Act, a contribution is not tax neutral if the contributed assets are sold within 7 years of the contribution, or if the shares obtained in exchange for the contribution are sold within that timeframe, if certain further prerequisites are met.

15 Under s. 1(2)(a) of the Real Estate Transfer Tax Act, changes in ownership in a partnership over a 5-year period can be aggregated to constitute a sale of the underlying real estate for tax purposes.

10. KEY CASES OF INTEREST

10.1 Current cases

The most controversial case dealing with alleged tax abuse relates to manufactured dividends in cum/ex-transactions. In these transactions, shares were purchased cum dividend but only delivered ex dividend in accordance with the general practice of the stock market and the OTC market. In lieu of a dividend, the purchaser obtained a dividend compensation payment totaling the net dividend (ie, the dividend net withholding taxes). At the same time, he obtained a tax withholding certificate from his bank. With the certificate, the taxpayer obtained a credit for dividend withholding taxes, despite the fact that no tax had been withheld. According to estimates from the Revenue, approximately EUR 12,000,000,000 of withholding taxes were paid to taxpayers that were never withheld at source. The main issue in the case was whether the purchaser in a cum/ex-transaction is entitled to a withholding tax credit, or whether such purchases are to be treated as an abuse of form. In a recent preliminary ruling, the Federal Tax Court declined to rule on the substantive issue.

10.2 Historic cases

In a series of cases, the Federal Tax Court expanded the application of GAAR in German tax law. The Court held that pursuant to the step transaction doctrine, a series of transactions undertaken with the objective of achieving the chosen structure through several steps should be treated in the same way as a single transaction.[16] Thus, the Federal Tax Court has held that a series of gifts made from one person to an intermediary, who is obliged to forward the gift to the ultimate recipient, is to be treated as a direct gift from the first donor to the ultimate beneficiary.[17] Whether or not this is part of the GAAR under s. 42 of the GTC or whether this is a separate legal instrument based on the substance-over-form approach stipulated in s. 39 of the GTC is being disputed among scholars.

Additionally, many of the most well-known cases in German tax law relating to the issue of tax abuse have been decided in favor of the taxpayer. For example, in one case, the court approved the use of a business loan for private purposes under a dual-account structure, which effectively permitted an interest deduction for funds used in private investments. As a consequence, legislation was enacted to override the case law and prohibit such structures. In another case, the Federal Tax Court held that dividend stripping did not constitute an abuse of law, even if the purchaser only owned shares in order to receive the dividend, and subsequently resold the shares to their previous owner.

11. PENALTIES

German anti-avoidance rules do not, per se, impose penalties. However, sanctions for an abusive structure can arise from subsequent tax filings,

16 See decisions BFH I R 8/05, BStBl. II 2007, 602; BFH I B 115/04, BStBl. II 2005, 528; BFH I R 112/03, BStBl. II 2004, 1085.

17 See Federal Tax Court II R 92/91.

which rely on the abusive structure to obtain a tax benefit. Where a potentially abusive tax structure has been chosen, the taxpayer must disclose the facts underlying the structure to the tax office. If the taxpayer fails to disclose all the facts and circumstances that are necessary for the tax office to determine the taxes owing, the taxpayer may be subject to criminal sanctions.

11.1 Legislative provisions

While GAAR and the specific anti-avoidance rules do not impose direct sanctions for the use of an abusive structure, the application of these rules will result in the structure being taxed as it would have been had the taxpayer chosen the appropriate structure. Additionally, s. 233a of the GTC provides for a 6 per cent interest charge on any adjustment, the interest starting to accrue 15 months after the end of the relevant fiscal year. Where tax fraud can be proven, the interest begins compounding immediately after the tax fraud was committed.

If the taxpayer is charged with tax fraud for failing to provide complete information regarding the chosen structure, a criminal sanction may be imposed. Additionally, other sanctions may be imposed including an exclusion from participating in public tenders, or a withdrawal of customs privileges. Finally, where accounting functions have been shifted abroad, the tax office may request that they be repatriated.

11.2 Examples of penalties imposed

The German Federal Supreme Court has ruled that in cases involving tax evasion where the amount of taxes withheld is in excess of EUR 1,000,000, a custodial sentence without probation should be imposed.[18] Further, a custodial sentence with probation may be appropriate where the amount withheld ranges from EUR 100,000 to EUR 1,000,000. Where the amount withheld is less than EUR 100,000, the Court has held that a fine is usually a more appropriate penalty. However, where unlawful tax refunds are obtained, the potential sanctions are higher; for instance, where an amount of EUR 50,000 is illegally obtained, a custodial sentence with probation may be imposed.[19]

In a recent tax fraud case involving the improper treatment of employees as self-employed persons, the ensuing wage tax and VAT resulted in a custodial sentence of 5 years and 6 months. However, this sentence included charges for the wrongful withholding of employee salaries, which accounted for approximately half of the sentence.[20] In another case involving the artificial interposition of a Swiss corporation into a royalties payment stream, resulting in EUR 2,000,000 of illegally obtained funds, a custodial sentence of 2 years and 10 months was imposed.[21]

---

18 See Federal Supreme Court 1 StR 525/11.
19 See Federal Supreme Court 1 StR 416/08; Federal Supreme Court 1 StR 116/11.
20 See Regional Court of Düsseldorf 014 KLs-130 Js 62/05-8/10.
21 See Federal Supreme Court 1 StR 492/11.

12. CURRENT TRENDS

International media has increasingly reported on the topic of corporate tax strategies and the tax rates paid by well-known multinationals, such as Starbucks and Google. The German media have taken up this topic, and since 2013, a public debate has been developing regarding the 'fair share' that international corporates should contribute to the German budget. The public debate has focused largely on the strategies employed by corporates that are subjected to a remittance-based taxation for their foreign undertakings, for whom there is a benefit to be gained by keeping funds off-shore in order to shelter them from taxes.

In contrast, German international tax law employs a world-income approach, where all global income is, unless exempted under a tax treaty, subject to German income tax, irrespective of whether or not it is distributed. Equally, German CFC rules target any income derived by a subsidiary of a German taxpayer that is subject to low taxation abroad, unless the taxpayer can show that it was derived from an eligible active business.

Therefore, most of the structures discussed as abusive in the current debate would not apply to a German parent. Measures aimed at such structures are somewhat difficult to integrate into national laws. At the same time, any measures aimed at increasing source-state taxation impede Germany's fiscal interests, as Germany still has a foreign trade surplus and is a substantial export nation, such that source-state taxation is more costly to the Revenue than residence-based taxation.

12.1 National policy and law

In recent national debates on the tax affairs of multinational corporations, calls for additional measures targeting international tax planning have increased. The debates highlight the perceived imbalances in the taxation of individuals and corporations, and impose pressure on the government authorities to act to prevent tax structuring strategies that may be used by corporations. Accordingly, the Bundesrat, Germany's second legislative chamber, passed a resolution on 'fighting international tax structures' in May 2014.[22] This resolution calls for the Government to introduce a pan-European registration requirement for international tax planning measures, and for the inclusion of a registration requirement for such structures in national German law. A similar registration requirement for tax structures has been discussed in previous legislative proposals.[23] For example, under a previous proposal, advisors marketing a tax structure were required to register it with the Federal Tax Office, and taxpayers were required to quote the registration number in their tax returns. The design of the current proposal has yet to be determined.

22 Bundesrats-Drucksache 205/14 dated 23 May 2014.
23 See Bundesrats-Drucksache 544/1/07 dated 11 September 2007.

12.1.1 The impact and role of the OECD and other international relations

Germany is an active member of the OECD, and is currently participating in the OECD BEPS Project.[24] Sources close to the German Ministry of Finance have, however, stressed that Germany aims not only at preventing profit shifting and base erosion, but also at preventing German multi-nationals from being hit with double taxation. Therefore, at technical level, there will be a balanced approach to this, aiming at achieving the targets set out in the Paris declaration on the one hand, whilst ensuring that this does not give rise to double taxation on the other hand. At the same time, Germany has already taken substantial national law measures aimed at curbing base erosion and profit shifting, such as the measures on shifting of functions.

Additionally, Germany is one of the most adamant supporters of the Common Corporate Consolidated Tax Base (the 'CCCTB') Project, aimed at curbing profit shifting within the EU.[25] Germany's position is that the CCCTB should be mandatory in order to prevent forum shopping by taxpayers. Although the EU has reached a general agreement on taking measures to curb unfair tax competition, there are substantial differences of opinion among the member states regarding the nature of fair and unfair tax competition. These differences are exacerbated by the fact that income tax law is not part of the common structure and jurisdiction of the EU, but rather, remains within the domain of the individual member states. As such, the current debate will likely continue, as it will take some time for the member states to agree on a unified approach. This will likely delay the introduction of a unified tax base for EU enterprises.

24 The project is a follow-up to the 'Declaration on Base Erosion and Profit Shifting' adopted 29 May 2013 at the Paris OECD Council.

25 As outlined in COM(2011 121/4): Proposal for a Council Directive on a Common Consolidated Corporate Tax Base (CCCTB).

Greece

Potamitisvekris Law Firm
Aspasia Malliou & Ifigeneia Efthimiou

PART ONE: TRANSFER PRICING

1. GENERAL OVERVIEW

Specific transfer pricing legislation has been in force in Greece since 2009.[1] Since then, it had been constantly changing and evolving until it was finalized with the new tax laws 4172/2013 (Greek Income Tax Code) and 4174/2013 (Tax Procedures Code).[2] Specific transfer pricing rules were officially introduced in Greece by the Greek Ministry of Development in 2009 but they were subsequently abolished in 2013.[3] Previously, the Greek Income Tax Code provided a general rule (article 39 of L.2238/1994) which was amended many times throughout the years and remained in force along with L.3728/2008 until 2013. The main aim of the provisions are to set out that where an agreement for the supply of goods or services concludes between Greek affiliate enterprises, or between Greek and foreign affiliate enterprises, and the agreed contractual consideration differs unjustifiably from what would have been agreed for a comparable transaction in similar market conditions if said enterprises were unrelated/independent enterprises, then any amount over or under the amount invoiced, according to the above, would be considered an accrued deemed profit for the respective local enterprise and, therefore, should be included in its actual (net) profits and be taxed accordingly. The above rule, as well as 39A of L.2238/1994 (TP documentation) were abolished on December 31, 2013 and were replaced by new provisions introduced in the new Greek Income Tax Code (L.4172/2014).

2. IDENTIFICATION OF LEGISLATIVE FRAMEWORK

The specific transfer pricing legislation sets a new regime for transfer pricing regulations in Greece. It is important to highlight that the existence of two laws (ie, article 26 of L.3728/2008 and articles 39 and 39A of Greek ITC) that implemented transfer pricing rules within the same time period have created many problems and discrepancies for MNEs, as well as Greek companies.[4] Therefore, as of January 1, 2014 onwards, the new provisions attempt to harmonize the issue by appointing the Ministry of Finance as the

1 Article 26 of L.3728/18-12-2008 Ministry of Development – Ministerial Decision A2 8092/31.12.2008-FEK 2709/B/31.12.2008.
2 Ministerial Decision POL 1097-FEK 883/9-04-2014 and POL 1144/2014.
3 L.4110/2013/FEK 17/ /23-1-2013 and 4170/2013 Ministry of Finance – Ministerial Circular POL 1179/18-7-2013 and 1120/ 26-9-2013.
4 Article 26 of L.3728/2008 – Article 39 of L.2238/1994 as amended by laws 3775/2009, 3842/2010, 4110/2013.

responsible body for transfer pricing tax audits. As a result, the legislation has been altered many times throughout these years and companies should be cautious because obligations and details on TP documentation may differ from year to year.

2.1 Federal and provincial legislation

No distinction between federal and provincial legislation exists in Greece.

2.2 State legislative interplay

The main points of the new transfer pricing legislation, which are introduced by the new ITC and Tax Procedures Code (L.4172/2013[5] and L.4174/2012[6]), are described below and have been effective since January 1, 2014:

- In principle, as provided in the relevant provisions of the new Greek transfer pricing legislation, intragroup transactions of Greek legal entities and foreign permanent establishments (ie, transactions with headquarters and related parties) seated in Greece are subject to Greek transfer pricing rules.
- A broader definition of the meaning of affiliated enterprises is provided. The new law defines the term 'associated person', which extends to legal persons, individuals and any other body of persons. The term encompasses two persons whereby: i) one of them holds directly, or indirectly, at least 33 per cent of shares, parts or quotas in the other, estimated on the basis of total value or number, or equivalent profit participation rights or voting rights, ii) another person participates directly, or indirectly, in any of the aforementioned ways, or iii) between them, there is direct or indirect management dependence or control or the possibility for one person to exercise decisive influence on the other, or of a third person to do so in both of them.
- Furthermore, the concept of 'business restructurings' is introduced. Specifically, a business restructuring must be effected in accordance with the arm's length principle. It is stated that in the case of an intercompany business restructuring, either local or cross-border, in which there is transferred goodwill or intangible assets or assigned their use, then such transfer should be performed at a price which shall be in compliance with the arm's length principle. Moreover, the reallocation of risks and functions in the context of this restructuring should be performed in accordance with the arm's length principle by taking into account other comparable cases.
- As regards to the transfer pricing methods used, apart from the traditional transaction methods (ie, comparable uncontrolled price, resale price and cost plus) and the transactional methods (ie, net margin and profit split) under FY 2008-2011, any other appropriate method was accepted if it was sufficiently documented. However, for FY 2012 and

[5] Articles 2 and 50 of L.4172/2013 – Definition for associated entities/intragroup transactions.
[6] Article 21 of L.4174/2013- Transfer Pricing Documentation File.

onwards, the Ministry of Finance makes references to the traditional and transactional transfer pricing methods.

- The new law includes enhanced obligations for Greek affiliated enterprises to maintain transfer pricing documentation for their intragroup transactions. In addition, the law includes specific deadlines for drafting of documentation and the electronic submission of a summarized table of transfer pricing information to the Greek Tax Authority. Within a four month deadline, taxpayers must electronically submit a summarized Information Table in relation to their intercompany transactions to the General Secretariat of Informative Systems of the Ministry of Finance.
- Exemptions from the transfer pricing documentation obligation are available in the following cases: a) Intragroup transactions or transfers of functions with one or more related parties not exceeding EUR 100,000 annually and in total, provided the taxpayer's turnover during the fiscal year does not exceed EUR 5,000,000 or b) Intragroup transactions or transfers of functions with one or more related parties not exceeding EUR 200,000 annually and in total, provided the taxpayer's turnover during the fiscal year exceeds EUR 5,000,000. If the intercompany transactions or transfers of functions (in total and not per category of transaction or per counterparty) exceed the EUR 100,000 or EUR 200,000 thresholds annually, then the documentation requirement is triggered for every separate intragroup transaction or transfer of function, irrespective of its value.

Apart from the main aspects of the new legislation listed above, there have been significant changes in Greek transfer pricing rules which can be summarized in the most crucial points:

- The definition of associated companies has been altered in the different laws introducing transfer pricing rules (two transfer pricing regimes as referred above);
- The threshold[7] of intercompany transactions for documentation or other reporting obligations has also changed;
- Penalties have varied between the two regimes (as provided in the two legislations which are currently aligned with the penalties provided by the Ministry of Finance); and
- Since the amendments in 2013, all types of intragroup transactions fall under the scope of transfer pricing, including loans and transfer of shares, parts and real estate property.

2.3 International treaties and agreements

Greece (a member of the OECD since 1961) has signed and ratified 54 bilateral conventions for avoiding double taxation with third countries.

It is widely accepted, that transfer pricing issues arise mostly on crossborder transactions. In this context, transfer pricing issues should be

[7] Threshold-Value of each type of intragroup transaction for every counterparty which is subject to TP documentation: For FY 2008–2009 over EUR 200.000 For FY 2010–2011 over EUR 100.000
For FY 2012–2013 over 20.000 For FY 2014 0.

examined in the framework of the Double Tax Avoidance Conventions and specifically, articles 9 and 25 of the OECD Model. Furthermore, transfer pricing methodology should be aligned with the Guidelines provided by the OECD.

(a) Taxation of associated enterprises

In particular, according to the provisions of article 9 of the OECD Model, where a) an enterprise of a Contracting State participates directly or indirectly in the management, control or capital of an enterprise of the other Contracting State, or b) the same persons participate directly or indirectly in the management, control or capital of an enterprise of a Contracting State and an enterprise of the other Contracting State, and in either case, conditions are made or imposed between the two enterprises in their commercial or financial relations which differ from those which would be made between independent enterprises, any profits which would, but for those conditions, have accrued by one of the enterprises, but, by reason of those conditions, have not so accrued, may be included in the profits of that enterprise and taxed accordingly.

The provisions of the Double Taxation Avoidance Agreements, which follow article 9 of the OECD Model Tax Convention, provide for the correction of profits of a company in the case of a breach of the arm's length principle. In this case, however, a respective reallocation of the profits of the connected company of the other country is required in order to avoid a double (financial) taxation. In this context, the reallocation takes place after the tax authorities of the contracting parties have been in contact/exchange of information for this particular case. The provisions of article 9 apply to associated enterprises of the two contracting parties. Therefore, there are two elements that outline the scope (subject) of the application of article 9: the definition of the company and the relation between enterprises.

The provisions of DTT in article 9 apply to cases where two companies implement conditions or terms on commercial or financial relationships between them which differ from those that would have prevailed between independent companies. As deemed from the wording of the provision, the existence of commercial or financial relations is an essential prerequisite for its application. The second prerequisite is a violation of the arm's length principle. The criterion for compliance with this principle is the financial terms of the transactions, not their price. The third prerequisite is that the violation of the arm's length principle should result in a reduction of taxable profit. Therefore, in order for the legal consequences to be enacted, there should be proof of the performance of reduced profit. In addition, the reduction of the profit should be attributed to the commercial or financial terms of the transaction. Hence, in order for an adjustment of profits to take place, the reduction of the profit should be attributed not to a specific commercial or financial relationship, but to their relationship as a whole. This is due to the fact that in a specific transaction, a deviation from the arm's length principle may occur but this deviation may be offset by an advantage of another transaction. In essence, there is no profit reduction in such a case, therefore, the provisions of profit adjustments will not be applied.

Double taxation avoidance is introduced in article 9, whereas article 25 mentions the process of the application of article 9.

(b) Mutual agreement procedure

The mutual agreement[8] is a well-established means through which tax administrations consult to resolve disputes regarding the application of double tax conventions. This procedure, described and authorized by article 25 of the OECD Model Tax Convention, can be used to eliminate double taxation that could arise from a transfer pricing adjustment. Article 25 sets out three different areas where mutual agreement procedures are generally used. The first area includes instances of 'taxation not in accordance with the provisions of the Convention' and is covered in paragraphs one and two of the article. Procedures in this area are typically initiated by the taxpayer. The other two areas, which do not necessarily involve the taxpayer, are dealt with in paragraph three and involve questions of 'interpretation or application of the Convention' and the elimination of double taxation in cases not otherwise provided for in the Convention. Paragraph nine of the Commentary on article 25 makes clear that article 25 is intended to be used by competent authorities in resolving juridical and economic double taxation issues arising from transfer pricing adjustments made pursuant to paragraphs 1 and 2 of article 9. Paragraph 5 of article 25, which was incorporated in the OECD Model Tax Convention in 2008,[9] provides that, in the cases where the competent authorities are unable to reach an agreement within two years of the initiation of a case under paragraph one of article 25, the unresolved issues will, at the request of the person who presented the case, be solved through an arbitration process. It is worth mentioning that Greece has incorporated the new arbitration clause of article 25 into recently concluded Double Tax Avoidance Treaties such as those with Mexico and Canada. Furthermore, it should be noted that on July 23, 1990, the Member States of the European Communities signed a multilateral Arbitration Convention to resolve transfer pricing disputes among themselves. The Arbitration Convention entered into force on January 1, 1995. In any case, for greater certainty, the taxpayer should protect their rights of domestic appeal since Greece (expressed with a reservation on the relevant clause of the OECD Model) associates the mechanism of MAP with the rights provided in Greek tax legislation. Thus, the procedure also relies on domestic law for implementation.

3. NATIONAL POLICY ISSUES

Historically, Greek law[10] provides that transactions between associated companies should be examined by comparing the corresponding

8 OECD Transfer Pricing Guidelines for Multinational Enterprises and Tax Administrations.
9 OECD Improving the resolution of tax treaty disputes (adopted by the Committee on Fiscal Affairs on 30 January 2007).
10 Greek IFA Branch Report on Transfer Pricing and Intangibles by Aspasia Malliou and Katerina Savvaidou, Cahiers de droit fiscal international, IFA 2007, Kyoto Congress.

transactions of those companies with independent third parties. In order, to ascertain the existence of an unjustifiable price in a transaction between associated companies, it is necessary to take into account the price that would have been agreed on in the case of a contract with another independent person, according to the prevailing market conditions at the time at which the contract under consideration was drafted. As a general remark, it should be noted that the Circulars (interpretative) issued by the competent Ministries[11] have focused mostly on the preparation of TP Documentation Files, references on the selection of the transfer pricing methodology and other procedural issues.

3.1 Overall national policy announcements

Definition for intragroup transactions as provided in article 50 of the new ITC

The new definition of intragroup transactions, as provided in article 50 of the Greek ITC, adopts a large portion of the wording of article 9 of the OECD Model Tax Convention on Income and Capital. When legal persons or legal entities perform one or more transactions – domestic or foreign – with associated persons, as defined in article 2 of ITC (Income Taxation Code mentioned above), with financial or commercial terms which are different to those that would have been agreed between non-related persons (independent enterprises) or between associated persons and third parties, the profits that would have been incurred by the legal person or the legal entity without these terms that were not realized due to the different terms (arm's length principle), are included in the profits of the legal person or the legal entity as far as they don't reduce the tax due. The previous provision is applicable and interpreted pursuant to the general principles and guidelines of the OECD for transfer-pricing.

As mentioned above in the relevant provision, it is now specified that the entities that are subject to compliance with the arm's length principle and, therefore, documenting of transactions, are considered legal entities **and other entities** when performing transactions with related entities. This addition seems to broaden the frame of application of the respective obligation, since it now expressly includes, aside from legal entities also, other entities in general.

3.2 National revenue authority initiatives

APA procedure

Article 22[12] of L.4174/13 introduces the provisions for concluding Advance Pricing Agreements to the Greek tax law. These agreements have been regulated and applied in seventeen (17) out of 28 state-members of the EU (Austria, Belgium, France, Germany, Denmark, UK, Ireland, Spain, Italy, Netherlands, Hungary, Poland, Portugal, Romania, Slovakia, Sweden, Czech Republic) and internationally in countries such as US, Japan, Russia

11 MoD A2 8092/31.12.2008-FEK 2709/B/31.12.2008-MoF POL 1179/18-7-2013 and POL 1120/ 26-9-2013.
12 Introductory interpretation on the provisions of the new tax procedures code L.4174/2013.

etc. The Advance Pricing Agreements contributes to the creation of a stable tax frame because, with them, costly and protracted tax controls of transnational transactions are avoided, the cost of compliance is reduced and, consequently, the double taxation is avoided. The EU guidelines for the Advance Pricing Agreements (Annex of the Announcement of the European Commission for the Transfer Pricing EU Forum for the avoidance and resolution of disputes 2007), for which Greece has been politically bound at ECOFIN, were applied for the creation of the proposed provisions.

The Europe Commission defines the guidelines for the Advance Pricing Agreements as an effective measure for the avoidance of tax disputes with important advantages both for the Tax Authorities and the tax payers. The guidelines explain which methods the state-members can apply this process to and provide guides for tax payers that are engaged in the process.

It has been mentioned that the proposed Agreements by the OECD and EU Guidelines, mentioned above, are agreements between the companies and the State. However, it is arguable as to whether the Greek law permits the direct signing of such an Agreement. For this reason, the General Secretary for Tax Affairs chooses to issue administrative acts.

In this framework, as of January 1, 2014, the Tax Procedures Code provides the possibility of an APA for Greek corporations in regards to their future intragroup pricing. An APA will cover any relevant criteria used for the determination of the intragroup pricing. These criteria mainly include the transfer pricing method, the comparable data to be used and any relevant adjustments to be made, as well as the critical assumptions under which the transfer pricing methodology approved will remain valid. An APA term cannot exceed four years and retroactive effect will not be possible. The Tax Procedures Code does not exclude the determination of the pricing or margin from the APA procedure. The APA may be revised, revoked or cancelled in the case that the taxpayer does not comply with the terms thereof, if the critical assumptions change or are proved incorrect, if a different outcome arising in the context of the mutual agreement procedure pursuant to the relevant bilateral tax treaty or in the context of the convention of the member states of the European Union on the correction of profits of associated enterprises. The publication of an APA decision does not prevent to initiate at a later stage the mutual agreement procedure, as provided in the relevant Double Tax Avoidance Treaty or the European Convention for the elimination of double taxation in connection with the adjustment of profits of associated enterprises (tax arbitration convention) for the identical transactions of the taxpayer.

(a) APA procedure as from 1.1.2014

The General Secretary of Public Revenues of Greece issued a Ministerial Decision POL 1284/31.12.2013, in relation to the procedures for the conclusion, amendment, revocation and annulment of an Advance Pricing Arrangement (APA). It is applicable for both unilateral and bilateral APAs and can be effective for cross border intercompany transactions from January 1, 2014 and onwards.

- The interested entity has the option to seek for preliminary consultation in order to investigate as to whether the application has the chance to be accepted by the tax authorities. In this respect, the interested party submits necessary information which is covered by tax secrecy rules.
- The next step is to file an application for an APA (if a preliminary hearing occurred the deadline is 30 days after its conclusion).
- Within the framework of the application, the interested party should file necessary data. As an example, for a company, the necessary data would be group structure, proposed transfer pricing method and in general, all available documentation as described in the relevant Decision, etc. Furthermore, any element that may play a significant role in the transactions and the trends of the relevant business (such as industry and market trends, description of the business strategy, functional analysis, financial data etc.) should be filed with the relevant authorities.
- The competent tax audit Directorate evaluates the application and has the right to ask for additional information from the applicant or to seek information from foreign tax authorities following the procedures on information exchange provided by the relevant Double Tax Treaties.
- After the completion of the evaluation procedure, the tax audit Directorate prepares a report presenting its conclusions. This report is provided to the applicant and for bilateral APAs, to the competent authority of the countries involved in the procedure.
- At the final stage, a hearing is arranged (within 10 days after the evaluation procedure) between the parties so as to reach to a mutually acceptable agreement on the terms of the APA. In the event that an agreement is achieved, a summary of the APA is drafted and signed by the relevant parties. If no consensus is attained, the summary will describe the rejection of the APA.
- Where the APA is concluded, the relevant APA decision should contain information such as the data of the applicant, the intercompany transactions covered, information on the counterparties, the conclusion of the tax authorities, the duration of the APA procedure, details on the methodology agreed for the pricing etc. The relevant applicant is also obliged to file an annual compliance statement/report presenting supporting data.
- The APA can be revised at the request of the applicant or revoked/ annulled by the competent tax authority.
- The fees to be attributed by the applicant, during the APA process, are provided in the relevant Ministerial Decision POL1284/2013. In particular, for a preliminary consultation a fee of EUR 1.000 should be paid, for filing an APA application, a fee of EUR 5.000 should be paid and finally, for consultations with foreign tax authorities the fees amount to EUR 10.000 for each country involved.

(b) Tax certificate (applicable until December 31, 2015)

As per the provisions of the previous Greek Income Tax Code (article 82 of L.2238/1994) and the relevant Ministerial Decision 1159/22-07-2011, (applicable for Greek corporations to financial years ending from June 30, 2011 and onwards and for branches of foreign companies for financial years ending after December 2012 and onwards) transfer pricing documentation should be prepared and provided by the Greek entities to their certified auditors before the issuance of the annual tax certificate. The annual tax certificate is conducted along with the statutory audit by certified auditors. Its aim is to examine any pending tax obligations or violations in several tax areas. According to the provisions of articles 65A and 66 of the Tax Procedures Code L.4174/2013, the tax certificate procedure will be applicable until January 1, 2016. In light of the above information, it is clear that very few tax audits in relation to transfer pricing have been carried out by the Ministry of Finance during the past years.

3.3 Administrative statements

There is no precedent or guidelines for the performance of tax audits as regards to transfer pricing conducted by the Greek Ministry of Finance. Additionally, the aforementioned article 39 of L.2238/1994 imposes, on the local enterprise, a distinct penalty of 10 per cent on any deemed profit (ie, any amount over or under invoiced according to the above would be considered as an accrued deemed profit for the respective local enterprise and, therefore, it should be included in its actual (net) profits), irrespective of any additional tax assessment or other penalties provided for by the law.

With respect to the definition of the term 'affiliate enterprises', when it comes to transactions between a local entity and foreign entity, the article itself provides a relevant clarification. The article states that the foreign enterprise must have the control of the Greek enterprise through a participation either to the share capital participation or the administration of the local entity. However, the Greek case law has accepted, by way of a broader interpretation, that the scope of application of the above article may cover cases of local and foreign entities without capital participation or administrative control, to the extent that these entities belong to the same group of companies.

In terms of the definition and identification of 'comparable transactions', the wording of article 39 implies that only similar transactions (ie, provided for the same or similar supply) between the local entity in question and third parties would serve as a measure of comparison. The same approach has been followed by the case law of the Greek Council of State (the Supreme administrative Court of Greece). The Greek Council of State has held that the comparison for the existence of unjustifiable pricing in the transactions between affiliate entities should be made in reference to the pricing that would have been applied if the same agreement had been concluded with a third party under market conditions prevailing at the time that the agreement in question was in place. Therefore, it results that the Greek tax framework adopted, in essence, the Comparable Uncontrolled Price (CUP) method for the determination of the arm's length range by using solely internal comparables ie, comparable agreements between the Greek entity and third counterparties (internal CUP).

Furthermore, the jurisprudence has not dealt extensively with the above matter so as to set some general guidelines for the interpretation of the subject parameter. For instance, the Council of State has held that the granting of significant discounts in the sale of products between local entities within the scope of a commercial co-operation agreement is justifiable since the purchasing entity has undertaken some expenses for the promotion of the products purchased, which (expenses) otherwise (under normal conditions) would have burdened the supplier.

The Greek Ministry of Finance has issued a ministerial decision that provides guidance on the contents of the transfer pricing documentation file, the parties subject to the transfer pricing rules and exemptions therefrom, language requirements, transfer pricing documentation methods and the content of the summary information table. The new ministerial decision POL 1097, issued April 9, 2014 and its amending POL 1144/2014 is, to a great extent, similar to a previous decision (POL 1179/2013), which provided guidance and clarifications on Greek transfer pricing rules and documentation requirements under the previous tax regime (Income Tax Code L.2238/1994). The older decision is still applicable for fiscal years ending on or before 31 December 2013. According to the new ministerial decision, the deadline for submission of the summary information table (SIT) remains the end of the fourth month following the taxpayer's fiscal year end. The SIT may only be filed electronically on the webpage of the General Secretariat of Information Systems (GSIS) of the Greek Ministry of Finance. Submission of the SIT requires the use of a special application (xml file), that is provided by the Ministry of Finance, and should meet the specifications set forth by the ministry in the new decision's appendix, also available on the GSIS website. It should be noted that the SIT is attached to the Greek transfer pricing file and is filed electronically with the tax authorities merely for information purposes. The SIT should not, by any means, be considered complete and sufficient transfer pricing documentation that supports the compliance of the taxpayer's intragroup transactions with the arm's length principle. Under the Code of Tax Procedures, taxpayers must prepare the transfer pricing documentation file within four months following the end of their fiscal year. The transfer pricing file must be kept at the taxpayer's premises, according to the provisions of the Code of Tax Recording Transactions. The transfer pricing documentation file must be made available to the tax authorities within 30 days following a request. Furthermore, the recent Ministerial Circular POL 1144/2014 states and implements the wording of the OECD Transfer Pricing Guidelines for MNEs and focuses on the update of the Documentation File when market conditions change or any other change or transaction might impact the function of the Group entity.

New issues posed by the latest Ministerial Circular POL 1097/2014

- An important provision of this ministerial decision is the newly enacted obligation to include a 'special chapter' in the transfer pricing documentation file, whereby the taxpayer is required to describe all

facts and events of the prior fiscal year that have an impact on the information and data included in the file and that are due to market condition changes. The taxpayer may use the existing transfer pricing documentation file to cover also the next fiscal year's transfer pricing documentation requirements, provided that file is updated and includes all necessary changes. The taxpayer must disclose all the sections of the existing documentation file that were updated with relation to the previous fiscal year. The documentation file must be updated within four months following the end of the fiscal year.
- A transfer pricing documentation file will be considered incomplete or inadequate by the local tax authorities if, during the course of an audit, it is not possible for the auditor to verify the correctness of the calculations or the transfer pricing documentation methods used, even after additional information has been provided to the auditor. When the documentation file is deemed incomplete or inadequate, a one-off penalty is calculated at the rate of 1 per cent on the taxpayer's revenues during the fiscal year under review, including any adjustments to the taxpayer's profits. This penalty cannot be less than EUR 10,000 or more than EUR 100,000.

3.4 Administrative guidelines

However, as from the first introduction of transfer pricing rules in Greece until today, the general principles and OECD guidelines have been applied as important resources for transfer pricing purposes in Greece. According to the recent interpretation by the Ministry of Finance, it seems that for FY 2012 and onwards, the accepted transfer pricing methods are the traditional transaction methods and transactional methods in comparison to the previous tax regime that accepted any other method as provided in the OECD 'Transfer Pricing Guidelines for Multinationals and Tax Administrations'.

The BEPS project initiated by the OECD focuses on developing new tax policy tools to address 'double non taxation' caused by current deficiencies in the international tax system. In particular the OECD Discussion Draft on TP Documentation and CbC reporting underlines the following aspects:
- Major transactions including intangibles, intercompany loans and business restructurings are proposed to be in the Master File.
- The local file should present the impact of major transactions to the local entity.
- CbC reporting in order to enable TP risk assessment.

4. CASE LAW

Case laws are not widely known since TP rules have only been recently adopted in Greece. Furthermore, from FY 2011 and onwards, the tax certificate audit by certified auditors covers also TP reporting and documentation as mentioned above. Nevertheless, we will enumerate cases in relation to the prior general arm's length principle (eg, tax adjustments on the revenues of Greek entities due to over or under pricing) provided in the previous tax regime (ie, article 39 of the previous ITC before the implementation of transfer pricing rules). A significant element that should be taken into consideration is the fact that, until now, the burden of proof lay with the tax authorities to substantiate the hidden profits deriving from over or under pricing. As of January 1, 2014, the new Tax Procedures Code provides that the burden of proof lies with the taxpayer in order to convince the tax authorities that they have not committed over or under pricing so as to avoid taxation in Greece. This shifting of the burden from the tax authorities to the taxpayer does not seem to comply with the fundamental principles of taxation as provided in the Greek Constitution.

However,[13] it should also be noted that the OECD guidelines on determining the arm's length price are followed to an extent, as the 'normal' price is determined on a transaction-by-transaction basis and therefore is not objectively defined for all transactions. Moreover, in order to distinguish an unjustifiable price from a 'normal' price, the specific transaction between associated companies is compared with corresponding similar transactions of the same companies with independent parties, taking into account the prevailing market conditions at the time that the contract was drawn up.

Indeed, Greek law also attempted to adhere to the OECD guidelines in regards to ascertaining the arm's length principle for the subjective features of the transaction under consideration. Specifically, the particular circumstances that characterize each transaction – a fact that could lead to differentiating the arm's length price from the real market price. This is expressly attempted through the condition set out in article 39 ITC. In applying 39 ITC, it is not sufficient to simply ascertain that the price covenanted in the sales and purchase agreements or service agreements between two companies is over or under the "normal" price, but that this divergence is not justifiable. Therefore, an attempt at considering the particular circumstances of each specific transaction is made by providing companies with the possibility f avoiding the application of article 39 ITC, by justifying the overpricing or under pricing. It should be noted, however, that Greek law did not determine the specific reasons that would be sufficient to justify overpricing or underpricing, but rather allowed this issue to be interpreted by the courts. Nevertheless, Greek law and court practice diverged from the OECD guidelines, as in determining the arm's length price the roles undertaken by the contractual parties are considered, and are determined, for example, by reference to the financial risk that each of the associated companies undertakes, etc.

Additionally, even though Greek law provided for the adjustment of the taxable profits of a company that has overpriced or accepted underpricing, it did not also provide – unlike article 9 of the OECD model – the possibility for the contracting company to adjust its profits. This may result in the double taxation of the relevant profits at group level. Therefore, this double taxation, which may occur due to the unilateral price change applied by a

13 Greek IFA Branch Report on Transfer Pricing and Intangibles by Aspasia Malliou and Katerina Savvaidou, Cahiers de droit fiscal international, IFA 2007 Kyoto Congress.

domestic company for a transaction within the group, without this being compensated by a corresponding price adjustment in the other Greek company, constitutes an indirect tax penalty for the companies of the group. It is not possible to resolve this issue in the context of the mutual agreement procedure provided by article 25 of the OECD model. Recourse to this procedure is possible with respect to transactions between a Greek and foreign company, with head offices in a state with which Greece has entered into a convention for the avoidance of double taxation and whose profits were adjusted by the foreign authorities or vice versa.

4.1 Current cases

Due to the recent implementation of transfer pricing rules, at the moment, no recent court cases have been released to the best of our knowledge.

4.2 Historical cases of note

According to case law, in order to consider a deviation between associated companies as an accounting difference, the divergence from 'normal prices' must be substantiated with evidence. Therefore, unlike the guidelines of the OECD, the explicit legal priority in this method, based on determining the normal price seems, to exclude the application of other methods in addition to price comparison. Indeed, this is demonstrated by the fact that the case law of the Greek courts has deflected the efforts of the tax authorities to apply a different method, such as the simple comparison of the gross or net profits of an associated company with the corresponding profit margin (profit rate determined by law) for professionals of the same category – a method that simulated the cost plus profit method, defined in the OECD guidelines.

Indeed, the Greek tax authorities have particular difficulties in identifying the comparable transactions required for determining real market prices, due mainly to their inability to access relevant databases in order to obtain the pertinent data. The application of article 39 ITC depended on the contracting companies' intent to avoid direct or indirect taxes. Specifically, article 39 ITC did not apply if the contracting parties proved that the overpricing, or the underpricing, did not occur with the intent of avoiding direct or indirect taxes. In accordance with the relevant circular of the Minister of Finance, the provisions of article 39 ITC did not apply if during the audit, no proof of hiding profits by over or under pricing came to light. In contrast to article 9 of the OECD Model, the purpose of which is to avoid double taxation, article 39 ITC is an anti avoidance clause. In practice, however, the case law of the Greek courts attempts to nullify this way of thinking, by accepting that the intent of taxation avoidance, in the sense of article 39 ITC, is presumed if there is proof of a tax advantage to the contracting parties arising from such over or under pricing.

In the past, the legislative scope of article 39 ITC did not determine the reasons that could justify overpricing or underpricing, nor have these been codified in case law to date with objective reasons or criteria that could suggest relevant indications. Conversely, the Council of State has formulated judgments on a case-by-case basis with respect to the reasons that led to applying or excluding the presumption of article 39 ITC (prior to the implementation of specific transfer pricing rules in Greece).

Indicatively, before the implementation of specific transfer pricing rules in Greece, the Council of State accepted that granting increased credits for the sale of products was justified if the expenses for promoting the seller's products were borne by the buyer[14]. At the same time, the Council of State judged that the claim that the seller was not an independent business unit was not a sufficient reason for deviating from the arm's length principle. This is because it had been established in order to serve and organise the production of the associated businesses which were the sole buyers of its products.[15] Furthermore, the Council of State judged that the tax authority bears the burden of proof in underpricing or overpricing by invoking specific actual circumstances, which substantiate the unjustifiable divergence from normal prices.[16] The relevant claims of the tax authority must refer to specific information of price setting. Information on cost is not considered sufficient.[17] The average discounts granted between associated and third businesses for the same time period, and under the same conditions, could be considered as information on cost.[18] The comparison of fees must be made with respect to third parties, and not with respect to the fluctuation of fees between associated companies.[19]

5. PENALTIES

As mentioned above, penalties varied between the two legislative frameworks (initiated by the Ministry of Development and the Ministry of Finance) and implemented in Greece as from FY 2008 and onwards.

As provided in the OECD Guidelines for transfer pricing, in order to eliminate double taxation in transfer pricing cases, tax administrations may consider requests for corresponding adjustments. A corresponding adjustment, which in practice may be undertaken as part of the mutual agreement procedure, can mitigate or eliminate double taxation in cases where one tax administration increases a company's taxable profits (ie, makes a primary adjustment) as a result of applying the arm's length principle to transactions involving an associated enterprise in a second tax jurisdiction. The corresponding adjustment, in such a case, is a downward adjustment to the tax liability of that associated enterprise, made by the tax administration of the second jurisdiction, so that the allocation of profits between the two jurisdictions is consistent with the primary adjustment and no double taxation occurs. It is also possible that the first tax administration will agree to decrease (or eliminate) the primary adjustment as part of the consultative process with the second tax administration, in which case, the corresponding adjustment would be smaller (or perhaps unnecessary). It

14 Greek Supreme Administrative Court Decision (STE) 660/1995.
15 Greek Supreme Administrative Court Decision (STE) 4413/1996.
16 Greek Supreme Administrative Court Decision (STE) 3803/1988.
17 Greek Supreme Administrative Court Decision (STE) 3455/1995.
18 Greek Supreme Administrative Court Decision (STE) 661/1995.
19 Greek Supreme Administrative Court Decision (STE) 4464/1997.

should be noted that a corresponding adjustment is not intended to provide a benefit to the MNE group that is greater than if the controlled transactions had been undertaken at arm's length conditions in the first instance.

It should be mentioned that, in the event of tax adjustments from income tax perspective,[20] penalties for inaccurate filing of a CIT return may be imposed. These penalties range from 10 per cent up to 100 per cent , depending on the difference (ie, tax assessed by the tax authorities – declared income on CIT return).

5.1 Types

Apart from the tax adjustments determined on a case by case basis, the other transfer pricing penalties on the non filing/late or inaccurate filing of Information Table/Documentation File imposed may be summarized and presented as follows:[21,22]

Penalties	FY 2008–2009	FY 2010–2011	FY 2012–2013	FY 2014
Penalty for non-filing of the table/list presenting intragroup transactions	10 per cent of the amount of intragroup transactions	10 per cent of the amount of intragroup transactions	1 per cent of the turnover (minimum EUR 10,000–maximum EUR 100,000)	
Penalty for inaccurate filing list/table	Inaccurate filing is considered as non-filing of the transactions	Inaccurate filing is considered as non-filing of the transactions	No provision exists	1 per cent of the turnover (minimum EUR 10,000–maximum EUR 100,000)
Penalty for late filing list/table	0.1 per cent of the turnover (minimum EUR 1,000–maximum EUR 10,000)			
Penalty for not submitting TP Documentation File	10 per cent of the amount of intragroup transactions	20 per cent of the amount of intragroup transactions	1 per cent of the turnover (minimum EUR 10,000–maximum EUR 100,000)	
Penalty for late submission of TP Documentation File	10 per cent of the amount of intragroup transactions	20 per cent of the amount of intragroup transactions	1 per cent of the turnover (minimum EUR 1,000–maximum EUR 10,000)	

[20] Article 58 of L.4174/2013 penalties for non or inaccurate filing.

[21] EY Presentation – Practical issues on the implementation of transfer pricing rules in Greece.

[22] Article 56 of L.4174/2013 – penalty for late or inaccurate filing of Intragroup Information Table or Transfer Pricing Documentation File.

Penalties for tax adjustments due to over- or under-pricing	10 per cent of the profit difference	20 per cent of the profit difference	No provision exists	No provision exists

5.2 Special or notable cases

The former competent Directorate of the Ministry of Development, which performed tax audits in relation to transfer pricing during the past years, has imposed penalties (for non compliance to the Greek transfer pricing legislation) amounting to approximately EUR 2.2 million on two MNEs in Greece. Furthermore, the Directorate has imposed over 300 penalties, amounting to EUR 2.3 million, for late filing of the list presenting the intragroup transactions.

As per recent press releases on an unofficial basis,[23] a common structure scrutinized by Greek tax inspectors on several occasions is the case of a Greek entity using the set up of intermediate companies (ie, offshore entities/established in privileged tax regimes/affiliate and non) aiming to overprice services or products from EU or third counties so as to shift profits outside of Greece and thus avoid taxation.

6. DISPUTE RESOLUTION MECHANISMS

During the past years, an Administrative Dispute Resolution Mechanism has been adopted by Greek tax legislation with the involvement of a Special Committee/Directorate. This procedure is new in Greece and its purpose, amongst others, was to reduce the amount of cases which ended in Administrative Courts for tax disputes. Thus far, the experience indicates that the procedure has been ineffective, since most cases continue to end in the courts due to the fact that an out of court settlement is not achieved. Furthermore, since a suspension of the execution of the penalty is not given in most cases, it seems that the taxpayers will be burdened according to the new tax regime to pay even 100 per cent of the imposed penalty plus surcharges (if any).

The new Administrative Dispute Resolution Mechanism should be examined by the Greek courts since it introduces a procedure by the tax authorities which may be considered as non compliant with the principles of the Greek Constitution (article 78).

6.1 Preferred national options

Since January 1, 2014, the competent Directorate for an out of court settlement has been the Directorate for Dispute settlement. According to the interpretative circulars issued and the relevant provisions (article 63 of tax Procedures Code), the relevant Directorate is the competent authority

[23] Article on offshore entities and relevant structures in Greek economy published by the officials of Greek Department for the Prosecution of Financial Crime.

for all tax disputes. In particular, the Code provides the filing of an out of court petition by the taxpayer for the review of the tax assessment act issued by the tax administration. The deadline for filing the relevant petition is 30 days from the notification of the act.

6.2 International options

The bilateral conventions for avoiding double taxation signed between Greece and other states contain a provision for setting in motion a MAP[24] (mutual agreement procedure), as per article 25 of the OECD Model. However, it should be remembered that Greece has expressed an explicit reservation in applying the prescription with respect to article 25. Greece[25] has made a reservation to the provisions of article 25 para. 2 of the OECD Model Tax Convention, expressing its view that 'the application of tax reliefs and tax returns after a mutual agreement should remain connected to the time periods provided by the national legislation'. However, the provision of article 25 para. 2 was adopted in the majority of tax conventions of Greece except for the agreements with Belgium, France, Germany, Denmark, Switzerland, USA, India, Italy, Cyprus, Mexico and Sweden.

As per the statistics published by the OECD, and the relevant unofficial information provided by the competent Directorate of International Economic Affairs, only few cases have initiated the process in Greece.

The Arbitration Convention (90/436/EEC) was ratified by Greece with L.216/1994, and the Protocol dated May 25, 1999 by L.3140/2003. As per article 25 of the OECD Model, following a relevant application of a taxpaying domestic company with relation to a foreign company in a state with which Greece has entered into a convention for avoiding double taxation and whose taxable profits were adjusted by the foreign tax authorities, the Greek authorities have never set a MAP in motion on their own initiative. However, this procedure has been set in motion following the initiative of foreign tax authorities in resolving double taxation issues, not necessarily linked to transfer pricing issues. With respect to the relevant procedures in the context of applying the Arbitration Convention, as per the information provided by the competent authority, Greece has not received numerous cases. In any event, Greece has not made use of the relevant provisions of the Arbitration Convention, mainly due to the difficulties in its application. The application of the Arbitration Convention by the Greek authorities is rendered even more difficult due to the interpretation of article 8. According to article 8, a company's right to apply the provisions of the convention depends on the condition of not having committed serious violations of the tax legislation in the past. According to a relevant statement by Greece, the meaning of serious tax violations is particularly broad. Therefore, by easily qualifying a tax violation as serious, Greece significantly reduces the company's rights to fall under the provisions of the Arbitration Convention.

24 Greek IFA Branch Report on Transfer Pricing and Intangibles by Aspasia Malliou and Katerina Savvaidou, Cahiers de droit fiscal international, IFA 2007, Kyoto Congress.
25 A. Tsouroufiis, Transfer pricing (Nomiki Vivliothiki, 2010).

PART TWO: TAX AVOIDANCE

7. ACCEPTABLE TAX PLANNING AREAS/SUBJECTS

A general anti avoidance tax rule was introduced in Greece on January 1, 2014 and has been effective since then. Until today, tax evasion was penalized in Greece in a general form with no particular provisions. In this respect, tax evasion was defined and interpreted as the shifting of profits to other jurisdictions that should have been taxed in Greece.

8. DEFINING ABUSIVE TAX AVOIDANCE

There is no other definition than the one described below.

9. THE LEGISLATIVE FRAMEWORK

A general anti abusive rule was introduced for the first time in Greece (article 38 of L.4174/26.07.2013, applicable as from January 1, 2014), as part of new measures to combat tax evasion, allowing tax authorities to disregard artificial arrangements set up for tax evasion purposes.

Upon assessing 'artificial arrangements' tax authorities should:

- Refer to the substance and business purpose of the arrangement, or lack thereof,
- Compare the tax burden triggered in the context of the potentially 'artificial arrangement', to the tax burden that would arise, in the absence of such arrangement. Please refer in detail to the relevant article below.

According to the aforementioned article 38 of L.4174/2013:

1. During the tax determination process the Tax Authority can ignore any artificial arrangement that aims at tax evasion and leads to a tax benefit. These agreements are treated, for tax purposes, according to their actual economical substance.
2. For the purposes of paragraph one, an arrangement means any transaction, scheme, action, operation, agreement, grant, understanding, promise, undertaking or event. An arrangement may comprise of more than one step or part.
3. For the purposes of paragraph one, an arrangement or a series of arrangements is artificial where it lacks commercial substance. In determining whether the arrangement or series of arrangements is artificial, the Tax Authority will examine whether they involve one or more of the following situations:
    (a) the legal characterisation of the individual steps which an arrangement consists of is inconsistent with the legal substance of the arrangement as a whole;
    (b) the arrangement or series of arrangements is carried out in a manner which would not ordinarily be employed in what is expected to be a reasonable business conduct;
    (c) the arrangement or series of arrangements includes elements which have the effect of offsetting or cancelling each other;
    (d) transactions concluded are circular in nature;

(e) the arrangement or series of arrangements results in a significant tax benefit but this is not reflected in the business risks undertaken by the taxpayer or its cash flows; or
(f) the expected pre-tax profit is insignificant in comparison to the amount of the expected tax benefit.

4. For the purposes of paragraph one, the purpose of an arrangement or series of arrangements avoids taxation where, regardless of any subjective intentions of the taxpayer, it defeats the object, spirit and purpose of the tax provisions that would otherwise apply.
5. For the purposes of paragraph one, a given purpose is to be considered essential where any other purpose that is, or could be, attributed to the arrangement or series of arrangements appears at most negligible, in view of all the circumstances of the case.
6. In determining whether an arrangement or series of arrangements has led to a tax benefit as referred to in paragraph one, the Tax Authority will compare the amount of tax due by a taxpayer, having regard to those arrangements, with the amount that the same taxpayer would owe under the same circumstances in the absence of the arrangement.

Furthermore, it should be underlined that expenses paid to natural persons or legal entities that are domiciled/seated in non cooperative States or States with privileged tax regime, as provided in the new ITC, would be considered as non deductible unless the Greek tax payer proves (ie, bears the burden of proof) that they are not connected with profit (income, capital) shifting or tax evasion or tax avoidance (articles 23 and 65 of L.4172/2013).

10. KEY CASES OF INTEREST

No case law is available since no particular anti avoidance provision existed in the past.

11. PENALTIES

In general, no guidelines have been given by the Ministry of Finance for the implementation of penalties in the event of anti-avoidance cases (article 38).

11.1 Legislative provisions

The legislative framework for penalties related with anti avoidance is provided in article 55 of L.4174/2013 (Tax Procedures Code). The penalties depend on each case (ie, fictitious invoices or direct and indirect taxation etc.) with reference on the thresholds for committing tax evasion and no specific indication on the actual penalties imposed. We enumerate below certain cases:

- Failure to submit or submission of an inaccurate tax income return (non-payment of a certain amount of tax >EUR 10,000 for single entry and >EUR 60,000 for double entry books).
- Failure to submit or submission of inaccurate VAT tax return or non-attribution of VAT or/and withholding taxes (non-payment of a certain amount of tax >EUR 10,000 for single entry and >EUR 60,000 for double

entry books). Obtain a tax refund after misleading the competent Greek authorities.
- Issuance of fictitious records (invoices) or distorted data: 100 per cent in value.
- Issuance and acceptance of fictitious invoices: 50 per cent in value (with a 15 per cent – 25 per cent reduction in some exceptional cases, or EUR 500 per data with fine up to EUR 50.000 per tax year under examination).
- Non-issuance or inaccurate issuance of documents of representing value >EUR 5.000 : 40 per cent of the transaction value with a minimum fine of EUR 2.500.
- Non filing or inaccurate filing of real estate tax/special property tax/ every other tax not included above.

Apart from the above, it should be mentioned that in the event of tax adjustments from an income tax perspective,[19] penalties for inaccurate filing of a CIT return may be imposed. These penalties range from 10 per cent up to 100 per cent , depending on the difference (ie, tax assessed by the tax authorities – declared income on CIT return). Also, the new Tax Procedures Code provides that in the case of a late payment of tax, the taxpayer is obliged to pay interest for the time period from the end of the legal deadline until the date of payment.

12. CURRENT TRENDS

As released in the Action plan of BEPS (BASE EROSION AND PROFIT SHIFTING 2013), countries around the world should agree on international rules that are clear and predictable. This will give certainty to both governments and enterprises aiming to eliminate tax evasion and profit shifting to low tax or no tax regimes.

12.1 National policy and law

CFC rules[26] are introduced for the first time in the Greek tax legislation with the aim of dealing with tax avoidance of Greek companies through shifting revenues to subsidiaries in low tax jurisdictions. Basically, these rules provide for the inclusion of undistributed 'passive' income (eg, interest, dividends, royalties etc.) of foreign subsidiaries in the taxable income of the Greek companies under the conditions stipulated in the law.

CFC rules are designed to combat the diversion by resident taxpayers of income to companies they control and that are typically resident in countries imposing low or no taxation. Pursuant to the new Greek CFC rules, the taxable income of a Greek tax resident entity could include the undistributed income of a foreign legal entity provided, amongst others, that the Greek tax resident holds (severally or jointly with affiliated persons) shares directly or indirectly, voting or dividend rights in the capital of such foreign entity exceeding 50 per cent and the latter entity is resident in a tax free or low tax jurisdiction.

26 Presentation of new Income Tax Code (L.4172/2013) by Zepos-Yannopoulos Law Firm.

As a general rule, EU entities fall outside the scope of Greek CFC rules (unless the legal entity is deemed to be an artificial arrangement generated for the purpose of tax avoidance – in line with EU case law). If deemed a CFC, all undistributed income would be considered as taxable (business) income of its Greek tax resident shareholder. The Greek CFC rules are effective as from January 1, 2014 and onwards.

12.1.1 The impact and role of the OECD and other international relations

From our analysis above, it is obvious that since January 1, 2014, Greek tax legislation makes an effort to keep up with the new trends taking into consideration that tax evasion in Greece has been a major and unsolved issue. In particular, for first time in Greece tax avoidance and CFC rules have been introduced and the transfer pricing legislation has been updated at a great extent. Thus, Greece being a member of OECD would have to follow the changes launched by OECD in terms of BEPS[27] and the global initiative to abolish base erosion and shifting of revenues.

[27] Action Plan on Base Erosion and Profit Shifting, OECD, 2013.

India

Singh & Associates, Advocates and Solicitors
Manoj K Singh

PART ONE: TRANSFER PRICING

1. GENERAL OVERVIEW

Transfer pricing refers to price setting strategies used by Multinational Enterprise ('MNE') groups in intragroup transactions to establish prices different from those that would have been obtained had the group members been dealing at arm's length. The concept of transfer pricing was first adopted by the US in 1968. Between 1979 and 1984, the Organisation for Economic Co-operation and Development (the 'OECD') prepared several reports on transfer pricing, and issued the Transfer Pricing Guidelines in 1995.

Transfer pricing, though an important part of India's income tax law, is not a defined term in the tax legislation. The Income Tax Act,1961, (the 'Income Tax Act' or 'Act') did not address transfer pricing per se, but disallowed 'excessive payments' between related parties. India formally adopted the OECD's concept of transfer pricing in 2000.

The term 'transfer price' refers to the actual price charged in a transaction between related entities that are part of the same MNE group. Since tax rates vary from country to country, there is an opportunity for MNE groups to set up transactions between group members to limit the tax liability of the group as a whole. This involves setting prices at a rate that is lower than that which would have been obtained had the enterprises been dealing at arm's length. The result is that less profit is recorded in countries with higher tax rates, thereby limiting the tax revenue of the host country.

To prevent the loss of tax revenue as a result of transfer pricing, new provisions were added to the Income Tax Act in April 2002. These provisions provide a detailed statutory framework for the computation of reasonable and equitable profits for multinational enterprises. Any income arising from an international transaction must be computed on the basis of the arm's length price. Further, expenses and interest deductions must also be determined having regard to the arm's length price.

2. IDENTIFICATION OF LEGISLATIVE FRAMEWORK

The key legislation in India dealing with transfer pricing includes:

- The Income Tax Act, read together with the Income Tax Rules, 1962 (the 'Income Tax Rules' or 'Rules'); and,
- The Double Taxation Avoidance Agreements ('DTAAs') entered into by India with various countries.

However, in order to understand the transfer pricing legislation in India, it is important to first understand the meaning of several key terms.

The term 'associated enterprise' is defined in section 92A of the Act. Two enterprises are deemed to be associated at any time during the previous year if they fall into any of the following categories:

- One enterprise holds, directly or indirectly, shares carrying not less than 26 per cent of the voting power in the other enterprise;
- Any person or enterprise holds, directly or indirectly, shares carrying not less than 26 per cent of the voting power in each of such enterprises;
- A loan advanced by one enterprise to the other enterprise constitutes not less than 51 per cent of the book value of the total assets of the other enterprise;
- One enterprise guarantees not less than 10 per cent of the total borrowings of the other enterprise;
- More than half of the board of directors or members of the governing board, or one or more executive directors or executive members of the governing board of one enterprise, is appointed by the other enterprise;
- More than half of the directors or members of the governing board, or one or more executive directors or executive members of the governing board of each of the two enterprises are appointed by the same person or persons;
- The manufacture or processing of goods or articles or business carried out by one enterprise is wholly dependent on the use of knowhow, patents, copyrights, trade-marks, licenses, franchises or any other business or commercial rights of a similar nature, or any data, documentation, drawing or specification relating to any patent, invention, model, design, secret formula or process, of which the other enterprise is the owner or in respect of which the other enterprise has exclusive rights;
- Ninety per cent or more of the raw materials and consumables required for the manufacture or processing of goods or articles carried out by one enterprise, are supplied by the other enterprise or by persons specified by the other enterprise, and the prices and other conditions relating to the supply are influenced by such other enterprise;
- The goods or articles manufactured or processed by one enterprise, are sold to the other enterprise or to persons specified by the other enterprise, and the prices and other conditions relating thereto are influenced by such other enterprise;
- Where one enterprise is controlled by an individual, the other enterprise is also controlled by such individual or his relative or jointly by such individual and a relative of such individual;
- Where one enterprise is controlled by a Hindu Undivided Family ('HUF'), and the other enterprise is controlled by a member of such HUF, or by a relative of a member of such HUF, or jointly by such member and his relative;

- Where one enterprise is a firm, association of persons or body of individuals, and the other enterprise holds not less than a ten per cent interest in such firm, association or body of individuals; or,
- There exists between the two enterprises any prescribed relationship of mutual interest.

An 'international transaction' is defined in s. 92B of the Income Tax Act as a transaction between two or more associated enterprises, either or both of whom are non-residents, in the nature of a purchase, sale or lease of tangible or intangible property, the provision of services, the lending or borrowing of money, or any other transaction having an impact on the profits, income, losses or assets of such enterprises. An international transaction includes a mutual agreement or arrangement between two or more associated enterprises for the allocation or apportionment of, or any contribution to, any cost or expense incurred or to be incurred in connection with a benefit, service, or facility provided or to be provided to any one or more such enterprises.

A 'deemed international transaction' under s. 92B(2) of the Act is a transaction entered into by an enterprise with a person other than an associated enterprise, which is deemed to be a transaction entered into between two associated enterprises as a result of a prior arrangement between the enterprise and the other person that determines the substance of the transaction.

An 'uncontrolled transaction' is defined in rule 10A(a) of the Income Tax Rules as a transaction between enterprises other than associated enterprises, whether resident or non-resident. It is also commonly referred to as 'contracting under uncontrolled conditions'. An uncontrolled transaction can occur between a resident and a non-resident, two residents, or two non-residents.

Section 92F(ii) of the Act defines the 'arm's length price' as the price which is applied or proposed to be applied in a transaction between persons other than associated enterprises, in uncontrolled conditions. Section 92C(1) of the Act stipulates that the arm's length price is to be determined by adopting the most appropriate of the following methods:

- The Comparable Uncontrolled Price Method (CUP method);
- The Resale Price Method (RPM);
- The Cost Plus Method (CPM);
- The Profit Split Method (PSM);
- The Transactional Net Margin Method (TNMM); or,
- Any other method as prescribed by the Board and provided for in the Rules.

2.1 Federal Legislation

The transfer pricing provisions in the Income Tax Act are applicable to a taxpayer if:

- He or she enters into an international transaction with an associated enterprise;

- He or she enters into a transaction where one of the parties to the transaction is a person located in a notified jurisdictional area; or,
- He or she enters into a specified domestic transaction ('SDT'), where the aggregate of the transactions entered into in the previous year exceeds Rs. 5 crores.

The following provisions of the Income Tax Act and Income Tax Rules deal with transfer pricing in respect of international and domestic transactions.

Relevant provisions of the Income Tax Act	Subject matter
92	Computation of income from international transactions having regard to the arm's length price
92A	Definition of associated enterprise
92B	Definition of international transaction
92C	Computation of arm's length price
92CA	Reference to transfer pricing officer
92CB	Power of Board to make safe harbor rules
92CC	Advance pricing agreements
92CD	Effect of advance pricing agreements
92D	Maintenance of information and documents by persons entering into an international transaction or specified domestic transaction
92E	Report from an accountant to be produced by persons entering into an international transaction or specified domestic transaction
92F	Definitions of terms relevant to the computation of the arm's length price
94A	Special measures in respect of transactions with persons located in the notified jurisdictional area
144C	Reference to dispute resolution panel
271AA	Penalty for failure to maintain information and documentation in respect of certain transactions
271BA	Penalty for failure to maintain information and documentation in respect of certain transactions
271G	Penalty for failure to record or produce information under section 92D

Relevant provisions of the Income Tax Rules	Subject matter
10A	Definitions of terms relevant to the computation of the arm's length price
10AB	Other methods to determine the arm's length price
10B	Determination of arm's length price under section 92C
10C	Most appropriate method for determining the arm's length price

10D	Information and documents to be maintained under section 92D
10E	Report from an accountant to be produced under section 92E

2.2 State and provincial legislative interplay

In India, there is no separate provincial legislative framework for transfer pricing. The Finance Act, 2012, introduced additional provisions regarding transfer pricing audits. Section 92E of the Act, as amended by the Finance Act, 2012, provides that every person who has entered into an international transaction or a SDT during a previous year must obtain a report from an accountant and file such report on or before the date specified in the prescribed form. According to rule 12(2), the audit report shall be filed electronically in Form No. 3CEB, along with the return of income. This audit report is the primary document relied on by the assessing officer (AO) to determine the details of the international transaction undertaken by the taxpayer.

Section 92C(3) of the Income Tax Act empowers the AO to require the production of information by the taxpayer. Section 92D(3) also permits the AO to require the production of information or documents from any person who has entered into an international transaction or a SDT within 30 days of the issuance of a notice. On the basis of the obtained information, the AO may initiate an audit and require the production of principal and supplementary documents to ascertain whether the price charged in the transaction satisfies the arm's length standard.

2.3 International Treaties and Agreements

India has entered into DTAAs with several other countries, which are binding on both the Government of India and the government of the other contracting state. In the event of a conflict with domestic law, the terms of the DTAA are binding.[1] Although DTAAs do not provide specific rules regarding transfer pricing, article 9 (associated enterprises) and article 27 (mutual agreement procedures) provide some guidelines on transactions between associated enterprises. Typically, the associated enterprise provisions of a DTAA will provide for an adjustment to profit where a transaction has been entered into between associated parties (eg, a parent and a subsidiary, two companies under common control, etc.).

With some exceptions, the DTAA typically provides that if the adjustment in the first state results in double taxation of the same income, the other state shall make an appropriate adjustment to relieve the double taxation. Further,the DTAA generally provides for consultation between the competent authorities of each state for the purposes of determining the required adjustment.

1 *CIT v P.V.A.L. KulandagonChettiar*, 2004 (267) ITR 654(SC).

Examples of some tax treaties that do not provide for an adjustment to prevent double taxation include India's treaty with Belgium, Finland, France, Germany, Italy and Norway.These treaties generally provide that:

- Where a taxpayer considers that the action of one or both states would result in taxation not in accordance with the tax treaty, the taxpayer may approach the competent authority of the state in which he or she is a resident;
- The competent authority shall endeavor, if it is not itself able to arrive at an appropriate solution, to resolve the discrepancy by mutual agreement with the competent authority of the other state.

3. NATIONAL POLICY ISSUES

With the increasing mobility of capital and technology, there has been a significant increase in businesses operating across national boundaries. These multinational companies carry on business activities in multiple tax jurisdictions, and frequently transfer resources and assets across jurisdictions. As a result, transfer pricing has emerged as one of the most significant areas of tax administration. The main objective of a multinational company engaging in transfer pricing is to minimize the tax liability of the entity as a whole. However, using the transfer pricing rules to reduce tax liability raises several ethical questions:

- Do corporations that use the transfer pricing rules to minimize taxes pay less than their fair share of taxes in some jurisdictions? Are such corporations bad corporate citizens?
- What duty do corporations have to pay taxes to various governments? Is society harmed when a corporation has structured their transfer pricing methods in order to minimize taxes?

3.1 Overall national policy announcements

Circular No. 6/2013 issued by the CBDT on June 29, 2013, clarified the functional profile of development centers engaged in R&D functions with insignificant risks for the purpose of transfer pricing. This circular is expected to increase consistency in the Indian Revenue Services' ('IRS') approach to accepting the functional profile of an R&D center that operates under a net margin-based pricing model. The circular is helpful as a reference guide in settling transfer pricing litigation.

In order to reduce the number of transfer pricing audits and lengthy transfer pricing disputes, the CBDT introduced the Safe Harbor Rules on September 20, 2013. The Safe Harbor Rules are effective for a 5-year period commencing in the 2013–14 taxation year. The rules require the income tax authorities to accept the transfer price declared by the assessee for certain specified industries.

The Advance Pricing Agreement ('APA') came into force on July 1, 2012, after being introduced in the Union Budget 2012. The APA is an arrangement between the taxpayer and the tax authority covering future transactions, with a view to resolving potential transfer pricing disputes in a cooperative manner.

3.2 National revenue authority initiatives

The Finance Act, 2012, introduced new mandatory transfer pricing documentation requirements, which apply to every person who has entered into an international transaction or a SDT.

3.3 Administrative statements

The Directorate of Income Tax regularly releases a publication entitled 'Let Us Share', comprising of best practices and recent orders of the Income Tax Department. This publication provides a valuable resource regarding the internal processes, investigative tools and decision-making mechanisms employed by the Income Tax Department. Through this publication, the Department attempts to build consensus on various taxation issues in order to reduce the frequency of tax litigation.

3.4 Administrative guidelines

The Indian tax authority imposes certain duties on the taxpayer and its accountants in regards to transfer pricing. Every person who enters into an international transaction must maintain such documents and information as may be prescribed by the AO or transfer pricing audit officer ('TPO'), in order to compute the income arising from the transaction having regard to the arm's length price. This requirement is consistent with the OECD's Transfer Pricing Guidelines. Additionally, every person who has entered into an international transaction or a SDT must obtain a report from an accountant and file such report in the prescribed form.

The accountant who is issuing the report to the enterprise must be duly appointed by the taxpayer. The accountant must also be given certain powers to require information and documents from the enterprise (eg, books of account, etc.), in order to fulfill his or her responsibility in a satisfactory manner. If an internal accountant conducts an audit, the accountant may rely on that audit.

4. CASE LAW

(a) Ranbaxy Laboratories Ltd v CIT (Delhi High Court)

The issue in this case was whether the AO was competent to determine the arm's length price of the international transaction without the assistance of the TPO, notwithstanding that the aggregate value of the transaction exceeded Rs. 5 crores.[2]

The Court held that whenever the aggregate value of an international transaction exceeds Rs. 5 crores, an AO is not competent to determine the arm's length price of the international transaction and it is compulsory to refer the matter to theTPO. As per CBDT Instruction No. 3/2003, the AO has a duty to refer the matter to the TPO. Since the AO in the case did not comply with this requirement, the Court held that the Commissioner was correct in holding that the order of the AO was *'erroneous and prejudicial to the interest of the Revenue.'*

2 (2012) 250CTR (Del) 33, [2012] 345ITR193 (Delhi), [2012] 204 TAXMAN294 (Delhi).

(b) Hinduja Ventures Ltd. v ACIT (ITAT Mumbai)

In this case, the taxpayer alleged that the values adopted by the TPO to determine the operating profit margin were erroneous because they included the value all units and all branches located within and outside India.[3] The TPO argued that the taxpayer had not submitted segmental accounts, and as a result,the TPO adopted the entire value instead of the value of the international transaction.

Since the taxpayer had subsequently submitted the segmental accounts for the international transaction, the tribunal referred the case back to the AO and the TPO to determine the operating profit margin. Additionally, the tribunal held that the computation of transfer pricing adjustments could be made using the comparable uncontrolled transactions of outside parties.

4.1 Current cases

(a) Yum! Restaurants (India) Private Limited V ITO

In this case, the taxpayer, Yum! Restaurants (India) Private Ltd. ('YRIPL'), was engaged in the business of franchising Pizza Hut and KFC restaurants in India.[4] The taxpayer had obtained franchisee rights from KFC International Holdings ('KFCIH') and Pizza Hut International LLC ('PHILLC'). The main issue in the case was whether the set of comparables selected by the TPO to compute the arm's length price were inappropriate. In rendering its decision, the Court stated:

'We find that [the] inclusion of Saket Projects Ltd. [the entity used as a comparable] in the comparable basis is not justified. The specific characteristics of services provided, assets employed and risk assumed, ie, the FAR of the comparable is decisive [in the] inclusion or exclusion of comparables. Saket Projects Ltd. is functionally different as it is organizing events with various kinds of sponsorships. The company in this division is earning revenue from selling event fees and offering space for rent, which cannot be compared with [the] provision of marketing and sales support services. Further, the segmental allocation of expenses was also not reliable. Keeping all these facts in view, we direct to exclude Saket Projects Ltd. from the comparables.

'In the case of M/s. Choksi Laboratories Ltd., we hold that it was engaged in chemical testing services, which are highly technical and not comparable to assessee. It has been held to be not comparable on the functional basis. In view of these facts, we also hold that Choksi, Rites and Wapcos are functionally different from the assessee company and cannot be held to be proper comparables, therefore, we direct to exclude these from the TPO adjustment while determining the ALP. As far as, M/s. Indus Technical & Financial Consultants Ltd. is concerned, it is engaged in rendering services pertaining to environment and energy conservation, which cannot be held to be different from the assessee company. Although the assessee's claim that as per the website of the company, M/s. Indus Technical & Financial Consultants Ltd. is a renowned manufacturer of TMT Bars, we find no

[3] ITA No. 886/Mum/2010(A.Y.:2006-07).

[4] ITA No. 6168/Del/2012.

substance in this claim and we dismiss this plea of the assessee. Accordingly, we direct to recompute the ALP.'

(b) ITO v Adani Port- Infrastructure Pvt Ltd.

In this case, the taxpayer made a payment of 40,635 GBP to HRJ Wallingford Ltd., United Kingdom.[5]The AO determined that the payment was in respect of Navigation Studies Phase-3 at Port of Dholera, and noted that no tax had been deducted when the payment was made. The taxpayer contended that the payment was not in the nature of 'making technical knowledge available to the taxpayer, and that technical knowledge, skill or know-how was not 'made available' to the service recipient pursuant to Article 13 of the DTAA between India and the UK.

The Court made the following statement in rendering its decision:

'There is [a] significant distinction between the definitions as prescribed [in section] 9 of [the] Income Tax Act of 'fees for technical services' as compared with the definition prescribed in Article 13 of [the] Indo-UK treaty. But the settled law is that the provisions of [the] DTAA override the provisions of [the] IT Act in the matter of ascertainment of taxability under the Income Tax Act. Therefore, we have to decide this issue in the light of [the] articles of [the] DTAA. Resultantly, Ground No 3 of the Revenue shall also not survive. At this juncture, it is worth [mentioning] a decision of [the] Apex Court pronounced in the case of Union of India v AzadiBachaoAndolan. *Further in the case of* GE India Technology, *it was decided that there was no obligation for withholding the tax on any person making [a]payment to a non-resident if the payment made to the non-resident is not chargeable under the provisions of [the] IT Act. In any case, the issue before us is limited to the applicability of the provisions of Article 13 of [the] DTAA between India and [the] UK and after considering the facts we hereby hold that the fees for technical services was not paid for making available the technical knowledge, experience, know-how to the assessee. Therefore, the payment made by the assessee to the said resident is out of the ambits of the provisions of section 195 of [the] IT Act.'*

4.2 Historical cases of note

Some landmark judgments on the subject of transfer pricing in India are summarized below.

(a) Aztec Software and Technology Service Ltd. V ACIT

In this case, a special bench of the Bangalore Income Tax Appellate Tribunal held that mere technical errors in the transfer price determined by the Revenue are not a basis for deleting a transfer pricing adjustment.[6] The Tribunal held that unless the arm's length price submitted by the taxpayer is specifically accepted, the appellate authority must determine the arm's length price itself, or direct a lower authority to do so. The Tribunal also rejected the use of industry averages as the Comparable Uncontrolled

[5] ITA No. 1405/Ahd/2009.
[6] [2007] 107ITD141 (Bang).

Price, since such an approach overlooked the factors relevant to examining comparability (eg, quality, market conditions, etc.).However, the Tribunal did not determine the computation of the arm's length price itself. Instead, the case was remanded back to the Revenue for a determination of the arm's length price.

(b) Maruti Suzuki India Limited v Addl. Commissioner of Income Tax, TPO, New Delhi

This case involved the payment of brand royalties by an Indian taxpayer to its foreign affiliate.[7] In rendering its decision, the Delhi High Court stated:

'If a domestic entity, which is an associated enterprise ('AE'), uses a foreign trademark on its products manufactured [or] sold in India, no payment to the foreign entity on account of such usage is necessary [if] the use of the foreign trademark is discretionary.If the domestic entity, which is an AE, is mandatorily required to use the foreign trademark on its products, appropriate payment in this regard should be made by the foreign entity to the domestic entity.

'Advertisement, marketing and promotion expenditure[s] incurred by an AE of a foreign entity using a foreign trademark do not require any payment or compensation by the owner of the foreign trademark if such expenses do not exceed the expenses incurred by a comparable independent domestic entity. If such expenses incurred are more, the foreign entity needs to suitably compensate the domestic entity.'

(c) Morgan Stanley & Co. Inc v Director of Income Tax

In this case, the Supreme Court of India ruled that the outsourcing of services, such as back-office operations to a captive service provider, did not per se create a permanent establishment of the parent company in India.[8] In its decision, the Court clarified the difference in the tax treatment of persons performing a stewardship and the deputation of employees. On the issue of transfer pricing, the Court accepted the single-entity approach for the attribution of profits to a PE, by ruling that the payment of an arm's length price by the non-resident to the PE extinguished any further attribution. Additionally, the Court reiterated the importance of identifying an economic nexus before imposing tax on a non-resident's global profits in India.

5. PENALTIES

The following table provides an overview of the legislative provisions, which establish the applicable penalties for transfer pricing.

7 WP(C) 6876/2008.
8 (2007) 210 CTR (SC) 419.

S. no.	Offense	Section of the Income Tax Act	Penalty amount
A	Failure to maintain prescribed information	271AA	2 per cent of the transaction value
	Failure to report any such transaction		
	Production of incorrect information		
B	Failure to produce information/ documents during assessment	271G	2 per cent of the transaction value
C	Concealment of particulars of income and producing inaccurate particulars of income	271(1)(c)	100 per cent to 300 per cent of tax on adjustment amount
D	Failure to produce accountant's report	271BA	INR 1,00,000

5.1 Types

Under the provisions of the Income Tax Act, stringent penalties have been prescribed for non-compliance with the transfer pricing regime. However, the Income Tax Act only imposes fines for a contravention of the transfer pricing rules; there is no possibility of imprisonment for a transfer pricing violation in India. This is different from other countries, such as Uganda, which specify both monetary penalties and imprisonment terms for transfer pricing violations.

5.2 Special or notable cases

Penalties under the Income Tax Act are imposed when a taxpayer fails to complywith his or her obligations under the transfer pricing rules. In*Hindustan Steel Limited v State of Orissa,* the Court stated:

'[A] penalty is not to be imposed because it is lawful to do so. Where a penalty should be imposed for failure to perform a statutory obligation is a matter of discretion to be exercised judicially and on consideration of all relevant circumstances. Even if [a] minimum penalty is prescribed, the authority competent to impose the penalty will be justified in refusing to impose the penalty, when there is a technical or venial breach of the provisions of the Act or where the breach flows from the bonafide *belief that the offender is not liable to act in the manner prescribed by the statute.'*[9]

In *CGT v Late H.H. Maharaja Bhagwat Singh,* the Court stated:

'Assessment[s] and penalt[ies] are different procedures. The evidences are also taken separately. In fact, in a penalty proceeding, the concerned authority has to consider the matter afresh on the matter available before it, and [a] necessary conclusion attracting [a] penalty has to be drawn and [a] specific finding has to be given.'

[9] (1972) 82 ITR 26 (SC).

In *Sankalp Exports Pvt. Ltd., Agra v Department of Income Tax,*[10] the Court held:

'If there is non-compliance with the requirement of maintenance of documentation, section 271AA, 271BA and 271G [may apply]. The matter is to be examined on [the] merits and in [an] objective manner. Once it is on record that requisitions have been complied with, there cannot be any basis to come to the conclusion that the records were not maintained. It is also elementary that the provisions of section 271AA and 271G are subject to the provisions of section 273B, which unambiguously sets out the legal position that where [an] assessee can demonstrate that there was a reasonable cause for failure to comply with the failure in question [a penalty cannot be imposed].'

Therefore, a penalty cannot be imposed if the taxpayer has reasonable cause for a failure to comply with the Act. If the taxpayer establishes such reasonable cause, a penalty cannot be imposed.[11]Further, in*IL & FS Maritime Infrastructure Co. Ltd. v Assistant Commissioner of Income Tax,* the taxpayer alleged that a penalty should not be imposed because the taxpayer had been under a mistaken but *bona fide* belief that section 92B was not applicable to the transaction in question.[12] The Court found in favor of the taxpayer and held that the explanation put forth by the taxpayer fell within the meaning of "reasonable cause" as provided under section 273B of the Act.

6. DISPUTE RESOLUTION MECHANISMS

Since its formal adoption in 2000, transfer pricing has become one of the most litigated tax areas in India. As a result, like many other jurisdictions, India has developed resolution mechanisms to facilitate the settlement of transfer pricing disputes. The two main dispute resolution mechanisms adopted in India include:

- The traditional approach; and,
- The alternative dispute resolution mechanism under section 144C of the Act.

6.1 Preferred national options

Section 144C of the Income Tax Act was introduced in response to the shortcomings of the traditional dispute resolution mechanism, which involved lengthy processes that lacked finality. Section 144C provides for the creation of a Dispute Resolution Panel ('DRP') to facilitate the timely resolution of transfer pricing disputes (see Figure 1).

6.2 International options

The United Nations Transfer Pricing Model released in 2012 included a chapter on India. This chapter detailed India's response to a variety of topics including the use of contemporary data; the treatment of contract R&D services; the 3 per cent variation in the arithmetic mean of the arm's length range; and comparability adjustments for working capital, capacity

10 ITA No. 310 and 311/Agr/2013.
11 *Cargill India Pvt. Ltd. v Dy. Commissioner of Income Tax,* (2008) 116TTJ (Delhi) 1.
12 [2013] 144ITD559 (Mum).

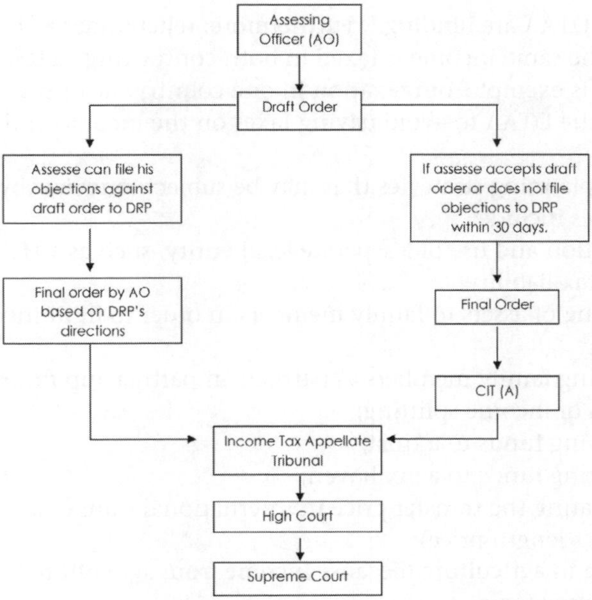

and risk. It also outlined India's response to issues such as location savings; royalties for brands and trademarks; development of marketing intangibles; intragroup services; and intercompany financial transactions. Although the chapter is not legally binding, it is frequently used as a reference point in transfer pricing litigation.

The Mutual Agreement Proceeding ('MAP') provides an option for international dispute resolution. The concept emerged from an India–US tax treaty, wherein both countries entered into a memorandum of understanding. The CBDT recently issued a circular extending the applicability of the memorandum of understanding to Indian resident entities in the course of a MAP invoked by a US resident. Accordingly, if an Indian subsidiary of US company incurs a transfer pricing adjustment and the US company initiates a proceeding under MAP, the Indian subsidiary can apply to stay the demand until the MAP is concluded.

PART TWO: TAX AVOIDANCE

7. ACCEPTABLE TAX PLANNING AREAS/SUBJECTS

The law of India treats tax offences, such as tax evasion, as criminal offences. Chapter XXII of the Income Tax Act sets out the legislative framework for criminal prosecution, including minimum and maximum sentences (eg, 7 years imprisonment). In contrast, tax avoidance through artificial devices such as holding companies and activities such as treaty shopping has become a common practice.

India has entered into several Double Taxation Avoidance Agreements ('DTAAs'), which bind both the Government of India and the government of the other contracting state. In the event of a conflict with domestic law, the terms of the DTAA are binding.[13] Furthermore, relief under a DTAA is only available if the same income is taxed in both contracting states. Therefore, if a taxpayer is exempt from taxation in one country, he or she cannot seek relief under the DTAA to avoid paying taxes on the income in the other country.

Some tax planning strategies that may be subject to review by the Indian tax authorities include:

- The creation and use of a separate legal entity, such as a HUF, to reduce income tax liability;
- The gifting of assets to family members in order to limit income tax liability;
- Appointing family members as partners in partnership firms for the purposes of income splitting;
- Transferring funds to a trust;
- Transferring funds to a tax haven;
- Manipulating the transfer price in international transactions (ie, using a non-arm's length price);
- Investing in agriculture (because income from agriculture is exempt from income tax);
- Investing in tax-free bonds;
- Adopting a different accounting method for different sources of income to reduce income tax liability; and,
- Selling assets after a prescribed period of time to take advantage of a long-term capital gain.

8. DEFINING ABUSIVE TAX AVOIDANCE

The tax legislation in India does not provide a definition of 'abusive tax avoidance'. However, the Supreme Court of India has stated:

'The shortest definition of tax avoidance that has come across is "the art of dodging tax without breaking the law". Much legal sophistry and judicial exposition have gone into the attempt to differentiate the concepts of tax evasion and tax avoidance and to discover the invisible line supposed to exist which distinguishes one from the other. Tax avoidance, it seems, is legal; tax evasion is illegal … We must recognize that there is behind taxation laws as much moral sanction as behind any other welfare legislation and it is a pretense to say that avoidance of taxation is not unethical and that it stands on no less moral plane than honest payment of taxation. In our view, the proper way to construe a taxing statute, while considering a device to avoid tax, is not to ask whether the provisions should be construed literally or liberally, nor whether the transaction is not unreal and not prohibited by the statute, but whether the transaction is a device to avoid tax, and whether the transaction is such that the judicial process may accord its approval to it … It is neither fair nor desirable to expect the legislature to intervene and take care of every device and scheme to avoid taxation. It is up to the Court to take stock to determine the nature of the new and sophisticated legal devices to avoid tax and consider whether the situation created by the devices could be related

13 *CIT v P.V.A.L. KulandagonChettiar,* 2004 (267) ITR 654 (SC).

to the existing legislation with the aid of emerging techniques of interpretation as was done in Ramsay *(1982 AC 300),* Burma Oil *(1982 STC 30) and* Dawson *(1984-1 All ER 530), to expose the devices for what they really are and to refuse to give judicial benediction.'*[14]

9. THE LEGISLATIVE FRAMEWORK

The General Anti-Avoidance Rule ('GAAR') was introduced into the Income Tax Act by the Finance Act, 2012, and was to come into effect in April 2014. However, the Finance Act, 2013, deferred the applicability of GAAR until the 2016–17 taxation year. As a result, India does not currently have GAAR in effect.

However, Chapter 10A has been added to the Income Tax Act and will come into force in April 2016. This chapter, comprising of ss. 95 to 102 of the Act, codifies the doctrine of substance over form. It provides that an arrangement that has been designed to obtain a tax benefit, and that satisfies at least one of the specified tests is an impermissible avoidance agreement. The burden of proving that there is an arrangement designed to obtain a tax benefit is on the tax authority.

The government has also extended the application of the transfer pricing provisions to specified domestic transactions, in order to prevent abusive tax avoidance. Other initiatives that have been undertaken to prevent abusive tax avoidance include:

- The creation of the Investigation Department of the Central Board of Direct Taxes (the 'CBDT'), to conduct searches of undisclosed assets and income;
- The execution of Tax Information Exchange Agreements ('TIEAs') between the CBDT and other countries;
- The establishment of Overseas Income Tax Units in other countries;
- The introduction of a compulsory reporting requirement for assets held abroad;
- New rules which permit the re-opening of assessments for a period of 16 years for international assets;
- The imposition of tax collection at source for cash purchases of bullion and jewelry, as well as trades in coal, lignite and iron ore;
- The levying of taxes at the highest rate (ie, 30 per cent) for unexplained cash, credits, investments, expenditures, etc.;
- The introduction of a reporting mechanism for assets and bank accounts in a foreign country; and,
- The prosecution of cases against taxpayers who fail to comply with the relevant tax laws.

10. KEY CASES OF INTEREST

Since GAAR will not come into force until April 2016, there are presently no GAAR cases in Indian jurisprudence. However, some cases dealing with the issue of abusive tax avoidance are summarized below.

---

[14] *Mcdowell and Co. Ltd. v Commercial Tax Officer AIR* 1986 SC 649.

(a) Commissioner of Income-Tax v Sri AbhayanandaRath Family

In this case, the Division Bench of the Orissa High Court made the following observations:

'Evading [the] payment of tax' is quite different from 'tax planning'. A person may plan his finances in such a manner, strictly within the four corners of the taxing statute, that his tax liability is minimized or made nil. If this is done ... strictly in accordance with and taking advantage of the provisions contained in the Act, by no stretch of [the] imagination can it be said that payment of tax has been evaded. In the context of [the] payment of tax, 'evasion' necessarily means, 'to try illegally to avoid paying tax'. But, as in the instant case, a trust has been created in accordance with law and [the] creation of such a trust is not hit by any of the provisions contained in the Act. [Therefore], one fails to understand how [the] creation of such a trust can be said to have been created 'illegally to avoid payment of tax.'[15]

(b) The Commissioner of Income Tax, Patiala v M/s Punjab State Electricity Board, Patiala Board

In this case, the taxpayer, the Punjab State Electricity Board, sold energy saving devices eligible for 100 per cent depreciation pursuant to s. 32 of the Income Tax Act and Rule 5 of the Income Tax Rules. The devices were leased and deduction was sought for the rental income. The Indian tax authority disallowed the deduction on the basis that the transactions entered into by the taxpayer were sham transactions.

The High Court of Punjab and Haryana decided the case in favour of the taxpayer and made the following observations:

'[The] only contention raised by the learned counsel for the revenue is that the machinery was [an] integral part of the boilers and continued to be with the assessee in spite of [the] sale. The fact remains that ... consideration was received by the assessee and lease rental was paid by the assessee. Merely because tax liability was reduced could not be conclusive of [an] arrangement being [a] sham.'[16]

10.1 Current cases

(a) Vodafone International Holdings v Union of India & Anr

One of the most important tax avoidance cases in India is Vodafone *International Holdings v Union of India & Anr,* decided by the Supreme Court of India on January 20, 2012.[17] In this case, the Court held that a transfer between non-residents involving shares of a foreign holding company with an Indian subsidiary was not a transfer of capital assets situated in India. As a result, the capital gains arising fromthe transaction were not taxable in India. Additionally, the Court made the following rulings:

- The transfer of a foreign holding company's shares didnot terminate the foreign company's right to control the Indian subsidiary, nor did it result in the transfer of assets situated in India;

15 [2002] 255 ITR 436 Orissa.
16 [2010] 320 ITR 469 (P&H).
17 [2012] 341 ITR 1 (SC).

- Section 9(1) of the Act does not deem shares of a foreign company that has a subsidiary in India to be situated in India;
- Section 9 does not apply to income arising from indirect transfers; and,
- The source of income is determined by where a transaction takes place, and not where an asset that was part of the transaction was acquired.

After the decision was released, the Indian Government amended s. 9 of the Income Tax Act to provide that income accruing to non-residents directly or indirectly through the transfer of a capital asset situated in India is to be taxed in India, effective retroactively from April 1, 1962.

10.2 Key historical cases

One of the key historical cases in India dealing with the issue of tax avoidance is the case of *Union of India and Anr v AzadiBachaoAndolan and Anr,* decided by the Supreme Court of India in 2003.[18] The Court made the following statements with regards to tax avoidance:

'We may in this connection usefully refer to the judgment of the Madras High Court in M.V. Vallipappan and others v ITO, *which has rightly concluded that the decision in* McDowell *cannot be read as laying down that every attempt at tax planning is illegitimate and must be ignored, or that every transaction or arrangement which is perfectly permissible under law, which has the effect of reducing the tax burden of the assessee, must be looked upon with disfavour. Though the Madras High Court had occasion to refer to the judgment of the* Privy Council in IRC v. Challenge Corporation Ltd., *and did not have the benefit of the House of Lords' pronouncement in* Craven, *the view taken by the Madras High Court appears to be correct and we are inclined to agree with it.*

'We may also refer to the judgment of [the] Gujarat High Court in Banyan and Berry v Commissioner of Income-Tax, *where, referring to* McDowell, *the Court observed: "The court nowhere said that every action or inaction on the part of the taxpayer which results in [a] reduction of tax liability to which he may be subjected in [the] future, is to be viewed with suspicion and be treated as a device for avoidance of tax irrespective of [the] legitimacy or genuineness of the act; an inference which unfortunately, in our opinion, the Tribunal apparently appears to have drawn from the enunciation made in [the]* McDowell *case(1985) 154 ITR 148 (SC)." The ratio of any decision has to be understood in the context it has been made. The facts and circumstances which lead to [the]* McDowell *decision leave us in no doubt that the principle enunciated in the above case has not affected the freedom of the citizen to act in a manner according to his requirements [and] his wishes in the manner of doing any trade, activity or planning his affairs with circumspection, within the framework of law, unless the same fall in the category of colorable device[s] which may properly be called a device or a dubious method or a subterfuge clothed with apparent dignity.'*

11. PENALTIES

As stated above, GAAR has not yet come into force in India. However, s. 98 in Chapter X-A of the Act sets out the consequences of an impermissible

[18] [2003] 263 ITR 706 (SC).

avoidance arrangement. Although this section does not include any penalties per se, where a transaction is held to be an impermissible avoidance arrangement, the tax authorities may:

- Disregard, combine or re-characterize any step in a part or the whole of the impermissible avoidance arrangement;
- Treat the impermissible avoidance arrangement as if it had not been entered into or carried out;
- Disregard any accommodating party or treat any accommodating party and any other party as one person;
- Deem related persons to be one person for the purposes of determining tax liability;
- Reallocate any receipt of a capital nature or revenue nature, orany expenditure, deduction, relief or rebate among the parties to the arrangement; or,
- Disregard the corporate structure of any arrangement.

11.1 Legislative provisions

The legislative provisions relating to GAAR are set out in ss. 95–102 in Chapter X-A of the Income Tax Act.

Section	Name of the Section
95	Applicability of GAAR
96	Impermissible avoidance arrangement
97	Arrangement to lack commercial substance
98	Consequences of impermissible avoidance arrangement
99	Treatment of connected person and accommodating party
100	Application of this Chapter
101	Framing of guidelines
102	Definitions

11.2 Examples of penalties imposed

Not applicable.

12. CURRENT TRENDS

Currently, the Government of India is attempting to prevent tax avoidance by identifying and closing loopholes in the taxation system. Additionally, GAAR is to come into effect for the 2016–17 taxation year.

At the international level, the issue of tax avoidance is being discussed and measures are being implemented to prevent companies from taking advantage of loopholes in taxation systems and transferring their profits to low-tax jurisdictions. For example, at the most recent OECD Annual Ministerial Council Meeting in Paris, India and 46 other countries agreed to implement a single global standard on the automatic exchange of information, in order to facilitate the international exchange of information on tax matters.

12.1 National policy and law

The Indian Government is proposing the introduction of a new Goods and Services Tax (GST), which would replace all indirect taxes levied on goods and services by the central and state governments. Additionally, GAAR is to come into effect for the 2016–17 taxation year.

The Indian Government has entered into DTAAs with several other countries. Additionally, the CBDT has executed TIEAs with several tax havens. These new government policies are likely to be effective in reducing abusive tax avoidance in India.

12.1.1 The impact and role of the OECD and other international relations

India is currently working with the OECD on several projects, including the Forum on Tax Administration; the Oslo Dialogue on Tax and Other Crimes; the Network on Fiscal Relations across Levels of Government; and the Advisory Group for Co-operation with Non-OECD Economies.

According to India's Joint Secretary of Foreign Tax and Tax Research, India plays a leading role in the work of the Global Forum on Transparency and Exchange of Information for Tax Purposes. In 2011, the OECD and India signed a three-year cooperation programme in the tax area, covering high-level policy dialogue, multilateral events on taxation in India, and a strengthening of India's participation in the OECD's Committee on Fiscal Affairs. India also recently signed and ratified the Convention on Mutual Administrative Assistance in Tax Matters, which was developed by the OECD and the Council of Europe. Additionally, at the most recent OECD Annual Ministerial Council Meeting in Paris, India and 46 other countries agreed to the Declaration on Automatic Exchange of Information in Tax Matters.

The OECD has also been very active in the development of the tax administration system in India, particularly in the areas of transfer pricing, international taxation, and the exchange of information through tax treaties. The involvement of the OECD has permitted tax auditors and their supervisors to learn and apply audit techniques and taxation principles consistent with international best practices. Additionally, since 2000, the OECD has held 30 bilateral and multilateral technical events in India. These events have provided a platform for Indian tax administrators to develop practical solutions to problems in the Indian tax system.

Indonesia

Ali Budiardjo, Nugroho, Reksodiputro
Freddy Karyadi & Anastasia Irawati

PART ONE: TRANSFER PRICING

1. GENERAL OVERVIEW

The regulation of transfer pricing in Indonesia has been changed several times over the past few years. It was first introduced in Law No. 7 of 1983 regarding Tax Incomes. In 1993, the Tax Office issued guidelines on the determination of transfer pricing adjustment. Following these guidelines, there were requirements introduced in 2002 that require the disclosure of related party transaction in corporate income tax returns. There were also specific references of the Tax Office made in relation to the transfer pricing documentation. From 2009 onward, the taxpayers have been required to disclose additional details of related party transaction in their annual tax returns and declare whether the relevant transfer pricing documentation is available. In 2010, the Tax Office issued two importance reference documents. The first was a set of detailed transfer pricing regulations. These regulations provided clear guidance on transfer pricing issues, including the applicability of the arm's-length principle; basic requirements to determine whether the prices are in compliance with the arm's-length principle; and documentation requirements. The second was a set of guidelines on the mutual agreement procedure (MAP) and advance pricing agreement (APA).[1]

2. IDENTIFICATION OF LEGISLATIVE FRAMEWORK

2.1 Federal legislation

(a) Income tax

For income tax purposes, the regulation regarding transfer pricing can be found in Article 18 and 18 paragraph (3) of Law No. 7 of 1983 regarding Tax Incomes, as amended by Law No. 36 of 2008 ('Income Tax Law').

Article 18 states that the tax authorities may adjust a taxpayer's taxable income for related party transactions that were not carried out on an arm's-length basis. The definition of 'Related Parties' will be met in any the following circumstances:

- where a taxpayer, either directly or indirectly, participates in 25 per cent or more of the capital of another taxpayer. Also, where a company participates in 25 per cent or more of the capital of two taxpayers, in which case the latter two taxpayers are also considered to be related;

1 Articles by Iwan Hoo and Wara Kertinigrum dated 14 March 2014: 'Indonesia: A light at the end of the tunnel for Indonesia?'

- where a taxpayer, either directly or indirectly, controls another taxpayer or where there are two or more taxpayers who are under common control;
- where there is a family relationship by blood or marriage between the taxpayers.

Paragraph (3) of Article 18 provides that the five arm's length pricing methodologies from the Organization for Economic Co-operation and Development ('OECD') Guidelines should be used to set or review the transfer prices. If the arm's length principle is not followed, the Directorate General of Taxation ('DGT') is authorized to recalculate the taxable income or deductible costs arising from a transaction by applying the arm's length principle.

(b) Value added tax

As for value added tax purposes, the regulation regarding transfer pricing can be found in Article 2 of Law No. 8 of 1983. The latter was last amended in 2009 by Law No. 42 regarding Value Added Tax on Goods and Services and Sales Tax on Luxurious Goods ('VAT Law').

(c) Other regulations

(a) Government Regulation 80 of 2007, regarding Implementation Procedures on Taxation Rights and Obligations based on General Tax Provisions and Procedures Law (GR 80/2007). This regulation was last amended in 2011 by Government Regulation 74 (GR 74/2011).

This regulation provides that in the event that taxpayers conduct related-party transactions, they are obliged to keep documents and/or additional information to support that the related-party transactions are in accordance with the principles of fairness and predominance of business. GR 74/2011 allows the Ministry of Finance ('MOF') to regulate the mutual agreement procedure ('MAP'), the advance pricing agreement ('APA'), and the exchange of information rules. Nevertheless, the MAP, APA, and exchange of information rules are issued under the DGT Regulation.

(b) Government Regulation 94 of 2010 governs the calculation and settlement of income tax during the fiscal year (GR 94/2010). This regulation clarifies various provisions in the Income Tax Law, including non-interest-bearing loans from shareholders.

(c) MoF Regulation 258/PMK.03/2008 (MoF Regulation 258) sets a rate of 25 per cent of the transaction value for deemed taxable gains derived from the disposal of shares in a foreign company, domiciled in a tax haven country, that acts only as a special purpose vehicle and holds shares representing 25 per cent or more ownership in an unlisted Indonesian company. The regulation entered into force 1 January 2009.

d) MoF Regulation 140/PMK.03/2010 (MoF Regulation 140) applies the look-through principle to any foreign special purpose vehicle (SPV) owned by a resident taxpayer that purchases shares in or receivables of another Indonesian tax resident. This regulation is designed to prevent so-called U-turn tax planning and will be imposed if the SPV lacks substance and the purchase price is not set at arm's length. As such, those shares or receivables would be considered the assets of the shareholder of the SPV rather than the assets of the SPV.

(e) MoF Regulation 17/PMK.03/2013 on tax auditing (MoF Regulation 17).

(f) DGT Regulation PER-22/PJ/2013 (DGT Regulation PER-22). DGT Regulation PER-22 governs transfer pricing auditing. The regulation outlines the procedure for transfer pricing auditing; the method used for transfer pricing auditing; and specific issues regarding intra-group services, intangible transactions and intra-group loans.

(g) DGT Regulation PER-43/PJ/2010 (DGT Regulation PER-43), as amended by DGT Regulation PER-32/PJ/2011 (DGT Regulation PER-32). DGT Regulation PER-32 provides basic transfer pricing rules and the framework for transfer pricing in Indonesia. The regulation provides guidance with respect to the preparation of transfer pricing documentation for taxpayers who conduct transactions with related parties. It also examines the arm's length nature of the transactions. Additionally, DGT Regulation PER-32 introduced the most appropriate method and replaced the hierarchy of alternative methods.

(h) DGT Regulation PER-48/PJ/2010 (DGT Regulation PER-48). DGT Regulation PER-48 provides the authority to exercise the MAPs of any tax treaty. The regulation is meant to aid investigation of cross-border transfer pricing cases that allegedly involve the illegal avoidance of Indonesian tax obligations. Under the regulation, the DGT will form a special transfer pricing team to correct transfer pricing transactions of resident taxpayers using the corresponding adjustment mechanism.

(i) DGT Regulation PER-69/PJ/2010 (DGT Regulation PER-69). DGT Regulation PER-69 introduces procedures for obtaining an APA in conjunction with the transfer pricing provisions in Article 18 of the ITL.

(j) DGT Regulation PER-39/PJ/2009, as amended by DGT Regulation PER-26/PJ/2013 (DGT Regulation 26). DGT Regulation 39 introduces a new format of the corporate income tax return (starting from fiscal years after 2009). Any declaration of related-party transactions would require the taxpayer to disclose such transactions in detail in the corporate income tax return.

(k) DGT Regulation PER-61/PJ/2009 (DGT Regulation 61), as amended by DGT Regulation PER-24/PJ/2010 (DGT Regulation 24). This regulation governs the procedures of application for tax treaties.

(l) DGT Regulation PER-62/PJ/2009 (DGT Regulation 62), as amended by DGT Regulation PER-25/PJ/2010 (DGT Regulation 25). This regulation governs anti-abuse of tax treaty provisions.

(m) Circular Letter SE-04/PJ/1993 (Circular Letter 04), which has been replaced by Circular Letter SE-50/PJ/2013 (Circular Letter 50). The latter provides technical tax auditing guidance for taxpayers in special relationships. The goal of this Circular Letter is to increase the number of multinational companies in the era of globalization. The national boundaries between jurisdictions have become blurred, which in turn impacted how multinational companies carry out investment transactions and cross-border trade. The corresponding high financial burden of production costs and the overcapacity of domestic markets have also pushed multinational companies to expand beyond their jurisdiction. Multinational companies generally prefer more favourable states that provide comparative advantages in production cost (location saving) and market share (market premium). The technical guidance in tax auditing provided by this Circular Letter provides convenience and uniformity for tax auditors conducting audits of taxpayers with special relationships and verifies the quality of these audits.

2.2 State and provincial legislative interplay

To date, the Indonesian provincial legislature has not issued a regulation on transfer pricing. In this regard, there is no state and provincial legislative interplay that is relevant for transfer pricing cases.

2.3 International treaties and agreements

International institutions such as the OECD, the United Nations, and ASEAN have significantly influenced the content of Indonesia's Tax Treaty. When negotiating its tax treaties, Indonesia tends to follow either the UN model or ASEAN model, depending on the type of treaty partner involved.

Indonesian transfer pricing rules have adopted many key concepts from the OECD Guidelines. Nevertheless, Indonesia's regulations are not as detailed and complete as the OECD Guidelines or UN TP Manual. For example, cost contribution agreements are mentioned as falling within the scope of the transfer pricing rules. However, the regulations do not provide any further guidance on the application of the arm's length principle.

3. NATIONAL POLICY ISSUES

The Indonesian Tax Office's goal of combating transfer pricing cases is primarily driven by their goal of fulfilling the country's target tax revenue. Because of this, the Indonesian Tax Office has an extensive working knowledge of transfer pricing matters.

3.1 Overall national policy announcements

On March 21, 2014, the DGT issued DGT Circular Letter No. SE-15/PJ/2014 which outlined a 2014 tax audit revenue goal of Rp 24 trillion (approximately USD 2.2 billion). This figure represents an increase of 30 per cent from the DGT's 2013 target. Based on its 2014 target, the DGT may issue tax audit instruction letters focusing on manual risk for taxpayers:

- who have a transaction with domestic related parties, including individuals related to the transaction;
- who have a transaction with related parties (transfer pricing audit apart from normal tax audit due to tax overpayment);
- who are engaged in oil and gas sectors; and/or
- who are subject to a joint audit between the DGT and external parties.

3.2 National revenue authority initiatives

Based on several recent audits by the Indonesian Tax Office,[2] the following examples represent transfer pricing arrangements that have been challenged by the Office as being improper:

- The disallowance of expenses incurred by Indonesian taxpayers relating to the payment of royalties and intra-group services without properly taking into account the taxpayer's business or economic circumstances. Rejections were often made because of trivial administrative matters, such as the lack of a patent certificate;
- The disallowance of using multiple-year data for benchmarking purposes and basing the conclusions on the results of the year under audit only. The use of a two or three-year analysis to achieve a desired outcome, while not taking into account the companies' business cycles, was also prohibited;
- An insistence on using public market data that may not be comparable to the terms of the transactions being reviewed;
- A greater emphasis on product comparability as a criterion for the selection of comparables under the transactional net margin method;
- The selection/application of a transfer pricing method based on a very generic understanding of the company's business under review;
- An oversimplification of a company's business characteristics. Generally, the Indonesian Tax Office categorizes the characteristics of a company as toll manufacturing, contract manufacturing or fully fledged manufacturing. Other business setups are often simply placed into one of these three aforementioned groups.

3.3 Administrative statements

See section 2.1 above.

3.4 Administrative guidelines

See section 2.1 above.

4. CASE LAW

At the moment, many transfer pricing-related cases are under review by the Tax Court. Following the initial implementation of the transfer pricing regulations, there were often delays in receiving a verdict from the Tax Court. Because of the Tax Court's lack of familiarity with transfer pricing issues, some commentators felt that the Court was not yet ready to effectively prosecute transfer pricing cases. Compared to these early years, the situation today has improved slightly. The Tax Court is currently completing most transfer pricing disputes at an ordinary pace, although the results of transfer pricing appeals are still less predictable than other types of tax disputes.

[2] Ibid.

4.1 Current cases

In 2013, the Tax Court decided an important transfer pricing case involving intangible property.[3] The object of the dispute was relating to the payment of royalty expense. The appellant subsequently deducted the cost of the licensing fee from their taxable income while pursuant to the appellee (Tax Authority), the payment of royalty expense was considered as a dividend distribution by the appellant to its principal. As such, it cannot be deducted in the calculation of taxable income.

Here, the judge concluded that the license agreement existed and the appellant was granted a license to sell and market, but not to manufacture, a product owned by an affiliated party. Therefore, the judge agreed that the non-payment of the royalty violated the Intellectual Property Rights Law as well as the Agreement on Trade-related Aspects of Intellectual Property Rights. Here, the appellee unsuccessfully argued that including this amount in their income effectively meant that they were paying the licensing fee twice. The Tax Court held that instead of considering Article 9 of the OECD Guidelines, the appellee erred by only examining the application of Article 18, paragraph 3 of Indonesia's Income Tax Law. Furthermore, the appellant could not demonstrate a connection between the production process and the use of the product's brand name. Based on these facts, the Court annulled the correction made by the appellee.

4.2 Historical cases of note

A significant case relating to transfer pricing involved a tax dispute with PT Toyota Motor Manufacturing Indonesia ('TMMI').[4] The dispute arose from TMMI's abnormal tax returns for the period of 2008. TMMI reported its sales as IDR 32.9 trillion. Conversely, the DGT estimated that the actual amount of TMMI's sales was significantly higher at IDR 34,5 trillion. Based on the DGT's calculations, this resulted in a tax deficit of IDR 500 billion (excluding the amount of the penalty for the late payment).

According to the DGT, TMMI's abnormal tax returns were due to illegal transfer pricing. During a period where TMMI claimed numerous business losses, PT Toyota Astra Motor ('TAM') recorded huge profits. While TMMI sold cars below the production cost, TAM sold the identical product to Auto 2000 for 50 per cent more than the production cost.

Although the trial between TMMI and DGT has concluded, the judge's decision has not yet been issued. As such, we can only wait for the result of the decision to find out whose calculation is correct. If the judge decides that TMMI's argument is not correct and finds them guilty, TMMI will be forced to pay the tax deficit of Rp 500 trillion (excluding the penalty for the late payment).

[3] Verdict number Put-44244/PP/M.VIII/15/2013.

[4] This case has been on trial since 2013 but has not yet been decided.

5. PENALTIES

In Indonesia, the penalties for violations of transfer pricing laws and regulations can be divided into two categories: (i) administrative sanctions; and (ii) general penal sanctions.

5.1 Types

(i) Administrative sanctions

There are several administrative sanctions that can be imposed on taxpayers who are deemed to have violated the prevailing laws and regulations regarding taxation in conducting their transfer pricing transaction. These include: (a) a fine of 2 per cent per month for late payment of tax, up to a maximum of 48 per cent of the unpaid tax; (b) interest penalties; and (c) an increase.

(ii) Penal sanctions

There are several penal sanctions that can be imposed on taxpayers. Among others, these include:

(a) imprisonment;
(b) confinement (*kurungan*);
(c) a fine; in criminal cases, fines of 200 per cent-400 per cent of the unpaid tax are possible.
(d) additional penal sanctions such as: (i) revocation of certain rights; and/ or (ii) forfeiture of certain goods.

5.2 Special or notable cases

Case Put.48364/PP/M.XI/15/2013

This case illustrates an overview of the application of the 'cost-plus method', which considers a comparability analysis to determine the arm's length mark-up. During the fiscal years of 2004, 2005 and 2006, the taxpayer's export transactions covered various regions, comprising: Taiwan, Philippines, Australia, Malaysia, Singapore, Thailand, USA and China. The adjustment proposed by the tax authorities was derived from the comparison of the profit earned from the taxpayer's related parties transactions and comparable companies' profit. In relation to the taxpayer business model, either the taxpayer or the tax authorities agreed to classify the taxpayer business characterisation as 'contract manufacturer'. Previously, in fiscal year 2005, the taxpayer conducted business restructuring in respect to the changes of the ownership structure.

As mentioned above, the cost-plus method was selected as the method to test the arm's length nature of the transactions under review. The selection of the cost-plus method by the tax authorities is based on consideration of the 'hierarchy method', as regulated in KEP-01/PJ.7/1993 (Guidance of tax audit for taxpayers with a special relationship). Meanwhile, as the panel of judges used dynamic interpretation in deciding this dispute, the judges claimed that the fundamental basis for choosing the cost-plus method should be based on the consideration of 'the most appropriate method', as stated in OECD Transfer Pricing Guidelines 2010 and PER-32/PJ./2011

(Implementation of the arm's length principle for taxpayers with a special relationship) as the current guidelines.

In regard to the implementation of the cost-plus method, different points of view regarding the 'cost-plus-mark-up' terminology caused dispute. Based on the analysis conducted by the tax authorities, the arm's length mark-up for the taxpayer should be 25.12 per cent, which is calculated by using the gross mark-up percentage (the ratio between the gross profit and the cost of goods sold/COGS), while the taxpayer implemented a 6 per cent mark-up of operating profit, in accordance with the taxpayer's group policies. Such mark-up was calculated by using the operating profit (after considering the operating expenses). In addition, there were also differences regarding the accounting consistency of interest expense between the two parties. The tax authorities calculated the interest expense as a component of COGS, whereas the taxpayer considered the interest expense as a component of the non-operating expenses. In relation to this matter, the panel of judges stated that the tax authorities should perform an accurate adjustment regarding the distinction of accounting consistency between the comparable companies and the taxpayer, and such adjustment shall be in accordance with the principles agreed internationally. Furthermore, the panel of judges argued that if the tax authorities had already made a correction, then the tax authorities should make an evaluation as to whether the correction made was in accordance with the arm's length principle as stated in the OECD Transfer Pricing Guidelines and agreed internationally, ie the tax authority bears the burden of proof. Thus it would be easier for the tax authorities to be held responsible for the correction made by it as stated in Point 18 OECD Transfer Pricing Guidelines.

In this case, in accordance with the OECD Transfer Pricing Guidelines, the panel of judges held that the tax authorities must perform a comparability analysis to challenge the arm's length pricing of the related party transactions of the taxpayer. However, based on the available evidence, the panel of judges claimed that tax authorities did not perform an in-depth and comprehensive comparability analysis regarding the economic circumstances and business strategies. Moreover, the panel of judges also claimed that the tax authorities did not perform an accurate adjustment in connection with the differences of accounting consistency between the comparable companies and the taxpayer. The panel of judges stated that the tax authorities had stressed the implementation of the arm's length principle only at the financial analysis and were less concerned with the non-financial analysis, ie the differences in accounting consistency.

Furthermore, in this case, the panel of judges used an expert witness. Although the involvement of expert witnesses, including lawyers, economists, engineers, experts in a particular industry and marketing experts, is not explicitly referred to in OECD Transfer Pricing Guidelines, in practice, in some developed countries, expert witnesses are always included in the transfer pricing audit. In America, the involvement of expert witnesses in a particular industry and specialists, including outside industry experts, is written firmly into the international audit manual (Chapter 61,

LMSB International Program Audit Guidelines, section 3, Development of RC section 482 Cases), including it being mandatory for international examiners to request the assistance of/a consultation with economist for particular audits, including where there is a potential underpayment of more than $500,000 (approx. IDR 4.5 billion). Expert witnesses should be used in the audit phase to do the functional analysis, to help obtain relevant facts and to determine whether a correction/adjustment is justifiable and could be defensible by law or according to the economic theory.

Taking into account the facts and data, as well as information on the above, the panel of judges concluded that the corrections made by the tax authorities did not properly apply the arm's length principle and did not consider the various matters outlined in the OECD Transfer Pricing Guidelines. Accordingly, the panel of judges concluded that the adjustment proposed by the tax authorities was not upheld.

Case Put.48154/PP/M.XV/15/2013

This case illustrates the importance of the application of the appropriate transfer pricing method in accordance with the regulations applicable at the time and the importance of the comparability analysis, as well as the ability to perform an accurate adjustment, since these factors affect the results of the transfer pricing analysis. The taxpayer chose the transactional net margin method as the most appropriate method, while the tax authorities chose the cost-plus method to determine the arm's length price of related party transactions. The selection of the underlying method chosen by the tax authorities is in accordance with the hierarchy of the transfer pricing method, which must be applied as pursuant to the regulations applicable at the time. In the implementation of the cost-plus method, the internal comparable was used to determine the arm's length price, as the taxpayer assumed that the tax authorities do not take into account the five comparability analyses, thus the related parties transactions and the independent transactions are not comparable. Regarding this, the tax authorities accordingly performed the adjustment related to the comparability factors of both transactions during the objection process, to ensure that the related party transactions were comparable with the independent transactions.

In this case, the panel of judges held in favour of the tax authorities, since there was not sufficient evidence to support the taxpayer's assertion that the transactions occurring between its affiliates and independent parties were not comparable. In other words, the taxpayer could not prove that there was a fault in the correction made by the tax authorities. This means that the burden of proof lies with the taxpayer. As such, the panel of judges concluded that the adjustment proposed by the tax authorities was upheld.

A dissenting opinion was also delivered by one of the judges in this case, who stated that the tax authorities had calculated a non-comparable arm's length price of the taxpayer's related party transactions. He stated that the tax authorities had compared the selling price of export transactions from affiliates to the selling price of export transactions combined with local transactions from independent parties, whereas these transactions has different levels of risk to bear since one was from a foreign market and the other was from the domestic market.

It should be added that the panel of judges paid inadequate attention to the application of the internal cost-plus method chosen by the tax authorities. The panel of judges did not consider the five comparability factors in the implementation of the internal cost-plus method, ie including functions performed, assets used and risk borne by the taxpayer in running its business, different levels of market due to taxpayer selling its product to foreign and domestic markets, and significant differences in the number of sales achieved from the export transactions, to be deemed internally comparable.

6. DISPUTE RESOLUTION MECHANISMS

In Indonesia, tax disputes are first heard in the Tax Court. The Court was established as an institution to settle tax disputes in Indonesia pursuant to Law No. 28 of 2007 regarding the Third Amendment on Law No. 6 of 1983 on the General Provisions and Guidelines on Taxations ('General Provisions').

6.1 Preferred national options

The hierarchy of courts in relation to tax disputes settlement in Indonesia consists of:

(i) Tax Court Law (as mentioned above)

There are two processes under the Tax Court:

- The Appeals Process: the process initiated by the taxpayer who objects to a decision issued by the Director General of the Tax Office; or
- The Lawsuit Process:[5]
  Taxpayers may initiate a lawsuit in the Tax Court in relation to:
  (a) the implementation of a coercive warrant, notice of seizure, or notice of auction;
  (b) a decision of prevention in the framework of tax collection;
  (c) decisions that relate to the execution of tax decisions, other than those stipulated in paragraph (1) of article 25, and article 26 of the General Provisions; or
  (d) the issuance of notice of tax assessment or a decision on objection which is not in accordance with the procedure as stipulated under the law.

(ii) Supreme Court

The Supreme Court is arranged to conduct civil review on some tax disputes settlements issued by the Tax Court.

[5] Article 23 of Law No. 28 of 2007 regarding the Third Amendment on Law No. 6 of 1983 on the General Provisions and Guidelines on Taxations.

In resolving the disputed cases, both parties to the dispute may use any references or resources that can be used as evidence to support their argument as laid down in the Tax Court.

6.2 International options

The international options for dispute settlement in the Indonesian tax system can be found under tax treaties. Most tax treaties do not allow for an arbitrator to remedy the dispute in situations where the MAP does not reach a clear decision. On the other hand, a decision by the Tax Court can terminate the requirement for a MAP decision under certain conditions. The Directorate General of Taxation is authorized to discontinue the MAP assistance and refer the matter to dispute resolution if the appellant has filed an appeal letter. If the taxpayer has filed the objection letter and they did not annul this process, the Directorate General of Taxation should deny the MAP assistance. In 2003, the International Fiscal Association clarified the formatting of tax treat arbitration with the Directorate General of Taxation.[6]

Even though MAP assistance may be an effective tool for resolving conflicts between two contracting states, the number of cases involving MAP are rare. As outlined above, Indonesia's domestic tax laws and tax treaties will remedy disputes.

In addition to the MAP, the APA is an alternative tool for international dispute resolution in relation to tax, especially in relation to transfer pricing. The APA is an arrangement where taxpayers and the Tax Office agree in advance on acceptable transfer pricing results for a fixed number of years. The APA can be: (i) unilateral, between the taxpayer and one jurisdiction only; (ii) bilateral, between the taxpayers and both jurisdictions; or (iii) multilateral, where several tax jurisdictions are involved. The APA is only allowed for a period of 3 years and may be rolled back for prior years, subject to fulfilment of certain conditions.[7]

PART TWO: TAX AVOIDANCE

7. ACCEPTABLE TAX PLANNING AREAS/SUBJECTS

Tax Planning can be described as certain acts that are conducted with the purpose of minimizing the payable income tax to Indonesian authorities in a legal way. Tax planning is usually conducted by utilizing loopholes within existing laws and regulations.

There are many ways or instruments that are deemed to be part of tax planning. These can be divided into: (i) national tax planning; and (ii) international tax planning.

6 See DGT Letter Number: S-142/PJ.31/2003 concerning the response of Tax Treaty Arbitration Draft.

7 Article by Ay-Tjhing Phan and Ravi Gupta regarding Indonesia: 'Transfer pricing in Indonesia: A whole new ball game', dated 27 June 2012.

(i) National Tax Planning[8]

National tax planning only takes into account the loopholes of prevailing laws and regulations regarding tax in the national jurisdiction of the taxpayer. Examples of national tax planning that can be conducted by an entrepreneur include the following:

- establishing a company which fulfills the criteria under the Tax Holiday Regulation to enjoy certain benefits;[9]
- a company whose payable income tax is more than IDR 100 million may change the distribution of *natura* to an employee into allowances in the form of money;
- a company with losses can change the allowances of an employee from money into distribution of *natura* since the latter is not an object of Article 21 of the Income Tax Regulation.

(ii) International tax planning[10]

International tax planning takes into account the national prevailing laws and regulations regarding taxation as well as tax treaties. One important planning consideration for Indonesian tax authorities is the so-called 'treaty shopping' among entrepreneurs. This popular method involves a preconceived effort to achieve the greatest possible benefit from the international tax treaties available. In general, taxpayers are interested in treaty shopping for the following reasons:

- claiming an otherwise unavailable reduction or exemption of withholding taxes in the source state of the income;
- claiming an otherwise unavailable tax exemption in the residence state; and
- claiming the benefit of a tax sparing credit.

The example of 'treaty shopping' among other is as follow: a person who resides in Country B sets up an entity in Country A to receive income in the form of a dividend from an offshore company who is located in Country C. The goal of this arrangement is to receive the income in a more tax-beneficial manner due to a tax treaty between Country A and Country C. In conducting their tax planning, entrepreneurs should consider the following:

- the tax planning does not violate any obligations under the prevailing tax laws and regulations;
- such tax planning is reasonable (in the long or short term), in the commercial view of the business;
- there is sufficient supporting evidence that the action was tax planning.

8 Article of Erly Suandy regarding Tax Planning in 2011.

9 Tax Holiday Regulation is Regulation 130/PMK.011/2011 concerning Granting of Corporate Income Tax Exemption or Reduction which provides certain benefits to 'pioneer industries', which is defined as 'industries having extensive interconnection, giving high value added and externality, introducing new technology, and having strategic value for the nation-wide economy.

10 Article in January–February 2009 edition of Asia Pacific Tax Bulletin prepared by Bart Koster.

8. DEFINING ABUSIVE TAX AVOIDANCE

There is no clear or exact definition of abusive tax avoidance in the prevailing laws and regulations in Indonesia. As such, there are numerous different interpretations on the definition of tax avoidance between the tax subject and the tax authority. This has resulted in legal uncertainty regarding the correct tax practice in Indonesia.

Despite to the lack of a clear definition, many tax practitioners define abusive tax avoidance as tax planning that violates the prevailing tax laws and regulations. Such planning is separate from the legal tax planning discussed above in point 7. Further, DGT Regulation number PER-62/PJ/2009 states that a tax treaty will abuse Indonesia's domestic legislation where:

(a) there is a transaction that has no economic substance, which is done by using the structure/scheme in such a way with a view solely to obtain tax treaty benefits;
(b) there is a transaction with a structure/scheme where the legal form differs from the economic substance with the sole view to obtain tax treaty benefits; or
(c) the recipient of the income is not the beneficial owner.

9. THE LEGISLATIVE FRAMEWORKS

Indonesia does not have a general anti-avoidance rule or related regulations. The rules and regulations on anti-avoidance are contained in several specific anti-avoidance provisions. The only provision in the rules and regulations that clearly discusses combating illegal or abusive tax avoidance is Article 32 A of Income Tax Law. This grants the government powers to enter into international treaties, providing that:[11]

'In efforts of promoting economic and trading relationships with other countries, it is necessary to have a special set of law (lex specialist) which regulates the taxing rights of each country covered in the law to provide legal certainty, to avoid double taxation and to prevent tax evasion. *The form and substance of such law refer to the international convention, other regulations, and also the national tax regulation of each country.'*

Specifically, the main anti-avoidance rules in Indonesian tax law are contemplated in Articles 2.6, 4, 18 and 26 of the Income Tax Law. Among other things, these cover the following:

- debt to equity ratios, ie, thin capitalization rules;
- constructive dividends;
- foreign controlled corporations;
- transfer pricing and advanced pricing agreements;
- the factual condition of tax residence;
- substance over form rules;
- wide definition of taxable objects;
- beneficial ownership definition and tests; and

[11] Elucidation of article 32A of the Income Tax Law No. 7 of 1983, as lastly amended by Law No. 36 of 2008 regarding Income Tax Law (author's translation).

- indirect transfer of shares (according to MOHF Regulation258/ PMK.03/2008, *'for transfer of shares, there is a specific regulation for transfer of shares between special purpose company or conduit company as regulated under Regulation of MOF number 258/PMK.03/2008 dated 31 December 2008, in which it is regulated that for the transfer of shares between the special purpose company or conduit company, the estimated net income will be subject to 20% of income tax; the amount of the net income is 25% of the selling price'*).

As mentioned earlier, there is no general regulation regarding illegal or abusive tax avoidance. As such, the Indonesian tax authorities usually issue specific regulations or circulars to attack specific transactions that they deem as abusive tax avoidance practices. Among other things, these un-codified and circulars include the following:

- DGT Regulation on the interpretation of the term 'beneficial owner' in relation to dividends;
- circulars on the interest and royalties paid to non-resident taxpayers from tax treaty countries;
- circulars on the unilateral increase of withholding tax on interest paid to Netherlands taxpayers; and
- regulation on what non-interest bearing loans are permitted.

In addition to the above-mentioned un-codified and circulars, the regulations relating to transfer pricing as mentioned in Section 2.1(c) will also apply to the abusive tax avoidance case (as relevant).

Further, the current framework of Indonesia's tax laws (which is influenced by United States tax law) adopts the principle of substance over form. There are two factors that are particularly relevant to the application of the substance over form principle in Indonesia:

(a) **Definition of Taxable Income:** The Income Tax Law defines 'taxable income' broadly to include income 'in whatever name or form'. By this definition, tax can be imposed in any economic gain received or earned by a taxpayer that can be used for consumption or for increasing the taxpayer's wealth. This definition is simply concerned as to whether the taxpayer has received an economic gain as opposed to the particular source of the gain. This specific provision in the Income Tax Law assumes that the earning or receipt of an economic gain is the best possible measure of the appropriate level at which the taxpayer should contribute to government funds.

(b) **Records and Book Keeping:** Article 28 of the General Provisions and Procedures of Taxation Law in Indonesia[12] states that all tax records and bookkeeping should follow the Indonesian accounting standards, unless any tax regulations require otherwise. These standards apply the substance over form principle.

Pursuant to the above, the tax officials in Indonesia frequently refer to the principle of substance over form in conducting tax audits and investigations. This also applies to the Tax Court in Indonesia since most of

[12] General Provisions and Procedures of Taxation Law No. 6 of 1983, as lastly amended by Law No. 28 of 2007.

the latter's judges are former tax officials. Nevertheless, the enforcement of this principle is not always consistent since it can be subjective. Therefore, there is no clear and general guidance on how to implement the principle of substance over form in Indonesian tax practices.

10. KEY CASES OF INTEREST

10.1 Current cases

(a) Decision of Indonesian Supreme Court No. 2239 K/PID.SUS/2012: This decision relates to the accusation of tax evasion conducted by the tax manager of Asian Agri Group. This allegedly caused a loss of approximately IDR 1,259,977,695,652 to the income of the State. Specifically, it was alleged that the accused engaged in the following methods of tax evasion:

- International Financial Engineering: The export of the products was manipulated so that the products were sent directly to the end buyer while the financial documents for the export (ie, letter of credit, invoice) recorded that the products were sold to companies in Hong Kong. The products were then sold to a company in Macau or the British Virgin Islands ('Intermediary Companies') before they were finally sold to the end buyer. The Intermediary Companies were proven to be special purpose vehicle companies that were used as facilitators to support the transaction and accommodate the different sales prices. There was under-invoicing to the Intermediary Companies compared to the alleged sales price to the end buyer. Therefore, the profit obtain by the seller in Indonesia was lower.
- Domestic Financial Engineering: There were certain mark ups of fees to decrease the tax amount owing by the company. These included:
  (a) Jakarta Fee: The markups were conducted by the accused party in Jakarta's office of the company and did not contain any real economical value. They were simply made to collect the expenditures of the company's account that was affiliated with Asian Agri Group to certain bank accounts.
  (b) Hedging Fee: This fictitious fee involved the creation of losses in the form of a washout/hedging loss. The mechanism for creating the loss was made by creating a fictitious contract for the export of crude palm OH/CPO to companies in Hong Kong where the delivery of the products was made on a later date. Before the date of delivery, there was a washout at a higher price by an affiliated company of Asian Agri Group. The difference between the sales price and the purchase price was then calculated as a Hedging Fee loss.
  (c) Management Fee: This fictitious fee was imposed as a general and administrative fee on a contract between the affiliated companies of Asian Agri Group (off shore or on shore). However, the progress and performance of the management services was either hardly seen or there was no evidence that the services were provided. This practice ultimately created a loss to minimize the payable income tax.

The panel of judges in the Supreme Court ruled that the accused was guilty of submitting an inconsistent report whose substance was either incorrect or incomplete. The accused was sentenced to a probationary imprisonment for two years on the condition that, within 1 year, Asian Agri Group's 14 affiliated companies pay a fine of twice the indebted underpayment amount.

(b) Decision Number 42749/PP/M.I/15/2013 and Number 42750/PP/M.I/15/2013

These related court decisions are regarding:

- appeal on tax underpayment assessment letter of corporation income tax; and
- appeal on tax underpayment assessment letter of value added tax of taxable goods and services.

Based on these decisions, the Indonesian Tax Court upheld the assessment of the Tax Office that a sale of business division between PT Siemens Indonesia and PT Nokia Siemens Network (formerly PT Nokia Networks) constitutes a related parties transaction.

A year before the sale of business division, foreign shareholders of the PT Siemens Indonesia and PT Nokia Siemens Networks entered into a framework agreement which was executed on 19th June 2006. The Original Framework Agreement regulates as follows:

- Nokia Corporation and Siemens AG agreed that Nokia Corporation would transfer its Nokia Network Business to Nokia Siemens Network BV and Siemens AG would transfer its Siemens Network Business to Nokia Siemens Network BV, with the shareholding composition in the Nokia Siemens Network BV being 50 per cent each;
- for the establishment and transfer of their network business to Nokia Siemens Network BV, Siemens AG and Nokia Corporation were acting on behalf of themselves and their affiliations;
- Siemens AG and Nokia Corporation (on behalf of themselves and their affiliations) shall deliver each of their operating net assets in the amount of EUR 1.6 billion to the Nokia Siemens Network BV;
- the network joint venture owned by Nokia Corporation and Siemens AG in various countries shall be transferred to the Nokia Siemens Network BV;
- Siemens Network Asset, which was transferred to the Nokia Siemens Network BV, shall be legally and beneficially owned by Siemens or a member of the Siemens Group and owned or under the control of Siemens or a member of the Siemens Group.

Siemens AG (the holder of 93.5 per cent of the shares of PT Siemens Indonesia) and Nokia Corporation (the holder of 95 per cent of the shares of PT Nokia Siemens Networks, which then transferred its shares to Nokia Siemens Networks Oy) then established and became shareholders of a joint venture company in the Netherlands, named Nokia Siemens Networks BV. After the transfer of the Communication Division of PT Siemens Indonesia to PT Nokia Siemens Networks, Nokia Siemens Networks BV proceeded to obtain the sharesof PT Nokia Siemens Networks' shareholders, and thus became the controller of PT Nokia Siemens Networks pursuant to the Local Share Transfer Agreement which regulated the transfer of the shares of Nokia Siemens Networks Oy held by Nokia Corporation to Nokia Siemens Networks BV.

In relation to this transaction, PT Siemens Indonesia argued that:

(i) the framework agreement is a memorandum of understanding which is still subject to fulfilment of certain conditions before a final and binding agreement is executed; and

(ii) at the time of transfer of the business division, PT Nokia Siemens Networks and PT Siemens Indonesia were not related parties in accordance with Article 18 paragraph (4) section (a) and (b) above, and the special relationship was only established after the joint venture company became controller of the PT Nokia Siemens Networks.

On the other hand, the Indonesian Tax Court decided that the framework agreement is a binding agreement on its parties and the sale of PT Siemens Indonesia's business division to PT Nokia Siemens Networks is a follow-up transaction of the framework agreement.

The Indonesian Tax Court interpreted that the existence of the framework agreement and the subsequent establishment of the joint venture company created a merger between PT Siemens Indonesia's and PT Nokia Siemens Networks's shareholders for this particular purpose. As such, the subsequent transfer of business division between PT Siemens Indonesia and PT Nokia Siemens Networks is a transaction between two related parties under common control, considering the legal fact that the shares of Nokia Siemens Networks BV were owned by Siemens AG and Nokia Finance International BV (subsidiary of Nokia Corporation) with the shareholding composition of 50 per cent each, thus the legal event that was the transfer of the Communication Division from PT Siemens Indonesia to PT Nokia Networks was not a business transaction that was conducted by two independent legal entities, but a business transaction that was legally bound by the terms and conditions of transaction which were determined by Siemens AG and Nokia Corporation, which control PT Siemens Indonesia and PT Nokia Networks *a quo*. Furthermore, the existence of another document, which is a decision of WIPO Arbitration and Mediation Center on a dispute concerning a 'domain name', which in its consideration stated that *'the new joint venture Nokia Siemens Oy, co-owned and co-founded by Nokia Corporation and Siemens AG, was publicly and officially announced by Nokia Corporation and Siemens AG on June 19, 2006'*, is further evidence strengthening the Panel of Judges' belief that, since 19 June 2006, there had been an agreement between Siemens AG and Nokia Corporation on the global level, the provisions of which bound the transfer of the Communication Division from PT Siemens Indonesia to PT Nokia Networks.

In conclusion, the Tax Court decided that the sale of Communication Division which was done by PT Siemens Indonesia was a transaction with a related party, and the determination of the fair market value of PT Siemens Indonesia's Communication Division done by the tax authority of the case was fair. Therefore the Panel of Judges concluded that the tax authority's correction of the fair market value of the Communication Division in the amount of Rp 1,591,654,000,155.00 should be upheld on the grounds of the statement of the tax authority, which stated that the independent appraisal of PT Siemens Indonesia had miscalculated by calculating the projected income without considering the historical value, and only used the periodic financial statement from October 2006 to March 2007, by the existence of a discount rate and by inconsistency in the use of the HCPT project, in that the HCPT project was omitted in the calculation of the growth of sales but was calculated in the EBIT.

Comments

It is understood that there are many transactions entered into by two or more Indonesian taxpayers which have been influenced by their respective shareholders or groups residing abroad. Although those Indonesian taxpayers have no ownership relationship and appear independent, their transactions which are not at arm's length must be done by them as per the guidance of their shareholders/groups residing abroad which have agreed to implement their arrangements globally.

The complexity of such transaction may have misled the tax authorities when calculating the tax due from PT Siemens Indonesia. As can be seen in the cases, there was a huge difference between the calculation of PT Siemens Indonesia and that of the tax authorities. If the tax authorities cannot see the relationship between the parties, they may lose a huge amount of income for the state.

The Indonesian capital market regulation defines a controller as follows:

(i) any person that owns more than a 50 per cent share of the total paid-up capital of either a public company or an equity issuer; or

(ii) any person that has the ability to determine, whether directly or indirectly, by any means, the management and/or policy of either a public company or an equity issuer.

Meanwhile, the Anti-Competition Regulation describes control as (i) ownership of shares or control of more than 50 per cent of the voting rights of a business entity or (ii) ownership of shares or control of less than 50 per cent of voting rights, but is able to influence and determine the management policy of a business entity and/or is able to influence and determine the management of a business entity.

Apparently the scope of the term 'control' in tax law as described in an earlier section is much broader than in capital market regulation and/or anti-monopoly regulation, thus the enforcement of the transfer pricing rule must be done more dilligently to capture any complex transaction structure.

10.2 Key historical cases

Introduction

This case involved the issuance of notes to Indah Kiat Pulp & Paper Tbk ('IKPP'). After Indah Kiat BV (the issuer of the notes) defaulted in May of 2001 and IKPP refused to honor its obligations as the guarantor of the payments, the noteholders took legal action in the State of New York against IKPP and Indah Kiat BV. Although the case was already before the courts in New York and the indenture and underwriting agreements provided New York courts exclusive jurisdiction, IKPP commenced a separate lawsuit in Indonesia. This was done in an attempt to declare the transaction documents in relation to the issuance of the notes (including the indenture and underwriting agreements, the intercompany loan, the documentation of collateral in Indonesia) null and void.

Several arguments were set forth by IKPP to support its contention that the transaction was 'a legal manipulation' and 'an engineered transaction' that invalidated the transaction documents. The reasons included the unlawful issuance of notes by a special purpose vehicle (SPV); the concept of a 'trust' which was unknown in Indonesia; non-compliance with the collateral laws of Indonesia; the laws of the jurisdictions concerned in this structure; and the evasion of tax through treaty shopping.

Facts

In June of 1994, Indah Kiat International Finance Company BV (Indah Kiat BV), a company incorporated in the Netherlands and fully owned by IKPP, issued the following notes to various international investors:

- one certificate amounting to USD 150 million, bearing an interest of 113⁄8 per cent and due in 1999;
- two certificates amounting to USD 100 million, bearing an interest of 117⁄8 per cent and due in 2002; and
- one certificate amounting to USD 150 million, bearing an interest of 121⁄2 per cent and due in 2006.

The funds received from the issuance of these notes were to be used as working capital for IKPP. The basic structure of this financing scheme involved two stages in which (i) the noteholders extended a loan to Indah Kiat BV based on an indenture, the repayment of which was guaranteed by IKPP; and (ii) Indah Kiat BV then passed on the funds that it obtained from the issuance of the notes to IKPP through a loan agreement.

IKPP also entered into an underwriting agreement with Morgan Stanley. The trustee was Bank of America National Trust Company (currently known as the US Bank National Association) and the security agent PT Bank Fuji International Indonesia (currently known as PT Bank Mizuho Indonesia). The various agreements entered into for the issuance of these notes are listed below:

- the Indenture Agreement between IKPP, the trustee and Indah Kiat BV. Based on the agreement, IKPP acted as a guarantor for the payment obligations of Indah Kiat BV;
- the Loan Agreement between Indah Kiat BV and IKPP;
- the Collateral Agency Agreement between the trustee and PT Bank Mizuho Indonesia (Bank Mizuho) for the appointment of Bank Mizuho as the security agent;
- security interest documents, as collateral for the payment obligations of the notes, ie, pledges over land and buildings and fiduciary security; and

- the Underwriting Agreement between Indah Kiat BV, IKPP and Morgan Stanley.

Decision

The case was filed at the District Court of Bengkalis and assigned the civil case registration number of 05/Pdt.G/2003/PN.BKS dated 13 November 2003. In the decision (No. 05/PDT.G/2003/PN.BKS) issued on 29 September 2004, the following was held:

- the Court approved IKPP's claim in part;
- the Court declared that the defendants (US Bank National Association et al.) had committed a tort;
- the contracts relating to the issuance of the notes were a tort and therefore null and void. According to the Court, a tort is an act that causes loss to others or an act that meets the following criteria: (i) an act that is against the law, (ii) an act that causes loss, (iii) an act wrongfully performed, and (iv) the existence of a relationship between the act and the loss;
- the Court also added that according to certain jurisprudence of the Supreme Court, fulfillment of one of the above criteria is sufficient to find that a tort exists (ie, the satisfaction all the four criteria is unnecessary);
- furthermore, acts which satisfy the following conditions are deemed to be against the law: the act (i) is against the legal obligation of the person committing the act, (ii) violates the subjective rights of the other person, (iii) violates ethical principles and/or norms, and (iv) is against the principles of appropriateness, care and prudence which parties should uphold when interacting with others;
- the Court nullified the agreements based on the reasoning that the transaction documents related to the issuance of the notes were entered into without any legal cause, and therefore did not meet the provision of Art. 1320 of the Indonesian Civil Code (ICC) in relation to the basic legal conditions required for an agreement to be valid under Indonesian law;
- the Court declared the attachment of the collateral was enforceable and valid; and
- the Court held that any claims with regard to the compensation must be rejected.

Some other considerations of the Court were, inter alia:

- In addition to the loan agreement between IKPP and Indah Kiat BV (where IKPP was the debtor of Indah Kiat BV), IKPP also acted as a guarantor on the payment obligations of Indah Kiat BV. The Court considered both of the above transactions as essentially one transaction, and that IKPP had acted both as a debtor and guarantor in the same transaction. Accordingly, the Court was of the view that this was in contravention with Art. 1820 of the ICC which prohibits the borrower from guaranteeing its own debt. Under Art. 1820 of the ICC, a guarantee is an agreement pursuant to which a third party agrees, for the benefit of the creditor, to fulfill the obligations of the debtor in the event that the debtor fails to fulfill its repayment obligations. Accordingly, a borrower cannot guarantee its own obligations and thus, the borrower cannot act as the guarantor in the same transaction.

- Indah Kiat BV (deemed as an SPV) was established for the sole purpose of circumventing Indonesian tax regulations and avoiding tax obligations in Indonesia. Indah Kiat BV was deemed as an SPV given that (i) it had no business activities or investments, (ii) it had no offices, office equipment or employees, other than its directors, and (iii) its paid-up capital was only USD 2. The court viewed that based on the Indonesia–Netherlands tax treaty, treaty protection was accorded to companies which had trading and investment activities. As Indah Kiat BV undertook neither trading or investment activities, its purpose other than an SPV could not be established.
- The structure also enabled Indah Kiat BV to issue the notes and avoid the Indonesian domestic requirement that notes issued were subject to approval from BAPEPAM (the Indonesian Capital Markets Regulatory Authority). The subsequent decision of the High Court of Pekanbaru (No. 40/PDT/2004/PTR) dated 16 June 2005 affirmed the decision of the District Court of Bengkalis. The Supreme Court's decision (No. 381K/Pdt/2006) upheld the decisions of both the District Court and High Court. The Supreme Court did not address any evidentiary issues but instead considered whether there had been a misapplication of the laws; a violation of prevailing laws; a failure to meet any conditions required by laws and regulations, the failure of which should nullify the decision; and the competency of the courts. Although the Supreme Court's decision has permanent legal force, a Judicial Review can reexamine the decision if new evidence comes to light.

Comments

The main reasons that IKPP used the Dutch SPV to issue the notes are discussed below:

Interest withholding tax: If the notes had been issued directly by IKPP, the applicable withholding tax rate would have been a maximum of 20 per cent. This rate could have been reduced, depending on the countries of residence of the noteholders and the applicable tax treaty provisions.

Under the financing scheme, the tax that IKPP was required to withhold on interest payments made in relation to the loan from Indah Kiat BV was reduced to 10 per cent based on the Indonesia–Netherlands tax treaty. Meanwhile, the payment of interest by the Dutch SPV to various international noteholders was not subject to withholding tax as the Netherlands generally does not levy withholding tax on interest payments.

Capital gains tax: If the notes had been issued directly by IKPP, the profits earned by various foreign noteholders from the disposal of notes would have been subject to withholding tax on capital gains at 20 per cent. The structure using the Dutch SPV circumvented Indonesian capital gains withholding tax unless of course, the noteholders were Indonesian tax residents or had a permanent establishment in Indonesia.

Avoiding public offering requirements: Under Indonesian Capital Market Law No. 8 of 1995 ('Law 8/1995'), a public offering is defined as an offering of securities by an issuer for the purpose of selling securities to the public in accordance with the procedure stipulated under Law 8/1995 and its implementing regulation. The following issuances of securities are subject to the regulations prescribed by Law 8/1995:

'Any offering of securities which is made (i) in the territory of the Republic of Indonesia; or (ii) to Indonesian citizens (wherever domiciled) by the use of mass media, offering of securities to more than 100 parties or selling the securities to more than 50 parties. The regulatory provisions also apply to domestic issuers making public offers abroad to Indonesian citizens.'

In order to avoid the regulatory approvals concerning public offerings (under Capital Market Laws), these issues can be made abroad.

11. PENALTIES

In Indonesia, the penalties for abusive tax avoidance by taxpayers can be divided into (i) administrative sanctions; and (ii) penal sanctions in general.

(i) Administrative sanctions

The administrative sanctions which can be imposed on taxpayers who are deemed to have violated the prevailing laws and regulations regarding taxation in conducting their tax planning include: (a) a fine; (b) an interest payment; and (c) an increase.

(ii) Penal sanctions:

The penal sanctions that can be imposed on taxpayers include:

(a) imprisonment;
(b) confinement (*kurungan*);
(c) a fine;
(d) additional penal sanctions, ie: (i) revocation of certain rights; and/or (ii) forfeiture of certain goods.

11.1 Legislative provisions

As discussed in section 9, Indonesia does not have a general anti-avoidance rule or related regulations. The regulations regarding anti-avoidance in Indonesia are spread among several specific regulations, which include:

- Article 4, 8, 18 (1), (2), (3), (3a), (3b), (3c), (3d), (4) and 32 A of Income Tax Law. These articles are focused on income tax objects, the government's authority to re-evaluate the transaction's value for the purpose of paying tax, taxable transitions, and the amended act on taxation procedure including the sanction;

- Circular Letter of Directorate General of Taxation No. SE-04/PJ.34/2005, as revoked by Circular Letter No. SE - 03/PJ.03/2008. This concerns the interpretation of the term 'beneficial owner' as mentioned in Decision regarding Avoidance of Double Taxation between Indonesia and the other countries;
- Regulation of Directorate General of Taxation No. PER 43/2010, as amended by PER-32/2011. This deals with the Application of the Principle of Fairness and Predominance of Business in Transactions Between Taxpayers and the Related Party;
- Regulation of Directorate General of Taxation No. PER/48/PJ/2010, regarding the Guidelines on the Implementation of Mutual Agreement Procedure Pursuant to the Agreement on Double Tax Avoidance;
- Regulation of Directorate General of Taxation No. PER-59/PJ/2010, regarding the Guidelines on the Notification for the Receipt of Dividends;
- Regulation of Directorate General of Taxation No. 69/PJ/2010, regarding the Advance Pricing Agreement;
- Regulation of Directorate General of Taxation No. PER-62/PJ/2009, regarding the Avoidance of Double Taxation;
- Decree of Minister of Finance No. 258/PMK.03/2008, regarding Tax on Disposal of Shares Through Special Purpose Vehicle;
- Decree of Minister of Finance No. 650/KMK.04/1994, as revoked by Decree No. 256/PMK.03/2008. This covers the determination on when the dividend is accrued by a domestic taxpayer on the capital participation in an offshore company other than the company whose shares are traded on the stock exchange;
- Regulation of Minister of Finance No. 140/PMK.03/2010. This regulates that there is a possibility for a determination that a taxpayer is a 'true taxpayer' who purchases a corporation's shares or assets through another party or a special purpose company. Both the former and the latter have a special relationship with other parties due to the irregularity on the determination of the price;
- Regulation of Minister of Finance 258/PMK.03/2008 (MoF Regulation 258) sets a rate of 25 per cent of the transaction value for deemed taxable gains. These gains are derived from the disposal of shares in a foreign company that is domiciled in a tax haven country and acts only as a special purpose vehicle to hold shares representing 25 per cent or more ownership of an unlisted Indonesian company. This regulation came into force on January 1, 2009;
- Regulation of Minister of Finance No. 139/PMK.03/2010 states that the income obtained by a domestic taxpayer in relation to work, activities, or services from an employer with a special relationship with an offshore company can be re-determined under certain circumstances. A re-assessment will occur where the employer transfers all or part of the taxpayer's income in the form of expense charging or other charging to the offshore company;
- Etc.

11.2 Examples of penalties imposed

As described in section 10, there are several types of penalties that may be imposed on entrepreneurs who engage in abusive tax avoidance. These include: (i) administrative sanctions in the form of a fine to the entrepreneur to pay back the indebted underpayment; and/or (ii) penal sanctions in the form of imprisonment or probationary imprisonment, where the defendant will not go to prison unless he/she conducts any criminal actions within a certain period.

12. CURRENT TRENDS

With transactions becoming increasingly complex as a result of globalization, certain taxpayers may attempt to engage in tax avoidance through the use of invisible 'control'. The Indonesian Government had already noted this trend and issued Circular Letter of DGT No. SE-26/PJ/2013 regarding Technical Guidelines on Group Tax Audit Procedures ('SE-26') and Circular Letter of DGT No. SE-50/PJ/2013 ('SE-50'). These circular letters will provide guidelines for tax auditing of transactions involving group (affiliated) entities and transfer pricing. It is expected that there will be more laws and regulations regarding these matters since the trend is increasing.

12.1 National policy and law

On April 1, 2014, the Minister of Finance issued Regulation No. 60/PMK.03/2014 ('PMK-60'). This further regulates the exchange of information ('EOI') procedure and is applicable for international tax agreements, such as:

- the Double Taxation Agreement (DTA/tax treaty);
- the Tax Information Exchange Agreement (TIEA); and
- the Convention on Mutual Administrative Assistance in Tax Matters (Convention), whether or not the Convention takes place before or after the effective date of PMK-60.

PMK-60 stipulates that EOI can be carried out through several channels. This may be initiated either by a relevant unit under the authority of the DGT or by a country/jurisdiction partner (foreign request). The scope of EOI includes:

(a) EOI upon request: This EOI may be triggered by a suspicion of tax avoidance or tax treaty shopping on cross border transactions. In regard to foreign requests, PMK-60 requires reciprocity where the country partner must also provide the information requested by Indonesia under similar circumstances. The Indonesian authority may reject such a request if the manner of gathering information requires administrative conduct that contradicts the prevailing regulations.

(b) Spontaneous EOI: The DGT may provide information spontaneously without any EOI request as a follow-up action from a tax audit, preliminary tax audit or tax investigation. This may lead to the following results:
   - there is an indication of significant tax loss in the country partner;
   - there were payments to a country partner that are suspected to not be reported there;

- there was a tax incentive available in Indonesia enjoyed by the foreign taxpayer that can increase its tax obligation in the latter's home country; and/or
- there were transactions between the domestic and foreign taxpayers structured to minimize tax due in Indonesia and/or the country partner.

(c) Automatic EOI: An automatic EOI is information maintained periodically by the DGT, such as: changes in a taxpayer's place of domicile, dividend, interest, royalty, capital gain, salary and remuneration.

The issuance of this PMK-60 has given more tools to the DGT to combat tax avoidance. We believe that more regulations providing the government with the tools to combat tax avoidance will be issued in the near future. This is in line with the desire of the government to combat illegal tax avoidance in Indonesia.

12.1.1 The impact and role of the OECD and other international relations

The Indonesian Tax Treaty has influenced the respective models of several international institutions. These institutions include the OECD, United Nations, and ASEAN. In negotiating tax treaties, however, Indonesia tends to follow the UN Model and the ASEAN Model (depending on the type of the treaty partner).

Between 1970 and 1999, Indonesia negotiated tax treaties with 26 OECD Member countries. These countries comprised of: the Netherlands, Japan, Belgium, Germany, the United Kingdom, Canada, France, Switzerland, Denmark, New Zealand, South Korea, the United States of America, Australia, Austria, Finland, Italy, Norway, Spain, Sweden, Czechoslovakia, Luxembourg, Poland, Hungary, Mexico, Slovakia and Turkey.

During the negotiation process, the following items have been included as the reference of tax treaty policy in Indonesia:[13]

(a) Permanent Establishment;
(b) Business Profit;
(c) Shipping, Inland Waterways Transport, and Air Transport;
(d) Dividends, Interest, and Royalties;
(e) Capital Gains; and
(f) Other Income.

With regard to the definition of a Permanent Establishment, only 4 tax treaties have followed the OECD Model. These are the treaties between Indonesia and Australia, Belgium, South Korea, and the United of Arab Emirates.

Indonesia has also referred to the UN Model's tax rates of 5 per cent, 10 per cent, 12.5 per cent 15 per cent and 20 per cent (not included the Saudi Arabia) for the taxation of dividends, interest and royalties. In the area of the Capital Gains on Movable Property, Indonesia has followed the

[13] Gunawan Pribadi, 'Rekontruksi Kebijakan P3B Indonesia', The Ministry of Finance of Republic Indonesia, Available at *http://www.kemenkeu.go.id/en/node/18660*.

OECD Model supported by 20 countries as opposed to the UN Model that no longer exists.

As part of an agreement with 15 other countries, Indonesia requires the taxation of gambling and prizes at their source. For every other country, the right to tax is granted to the residence state for 6 countries.[14] Apart from the provision on gambling and prizes, Indonesia's tax treaty is consistent with the OECD Model as opposed to the UN Model.

14 The Tax Treaty can be found at *http://www.ortax.org/ortax/?mod=treaty*.

Ireland

Matheson Joe Duffy & John Ryan

PART ONE: TRANSFER PRICING

1. GENERAL OVERVIEW

Ireland introduced formal transfer pricing legislation for the first time in 2010. The *Finance Act*, 2010 introduced a new transfer pricing regime to Ireland for accounting periods commencing on or after 1 January 2011, for transactions the terms of which were agreed on or after 1 July 2010 (the 'Transfer Pricing Rules').

Broadly, the Transfer Pricing Rules require domestic and international transactions between associated persons undertaken in the course of trading activities to be entered into at arm's length. Where an arrangement between associated entities is made otherwise than at arm's length, an adjustment may be made to the Irish profits. An adjustment is only made where income is understated or expenses are overstated.

The transfer pricing legislation specifically provides that the Transfer Pricing Rules should be construed in accordance with the 2010 OECD Transfer Pricing Guidelines for Multinational Enterprises and Tax Administrations (the 'OECD Guidelines').

2. IDENTIFICATION OF LEGISLATIVE FRAMEWORK

Part 35A of the Taxes Consolidation Act 1997 (the 'TCA') sets out the relevant transfer pricing legislation. We set out below the circumstances in which the Transfer Pricing Rules apply, the arrangements that are specifically excluded from the application of the Transfer Pricing Rules, and the consequences of the application of the Transfer Pricing Rules.

The Transfer Pricing Rules apply in the following circumstances:

(a) There is an 'arrangement' involving the supply and acquisition of goods, services, money or intangible assets. *'Arrangement'* is defined very broadly and means *'any agreement or arrangement of any kind (whether or not it is, or is intended to be, legally enforceable).'*[1]

(b) At the time of the supply and acquisition, the supplier and acquirer are 'associated'. Two persons are associated if (1) one person participates in the management, control or capital of the other, or the same person participates in the management, control or capital of each of the two persons, and (2) the first person is participating in the management, control or capital of the other person if that other person is a company controlled by the first person.[2]

1 Section 835C TCA.
2 Section 835B TCA.

(c) The profits or gains or losses arising from the relevant activities are in respect of 'trading' activities.[3] *'Trading'* is defined in Irish legislation as including *'every trade, manufacture, adventure or concern in the nature of a trade.'* This is a key characteristic of the Transfer Pricing Rules that is quite unusual.

There is no definition of 'trade' in Irish tax legislation. Generally, to be trading, the Irish company should be engaged in the key profit-making commercial activity and should have the persons in Ireland with the requisite skill and expertise to perform that activity.[4] Certain activities may be subcontracted to third parties; however, the directors must be involved in managing the commercial activity and strategic policy of the company.

In most cases, there will be little doubt about whether a company's activities constitute trading. Guidance as to what constitutes 'trading' is derived from case law and by reference to a set of rules known as the Badges of Trade. These rules were drawn up in 1955 by the UK Royal Commission on the Taxation of Profits and Income and have been approved by Irish courts. The Badges of Trade, and matters to be considered in determining whether a particular activity constitutes a trade, include the following: (i) subject matter; (ii) length of ownership; (iii) frequency of transactions; (iv) supplementary work; (v) circumstances for sale; (vi) motive for transaction.

These issues have been considered extensively in the courts. In *IRC v Fraser,*[5] the taxpayer bought and sold a large quantity of whiskey and was held to be trading on the basis that the whiskey acquired was more than he could personally use. In *Leach v Pogson,*[6] over the course of 4 years, the taxpayer set up and disposed of 29 driving schools and was held to be trading. In *IRC v Livingston,*[7] the taxpayers acquired a cargo vessel and sold it at a profit and were held to be trading on the basis that even though it was an isolated transaction, substantial work was undertaken with a view to a subsequent disposal. In the UK High Court case of *Noddy Subsidiary Rights Company Limited v CIR,*[8] a company was formed to exploit the name and image rights of a character from a children's book. It was held that, in certain circumstances, the exploitation of these rights could constitute a trade. In this case, considerable weight was placed on the evidence of a high degree of activity associated with trying to promote the brand in question, seeking out and evaluating licensees, and of dealing with third parties.

A guidance note on the classification of activities as trading has been issued by the Irish Revenue Commissioners ('Irish Revenue') and states that they may be prepared to express a view as to whether a particular

---

3 Section 835C TCA.
4 This is based on relevant case law in the area as well as the Revenue Guidance on the Classification of Activities as Trading (19 August 2010); available at: *http://www.revenue.ie.*
5 24 TC 498.
6 40 TC 585.
7 11 TC 538.
8 43 TC 458.

transaction or operation amounts to a trade or will qualify for the 12.5 per cent rate. In arriving at a decision, Irish Revenue endorse the *Noddy* case and have stated that the key considerations in their view are:

(i) Is there any commercial rationale for the type of situation proposed?

(ii) Is there any real value added in Ireland?

(iii) Are there employees in Ireland with sufficient levels of skill to indicate that the company is actively carrying on a trade?

Irish Revenue have also published details of cases submitted and opinions issued in the period from December, 2002 to December, 2011 on the classification of activities as trading activities.[9] Irish Revenue have stated that opinions on the classification of activities as trading are arrived at with reference to the specific facts and circumstances of each case. The key issues in the decision-making process are the activity, authority and skill levels within the company.

(d) Transactions undertaken otherwise in the course of a trade are not subject to the Transfer Pricing Rules. However, for Irish capital gains tax purposes, transactions between connected persons are deemed to be otherwise than a bargain at arm's length and are therefore deemed to be for a consideration equal to the market value[10].

The Transfer Pricing Rules are excluded in the following circumstances:

(a) The arrangement is concluded within a 'small or medium-sized enterprise'. A small or medium-sized enterprise means an enterprise which would fall within the category of micro, small and medium-sized enterprise as defined in the Annex to the Commission Recommendation 2003/361/EC of 6 May 2003 (OJ L124, 20 May 2003, p. 36 (broadly, less than 250 employees and either a turnover of less than EUR 50 million or assets of less than EUR 43 million on a group basis).[11]

(b) The arrangement was agreed before 1 July 2010. The transfer pricing legislation includes a 'grandfathering clause',[12] which seeks to ensure that arrangements in place before 1 July 2010 are not subject to the Transfer Pricing Rules. This creates some uncertainty for taxpayers where a pre-1 July 2010 arrangement is varied, though the arrangement itself may remain in place as to whether the arrangement remains grandfathered. The view of Irish Revenue, although not published officially, is that for an arrangement to remain grandfathered, the arrangement existing as at 1 July 2010 should be able to 'deliver the terms' of the ongoing arrangement.

(c) The arrangement relates to a section 110 securitization special purpose vehicle. Section 110 of the TCA contains a specific legislative requirement that the transactions entered into by a qualifying company should be by way of bargain at arm's length, except in respect of profit participating loan notes issued by a qualifying company.

---

9 Revenue Guidance on the Classification of Activities as Trading (19 August 2010); available at: *http://www.revenue.ie*.

10 Section 547 TCA.

11 Section 835E TCA.

12 Section 42 Finance Act 2010.

The consequences of the application of the Transfer Pricing Rules are as follows:

(a) Where an arrangement between associated entities is made otherwise than at arm's length, an adjustment may be made where the Irish company has understated income or overstated expenses. 'Arm's length amount' is defined as the amount of the consideration that independent parties would have agreed to, had those independent parties entered into that arrangement.[13]

(b) The relevant person to which the Transfer Pricing Rules apply must have available such records as may be reasonably required for the purpose of determining whether the trading profits have been computed on an arm's length basis in accordance with the Transfer Pricing Rules.[14]

2.1 Federal legislation

Ireland does not have applicable federal and state/provincial legislation.

2.2 State or provincial legislation

Ireland does not have applicable federal and state/provincial legislation.

2.3 International treaties and agreements

The primary source of international law impacting transfer pricing in Ireland are the 70 double tax treaties entered into by Ireland. For Irish tax purposes the provisions of double tax treaties take precedence over domestic law.[15] In addition the transfer pricing legislation specifically provides that the Transfer Pricing Rules should be construed in accordance with the OECD Guidelines.[16]

(a) Double tax treaties

From a transfer pricing perspective, double tax treaties are typically most relevant where there is an allocation of profits to a permanent establishment in accordance with Article 9 of the OECD Model Tax Convention on Income and Capital Gains (the 'OECD Model Convention').[17]

In situations where there is a dispute about the profits allocable to a permanent establishment most Irish double tax treaties include a mutual agreement procedure article in accordance with Article 25 of the OECD Model Convention.

Almost all Ireland's double tax treaties contain an exchange of information provision. This is particularly important in the context of transfer pricing audits and it is important to note that Irish Revenue have wide information gathering powers and this information can be provided to tax treaty partner countries.

---

13 Section 835C TCA.
14 Section 835F TCA.
15 Section 826 TCA.
16 Section 835D TCA.
17 22 July 2010.

(b) OECD guidelines

The transfer pricing legislation specifically provides that the Transfer Pricing Rules should be construed in accordance with transfer pricing guidelines. The *'transfer pricing guidelines'* are defined quite broadly and includes *'such additional guidance, published by the OECD on or after the date of passing of the Finance Act 2010, as may be designated by the Minister for Finance ... by order ...'*

In effect this means that the Transfer Pricing Rules must be construed in accordance with all relevant, current and future OECD guidelines. Furthermore, it means that transfer pricing discussions with Irish Revenue are typically framed and discussed in the context of OECD guidelines.

3. NATIONAL POLICY ISSUES

Ireland's overarching policy with respect to transfer pricing is that it should be construed in a manner that is consistent with the OECD guidelines. Furthermore Ireland has sought to link the application of the Transfer Pricing Rules to the availability of the 12.5 per cent tax rate on trading income.

3.1 Overall national policy announcements

In recent years the key national policy announcement was the introduction of transfer pricing legislation taking effect from accounting periods commencing on or after 1 January 2011. Irish Revenue has since stated that they intend to apply a collaborative approach to transfer pricing audits.

3.2 National revenue authority initiatives

In November 2012, in the context of a collaborative approach to transfer pricing, Irish Revenue announced that Transfer Pricing Compliance Reviews ('TPCRs') would form the cornerstone of monitoring compliance with the transfer pricing legislation.[18] The TPCR process was seen as an appropriate mechanism to optimize the use of resources in Irish Revenue's transfer pricing intervention program having regard to the complex and time-consuming nature of transfer pricing audits. It is hoped that the TPCR would represent a collaborative approach to monitoring compliance with the transfer pricing rules. The TPCR program is discussed in more detail in section 6 below.

3.3 Administrative statements

In conjunction with the publication of the relevant transfer pricing legislation in the *Finance Bill*, 2010 Irish Revenue published a Q&A paper providing background to the introduction to the Transfer Pricing Rules,[19] what is meant by transfer pricing and the arm's length principle, how it would apply and what it would mean in practice for businesses operating in Ireland.

---

18 *www.revenue.ie/en/about/foi/s16/income-tax.../35a-01-01.pdf.*

19 *www.revenue.ie/en/practitioner/law/bills/archive/.../transfer-pricing.pdf.*

3.4 Administrative guidelines

(a) Notes for guidance on legislation

Irish Revenue have published the Notes for Guidance on Part 35A of the TCA which summarises the relevant legislative provisions and Irish Revenue's interpretation of the legislation in an easy-to-read format.[20]

(b) Freedom of information material published

Irish Revenue's operations manual contains an overview of the approach to transfer pricing and includes information regarding the overall structure of the legislation, the TPCR process and documentation requirements.[21]

(c) Transfer pricing documentation

Section 835F of the TCA imposes an obligation on companies to have available records as may reasonably be required for the purposes of determining whether the trading income of the company has been computed on an arm's length basis; however, Irish tax legislation is not prescriptive as to the form of that documentation. Irish Revenue have provided some guidance on documentation requirements.[22] The following is an overview of Irish transfer pricing documentation guidance:

(i) There is no standard or required form of transfer pricing documentation. However, the EU Council code of conduct, EU Transfer Pricing Documentation,[23] and Chapter V of the OECD Guidelines are considered good practice.

(ii) Documentation should be available at the time the relevant tax return is made although it is best practice that the documentation is prepared at the time of the transaction in question.

(iii) Suitable documentation may already be held by another group company.

(iv) The extent of documentation depends on the facts. The cost and administrative burden of preparing documentation should be commensurate with the risk involved. For example, it would be expected that complex and high-value transactions would generally require more detailed analysis and related documentation than simple, easily understood and comparable, high-volume transactions.

(v) The quality of the documentation will be a key factor in determining whether an adjustment on audit should be regarded as correcting an innocent error or a technical adjustment. The quality of the documentation will depend on its suitability for purpose. Again, for complex high-value transactions the benchmark for what represents quality documentation will be higher.

(vi) At a minimum, the transfer pricing documentation should identify:
   (1) the associated persons for the purposes of the legislation;

---

20 *www.revenue.ie/en/practitioner/law/notes-for-guidance/tca/part35a.pdf.*
21 *www.revenue.ie/en/about/foi/s16/income-tax.../35a-01-01.pdf.*
22 Tax Briefing 07/2010.
23 OJ No. C176, 28.07.2006, p.1.

(2) the nature and terms of transactions within the scope of the legislation;
(3) the method or methods by which the pricing of transactions were arrived at, including any study of comparables and any functional analysis undertaken;
(4) how that method has resulted in arm's length pricing (this will usually include an analysis of market data or other information on third-party comparables);
(5) any budgets, forecasts or other papers containing information relied on in arriving at arm's length terms; and
(6) the terms of relevant transactions with both third parties and associates.

4. CASE LAW

As Ireland has only recently introduced the Transfer Pricing Rules there are no litigated Irish transfer pricing cases. Furthermore, Irish Revenue are currently trying to position transfer pricing as a collaborative rather than confrontational matter and therefore transfer pricing litigation is not seen as a policy priority right now.

4.1 Current cases

There are no transfer pricing cases currently before the Irish courts.

4.2 Historical cases of note

Ireland only introduced transfer pricing legislation with effect from accounting periods commencing on or after 1 January 2011. However, *Belville Holdings v Cronin*,[24] a High Court case that predates the introduction of the transfer pricing legislation, is often quoted as supporting the proposition of a general transfer pricing rule in Irish law outside the transfer pricing legislation. In this case the taxpayer was a holding company that also carried on the trade of managing and financing its subsidiaries. The holding company recharged only a part of its operating expenses to the subsidiaries thereby generating a trading loss which it sought to set off against dividends received by its subsidiaries. The High Court held that, effectively, a charge should be made by the holding company for the service it provided and the charge should be an amount to bring the transaction within the realm of being a bona fide transaction in the ordinary course of business. However the court did not give any view as to what the appropriate charge should be and it is not certain how widely the *Belville* case can be interpreted. It is not certain that *Belville* requires an 'arm's length charge' (rather it requires a charge to bring it 'within the realm of being a bona fide transaction').

[24] III ITR 340.

5. PENALTIES

The Transfer Pricing Rules do not prescribe a separate penalty regime and therefore general tax legislation[25] and the Code of Practice for Revenue Audit[26] will be applicable.

5.1 Types of penalties

In a case where a penalty arises, the amount of the penalty due is generally computed by the Irish Revenue auditor, agreed with the taxpayer and paid. Where there is no agreement between Irish Revenue and the taxpayer on the amount of the penalty, or where an agreed penalty is not paid, the penalty due will be determined by a court.

The applicable penalty is a tax-geared penalty, as set out in the TCA,[27] and can vary depending on (i) the category of default giving rise to the penalty, (ii) whether the taxpayer has made voluntary qualifying disclosure of the underpayment of tax and (iii) whether the taxpayer co-operates during the course of the audit.

The relevant categories of default are (a) deliberate behaviour; and (b) careless behaviour, (i) with significant consequences; or (ii) without significant consequences.

(a) Deliberate behaviour penalties

Deliberate behaviour is not defined in the TCA and is, therefore, given its normal meaning. In general, deliberate behaviour involves either a breach of a tax obligation with indicators consistent with intent on the part of the taxpayer or a breach that cannot be explained solely by carelessness. For deliberate behaviour penalties to apply, the auditor must be satisfied (i) that the facts of the case are consistent with intent to default, or (ii) that the taxpayer's actions or omissions were likely to result in a tax default and those actions or omissions cannot be explained solely by carelessness.

(b) Careless behaviour penalties

Taxpayers must exercise care in fulfilling their tax obligations. Careless behaviour means a lack of due care rendering tax liabilities returned by the taxpayer, or repayment claims made, incorrect. Careless behaviour is distinguished from deliberate behaviour by the absence of indicators, in the facts and circumstances of the default, consistent with intent.

'Carelessly' is defined in the Acts as meaning the *'failure to take reasonable care.'* The test of reasonable care is *'whether a taxpayer of ordinary skill and knowledge, properly advised, would have foreseen as a reasonable probability or likelihood the prospect that an act (or omission) would cause a tax underpayment, having regard to all the circumstances.'* The taxpayer cannot devolve the responsibility of making a correct return to an agent. If all relevant matters have not been brought to the attention of the agent, the taxpayer has not taken due care.

---

25 Part 47 TCA.
26 *www.revenue.ie/en/practitioner/code-of-practice-revenue-audit.pdf.*
27 Section 1077E TCA.

Where there is careless behaviour, the appropriate penalty depends on whether that careless behaviour gave rise to significant consequences.

(i) Careless behaviour with significant consequences is distinguished from careless behaviour without significant consequences by reference to the size of the shortfall relative to the correct tax liability concerned.

(ii) Significant consequences: this phrase is not defined in the TCA but is used to describe the statutory penalty applicable where the tax underpaid exceeds 15 per cent of the tax correctly payable. The 15 per cent test is to be applied separately to each tax type and period in respect of which a return or statement of liability is required to be made by the taxpayer. In the case of a reduction in a repayment made, if any, compared with the repayment claimed, if the reduction exceeds 15 per cent of the amount of the repayment claimed by the taxpayer, a penalty in the category of careless behaviour with significant consequences will apply if the incorrect claim arose from a lack of due care by the taxpayer.

Penalty Mitigation Table in respect of penalties imposed after 24 December 2008.

Qualifying disclosure	**Category of default**	**Co-operation**	
		Prompted	**Unprompted**
All qualifying disclosures in this category	Careless behaviour without significant consequences	10 per cent	3 per cent
First qualifying disclosure in these categories	Careless behaviour with significant consequences	20 per cent	5 per cent
	Deliberate behaviour	50 per cent	10 per cent
Second qualifying disclosure in these categories	Careless behaviour with significant consequences	30 per cent	20 per cent
	Deliberate behaviour	75 per cent	55 per cent
Third or subsequent qualifying disclosure in these categories	Careless behaviour with significant consequences	40 per cent	40 per cent
	Deliberate behaviour	100 per cent	100 per cent
No qualifying disclosure	**Category of default**	**No co-operation**	**Co-operation only**
All defaults where there is no qualifying disclosure	Careless behaviour without significant consequences	20 per cent	15 per cent
	Careless behaviour with significant consequences	40 per cent	30 per cent
	Deliberate behaviour	100 per cent	75 per cent

5.2 Special or notable cases

There are no Irish court cases that discuss the imposition of penalties. However the imposition of penalties and the opportunities to mitigate are discussed in detail in the Code of Practice for Revenue Audit published by Irish Revenue.

6. DISPUTE RESOLUTION MECHANISMS

In the first instance Irish Revenue prefers to handle transfer pricing investigations by way of TPCR. Cases may escalate from TPCR to full transfer pricing audit. International transfer pricing matters (eg, seeking correlative relief in Ireland for transfer pricing adjustment made in another jurisdiction) may be resolved either unilaterally, through the mutual agreement procedure under the relevant double tax treaty or under the European Arbitration Convention. Transfer pricing matters may be agreed in advance by way of bilateral Advance Pricing Agreements ('APAs'). Current policy is that Irish Revenue will not provide a unilateral APA.

6.1 Preferred national options

(a) TPCR

Taxpayers are selected on a risk assessment basis to conduct a self-review on their transfer pricing for a specified period. Taxpayers have three months to conduct the self-review and to provide a report to Irish Revenue.

TPCRs are not formal audits and adjustments may be agreed upon under the TPCR without the imposition of any penalties. If Irish Revenue is satisfied with the results of the TPCR, a letter confirming that they have no further enquiries will be issued, giving taxpayers comfort that their transfer pricing policy for that period has been accepted by Irish Revenue. Where Irish Revenue is not satisfied with the level of information received, or with the transfer pricing, TPCRs may be escalated to more formal audits (with the related risk of penalties). However, Irish Revenue considers the TPCR to be a substantial compliance check in its own right and not normally a precursor to a transfer pricing audit. While the TPCR process is in its infancy, the approach to date, in respect of the TPCRs, has been cooperative and open.

The report to Irish Revenue under the TPCR should provide the following information:

(i) The group structure
(ii) Details of transactions by type and associated companies involved
(iii) Pricing and transfer pricing methodology for each type of transaction
(iv) The functions, assets and risks of parties
(v) A list of documentation available/reviewed
(vi) The basis for establishing how the arm's-length standard is satisfied

The information does not have to be provided in a particular format and Irish Revenue has confirmed that where a transfer pricing study or report already exists, that study will suffice, provided it contains the information listed above.

(b) Full transfer pricing audit

A transfer pricing audit is conducted in the same manner as a regular corporation tax audit. The tax audit and appeal procedure can be summarised as follows:

(i) Cases are selected for audit by Irish Revenue primarily on a risk assessment basis though some random audits are conducted. In addition a full audit may escalate from the conduct of a TPCR.
(ii) Typically Irish Revenue will provide 21 days' notice of an audit setting out the scope and nature of the audit.
(iii) Following notification of the audit, the taxpayer is still entitled to file a prompted qualifying disclosure of any underpayment of taxes which can ultimately result in a mitigation of penalties.
(iv) Following the audit Irish Revenue may issue a notice of assessment to corporation tax setting out the underpayment of tax together with interest and penalties payable by the taxpayer.
(v) The taxpayer must lodge an appeal to an assessment within 30 days. Appeals are heard by the Appeal Commissioners.
(vi) If the Appeal Commissioners determine the appeal the matter may be reheard before the Circuit Court and ultimately appealed to the High Court and Supreme Court.
(vii) If the Appeal Commissioners dismiss the appeal the taxpayer can only appeal to the High Court or Supreme Court if he considers that having regard to the available evidence, the dismissal of the appeal was unreasonable.

6.2 International options

(a) Unilateral Relief

From a transfer pricing perspective, double tax treaties are typically most relevant where there is an allocation of profits to a permanent establishment in accordance with Article 9 of the OECD Model Convention. Irish Revenue may accept a transfer pricing adjustment under Article 9(2) without formally engaging in a MAP.

Many of Ireland's double tax treaties do not include an equivalent to Article 9(2) of the OECD Model Convention. This means that there is potentially double taxation where an adjustment is made to profits in accordance with such double tax treaties, because Irish domestic law requires that a corresponding adjustment can only be taken in such instances where the adjustment is taken in accordance with a double taxation agreement. However, although not legally obliged to allow a corresponding adjustment where there is no equivalent to Article 9(2) of the OECD Model, Irish Revenue generally allow for relief from double taxation on the basis of a claim under the MAP article of the relevant double tax treaty or EU Arbitration Convention.

(b) Mutual agreement procedure

There is no formal procedure for undertaking a MAP under Irish law however the MAP request should (i) quote the legal basis for the MAP ie, the relevant Article in Ireland's double taxation treaties/agreements or EU Arbitration Convention; (ii) explain why a MAP is considered necessary; (iii) explain the issues involved (attaching relevant background documentation); and (iv) set out what the requester considers to be the correct outcome (attaching any documents, case law, etc, backing up the requester's view). Furthermore if the MAP request(s) is being made to more than one Competent Authority, the Irish Competent Authority should receive the same information as the other Competent Authority(ies).

(c) EU Arbitration Convention

In the MAP Article 25, there is typically no obligation on the respective Competent Authorities to reach a binding decision. They are typically only required to endeavour to resolve the case and find a solution. As such, binding arbitration procedures are useful in coming to a final solution for the taxpayer where the MAP process has proved unsuccessful.

The EU Arbitration Convention[28] currently applies in all EU Member States and provides for a process to resolve disputes arising in connection with the adjustment of profits between associated enterprises (ie, transfer pricing adjustments).

Where a taxpayer believes that there is double taxation as a result of a transfer pricing adjustment, a claim must be presented to the Competent Authority of the country in which it is resident (eg, Ireland) within 3 years of adjustment being made. If Irish Revenue consider that the claim is well-founded and if Irish Revenue cannot solve the issue unilaterally, it will be obliged to attempt to resolve it by mutual agreement with the Competent Authority of the other EU Member State.

Where no agreement has been reached between the two Competent Authorities within two years, the matter is sent to an arbitration commission for an opinion regarding how to eliminate the double tax. The arbitration commission board usually consists of two independent 'persons of standing' from the arbitration panel, a chairperson and the representatives of the Competent Authorities. The decision of the arbitration commission shall be reached within a six month period; however, this decision is not binding on the parties involved. The Arbitration Convention merely requires the Competent Authorities to reach a final binding decision within a further six months after the conclusion of the proceedings of the arbitration panel.

(d) Advance pricing agreement

Irish Revenue will consider bilateral or multilateral APAs. However, as a policy matter, they will generally not consider unilateral APAs. The APA process is similar to the MAP process described above.

PART TWO: TAX AVOIDANCE

7. ACCEPTABLE TAX PLANNING AREAS/SUBJECTS

The scope of acceptable tax planning in Ireland has narrowed over the last number of years. Most recently the Irish Supreme Court has held in *O'Flynn*

[28] Convention 90/436/EEC

Construction Limited v Revenue Commissioners[29] that the Irish general anti-avoidance rule ('GAAR') should be broadly interpreted.

There is no comprehensive list of transactions which Irish Revenue consider to be abusive. However the *Finance Act*, 2010 introduced a mandatory disclosure regime for certain transactions.[30] Irish Revenue emphasise in published guidance notes that, just because a transaction falls within the mandatory disclosure regime, does not mean that it falls afoul of the GAAR. However the type of transactions which are identified as being subject to mandatory disclosure are indicative of the type of transaction that Irish Revenue regard as undesirable and may fall afoul of the GAAR.

A disclosable transaction is a transaction or a proposal for a transaction which gives rise to a tax advantage (being the main or one of the main benefits expected from the transaction) and which also falls within one of the following specified descriptions:

(a) There is a desire to keep the scheme confidential from other promoters or from Irish Revenue.
(b) It would be reasonable to expect a premium fee to be charged on the basis of how it gives rise to the expected tax advantage.
(c) The scheme is a standardised tax product that does not require tailoring to client's specific circumstances to any material extent.
(d) The scheme creates a tax loss that can be used by more than one individual client and the main outcome of the transaction, to an informed observer, is the provision of tax losses.
(e) A transaction structured so as to create a loss buying scheme for corporates.
(f) Employment schemes that generate a tax advantage for an employer, employee or any other person. This does not include routine schemes that already involve Irish Revenue oversight (eg, retirement benefit schemes).
(g) Schemes that convert income (taxable at a higher rate) into capital gains (taxable at a lower rate). This does not include routine schemes that already involve Irish Revenue oversight (eg, share ownership trusts).
(h) Schemes that convert income (taxable at a higher rate) into a gift (taxable at a lower rate).

It is important to note that Irish Revenue do not consider that routine day to day tax advice and the routine use of statutory exemptions and reliefs for bona fide purposes should be regarded as disclosable transactions.

8. DEFINING ABUSIVE TAX AVOIDANCE

(a) GAAR

Section 811 TCA contains Ireland's GAAR for tax purposes. It is intended to defeat the effect of transactions which have little or no commercial reality but are intended to reduce or avoid a tax charge or to artificially create a tax deduction or a tax refund.

29 14 December 2011.
30 Part 33, Chapter 3 TCA and related regulations.

The GAAR applies where Irish Revenue form the opinion that a transaction is a 'tax avoidance transaction'. A tax avoidance transaction is a transaction that gives rise to a tax advantage and was not undertaken or arranged primarily for purposes other than to give rise to a tax advantage. In considering whether a transaction is a tax avoidance transaction Irish Revenue should consider the results of the transaction, its use as a means of achieving those results and any other means by which the results or part of the results could have been achieved.

The GAAR directs that a transaction should not be a tax avoidance transaction where either (a) it was undertaken with a view to the realisation of profits in the course of the business and was not undertaken primarily to give rise to a tax advantage, or (b) it was undertaken to obtain the benefit of a relief/allowance/abatement provided in the TCA and was not a misuse or abuse of that provision.

In determining whether a transaction is a genuine commercial transaction or the legitimate use of a tax relief, Irish Revenue can give regard to the substance of a transaction and related transactions so as to get behind the mere form of the transaction. The GAAR is considered in more detail below.

(b) Case law

The GAAR was introduced in 1987. However, there has only been one material case decided by the Irish courts in respect of its meaning, namely the *O'Flynn* case. This case was recently decided by the Irish Supreme Court, which delivered an instructive majority judgment on the way in which section 811 of the TCA should be applied. The facts in question involved a series of pre-planned steps designed to permit a building and construction business access to a tax relief intended to promote export sales. The Supreme Court held against the taxpayer, and the majority judgment offered some trenchant criticism of aggressive tax planning. The *O'Flynn* case is considered in more detail below.

(c) Mandatory disclosure regime

As outlined above a mandatory disclosure regime was introduced in the *Finance Act*, 2010 as part of an attempt to identify and shut down unacceptable tax planning.

9. THE LEGISLATIVE FRAMEWORK

(a) Tax Avoidance Transaction

The concept of a 'tax avoidance transaction' is the key concept in the GAAR. It is defined as a transaction which meets two conditions:

(i) The transaction must give rise to (or but for section 811 of the TCA would give rise to) a 'tax advantage'.

(ii) The transaction must not have been undertaken or arranged primarily for purposes other than to give rise to a 'tax advantage'.

It was observed by the Supreme Court in the *O'Flynn* case that this test is directed towards 'making the difficult distinction between a commercial transaction which has been legitimately structured in such a way as to mitigate the tax due on the one hand, and a purely tax-driven transaction designed to give rise to a tax advantage on the other'. The Supreme Court acknowledged that this is a distinction 'more easily described than applied'.

There are two initial points to address. First, the matter in question must constitute a 'transaction'. A *'transaction'* is defined to include any *'course of action'* or *'course of conduct'*. Second, the transaction must give rise to a 'tax advantage'. A *'tax advantage'* includes a *'reduction or avoidance or deferral'* of any charge to Irish tax or to any *'potential or prospective'* charge to Irish tax.

(c) Matters which must be considered

In determining whether a transaction is a 'tax avoidance transaction', there are various features of the transaction required by section 811 of the TCA to be considered by Irish Revenue.

First, Irish Revenue must have regard to 'any one or more' of the following:

(i) The results of the transaction.
(ii) The use of the transaction as a means of achieving those results.
(iii) Any other means by which the results (or any part of the results) could have been achieved.

Second, Irish Revenue must have regard to all of the following:

(i) The form of the transaction.
(ii) The substance of the transaction.
(iii) The substance of any other transaction or transactions with which that transaction may reasonably be regarded as being directly or indirectly related to or connected.
(iv) The final outcome and result of that transaction and any combination of those other transactions which are so related or connected.

In considering the 'substance' of a transaction, the Supreme Court in the *O'Flynn* case took a very broad approach. In that case, the Supreme Court reviewed the 40-plus steps involved and then considered, analysed and concluded on them in the whole. The Supreme Court looked at the starting point and the end point, and drew conclusions with respect to the overall effect of the arrangement. The Supreme Court did not focus on any particular step, nor did the Supreme Court identify any single step as the transaction in respect of which the desired relief could be dis-applied.

(c) Safe-harbours

The legislation also provides for two safe-harbours, where a transaction will not be a 'tax avoidance transaction':

(i) The first safe-harbour is for 'business profits'. This applies where a transaction was undertaken with a view (directly or indirectly) to the realisation of profits in the course of the business activities of a business carried on by a person. The transaction in question must not have been undertaken or arranged primarily to give rise to a tax advantage. This safe-harbour applies even if the purpose or purposes of the transaction could have been achieved by some other transaction which would have given rise to a greater amount of tax being payable.

(ii) The second safe-harbour is for the 'proper use' of a tax relief. This applies where the transaction was undertaken or arranged for the purpose of obtaining the benefit or any relief, allowance or other abatement and that transaction would not result (directly or indirectly) in a *'misuse of the provision or an abuse of the provision, having regard to the purposes for which it was provided.'*

10. KEY CASES OF INTEREST

The GAAR was introduced in 1987. However, there has only been one material case decided by the Irish courts in respect of its meaning, namely the *O'Flynn* case.

The *O'Flynn* case is analysed in detail below. However, at this stage it is worth highlighting that the Supreme Court held that the purpose of section 811 of the TCA was to reverse the *Duke of Westminster* case[31] in Ireland. The *Duke of Westminster* case was a United Kingdom House of Lords case decided in 1936, which had (broadly) supported a 'form over substance' approach to the application of tax legislation. In the leading judgment of the Duke of Westminster, it was held that *'[e]very man is entitled if he can to order his affairs so as that the tax attaching ... is less than it would otherwise be. If he succeeds in ordering them so as to secure this result, then, however unappreciative the Commissioners of Inland Revenue or his fellow taxpayers may be of his ingenuity, he cannot be compelled to pay an increased tax.'* This decision had effectively been overturned by the United Kingdom courts in 1982 but had been endorsed by the Irish courts in the decision of *O'Sullivan v P Ltd.* The *O'Flynn* case now effectively marks the end of such a taxpayer-friendly approach in Ireland.

(a) Current cases

Following the successful outcome for Irish Revenue in the *O'Flynn* case, they have been actively issuing notices to taxpayers where they form the opinion that a transaction is a tax avoidance transaction. These cases have not yet been litigated through the Irish courts on the substantive point of whether or not they constitute tax avoidance. However, it is safe to say that even though it took 25 years for the first GAAR case to be heard in the Irish Supreme Court, we will not have to wait 25 years for the next case.

The High Court case of *Ronan McNamee v Revenue Commissioners*[32] involved a judicial review of the process Irish Revenue deployed in challenging transactions under the GAAR. The judge found in favour of Irish Revenue and found the Applicant was not entitled to any of the reliefs sought. The Applicant had sought an order quashing Irish Revenue's notice of opinion, issued by a nominated officer of Irish Revenue, that a number of transactions entered into by the Applicant and his wife together constituted a tax avoidance transaction for the purposes of the GAAR. The issuing of the

[31] 19 TC 490.
[32] 27 November 2012.

notice of opinion had the consequence of the withdrawal of a tax advantage of over EUR 6 million.

The judge found that the notice of opinion issued by the nominated officer of Irish Revenue concerning these series of transactions complied with the procedural requirements of section 811 of the TCA. He further found that there was no evidence that the officer who had formed the opinion was tainted by pre-judgment or bias and there was no breach of natural or constitutional justice.

(b) Key historical cases

The *O'Flynn* case focused on whether a claim for a particular tax relief should be denied by virtue of section 811 of the TCA, notwithstanding that the technical conditions for the relief itself were satisfied. Much of the case related to the second safe-harbour, and whether the claim for the tax relief in question was a 'misuse or abuse' of the tax relief.

The majority judgment in the Supreme Court indicated that this safe-harbour must be considered in light of the general purpose of section 811 of the TCA namely to reverse the *Duke of Westminster* case in Ireland. The Supreme Court offered two (somewhat informal) tests of whether section 811 of the TCA should deny a claim for a tax relief:

(i) was the claim a 'proper and intended use' of the relevant tax relief?
(ii) was the claim an 'appropriate use' of the relevant tax relief?

In ascertaining the 'intention' or 'appropriate use' of any particular tax relief, the Supreme Court indicated that this was to be derived from the legislative words used in their context ('deploying all the aids to construction which are available, in an attempt to understand what the Oireachtas intended.').

The Supreme Court gave examples of situations where section 811 of the TCA may not be applied:

(i) where the Irish parliament has not contemplated at all the scheme subsequently constructed;
(ii) where there was a gap that the Irish Parliament had neglected;
(iii) where an intended scheme was not foreseen;
(iv) where the tax relief is 'so technical and detailed so that no broad or general purpose can be detected'; and
(v) where a tax relief has its own explicit anti-avoidance provision.

In respect of the first three bullet points, the Supreme Court held that the courts would *'not [be] empowered to disallow a relief ... since to do so would be to exceed the proper function of the courts in the constitutional scheme.'*

In respect of the last two bullet points, the Supreme Court held that *'there may be no room for the application of section [811] since it may not be possible to detect a purpose for the provision other than the basic one that the Oireachtas intended that any transaction which met requirements of the section should receive the relief.'*

To contrast these situations, the Supreme Court held that section 811 of the TCA should be applied where it could be said *'with some confidence'* that the result is *'not the sort of relief'* that the legislation intended to result.

The Supreme Court acknowledged that such an evaluation *'may be difficult and can create some uncertainty.'* However, that was not a reason *'to avoid the task.'* The Supreme Court held that *'the desire to provide certainty to those who wish to avoid a taxation regime which applies to others similarly situated to them, is something which ranks low in the objectives which statutory interpretation seeks to achieve.'* Certainty could be achieved, the Supreme Court observed, by paying tax.

To ascertain the 'purpose' of a tax relief, the Supreme Court was quite clear that it was not sufficient to simply consider the 'general purpose' of the tax relief provision. Instead, it was necessary to ascertain the purpose of the 'particular scheme'. In other words, the focus should not be on an attempt to define the overall parameters of tax relief in question (which could descend into 'rhetoric'), but should instead be on an attempt to conclude whether the transaction in question fell within the tax relief.

The Supreme Court held that *'the important guides'* in determining whether there was a *'misuse or abuse'* of a tax relief in the context of a particular transaction were the matters set out in section 811 of the TCA itself, namely:

(i) The form and substance of the transaction.
(ii) Whether the transaction was undertaken for the realisation of profit in the course of business activities carried out by any person.
(iii) Whether it was undertaken primarily for purposes other than to give rise to a tax advantage.

The Supreme Court emphasised that, in ascertaining whether a tax relief was being *'misused or abused',* Irish Revenue should have regard to all these matters to which attention is directed under section 811 of the TCA itself.

Nevertheless, the Supreme Court did also review some technical aspects of the tax relief in question in the *O'Flynn* case, namely:

(i) its interaction with company law;
(ii) its requirement for profits (as opposed to revenues);
(iii) its requirement for the company's capacity to declare a dividend; and
(iv) its silence on the ability to sell or transfer these tax-free reserves.

11. PENALTIES

The penalties provided for in general tax legislation and the Code of Practice for Revenue Audit outlined in section 6 above apply equally to tax avoidance transactions. However an additional 20 per cent surcharge can apply to tax avoidance transactions. Furthermore, the most serious tax offences can be punished by a fine or imprisonment or both (in addition to paying tax, interest and penalties).

(a) Legislative provisions

Section 811A of the TCA provides that, where the opinion of Irish Revenue that a transaction is a tax avoidance transaction (within the meaning of the GAAR) becomes final, interest and a 20 per cent surcharge will be payable on the tax that the taxpayer unsuccessfully attempted to avoid paying.

The section also provides that, by making a protective notification to Irish Revenue in respect of a transaction within 90 days of beginning a transaction, the taxpayer can, on a wholly non-prejudicial basis, obtain protection from the possibility of such interest or surcharge arising in the event of Irish Revenue successfully challenging the transaction. In addition, where a full protective notification has been made, the time period within which Irish Revenue must form an opinion that a transaction is a tax avoidance transaction under section 811 of the TCA is limited to a period of two years from the date of the notification. A notice of opinion under section 811 of the TCA can otherwise be made at any time.

Criminal proceedings can be initiated where serious tax evasion is suspected.[33] The types of offences that are most likely to be prosecuted include (i) deliberate omissions from tax returns; (ii) false claims for repayment; (iii) use of forged or falsified documents; (iv) facilitating fraudulent evasion of tax; (v) systematic schemes to evade tax; (vi) use of offshore bank accounts to evade tax; (vii) insidious schemes of tax evasion; (viii) failure (as distinct from minor delays) in remitting fiduciary taxes.

(b) Examples of penalties imposed

As part of any audit settlement Irish Revenue will insist that full tax and interest is paid. Tax geared penalties may be mitigated in accordance with the discussion at section 6 above. Although Irish Revenue publishes a list of tax defaulters on a quarterly basis, the settlement amount disclosed does not distinguish between tax, interest and penalties. Tax defaulters who make a qualifying disclosure are not published in the list of tax defaulters.

12. CURRENT TRENDS

12.1 National policy and law

Current Irish policy is to very firmly target and narrow the scope of aggressive tax planning and abusive tax avoidance. Irish Revenue have wide powers of investigation, a GAAR that is only recently being utilised to full effect, a broad based mandatory disclosure regime and a judiciary that are prepared to look at substance over form.

The reaction of the Revenue Chairman, Josephine Feehily, following the judgment in the *McNamee* Case is instructive: *'The judgment of the High Court, delivered this morning, is an important one in confirming the efficacy of Revenue's procedures around section 811. Challenging transactions which we believe have little or no commercial reality is an important part of our strategy. At the end of last year, 50 avoidance schemes were being challenged by Revenue. Aggressive tax planning and abusive avoidance schemes are very damaging to the Exchequer and to the fairness of the tax system. We will continue to challenge taxpayers, and the promoters/advisers who market these schemes, where we can, and will recommend legislative changes to the Minister for Finance where we consider that is the best course of action.'*

[33] Section 1078 TCA; s. 531 TCA; s. 1056 TCA.

As part of Budget 2013, the Irish Department of Finance published a document entitled 'Ireland's International Tax Strategy'. Included within this tax strategy paper was a statement that *'Aggressive tax planning by companies is a major issue across the world and it needs to be addressed. Ireland is very much involved in the process of addressing the issue.'*

In May 2014 the Department of Finance launched a public consultation paper entitled 'OECD Base Erosion and Profit Shifting Project in an Irish Context'. This consultation paper was issued in the context of the on-going OECD BEPS process, as a basis for encouraging debate on the options for Ireland's tax system in responding to a changing international tax environment.

Recent domestic legislation enacted to target perceived aggressive tax planning included the introduction of a change to the corporate tax residency rule under Irish law, which essentially means that an Irish incorporated company would be tax resident in Ireland if it was not otherwise resident anywhere else. This was an effort to remove the so-called 'stateless companies' ie, Irish incorporated companies that were tax resident nowhere. It is important to note that domestic Irish legislation still permits Irish incorporated companies in certain circumstances to be tax resident in another jurisdiction (even a so-called tax haven) where they are managed and controlled in that jurisdiction.

12.2 Impact and role of the OECD and other international relations

As well as highlighting Ireland's domestic response to countering aggressive tax planning, the Tax Strategy Paper commits Ireland to the international effort. Ireland's activities in countering aggressive tax planning can be summarised as follows:

(a) Through the OECD

Ireland is an active participant in the OECD/G20 Base Erosion and Profit Shifting (BEPS) project.

From Ireland's perspective, the key purpose of the project is to better align the right to tax with real economic activity. Ireland already does this (profits charged in Ireland reflect substantive operations here), and in this regard Ireland is fully supportive of solutions that would extend the alignment of tax and real economic activity internationally. Ireland does view BEPS as a project to be addressed collectively and as such it requires a co-ordinated effort and should not necessarily require immediate unilateral action on the part of any particular country.

(b) Through the EU

On 30 June 2013 Ireland finished its seventh Presidency of the Council of the European Union. Ireland's Presidency coincided with tax policy issues taking centre stage in the international arena. Against this elevated profile for taxation, the Irish Presidency's plan to focus on tackling tax fraud and tax evasion was very much in line with international developments. At a practical level our Presidency prioritised work in the following areas: tackling tax fraud and tax evasion, achieving a mandate to negotiate with third countries on the Savings Taxation agreements, tackling hybrid mismatches and enhancing administrative cooperation on tax. In addition Ireland carried forward the work on the Financial Transaction Tax (FTT), Energy Tax Directive and the Common Consolidated Corporate Tax Base (CCCTB).

Israel

Barnea & Co Henriette Fuchs

PART ONE: TRANSFER PRICING

In May 2010, when the OECD invited Israel to become a member, Israel was particularly welcomed in light of *'its scientific and technological policies having produced outstanding outcomes on a world scale.'*[1] The economic growth of Israel, a 'new' country at only 66 years young, with a current population over 8 million people, became evident at the start of 2009 with 65 Israeli companies listed on the NASDAQ;[2] more than any other foreign country. The greater area of Tel Aviv is currently home to over 700 early-stage startups, and as many as 5,000 start-ups overall. Tel Aviv ranks second to Silicon Valley as a leading tech center. Israel's high-tech and industrial capabilities, combined with its long standing tax benefits for new initiatives and high-tech companies,[3] have attracted large foreign investors and venture funds to the country, contributing to its reputation as a high-tech and industrial powerhouse. In 2013, mergers and acquisitions in Israel, excluding public offerings, amounted to an aggregate $6.5 billion deal. In addition, Israel's energy market is picking up steam as participants prepare to exploit the oil and gas reserves discovered only in 2011 in the Tamar and Leviathan sites off the coast of Haifa. The cross border nature of Israel's technological economy and booming energy market add a special dimension to Israel's anti-avoidance and transfer pricing legislation and policies.

1. GENERAL OVERVIEW

In 2003, a major Tax Reform came into effect in Israel,[4] and a special section on transfer pricing[5] was introduced to the Income Tax Ordinance of Israel. Before the acceptance of the legislative introduction of arm's length requirements importance had already been placed on transfer pricing principles.

The focus of transfer pricing legislation in Israel is on the prevention of a shift of profit to other jurisdictions, not primarily on the transfer of income to lower tax jurisdictions. Transfer pricing legislation and Regulations in Israel demand that in *'international transactions where there are special relationships between the parties ... must be reported according to market*

[1] *http://www.oecd.org/israel/israelsaccessiontotheoecd.htm*
[2] 'Start-up Nation: The Story of Israel's Economic Miracle' (2009) bestseller by Dan Senor and Saul Singer
[3] Law for Encouragement Capital Investment 5719-1959; Law for Encouragement Industrial Research & Development Law 5744-1984; Sections 14 & 97 ITO for new & returning residents; Benefits for Angels Section 20 'Law for Economic Policy 2010–2011'.
[4] Accepted in Israeli Parliament (the 'Knesset') on 24 July 2002, published on August 11, 2011 as Amendment 185 to the ITO.
[5] Section 85A Income Tax Ordinance 1969.

conditions.' The profit reported may not be less than the price or conditions which would have been agreed between unrelated parties.

2. IDENTIFICATION OF LEGISLATIVE FRAMEWORK

National tax law governs transfer pricing issues, and there are no state or municipal income taxes that reference dealings between related parties.

2.1 National legislation

The governing legislation for income tax in Israel, contemplating both individuals and corporate entities, is the Income Tax Ordinance[6] (the 'ITO'). The historic foundation of Israel's first Income Tax Ordinance[7] was the 'Model Tax Ordinance'[8] as developed in the 1920's by the United Kingdom and issued in Israel in 1941. Since the 1961 major re-draft, over 100 additional amendments to the ITO followed. The 2003 Tax Reform changed Israel's tax system from a system of 'territoriality' to one of 'personal taxation' based on world-wide income.

Therefore, at the time of the 2003 Tax Reform, a general transfer pricing requirement was introduced to the ITO; s. 85A.

Pursuant to the authority given to him thereto by ss. 85A ITO, 243 and 244(A) ITO, the Minister of Finance issued the Transfer Pricing Regulations on 29th of November 2006, thus bringing transfer pricing reporting requirements into operational effect. A two-year transition period was announced, beginning in 2006, during which taxpayers were allowed to rely on prior documentation prepared for foreign transfer pricing purposes provided it was in accordance with OECD Transfer Pricing Guidelines. The Regulations, a combination of s. 482 of the United State Revenue Code and the OECD Transfer Pricing Guidelines, determine, in a hierarchical order, the 'best methods' acceptable in Israel for determining fair market value.

The preferred method is the price comparison of a similar international transaction between unconnected parties (CUP). A local adjustment may be required to cover the interquartile range, which is comparable either in the EU or the US. If this method cannot be used, the Profitability Method (PM), the Cost Plus Method (CPM), or the Resale Price Method (RPM) may be considered (in this order). The Comparable Profit Method (CPM) may be applied in case the CPM or RPC are not suitable. The Profit Split Method (PSM) may be considered after testing the foregoing, while any other methods may only be operated if none of the foregoing are suitable.

Starting 2007, the annual tax return of a taxpayer must include a special transfer pricing Form[9] identifying each intercompany dealing, its volume, details of the related party and its residency. This Form requires the explicit signature of responsible management of a corporate body taxpayer.

'Related party transactions' cover a wide range of dealings, including financing transactions while only excluding qualifying 'capital notes'.

6 Income Tax Ordinance [NEW VERSION] 5721-1961.
7 The Palestine Income Tax Ordinance – 1941.
8 This Model Tax Ordinance was intended for in the UK colonies and 'mandates'.
9 Form 1385.

No 'safe haven' or relief from documentation requirements have been provided, while only certain 'one time transactions' may be excluded from documentation requirements (but must still be reported on the Form).

If requested by the Tax Assessor, a taxpayer must, within 60 days, submit relevant transfer pricing documentation including explanations of its activities, group structure, parties to the relevant transactions, their respective residency and of any special relations with other parties. A description of the economic environment where the taxpayer is active and an economic analysis of the transfer pricing assessment must also be included. Certain documents may need to be submitted to substantiate the data declared, ie, contracts or tax returns filed with foreign tax authorities.

The tax authorities have published various position papers on subjects connected to transfer pricing on restructuring, interest free capital notes,[10] and the recognition of stock option expenses when dealing with an Israeli entity reporting on the basis of cost plus (mainly R&D companies).[11]

2.2 International treaties and agreements

To the extent that the determinations of national tax law conflict with a treaty,[12] the treaty content shall override domestic tax law.[13] In case of a conflict, a taxpayer who is an interested party to a treaty may request for activation of the *mutual agreement procedure* (MAP) (see further section 6(b)). The ITA published its MAP guidelines in 2001,[14] posing that the tax authorities have full discretion whether to award the commencement of a MAP procedure or not. The District Court has judged that a taxpayer has the right to demand that the competent authority properly use its discretionary powers when deciding whether or not to allow the MAP procedure, but does not see the activation by ITA of the procedure as an obligation.[15] At the end of 2010, Israel reported 4 cases to the OECD over the preceding 4 years where taxpayers had invoked a MAP.[16] Compared to similar reports by other OECD member countries, this number is relatively low. This may be explained, *inter alia*, by Israel's recent joining of the OECD.

Israel has included an *arbitration* procedure in a number of its tax treaties. The first treaty containing an arbitration option was signed in 1995 with Ireland,[17] followed by Mexico.[18] Israel has continued to (re-)negotiate treaties, for instance, with Belgium, Denmark, Germany, and Great Britain, inclusive of the arbitration option consistent with the 2008 amendments to the OECD Model Treaty. Note that Article 25(5) of the OECD Model Treaty offers relief by arbitration, limiting the time for reaching an agreement to 2 years and arbitration may be activated without prior agreement of the

---

10 March 2008.
11 July 24, 2011.
12 Currently Israel is a party to over 50 treaties for prevention of double taxation.
13 Section 196 ITO
14 Instruction 23/2001 December 16, 2001
15 See Income Tax Appeal 1255/02 Jeteck Technologies Ltd. v Assessing Officer Kfar Saba (Tel-Aviv District Court, April 7, 2005 regarding MAP treaty with Japan.
16 *http://www.oecd.org/israel/countrymutualagreementprocedurestatistics2006-2010.htm#isr*
17 *http://ozar.mof.gov.il/hachnasot/Ireland_eng.pdf*
18 1999.

tax authorities, whereas Israel's approach to arbitration in its treaties is, conversely, of a *voluntary* character and not mandatory on the ITA.

Section 9(2) to the OECD Model Treaty requires contracting countries to provide a compensating income adjustment in a case where the other country has made an appropriate adjustment. Some 16 treaties signed by Israel do not include the *associated enterprises clause*.[19]

Most of the tax treaties signed by Israel do contain provisions regarding exchange of information and collection of taxes.

3. NATIONAL POLICY ISSUES

In light of the fact that Israel only made its statutory transfer pricing reporting requirements functional in 2008, the reporting of proper income and profit regarding related party transactions has gained momentum over the last couple of years. In-depth experience has accumulated while a symbiosis with other taxing jurisdictions has yet to find more recognition in determinations policies, compliance, and the multinational understanding of Assessing Officers.

(a) Overall national policy announcements

Following the publication of the Report on Transfer Pricing Aspects of Business Reorganizations[20] by the OECD, the ITA, enthused over Israel's new membership to the organization, issued an instruction[21] explaining to its Tax Assessors in great detail how to keep a close eye on value escaping Israel in cross border mergers and acquisitions. The instruction focuses on shifts in value of newly acquired domestic companies, where no transfer of value is visible. A change in the business model regarding the local activities, for instance from that of a business comprehensively run from Israel to that of a mere R&D center, will provide the ITA with arguments that there has been an transfer of 'intangible value'. A good number of post-acquisition companies were, over the last 3 years, subjected to stern transfer pricing audits, where the actual transfer of an intangible was argued subject to transfer pricing reporting and potentially tax.

(b) National revenue authority initiatives

The Transfer Pricing Regulations offer a taxpayer the possibility to approach the tax authorities for an Advance Pricing Agreement (APA).[22]

Oftentimes it is the specialist transfer pricing unit of the Income Tax Commissioner's Office that considers such requests and may eventually issue a unilateral confirmation – as if agreement has been reached contractually – as to the acceptable arm's length pricing. Also may the Tax Assessor be approached. An APA request must be accompanied by supporting documentation including intercompany agreements and any documents or explanations supporting the transfer pricing position taken in the request.

---

19 Austria, Belgium, Brazil, Denmark, Germany, Greece, Hungary, Ireland, Netherlands, Norway, Poland, Romania, Sweden and Thailand.

20 *http://www.oecd.org/tax/transfer-pricing/45690216.pdf.*

21 *http://taxes.gov.il/IncomeTax/Documents/HanhayotMikzoiyot/mikzoiyot080710.pdf.*

22 Section 85A (d) ITO.

Should no answer be forthcoming from the tax authorities within 120 days (which may be extended to 180 days under certain circumstances), the proposal of the taxpayer as filed will be considered 'at arm's length'.

(c) Administrative statements

The ITA has issued a detailed 27-page Circular[23] following the implementation of the statutory Transfer Pricing Regulations intended to further clarify the Regulations. The Circular has a wide scope and addresses the following issues, though not exclusively:

'Special relations' – interpreted not only as family relations or control within a group of companies, but any 'other' relations that may influence pricing policies between parties. Special relations may also exist where there are mutual economic interests between the parties, or where parties are guided by the same interest and therefore choose not to set a 'market price' (a transaction between a senior employee and his employing entity, for example).

'One-time transaction' – the Regulations release a one-time transaction, if authorized by the ITA, from the determination of an arm's length price between related parties. The Regulations and the ITO do not provide a definition. The Circular alludes to situations where there is a low frequency of transactions which have a limited economic scope (transaction does not exceed 10 per cent of the annual income amount of the taxpayer in the specific business area and the actual amount is up to 4 million New Israeli Shekels).

Reporting and documentation requirements – the Regulations require reporting and submission of relevant transfer pricing documentation (read 'report') with respect to all cross-border 'transactions' between related parties within 60 days of a request by the ITA. The term 'transaction subject to report' is not defined and, where transactions are performed on a routine basis between related entities, each and all should be reported. This has already proven to be an extensive and disproportionate administrative burden on the taxpayer and will most likely be a similar burden on the ITA.

The Circular may have actually widened the scope of the statutory transfer pricing provisions on certain points; this raises questions as to the legal effects of the Circular to the extent it exceeds the statutory legal determinations, and the enforceability thereof. At the same time, tax experts have argued that the Circular, as issued by the ITA, missed the chance to contribute to a more unequivocal understanding of the statutory transfer pricing rules in Israel.

(d) Administrative guidelines

The Regulations refer to the OECD Transfer Pricing guidelines as a main resource. Where the Regulations are silent OECD transfer pricing guidelines may be consulted and followed.

23 Circular 3/2008.

(e) Other developments of interest

The reading of a legislative proposal is pending in the Israeli Parliament,[24] which aims to tackle the general problems tax authorities face when taxing players in the digital economy. There is, in addition, an inherent difficulty from a transfer pricing perspective regarding commercial activity on the internet. The proposal is to tax 'content providers' at 7 per cent on revenues from search engine advertising services. The proceeds of this tax would be reserved in a special fund and are to be used for the benefit of Israeli content providers. Whether this legislation will find favor with the finance committee and the Israeli parliament is difficult to predict; opinions have been divided and the law as proposed seems difficult to administer. In parallel, the tax authorities are expected to publish a Circular addressing relevant aspects of internet trading and e-commerce, both from a direct as well as an indirect tax perspective

A much discussed draft bill, which paves the way for requiring public corporations to annually disclose their income in other countries of activity in their annual reports (somewhat similar to Country by Country reporting), may also come under parliamentary discussion. Legislation as proposed would not exactly belong to the domain of tax legislation, and is mainly driven by socio-economic considerations against the backdrop of the current global desire to combat corporate tax planning. It is not clear when and if the bill will reach its reading and whether many companies would oppose its implementation. Its acceptance will cause serious extra compliance and administrative burdens on top of the already rather unbridled compliance requirements of existing Israeli transfer pricing obligations in the lack of any transfer pricing 'safe haven'.

4. CASE LAW

At this stage, though various disputes are moving towards the scrutiny of the court, there has only been one case in Israel relating to transfer pricing that has reached the court.[25] This specific case was ruled long before transfer pricing became of relevance in Israel, and well before the implementation of transfer pricing legislation.

It is important to point out that tax litigation in the first instance is heard by the District Court in Israel. To date, going to court is lengthy and time consuming. Until recently District Court had only few judges versed in tax law on the bench. Recently, additional judges have been appointed to the bench of the District Courts in Tel Aviv and in Central Israel, who have substantial experience and a long standing reputation in tax matters. It is expected that the partial removal of a bottleneck within the judiciary will provide for swifter expertise judgments. This may lower the threshold for taxpayers to address the courts more frequently regarding all tax matters and surely including challenging transfer pricing matters.

---

24 Generally referred to as 'Google-law'.
25 Ideal Tours – Ideal Tours (1982) Israel Ltd v Jerusalem 1 Assessing Officer (Tax Appeal 9054/05).

5. PENALTIES

No special penalties apply in matters regarding transfer pricing, other than as described in section 11. The general penalties anchored in tax law, which apply when a deficit of tax payment occurs, also cover transfer pricing-related tax loss.

It should be noted that a false declaration on Form 1385 could bring the relevant corporate officer who signed on the Form within the scope of criminal law.

6. DISPUTE RESOLUTION MECHANISMS

(a) Preferred national options

Where a taxpayer files an annual tax return, the tax report is a self-assessment of income. The Assessing Officer examines the return to which transfer pricing issues are an integral part. The Tax Assessor may challenge the return within 3 years[26] (4 years if special permission was obtained by the Assessor from the Income Tax Commissioner) following the end of the tax year in which it was filed. The Tax Commissioner may re-open the assessment up to 10 years (or more) thereafter under certain circumstances.

When a dispute rooted in transfer pricing issues arises, the taxpayer must follow the regular administrative venues. A written objection requesting that the Assessor review and change his tax assessment must be submitted within 30 days after the day of assessment.[27] When the Assessing Officer receives the 'writ of objection', he may request the delivery of all particulars and documents relating to the income. The Assessing Officer may determine the tax by written order, confirming, increasing or reducing the assessment. A taxpayer may appeal the decision to the District Court.[28]

The complex matters of transfer pricing have been entrusted solely to the Income Tax Assessor, who frequently chooses not draw on support by the expert unit in transfer pricing matters of the Tax Commissioners Office. Consequently, taxpayers often compromise to prevent costly and lengthy tax litigation (see section 4).

(b) International Options

Where disputes arise between the tax authorities and a taxpayer in relation to transfer pricing matters, which potentially cause double taxation, eligible taxpayers may draw on the mutual agreement procedure present in any of Israel's tax treaties. See section 2.2.

PART TWO: TAX AVOIDANCE

7. ACCEPTABLE TAX PLANNING AREAS/SUBJECTS

Taxpayers are free to handle their business affairs the way they see fit, within the framework of applicable legislation, while respecting the general prohibition from engaging in illegal activities.

26 Section 145 ITO.
27 Section 150 ITO.
28 Section 153 ITO.

The importance of the opportunity, and even the basic 'right', of a taxpayer to plan his tax position has been widely acknowledged and oftentimes closely associated with the basic constitutional right to one's property.[29] Case law has repeatedly recognized the essential importance of the ability, and even the obligation, for the management of a business to optimize its tax position, while professional literature in Israel has subscribed to this.

8. DEFINING ABUSIVE TAX AVOIDANCE

Distinction is made between undesirable tax avoidance and criminally driven tax evasion by Israeli tax legislation and authorities. When a taxpayer achieves his goal by misrepresentation or by intentionally concealing facts, there is a fraud. A tax avoider who does not operate with criminal intent will disclose the facts and his tax planning goals, which should not be in blatant conflict with legislation. The actions of a taxpayer, who structures his dealings in a certain way that this constitutes undesirable tax planning, may have also crossed over into the territory of deeds that are explicitly qualified as illegal tax planning.

No statutory definition has been provided in reference to 'illegitimate tax planning'. The ITA and the judicature consider certain tax planning as 'aggressive', and thus undesirable, when the planning or actions are explicitly contrary to the spirit, norms, and intention of the law. The High Court of Justice explained that the crux of the question, whether the tax planning is unacceptable, depends on whether the specific tax planning is *in contradiction* with the normative framework of applicable tax law.[30] Case law has contributed to the development of a set of tests to establish whether undesirable anti-planning has occurred; the courts will assess *'essence over form'* in judging the circumstances based on their economic significance, *'re-classification of the transaction'* in assessing a transactions real significance, and using a *'business purpose'* test in situations where transactions lack a commercial or credible business motive. A Committee appointed in 2004,[31] which was to offer its recommendations regarding the introduction of legislation to counter undesirable tax planning, described in its report the characteristics of 'illegitimate tax planning' along the same lines.

In the absence of a statutory definition of 'illegitimate tax planning', tax legislation in Israel contains a number of explicit anti-abuse sections, while certain regulations require a taxpayer to report his connection to certain transactions in his annual tax return. These situations are labelled as 'aggressive tax planning'.

9. THE LEGISLATIVE FRAMEWORK

When considering Israel's anti-abuse tax legislation, it is important to remember that its tax legislation was only converted into a personal

29 Section 3 Basic Law: Human Dignity and Liberty (1992).
30 State of Israel v Promedico Ltd Criminal Case 55/96.
31 The Israel Tax Authority, Report of the 'Committee on Aggressive Tax Planning' (2005) available in the Hebrew language link *http://ozar.mof.gov.il/taxes/taxesplan07-2005.pdf*.

system of tax on a world-wide basis in 2003. Since then, specific anti-abuse legislation and the definition of 'illegitimate tax planning' have gained significant importance. These developments coincide with the current global discussion on permissible tax planning.

The ITA is led by a mission to levy 'proper tax'. This principle, which is recurrent in Israeli case law, reflects that correct tax should be levied and paid on relevant income. The avoidance of tax and the reduction of taxes could be viewed as 'illegitimate' even if they do not explicitly or otherwise violate tax law.

Section 86,[32] as a more general anti-avoidance provision, affords the Tax Assessor the tools to disregard certain transactions where he can establish 'artificiality' of 'fictitiousness' allowing him to tax ignoring the sham transaction. Only when avoidance or other minimization of the tax charge is the main motive for a transaction, or a constellation of transactions, may the Tax Assessor invoke his authority. The burden of proof is on the Tax Assessor, and the taxpayer is absolved when the transaction is driven by a business motive and not merely a tax motive. The significance of a business motive, or business motives, must stand alone from any possible tax saving attained.

Since 2003, various anti-abuse measures have been introduced to the ITO. A new section, in effect since 2003,[33] provides an anti-deferral rule applicable to qualifying resident taxpayers who own qualifying means of control in a foreign controlled company, mainly showing passive income taxed against relatively low rates (CFC legislation). Undistributed profits may need to be reported by the Israeli resident shareholder, whether individual or corporate, as if these profits had been distributed as dividend. Another provision – accepted in 2006[34] – aims at tax income accumulating in trust arrangements. Before this amendment, income accumulating in a trust could not easily be taxed. Further, the practitioner of a certain profession who exercises his vocation through a foreign company – which is under at least 75 per cent control by Israeli residents – may find the income of the foreign company subject to tax in Israel.[35] Lastly, the ITO allows for a foreign company, managed and controlled from Israel, to be taxed as a 'resident company',[36] subject to taxation on world-wide income. Transfer pricing legislation is considered a substantial part of Israel's explicit statutory blockade against undesirable tax planning.

Following the Report of the Committee on Aggressive Tax Planning, legislation was conceived and accepted,[37] giving the Minister of Finance[38] the opportunity to list situations considered 'abusive' requiring reporting by the taxpayer. Upon the issuance of the initially 'transitional' Regulations[39]

32 Initially s. 22B in The Palestine Income Tax Ordinance of 1941, s. 28 in the newly issued ITO of 1947 and s. 86 in the ITO of 1961.
33 Section 75 B ITO.
34 Section 75C-R ITO.
35 Section 5 (5) ITO.
36 Section 1 Definitions ITO.
37 As part of Amendment 147 to the ITO taking effect on January 1, 2006.
38 Section 145 A 2 ITO.
39 Regulations (Aggressive Tax Planning to be Reported) 2006, published on December 3, 2006

in 2005, a Circular[40] was published by the tax authorities explaining how taxpayers should deal with the reporting of obligations regarding certain suspect situations. These Regulations, which became permanent and were expanded in December 2009, require that a taxpayer report his involvement in certain 'tax planning' set up as an integral part of his obligatory annual tax filings.[41] The reporting of such potentially abusive situations is by special Form,[42] and an integral part of a taxpayers' annual tax return.[43]

The tax planning situations[44] are:

- The recognition of expenses for management or advice relating to 2 million NIS or more in favour of a relative, if these charges effectively reduce the payable tax;
- The sale of an asset to a relative resulting in a loss of NIS 2 million or more, which is partly or entirely offset within a period of 24 months after the year of sale;
- The transfer of an asset, received by way of a gift from a related party, which was exempt from tax in Israel to a third party within three years of the gift generating a loss eligible for offset against other income of NIS 2 million or more;
- The transfer of an asset, received by way of a gift from a related party, which was exempt from tax in Israel to a third party within three years of the gift generating a gain against which an eligible loss of NIS 2 million or more was offset;
- The waiving of a claim of a related party by an entity of more than 1 million NIS, when because of the waiver, the tax payable on the amount of the waiver was less than it would have been without the waiver.
- The acquisition of 50 per cent or more of the means of control of an entity with losses of at least NIS 3 million, eligible by applicable tax law for offset;
- The acquisition or holding of 25 per cent of a foreign entity in a country that does not have a tax treaty with Israel where income is taxed at a rate less than 20 per cent, or if income is received of NIS 1 million from that entity;
- Repayment of all or part of the debt of a substantive individual shareholder to an entity, in an amount of at least NIS 1 million, in the last quarter of a tax year, provided that the amount of the substantive shareholder's debt to the body – or that of his relative – increase by not less than 25 per cent of the said repaid amount of debt in the first quarter of the following tax year.
- The transfer of control in an entity, while another person's rights to the entity were endorsed to the acquirer or a relative, and an obligation of individuals was paid by the acquirer or seller of the means of control, and/or a debt of the individuals to the acquirer of the control in the

[40] Circular 2/2008.
[41] Section 131 (a) 5 d ITO.
[42] Form 1213 to annual tax return.
[43] Section 131 (g) ITO.
[44] *http://taxes.gov.il/TaxesFormsList/itc1213.pdf*

body was created, which derives from the right that was endorsed to a greater amount than that of the obligation paid.
- The acquisition or holding by an Israeli resident of 25 per cent of a treaty-country entity, or the receipt of NIS 1 million from such an entity.
- Payment by a family company to a taxpayer, which was claimed as an expense in the tax year and was deemed a loss for the taxpayer, to an amount of more than 500,000 NIS;
- The contracting with the holder of a real estate right for the provision of construction services on the real estate or the provision of financial services for the said construction, for which all or part of the consideration is calculated according to the consideration for sale of the real estate right;
- The contracting with the holder of a real estate right for the sale thereof with a group of purchasers who organized themselves as a group in order to eventually purchase the right to build;

10. KEY CASES OF INTEREST

Throughout the years, the Israeli Supreme Court has consistently agreed that even though the letter of the law may not prohibit a certain tax planning approach, it may still not be legitimate.

The **Rubinstein Case** (*Assessing Officer v Yoav Rubinstein & Co.* 3415/97) was considered by the Supreme Court of Israel in the nineties when there was no legislated limitation on the offset of losses. A company, with significant tax relevant losses and without any continued activity or remaining assets, was acquired by new owners. The new owners changed the name of the company, and turned the company into a successful construction business. The company subsequently claimed the offset of past losses from its former activities against profits of its 'new' activities. The Supreme Court ruled the acquisition of the shares in the company 'artificial', driven solely by the potential for offset of the losses for tax purposes. The Israel Supreme Court stressed that the transaction was (1) aimed to reduce tax, (2) had no real commercial purpose, and (3) was not in accordance with normal patterns of business behaviour.

In the **Promedico Case** (*Promedico Ltd. v The State of Israel* 1182/99, 1493/99, 2606/99) the Supreme Court considered the legitimacy of a tax planning. Foreign related offshore companies had supplied, in 1980, pharmaceutical products to an Israeli importer, which paid a commission on each transaction to those companies. The Israeli Supreme Court ruled that the commissions might have been excessive, but the court ruled this to be a matter in the domain of civil legal matters (though today, this issue would be subject to the scrutiny of the 2006 'transfer pricing' legislation). The court did not deem the commissions fictitious, which, if established, could have qualified as a criminal act of a committed by the management of the tax paying body. The Supreme Court balanced the right of the taxpayer to perform reasonable tax planning against the public interest that is served by protecting an equitable and fair tax system. The Supreme Court subscribed to the freedom to tax planning and did not endorse criminal charges.[45] While the District Court had not accepted the defense's argument that the accused could rely in good faith upon advance consultation with a tax expert, the Supreme Court instead examined whether the defendants acted in good faith according to the advice they received from a legal professional who knew the facts.

In another case, an architect liquidated a profitable company and moved its business, premises and employees into a newly established company thus hoping to enjoy a special reduced tax rate on income from the liquidation of the old company. The District Court (*Shitreet v Tax Assessor 2006* 1125/00) ruled that an acceptable transaction has 'commercial purpose' and that liquidation of the company by the architect was void of any commercial purpose, making the constellation 'artificial'. The Supreme Court agreed with the District Court.[46]

In the case of *Doron Reuveni Holdings (1993) Ltd v Tel-Aviv Assessing Officer* (Civil Appeal judgment 4374/05 September 19, 2007) an insurance brokerage company owned by a taxpayer sold 40 per cent of its goodwill to an investor for NIS 2.6 million in cash. Immediately, the investor and seller together formed a new company and contributed their respective stakes in the goodwill in return for shares under a tax deferral arrangement.[47] The new company continued the business to later become a tax transparent 'family company' for Israeli tax purposes resulting in the NIS 2.6 million sale to be taxed at around only 10 per cent, instead of a 50 per cent progressive rate which should have applied had the taxpayer directly sold his shares in the company to the investor. The Supreme Court sanctioned reclassification of the artificial transaction pursuant to s. 86 (see above), undoing the improper reduction of tax in the absence of convincing commercial rationale.[48]

To date, no cases with regards to the Regulations as to Tax Planning that must be reported have been put to the judgment of the Courts.

11. PENALTIES

11.1 Legislative provisions

When the Assessing Officer establishes that artificial transactions were the motive for certain behaviour, he may issue a best judgment assessment of adjusted income and subsequent taxes due, disregarding actions and transactions.

An omission by a taxpayer to report his connection to any of the transactions required to be reported as in section 9 above is considered an offence,[49] comparable to the non-filing or faulty filing of a tax return.[50]

If the shortfall tax of an 'artificial' or 'fictitious transaction' was more than 50 per cent of the tax that the taxpayer was already liable to without adjustment of his assessment, and the taxpayer does not succeed in

45 Horvitz vs State of Israel, Criminal Appeal 1182/99.
46 Shitreet vs Tax Assessor 2006 10666/03.
47 Section 104 ITO
48 *'A deal done by very intelligent people and which, without the tax considerations, would be a very silly deal.'*
49 Section 217 ITO filing of an Incorrect Tax Return and Provision of Information.
50 Section 131 b (1) ITO.

convincing the Tax Assessor that he was not negligent, a fine of 15 per cent of the shortfall tax may be issued against the taxpayer.

If, for a tax year, a shortfall tax fine of 500,000 NIS or more was issued to a taxpayer and the shortfall tax was more than 50 per cent of the tax that the taxpayer was already liable to (without adjustment of his assessment) the tax assessor is authorized to impose a fine of 30 per cent of the missing tax. He can only charge the 30 per cent if the tax deficiency results from an artificial act,[51] or a tax planning act that should have been reported.

Fines, as above, may be enforced as part of the actual tax assessment. In addition to any fines, the filing of any incorrect return may result in imprisonment for 2 years or a criminal fine of up to 75,300 NIS.[52]

Fraud, when a person maliciously commits an offense under tax legislation, is liable to up to seven years imprisonment or a fine of up to 452,000 NIS and double the amount of income which he concealed, intended to conceal or helped to conceal, or to both penalties. [53]

12. CURRENT TRENDS

12.1 National policy and law

As part of the draft budget law 2013–2014, in 2013 the Israeli Ministry of Finance proposed[54] that taxpayers be required to disclose opinions and advice from a professional advisor used or relied on by them. Such disclosure would have to include the presumed tax effect of advice received. The draft of this disclosure requirement sought to cover also verbal advice regarding future transactions, and would have applied to all taxes, including VAT and land-appreciation tax. Failure to disclose would have triggered a fine of three times the tax saving, or NIS 50,000, whichever the higher. This part of the budget law did not pass into legislation.

On the same occasion, proposals were tabled that the filing of incorrect tax returns and information[55] and the malicious commitment of an offence[56] specified in the ITO would become an offense categorized as part of the Law on Prohibition of Money Laundering.[57] In the case of offenses as defined in the law on money laundering, the Financial Intelligence Unit, which is responsible for enforcing the law and receives real-time reports from Israel's banks regarding suspicious transfers of money, would have been allowed to transmit its intelligence to the Tax Authority.

This proposal was also removed from the budget law and awaits further discussion.

Both proposals however, reflect the increasing readiness of the national policy developers to continue finding more advanced ways to discourage abusive tax avoidance.

---

51 According to Section 86 ITO.
52 Section 217 ITO.
53 Section 220 ITO.
54 Economic Arrangements Law 2013–2014.
55 Section 217 ITO.
56 Section 220 ITO.
57 Prohibition on Money Laundering Law 5760-2000.

12.2 The impact and role of OECD and other international relations

As mentioned at the beginning of this Chapter, Israel joined the OECD in 2010. The BEPS action Plan launched by the OECD has influenced the thinking of finance officials and tax officials in Israel.

In the international arena, Israel has not yet sought to limit treaty application by limitation of benefits other than by its national interpretation of 'beneficial owner' and 'beneficial ownership', and the prohibition of 'treaty shopping'. However the Court decision in *Yanko Weiss v the Tax Assessor of Holon* ('*Yanko Weiss*')[58] explained that a general anti-avoidance rule, such as the one regarding prohibition of artificiality, as mentioned in s. 86 of ITO, may apply in tax treaty situations and does not contradict a treaty but rather complements a treaty. The question was whether a treaty can override the ability of the Tax Assessor to claim 'artificiality'. In this case, a company was incorporated in Israel, but registered in 1999 as a Belgian resident company and claimed to have moved its management and activities to Brussels. The company received confirmation of Belgian tax residency from the local tax authorities. Subsequently, the company claimed benefits under the Israel–Belgium Tax Treaty on income from an Israeli resident subsidiary company. The District Court made reference to Article 31 of the Vienna Convention on the Law of Treaties of May 23, 1969, reminding that *'A treaty shall be interpreted in good faith in accordance with the ordinary meaning of the treaty in their context and in the light of its objects and purpose.' 'The intention expressed in Section 86 ITO by reference to "improper" matches "good faith" doctrine of Article 21 of the Vienna Convention. Section 86 is not governed by the instructions of any tax treaty, but exactly fits in with the understanding that treaties should not be abused. It is also a purpose of tax conventions to prevent tax avoidance and evasion.*[59] *Tax treaties are not intended and cannot be construed as intended to be used in an abusive way, only in good faith and in the usual way, whether or not they contain express rules in this regard.'* The ITA was allowed to raise a claim of artificiality, notwithstanding the applicability of a tax treaty.

58 Tel Aviv District Court judgment December 30, 2007 (Income Tax Appeal 1090/06),
59 OECD commentary OECD Model Tax Treaty.

Italy

Chiomenti Studio Legale
Massimo Antonini & Paolo Giacometti

PART ONE: TRANSFER PRICING

1. GENERAL OVERVIEW

The current Italian transfer pricing framework is not extensively detailed. It consists of few legal provisions supplemented by some guidance provided by the Italian Tax Authorities in Circular Letters and Rulings.[1] Furthermore, it must be borne in mind that some of these documents have been issued in a different historical context, ie, 1980 and 1990.

That being said, transfer pricing has gained increased attention in recent years. This is due to the fact that the Italian Tax Authorities have been focusing their audit and assessment activities on dealings between associated enterprises. This has resulted in the Tax Authorities serving a significant number of notices of assessment grounded on transfer pricing provisions.

This new attitude to the matter has been balanced by penalty protection rules. Introduced in 2010, the taxpayers may benefit from this protection by providing the Tax Authorities with the relevant transfer pricing documentation, drafted according to certain patterns and criteria. In addition, taxpayers willing to gain the penalty protection are required to report the total amounts of intercompany transactions in their annual tax return.

These developments have significantly enhanced the transfer pricing field in Italy and contributed to the creation of a broader level of awareness among taxpayers and tax officers. In light of these developments, Law 27 December 2013, No. 147 (the '2014 Budget Law') has introduced a number of important transfer pricing-related changes aimed at:

- counteracting certain aggressive tax planning schemes and the profit shifting within MNEs of the internet and e-commerce industries; and
- clarifying that transfer pricing legislation applies not only to IRES (ie, the Italian corporate income tax), but also to IRAP (ie, the Italian regional tax on business activities).

2. LEGISLATIVE FRAMEWORK

According to Article 110(7) of Income Tax Consolidated Act (ITCA),[2] transactions between resident and non-resident enterprises belonging to the same group should be carried out at their 'fair value'.

---

[1] The legal provisions and the various guidance documents issued by the Italian Tax Authorities will be referred to also as 'transfer pricing legislation' or 'transfer pricing provisions'.

[2] Article 110 (7) Presidential Decree 22 December 1986, No. 917: '*Items of income arising from transactions with non-*

Within the Italian tax system, the definition of 'fair value' is provided by Article 9(3) of ITCA and corresponds, in principle, to the definition of arm's length price. Generally speaking, this is the average price or consideration:

- paid for goods and services of the same or similar type;
- at free market conditions and at the same level of commerce; and
- at the time and place at which the goods were purchased or the services performed.

In order to determine the fair value, reference should be made, if possible, to the price list of the provider of goods or service. Absent such a price list, reference should be made to the price list issued by the Chamber of Commerce and to professional tariffs, taking into account usual discounts.

The above-mentioned 2014 Budget Law has introduced a number of provisions that may affect both procedural aspects and fundamental concepts of transfer pricing.

In particular, article 1(281) of that Law provided an authentic interpretation according to which transfer pricing legislation applies also to IRAP.

As an authentic interpretation provision, this rule will operate retrospectively starting from January 1, 2008. Given the uncertainty in the area, however, paragraphs 282 and 283 specify that potential penalties shall not be requested in connection with IRAP adjustments potentially arising for tax years ending on December 31, 2012 or earlier.

Italy has also introduced a new regime for taxpayers involved in the digital economy, which is currently being discussed by the OECD as part of the BEPS project. Pursuant to article 1(177) of 2014 Budget Law, taxpayers belonging to the digital economy business are not allowed to determine the fair value of their online advertising services (including any auxiliary services) by means of the cost plus method, unless an international standard ruling has been entered into.

2.1 Federal legislation

None.

2.2 State and provincial legislative interplay

None.

2.3 International treaties and agreement

(a) Exchange of information

The Legislative Decree 4 March 2014, No. 29, has implemented the Mutual Assistance Directive on administrative cooperation in the field of taxation.[3]

resident companies which control—directly or indirectly—the enterprise, or are controlled by the enterprise or by the same person controlling the enterprise, are evaluated … on the basis of the fair value of the goods supplied, the services rendered and the goods and services received, if they increase the taxable income; this provision shall also apply if the result is a decrease in taxable income, but only in compliance with agreements concluded by the competent authorities of foreign States in accordance with the mutual agreement procedures provided for by international conventions for the avoidance of double taxation. This provision applies also to goods supplied and services rendered by non-resident companies on behalf of which the enterprise carries out the sale and marketing of raw materials or manufactured goods or the manufacturing or processing of products …' (unofficial translation).

[3] Directive 15 February 2011, No. 2011/16/EU.

This Directive laid down new rules and procedures for administrative cooperation between EU countries with regard to the exchange of information between tax authorities. In this context, the above-mentioned Decree might have a significant impact on transfer pricing issues because through the exchange of information, the Italian Tax Authorities may request and obtain information relating to, for example, the profile of a company used as a tested party in an intercompany transaction.

(b) Mutual agreement procedure

Whereas economic double taxation arises as a consequence of transfer pricing adjustments, many double tax conventions entered into by Italy provide for a Mutual Agreement Procedure (MAP). On June 5, 2012, the Italian Tax Authorities published Circular Letter No. 21, which provided important clarifications with reference to the MAP procedure under article 25 of the OECD Model Tax Convention on Income and on Capital and under the EU Arbitration Convention of 23 July 1990 No. 90/436/CEE.[4] These clarifications may prove to be very useful in order to prevent double taxation for all MNEs with affiliates in Italy that have been assessed on transfer pricing issues.

3. NATIONAL POLICY ISSUES

To the greatest extent possible, the Italian Tax Authorities' policy is aimed at reducing the risk that taxpayers shift income from Italy to other countries with lower taxation. In order to do that, some specific procedures have been implemented; in detail, such procedures are aimed at ensuring a higher level of fairness between the taxpayer and the Italian Tax Authorities.

3.1 Overall national policy announcements

None.

3.2 National revenue authorities initiatives

(a) International ruling procedure[5]

This procedure is similar to an Advance Pricing Agreement procedure. In particular, companies engaged in international activities[6] have access

[4] The MAP under article 25 of OECD Model Tax Convention on Income and on Capital can be used in order to prevent double taxation between Italy and other contracting States. In principle, such procedure does not ensure the relief from double taxation as it does not bind the different tax authorities to reach an agreement, unless a specific arbitration clause is provided for by the relevant treaty. The Circular Letter clarified that taxpayers must request to start this type of MAP process within two years from the date of the notification of the notice giving rise to the double taxation. On the contrary, the MAP under the EU Arbitration Convention can only be used to relieve double taxation arising from transfer pricing adjustments, and obliges the tax authorities to reach an agreement in order to remove the double taxation. Taxpayers must request to start this type of MAP process within three years from the date of the notification of the notice with the adjustment leading to the double taxation.

[5] Article 8 of Legislative Decree 30 September 2003, No. 269, converted into Law 24 November 2003, No. 326.

[6] Pursuant to article 1(1)(a) of the Implementing regulation issued by the Italian Tax Authorities' Director on 23 July 2004, the procedure may be started by the following taxpayers: (i) resident companies subject to transfer pricing legislation; (ii) resident companies owned by a non-residents or holding a participation in non-resident companies; (iii) resident companies paying or receiving dividends, interest or royalties, to or from non-residents; (iv) non-resident companies that carry out their activities in Italy through a permanent establishment (PE) with regard to attribution of profits to such PE. Moreover, it must be stressed that article 7 of Law Decree 23 December 2013, No. 145, converted into Law 21 February 2014, No. 9, has extended the scope of international ruling procedure: in particular, companies would be allowed to ask the Italian Tax Authorities whether their operations exceed the PE threshold or not.

to an international standard ruling procedure with regard to certain international tax issues, including transfer pricing. Companies shall initiate the international ruling procedure by filing a request with specific offices of Italian Tax Authorities. The procedure is concluded with a binding agreement between the Italian Tax Authorities and the company for the tax period of the agreement and the four[7] subsequent tax periods, unless changes occur in the relevant factual or legal circumstances. Recourse to such a procedure allows the prevention of possible future conflicts between the tax authorities and the company with regard to transfer pricing matters or any other issues falling within the scope of this procedure.

The tax authorities have informed that since the end of 2010, they have begun to accept the possibility of concluding bilateral or multilateral agreements. The tax authorities have also indicated that, as of December 31, 2012, negotiations for 19 bilateral APAs were in progress.

(b) Cooperative compliance project

This project aims at identifying the main features of a new form of relationship between 'large business taxpayers' and the Italian Tax Authorities in order to develop the current risk management monitoring activity[8] into a more advanced project that is consistent with the recent recommendations released by the OECD.[9]

The new regime implies a commitment for taxpayers to adopt compliant behaviors, based on transparency and disclosure in dealing with the Tax Administration.

In exchange for a higher level of fairness, the Italian Tax Authorities should be available to meet taxpayers' needs and to settle issues in a timely and effective manner.

The underlying purpose of this approach is to implement an *ex ante* as opposed to the traditional *ex post* approach, with related benefits in terms of taxpayers' compliance and certainty.

The 'large business taxpayers' that will be admitted[10] to the project will engage with the Italian Tax Authorities in *ad hoc* technical tables to examine several issues jointly on mutual cooperation. These taxpayers will also participate in an open and a fully transparent dialogue targeted at promoting voluntary compliance.

---

7 Article 7 of Law Decree 23 December 2013, No. 145, converted into Law 21 February 2014, No. 9, has extended the time period under which the agreement is binding from three to the current five years.

8 Provided by article 27(9-12) of Law Decree 29 November 2008, No. 185, converted into Law 28 January 2009, No. 2.

9 See the document published by the OECD, 'Co-operative Compliance: A Framework. From Enhanced Relationship to Co-operative Compliance', at *http://www.oecd.org/tax/administration/co-operative-compliance.htm*.

10 The Italian Tax Authorities reserve the right to select the applications, based on the following mandatory requirements: (i) being qualified as a 'large business taxpayer' (ie, taxpayers with overall turnover or operating revenues not less than EUR 100 million pursuant to article 27(10) of Law Decree 29 November 2008, No. 185, converted into Law 28 January 2009, No. 2); (ii) having implemented an organizational model pursuant to article 6 of Legislative Decree 8 June 2001, No. 231 or having adopted a 'tax control framework' to manage tax risks. Moreover the Italian Tax Authorities should select the applications based upon some optional requirements such as: (i) belonging to a multinational group of companies, or to carry out its business activity in Italy or abroad through permanent establishments; (ii) having adopted similar cooperative compliance project in foreign jurisdictions or having subscribed a code of conduct with other tax administrations; (iii) having already entered into initiatives falling within the concept of cooperative compliance in Italy, such as the international ruling procedure or having adopted the transfer pricing documentation requirements regime.

Once this testing phase is concluded and the regime has been implemented through appropriate legislative measures, this project should provide taxpayers with several key advantages. In addition to reducing compliance duties, taxpayers should also benefit from advance legal certainty on the specific transactions performed.

3.3 Administrative statements

The above mentioned legislative framework has been supplemented by operating guidelines published by the Ministry of Finance through Circular Letters 22 September 1980, No. 32/9/2267 and 12 December 1981, No. 42/12/1587. The 1980 Circular Letter provided principles and methods to be used in determining the 'fair value'. Even though these guidelines were based upon the 1979 OECD Transfer Pricing Report, tax officers have grounded their claims on the 1980 Circular Letter for many years and, in some cases, continue to do so, notwithstanding the fact that the Italian Tax Authorities have officially discouraged this approach. As mentioned above, the Italian Tax Authorities have significantly improved their knowledge and awareness of transfer pricing issues over the past decade. The increase of attention and awareness can be gathered from:

- Circular Letter 20 October 1998, No. 1. This Circular Letter outlined the general guidance for tax investigations and included transfer pricing auditing in the framework of regular investigations of multinational enterprises;
- the possibility to report to the Italian Tax Authorities that the transfer pricing documentation (ie, a country-file and a master-file) has been pre-arranged. The taxpayer must also report the overall amount of intercompany transactions. Most importantly, the pre-arrangement of the transfer pricing documentation is connected with the penalty protection rules: in order to benefit from this regime, the company must check a box in the tax return;
- Circular Letter 15 December 2010, No. 58. This Circular Letter concerned the content of transfer pricing documentation and clarified the scope of the penalty protection regime set forth under article 1(2-ter) of Legislative Decree 18 December 1997, No. 471;
- Circular Letter 5 June 2012, No. 21. This Circular Letter provided some guidance on the MAP procedures.

3.4 Administrative guidelines

(a) OECD Guidelines

The OECD Transfer Pricing Guidelines have had a significant impact on the Italian transfer pricing framework.

On the other hand, the out-of-date domestic legislative framework and the lack of detailed guidance from the Italian Tax Authorities leave significant gaps and uncertainty in transfer pricing matters.

The OECD Guidelines, used by both tax officers and MNEs, extensively supplement the Italian transfer pricing legislation.

(b) Regulation issued by the Director of Italian Tax Authorities

The requirements of the transfer pricing documentation have been set forth by article 26 of Law Decree 31 May 2010, No. 78, converted into Law 30 July 2010, No. 122, and they have been implemented by the Regulation 29 September 2010, issued by the Italian Tax Authorities' Director. This Regulation provided for the contents and the pattern of the transfer pricing documentation in order for the taxpayer to gain the penalty protection. The fulfillment of the documentation requirements is subject to the evaluation of the Tax Authorities that may be eventually challenged before the competent Tax Court.

4. CASE LAW

In the past, the jurisprudence of the Supreme Court and of Provincial and Regional Tax Courts has been inconsistent and some judges were not experienced in transfer pricing matters. Nevertheless, appeals filed by taxpayers against transfer pricing claims were likely to be allowed. In recent years, however, the tax authorities' increased attention to transfer pricing issues and judges' improved familiarity with the field has produced mixed results. On the one hand, judicial decisions have become increasingly technical and complex; on the other, taxpayers have been less likely to succeed in litigation.

With that in mind, the most important decisions of the Supreme Court will be summarized below.

4.1 Current cases

(a) Decision of the Supreme Court 27 February 2013, No. 4927

According to an intercompany software license agreement, a US holding company had recharged an Italian subsidiary by applying a 30 per cent royalty fee on revenues. The tax officers claimed that such a rate was not at arm's length and were only prepared to recognize a 7 per cent royalty fee. This position was in line with the guidance provided in the Circular letter 22 September 1980, No. 32/9/2267.

The Supreme Court accepted this rationale and clarified that the above-mentioned Circular Letter laid down some arm's length determination criteria that companies should apply in uncontrolled transactions. This Circular Letter specified that in the event of a transfer of the right to use an intangible, the royalty fee depends upon the specific industry to which the intangible asset refers to. In this respect, the Circular letter provided the following guidance:

- royalty rates applicable to intangibles related to the iron and steel industry may range from 1 per cent to 5 per cent on the annual revenues generated by the use of the intangible;
- royalty rates applicable to intangibles related to technology-intensive industries (eg, electronic, chemistry) may rise up to 7 per cent.

The Circular letter also specified that these are mere starting points for the determination of the most appropriate royalty rate, which must always take into account the specific circumstances of the transactions at issue.

It is worth noting that the Supreme Court should have considered that a royalty fee above 7 per cent might be at arm's length if the taxpayer is able to prove and support the correctness of the adopted transfer pricing policy. Moreover, it should be pointed out that the above-mentioned Circular Letter is currently obsolete and may no longer be useful to adequately represent the today's market conditions.

(b) Decision of the Supreme Court 24 July 2013 No. 17955

Italy's Supreme Court recently held that transfer pricing rules must also be applied to domestic intragroup transactions, even though such transactions fall outside the scope of article 110(7) ITCA.

The Supreme Court stated that the transfer prices of intercompany transactions between companies resident in Italy must comply with the arm's length principle set forth in article 9 of ITCA.

The judges *de facto* extended the scope of article 110(7) beyond its literal meaning, providing the transfer pricing regime with an anti-abuse function. In particular, the Supreme Court stated that 'anti-avoidance principles aimed at preventing that profits are shifted within corporate groups [...] are rooted in EU law and in anti-avoidance clauses of domestic law [...]. Thus [...] the tax authorities are entitled to challenge also 'domestic' intercompany prices and to adjust them, if not deemed at arm's length, provided that the underlying operation resulted in a tax saving'.

(c) Decision of the Supreme Court 13 July 2012, No. 11949

This case concerned the burden of proof in transfer pricing disputes. The Supreme Court acknowledged that the arm's length principle must be considered as an anti-avoidance provision. Consequently, the burden of proof rests with the Italian Tax Authorities.

Nevertheless, since this case concerned costs borne by the Italian taxpayer, it was for the taxpayer to prove that such costs were necessary for its business activity.

4.2 Historical cases of note

(a) Decision of the Supreme Court 31 March 2011, No. 7343

The Supreme Court addressed a specific issue in the context of transfer pricing, namely the lower revenue following the discounts applied by an Italian company for the exclusive benefit of its associated companies.

In particular, the Italian company had sold goods to its foreign associated companies at a lower price than the one charged to independent companies even though the goods sold were identical.

The Supreme Court held that the function of transfer pricing rules is to prevent a shift of domestic income abroad and, accordingly, solely on an ancillary basis, transfer pricing rules have an anti-avoidance character. As a consequence, it is not necessary to provide proof of a tax saving in order to support the notice of assessment.

It must be noted that this decision partially amended previous decisions where the Supreme Court had expressly attributed an anti-avoidance role to article 110(7). In these decisions, the Court had stated that the Italian Tax Authorities should have verified whether the tax burden borne in the State of residence of the foreign associated company was lower than the one applied in Italy.

The Supreme Court also reiterated that reference must be made to article 9 of the ITCA when determining the method for calculating transfer prices. This provision makes a selection among the criteria laid down by the OECD Guidelines and favors the traditional 'comparable uncontrolled price' (CUP). Therefore, the Supreme Court stated that the discounts applied to transactions between the associated companies did not constitute the usual discounts pursuant to Article 9(3) of the ITCA, given that solely discount conditions applied to third parties can be considered at arm's length and accordingly admitted also between companies belonging to the same group.

(b) Decision of the Supreme Court 13 October 2006, No. 22023

This judgment sets out the important principle according to which it is for the Italian Tax Authorities to prove that a transfer pricing policy is not compliant with the arm's length standard.

The Supreme Court decided in favor of the taxpayer because the Italian Tax Authorities had not demonstrated that the group's transfer pricing policy was not at arm's length. Moreover, the judges referred to the OECD Guidelines, which expressly state that the local tax authorities should set out the reasons for any transfer pricing adjustment. Therefore, taxpayers are not obliged to prove that intra-group transactions are at arm's length unless the Tax Authorities have proved that the arm's length principle has been violated.

5. PENALTIES

As a general rule, transfer pricing claims may give rise to the application of penalties for unfaithful tax returns (*'dichiarazione infedele'*).

Pursuant to article 1(2) of Legislative Decree 18 December 1997, No. 471, if an unfaithful tax return is filed, penalties will range from 100 per cent to 200 per cent of the higher income assessed by the Tax Authorities. Pursuant to article 1(3) of the same Legislative Decree, penalties may be more burdensome, ranging from 133 per cent to 266 per cent, if the higher income is foreign sourced.

If the taxpayer fails to file the annual income tax return (*'omessa dichiarazione'*), penalties ranging from 120 per cent to 240 per cent of the unreturned amount will be applicable.

In the event of a missed payment of taxes reported as due in a tax return, a penalty of 30 per cent of the unpaid amount is applied under article 13 of the Legislative Decree 18 December 1997, No. 471.

Finally, where multiple violations have triggered the application of more than one penalty, Article 12 of the Legislative Decree 18 December 1997, No. 472 will apply. This provides for a single cumulative penalty (*'cumulo giuridico'*), determined according to certain criteria, where the cumulative penalty is lower than the sum of all the applicable penalties in connection with the various violations on a stand-alone basis.

5.1 Types

As mentioned above, taxpayers may benefit from the transfer pricing penalty protection regime as long as they have pre-arranged their transfer pricing documentation. Pursuant to article 1(2-*ter*) of Legislative Decree 18 December 1997, No. 471,[11] transfer pricing adjustments claimed by the tax officers will not trigger the relevant penalties to the extent that the taxpayer has provided the tax officers with the proper transfer pricing documentation.

On September 29, 2010, the Director of the Italian Tax Authorities issued a Regulation clarifying the content of both country-file and master-file.[12] This Regulation was intended to assist taxpayers in drafting their documentation, and outlined the necessary requirements, also in terms of drafting patterns and criteria.

Furthermore, penalties outlined under article 1(2) of Legislative Decree 18 December 1997, No. 471[13] are not applicable when both of the following requirements are met:

- the taxpayer has checked the box of the tax return reporting to the Italian Tax Authorities that transfer pricing documentation has been pre-arranged; and
- in the event of a tax assessment, the taxpayer has provided the tax officers with the proper transfer pricing documentation. This documentation must be drafted according to the guidelines listed in the Director's above-mentioned Regulation and made available within ten days from a formal request.

Given the above, preparing a detailed and suitable transfer pricing documentation is strongly advisable.

5.2 Special or notable cases

(a) Decision of the Provincial Tax Court of Milan, 29 March 2012, No. 99

The case concerned a tax assessment where the Italian Tax Authorities applied penalties in connection with transfer pricing claims.

The Provincial Tax Court of Milan clarified that no penalty should be imposed if the taxpayer has cooperated with the Tax Authorities in order to outline and detail all the intercompany transactions, irrespective of the fact that any transfer pricing documentation had been pre-arranged. Such principle is consistent with the 'favor rei' principle under article 3, Legislative Decree 18 December 1997, No. 472.

Moreover, the judges clarified that cooperative conduct is satisfied where the company provides the tax auditor with all of the necessary

---

[11] Such provision was introduced through article 26 of Law Decree 31 May 2010, No. 78, converted Law 30 July 2010, No. 122.

[12] Such 'guidelines' are basically consistent with the principles set out in the Code of Conduct issued by the EU Joint Transfer Pricing Forum.

[13] Which, as mentioned, provides for the application of penalties ranging from 100 per cent to 200 per cent of the unreported income claimed by the tax officers.

documentation in order to prove its compliance with the arm's length principle.

Please note that this decision covered a tax year previous to the enactment of the penalty protection regime.

6. DISPUTE RESOLUTION MECHANISM

In terms of dispute resolution mechanisms, there is no specific procedure for transfer pricing. However, there are several procedures available under the Italian tax system aimed at settling claims raised by tax officers or notices of assessment. The scope of these procedures is general and covers also transfer pricing disputes. This helps the taxpayer to reduce the time and expense invested in a potential tax appeal. In certain cases, it may also allow for a reduction of tax penalties.

These procedures may take place at different stages during a tax audit and tax proceedings. The key features of the most relevant dispute resolution procedures are analyzed below.

6.1 Preferred national options

(a) Ruling ('interpello')

The 'Ruling' consists of a request filed by the taxpayer with the Italian Tax Authorities to receive a clarification on the correct interpretation of a tax rule that applies to the taxpayer's situation.[14]

(b) Settlement of the tax audit report ('Adesione al processo verbale di constatazione')[15]

This procedure is aimed at settling the tax obligation before the formal notification of a notice of assessment. The taxpayer's settlement is unconditional and must cover all of the claims raised by tax officers in the tax audit and included in the tax audit report. Within 30 days from the delivery of the tax audit report, the taxpayer must provide the competent Office of the Italian Tax Authorities with an *ad hoc* communication. If the taxpayer meets this requirement, they will benefit from having their penalties reduced to one-sixth of the minimum applicable penalties. This procedure is not available to taxpayers that have pre-arranged the transfer pricing documentation.[16]

(c) Settlement of the 'cross-examination notice of assessment' ('Adesione agli inviti a comparire')

Under this procedure, the Italian Tax Authorities provide the taxpayer with an *ad hoc* notice of assessment (ie, a cross-examination notice of assessment). This notice entitles the taxpayer to attend a hearing where a cross-examination on the matter will take place. The cross-examination notice of assessment includes all of the details of the claims raised by the

14 Italian tax law knows various types of ruling: in principle, ordinary ruling, CFC ruling and anti-avoidance ruling. Ordinary ruling is the most common and is provided for by Article 11 of the Law 27 July 2000, No. 212 (so-called Taxpayer's Chart of Rights).

15 Article 5-*bis*, Legislative Decree 19 June 1997, No. 218.

16 See Circular letter 15 December 2010, No. 58.

Italian Tax Authorities. The taxpayer is entitled to settle the claim by paying the amount requested by the Italian Tax Authorities and a reduced penalties no later than 15 days prior to the date scheduled for the hearing. Using this procedure, the taxpayer will benefit from having their penalties reduced to one-sixth of the minimum applicable penalties.[17]

(d) Tax settlement ('Accertamento con adesione')[18]

The tax settlement allows the taxpayer to settle a notice of assessment before filing a tax appeal. Both the taxpayer and the Tax Authorities can initiate this procedure. The taxpayer must file a tax settlement procedure request within 60 days from the notification of the notice of assessment. In this case, the deadline for filing the appeal against the notice of assessment is extended for 90 days. During this lapse of time, the Tax Authorities and the taxpayer may cross-examine the matter. If an agreement is reached, a tax settlement act is executed and signed by the Tax Authorities and the taxpayer. The taxpayer will benefit from having their penalties reduced to one third of the minimum applicable penalties.

(e) Settlement of tax penalties ('Definizione agevolata delle sanzioni')[19]

This procedure allows the taxpayer to settle solely the penalties by paying one-third of the penalties applied in the notice of assessment. The payment must be made within sixty days from the notification of the notice of assessment (ie, the same deadline for filing the appeal). The settlement concerns only the penalties and the taxpayer remains entitled to appeal the claims raised in the notice of assessment with regard to the higher taxes requested. However, if the appeal is allowed, the taxpayer will not have title to recover the penalties previously settled.

(f) Judicial settlement ('Conciliazione giudiziale').

Judicial settlement allows the parties to settle their dispute before a decision is issued by the Tax Court. This procedure can apply to all tax disputes as long as it is not initiated later than the first hearing before the Provincial tax court. Judicial settlements can also occur during the public hearing or before the public hearing. The taxpayer, the Tax Office, or a Tax Court Judge can initiate the procedure. In the event of Judicial settlement, the amount of taxes is set in order to discontinue the dispute. If successful, the penalties can be reduced to 40 per cent.

6.2 International options

As far as the international dispute resolution mechanisms are concerned, reference should be made to section 2.3 above on MAP.

17 As mentioned above, in the event of transfer pricing adjustments made by the tax auditors, penalties should apply only if the taxpayer has not pre-arranged the transfer pricing documentation or if the latter is not considered suitable by the tax officers.

18 The various tax settlement procedures are governed by Legislative Decree 19 June 1997, No. 218.

19 Articles 16–17 of Legislative Decree 18 December 1997, No. 472.

PART TWO: TAX AVOIDANCE

7. ACCEPTABLE TAX PLANNING AREAS/SUBJECTS

The Italian tax law allows taxpayers to minimize their tax burden by selecting among several legal instruments the most appropriate for their specific circumstances. Although this principle should be inherent in the Italian tax system, the Italian Tax Authorities have challenged this by carrying out tax assessments that found tax avoidance schemes in fully lawful operations.

There are several Supreme Court cases that clarified the difference between tax avoidance and legitimate tax savings.[20] According to the Supreme Court, tax avoidance occurs where a taxpayer has complied with the letter of the law but nevertheless arranges their affairs so as to contravene the law's goals and minimize their tax burden. On the other hand, no avoidance occurs where the taxpayer arranges their affairs so as to benefit from the least possible tax in a way that the tax system recognizes as legitimate.

8. DEFINE ABUSIVE TAX AVOIDANCE

The introduction into the Italian tax system of a general anti-avoidance rule has been debated since early 1980's.

In 1997, Presidential Decree 29 September 1973, No. 600, was amended to fill this gap and article 37-*bis* was introduced with a scope limited to specific operations.[21]

Although this provision has never been a general anti-avoidance rule, several decisions of the Italian Supreme Court[22] have significantly extended its scope and reached the conclusion that a general anti-abuse clause in the Italian tax system can be gathered from the ability to pay principle.

9. THE LEGISLATIVE FRAMEWORK

The Italian tax system does not feature a general anti-avoidance rule. However, several specific anti-avoidance rules are provided. The most relevant are described below:

(a) Article 37-bis of Presidential Decree 29 September 1973, No. 600

Pursuant to Article 37-bis, paragraph 1:

'The tax authorities may disregard acts, facts and agreements, even connected among themselves, lacking of valid economic reasons, which are aimed at circumventing obligations or prohibitions set forth by the tax laws, and at obtaining tax reductions or refunds that are otherwise undue.'

According to this provision, the tax authorities may re-characterize a given transaction for tax purposes and apply the taxes on the basis of the specific rules that have been avoided.

---

20 For example, decisions of the Supreme Court 17 October 2008, No. 25374; 21 January 2011, No. 1372.

21 See *infra*.

22 For example, decisions of the Supreme Court 11 February 2013, No. 3243; 27 February 2013, No. 4901. See also *infra*.

In order for Article 37-*bis* to apply and for the tax authorities to challenge and disregard the tax benefits deriving from a transaction, the following conditions must be simultaneously met:

(i) the transaction shall be aimed at circumventing tax obligations or prohibitions set out by tax law provisions;
(ii) the transaction shall be aimed at obtaining tax benefits (eg, reductions, exemptions or refunds) which would otherwise be undue;
(iii) the transaction shall not be grounded upon valid business reasons.

Based on the above provision, the tax authorities may disregard any tax advantage obtained as a result of the above-mentioned acts, facts and transactions. Accordingly, the authorities may recover the taxes determined on the basis of the provisions that have been avoided.[23]

In terms of the provision's scope of application *ratione materiae*, article 37-*bis* only applies where one or more of the following transactions are involved:

- conversions, mergers, demergers, winding-up and distribution to the shareholders of reserves other than profit distribution;
- corporate contributions, as well as contracts concerning the transfer of the use of enterprises and going concerns;
- assignments of debt claims or tax credits;
- assignments of tax credits;
- transactions (including accounting classifications and evaluations) related to financial instruments;
- transfers of goods and/or services between companies belonging to the same tax consolidation;
- transactions under legislative decree no. 544 dated 30 December 1992 regarding the harmonization with EU directives for mergers, demergers, contributions of assets and share exchanges;
- payments of interest and royalties if such payments are made to controlled entities (directly or indirectly) by one or more persons that are not resident in one Member State of the European Union;
- payments of liquidated damages, advance payments /break up fees, contractual indemnification to/from related companies resident in black listed countries.

(b) Article 37(3) of Presidential Decree 29 September 1973, No. 600

Another provision that is used to prevent tax avoidance is article 37(3) of Presidential Decree 29 September 1973, No. 600. Here, the Italian Tax Authorities can allocate income to a certain taxpayer that appears to belong to another taxpayer if it can be proved that the latter taxpayer is the effective beneficiary of the income.

(c) Article 110 (10) ITCA

Another relevant anti-avoidance provision used by the Italian Tax Authorities is article 110(10) of ITCA. This outlines the tax regime for Italian

[23] Article 37-*bis*(2) of Presidential Decree 29 September 1973, No. 600

resident companies that carry on transactions with companies resident in black-list countries. Pursuant to article 110(10) ITCA, costs and expenses borne in connection with transactions carried on with a company resident in a black-list country are not deductible. Article 110(10) ITCA does not apply if one of the conditions set forth in paragraph 11 of the same article is met. In other words, article 110(10) will not apply if the resident company proves that either: (a) the foreign company primarily and actually carries on a commercial activity; or (b) the transaction has a genuine business purpose.

(d) CFC rule

Article 167 ITCA lays down the Italian controlled foreign company regime (the 'CFC regime'). This provides for that if an Italian resident (directly or indirectly) controls a foreign entity located in a black-list country, any income derived by the CFC is taxed on an accrual basis by way of a look-through approach in the hands of the resident taxpayer, in proportion to the participation held. The look-through approach laid down under the CFC regime is not applicable where the Italian shareholder can prove that either:

- the CFC mainly carries out a genuine commercial activity in the State where it is located (business test exemption); or
- the participation in the CFC does not have the effect of locating its income in a low tax jurisdiction (income test exemption).

The CFC rule also applies to any CFC regardless of whether it is listed among the black-list countries. As a result, this has the potential of including EU subsidiaries. The CFC regime will apply where both of the following conditions are met: (i) the controlled company is subject to an effective taxation lower than one half of that which would be levied if the company were considered resident in Italy for tax purposes; and (ii) more than 50 per cent of its income is either made of passive income, or derives from intra-group services. However, this provision does not apply if the Italian taxpayer is able to prove that the establishment of the CFC was not an artificial arrangement aimed at gaining an undue fiscal advantage.

10. KEY CASES OF INTEREST

10.1 Current cases

(a) Decision of the Supreme Court 22 November 2011, No. 7739

The Italian Supreme Court has finally stated its position on the relevance of tax avoidance in relation to criminal law. The Supreme Court stated that in the event of tax crimes such as an unfaithful[24] or omitted[25] tax return, a criminal charge connected to tax avoidance cannot be excluded. The judges also clarified that such crimes may be committed through conducts similar

[24] Under article 4 of Legislative Decree 10 March 2000, No. 74, if in a given fiscal year unpaid tax is higher than (i) EUR 50,000.00, and (ii) 10 per cent of the total items of income reported in the tax return or, in any event, higher than EUR 2,000,000.00, such violation would amount to the crime of unfaithful tax return (*'dichiarazione infedele'*), and the prison term ranging from 1 to 3 years.

[25] Under article 5 of Legislative Decree 10 March 2000, No. 74, if a taxpayer does not file, in a given fiscal year, the tax return and unpaid tax is higher than EUR 30,000.00, such violation would amount to the crime of omitted tax return (*'omessa dichiarazione'*) and the prison term would range from 1 to 3 years.

to those expressly provided by article 37(3) and article 37-*bis* of Presidential Decree 29 September 1973, No. 600.

10.2 Key historical cases

(a) Decisions of Supreme Court of 23 December 2008, Nos. 30055, 30056 and 30057

Grounding its interpretation on the Halifax case of the European Court of Justice (C-255/02), the Italian Supreme Court held that the existence of a general anti-abuse clause flows directly from the prohibition of abuse of law developed by the European Union. This prohibition is derived from the principles of effectiveness and loyal cooperation. The Supreme Court extended the European Court of Justice's literal interpretation in holding that the European Union principles of effectiveness, loyal cooperation and non-discrimination should be a general 'interpretation canon' of the Italian tax system that applies beyond the limited harmonized sectors of tax law. The Supreme Court based the existence of a general anti-avoidance rule on the tax principles of the Italian Constitution, ie, the principles of ability to pay and progressivity of taxation (article 53 of the Italian Constitution). Consequently, the Supreme Court has stated that the principle according to which the taxpayer cannot unduly benefit, for tax purposes, from the misuse of legal instruments (those which, although not forbidden by a specific rule, lack of any economically sound reason, except for tax savings) is a direct and essential consequence of article 53 of the Constitution.

To date, this decision has been applied to VAT, income taxes, registration taxes, and various other ancillary taxes.

11. PENALTIES

11.1 Legislative provisions

There are no specific penalties associated with anti-avoidance rules. In the event of a tax avoidance conduct challenged by tax auditors, the applicable penalties are those provided for by Legislative Decree 18 December 1997, No. 471. As mentioned above, in the event of an unfaithful tax return, penalties generally range from 100 per cent to 200 per cent of the higher unreported taxable income claimed by the Tax Authorities. If the taxpayer does not file the tax return, penalties may range from 120 per cent to 240 per cent of the unreturned amount.

11.2 Examples of penalties imposed

(a) Decision of the Supreme Court 30 November 2011, No. 25537

This dispute concerned the entitlement to disregard under article 37-*bis* the effects resulting from a complex business restructuring. The Supreme Court affirmed that Italian law provides for the application of penalties, notwithstanding the fact that a violation of law or a tax avoidance arrangement have occurred, being it necessary for the application of such penalties solely that the income reported in the tax return be lower than the one challenged by the tax auditors. In substance, penalties are applicable as long as a tax return is incorrect.

12. CURRENT TRENDS

12.1 National policy and law

On 11 March 2014, the Italian Parliament issued Law No. 23. Pursuant to article 5, the Government has been authorized to implement the review of all the existing anti-avoidance rules in order to unify them under one general anti-avoidance principle whose source can be found in article 53 of the Constitution.[26] In particular, the Parliament has appointed the Government with the task of defining the concept of 'abuse of law'. According to article 5, the Government is responsible for issuing Legislative Decrees that define the abuse of law as the misuse of legal instruments for the primary goal of gaining an undue tax advantage, even if such conduct does not violate any specific provision.

12.1.1 The impact and role of the OECD and other international relations

On 19 July 2013, the OECD released the Base Erosion and Profit Shifting (BEPS) Action Plan. Since then, several 'actions' identified by the BEPS Action Plan in order to counteract and prevent tax avoidance have been implemented by some recent provisions. In particular, the Italian Parliament has attempted to set specific tax rules on web advertising by requiring Italian companies to purchase their internet advertising spaces only from locally registered companies. Because this provision was likely against EU Law, it has been subsequently repealed. However, the 2014 Budget Law discussed above has laid down a relevant provision in order to counteract base erosion and profit shifting enacted by e-commerce companies. In particular, article 1(177) of Law 27 December 2013 No. 147 expressly prevents such companies from determining their PLI (including any auxiliary services) according a transfer pricing method based on costs borne. An exception to this rule is where an international standard ruling has been entered into.

Moreover, Law 11 March 2014, No. 23 has also provided:

- a general review and a reinforcement of anti-avoidance rules; and
- an innovative relationship between the Italian Tax Authorities and taxpayers in order to improve and grow a culture of tax compliance. This innovative project has been anticipated by the announcement of the Cooperative Compliance Project.

[26] Article 53 of the Constitution contains the ability to pay principle.

Japan

Hashidate Kenji Hashidate, Michihiro Matsumoto, Michiko Hashidate, Eiko Minowa, Makoto Sato & Erwin Condez

PART ONE: TRANSFER PRICING

1. GENERAL OVERVIEW

The Japanese transfer pricing taxation system was introduced in 1986, which is more recent when compared with other countries. The Japanese transfer pricing taxation system is based on the Transfer Pricing Guidelines for Multinational Enterprises and Tax Administrations ('OECD Transfer Pricing Guidelines'). The Japanese Acts, circular notices, and other stipulations that are relevant to the OECD Transfer Pricing Guidelines are amended or revised in accordance with any amendments or revisions of the said Guidelines.

In Japan, most disputes related to transfer pricing taxation are resolved by Mutual Agreement Procedures ('MAPs'), and there are few cases that proceed to litigation. However, the Japanese tax authority aggressively imposes transfer pricing taxation and the numbers of such cases increases yearly.

2. IDENTIFICATION OF LEGISLATIVE FRAMEWORK

2.1 Federal legislation

Japanese transfer pricing taxation is based on the arm's length principle. Transactions between domestic Japanese corporations and their foreign affiliated enterprises should be priced as if done at arm's length between unrelated companies. If a domestic Japanese corporation receives a payment from an affiliated foreign enterprise that is less than an arm's length price, or makes payment to an affiliated enterprise that is greater than an arm's length price, the tax authority may adjust those transaction amounts to reflect arm's length pricing and assess taxes on the resulting additional income (Special Taxation Measures Law ('STML') article 66-4 I).

Japanese transfer pricing taxation is applicable only to corporations and is not applicable to individuals. Foreign affiliated enterprises are considered to have 'a special relationship' with the corporation if at least one of several conditions applies. 'A special relationship' occurs when the corporation directly or indirectly holds 50 per cent or more of the foreign enterprises' share holdings, or if substantial control exists due to business, financial, or other dependence (Special Taxation Measures Law Enforcement Order ('STMLEO') article 39-12 I). 'Controlled transactions' are transactions between domestic Japanese corporations and their foreign affiliated enterprises for the sale and purchase of assets, the rendition of services, or other similar transactions. There are two exceptional cases. Firstly, a transaction between a foreign enterprise and its permanent establishment ('PE') in Japan, that is obliged to pay Japanese corporation tax, is not considered a controlled transaction. Secondly, when a transaction between a corporation and its foreign affiliate is performed using a non-related enterprise as an intermediary, the transaction between the corporation and the non-related enterprise may still be deemed to be a controlled transaction. There is no definition of what constitutes an arm's length price in the Japanese Acts, although the methods of calculating an arm's length price are stipulated in STML article 66-4 II(i), wherein the CUP Method (STML article 66-4 II(i)(a)), RP Method (STML article 66-4 II(i)(b)), CP Method (STML article 66-4 II(i)(c)) and other methods equivalent to those stated in STML article 66-4 II(i)(a)–(c) are prescribed. Other methods are prescribed in a Cabinet Order. (STML article 66-4 II(i)(d)). An arm's length price is calculated by using the most appropriate method, taking into consideration the particular facts and circumstances of the specific case. In the event that a corporation engages in transactions that can be considered controlled transactions, if the relevant price applicable to such transaction falls within the range of the applicable arm's length price(s), the corporation should be able to avoid transfer pricing taxation (article 66-4(3)-4 of the administrative statement of STML).

2.2 State and provincial legislative interplay

Japanese transfer pricing taxation does not apply to domestic transactions, as the local tax rate is uniform throughout the nation.

2.3 International treaties and agreement

Presently, the Japanese government is a party to 51 tax conventions for the avoidance of double taxation and the prevention of fiscal evasion, covering 62 jurisdictions; eight Tax Information Exchange Agreements covering eight jurisdictions; and 32 Conventions on Mutual Administrative Assistance in Tax Matters, covering 32 jurisdictions, excluding Japan.

Previously, these tax treaties were based on the OECD Model Tax Convention, but a significant shift in guiding principles occurred with the 2013 amendments to Japan's tax treaty with the United States. In the 2013 amendments, so as to encourage the promotion of bilateral investment, a generous tax cut was allowed in the withholding income tax of the source country. Provisions governing limitations on such benefits and other provisions for the prevention of abuse of the treaty were also introduced. Such tax benefits, as well as the limitations on such benefits, have been introduced in the amendments to tax treaties with certain other countries.

3. NATIONAL POLICY ISSUES

According to recent statistics announced by the National Tax Agency of Japan (hereinafter referred to as the 'NTA'), the number of transactions taxed as transfer pricing cases was 222 in 2012, an increase of 22 per cent over the previous year (182 cases in 2011). The collective amount of taxable income in these cases being JPY97.4 billion in 2012, leading to an increase of 16.4 per cent over the previous year (JPY83.7 billion in 2011).[1] One of the reasons for this clear upward trend is that, in recent years, the NTA has begun actively applying transfer pricing taxation not only to transactions made by large companies, but also to transactions by small and medium-sized companies. Therefore, taking appropriate action to prevent or mitigate transfer pricing taxation has become even more important, regardless of the size of the company or transaction.

3.1 Administrative statement

In Japanese law, STML and the Order and Ordinance for Enforcement of STML outline the transfer pricing taxation rules and the calculation method for arriving at an arm's length price. Administrative statements provide further details and guidance. The administrative guidelines take into account the revisions of OECD Transfer Pricing Guidelines, in order to ensure conformity with international standards.

For example, the NTA issued an administrative statement in 2011 that stipulated four points to consider in determining an appropriate calculation method for an arm's length price. The four points included the relative strengths and weaknesses of each calculation method, the availability of the information required to calculate an arm's length price, etc. This administrative statement was created following the revision of STML, and also references Paragraph 2.2 of the 2010 OECD Transfer Pricing Guidelines.

3.2 Administrative guidelines

The NTA issued the following three administrative guidelines, which stipulate as to the NTA's investigation policy, points of attention regarding any Advance Pricing Agreement, the calculation method for arm's length prices of intangible asset transactions, mutual agreement procedures, and other related matters.

- Commissioner's Directive on the Operation of Transfer Pricing (Administrative Guidelines)
- Reference Case Studies on the Application of Transfer Pricing Taxation
- Commissioner's Directive on the Mutual Agreement Procedure

4. CASE LAW

As previously discussed, there have been few lawsuits dealing with transfer pricing taxation in Japan, since most transfer pricing taxation cases tend to be resolved through MAPs. Nevertheless, legal precedents are expected to be established in the future as more cases work their way through the court system.

4.1 Current cases

The case receiving the most attention from among several recent transfer pricing taxation cases is *Takeda Pharmaceutical Company Limited* ('Takeda'). In this case, about JPY57.1 billion of back taxes were imposed on Takeda

[1] See *http://www.nta.go.jp/kohyo/press/press/2013/hojin_chosa/03.htm* (in Japanese only).

because the tax authorities determined that the sale price of products sold by Takeda to a joint venture company it had established in the US was too low. Takeda requested that the issue be resolved through MAPs, but Japan and the US failed to reach agreement through the process. Therefore, Takeda filed an objection with the tax authority. Ultimately, the tax authority accepted Takeda's arguments and rescinded all the taxes charged to the company, eventually refunding the full amount to Takeda. With a disputed back tax amount of approximately JPY57.1 billion, this case is presently the largest transfer pricing case in Japan. As time goes on, Takeda is likely to have an impact on transfer pricing taxation enforcement by the tax authority.

4.2 Historical cases of note

(a) *Imabari Shipbuilding* case (Takamatsu High Court judgment dated October 13, 2006 (Case No. 17 (*Gyou-ko*) 2004/Takamatsu High Court))

The taxpayer, *Imabari Shipbuilding Co., Ltd.* ('Imabari'), was a shipbuilding company constructing ships for its foreign affiliated enterprise located in the Republic of Panama. The tax authority applied the CUP method and determined that the price agreed to in the transaction between Imabari and its foreign affiliated enterprise was less than what the arm's length price would have been if the transaction were between Imabari and a non-affiliate. Therefore, the tax authority applied transfer pricing taxation to the transaction with the foreign affiliated enterprise and made a reassessment. Following this reassessment, Imabari filed a lawsuit seeking the revocation of the reassessment.

At trial, Imabari claimed that it was not appropriate for the tax authority to have calculated an arm's length price without considering the significant differences between the transaction Imabari engaged in with its foreign affiliated enterprise and the 'comparison purpose transaction' selected by the tax authority. Because each shipbuilding contract is unique, no similar comparison purpose transaction could have existed in this case. However, the Takamatsu High Court rejected Imabari's claim and held that the tax authority's analysis could be limited to the factors which clearly affected the price, and that not all differences between the transaction and the comparison purpose transaction were required to be considered in the calculation of the arm's length price.

Aside from the above, Imabari also claimed that the concept of 'arm's length range' should be applicable even if the application of the CUP method was appropriate. It is important to note, that at the time of the transaction, the arm's length range was not yet stipulated under the relevant laws and regulations of Japan but was later introduced via the administrative statement described below. The court rejected this claim, holding that it was unnecessary to adopt the concept of arm's length range. At the present time, article66-4(3)-4 of the administrative statement of STML clarifies that arm's length range is applicable under certain conditions.

(b) *Adobe* case (Tokyo High Court judgment dated October 30, 2008 (Case No. 20 (*Gyou-ko*) 2008/Tokyo High Court))

Adobe Systems Co. ('Adobe'), the Japanese affiliate of the US company Adobe Systems Inc., received remuneration from its Dutch and Irish affiliate companies, comprising an amount equivalent to its general administrative expenses plus 1.5 per cent of the net sales accrued in Japan of Adobe products. The remuneration was received as consideration for the services Adobe provided in the promotion and marketing of Adobe computer graphics software, etc., sold in Japan. The tax authority selected a transaction in which a seller resold the same or similar software as a comparison purpose transaction in the calculation of the arm's length price. Then it applied transfer pricing taxation to the transactions with the foreign affiliated enterprises and made a reassessment. Adobe then filed a lawsuit seeking revocation of the reassessment.

The Tokyo High Court held that the reassessment should be revoked, finding that the arm's length price calculation method used by the tax authority did not fall under the definition of 'a method equivalent to a method consistent with the resale price method'. The resale price method, or a similar method, should have been adopted in this case because of the differences between Adobe and the selected comparison purpose enterprise in terms of the functions and risks in each respective transaction, as described in the below table. This case marked the first complete victory for a taxpayer in a transfer pricing lawsuit in Japan.

	Adobe's transaction	**Comparison purpose transaction**
Function	**Services** related to the promotion and marketing of graphics software → Adobe's remuneration included only the consideration for such services and did not include any profit gained from the resale of such software.	**Resale** of computer software → The gross income of the comparison purpose enterprise included the profit gained from the resale of such software.
Risk	Adobe did not bear any risk of loss, as the amount of its remuneration would never have fallen below its costs and expenses, regardless of sales figures.	The comparison purpose enterprise bore a risk of a loss if its sales figures ended up lower than its costs and expenses.

5. PENALTIES

5.1 Criminal Sanctions

If a taxpayer is exempted from a tax or receives a tax refund by means of deception or other wrongful conduct, such taxpayer may be punished by imprisonment with labor for a period of not more than 10 years, or a fine of not more than JPY 10 million. In the event that a simple failure to file a tax return is not connected with deception or other wrongful conduct, such a failure is not regarded as tax evasion; however, a taxpayer may be punished for his or her simple failure to file a tax return by imprisonment with labor for a period of not more than a year, or a fine of not more than JPY 500,000. Corporations are punished for the above acts by the levying of fines applicable to each respective article, in addition to punishment that may be applied to individual offenders (Corporation Tax Act ('CTA') article 159 to 163).

5.2 Additional tax

If a taxpayer does not comply with required tax obligations, 'an additional tax' will be imposed on top of the delinquent tax. In the event that a taxpayer files a tax return by the due date but the amount paid in the tax return is found to be less than the amount due to be paid, the taxpayer is required to pay an amount equivalent to 10 per cent of the difference as an 'additional tax for understatement' on top of the tax itself. Five percent is further added as an additional tax for understatement if the unpaid tax exceeds a certain amount. In the event that a taxpayer does not file a tax return by the due date, the taxpayer is required to pay an 'additional tax for failure to file', which is an additional 15 per cent of the tax amount to be paid. In the event that a person who deducts withheld taxes and is obliged to pay the tax does not pay such tax by the due date, 10 per cent of the delinquent tax amount is imposed as an 'additional tax on non-payment'. In the event that a taxpayer does not pay, or reduces payment of tax by concealing or falsely representing all, or part, of the facts that should be the basis for the calculation of the tax amount, a penalty of 35 per cent of the tax amount to be paid is imposed as a 'heavy additional tax' instead of an additional tax for understatement. A penalty of 40 per cent of the tax amount to be paid is also imposed, instead of the normal 15 per cent 'additional tax for failure to file' (General Law of National Taxes ('GL') article 65 to 68).

5.3 Special sanctions in transfer pricing taxation

(a) Presumptive tax imposition

Where the tax authority has requested that a corporation present or submit documents prescribed by an Ordinance of the Finance Ministry as being necessary to calculate an arm's length price, and the corporation fails to present or submit such documents, the tax authority may make a correction or determination with respect to the amount of income or net loss for the accounting period of the corporation. This correction or determination will be made on the presumption that the arm's length price would be the amount computed by the methods stated in STML article 66-4 II(i)(a)–(d).

(b) Right to question and inspect

Where a corporation has failed to submit the documents needed to calculate the arm's length price, the tax authority may, to the extent necessary to perform said calculations, question persons who are engaged in business of the same type or nature as the target corporation. The tax authority may also inspect the similar corporation's documents that are relevant to the line of business of the target corporation (SMTL article 66-4 VIII). Any similar corporation who fails to answer questions and/or cooperate with inspectors from the tax authority will be punished with a fine (SMTL article 66-4 XII).

6. DISPUTE RESOLUTION MECHANISM

For taxpayers who wish to dispute a transfer pricing assessment, there are generally two avenues to do so: domestic appeals and, in the case of transactions with countries that have a double taxation treaty with Japan, MAPs. A taxpayer can choose to pursue one or both of these options. Generally, most taxpayers pursue both options simultaneously, as domestic appeals have a strict limitations period and MAPs usually take a long time to complete. If a taxpayer settles a dispute through a MAP, a domestic appeal will be unavailable as a remedy.

6.1 MAPs

In the case of international double taxation caused by transfer pricing taxation, a taxpayer may request a MAP. A taxpayer cannot participate in mutual consultation directly. Mutual consultations are consultations between the competent tax authority of Japan and the competent tax authority of a treaty partner nation pursuant to the relevant tax treaty provisions. When mutual consultation results in an agreement, one/both of the tax authorities will follow and take the necessary steps to implement the agreement. If the competent Japanese authority accepts a treaty partner's claims, the Japanese tax authority will issue a correction notice and will refund the amount that corresponds to the reduction in the initial assessment to the taxpayer. If the taxpayer declines the proposed agreement between the two tax authorities, and further MAP consultations prove unproductive, the MAP may be terminated. From July 1st, 2012 to June 31st, 2013, 167 MAP cases were brought in Japan, including 131 MAP/APA[2] cases. During the same time period, the NTA initiated 170 MAP cases, with each MAP case taking an average of 29.3 months to reach resolution.

6.2 Domestic Appeals

(a) Reinvestigation

A taxpayer may request that the tax authority reinvestigate the determination of the taxpayer's tax liability, whether the initial determination or a subsequently corrected one, by filing a written reinvestigation request within two months of receipt of the initial notice or correction (GL article 75, 77).

(b) Reconsideration (National Tax Tribunal)

If a taxpayer objects to the tax authority's decision, he/she may request that the National Tax Tribunal reconsider the taxpayer's tax liability.

[2] See section 6.3(a).

This request must be made within one month of the taxpayer's receipt of the decision by the tax authority concerning the taxpayer's prior request for a reinvestigation. Generally, a person who has an objection to an administrative agency's exercise of authority would first request a reinvestigation. However, a taxpayer may bring his/her case to the National Tax Tribunal directly, without first requesting a reinvestigation, if the taxpayer's case falls into one of several situations provided for in the Acts (such as, for example, a rectification and decision by the tax authority). In such case, a taxpayer should submit a written reconsideration request within two months after receiving notice of such determination or correction (GL article 75, 77).

(c) Court decision

A taxpayer who objects to the decision of the National Tax Tribunal with regard to his/her request for reconsideration may appeal to the courts for a remedy within six months after receiving notice of a decision (Administrative Case Litigation Act article 14).

6.3 Preferred national options

(a) Advance pricing arrangement

It is advisable for taxpayers to utilize an Advance Pricing Arrangement ('APA') for avoiding disputes as to transfer pricing taxation. The APA is an administrative procedure based on a circular notice. Once the relevant tax authority examines and confirms the reasonableness of the transfer pricing methodology, etc., submitted by the taxpayer, the tax authority will not impose transfer pricing to the extent that the taxpayer complies with the terms of the taxpayer's application. An APA can be arranged to be either unilateral or between two or more nations. A unilateral APA is an agreement between the taxpayer and the NTA, while an APA between two or more nations is an agreement between the taxpayer, the NTA, and the relevant overseas tax authority in a country which is a signatory to the applicable tax treaty. The latter APA, known as an 'MAP/APA', is an approval system established in conjunction with the mutual agreement procedures found in tax treaties.

(b) Documentation

Mirroring requirements found in other countries, the FY 2010 tax reforms mandated that taxpayers prepare and preserve documents that are considered to be necessary for the calculation of arm's length prices. This reform was implemented to facilitate investigations against the taxpayer, allow taxpayers to more easily respond to investigatory inquiries, and allow clarity as to the ultimate results of any investigation (STML article 66-4 IV, STMLEO article 22-10). This provision works to both the taxpayers' and the tax authoritys' benefits, as it allows taxpayers the possibility of avoiding being charged with a larger tax bill, while allowing tax authorities some relief with respect to the cost and expense involved in a tax investigation.

6.4 International options

From a tax treaty perspective, a ratifier of a tax treaty has no legal obligation to reach a settlement, and the MAPs are somewhat limited in their ability to resolve double taxation disputes. Therefore, the need for arbitration, which would lead to a decision of some sort, has been discussed and negotiated with other countries. In Article 24 V of the Convention between Japan and the Kingdom of the Netherlands for the Avoidance of Double Taxation and the Prevention of Fiscal Evasion with Respect to Taxes on Income ('Convention'), arbitration procedures between the tax authorities of the signatories were introduced into Japan for the first time. In the Convention, arbitration procedures are given the same status as that of MAPs. An arbitration decision shall be deemed a settlement by the relevant tax authorities as if completed through MAPs, and shall bind both contracting countries, unless the taxpayer refuses to accept the arbitration decision. If the taxpayer accepts an arbitration decision but is in the process of either litigating or has requested an administrative review of the taxpayer's case, the taxpayer is required to withdraw the litigation or the request. In addition, in the Protocol Amending the Convention Between the Government of Japan and the Government of the United States of America for the Avoidance of Double Taxation and the Prevention of Fiscal Evasion with Respect to Taxes on Income, executed on January 25, 2013, it was stipulated that an arbitration process will be introduced as part of the mutual agreement procedures. As more tax treaties are executed or amended, it is likely that arbitration clauses will be more commonplace in Japanese law.

PART TWO: TAX AVOIDANCE

7. ACCEPTABLE TAX PLANNING AREAS/SUBJECTS

The effective Japanese corporate income tax rate is 35.64 per cent (23.71 per cent national tax and 11.93 per cent local tax), which is relatively high when compared with the rate found in other countries. However, there are a wide variety of special taxation options in Japan which taxpayers can take advantage of to reduce their tax liabilities. For example, a reduced corporation tax rate is available for small and medium-sized enterprises (STML article 42-3-2 and STML article 68-8), whereby a business earning income of under JPY 8 million in a business year (April 1, 2013 to March 31, 2014) is eligible for a reduced corporate tax rate of 15 per cent (as opposed to the regular figure of 19 per cent) on income earned for such business year. Enterprises engaged in research and development are also eligible for a special corporate tax rate (Tax System for Promoting Research and Development). Enterprises engaged in research and development are allowed to deduct 8~10 per cent of experimental research costs from income, up to a limit of 20 per cent of what their corporate taxes would have been. In addition, there are particular tax schemes for corporate reorganization (CTA article 62-2), by which enterprises may defer capital gains or losses of transferred assets and debts, as well as tax credits for foreign tax paid

(CTA article 69 and 81-15). Other options are available to business entities such as voluntary associations, anonymous partnerships, and limited liability partnerships, which are all eligible for pass-through taxation. However, it should be noted that the above-mentioned options or schemes may be considered inapplicable in a particular case by the relevant tax authority, with additional tax possibly imposed, where the tax authority has determined a particular privilege has been abused.

Cooperation with an appropriate expert who is familiar with the Japanese legal system and with prior precedent will be essential in planning tax strategy.

8. DEFINING ABUSIVE TAX AVOIDANCE

'Tax avoidance' is defined as the 'reduction or exemption of a tax burden while attaining an economic objective or economic outcome by being exempted from commonly-applicable tax requirements through the selection of not commonly used law without reasonable reasons'[3]. In the event that tax avoidance or any other similar activity occurs and there are specific provisions in the law that allow for tax authorities to restrict such activity, such activities will be prohibited pursuant to said provisions. However, there is a difference of opinion among the courts on the question of whether restricting tax avoidance activity can be done in the absence of a specific provision. Below are examples in which a court has determined that restrictions can be imposed even without specific authorizing provisions:

(1) where an inordinately unnatural or unreasonable act or accounting process is conducted with the objective of avoiding or reducing corporate tax, or where unfair tax avoidance is conducted through the adoption of an abnormal or unnatural act or accounting process (including, but not limited to, acts or accounting processes that are obviously contrary to economic rationality). For example, in a situation where a small company with impaired capital absorbs a company that has large scale interests, and the company surviving the absorption-type merger later changes its trade name to the name of the acquired company, a court determined the merger to be abnormal. The court found that it constituted tax avoidance, with the only objective in the transaction being the accrual of deductible expenses;[4]

(2) cases in which a court found an abuse in the decision as to the type of applicable law (such as Case No. 215 (*Gyou-hi*) 2003/ Supreme Court, mentioned in section 11.1.2(2) below); and

(3) cases where a court found the existence of tax avoidance in light of a taxpayer's series of actions, even if the individual actions by themselves would ordinary pose no problem. For example, a situation where a first company, formed with substantial loans, and a second company, formed with investments in such loans, was judged to be a situation that constituted tax avoidance.[5]

---

[3] Hiroshi Kaneko, *Tax Law* (Japan, 2013), p. 121.

[4] Judgment rendered by the Tokyo High Court on 10 December, 1962 (Case No. 467 (*Ne*) 1961/ Tokyo High Court).

[5] Judgment rendered by the Tsu District Court on 23 June 1997 (Case No. 3(*Gyou-u*)1996/ Tsu District Court).

9. THE LEGISLATIVE FRAMEWORK

There are no general statutory provisions restricting tax avoidance. There are, however, relatively general provisions, such as provisions applicable to acts and accounting processes of a taxpayer's affiliated company (CTA article 12) and provisions providing principles for the taxation of a real income earner (Income Tax Act ('ITA') article 12, CTA article 11 etc.,). There are also many specific provisions disallowing tax avoidance, such as a provision excluding a director's salary from being counted as part of gross expenses (CTA article 35) and a provision excluding contributions from deductible expenses (CTA article37). The provisions preventing international tax avoidance are as follows:

(1) Corporate Reorganization Taxation System

The Corporate Reorganization Taxation System was enacted in 1978 to prevent income transfers from a company located in Japan to any of its subsidiaries/parent companies located in countries where no corporate tax would be imposed on any such subsidiary/parent company (STML article 66-6 to 66-8);

(2) Transfer pricing taxation (see Part One); and

(3) Thin capitalization taxation system

A thin capitalization taxation system was enacted to prevent companies from engaging in tax avoidance by borrowing substantial funds in place of share issuances in cases where such companies receive funds from foreign affiliated companies. This system stipulates that where the ratio of investments to loans exceeds a certain percentage, any interest expense corresponding to the excess portion shall not be included in deductible expenses (STML article 66-5).

10. KEY CASES OF INTEREST

10.1 Current cases

(a) Judgment rendered by the Tokyo High Court on 29 May, 2013 (Case No. 421 (*Gyou-ko*) 2013/ Tokyo High Court)

In this case, the court dealt with the issue of whether Controlled Foreign Company Taxation should be applied to an individual shareholder of a certain legal entity established under the laws of Singapore. The court held that the following two requirements were met: (a) a specified foreign subsidiary company, etc., has a fixed facility (for example, an office, a shop, a factory., etc.) needed to operate its main business in the state or territory where its head office or principal office is located ('Substantial Criteria'), and (b) a specified foreign subsidiary company, etc., administers, controls and conducts its business by itself in the state or territory where its head office or principal office is located ('Administration-Control Criteria'). These two requirements comprise the requirements for the exemption from said taxation, therefore, taxation should not occur.

There are few cases pertaining to Substantial Criteria and/or the Administration-Control Criteria as applicable to Controlled Foreign Company Taxation in Japan. From among these cases, the above case is the sole case in which a taxpayer prevailed, having met such criteria.

Recently, more and more Japanese companies are establishing mid-holding subsidiaries in a state or territory where the tax burden to be imposed on the income of a corporation is significantly lower than in Japan. The above case is highly worth referring to when considering strategies to free mid-holding subsidiaries from the application of Controlled Foreign Company Taxation.

10.2 Key historical cases

(a) Case No. 133 (*Gyou-hi*) 2000/Supreme Court (the '*Film Lease* case')

A certain partnership (Kumiai) established under the Civil Code of Japan (Minpou), a portion of whose interests a real estate company ('X') holds, purchased a film (the 'Film'), and assigned the rights of distribution to a separate distributor. X declared its earnings to the tax office, with the Film recorded as an asset, and depreciation charges for the Film recorded as expenses in proportion to X's portion of the partnership. The tax authority in this case refused to allow the depreciation charge to be recorded as an expense and made a reassessment. The Supreme Court of Japan likewise refused to allow the depreciation charge for the Film to be recorded as an expense for X, reasoning that the Film was not a source of income originating from the partnership's business, and is therefore not used for the partnership's business. Specifically, the Supreme Court of Japan took the following two facts into consideration: (a) even if the partnership obtains ownership or title to the Film, the partnership lost a substantially all of its rights to use, obtain profit from, and dispose of the Film after assigning the rights of distribution to a distributor, and (b) the partnership was wholly absolved of responsibility for repayment of debts for the purchase of the Film, and no member of the partnership in this case sought any income that originated from the distribution of the Film.

(b) Case No. 128 (*Gyou-hi*) 2004/Supreme Court (the '*Obunsha Holdings Co., Ltd.* case')

In this case, a certain Japanese company ('X') established a subsidiary in the Netherlands ('A') whose shares were wholly owned by X. X made A issue a large amount of new shares and allot them to a related company ('B') of X in the Netherlands at a price especially favorable to B. The tax authority decided that through the above actions, X transferred a valuable asset in the form of shares from A to B, and made a reassessment whereby a value corresponding to the transferred shares of A was deemed to be a 'donation' (Kihu-kin) to B. X sought a revocation of the reassessment. The Supreme Court of Japan judged that even if the series of actions outlined above were based on resolutions passed during shareholders meetings of A, such resolutions were made by X (the sole shareholder of A) and the relevant parties (the directors of X, A, B, and the sole shareholder company of B) with the intention of realizing the transfer of a valuable asset through mutual communication, and thus, the series of actions fall into a category of 'transactions' (Torihiki) stipulated in Article 22 II of the CTA. The amount to be included in the gross profits of X would be any amounts related to said series of actions.

In the above cases described in (1) and (2), the Supreme Court of Japan judged, though close and comprehensive consideration of the respective transactions and actions of the taxpayers in these cases, whether the imposition of taxes should take place by determining the application of specific provisions of the tax laws.

11. PENALTIES

11.1 Legislative provisions (see section 5)

11.2 Examples of penalties imposed

(1) An example of criminal tax evasion (Case No. 1528 (*A*) 1985/Supreme Court). A company (X), which was a business involved in the purchase and sale of real estate, concealed its profits by means of recording fictitious sales, costs., etc., and submitting such fictitious information on its final returns to the tax office. As a result, X avoided approximately JPY 260 million in taxes. The court judged that purposefully concealing the true profits and submitting a final return to the tax office that included only a portion of the company's income fell into the category of 'fraud and any other unfair actions' stipulated in Article 159 I of the CTA and thus, constituted a criminal act. X was punished with a JPY 240 million penalty.

(2) An example of a court imposing additional tax (Case No. 215 (*Gyou-hi*) 2003/Supreme Court). The foreign tax credit is a system established for the avoidance of international double taxation whereby the amounts imposed by and paid to foreign governments are, to a certain extent, deducted from the amount to be imposed by Japanese tax laws (ITA article 95 or CTA article 69). Under Japanese tax laws, a Resident (defined in ITA article 2 (iii)) or a Domestic Corporation (defined in CTA article 2 (iii)) has, in principle, taxes imposed on all income, regardless of where in the world the income was generated (i.e., domestic sources of income as well as foreign sources). In such situations, when a Resident or a Domestic Corporation has taxes imposed on its foreign sourced income by foreign governments, it would, in the absence of a foreign tax credit, suffer from double taxation. In this case, the bank ('A') operated a business under which it paid foreign taxes on behalf of foreign companies in return for compensation from the foreign companies. Thereafter, A deducted the amounts it paid, from the amount to be imposed by Japanese tax laws, within the limits of the foreign tax credit. In this case, the tax authority denied the deductions made by A, making a reassessment and imposing upon A additional tax for its deficient returns. This decision was upheld by the Supreme Court of Japan, with the court finding that A's business practice was an abuse of the foreign tax credit.

12. CURRENT TRENDS

Succession by corporate successors of a predecessor's unpaid tax deficits is one of the issues that has been recently addressed in the Corporate

Reorganization Taxation System. In February 2009, *Yahoo Japan Corp.* ('Yahoo') acquired *IDC Frontier Inc.* ('IDC') from SoftBank Corp. for JPY 45 billion, with IDC being subsequently merged into Yahoo. At the time, both Yahoo and IDC belonged to the same corporate group controlled by SoftBank Corp. The tax authority decided that Yahoo's succession to the deficit of approximately JPY 22 billion carried forward by IDC by the above acquisition and merger was an 'unusual and anomalistic' transaction carried out for the purpose of tax avoidance. Therefore, the tax authority imposed approximately JPY 26.5 billion in taxes (including additional taxes) on Yahoo as a reassessment. Yahoo sought a revocation of the reassessment, but the Tokyo District Court on March 18, 2014 rejected the relief sought by Yahoo.

12.1 National policy and law

Under the tax laws of Japan, a Foreign Corporation (defined in CTA article 2(iv)) has taxes imposed upon its Domestic Sourced Income (defined in CTA article 138) ('Comprehensive Method'). However, on the other hand, Japan is a party to numerous tax treaties with many other countries (under which foreign corporations have taxes imposed only on the profits attributable to their PE), as well as the model Tax Convention ('Attribution Method'). Such tax treaties supersede the Comprehensive Method found in the tax laws of Japan.

Recently, discussions in Japan have focused on whether or not the Attribution Method as opposed to the Comprehensive Method should be applied to Japan's internal tax laws. If the Attribution Method were to be applied, profits attributable to the PE of foreign corporations would be recognized as profits that the PE would accrue if it were separated from, and independent of, any foreign corporation, with internal transactions between foreign corporations and their respective PE's being deemed to exist. In addition, the foreign tax credit system would be needed in order for the PE to avoid any double taxation that may occur when other countries impose taxes on the PE.

12.2 The impact and role of the OECD and other international relations

Japan strongly endorses the plan for Base Erosion and Profit Shifting ('BEPS') prepared by OECD's Committee on Fiscal Affairs. Japan has appointed Mr. Masatsugu Asakawa to be chairman of the committee and to lead discussions concerning international taxation in OECD meetings and other venues. Japan's goal will be to continue and encourage productive discussions concerning international taxation.

Luxembourg

MNKS Raquel Guevara

PART ONE: TRANSFER PRICING

1. GENERAL OVERVIEW

The Luxembourg tax system does not contain a set of rules that could strictly speaking be qualified as transfer pricing legislation.

Nevertheless, the principle of 'arm's length' is recognized in the Luxembourg tax system and the tax practice as well as the case law seem to follow the approach taken by the OECD transfer pricing guidelines as amended from time to time[1].

2. IDENTIFICATION OF LEGISLATIVE FRAMEWORK

2.1 National legislation

(a) Article 56 of the Luxembourg Corporate Income Tax Law ('CITL'), foresees that the tax authorities may re-calculate the taxable basis of a Luxembourg resident company if (i) a transfer of result is made possible or derives (ii) from particular economical relationships, direct or indirect, (iii) with a non-resident.

- (i) Only a tax inspector of a certain degree, having been explicitly empowered by the director of the tax services, is empowered to estimate the transfer of result and carry an adjustment of the taxable basis according to this provision. According to the parliamentary working papers of the CITL,[2] this should ensure a certain consistency when analyzing the potential cases where adjustments may be necessary. However, neither the CITL, nor the parliamentary documents foresee any particular guidelines as to the method that the tax authorities may follow to apply such empowerment;
- (ii) This provision leads to the fact that the burden of proof is with the tax payer, since the tax authorities do not particularly need to justify their assumption in cases in which they suspect a transfer of results;
- (iii) This provision does not cover transactions amongst Luxembourg tax residents, but solely transactions with non-Luxembourg residents (whether any kind of entity or individual);

[1] Charles Duro, René Faltz, Détermination des prix de transfert en l'absence de prix de marché comparables, Rapport Luxembourgeois, Cahier de Droit fiscal International, vol. 82a (Kluwer 1982). Jean Schaffner, Droit fiscal international (Promoculture-Larcier, 2014).

[2] Parliamentary Document no. 571/4, p.94 and ff.

(iv) As to the *'particular economical relationships'*, the tax law does not provide any guidance and thus, the coverage is quite large – it certainly covers any situation in which the control of one of the parties over the other party could make possible such a transfer of result. It also covers almost any relation except for relationships that would generally be considered typical commercial ones.

(b) Article 164 (3) of CITL covers the hidden dividend or so called constructive distributions. Indeed, according to this provision, hidden dividend distributions are part of the taxable basis of a Luxembourg company. A constructive distribution covers, in particular, but not exclusively, the case of a shareholder receiving an advantage that he would not have received if he would not have been shareholder of the company. As a general matter, it covers the situation in which a company grants an advantage that it would have never granted to a third/unrelated party under the same conditions. The consequences of this provision are that a constructive distribution is not tax deductible for the Luxembourg company granting the advantage and furthermore, the advantage may be subject to withholding tax (currently 15 per cent or 17,5 per cent if taken in charge by the distributing company, as would generally be the case in a constructive distribution), unless such withholding tax would be mitigated or reduced to zero by the application of the domestic rules implementing the EU Parent-Subsidiary Directive or a Treaty for the avoidance of Double Taxation ('DTT'), if applicable at all.

(c) Articles 56 and 164 (3) of CITL both have different scopes but are, to a certain extent, complementary to each other:

(i) As article 56 CITL rules the adjustment to be made to the taxable basis of a Luxembourg company having created a situation in which the transfer of result is made possible. The tax treatment applicable to such transfer, and its tax qualification from a Luxembourg tax perspective, is indeed ruled by article 164 (3) of CITL.

(ii) Contrary to article 56, article 164 (3) of CITL covers domestic and cross border transactions. Indeed, and as a matter of fact, article 56 of CITL deviates slightly from current European Law as it excludes Luxembourg domestic transactions from transfer pricing considerations and the duty to comply with the arm's length principle.[3]

(iii) As mentioned above, article 56 CITL sets the burden of proof of particular economical relationships which have supposedly led to a transfer of result in the hands of the tax payer. The tax inspector does not necessarily need to prove the character of such relationship or the methods that lead to his suspicion. On the contrary, Article 164(3) of CITL is only applicable if the conditions for its application

---

3 This approach is derived from (already outdated) German tax law. Indeed the *Bundesfinanzhof* ruled on August 18, 2004 that the German transfer pricing regulations were not applicable to domestic transactions. In the meantime, German tax law and doctrine, particularly in terms of Transfer Pricing matters, has evolved very differently from Luxembourg.

are given, which must be proven by the tax authorities. It is worth noting that the application of article 164(3) of CITL is not restricted to an inspector vested with a certain degree, or special empowerment, by the director of the service;

(iv) Since the delegation of power to which article 56 of the CITL refers has never, or very rarely been granted, the application of article 56 is minimal in practice. On the contrary, article 164(3) of CITL has triggered a more elaborate case law and tax practice due to the above explained consequences that are, as you may appreciate, more severe. This is also due to the fact that the tax authorities consider this rule to be the basis of Luxembourg's adherence to the OECD Transfer Pricing Guidelines.[4]

(d) The Circular nr. 164/2 of January 28, 2011, concerning intra-group financing activities (the 'Circular'), constitutes the first transfer pricing rule integrated in the Luxembourg tax system. Moreover, the Circular recognizes the adherence of Luxembourg to the OECD Transfer Pricing Guidelines. It is therefore to be interpreted as a sign of the importance of transfer pricing regulations for the Luxembourg tax authorities, even if the OECD Transfer Pricing Guidelines have not (yet) been formally transposed into the Luxembourg tax system (and, as such, are not enforceable). The Circular rules the conditions under which a Luxembourg resident company carrying out intra-group financing activities can obtain an Advanced Price Agreement ('APA') on the margin to be realized on such activity. According to the Circular, intra-group financing activity is to be defined as activities consisting of granting loans or advancing funds to associated companies, where such loans or monies have been financed by means of public offerings, private loans, bank loans or any other financial instrument, and where associated companies means that one of the parties participates, directly or indirectly, in the management or capital or otherwise controls the other company, or if the same persons participate, directly or indirectly, in the management or capital or otherwise controls both of the companies. The conditions under which a Luxembourg company carrying out the above described activities can obtain an APA from the Luxembourg tax authorities are as follows:

(i) The company must fulfill certain substance requirements;

(ii) The company must bear its own risks, in particular, the ones related to its financing activity; and

(iii) A fully fledged transfer pricing study, substantiating the margin, in accordance with the OECD Transfer Pricing Guidelines must be filed together with the request.

(e) In the frame of the application of the so-called 'IP Box regime', consisting of the application of an 80 per cent exemption to the net revenues derived from certain IP, article 50bis of CITL foresees that

[4] As per the introduction to the text of the Circular nr. 164/2 of January 28, 2011, concerning intra-group financing activities. See section (d).

the evaluation of the intellectual property rights must comply with internationally recognized methods, without specifying any particular or preferred method. This is quite consistent with the current approach of the tax authorities who have, so far, not expressed a general preference for one valuation method over the other. Note: it is the duty of the tax payer to explain the method used – upon an eventual request from the tax authorities – and its compliance with internationally recognized methods.

2.2 International Treaties and Agreements

Luxembourg, as a OECD Member has approved the OECD Transfer Pricing Guidelines as well as the Model of OECD Convention to avoid Double Taxation (the 'OECD Model'), serving as a model to sign the more than 70 DTTs currently entered into by Luxembourg. However, while the DTTs are part of the Luxembourg legal and tax system and are at the top of the hierarchy by means of the publication of a law transposing such DTT into the domestic legal system, the OECD Transfer Pricing Guidelines are not part of the Luxembourg domestic tax system. They are therefore, not able to modify the obligations and duties of the Luxembourg resident tax payers and are not enforceable by the tax authorities in front of the Luxembourg courts of justice.

As regards the OECD Model, its article 7 rules the attribution of profits to a permanent establishment of a company located in the other contracting state. As a result of several decades of discussion, the current position is that the permanent establishment needs to be attributed a profit according to the arm's length principle as if the permanent establishment would be a separated entity from its head office. This would imply that the transactions between the head office and the permanent establishment need to be regarded as if they would have been carried by unrelated and functionally differentiated parties (irrespective of the total profit realized by the head office). Criteria such as the risks borne, assets used and activities carried, should drive the attribution of profits, irrespective of the total profits of the company. This principle is explicitly reproduced in the DTTs signed by Luxembourg with Germany (2012), the USA and the UK (2001). On the other hand, and as an exception to this now broadly accepted approach, for example the DTT between Luxembourg and Belgium (2003) and between Luxembourg and Uzbekistan (2003) foresee, under certain conditions, the allocation of a lump-sum amount of profit and expenses to the permanent establishment out of the total profit of the company (including the permanent establishments').

3. NATIONAL POLICY ISSUES

Luxembourg's priority in this respect is the establishment of a full set of transfer pricing rules.

This has been recognized by the government, specifically the government finance department. As a result, the Luxembourg tax authorities are participating in the working groups of the OECD regarding (amongst others) transfer pricing matters.

Further, at the European level, the European Commission has developed a code of conduct regarding transfer pricing matters. The code contains guidelines regarding the means and burden of proof. The code also contains recommendations to establish a set of documentation to cover, first, the group's transfer pricing policies and, second, specific reports covering where the group is active in each of the EU countries. The code foresees that the documentation is able to provide not only the methodology used, but also, comparable elements and data covering preceding years and forecasts, cash flows, terms and conditions of the relevant agreements, economical background to the transactions, and *in fine*, any information that would be able to be factored in and support the transfer policy applied. This code is of voluntary application and, as far as Luxembourg is concerned is also not enforceable in court.

At a national level, and as of the date of this report, there are no legislative initiatives. It is however not to expect that Luxembourg deviates from the OECD Transfer Pricing Guidelines, that have already been recognized by the tax authorities at several occasions (see above). Furthermore, it is likely that the Luxembourg government will incorporate the OECD Transfer Pricing Guidelines into Luxembourg's legal framework to ensure 100 per cent compliance. This is similar to what The Netherlands did some years ago.

Finally, in the past years, the tax authorities have created a new division stemming from the Director of the tax authorities, named the Economic Division. Where needed, the Economic Division was initially in charge of the review and signature and/or discussion of the APAs filed by the tax payers in the frame of the Circular (see section 2.1.(d)). The Economic Division has, however, the vocation to broaden its activities to generally cover transfer pricing matters, and in the fulfillment of this duty, according to the Activity Report of 2013 issued by the Luxembourg tax authorities, it treated 590 files in 2013.

3. CASE LAW

There is very little case law in Luxembourg in regards to transfer pricing. Bearing in mind the legal framework explained above, this was to be expected.

The *Conseil d'Etat* ('CE') on May 5, 1965: the tax authorities analyzed the prices applied to petrol products in a transaction amongst related parties and established significant differences as to what the tax authorities would have considered market practice. The tax payer was not able to justify the differences nor the method applied to determine the prices applied to the transaction. In their sentence, the CE recognized the need to demonstrate that the prices used correspond to the ones that would have been used amongst unrelated parties. Due to the fact that the tax payer was not able to demonstrate the nature of the differences identified by the tax authorities, the CE concluded that the prices were not respecting the arm's length principle.

As was ruled by the CE on June 25, 1974, if the tax payer is not cooperative with the tax authorities, for example in having a correct accounting, or furnishing supporting documentation and/or clarification of the facts and the tax position taken, the tax authorities have a broader power to make an indirect estimation of the taxable basis of the tax payer.

Indeed, if the tax payer is cooperative, the tax authorities need to prove that the pricing method applied by the tax payer does not respect the market practice/the arm's length principle (according to para. 271 *Abgaben Ordnung*, 'AO')).

On September 10, 2008, the *Tribunal Administratif* ('TA') went a bit further when it ruled that the tax authorities can apply out of a range of transfer prices, which are less favourable to tax payers, to avoid granting advantages to a non-cooperative tax payer, as it could not be justified with respect to the remaining tax payers and the duties imposed on them.

On May 7, 2007, the TA intended to estimate the fulfillment of the arm's length principle by the conditions under which a loan had been granted. In order to determine the compliance with this principle, the court relied on the principles that should drive a prudent and diligent director ('*ordentlicher und gewissenhafter Geschäftsleiter*'). Following the views of the TA from October 16, 2007, the *Cour Administrative* ('CA') confirmed the legality of such method. This principle had previously been recognized by the TA on March 29, 1999, and was likely inherited pursuant to the German origins of our tax system. As an example, the German tax court, *Bundesfinanzhof* ('BFH'), recognized this principle in case law dated October 17, 2001.

On June 28, 2000, the TA ruled on the case of the company Foreign Trade Corporation (Fotraco): the tax authorities had denied the tax deductibility of a commission paid by Fotraco to a Cyprus company to which it was related. The tax authorities denied the tax deductibility on the basis that the expenses were not made for, and on the benefit of, Fotraco. The TA accepted the recourse interposed by Fotraco, as it estimated that the tax authorities could not sufficiently prove the absence of an economical background to the transaction. In particular, this case law reveals the difficulty of the application of the arm's length principle in the case of groups, as the Luxembourg tax and legal system does not recognize the concept of 'group interest'. The court also validated Fotraco's approach in applying the cost-plus method.

Article 164(3) of CITL, as well as the administrative practice related to hidden distributions, have been largely modeled on the case law generated by the German BFH or its predecessor *Reichsfinanzhof*. As mentioned above, the application of article 164(3) of CITL has generated more case law than the remaining legal and administrative provisions, partly due to its more severe consequences. Below is a brief description of some of the most relevant cases:

On March 29, 1999, the TA concluded that some amounts settled by a Luxembourg company to its shareholder were not in the benefit of the company and that the payment of such amounts had no consideration or other reason of being, other than to help the shareholder settle and shorten the term of some of his contracted liabilities. The TA based its decision on the obligation of a director to be prudent and diligent and thus, not to enter into transactions that are not in the best interest of the company (see above).

On January 13, 1987, in the affaire S.A. Overseas Development Bank vs. the tax authorities, the CE explained that the finality of article 164(3) of CITL must be to assist the tax authorities to reestablish the true nature of transactions and (the said article) must be interpreted along these lines. As a result, the CE concluded that transfers from the patrimony of a company to the patrimony of the shareholder(s) that are made possible by the company act underlying the relationship and are to be treated as hidden dividend distributions. The same doctrine was praised by the TA in July 19, 2000.

Some of the court cases referred to above, as well as the TA on February 21, 2001, confirmed that '*The tax authorities can assume a reduction of the profits of the company (for the benefit of another entity) if the circumstances are favourable to it, without needing to prove this with precision. The burden of proof is therefore reversed to the tax payer, who needs to prove that either there is not a reduction of the profits of the company or if there would be one, that it is not due to the particular relationship between the two companies.*'[5]

In particular, in June 2004, the TA already reminded the tax payer that a set of documentation to be furnished to the tax authorities in case of requests is essential to allow for the deduction of expenses. Indeed, in the case at hand, the TA had denied the tax deductibility of some expenses paid to a related entity as it concluded that it was not sufficiently proven that the expenses were arm's length.

A more recent decision made by the TA on June 6, 2005 seems to soften the above doctrine and reiterates that according to article 59 of CITL '*the proof of the facts leading to a tax event is with the tax authorities, (whereas) the proof of the facts reducing the tax burden or exempting from taxation is with the tax payer*'. Based on this case law, it should be concluded that '*the tax authorities must perform an objective and impartial analysis of the declarations made by the tax payer, and it is only in case the tax payer would not sufficiently clarify the aspects that may appear doubtful to the tax authorities or in the absence of elements put at the disposal of the tax authorities, that the latter can question the economic reality of the transactions.*'[6]

This decision law was confirmed by the TA on May 31, 2006.

However, the TA returned to the previous doctrine of the reversal of the burden of proof to the tax payer on November 27, 2006. The CA also returned to this doctrine on October 26, 2007.

On February 17, 2011, the TA confirmed that, in first instance, the tax authorities have the burden of proof in showing there is a hidden dividend distribution. It is further confirmed that the tax authorities need to do an

---

5 Courtesy translation from Jean Schaffner, Droit fiscal international (Promocultire-Larcier, 2014), p.141.
6 Courtesy translation from Les Cahiers de Droit Luxembourgeois no. 14, October 14, 2001, Oliver R. Hoor.

objective and impartial analysis of the facts and information at their disposal and, in particular, of the facts that could appear doubtful (potentially leading to a hidden dividend distribution). Furthermore, in the frame of such an analysis, the tax authorities may be able to identify a series of facts and/or circumstances that make a hidden dividend distribution likely where such facts and circumstances have not been clarified by the tax payer. In that case, the tax authorities can assume a reduction of the benefits of the company (for the benefit of another entity), without being obliged to prove it. The burden of proof is then reversed to the tax payer, who must demonstrate that there was no shift of profits or that if there was one, it was not rendered possible by the particular economic relations between the two entities.[7]

On February 16, 2009, the TA reinforced that the conditions for the existence of a hidden distribution require not only a 'loss' on the hands of the company, but also a benefit in the eventual recipient of the distribution. Without this benefit, there would be no distribution of profits. In regards the burden of proof, the court case followed the above explained doctrine from the TA (November 27, 2006) and the CA (October 26, 2007). The court accepted the possibility of shifting the burden of proof to the tax payer, and in the case at hand, concluded that there had been a hidden distribution to the sole shareholder, since being continuously and permanently in a loss position is not consistent with the nature of a joint stock corporation whose nature is *per se* profit seeking. In the case at hand, the sole asset was a boat. The tax authorities decided that they had not received enough supporting documentation as to the purpose of the company and the use of the boat for the group of companies.

On March 25, 2010, the TA explained that the advantage granted by a company to their shareholder framed as a hidden dividend distribution could be of a direct or indirect nature.

5. PENALTIES

Since Luxembourg has not implemented any Transfer Pricing regulations in the strict sense of the term, there are no major penalties imposed by the Luxembourg tax system, other than the consequences of the potential adjustments as previously described:

(a) As a general rule, the tax authorities are allowed to re-assess the taxable basis of the tax payers within the limits and provisions of article 56 of CITL;
(b) Article 105(1) of CITL foresees that only expenses that are made with the aim of maintaining or increasing the revenues of the company can be tax deductible, allowing for adjustments in the case of unnatural business relationship(s);
(c) In the case of a hidden dividend distribution following the application of article 164(3) of CITL, the amount considered as a constructive distribution will not be tax deductible for the distributing company and

7 In the same sense, Les Cahiers de Droit Luxembourgeois no. 14, October 14, 2001, Oliver R. Hoor.

will be furthermore subject to the general withholding tax to which dividend distributions are subject. Unless, an exemption or reduction would be available, either by application of a domestic rule or by the rules implementing the EU Parent-Subsidiary Directive or a DTT, if applicable at all;

(d) In the frame of the Circular, and in case the concerned companies do not fulfill the substance requirements, the tax authorities would not grant an APA. Furthermore, they may deny the delivery of tax residency certificates and may equally spontaneously communicate this situation to the tax authorities of the involved foreign companies' country of residency.

6. DISPUTE RESOLUTION MECHANISMS

The Luxembourg law does not foresee any particular mechanism applicable to transfer pricing matters. As a result, the same legal procedures and recourses against the tax authorities exist as in any other tax matter.

In the case of cross border matters, we refer to the DTTs in force and the DTT Model of OECD and its commentaries.

PART TWO: TAX AVOIDANCE

7. ACCEPTABLE TAX PLANNING AREAS/SUBJECTS

Luxembourg tax law recognizes the possibility of tax payers choosing to structure their tax affairs in the most advantageous manner, even with a view to minimizing the tax liability. One of the consequences of the application of this doctrine to enterprises, is the principle of non-interference of the tax authorities in the administration, and choices made by the enterprise.

This principle is, however, limited by the concepts of Abuse of (Tax) Law and Simulation.

It is sometimes difficult to discern when we are in the presence of acceptable tax planning or an abusive arrangement.

Options at the disposal of the tax payer may be made available by the tax law itself. For example, the tax law may allow the tax payers to opt for the deferral of the taxation of gains realized upon a transfer under certain conditions[8]. It is generally accepted, and there is no doubt, that such provisions are a planning tool and their use does not constitute tax evasion or avoidance.

The limits may become more difficult to identify when the options are made possible because of the general provisions of law, as the liberty of the parties is generally recognized under private law.

Under old Luxembourg case law,[9] 'disguised' donations were, for example, not considered abusive but rather the result of the tax payer choosing the, legally accepted, less taxed choice.

---

8 Article 22 Bis CITL, implementing the neutrality regime of the EU Merger Directive.

9 Cour Supérieure de Justice (en cassation), July 8, 1892, Pasicrise Lux. Tome 3.

In fact, such concepts, like Abuse of Law and Simulation, are also limited by the legality of the tax law (meaning broadly speaking that taxes cannot be imposed without a law that rules it and that analogy in tax matters is prohibited) and the restrictive interpretation generally recognized to tax law (meaning that tax laws are to be interpreted restrictively and that facts that are not explicitly covered by the law should not be considered – this applies even to the concepts of Simulation and Abuse as long as they refer to the tax system).

8. DEFINING ABUSIVE TAX AVOIDANCE

The Luxembourg tax system does not contain a definition of Abusive Tax Avoidance. However, since, under certain circumstances, transactions may be considered as being either simulated or in Abuse of the law, we would assume for the purposes of this publication/chapter that Abusive Tax Avoidance is referencing what is currently punished by the Luxembourg tax system.

In the next section, we refer to several fact patterns that could give rise to abusive tax avoidance.

9. THE LEGISLATIVE FRAMEWORK

As mentioned above, the Luxembourg tax system does not recognize the principle of Abusive Tax Avoidance, but instead defines the Simulation and Abuse of tax law or simply Abuse. Whether the Fraud to the tax law is recognized by the Luxembourg tax system is a debated question.

Please see below a summary of the definition as well as the main features of each of these mechanisms.

9.1 Simulation

The concept of Simulation is mainly contemplated by § 5 of the *Steueranpassungsgesetzt* of October 16, 1934 ('StAnpG').[10]

It is important to note that this provision is solely applicable in direct taxation matters, therefore, taxes that are under the supervision of the direct tax authorities.

A specific law dated January 28, 1948, covers the Simulation for registration duty and inheritance taxes. The law applies to acts that intend to hide a part of the price in transactions for the transfer of real estate. Additional provisions of prior laws, which include the Civil Code, cover the impact of simulated transactions for the purposes of registration duties and other taxes.[11]

For simplification reasons and with a view to the (in comparison) reduced scope of the latter 1948 Law, we will refer exclusively to § 5 StAnpG.

This paragraph is derived from the German tax system implemented in Luxembourg during the occupation in WWII. The German definition of

[10] *'(1) Scheingeschäfte und andere Scheinhandlungen (zum Beispiel die Begründung oder die Beibehaltung eines Scheinwohnsitzes) sind für die Besteuerung ohne Bedeutung. Wird durch ein Scheingeschäft ein anderes Rechtsgeschäft verdeckt, so ist das verdeckte Rechtsgeschäft für die Besteuerung massgebend. (...).'*

[11] Law dated January 28, 1948; Loi du 22 frimaire an VII; article 1.321 Civil Code.

Simulation derives itself from the German Civil code[12] and both, the tax and civil Simulation, deny the effects to the simulated transaction and consider the 'real' transaction which the parties intended to hide.[13]

This differs slightly under the Luxembourg Civil Code, as simulated transactions may be opposable against third parties that may rely on the documents implementing a transaction. Nevertheless, according to § 5 StAnpG the tax authorities will ignore the 'apparent' transaction and will tax the 'hidden' one that intended to be (di)simulated.

As a general rule, a transaction is simulated when the parties' intention differs from the documents entered into or the transaction carried out.

9.2 Abuse

The concept of Abuse of the (direct) tax law is contemplated by § 6 StAnpG[14].

The general cumulative elements recognized by the Luxembourg doctrine to the Abuse of (tax) Law are as follows:

(i) There must be an abuse of the provisions generally foreseen by the law, such that the tax payer decides to use provisions that are not designed to reach the result sought by the tax payer and thus, are 'misused';

(ii) Such provisions chosen by the tax payer are in detriment of other provisions that would normally be considered as adequate to reach the result sought,
Indeed, this figure assumes equally that there are several means to achieve a result and that the one chosen by the tax payer is not adequate as opposed to the one commonly and reasonably used in these cases;

(iii) The described misuse of the law to carry a transaction for which the provisions were not designed, leads to tax savings,
If no tax savings are reached, there is no point in applying this provision. This means that it can only be applied against the tax payer, but not in cases where its application would lead to a lower taxation; and

(iv) There are no reasons, other than the tax savings, that support the choice made by the tax payer.
Traditional case law interprets this as a *senso contrario*, ie, if the tax payer can demonstrate that there may be other reasons, for example economic reasons, driving the choice, this would be an argument against the Abuse of law and the transactions would not be considered abusive.

In the event that the tax authorities decide that the transaction features the above elements, the transaction would be taxed according to the tax

12 § 117 BGB: *'(1) Wird eine Willenserklärung, die einem anderen gegenüber abzugeben ist, mit dessen Einverständnis nur zum Schein abgegeben, so ist sie nichtig. (2) Wird durch ein Scheingeschäft ein anderes Rechtsgeschäft verdeckt, so finden die für das verdeckte Rechtsgeschäft geltenden Vorschriften Anwendung.'*

13 At the time of the incorporation of these provisions into the Luxembourg tax system. In the meantime, the German tax law has equally evolved and there are circumstances in which a transaction may be declared null and void but may, nevertheless, be considered as a tax event.

14 *'(1) Durch Missbrauch der Formen und Gestaltungsmöglichkeiten des bürgerlichen Rechts kann die Steuerpflicht nicht umgangen oder gemindert werden. (2) Liegt ein Missbrauch vor, so sind die Steuern so zu erheben wie sie bei einer den wirtschaftlichen Vorgängen, Tatsachen und Verhältnissen angemessenen rechtlichen Gestaltung zu erheben wären. (...).'*

rules applicable, as if the choice made by the tax payer would have been the one corresponding to the 'adequate' alternative.

The tax authorities have the duty to prove the existence of an Abuse of law, but in practice, this duty is easily reversed as the courts, and the most extended doctrine, defend that the presence of the above elements suggests *per se* that there is a fraud intention in the tax payer's actions, and it is then the tax payer that needs to justify his choice.

9.3 Tax Fraud

The existence or not of Tax Fraud in the Luxembourg tax system is debatable. Some authors[15] consider that the fraud exists in any sector of the legal system, and that tax law is not an exception. Other authors[16] consider that this view ignores the nature of tax laws and argue that since no Luxembourg courts have estimated the existence of tax fraud, they have equally supported this view[17].

The main reasons that support the non-existence of tax fraud are the following:[18]

(i) The tax law must be interpreted strictly, and because this is a principle that admits no doubts, where the legislator desires to cover a particular fact pattern, this must be explicitly covered by the law;
(ii) The civil/private law focuses on the means to achieve a transaction whereas the tax law imposes a certain tax burden to a result – the tax law is not able to oblige the tax payers to follow one path over the other;
(iii) Moreover, according to such private law, the choice of the tax payer amongst the several instruments that may be available to him, may even (legally) be driven by the aim of saving taxes; and
(iv) The existence of § 6 StAnpG would make no sense if the analogy in tax matters would be allowed.

9.4 Others

Further, the Luxembourg CITL contains several anti-abuse provisions for particular situations that, generally speaking, apply the substance over form principle. The substance over form principle is aimed at ignoring a particular legal situation where the economic reality is presumed to be another with a view to certain circumstances.[19] For example, article 156.8 of CITL ignores the loss of the Luxembourg-tax-resident status if within the five years following the move that leads to the loss of his Luxembourg tax residency, the tax payer sells an important participation in a Luxembourg company.

For example, in the frame of international conventions, article 4 of the OECD Model of DTT foresees that the provisions of a DTT only cover

15 For example Schaffner, Krecké, Steichen.
16 Winandy.
17 L'abus de droit et la simulation en droit fiscal luxembourgeois, Jean-Pierre Winandy (Publications de L'Université du Luxembourg, 2004).
18 L'abus de droit et la simulation en droit fiscal luxembourgeois, Jean-Pierre Winandy (Publications de L'Université du Luxembourg, 2004).
19 Jean Schaffner, Droit Fiscal International (Promoculture-Larcier, 2014), p.989,.

residents of the contracting states as far as they are subject to tax in that contracting state. This allows entities that are not subject to tax, like Luxembourg Holdings incorporated under the 1929 law or Irish or UK companies, to avoid tax on a remittance basis. Luxembourg has entered in several DTTs where such a clause (or a similar one) would be applicable. For example, the DTT signed with Malta, which excludes the Maltese companies subject to the Malta International Business Activities Act of 1988. The DTT with Mauritius excludes the Mauritius entities that are not subject to a certain tax rate under Mauritius rules. The so-called 'Limitation of Benefits Clause' included in many DTTs, constitutes *in fine*, an anti-abuse measure. The USA DTT treaty is a particularly complex example but is not an isolated case.

As mentioned above, the liberty of the parties is limited by anti-abuse provisions, but these are generally to be interpreted strictly under Luxembourg tax law. The strict interpretation entails the prohibition of using an analogy from a tax perspective. The principle of legality of the tax laws also requires a Law for the application of taxes to a transaction (and thus prohibit the application of taxes to a fact pattern that is itself not covered by the tax law). Please see below for some examples of the application of these limits by the courts.

10. KEY CASES OF INTEREST

On July 12, 2012, the TA concluded the existence of Abuse according to § 6 StAnpG. The fact pattern was considered to sufficiently demonstrate that the parties had acquired a company with tax losses with the sole purpose of illegally benefiting from these losses. The TA estimated that the tax payers had not sufficiently proven the economic reasons that could eventually be the driver of the transaction and constitute *in fine* a kind of 'safe harbor'. It is also to note that the TA invited the tax payer to use the so-called '*wirtschaftliche Betrachtungsweise*'.[20] Indeed, the economical approach to transactions is, as mentioned above, one of the most common means to demonstrate the legality of the choices made by the tax payers.

Special attention needs to be paid since § 6 StAnpG and the *wirtschaftliche Betrachtungsweise* should not be identified. Indeed, the *wirtschaftliche Betrachtungsweise* is 'solely' a doctrine that eases the interpretation of Luxembourg tax rules under an economical perspective. This doctrine, unlike § 6 StAnpG, can be used in favour or against the tax payer and its application does not necessarily result in a re-qualifiation of a transaction as is the case in the application of § 6 StAnpG. As mentioned above, the application of § 6 StAnpG requires the intention of the parties to use the legal means at their disposal to achieve tax savings. The application of the *wirtschaftliche Betrachtungsweise* does not require or presume any type of intention and the existence of an intention to deviate from the law would not necessarily change the outcome of an application of this

20 This entails the recognition of the economical background and drivers of transactions as a means to understand the transactions and qualify them from a tax perspective (§ 1 Alinéa (2) and (3) StAnpG in its 1941 version).

economic interpretation. Finally, as in this case, both the *wirtschaftliche Betrachtungsweise* and § 6 StAnpG may be used in a combined manner, but it must be kept in mind that they do not represent the same principle.

A similar decision was taken by the CA on February 7, 2013. Again, in these cases, the tax authorities and the court requested the tax payer to substantiate the choices made and transactions entered into, where the fact pattern delivered (in the eyes of the tax authorities/the court) enough elements to presume a voluntary Abuse of the tax laws. Thereby, constituting a reversal of the burden of proof from the tax authorities to the tax payers.

Similar reasoning was shown in the TA's decisions on May 21, 2013 and June 27, 2013.

The reasoning of the above affairs show that the limits to the liberty of the entrepreneurs/tax payers and the Abuse of law is a thin and grey zone that has unfortunately, not been sufficiently clarified by the court cases. However, compared to the very few court cases in Luxembourg since the implementation of such clauses back in the nineteen-forties, the provisions of § 6 StAnpG gave rise to quite a few court cases in a relatively short period of time. This reveals the potential state of mind of the tax authorities but also an unfortunate trend to the use of the Abuse of law doctrine to limit the liberty of the parties granted by the civil law. The application of the Abuse of law doctrine should remain the exception and not the rule.

The TA explained on January 29, 2014, that the tax payer has the obligation to prove the transactions he declares (in the case at hand, the reality of services received in the frame of his activity for which he intended to deduct expenses incurred). In this context, the tribunal considered that the explanations given by the tax payer triggered reasonable doubts (that they were not justified) and confirmed the pertinence of the additional requests made by the tax authorities with the view to clarify the facts. In this context, the court ruled that the tax payer should substantiate the transactions and expenses under the principle of the *wirtschaftliche Betrachtungsweise* and added that such considerations should exclude the existence of other considerations of different nature.

Once again, the application of § 6 StAnpG together with the economical interpretation is required and seems to be the common characteristic of the most recent court cases.

11. PENALTIES

11.1 Legislative provisions

§ 5 and 6 of the StAnpG (Abuse and Simulation) are not particularly punished. However, the tax authorities are able to (i) ignore the documents entered into in order to tax the hidden transaction (in the case of the Simulation); or (ii) to ignore the transaction entered into to tax the transaction that better fits to the result that the parties wanted to achieve (Abuse of tax law).[21]

12. CURRENT TRENDS

12.1 National policy and law

As mentioned above, Luxembourg has actively taken part in the international community's raising interest on abusive tax planning. The number of court cases have significantly increased in the last few years and we should expect a further increase in litigation activity as the tax authorities seem to take strict positions on the concept of Fraud and Abuse of tax law.

Luxembourg's domestic legislation will equally be impacted by the anti-abuse measures required by the international community. As an example, the amendments to the domestic provisions implementing the EU Parent-Subsidiary Directive[22] have been made to avoid cases of double 'not taxation'. In particular, they have been made to avoid the exemption of income under the 'participation exemption' in the hands of the recipient company if the payment had been considered tax deductible by the company making such distribution.

12.2 The impact and role of the OECD and other international relations

The impact of the OECD and other international relations has already been noticed in recent developments but will continue to grow as the OECD expands its action plans. The extent to which the OECD is supported (or instructed) by other supranational establishments, like the G-20, the Ecofin, the global Forum for Transparency and many others, will also have an impact.

In the 2003 revisions of the OECD DTT Model of Convention and the commentaries, the OECD appraised a new function of the DTTs as the fight against tax evasion.[23]

As far as Luxembourg is concerned, Luxembourg made a reservation regarding the use of the DTT to fight against fraud and evasion in the sense that Luxembourg accepts the application of anti-abuse measures only if such measures are provided for in the DTT that is being applied.

In line with the OECD, the new DTT Luxembourg– Germany states that the DTT cannot be interpreted in such a way that it hinders the application of domestic anti-abuse/anti-fraud legislation.

Also, the DTT Luxembourg–Poland[24] foresees that where 'artificial arrangements' are put in place for the exclusive purpose of benefiting from the provisions of the DTT, such benefits will be denied.

---

21 Other provisions, as referred to above, in relation to indirect taxes, Registration duties and inheritance taxes may vary depending on the law abused and/or the transaction targeted.

22 Currently under discussions following to the initiatives against Hybrids at OECD level.

23 Brian J. Arnold, Tax treaties and Tax Avoidance: the 2003 revisions to the commentary of the OECD Model, Bulletin for International Fiscal Documentation, June 2004, p. 244. and Jean Schaffner, Droit fiscal international (Promoculture-Larcier, 2014), p. 996.

24 Signed in 2012 but in force since January 1, 2014.

The wording of such clauses is debatable as it opens the door to domestic rules which are out of Luxembourg's control. The concept of 'artificial arrangement' may also be difficult to interpret as each country may appreciate it differently.

Other DTTs foresee only a refusal of the application of the DTT upon common agreement of the tax authorities of each of the contracting states (eg, DTT Luxembourg–Taiwan).

The European Union also issued a Code of Conduct that targets the fight against tax regimes that have been identified as damaging the European market and the principles of the EU as far as corporate taxes are concerned. This Code of Conduct targets harmful tax competition amongst the EU member States but does not seem to be capable of systematically dismantling any type of tax practices by the EU members States that could eventually distort the competition.

Finally, and as far as the future is concerned, the G-20 and OECD initiatives, such as the one against BEPS which involve several working groups targeting the fight against tax fraud, aggressive tax planning and tax evasion, may not be excluded as a source of new domestic legislation to fight against tax fraud and tax evasion. A first, but nonetheless immense step, has already been forced by abolishing the bank secrecy and establishing the automatic exchange of information.

Malaysia

Lee Hishammuddin Allen & Gledhill S Saravana Kumar, Siti Fatimah Mohd Shahrom & Kho Chin Chau

1. GENERAL OVERVIEW

Prior to January 1, 2009, there was no specific transfer pricing legislation in Malaysia. The Inland Revenue Board of Malaysia ('MIRB') relied on the general anti-avoidance provision under s. 140 of the *Malaysian Income Tax Act 1967* ('ITA') for the purposes of transfer pricing adjustments. In July 2003, the MIRB issued the first Transfer Pricing Guidelines, which aimed at providing multinational enterprises ('MNEs') with the necessary information pertaining to the transfer pricing policy in this country. It also assisted MNEs to determine transfer prices which are consistent with the arm's length principle and in compliance with Malaysian tax laws as well as the administrative requirements of the MIRB.[1]

In January 2009, a specific transfer pricing legislation (s. 140A of the ITA) was introduced into Malaysian tax laws and took effect from 1 January 2009. The arm's length principle is set out in s. 140A and it requires taxpayers to determine and apply the arm's length price for their transactions with an associated person for the acquisition or supply of property or services.[2]

In line with the introduction of s. 140A of the ITA, in May 2012, the Income Tax (Transfer Pricing) Rules 2012 ('the Rules')[3] were gazetted and have a retrospective effect from 1 January 2009. To date, it remains a controversial issue as to the impact of the retrospective effect on taxpayers who may not be in compliance with the Rules from 1 January 2009.

In this context, the MIRB issued the new Transfer Pricing Guidelines 2012 ('the Guidelines') in July 2012. The Guidelines replaced the 2003 Transfer Pricing Guidelines and provided guidance on the administrative requirements pertaining to s. 140A of the ITA and the Rules.[4] The Guidelines are largely based on the governing standard for transfer pricing which is the arm's length principle as set out under the Organisation for Economic Co-operation and Development ('OECD') Transfer Pricing Guidelines. Nevertheless, the Guidelines may differ in certain areas to adhere to the ITA and MIRB procedures as well as domestic circumstances.[5] It must be noted that the Malaysian courts have ruled that internal rulings and guidelines issued by the MIRB have no legal effect. In this regard, the Guidelines have

1 MIRB Transfer Pricing Guidelines issued in 2003, *Garis Panduan Pindahan Harga (Transfer Pricing)* (2 July 2003) at page 2, paragraph 2, online: MIRB *http://www.hasil.gov.my/pdf/pdfam/garispanduanpindahanharga_bm.pdf.*

2 Section 140A(2) of the ITA.

3 PU (A) 132.

4 Transfer Pricing Guidelines 2012 (LHDN.01/46/197-1), online: MIRB *http://www.hasil.gov.my/pdf/pdfam/MalaysianTransferPricingGuidelines2012.pdf.*

5 Ibid., at p. 1, para. 1.

no legal effect and merely serve as a guidance to taxpayers in respect of the MIRB's transfer pricing policy and practice.

2. IDENTIFICATION OF LEGISLATIVE FRAMEWORK

2.1 Federal Legislation

Section 140A of the ITA encompasses the transfer pricing provisions. The following is a summary of the subsections contained within s. 140A.

Section 140A applies to transactions for the acquisition or supply of property or services with associated persons, so long as one of them is assessable or chargeable to tax in Malaysia. This controlled transaction is referred to in subss. 140A(2) and (5) of the ITA as follows:

Subsection 140A(2) reads:

'Subject to subsections(3) and (4), where a person in the basis period for a year of assessment enters into a transaction with an **associated person** *for that year for the acquisition or supply of property or services, then, for all purposes of this Act, that person shall determine and apply the arm's length price for such acquisition or supply.'*

Subsection 140A(5) reads:

'The **transactions**[6] *or the* **financial assistance** *referred to in subsection (2) or (4) respectively, shall be construed as a transaction or financial assistance between –*

(a) persons one of whom has control over the other;
(b) individuals who are relatives[7] *of each other; or*
(c) persons both of whom are controlled by some other person.'

Subsection 140A(3) provides that the Director General of Inland Revenue ('DGIR')[8] has the power to substitute the price of a transaction with a price it considers to be an arm's length price if it has reason to believe that the transaction does not reflect the current market price between independent parties.

Subsection 140A(3) reads:

'Where the Director General has reason to believe that any property or services referred to in subsection (2) is acquired or supplied at a price which is either less than or greater than the prices which it might have been expected to fetch if the parties to the transaction had been independent persons dealing at arm's length, he may in determination of the gross income, adjusted income or adjusted loss, statutory income, total income or chargeable income of the person, **substitute the price in respect of the transaction to reflect an arm's length price for the transaction.**'

Further, Subsection 140A(4) provides that:

6 For these purposes, 'transaction' has the same meaning assigned to it under subs. 140(8) of the ITA (see: s. 140A(6) of the ITA). Section 140(8) of the ITA defines 'transaction' to mean any trust, grant, covenant, agreement, arrangement or other disposition or transaction made or entered into orally or in writing (whether before or after the commencement of this Act), and includes a transaction entered into by two or more persons with another person or persons.

7 For these purposes, 'relative' has the same meaning assigned to it under subs. 140(8) of the ITA (see: s. 140A(6) of the ITA). Section 140(8) of the ITA defines 'relative' to mean a parent, a child (including a stepchild and a child adopted in accordance with any law), a brother, a sister, an uncle, an aunt, a nephew, a niece, a cousin, an ancestor or a lineal descendant.

8 The 'Director General' means the Director General of Inland Revenue referred to in s. 134 of the ITA (see: s. 2(1) of the ITA).

'Where the Director General, having regard to the circumstances of the case, is of the opinion that in the basis period for a year of assessment the value or aggregate of all financial assistance granted by a person to an associated person who is a resident, is excessive in relation to the fixed capital of such person, any interest, finance charge, other consideration payable for or losses suffered in respect of the financial assistance shall, to the extent to which it relates to the amount which is excessive, be disallowed as a deduction for the purposes of this Act.'

2.2 Income Tax (Transfer Pricing) Rules 2012 and the Transfer Pricing Guidelines 2012

The significant implications of the Rules can be summarised as follows:

(a) The requirement for contemporaneous transfer pricing documentation;[9]
(b) The application of methods to determine the arm's length price of a controlled transaction;[10] and
(c) The recognition of concepts such as intra-group services, cost contribution arrangement and intangible property in the context of transfer pricing.[11]

The Guidelines apply to businesses exceeding RM 25 million in gross income and where the total amount of related party transactions exceeds RM 15 million.[12] For individuals providing financial assistance, the Guidelines only apply if the transaction exceeds RM 50 million.[13] In order to ease the compliance burden, taxpayers falling outside these thresholds may opt to comply with limited provisions of the Guidelines.[14]

Both the Rules and Guidelines state in detail the specific documentation which should be included in the contemporaneous transfer pricing documentation.[15] They also list the documentation that should be prepared at the time when a taxpayer is developing or implementing any controlled transaction.[16] Lastly, they outline the documentation that should be updated prior to the due date for furnishing a return for that year of assessment if the controlled transaction is reviewed and there are material changes[17].

The Rules and Guidelines also prefer applying the traditional transactional methods to determine the arm's length price of a controlled transaction,[18] such as the compared uncontrolled price method, resale price method or cost plus method.[19] Where the traditional transactional methods stated above cannot be reliably applied,[20] the transactional profit methods shall be applied. This involves either the profit split method or transactional net margin method.[21]

9 The Rules, at para. 4.
10 Ibid., at paras 5, 6 and 7.
11 Ibid., at paras 9, 10 and 11.
12 The Guidelines, at para. 3.1(a).
13 Ibid., at para. 3.1(b).
14 Ibid., at para. 3.2.
15 The Rules, at para. 4(2) and the Guidelines, at para. 25.
16 The Rules, at para. 4(3)(a) and the Guidelines, at para. 25.
17 The Rules, at para. 4(3)(b) and the Guidelines, at para. 25.
18 The Rules, at para. 5(1).
19 The Rules, at para. 5(4).
20 The Rules, at para. 5(2).
21 The Rules, at para. 5(4).

Pursuant to the Guidelines, a penalty regime for transfer pricing adjustments has been introduced. Taxpayers without contemporaneous transfer pricing documentation will be subject to a 35 per cent penalty. This penalty may be reduced to 25 per cent if the transfer pricing documentation has been prepared but is not in accordance to the Guidelines.[22]

2.3 International treaties and agreements

Section 138C of the ITA introduces unilateral and bilateral advance pricing arrangements ('APA') in Malaysia and allows taxpayers to reach an agreement with the MIRB on the price of goods and services that would be transacted in the future with associated persons.[23] There are 3 categories of APA, namely:

(a) Unilateral APA, which is an APA between the taxpayer and the MIRB;
(b) Bilateral APA, which is entered into by 2 tax administrations provided for by the relevant double taxation agreements between Malaysia and the other contracting state; and
(c) Multilateral APA, which is an APA entered into between more than 2 tax administrations.

3. NATIONAL POLICY ISSUES

3.1 Overall national policy announcements

The MIRB continues to scrutinize the traditional related party transactions involving sales and purchases of goods and provision of intra-group services. They also scrutinize matters relating to royalty and trademark payments, as well as intra-group financing arrangements. In addition, they have developed new concepts on marketing intangibles. Following the issuance of the Guidelines and Rules, the MIRB has intensified its transfer pricing audits year-by-year in order to ensure that taxpayers will comply with the rules and legal provision concerning transfer pricing.[24]

In particular, the payment of significant intra-group charges has become a very contentious area in a number of transfer pricing audits. Many taxpayers are currently fighting an uphill battle during audits due to the lack of documentation or evidence to support the arm's length nature of the charges.[25]

3.2 Administrative guidelines

The Rules and the Guidelines have stated a number of requirements that bind taxpayers. In particular, focus is placed on the following key issues:

(i) Requirement for the preparation of contemporaneous transfer pricing documentation;
(ii) Application of methods to determine arm's length price; and

[22] The Guidelines, at para. 26.
[23] See the Income Tax (Advance Pricing Arrangement) Rules 2012 (P.U.(A) 133) and the Advance Pricing Arrangement Guidelines 2012 (LHDN.01/46/198-1), online: MIRB *http://www.hasil.gov.my/pdf/pdfam/MalaysianAPAGuidelines2012.pdf*.
[24] Global Transfer Pricing Review 2013 by KPMG International Cooperative.
[25] Ibid.

(iii) Recognition of cost contribution arrangements and intangible property within the context of transfer pricing.

It is particularly important that contemporaneous documentation is completed for transactions between inter-related parties when the transaction actually takes place. Rule 4 of the Rules states that 'a person who enters into a controlled transaction shall prepare a contemporaneous transfer pricing documentation'. These include, among others:

(a) Organisational structure, including organisational chart covering persons involved in a controlled transaction;
(b) Nature of the business or industry and the market conditions; and
(c) The controlled transaction.

Based on the rule stated in the Guidelines, it is important for taxpayers to prepare contemporaneous documentation for every transaction entered into.

The next concern is the determination of the arm's length price. The principles and procedures involved in determining the arm's length price are largely in line with the approaches taken in the OECD Transfer Pricing Guidelines. These include a functional analysis to determine the characterisation of the various parties in the controlled transaction; selection and application of transfer pricing methods; selection of profit level indicator ('PLI'); application of the 5 factors of comparability; and the selection of the tested party. With regards to the tested party, the MIRB would give priority to the availability of sufficient and verifiable information on both the tested party and comparables. Foreign tested parties where information is neither sufficient nor verifiable are not accepted. If the MNE has conducted a transfer pricing study on the provision of services by the foreign entity to the Malaysian entity at the foreign level using the foreign company as the tested party and the information is insufficient or unverifiable, the MNE may still be required to prepare a contemporaneous transfer pricing documentation for the Malaysian entity.

Last but not least, the MIRB is also concerned with the comparability analysis. Based on the Rules, year-to-year data comparisons should be used in comparing the results of a controlled transaction with the results of uncontrolled transactions during the same year. This is mandatory unless the data in the particular year does not provide the most reliable comparison.

4. CASE LAW

The first transfer pricing case in Malaysia was heard before the Special Commissioners of Income Tax ('SCIT') in 2013. Prior to the case of *MM Sdn Bhd v Ketua Pengarah Hasil Dalam Negeri*,[26] there were no transfer pricing cases in Malaysia. Since this was the only case on transfer pricing in Malaysia, it is rather difficult to pin-point the general position or treatment which will be adopted by the courts with regard to transfer pricing cases in this jurisdiction. In *MM Sdn Bhd*,[27] the SCIT ruled in favour of the taxpayer.

26 (2013) MSTC 10-046.
27 Supra.

Aggrieved by the decision of the SCIT, the DGIR appealed to the High Court of Malaya. The DGIR's appeal is currently pending before the High Court of Malaya.[28]

4.1 Current cases

The current pending appeal of *MM Sdn Bhd*[29] will see the first transfer pricing case being heard in the High Court after the SCIT ruled in favour of the taxpayer. The taxpayer in this case was principally engaged as a shipping agent for a Danish shipping company, AP. The taxpayer was effectively part of a division of AP, who appointed the taxpayer as its agent in Malaysia. Although AP was a wholly owned subsidiary, it owned 70 per cent of the taxpayer. All customers entered into a contract with AP, which was the principal. AP then appointed the taxpayer as its agent in Malaysia to manage the customers. The taxpayer only contracted with AP and no other parties. The taxpayer basically assisted AP in managing AP's client shipments in Malaysia. For the agency work undertaken, the taxpayer received a commission from AP, which was treated as the taxpayer's income and taxed as business income. Between 1998 and 2001, the commission rate paid by AP to the taxpayer was an export commission (also known as outward commission) of 3.25 per cent and an import commission (also known as inward commission) of 1.25 per cent. The export commission comprised of 1.625 per cent for receipt and bookings respectively. The import commission was essentially commission for delivery tasks undertaken by the taxpayer in delivering the goods to the customers in Malaysia. An Agency Agreement entered into between the taxpayer and AP was amended by an Addendum, whereby the commission rate paid by AP to the taxpayer was respectively reduced to 3 per cent for export commission and 1 per cent for import commission. This case presented several important questions. Firstly, did the DGIR have any legal basis to invoke s. 140(1) of the ITA and adjust the commission rate received in assessments between 2002 and 2005 by the taxpayer from its related principal? This was achieved by increasing the commission rate by 0.25 per cent subsequent to a transfer pricing audit. Secondly, did the DGIR have any factual basis to allege that the BPI services and Regional Services were never provided? As a consequence, the DGIR disregarded the BPI services and Regional Services charges paid by the taxpayer to its sister company in Singapore in the years of assessments between 1998 and 2005 subsequent to a transfer pricing audit. The DGIR had also imposed penalty on the taxpayer under s. 113(2) of the ITA.

Section 140(1) of the ITA provides 4 circumstances where the DGIR may invoke s. 140(1) and disregard or vary a transaction. The first circumstance arises where the DGIR has reason to believe that any transaction has the direct or indirect effect of altering the incidence of payable tax. The second involves relieving any person from liability that has arisen or would otherwise have arisen to pay tax or to make a return. The third involves

[28] As at 19.5.2014, Appeal No: R2-14-5-04/2013

[29] Supra.

evading or avoiding any duty or liability that is imposed by this Act. The fourth circumstance involves hindering or preventing the operation of the ITA in any respect. It is pertinent to note that the Parliamentary Debates established that the phrase 'he has reason to believe' was inserted to indicate that the DGIR should not exercise its jurisdiction arbitrarily. The judges sitting in the Special Commissioners of Income Tax found that the DGIR had failed to demonstrate that it had formed the belief under s. 140(1). The DGIR also lacked the relevant material upon which it could have formed the belief. Further, the SCIT held that the DGIR conducted the transfer pricing audit based on its Guidelines. These Guidelines have no legal effect as they are not an instrument prescribed under the law. By applying the Guidelines, it was held that the DGIR had acted *ultra vires*, illegally, without jurisdiction and contrary to the intention of Parliament. The DGIR adjusted the commission rate based on the Guidelines. The DGIR conceded that TP laws were not contained under the ITA. The application of the Guidelines was not provided for by the ITA, but was held by the SCIT to have been imposed unilaterally and without any legal authority by the DGIR. It was also held that the DGIR had failed to appreciate that the commission rate paid by AP to the taxpayer was at arm's length, despite the reduction. In fact, the taxpayer's operating profit margin was substantially higher than the average market. The DGIR failed to appreciate the manner and circumstances in which the taxpayer's business operated.

The SCIT also held that penalty imposed pursuant to s. 113(2) of ITA was not mandatory. This provision clearly confers discretion on the DGIR on whether penalty should be imposed. The penalty is designed to punish taxpayers who deliberately submit incorrect information and tax returns. In exercising its discretion, the DGIR must take into account all factors and circumstances of the case and should not act mechanically. No penalty should be imposed where an adjustment is purely technical or where the taxpayer did not intend evade taxes.

4.2 Historical cases of note

Our jurisdiction has no earlier cases and thus, no theme can be outlined.

5. PENALTIES

5.1 Types

There are no specific provisions in the ITA in respect of penalty on transfer pricing matters. In general, penalties are covered under s. 113(2) of the ITA. Section 113 of the ITA states that a person commits an offence when he/she submits an incorrect return or gives any incorrect information to the DGIR.[30]

Section 113(2) of the ITA functions as a penalty provision for understatement of tax liabilities. It carries a maximum penalty of 100 per cent and the discretion to impose a lower penalty lies in the hands of the DGIR.

30 Section 113(2) of the ITA

Before the issuance of the Guidelines by the MIRB, the unofficial penalty rate imposed by the DGIR was 45 per cent. Be that as it may, the issuance of the Guidelines prescribes a two-tier penalty rate as follows:

Scenario	Penalty rate
No contemporaneous transfer pricing documentation	35 per cent
Transfer pricing documentation not prepared according to requirements in the Guidelines	25 per cent

Additionally, a penalty at an increased rate of 20 per cent will be imposed on repeated offenders compared to the last penalty rate imposed for the previous offence. This circumstance would occur in the following scenarios:

(i) The taxpayer obstructs or interferes with a transfer pricing audit; or

(ii) The taxpayer fails to comply with the arm's length principle after the previous transfer pricing audit(s).[31]

In order to avoid the imposition of penalties by the DGIR, the Guidelines clearly require taxpayers to prepare contemporaneous transfer pricing documentation for every inter-related party transaction.

Section 113(2) of the ITA is not a mandatory provision. This section clearly confers discretion on the IRB on whether penalty should be imposed.

At this juncture, it is pertinent to note that in Malaysia's first transfer pricing case, *MM Sdn Bhd*,[32] the SCIT held that s. 113(2) of the ITA is not a mandatory provision. This provision clearly confers discretion on the DGIR on whether a penalty should be imposed. A penalty is designed to punish taxpayers who deliberately submit incorrect information and tax returns. In exercising its discretion, the DGIR must take into account all of the factors and circumstances of the case. The DGIR must not act mechanically in imposing a penalty on the taxpayer. It was also held that no penalty should be imposed where the adjustment is purely technical as it does not involve any intention to evade taxes.[33] Section 113(2) of the ITA is a provision that *'cannot be exercised at whim or fancy but after due consideration of all relevant facts and circumstances.'*[34]

6. DISPUTE RESOLUTION MECHANISMS

6.1 General overview

Transfer pricing matters in Malaysia are governed under the ITA. Prior to 2009, the DGIR had the power to disregard any transaction which he or she felt was not made on terms which might fairly have been expected to have

31 The Guidelines, at para 26.3.
32 Supra.
33 Supra.
34 KetuaPangarahHasilDalamNegeri v Kim Thye & Co[1992] 2 MLJ 708.

been made by independent persons engaged in the same or similar activities dealing with one another at arm's length.

Malaysia's transfer pricing laws were subsequently amended by s. 140A of the ITA, which came into effect on January 1, 2009. Section 140A allows the DGIR to substitute the price in respect of a transaction to reflect an arm's length price where there is reason to believe that the transaction was not made at the price which it might have been expected to fetch if the parties had been independent persons dealing at arm's length.

6.2 Preferred national options

In Malaysia, the dispute resolution mechanism relating to transfer pricing issues is identical to the dispute resolution mechanisms for other issues governed under the ITA. The dispute resolution mechanism operates via an appeal by an aggrieved taxpayer to the SCIT, which is provided under s. 99(1) of the ITA.

The appeal is made by lodging a 'Form Q', the prescribed form under the ITA, to the DGIR. The appeal must be made within 30 days after the service of the notice of assessment on the aggrieved taxpayer.[35] Under s. 100(1) of the ITA, the aggrieved taxpayer seeking an appeal can also make an application in writing to extend the time for an appeal beyond the prescribed 30 days.

Upon the receipt of the Form Q, the DGIR has one year to review the form.[36] During this period, the DGIR may request additional information such as the aggrieved taxpayer's books or other documents in the taxpayer's custody. Alternatively, the parties may also reach a settlement.

Where the DGIR needs more time to review Form Q, the DGIR may request an extension of time from the Minister of Finance.[37] Where the DGIR and the aggrieved taxpayer are unable to resolve the issue or issues on appeal during the revision period, the DGIR must forward Form Q to the SCIT.[38] Upon receipt of the Form Q, the SCIT will fix the matter for a hearing.

In the event where Form Q has been sent to the SCIT and a hearing has been fixed, the aggrieved taxpayer may at anytime withdraw the appeal where both parties have reached a settlement.[39]

It is of paramount importance for any aggrieved taxpayer appealing under s. 99(1) of the ITA to note that by virtue of s. 103(1) of the ITA, tax payable under an assessment shall be due and payable on the due date notwithstanding the aggrieved taxpayers' appeal.

The unsuccessful party can also appeal the matter to the High Court and further appeal to the Court of Appeal.

35 Section 99(1) of the ITA.
36 Section 101(1) of the ITA.
37 Section 101(1A) of the ITA.
38 Section 102(1) of the ITA.
39 Section 102(5) of the ITA.

7. ACCEPTABLE TAX PLANNING AREAS/SUBJECTS

Direct taxes account for 57.6 per cent of the Malaysian Treasury's revenue for 2013,[40] a staggering percentage by world standards. Inevitably, the extent of tax evasion and avoidance amongst Malaysian taxpayers will either make or break the nation in view of its heavy reliance on direct tax revenue.

In light of these numbers, Malaysia also had one of the highest cumulative illicit financial outflows between 2002 and 2011. This amount totaled US$370.38 billion globally.[41] For this reason, Malaysia can ill-afford to take lenient and soft approaches in tackling tax avoidance.

In past decades, Malaysia's lenient approach was exemplified by the insufficiency of specific anti-avoidance legislation and under-invocation of the general anti-avoidance provision of s. 140 of the ITA. More recently, however, Malaysia has introduced transfer-pricing legislation and by-laws (highlighted in Chapter 2.1) in addition to the goods and services tax in order to broaden its tax base and to combat tax evasion and avoidance.

Two important pieces of anti-avoidance legislation are s. 140 of the ITA and s. 25 of the Real Property Gains Tax Act 1976. Malaysia has also enacted other specific anti-avoidance provisions in the likes of transfer pricing provisions.

Section 140 of the ITA has received a notable amount of judicial pronouncements in Malaysian Courts. The most significant case was the landmark Court of Appeal decision of *Sabah Berjaya Sdn Bhd v Ketua Pengarah Jabatan Hasil Dalam Negeri,*[42] which ought to form the starting point of any anti-avoidance discussions in Malaysia. In this case, the Malaysian Court of Appeal held that only a tax mitigation scheme ought to fall outside of the ambits of s. 140 of the ITA and is deemed to be a legal transaction. However, tax evasion and tax avoidance schemes take different forms in the Malaysian context. The Court of Appeal went on to recognise the difference between tax evasion, tax avoidance and tax mitigation. The Court held that tax evasion involves wilful and fraudulent elements whilst tax avoidance involves a transaction where the dominant purpose of has no commercial purpose.

According to the Court of Appeal, the only legal form of arrangement allowed is a tax mitigation scheme where tax savings arise from a commercial transaction that is implemented or structured. In this regard, the Court of Appeal then held that a taxpayer company making donations to its shareholders in lieu of paying dividends was within the boundaries of the law and the anti-avoidance provision in the ITA. The Court of Appeal further held that the taxpayer in question did not do anything which did not reduce its income or suffer a loss, notwithstanding that it had obtained a reduction in its tax liability. For this reason, the taxpayer had not engaged in a tax avoidance scheme.

---

40 Treasury, Ministry of Finance Malaysia Economic Report 2013-2014, Table No. 6.3.
41 Global Financial Integrity – Illicit Financial Flows from Developing Countries: 2002-2011 Report
42 [1999] 3 CLJ 587.

8. DEFINING ABUSIVE TAX AVOIDANCE

Like other jurisdictions, the Malaysian courts have been eager to strike down abusive or aggressive tax avoidance schemes carried out by taxpayers by invoking the general and specific anti-avoidance provisions in the ITA. That said, it is worth noting that the term 'abusive tax avoidance' is uncommon within Malaysian context and is simply referred to as 'tax avoidance'. There is also an absence of any express definition of this term in Malaysian legislations or by-laws.

Over the years, Malaysian Courts have nevertheless highlighted various tax avoidance schemes which ought to be seen as aggressive or abusive. It is also worth noting that the Malaysian courts have been taking similar approaches to other Commonwealth jurisdictions in the interpretation of tax avoidance.

In delivering the Malaysian Supreme Court judgment of *Lim Kar Bee v Duofortis Properties (M) Sdn Bhd*,[43] Justice Peh Swee Chin stated that *'tax avoidance does not necessarily indicate an unassailable hallmark of legitimacy.'* In the same judgment, Justice Peh Swee Chin also held that the real test to determine whether a transaction is illegal or not is whether the primary purpose of the scheme or transaction is to avoid the payment of taxes. If it is in the affirmative, then the scheme or transaction is dubbed as being transacted 'for an illegal purpose' and therefore ought to be an illegal transaction in the eyes of the law. Based on this principle, the Supreme Court held that the scheme of a landowner to enter into an agreement to sell land to a prospective transferee and sign a trust deed declaring that he held the land in trust for the prospective transferee was illegal. This finding was based on the premise that the ultimate aim of such scheme was to avoid payment of the estate duty. In this regard, the scheme was held to be illegal and seen as a form of illegal tax avoidance scheme.

Besides judicial pronouncements like the one indicated above, Malaysia's executive branch (the Government of Malaysia) recently voiced its dissatisfaction with the rising rate of tax evasion and aggressive tax avoidance. Over the past decade, the country and its tax authorities have focussed on combating tax evasion and aggressive tax avoidance within the country. This is due to the rise of innovative methods by taxpayers in mapping out schemes and transactions that deliberately avoid tax. In light of this, the Prime Minister of Malaysia, Datuk Seri Mohamad Najib bin Abdul Razak, officially dubbed tax evasion and illegal tax avoidance as a *'treasonous act'* and likened paying taxes as *'the veins of patriotism.'*[44] While it is hoped that the Malaysian government's commitment will reduce the number of aggressive tax avoidance schemes, the results will remain to be seen in the next few years.

---

43 [1992] 2 MLJ 281.

44 *http://www.nst.com.my/nation/general/pm-tax-evasion-akin-to-treason-1.411200*

9. THE LEGISLATIVE FRAMEWORK

Section 140 of the Income Tax Act 1967 is the general anti-avoidance provision and was enacted by Parliament to target abusive tax avoidance schemes. This provision confers the DGIR with vast powers to disregard, vary or adjust any transaction where the taxpayer attempted to reduce their tax payable. The DGIR may also target taxpayers that attempt to evade or avoid duties or hinder the operation of the Malaysian income tax legislation as a whole. The DGIR can also relieve any person from any liability which has arisen. As such, s. 140 covers a very extensive and wide-ranging number of transactions carried out by the taxpayers. For this reason, the Malaysian Courts have examined the extent of enforceability of this anti-avoidance provision on taxpayers.

In *SBP Sdn Bhd v DGIR* [1988] 1 MSTC 2053, the SCIT outlined the test for a transaction to be categorised as a tax avoidance scheme and therefore fall under the ambit of s. 140 of the Income Tax Act 1967. The SCIT held that transactions must be carried out for *bona fide* commercial reasons or in the ordinary course of a business. Transactions involving the purchase of shell corporations whose sole asset consists of unabsorbed losses is tantamount to tax avoidance and falls afoul of s. 140.

Another significant case was decided by Justice Yusoff of the High Court of Malaysia in *LD Timber v Director General of Inland Revenue* [1978] 1 MLJ 203. To determine whether a taxpayer had entered into a scheme that altered the tax payable, it must be shown that the transaction cannot be explained by reference to ordinary business dealings without being labelled as a means to avoid tax.

Based on the above cases, the Malaysian Courts appear to have taken the view that transactions whose dominant purpose lacks any commercial goal will be labelled as tax avoidance schemes and disregarded or varied by the tax authorities. In order to fall outside the ambit of the general anti-avoidance rule, taxpayers must demonstrate that a transaction has a commercial purpose and is not undertaken for the sole purpose of reducing tax. As the Malaysian Court of Appeal discussed in *Sabah Berjaya Sdn Bhd,*[45] tax migration occurs where a tax savings occurs as a result of the manner by which a commercial transaction is implemented or structured.

In addition to s. 140, there are other specific anti-avoidance provisions in the ITA. Section 65 of the ITA provides that, pursuant to any settlement, any income from a source or assets that will become payable by a relative of the settlor will be deemed to be the settlor's income. This provision is intended to negate any settlement schemes which have an income-splitting effect by deeming any income to be the settlor's income.

Section 29(1) of the ITA covers income that becomes payable on demand by the taxpayer in relation to rent, discounts, annuities, royalties, interest or pensions. According to s. 29, such income ought to be taxable even when it has not been received. Without this anti-avoidance provision, any income obtainable on demand would only become taxable once it was received.

---

[45] Supra.

Section 24(2) of the ITA also covers the situation where a taxpayer withdraws a corporation's stock for personal use without paying any consideration. In this case, an amount equal to the market value of that stock shall be added to the taxpayer's gross income.

10. KEY CASES OF INTEREST

10.1 Current cases

The distinction between tax evasion, tax avoidance and tax mitigation was succinctly discussed in a Privy Council appeal from New Zealand (see *Commissioner of Inland Revenue v Challenge Corporation Ltd*[46]). The case is worth noting because New Zealand has a similar provision to s. 140(1) of the ITA. In delivering the majority decision, Lord Templeman stated:

'Income tax is **mitigated** *by a taxpayer who reduces his income or incurs expenditure in circumstances which reduce his assessable income or entitle him to reduction in his tax liability. Section 99 does not apply to tax mitigation because the taxpayer's tax advantage is not derived from an arrangement but from the reduction of income which he accepts or the expenditure which he incurs*

... Income tax is **avoided** *and a tax advantage is derived from an arrangement when the taxpayer reduces his liability to tax without involving him in the loss or expenditure which entitles him to that reduction.*

The taxpayer engaged in tax avoidance does not reduce his income or suffer a loss or incur expenditure but nevertheless obtains a reduction in his liability to tax as if he had.'

Lord Templeman's view was subsequently adopted by the Malaysian Court of Appeal in *Sabah Berjaya Sdn Bhd*.[47] The Court held that where a taxpayer makes a settlement, their income should be reduced because they have effectively deprived themselves of a source of capital. If the settlement is irrevocable and satisfies certain other conditions, this reduction will reduce the taxpayer's assessable income. The mere fact that there is a reduction of income resulting from the tax treatment adopted by the taxpayer does not amount to tax avoidance as it is simply a tax advantage received by the taxpayer. For example, premiums paid on a qualifying insurance policy by a taxpayer will reduce their tax payable under the ITA. Furthermore, this will not constitute tax avoidance since the tax reduction was only incidental to their purchase of the insurance policy. However, should there be a fictitious purchase involved, it will amount to tax avoidance (*Paramount Malaysia SdnBhd v Pesuruhjaya Khas Cukai Pendapatan & Anor*).[48]

10.2 Key historical cases

There is a limited amount of historical jurisprudence concerning tax avoidance in Malaysia. This is partly because aggressive tax avoidance does not play a major role in the tax planning industries in Malaysia. It may also be due to the fact that the MIRB has not aggressively pursued and

46 [1986] STC 548.
47 Supra.
48 (2002) MSTC 3908.

investigated these cases in the past. Although the amount of cases brought forward to courts has increased in recent years, there are very few cases in the field of aggressive tax avoidance. Not only is s. 140 of the ITA modelled after Australia's general anti-avoidance provision but s. 140(1) of the ITA also shares many features with other jurisdictions. In *MM Sdn Bhd,*[49] the MIRB invoked s. 140(1) of the ITA and increased the commission received by the taxpayer by 0.25 per cent. When this case was decided, however, Malaysia's legislature had yet to include the transfer pricing clauses.

The SCIT has also adopted a 'form over substance' approach. This involves considering an entity on its own without exploring the relationship with another entity. This approach is best demonstrated by the decision in *Sabah Berjaya Sdn Bhd.*[50] Like *CIR v Challenge Corporation Ltd,*[51] the Privy Council specified that a tax mitigation scheme is one that has an actual outlay that reduces the taxable liability. On the other hand, tax avoidance occurs where a taxpayer reduces their tax liability without making an expenditure entitling them to the reduction.

Another case worth noting is *YEHHSB v Ketua Pengarah Hasil Dalam Negeri.*[52] Here, the SCIT held that the interest earned from a fixed deposit made by a corporation's directors were taxable since the interest payments belonged to the taxpayer. As such, the respondent was correct to invoke the anti-avoidance section.

In conclusion, Malaysian courts will determine whether the general anti-avoidance provision in s. 140 of the ITA has been correctly invoked by examining whether the effect of a transaction results in an overall loss of revenue to the Government. If there is no commercially sound reason to support the transaction undertaken by the taxpayer, the anti-avoidance provision could and should be applied.

11. PENALTIES

11.1 Legislative provisions

There are no specific provisions in the ITA for tax avoidance. In general, penalties are covered under s. 113(2) of the ITA.

As discussed in Chapter 5, s. 113(2) of the ITA is a penalty provision for the understatement of tax with a maximum penalty of 100 per cent of the outstanding amount. However, the DGIR has discretion to impose a lower penalty.

The unofficial penalty rate imposed by the DGIR is 45 per cent where they are satisfied that one of the criteria listed in s. 140 has occurred. A taxpayer commits an offence under s. 113(2) if an incorrect return is made or incorrect information is furnished to the MIRB.

In 2013, the MIRB issued a Tax Audit Framework[53] stating that concessionary penalty rates may be imposed where the taxpayer makes voluntary disclosure before the MIRB commences its tax audit. The

49 Supra.
50 Supra.
51 (1986) STC 548.
52 (2010) MSTC 10-007.
53 Came into effect on 1st April 2013.

concessionary rates for voluntary disclosure range from 10 per cent to 35 per cent, depending on the time when the voluntary disclosure is made.[54]

Further, it is worth noting that no proceedings under s. 113 of the ITA can be initiated more than 12 years after the offence was committed.[55] Additionally, any person who aids, abets or incites another person to commit an offence under s. 113 of the ITA will be deemed to have committed the same offence and will be liable to the same penalty.[56]

Despite the concessionary penalty rates indicated by the MIRB, Malaysian courts have ruled that s. 113(2) of the ITA is not a mandatory provision. This section clearly confers discretion on the DGIR on whether penalty should be imposed or not.

11.2 Notable cases

In *Office Park Development Sdn Bhd v Ketua Pengarah Hasil Dalam Negeri*,[57] the High Court of Malaya affirmed the SCIT's decision to set aside the penalty imposed under s. 113(2) of the ITA. This was made on the basis that the taxpayer had acted in good faith at all material times, took professional advice, made full disclosure and that the dispute arose as a result of a technical adjustment.

In *Ketua Pengarah Hasil Dalam Negeri v Kim Thye & Co*,[58] the Supreme Court held that s. 113(2) is not a mandatory provision. The Supreme Court ruled that s. 113(2) clearly confers discretion on the Respondent as to whether penalty should be imposed or not.

It is pertinent to note that, in exercising the discretion, the DGIR must take into account all factors and circumstances of the case and should not act mechanically. At this juncture, reference is made to the decision of Justice Richard Malanjum in *Awang Tengah Ag Amin v Sabah Public Service v Sabah Public Service Commission & Anor*.[59] Here, his Lordship had the occasion to endorse a passage from the authoritative work of Professor M P Jain: *'When discretion is conferred on an authority, it must personally exercise the same; it must apply its own mind to the facts and circumstances of each case and come to its own decision. If authority acts without applying its mind to the case before it, then the action or decision taken by it will be bad because the authority has not exercised its discretion.'*[60]

During the Dialogue Sessions between the MIRB and the professional bodies on June 17, 2012 and October 2, 2013, the MIRB stated that *'a technical adjustment generally arises due to a differing interpretation of the tax legislation by the taxpayer, either due to a provision not being clearly defined or due to the existence of conflicting case law.'*[61] The MIRB confirmed that no penalty will be imposed in the event of a pure technical adjustment as this would not involve an intention to evade taxes.

---

54 See Tax Audit Framework 2013 issued by the MIRB.
55 Section 121(1) of the ITA.
56 Section 121(2) of the ITA.
57 [2011] 9 MLJ 479.
58 [1992] 2 MLJ 708.
59 [1998] 2 CLJ Supp 409.
60 Administrative Law of Malaysia and Singapore (3rd Ed).
61 http://www.micpa.com.my/micpamember/cpa_review/02.pdf.

12. CURRENT TRENDS

By virtue of s. 140(1) of the ITA, the MIRB has the authority to disregard or vary a transaction and make such adjustment as it thinks fit. This is done with a view to counteracting the effect of the transaction if the MIRB has reason to believe that the transaction has the effect of:

(a) altering the incidence of tax which is payable or suffered by or which would otherwise have been payable or suffered by any person;
(b) relieving any person from any liability which has arisen or which would otherwise have arisen to pay tax or to make a return;
(c) evading or avoiding any duty or liability which is imposed or would otherwise have been imposed on any person by this Act; or
(d) hindering or preventing the operation of the ITA in any respect.

The Malaysia position in this area is similar to Australia. If the dominant purpose of a transaction has no commercial purpose, that transaction will be disregarded or varied on the basis of tax avoidance by the tax authority. Therefore, the objective of the exercise must be to achieve a commercial purpose and not to enjoy tax efficiency without any other commercial purpose for the transaction. However, if tax savings arise by the manner in which the commercial transaction is implemented or structured, that is to be regarded in law as tax mitigation.

12.1 National policy and law

Malaysia has yet to issue any distinct government policies. The trends in the law suggest that taxpayers are favouring a more combustive tax avoidance technique that may see the government acting in a more aggressive manner by invoking s. 140(1) of the ITA. However, the MIRB has yet to conduct audits to identify aggressive tax avoidance methods currently used by both government-linked companies and multinationals company.

12.1.1 The impact and role of the OECD and other international relations

Malaysia has yet to become a member of the OECD. However, the case of *Damco Logistic Malaysia SdnBhd v Ketua Pengarah Hasil Dalam Negeri*[62] demonstrates that the Malaysian courts have observed the persuasiveness of the OECD's commentaries.

[62] (2011) MSTC 30-033.

Mexico

Basham Ringe y Correa, SC Mario Barrera-Vazquez

PART ONE: TRANSFER PRICING

1. GENERAL OVERVIEW

Mexico follows the arm's length standard. Accordingly, for income tax purposes, income and deductions derived from transactions entered into by and between taxpayers and their related parties (both Mexican residents and non-Mexican residents) must be calculated considering the amount of income and deductions that would result from comparable transactions entered into by and between independent parties. Otherwise, the tax authority may re-determine such income and deductions.

In order to calculate the arm's length price, six methods are available under the *Income Tax Law*, namely: (i) the comparable uncontrolled price; (ii) the cost plus, the resale price; (iii) the profit split; (iv) the residual profit split; and (v) the transactional net margin. The comparable uncontrolled price method must be used in all cases except when it is not suitable to determine the arm's length price, in which case the most appropriate method of the other five should be used.

These methods may yield a range of arm's length prices, which may be adjusted using statistical methods. Under the Regulations of the *Income Tax Law*, interquartile ranges are used.

It is important to mention as well that an independent transaction is deemed comparable to a controlled transaction when there are no differences between the two that may significantly affect the relevant consideration, or when there are such differences, but they may be eliminated through reasonable adjustments. To this end, factors such as features of a transaction, functions and risks assumed, contractual terms and economic circumstances are considered to determine comparability.

Finally it is noteworthy that: (i) Mexico uses the OECD's Transfer Pricing Guidelines as a tool to interpret transfer pricing provisions; and (ii) safe harbor rules are available to toll manufacturers (*maquiladoras*), which are a large industry in Mexico.

2. IDENTIFICATION OF LEGISLATIVE FRAMEWORK

2.1 Federal legislation

The core of transfer pricing rules are set forth in articles 76(XII), 179, 180, 181, 182 and 184 of the Income Tax Law. Further, some documentation obligations are set forth in articles 76(IX) and (X) of the same statute.

In addition, it is possible to request a letter ruling, concerning the transfer pricing method used by a taxpayer under article 34A of the Federal Fiscal Code.

2.2 State and provincial legislative interplay

The States of Mexico have no transfer pricing legislation.

2.3 International treaties and agreements

Currently, Mexico has 53 tax treaties in force. Typically, article 9 of those treaties, which replicates article 9 of the OECD's Model Tax Convention to a large extent, allows Mexico to impose a tax whenever conditions set between residents of Mexico and residents of the relevant treaty country are inconsistent with the arm's length standard.

Further, such an article establishes the possibility for both Mexico and its treaty partners to re-adjust profits of their respective residents when a portion of such profits has been taxed by the other country concerned, due to a transfer pricing adjustment.

In addition, double taxation issues that may result from such readjustment may be solved through the mutual agreement procedure set forth in those treaties.

It is necessary to mention that given our intensive trade with the US, it is the tax treaty that is most commonly used in Mexico. Nonetheless, other tax treaties are heavily used as well, such as that entered into with Canada.

Finally, it is noteworthy that the Supreme Court of Justice has determined that international treaties (such as tax treaties) are the highest law of the land, just below our Constitution, but above Federal law. Thus, tax treaties have great weight in Mexico.

3. NATIONAL POLICY ISSUES

Mexico is fully committed to raise tax revenues to become less dependent on oil revenues in order to boost the oil industry, which is regarded as the central piece in the current Administration's plan to accelerate Mexico's economy.

The impact of this policy is not only reflected in statutory amendments aimed to raise revenue, but also in more aggressive audit programs.

3.1 Overall national policy announcements

Mexico has publicly welcomed the OECD's BEPS report and the action plan, which may have a deep impact on both domestic and international rules governing transfer pricing. Further, Mexico is not only willing to participate in international efforts to tackle BEPS, it has already introduced some domestic rules which are clearly inspired by the BEPS report and may have an impact on related-party transactions.

3.2 National revenue authority initiatives

Some senior officials from the Tax Administration Service have mentioned that a program will be implemented to audit multinational enterprises and their related party transactions, particularly in areas such as corporate reorganizations, even if they have letter rulings. This effort is inspired to some extent by the BEPS report.

3.3 Administrative statements

In general, there is no guidance concerning transfer pricing audits. There are only a few internal revenue rulings, which include some rules regarding sham transactions over Mexican related parties. It is noteworthy, however, that the Supreme Court of Justice recently resolved a case concerning the deductibility of payments made under cost sharing agreements, which outlines some transfer pricing aspects thereof that must be analyzed by the tax authority when auditing that type of agreement. The Tax Administration Service has announced that it will follow the Supreme Court's guidance on this subject whenever it audits cost sharing agreements.

3.4 Administrative guidelines

As mentioned earlier, there is no guidance concerning transfer pricing audits, except for that concerning cost sharing agreements described above.

4. CASE LAW

Transfer pricing rules have been in place for more than 20 years in Mexico. Nevertheless, there is not much judicial experience on this matter. This is due to many factors, including the fact that in the past, transfer pricing audits were not very common. We do have some case law dealing with the constitutionality of transfer pricing rules, as well as case law dealing with very specific transfer pricing issues.

Nevertheless, this trend is likely to change, as the tax authority is now much more active in auditing transfer pricing matters and, therefore, it is more likely that tax deficiencies derived therefrom will be challenged in court.

4.1 Current cases

Recently, the Supreme Court of Justice ruled upon a case where a taxpayer challenged on constitutional grounds a provision of the *Income Tax Law* that disallows the deduction of payments made in connection with cost contribution agreements entered into with parties that are not subject to income tax.

The Supreme Court's decision ruled that the deduction of payments made in connection with cost contribution agreements entered into with foreign related parties should be allowed, provided that certain requirements are met, including compliance with the arm's length standard, which should be analyzed under the provisions of the Income Tax Law and the OECD's Guidelines on Transfer Pricing; particularly the chapter concerning cost contribution arrangements.

Although this case does not deal directly with transfer pricing, it allows a deduction of payments that are quite common in today's world, under the guise of transfer pricing.

4.2 Historical cases of note

As mentioned earlier, there is no significant case law concerning transfer pricing. The cases available essentially challenged the constitutionality of transfer pricing rules; however, courts have consistently ruled that the system is constitutional.

5. PENALTIES

In general, the greatest concern in transfer pricing matters is failure to comply with the arm's length standard, which may lead to a re-adjustment of income or deductions up to the median of the range, and, ultimately, to a tax deficiency, which typically includes the amount of unpaid tax, inflation adjustment, interests and a penalty of up to 75 per cent of the unpaid tax.

There are some other formal obligations that may lead to the imposition of penalties if not properly met. For example, taxpayers are required to file an annual information return on their transactions with foreign related parties. Likewise, they are required to keep documentation showing compliance with the arm's length standard in their related party transactions, which is typically a transfer pricing inquiry. Failure to file such an information return may result in a fine of up to $9,173.00; and failure to keep such documentation results in a fine of up to $225.00 for every transaction not supported with documentation.

5.1 Types

There are no other penalties specific to transfer pricing, other than those described above.

5.2 Special or notable cases

There are no major cases dealing with penalties. However, case law does provide some tests that penalties have to meet in order to be deemed constitutional. For example, for every violation, the law must provide a range of penalties, so that the authority in charge of punishing a violation may individualize the penalty, considering the particular facts and circumstances of the case. Accordingly, fixed penalties are unconstitutional.

6. DISPUTE RESOLUTION MECHANISMS

Under Mexican law, there are several dispute resolution mechanisms. The traditional domestic mechanisms are an administrative appeal which is heard by the tax authority, and a trial heard by the Mexican Tax Court. In addition to those mechanisms, we now have the possibility to enter into settlements with the tax authorities during audits.

Aside from those domestic options, we have the mutual agreement procedures under which Mexico and its treaty partners may agree on solutions to eliminate double taxation that may arise in many instances, including transfer pricing.

6.1 Preferred national options

In general, there is some reluctance to solve transfer pricing disputes in court for many reasons, including the cost of securing the relevant tax assessment during proceedings. As a result, a trial is typically seen as the last resort.

It is quite common, as a first resort, for taxpayers to request letter rulings or mutual agreement under a tax treaty as a preventive measure to avoid future transfer pricing disputes.

In cases of audits where the tax authorities' point of view may be different from the taxpayers', it is common to be involved in discussions with the authorities throughout the process to solve as many issues as possible; and when a tax assessment is inevitable, to challenge it through an administrative appeal or request a mutual agreement procedure under a tax treaty.

Given this trend of not resorting to our courts, we expect that this new possibility of entering into settlements with the tax authorities will be heavily used to solve transfer pricing disputes. Since this provision was only enacted last January, we will see how it will be implemented by the authority in the coming months.

6.2 International options

As mentioned earlier, mutual agreement procedures under tax treaties are often used either to avoid a future contingency with the tax authority or to solve a dispute with the tax authority. The reasons for the popularity of this alternative are many, including: legal certainty of the resulting agreement; flexibility, as the procedure may be requested within a very large time frame; and the possibility to still resort to domestic dispute resolution mechanisms.

The downside of these procedures is that taxpayers are not really a party thereto and therefore, they are not in control. Additionally, there is no timeframe within which a resolution must be issued. Under a mutual agreement procedure, Mexico and the relevant treaty country enter by themselves into discussions, negotiations and ultimately, into an agreement. In addition, Mexico or the relevant treaty country may refuse to engage in this procedure.

PART TWO: TAX AVOIDANCE

7. ACCEPTABLE TAX PLANNING AREAS/SUBJECTS

In Mexico, there are no legal definitions of tax planning or aggressive tax planning. Taxpayers may arrange their transactions as they see fit, which also means that they are able to legitimately minimize the payment of tax.

Naturally, taxpayers may not engage in fraudulent activities or enter into sham transactions to minimize their tax burden, as those situations may result in administrative and criminal liabilities.

Likewise, there are certain tax provisions aimed to limit some potential abuses by taxpayers in specific areas such as transfer pricing rules, thin capitalization rules, and CFC rules.

Tax authorities are increasingly requesting taxpayers prove that their transactions are supported by a business reason other than taxation, despite the fact that they may be structured legally. Likewise, they have developed programs to audit taxpayers who show low effective tax rates or who show sudden drops in their effective tax rates. This trend is likely to be boosted by the BEPS report.

Such reports will probably encourage the tax authorities to develop theories or mechanisms aimed to challenge the tax treatment given to structures they may consider abusive, even if they are lawful.

8. DEFINING ABUSIVE TAX AVOIDANCE

In Mexico, there is no definition of abusive tax avoidance. The tax authority, however, has identified specific transactions which are deemed abusive tax practices. Periodically, the tax authority publishes a description of such transactions.

Such publications are not binding on taxpayers. However, tax advisors who recommend structures that are regarded as abusive tax practices under such publication, and fail to reveal such situation in the relevant opinion letter may be subject to a penalty.

In addition, such publications serve as a guide for taxpayers as to what type of tax planning devices are likely to be challenged by the tax authority.

9. THE LEGISLATIVE FRAMEWORK

As mentioned earlier, we have no general anti-avoidance rule. We only have provisions aimed at tackling abusive tax avoidance in specific circumstances, such as CFC rules and thin capitalization rules.

Further, this year the Mexican Congress enacted certain provisions aimed at preventing tax treaty abuse. For example, in cases of payments between related parties which are deemed Mexican source income and may benefit from a tax treaty, the Mexican tax authority may request from the payee who resides in the relevant treaty country a document in writing and signed under oath by its legal representative, attesting that such items of income will be subject to income tax in their home country. Another example is the impossibility of deducting expenses paid to a related party located in a preferential tax regime, unless the consideration meets the arm's length standard, and such circumstances are proven by the Mexican taxpayer.

As mentioned earlier, the Mexican government is likely to try to enact similar statutory or regulatory provisions in light of the BEPS report. In fact, in the past it has tried to enact a GAAR, but such attempts have not yet passed in Congress.

10. KEY CASES OF INTEREST

10.1 Current cases

Recently, we have seen that the tax authority more often uses its powers to determine that a transaction is a sham for tax purposes, particularly in cases of corporate reorganizations. Likewise, it has become common for the tax authorities to review taxpayers' letter rulings in order to confirm the reality of the considerations paid between related parties. In fact, we have seen instances where it attempts to apply the relevant provisions dealing with sham transactions to cases that do not exactly fall within the scope thereof, which may of course be challenged in court.

Likewise, it is quite common for the tax authority to request documentation evidencing that transactions under audit had a business purpose, and that such business purpose was somehow materialized throughout the years. Sometimes, such requests may be illegal and therefore, they may ultimately be challenged.

10.2 Key historical cases

Unfortunately, we do not have much case law concerning abusive tax avoidance. In fact, much of the case law available on sham transactions is based on civil law, the area of the law where such concepts were originally conceived.

11. PENALTIES

11.1 Legislative provisions

As mentioned earlier, Mexico does not have a GAAR, therefore, it does not have a penalty in connection therewith. Nonetheless, the tax authority is empowered with imposing certain penalties for other reasons that may be quite burdensome, as described above.

In general, if the tax authority assesses a deficiency for any reason, including the application of an anti-avoidance rule, such as the CFC or thin capitalization rules, a penalty may be imposed, which may range between 55 per cent and 75 per cent of the unpaid tax, pursuant to article 76 of the Federal Fiscal Code.

In addition, articles 89 and 90 of the Federal Fiscal Code provide that tax advisors who recommend structures to reduce or eliminate payment of taxes that are regarded as abusive tax practices under the publication described above, and who fail to reveal such information in the relevant opinion letter may be subject to a penalty of up to $70,110.00 pesos (approximately $5,270.00).

11.2 Examples of penalties imposed

Typically, whenever the tax authority assesses a tax deficiency, a penalty equivalent to 55 per cent of the deficiency is imposed. It is rare to see a penalty higher than 55 per cent, because it would require a justification of the gravity of the case, whereas the 55 per cent penalty merely requires proving that the tax was not paid, because it is the minimum penalty under the law. It is also very rare to see a case where no penalty is imposed.

There may be cases when additional penalties are imposed for specific reasons, such as a failure to file a certain information return.

12. CURRENT TRENDS

12.1 National policy and law

The Minister of Finance has publicly announced that no further amendments will be introduced into our tax laws during the current administration, which ends in 2018. This does not mean that Congress cannot enact some amendments to our tax laws during that period, nor does it mean that the tax authorities cannot introduce amendments to the regulations or the general rules that may affect taxpayers. They may try to tackle what they regard as 'abusive tax avoidance', particularly in light of the BEPS report, discussed below.

It is difficult to anticipate what these changes will look like, if they happen. Nevertheless, there is much certainty that the tax authority will heavily audit all the issues covered by the BEPS report in the coming years, such as transfer pricing, because it has publicly announced that it will do so.

12.1.1 The impact and role of the OECD and other international relations

The OECD has always had a great impact upon Mexico's tax system. For example, our tax treaties are heavily inspired by the OECD's Model Tax Convention, the OECD Commentaries are a valid interpretive aid of Mexico's tax treaties, and the OECD's Transfer Pricing Guidelines are a source of interpretation of Mexico's transfer pricing rules.

This trend is not likely to change. To the contrary, Mexico gave a very warm welcome to the BEPS report and associated action plan. Further, Mexico has announced that it will actively participate with other countries in the implementation of measures to tackle BEPS and it has already enacted BEPS-related provisions, as discussed above. In May, 2014, during the OECD's annual Ministerial Council Meeting, Mexico signed the 'Declaration on Automatic Exchange of Information in Tax Matters', which should yield more information from taxpayers regarding related party transactions.

Though Mexico may be influenced by other sources, the OECD is certainly the most influential source, and will continue to be for the foreseeable future.

The Netherlands

Loyens & Loeff NV Lucia Sahin

PART ONE: TRANSFER PRICING

1. GENERAL OVERVIEW

The arm's length principle was codified in Dutch legislation in 2002. The OECD Model Tax Convention and Guidelines play an important role in interpreting this principle in the Netherlands. The State Secretary of Finance recently underlined this once again in his transfer pricing decree of 14 November 2013.

In the past, transfer pricing disputes were generally settled through a compromise with the tax authorities. Furthermore, the Advance Pricing Agreement practice works reliably whereby taxpayers can obtain an APA within a couple of months. Consequently, for many structures, certainty in advance is requested from the tax authorities. As a result, there is not much case law available on transfer pricing disputes. The worldwide trend of tax authorities being more and more focussed on transfer pricing, can also be seen at the Dutch tax authorities. Specifically, this can be seen in the increasing number of transfer pricing audits taking place.

2. IDENTIFICATION OF LEGISLATIVE FRAMEWORK

Since 1 January 2002, the arm's length principle has been codified in article 8b of the corporate income tax act ('CITA'). The codification, except for some slight differences, can be seen as a translation of the arm's length principle as set out in article 9 of the OECD Model Tax Convention ('OECD MC'). In addition, paragraph three of article 8b CITA provides for documentation requirements. Besides article 8b CITA, several decrees have been issued by the State Secretary of Finance, which serve as a clarification of Dutch policy regarding transfer pricing.

The Netherlands only has transfer pricing legislation at a state level.

2.1 Article 8b CITA

After providing the wording of article 8b CITA, I address various important elements of Dutch transfer pricing legislation, including the definition of 'related entities', transfer pricing documentation requirements and adjustments.

Article 8b CITA reads as follows:[1]

(1) If an entity, directly or indirectly, participates in the management or supervision, or in the capital of another entity, and the agreed or

[1] This is an unofficial translation of the Dutch text of article 8b CITA.

imposed conditions (transfer prices) of the transactions between these entities deviate from the conditions that would have applied in the market between independent parties, the entities' profit is determined as if the arm's length conditions had been agreed upon.

(2) The first paragraph applies in a similar manner if a person, directly or indirectly, participates in the management or supervision, or the capital of the one and the other entity.

(3) The entities mentioned in the first and second paragraph shall include information in their administration, which shows the manner in which the transfer prices that are referred to in the first paragraph were established, and from which it can be deduced if, in the market, the transfer prices that were established would have been agreed upon between independent entities.

(a) Related entities

Article 8b CITA only applies to entities.[2] Entities include companies, partnerships, associations, trusts, etc. The article does not apply to non-arm's length dealings between a shareholder and his company. For such transactions, article 3.8 of the personal income tax act ('PITA') prescribes that (dis)advantages that originate from the shareholders' relationship are eliminated from the profit of the taxpayer. Prior to the codification of the arm's length principle in the Dutch CITA, transfer pricing adjustments, both for personal as for corporate income tax purposes, were made based on article 3.8 PITA, (which through article 8 CITA also applies to corporate taxpayers).

The tax code does not define what qualifies as a related entity. From the parliamentary proceedings,[3] it follows that the shareholder, supervisor and/or manager should have sufficient authority to influence the transfer prices used for the transactions among the entities involved. On a case-by-case basis it should be determined whether sufficient authority is present. If the taxpayer believes there is not sufficient authority to influence the conditions agreed upon, he can request for the inspector's certainty in advance that the entities should not qualify as related entities.

Article 8b CITA covers both transactions among domestic related entities and among internationally related entities. Cross-border transactions are therefore treated in the same manner as domestic transactions, though they are clearly more often under the scrutiny of the tax authorities.

(b) Transfer pricing documentation

The obligation to keep transfer pricing documentation is needed so sufficient information is available for the tax authorities to judge whether the transfer price applied is at arm's length. The documentation should consist of a comparability[4] analysis as provided for in Chapter 1 of the OECD Transfer Pricing Guidelines for Multinational Enterprises and Tax Administrations

2 Entities as defined in article 2 paragraph 1 sub b of the General Tax Act.
3 Parliamentary proceedings, Second Chamber, 2001–2002, 28 034, nr. 5, p. 34.
4 This is not the extensive comparability analysis as required when filing for an APA.

('OECD Guidelines'). Based on the comparability analysis, taxpayers should be able to motivate their choice for a certain transfer pricing method. The best method rule[5] is not to be used in the Netherlands.[6] Nor is the taxpayer required to perform a study on the prices that would have been set for comparable independent transactions, ie, a benchmark analysis is not needed.[7] The absence of such a study does not lead to the reverse of the burden of proof. However, if the taxpayer does not carry out an explicit comparison of comparable transactions between independent entities, the tax authorities can test the transfer price against the arm's length principle by passing their opinion with respect to the transacting of independent entities under comparable circumstances.[8] To prevent the tax inspector from forming an opinion with respect to the actions of independent entities in similar situations as theirs, it is conceivable that taxpayers will prepare a full comparability analysis, including a benchmark analysis, themselves.

In the absence of any documentation, the burden of proof may shift to the taxpayer. In that case, the taxpayer has to show that it is plausible that the transfer price used is at arm's length. The burden of proof will not be increased when it is shifted to the taxpayer, ie, the taxpayer does not have to convince the tax inspector that the transfer price used is at arm's length; making it plausible will suffice.

The transfer pricing documentation should, in principle, be available to the taxpayer at the moment that the transaction is carried out. However, if the taxpayer does not avail of the required transfer pricing documentation, the tax inspector will give them a reasonable period in order to prepare the required transfer pricing documentation. The period a taxpayer is given to provide the required transfer pricing documentation may range from four weeks for simple cases, up to three months for more complex transactions.[9]

(c) Adjustments

According to the Explanatory Memorandum,[10] applying the transfer pricing methods will result in a range of values. In order to increase the reliability of the comparables, statistical methods like determining the interquartile range can be applied. If the transfer price used falls within the interquartile range, no adjustment will be made. If the transfer price falls outside the interquartile range and the taxpayer cannot substantiate such deviation, an adjustment is made. An adjustment will only be made if the remuneration falls outside the interquartile range that has been determined for the specific year, as well as outside of the interquartile range that has been determined by using multiple year data, ie, data of the specific year and prior years.[11] Subsequently, if it is reasonable that one point within the interquartile range corresponds best with the conditions of the inter-company transaction, an

5 The best method rule implies that the taxpayer should judge all methods and subsequently substantiate why the chosen method leads to the best result under the given circumstances.
6 Parliamentary proceedings, Second Chamber, 2001-2001, 28 034, nr. 3, p. 22.
7 Parliamentary proceedings, Second Chamber, 2001-2001, 28 034, nr. 5, p. 36.
8 Parliamentary proceedings, Second Chamber, 2001-2001, 28 034, nr. 5, p. 34.
9 Parliamentary proceedings, Second Chamber, 2001-2001, 28 034, nr. 5, p 36–37.
10 Parliamentary proceedings, Second Chamber, 2001-2001, 28 034, nr. 3, p. 21.
11 Decree State Secretary of Finance of 14 November 2013, nr. IFZ2013/184M, paragraph 2.4.

adjustment takes place to this point. If no such point can be indicated, the Netherlands takes the position that an adjustment should take place to the median value of the interquartile range. Further, if and to the extent the transfer price is already within the range, an adjustment of this transfer price to a new point within the range is only possible if the taxpayer substantiates the reasons for the adjustment and if it is contractually agreed upon and paid.[12]

A transfer pricing adjustment always results in a secondary transaction. This can take the form of an adjustment in current account, a deemed dividend distribution or an informal capital contribution. A secondary transaction may result in a secondary adjustment, ie, taking into account interest income or the imposition of dividend withholding tax. However, not all countries employ the same system. If the taxpayer demonstrates that (i) the other state does not recognise the secondary transaction as a result of which it does not give a credit for the dividend withholding tax, and (ii) there is no abuse of the rule on evading dividend withholding taxation, a secondary adjustment does not take place.[13] A comparable relief is not provided to the taxpayer if the interest deduction is denied in the other state.

2.2 International treaties and agreements

As a member of the OECD and the European Union, the Netherlands is influenced by these institutions when it comes to transfer pricing. In the following paragraphs, I discuss the position of the OECD MC and Guidelines and the EU Joint Transfer Pricing Forum ('EU JTPF') in Dutch tax law.

2.2.1 OECD MC and Guidelines

The arm's length principle is laid down in article 9 of the OECD MC. The application of the arm's length principle is elaborated in the commentary to the OECD MC and in the OECD Guidelines. The Netherlands, as a member of the OECD, endeavours to include a clause in accordance with article 9 OECD MC in its bilateral treaties. Moreover, the Dutch model tax convention[14] contains a comparable clause. In an international context, the OECD Guidelines play an important role when applying treaties and avoiding double taxation.

In the Explanatory Memorandum[15] it is said that the OECD Guidelines impact the Dutch legal practice. The legislator clarified this statement by saying that he considers the OECD Guidelines to be equivalent to the opinions of authoritative writers and the conclusions of the Advocate General of the Supreme Court.[16] However, the OECD Guidelines were incorporated in policy rules for the Dutch tax authorities by means of the 2004 Decree.[17] In the 2004 Decree, the State Secretary concluded that based

12 Decree State Secretary of Finance of 14 November 2013, nr. IFZ2013/184M, paragraph 2.3.
13 Decree State Secretary of Finance of 14 November 2013, nr. IFZ2013/184M, paragraph 4.
14 Dutch standard treaty 1987.
15 Parliamentary proceedings, Second Chamber, 2001-2001, 28 034, nr. 3, p. 8.
16 Parliamentary proceedings, Second Chamber, 2001-2001, 28 034, nr. 5, p. 47–48.
17 Decree State Secretary of Finance of 21 August 2004, nr. IFZ2004/680.

on article 3.8. PITA, in principle, the OECD Guidelines have direct effect in the Netherlands. In the 2013 Decree, the State Secretary repeated that he assumed the OECD Guidelines, in principle, have a direct effect on Dutch tax law.[18] These conclusions of the State Secretary of Finance with respect to the direct application of the OECD Guidelines in Dutch practice could be considered questionable, given the earlier mentioned considerations of the legislator as well as case law.[19]

2.2.2 EU joint transfer pricing forum

An important objective of the EU JTPF is to remove double taxation and administrative burdens that impede an efficient implementation of transfer pricing rules. The Netherlands – to a large extent – follows the recommendations of the EU JTPF, unless the Netherlands has expressed its reservations.[20]

3. NATIONAL POLICY ISSUES

Since 2001, the State Secretary of Finance has issued several decrees relating to transfer pricing. The decrees provide guidance on the interpretation and application of the statutory regulation on transfer pricing and related issues in specific situations. The Dutch tax authorities ('DTA') are bound by the decrees, but taxpayers may appeal to the courts on any provision applied by the tax authorities that originate from the decrees. If taxpayers do take positions that deviate from those taken in the decrees, they may expect discussions with the DTA which may lead to controversy and potentially to litigation.

The most recent transfer pricing decree is the 2013 Decree, which replaces the transfer pricing decrees from 2001 and 2004.[21] The 2013 Decree explains the view of the DTA on recent Dutch case law in relation to financial transactions. The 2013 Decree also documents certain positions of the DTA that were already taken in tax audits and advance pricing agreement ('APA') processes. The 2013 Decree links many of these positions to the OECD Guidelines but it also includes elements of the second draft of the OECD Report in relation to Intangibles ('Draft OECD IntangiblesReport')[22] and the DTA's desire to avoid (re)allocation of profits to tax havens. Several other decrees have recently been updated, such as the Advance Pricing Agreement Decree (DGB2014/3098), the Decree on Financial Service Entities (DGB2014/3101) and the Question and Answer Decree (DGB2014/3102).[23]

In the following paragraphs, I address the main policy announcements made in the 2013 Decree.

18 Decree State Secretary of Finance of 14 November 2013, nr. IFZ2013/184M, paragraph 2.1; his words, however, do not show much self-confidence.

19 Supreme Court 28 June 2002, nr. 36 446, BNB 2002/343.

20 Decree State Secretary of Finance of 14 November 2013, nr. IFZ2013/184M, paragraph 1.5.

21 Decree State Secretary of Finance of 30 March 2001, nr. IFZ2001/295M and Decree State Secretary of Finance of 21 August 2004, nr. IFZ2004/680M.

22 Revised Discussion Draft on Transfer pricing Aspects of Intangibles, dated 30 July 2013

23 These decrees date from 12 June 2014.

3.1 Overall national policy announcements

The 2013 Decree displays various themes that reflect the position the DTA take in conducting audits and reviewing APA requests. These four themes are the following:

1. Every transaction should add value;
2. People are the most important;
3. The two-sided perspective; and
4. The (economic) behaviour of the parties is decisive, the content of contracts is secondary.

In the following sub-paragraphs I deal with these themes based on statements and examples given in the 2013 Decree.

3.1.1 Every transaction should add value

In Chapter 2 of the 2013 Decree, the State Secretary indicates that each taxpayer needs to clearly consider more attractive alternatives before entering into a transaction with an affiliated party. In extreme cases, it is said to be possible to disregard transactions, if more attractive alternatives are available, whereby he refers to paragraph 1.65 of the OECD Guidelines. In his analysis, he refers to various paragraphs of Chapter 9 of the OECD Guidelines (inter alia 9.38, 9.173, 9.174 and 9.175). The State Secretary appears to assume that both parties have all the relevant information at their disposal and that they will act according to a specific economic theory (the 'contract theory').[24] Unfortunately, third parties often act less rationally and also enter into agreements if the 'total amount of cake' does not increase, but their share of the cake does.

Furthermore, the economic rationality of risk allocations should be reviewed, where elements of the degree of control and financial capacity to incur the risks play an important role. If risks cannot be controlled, they are said to be assumed by the most diversified entity.

An example is given in relation to the transfer of intangible assets. The State Secretary takes the position in Chapter 8 of the 2013 Decree that if, and to the extent, tangible or intangible assets are transferred to an affiliated party whereby this affiliated party does not add value to these assets due to the fact that it does not have the appropriate functionality to control the risks in relation thereto, such transaction cannot be considered to be at arm's length. Such transfer of assets will only take place if both parties to the transaction aim at an overall increase in profitability and if both parties are capable of controlling the risks they are said to assume. The fact that a transfer of assets can lead to an overall increase in net profitability because the transferee is subject to a lower effective tax rate than the transferor should not lead to a different conclusion according to the State Secretary, as the transferee will, in such a scenario, be fully dependent on the knowledge and skills of the transferor. In connection with this analysis, the State Secretary refers to paragraph 9.190 of the OECD Guidelines, where

[24] See interpretation of contract theory by P. Bogetoft and H.B. Olesen, 'Design of Production Contracts: Lessons from Theory and Agriculture', Copenhagen Business School Press, Denmark 2004.

an example of the transfer of intellectual property rights ('IPRs') to a 'shell' company is given. I appreciate that the State Secretary wants to scrutinise situations where IPRs are transferred by Dutch taxpayers to foreign (low-taxed) group companies which have limited substance. However, the State Secretary's argument appears questionable and unfounded. He seems to assume that the transferee should have his own qualified personnel that has the required expertise to control the associated risks. In practice, transfers of IPRs between third parties are observed, while such parties do not have such relevant expertise themselves, but rather engage experts from outside.

3.1.2 People are the most important

The location of people is the most important element when allocating risks, returns and even capital.

The statement that people, and more specifically 'own employees', are most important is also reflected in the example of the transfer of IPRs to a group company that misses the functionality.

When discussing intra-group procurement activities in Chapter 9 of the 2013 Decree, the State Secretary indicates that a routine remuneration, ie, a cost-based remuneration is most appropriate in the case of determining the transfer prices used for a procurement office that has a routine character. The profit-split method can be used when the activities are part of the core activities of the MNE. If the procurement office realises high volume discounts, it is to pass these on to the group companies for whom the procurement activities are carried out, unless the discounts are due to the specific knowledge and skills of the procurement office. This is in line with the position that is taken by the DTA in practice. In my view, however, such a position deviates from the contents of the relevant chapters of the OECD Guidelines and the position taken by many foreign tax administrations. This position of the DTA may therefore potentially lead to double taxation.

3.1.3 The two-sided perspective

With reference to paragraph 9.63 of the OECD Guidelines, the State Secretary indicates that a comparison of the conditions takes place from the perspective of all parties involved in the transaction. The State Secretary notes that in practice, transactions among unrelated entities will only take place if each party expects an increase in its profit.

The two-sided perspective is explicitly mentioned in Chapter 12 of the 2013 Decree, where financial transactions are discussed. The State Secretary takes the position that loans that are provided to group companies that have a credit rating which is lower than BBB– (or becomes lower than BBB– due to entering into the financial transaction) are deemed to lead to non-arm's length results, unless the taxpayer makes it plausible that entering into the financial transaction leads to an arm's-length result for *both* the lender and the borrower. From the perspective of the lender among other things, it is important to take into account whether it has a diversified portfolio. From the borrower's perspective, it should be determined whether the leverage has a negative effect on the financing expenses of the company and as a result decreases the return on equity. A third party is said not to attract debt financing if this would result in a fall of its credit rating below BBB- ('Investment Grade'). If, and to the extent that as a result of an intragroup financial transaction the credit rating of a group company falls below Investment Grade, this is deemed to lead to a non-arm's-length outcome unless the taxpayer proves otherwise.

3.1.4 The (economic) behaviour of parties is decisive, the content of contracts is secondary

Finally, attention should be given to the manner in which third parties would transact under comparable circumstances. The State Secretary explains in Chapter 2 of the 2013 Decree that a transfer pricing analysis starts with the transaction that is executed between affiliated parties (paragraph 1.64 OECD Guidelines). In his view, the contents of legally binding agreements are the starting position, unless the factual behaviour or the behaviour under the contract theory would deviate from the contents of these agreements.

3.2 National revenue authority initiatives

Due to the open relationship many Dutch taxpayers have with the DTA, not many transfer pricing conflicts reach court. Besides, the Netherlands is known for its well-functioning APA practice, where the DTA has a preference to conclude APAs.[25] APA procedures are efficient and are usually finalised within a couple of months. As a result, many transfer pricing issues are dealt with in advance.

Furthermore, over the last number of years, the DTA has pursued a high level of transparency towards taxpayers through horizontal monitoring. The key principles of horizontal monitoring are mutual trust, understanding and transparency. In return for the taxpayers' transparency, the DTA is prepared to commit itself to solve material issues including transfer pricing issues at a quicker pace and 'real time'. A precondition for horizontal monitoring is that the taxpayer is 'in control' (through the establishment of a 'tax control framework'). Transfer pricing is an important element of taxpayers being in control. Some taxpayers choose not to enter into a formal 'horizontal monitoring' agreement with the DTA but act 'horizontal monitoring compliant'.

Finally, the DTA announced recently that they will expand their capacity in order to further increase the number of audits. In the past, some industry-specific audits have taken place, for example, within the car and pharmaceutical industries. These sector specific audits have led to 'default' solutions. No specific announcements have been made concerning what transfer pricing audits they will target in the future. The Netherlands follows the best practices of the OECD laid down in its 2012 report 'Dealing Effectively with the Challenges of Transfer Pricing'.

25 Parliamentary proceedings, Second Chamber, 2001-2001, 28 034, nr. 5, p. 37.

4. CASE LAW

In the Netherlands, transfer pricing disputes are often settled in a compromise. Further, many taxpayers agree with the DTA upfront on the transfer pricing through concluding an APA. This explains the scarce amount of Dutch case law that exists on transfer pricing disputes. I cannot conclude that there is more transfer pricing litigation in one specific sector over another. Historically, many cases were won by the taxpayer due to the division of the burden of proof. However, recently, various cases were decided in favour of the authorities. These cases concerned aggressive structures, with little substance, where transfer pricing arguments did not uphold. These cases went more in the direction of abuse.

In this chapter, I discuss the latest case law regarding transfer pricing disputes in 4.1 and in 4.2. I discuss historical cases of note, which may also give foreign tax practitioners a better understanding of the positions taken by the DTA in transfer pricing discussions in the Netherlands. Since transfer pricing methodology and valuation is outside the scope of this book, I will not address jurisprudence on these topics. Case law from the lower courts is not addressed in this chapter.

4.1 Current cases

4.1.1 Swiss paper trader[26]

The taxpayer ('A BV') was involved in purchasing and selling of paper. The purchasing and selling activities were carried out by E. E, who was the director of A BV, and, together with his wife, he held all the shares in A BV. A couple of years later, in 1994, a Swiss company was established. The sole director of the Swiss company was a tax adviser that also served as director of various other companies that were registered at the same address. The functions of the Swiss director consisted of preparing the administration, corresponding, invoicing and filing corporate income tax returns.

As of 1996, part of the purchasing and selling of the paper was carried out through the Swiss company. The factual purchasing and selling was conducted by E, while using the same office space and phone line as was used for A BV. E was not an employee of the Swiss company nor had he received an order from the Swiss company to purchase and sell the paper. After the inception of the Swiss company, E determined on a case-by-case basis whether a transaction took place from the Swiss company or from A BV. Both entities had the same suppliers of paper, the same products, the same customers and the same carriers. The only difference lay in the invoicing and payment.

As confirmed by the Supreme Court, the Court of Appeal ruled that the income generated by the Swiss company should be taken into account at the level of the Dutch taxpayer under the deduction of an administrative fee for the Swiss company's services based on a cost-plus 15 per cent. Certain expenses were not to be included in the cost basis, ie, factoring and insurance fees.

26 Supreme Court 4 January 2013, nr. 11/00762, BNB 2013/77.

In my view, this decision is in line with the approach taken by the DTA where group companies that do not avail of sufficient substance are remunerated based on the cost-plus method where the residual profit is allocated to the Dutch taxpayer. It is remarkable that in the Swiss Paper Trader case, the DTA did not take the position that the Swiss company had a permanent establishment in the Netherlands or that it was effectively managed from the Netherlands.

4.1.2 Non-business-like loan case[27]

In this landmark case, the Supreme Court ruled that in order to qualify a loan as (non-)business-like, it should be determined whether the interest rate is at arm's length or can be adjusted to an arm's length rate without becoming profit participating. The analysis should be made at the moment that the loan is granted, based on the existing terms, conditions and circumstances of the loan agreement. If a loan is considered to be non-business-like, the following consequences exist:

(i) The arm's length interest rate on a non-business-like loan is set at the rate that the debtor would have paid if they had attracted the loan from a third party under a guarantee for the actual creditor, ie, under a deemed guarantee; and

(ii) A write-off on a non-business-like loan is not tax deductible for the lender.

Neither in this case, nor in later case law on non-business-like loans, has any detailed guidance been given as to when a loan should be considered to be non-business-like. In the 2013 Decree, the State Secretary indicated that, in his view, a loan is deemed to be non-business-like if the debtor has a credit rating that is worse than BBB– (or becomes less than BBB– as a result of the loan) unless the taxpayer proves otherwise. Furthermore, in his view, if the credit rating of the lender is worse than that of the borrower, a risk-free interest rate should be considered arm's length, since no value can be attributed to the deemed guarantee.

4.2 Historical cases of note

4.2.1 Car importer's case[28]

In this case, a Dutch taxpayer was involved in the import and sale of cars and other products to the distributive trade. The Dutch taxpayer was a subsidiary of a Japanese group. The DTA started an audit to verify whether the appropriate transfer prices were used for the car imports. Following the tax audit, the DTA imposed a higher tax assessment. The taxpayer objected to the higher profit following the transfer pricing adjustment. Reference was made to article 10 of the double tax treaty between the Netherlands and Japan, that is in accordance with article 9 OMC, making the case relevant for more or less all Dutch treaty situations.

---

27 Supreme Court 25 November 2011, nr. 08/05323, BNB 2012/37.

28 Supreme Court 28 June 2002, nr. 36 446, VN 2002/34.9.

The Supreme Court notes that while the parent company can autonomously decide on the transfer prices used, this does not necessarily mean that the transfer prices used should not be considered arm's length. Further, the Supreme Court noted that the inter-company relation does not have to be reviewed at a transaction level to determine if they have transacted at arm's length. A margin that is too low on product A could be compensated by a high margin on products B, C, D and E. The Supreme Court decided in favour of the taxpayer.

4.2.2 Sale and lease back case[29]

This case concerns the question whether goodwill should be realized in the case of a sale and lease back. A Dutch taxpayer sold business assets (machinery) to his foreign subsidiary which the foreign subsidiary subsequently leased back. Among other things, at issue was whether a transfer of profit potential, ie, goodwill, had taken place. The Court ruled that no goodwill realization should be considered to have taken place. Elements that were deemed important were the fact that prior to the transfer of the machinery, the Dutch parent company was not involved in renting out machinery and that no other business assets, nor personnel to carry out this activity, were transferred to the foreign subsidiary. New personnel who were hired by the subsidiary had not previously worked for the Dutch parent prior to the transfer. Consequently, the court ruled that there was no goodwill realization.

In my view, the judgment of the Court is in line with the remarks that were made in Chapter IX of the OECD Guidelines. In Chapter IX, it is specifically mentioned that the transfer of profit potential does not necessarily result in a realization of goodwill.

4.2.3 Slubcatcher case[30]

Although this case was decided in 1969, it was only published in 2010. Thus, between 1969–2010, taxpayers and their advisers were not able to take into account the decision of the Supreme Court.

In this case, the taxpayer outsourced the development of a machine, ie, a slubcatcher, that he would use for his business enterprise and for further exploitation to a third party. The application for a patent for the slubcatcher was transferred to an Antilles group company in 1953 against a compensation for the development costs. In the years 1958 and 1959, patents in relation to the slubcatchers were also transferred to the Antilles company. In 1960, the Antilles company received royalties and in 1961, the patents relating to the slubcatcher were sold to a third party. The tax inspector took the position that the transfer of the patents lacked economic substance. Consequently, the Dutch taxpayer should still be considered to be entitled to the royalty income and sales proceeds. The lower court followed this position.

---

29 Court of Appeal Amsterdam, 11 February 2009, nr. 04/04338.

30 Supreme Court, 25 June 1969, nr. 16 016, BNB 2010/93.

However, the Supreme Court ruled that the Antilles group company should be considered the owner of the patents, even though it missed every independent involvement in the patents. As a result, the Dutch taxpayer was not entitled to the royalty income and the new sales proceeds. The Supreme Court ruled that the prior transfers of the patents in the years 1953, 1958 and 1959 should have been executed under arm's length conditions, where the transfer price did not necessarily have to amount to the future royalty income or sales proceeds, but should have been the price that a third party would have requested in those years or, what a specialist could have declared.

5. PENALTIES

5.1 Types

Dutch legislation does not contain specific penalties relating to transfer pricing. However, the general penalties put down in the General Tax Act ('GTA') apply. Further guidance can be found in the Decree Administrative Penalties Tax authorities[31] with respect to the imposition of penalties.

Depending on the degree of intent to avoid tax or the gross negligence of the taxpayer, penalties may vary from zero to 100 per cent of the additional tax due. If the taxpayer wilfully misrepresented the profit reported in his tax return, ie, in case of fraud, or the taxpayer can be blamed for the misrepresentation, ie, in case of gross negligence, a penalty may be imposed of 50 per cent and 25 per cent, respectively, of the additional tax due. In special circumstances this penalty may be increased to 100 per cent and 50 per cent, respectively.

The State Secretary indicated[32] during the parliamentary proceedings that due to the complexity of the issues, penalties would only be imposed in cases where it can be demonstrated that a transfer price has been agreed to that is not at arm's length as a result of a pure wilful act. Therefore, no penalty would be imposed in the case of gross negligence or conditional intent.

Penalties are a non-deductible item for Dutch tax purposes.

5.2 Special or notable cases

In transfer pricing case law, penalties are not often imposed. However, in a recent court case of the lower court of Zealand–West Brabant,[33] a quite substantive penalty was imposed. The court held that by setting up the captive in Switzerland, the Dutch taxpayer was culpable in evading Dutch taxation. The penalty amounted to EUR 125,000 per year. The taxpayer filed an appeal against the decision.

6. DISPUTE RESOLUTION MECHANISMS

As stated previously, in the Netherlands, transfer pricing disputes are often settled through compromise. Alternatively, parties can choose to enter into

31 Decree of 16 December 2013, Stcrt. 2013, 35876.
32 Second Chamber, 28 034, nr. 5, p. 46–47
33 Lower Court Zealand-West Brabant, 17 January 2014, nr. AWB-11_3737.

a mediation process. This explains the scarce amount of Dutch case law on transfer pricing disputes. If a taxpayer is confronted with double taxation because the other state has imposed a transfer pricing correction, the Dutch competent authorities are willing to cooperate at an early stage in order to remove the double taxation either through a Mutual Agreement Procedure ('MAP') or an arbitrage procedure.

6.1 Preferred national options

Many transfer pricing disputes in the Netherlands are solved in personal discussions with tax inspectors. In transfer pricing discussions, the tax inspector of the Dutch taxpayer is accompanied by a member of the transfer prices Coordination Group of the DTA. The DTA's starting point is often to come to a compromise. Thus, Dutch taxpayers frequently settle a discussion by entering into a settlement agreement with the Dutch tax authorities. In these settlement agreements, parties agree upon the transfer pricing method and margin to the transaction(s) under consideration. In order to avoid disputes in the future, the taxpayer frequently files for an APA for subsequent years.

If the DTA and taxpayer do not come to a compromise on their transfer pricing dispute, the taxpayer has the possibility of filing an objection to the assessment, and if denied, of bringing its claim to the lower court. The court proceedings are comparable to any other Dutch tax litigation. In the court proceedings, the starting point of the DTA will be their initial position prior to the settlement agreement discussions. This means their last bid in the settlement discussions is no longer on the table. This evidently makes it less interesting for taxpayers to litigate.

6.2 International options

If taxpayers are confronted with double taxation as a result of a transfer pricing correction either imposed by the DTA or the foreign tax authorities, they can either choose to file for a MAP, if the Netherlands has concluded a bilateral tax treaty that provides for MAP, or start an arbitrage procedure for EU situations,[34] as well as situations where the double tax treaty contains an arbitrage provision. The difference between a MAP and arbitrage procedure is that, in the first case, states have the obligation to make an effort to solve the double taxation issue, while in the latter case, in most treaty situations[35] and in an EU context, they have to remove the double taxation. In practice, this difference makes arbitration the more desired procedure.

The directorate International Fiscal Affairs of the Dutch Ministry of Finance is the competent authority to assist taxpayers that are confronted with taxation that is not in accordance with a treaty.[36] The DTA's policy has always been to proactively avoid such a situation and to initiate consultations with taxpayers and foreign tax authorities at an early stage.

34 EU Arbitrage treaty, inter-governmental Convention signed on 23 July 1990, Convention 90/436/EEC on the elimination of double taxation in connection with the adjustment of profits of associated enterprises .

35 Provided the arbitrage provision of the double tax treaty provides for the obligation for the treaty states to remove the double taxation. The Netherlands endeavours to include such provision in its treaties.

36 Decree State Secretary of Finance of 14 November 2013, nr. IFZ2013/184M, paragraph 15.

This implies that such consultations can be started before the national legal procedures have been applied. The Netherlands has confirmed this in a specific decree on MAPs.[37] The Dutch competent authorities are endeavouring to finalise a MAP within a period of two years.

In the experience of the State Secretary, in several cases, double taxation can be fairly easily removed in a consultation process by exchanging facts and circumstances which are relevant for the case with the other state. Consequently, the Dutch tax authorities are willing to start talks with a treaty partner at an early stage, when the taxpayer expects that because of a transfer pricing correction imposed by the other state, they will be confronted with double taxation. Taxpayers can file a request to have this done when they think there is a situation in which double taxation may arise.[38] This welcome approach has already been applied in practice.

PART TWO: TAX AVOIDANCE

7. ACCEPTABLE TAX PLANNING AREAS/SUBJECTS

In this section, I address transfer pricing-related tax-efficient structures called 'informal capital structures'.

Informal capital structures have proven to be effective structures to reduce the taxable basis in the Netherlands and consequently, the effective tax rate of the Dutch taxpayer. The principle entails that the commercial results of the taxpayer should be reduced for tax purposes, since the taxpayer received a wilful benefit from the group company (parent) with whom it entered into a transaction. This reduction of the commercial profit is treated as an informal capital contribution which is not taxable in the Netherlands. If the benefit is derived from a transaction entered into with the Dutch taxpayers' foreign subsidiary, the correction takes the form of a deemed dividend distribution which would be exempt under the participation exemption.

The legal basis for deviating from the accounting results for tax purposes can be found in article 3.8 PITA, in conjunction with articles 8 and 8b of the CITA. These principles were confirmed in two Supreme Court cases. In the first case[39], the Dutch taxpayer purchased goods from his subsidiary at a price below the market price. The Supreme Court ruled that the benefits derived by the taxpayer in relation to transactions with his subsidiary should be excluded from the taxable basis in the Netherlands if this benefit had been wilfully allocated to the taxpayer as a result of the shareholder's relationship. The difference between the arm's length price and the transfer price applied to the purchases, should be considered a deemed dividend distribution from the subsidiary to the Dutch shareholder.

In the 'Swedish Grandmother' case[40], the Swedish indirect shareholder issued a non-interest bearing loan to his Dutch subsidiary. The Supreme Court ruled that benefits derived by a taxpayer in transactions with his

[37] Decree State Secretary of Finance of 29 September 2008, nr. IFZ2008/248M, paragraph 1.2.1.1.
[38] Decree State Secretary of Finance of 14 November 2013, nr. IFZ2013/184M, paragraph 15.
[39] Supreme Court, 23 April 1958, nr. 13 509, BNB 1958/179.
[40] Supreme Court, 31 May 1978, nr. 18 230, BNB 1978/252.

(indirect) shareholder should be excluded from the Dutch taxable basis, if such benefits had been wilfully allocated to the Dutch taxpayer because of the shareholder relationship. The Dutch taxpayer was able to deduct an arm's length interest and such interest was considered an informal capital contribution from the Swedish grandparent company to the Dutch taxpayer.

In practice, informal capital contribution structures often have to do with trading structures or IP structures. The following illustrates the informal capital structure based on a trading structure. A Dutch taxpayer purchases products from his foreign shareholder at a relative low transfer price. The Dutch taxpayer sells the products to third parties or group companies. The difference between the transfer price used and what should be considered an arm's length price for the purchases, or the difference between the accounting profit and the profit that follows from a benchmark study conducted for (limited risk) traders, is considered to be an informal capital contribution by the foreign parent to the Dutch taxpayer, which is not taxable in the Netherlands.

The Dutch tax authorities are generally willing to grant rulings to Dutch taxpayers confirming the treatment of the informal capital contribution.

8. DEFINING ABUSIVE TAX AVOIDANCE

Dutch tax law contains the abuse of law doctrine, *fraus legis*, which has been crystallised in case law. The Supreme Court[41] ruled that for *fraus legis* to be present, two cumulative requirements should be met:

(i) the sole or predominant motive for the transaction is the avoidance of tax, ie, apart from the tax benefit, there are no meaningful business reasons for the transaction under consideration; and

(ii) if the tax consequences of the transaction were allowed, they would be in conflict with the purpose and rationale of the relevant tax law.

If a taxpayer wants to make it plausible that the first requirement is not met, the court will look at whether considerations other than tax have played more than a secondary role.[42] If that is the case, then there should be no *fraus legis*. If *fraus legis* is present, this may have two consequences. Either (a) the transaction is eliminated, or (b) the transaction is substituted by an adjacent fact pattern that does fall under a specific rule.

So far, the Supreme Court has not applied *fraus tractatus*, ie, that the tax consequence of a transaction was in conflict with the purpose and rationale of a tax treaty, where the predominant motive for the transaction was the avoidance of tax.

9. THE LEGISLATIVE FRAMEWORK

In Dutch tax law, tax avoidance is dealt with in various ways. Dutch tax law contains both general anti-abuse rules ('GAARs') and specific anti-abuse provisions.

---

41 *See among others Supreme Court 21 November 1984, nr. 22 092, BNB 1985/32.*

42 Supreme Court*21 September 1983, nr. 22 060, BNB 1983/316.*

As to GAARs, as discussed in paragraph 8, the *fraus legis* principle applies in Dutch law.[43] This has proven to be the most successful GAAR in Dutch legislation. Further, the DTA may take a substance-over-form approach or consider the transaction to be a sham[44].

Furthermore, the Dutch CITA contains various specific anti-abuse provisions. These include among other things, the application of anti-base erosion rules and the restriction of utilising carry forward losses, thus restricting the trade in loss companies. In most cases, the specific anti-abuse provisions have been codified following case law where the taxpayer won the case or where the State Secretary of Finance stated that the transactions entered into by the taxpayer were abusive, ie, that there was *fraus legis*.[45]

10. KEY CASES OF INTEREST

In paragraph 10.1, I discuss the recent landmark cases of the Supreme Court where *fraus legis* was claimed by the State Secretary of Finance. In paragraph 10.2, I deal with the historical case law where abuse of law was claimed.

10.1 Current cases

The most recent Supreme Court landmark cases, where *fraus legis* was claimed by the State Secretary of Finance, are two cases from 7 February 2014. In these cases, our firm successfully represented the two taxpayers on the issue of whether shares can be classified as debt for Dutch tax law purposes. The Supreme Court ruled that the classification of shares under Dutch civil law – whether contributions on shares are available for recourse by creditors – is decisive. These cases were the Banking syndicate case[46] and the Australian RPS case.[47]

10.1.1 Banking syndicate case

In this case, a Dutch banking syndicate provided a loan to a Dutch holding company. The holding company used the proceeds of the loan to acquire shares of a Dutch listed company. The acquired shares qualified for the participation exemption regime, which provides for a full exemption from Dutch corporate income tax for benefits derived from a qualifying shareholding. The holding company was unable to offset the deductible interest expenses under the loan against taxable profits. However, the income derived by the banking syndicate from the loan was regularly subject to Dutch corporate income tax. Therefore, effectively a mismatch existed for Dutch tax law purposes.

To neutralise this mismatch, the holding company contributed his shares in the listed company to a new Dutch company in exchange for, among other things, shares with the characteristics of cumulative preference shares

---

43 Besides, the *richtige heffing* doctrine is still codified in article 31 of the GTA, but is no longer applied due to its limited scope. Instead, the tax authorities and Ministry of Finance claim *fraus legis*.

44 See, for instance, Supreme Court 27 June 1973, nr. 17 146, BNB 1973/187.

45 See for the case law that was the cause of implementing anti-base erosion rules: Supreme Court 23 August 1995, nr. 29 521, BNB 1996/3, Supreme Court 6 September 1995, nr. 27 927, BNB 1996/4, Supreme Court 20 September 1995, nr. 29 737, BNB 1996/5 and Supreme Court 27 September 1995, nr. 30 400, BNB 1996/6.

46 Supreme Court 7 February 2014, nr. 12/04640, BNB 2014/80 .

47 Supreme Court 7 February 2014, nr 12/03540, BNB 2014/79.

('CPS'). The holding company subsequently sold the CPS to a banking syndicate. The holding company used the proceeds of the sale to repay the loan from the banking syndicate. The return on the CPS was pre-determined. Furthermore, the banking syndicate and the holding company entered into contractual arrangements, allowing the banking syndicate to request the liquidation of the new Dutch company. The banking syndicate argued that benefits derived from the CPS were exempt from Dutch corporate income tax by virtue of the participation exemption. The tax authorities challenged this position by arguing that the CPS, in conjunction with the contractual arrangements, should be regarded as debt for Dutch tax law purposes, in which case benefits derived from the CPS would be regularly subject to Dutch corporate income tax.

The Supreme Court ruled that shares for Dutch civil law purposes cannot be regarded as debt for Dutch tax law purposes. Under Dutch civil law, a holder of shares is subordinated to all creditors, and any contributions made by shareholders are therefore available for recourse by creditors of the company. This characteristic of shares is not affected if (i) the shareholder has the right to terminate his capital financing after a certain period and (ii) such capital financing has certain (economic) similarities with a loan. Therefore, if a shareholding exists for Dutch civil law purposes, such shareholding should be respected as such for purposes of the participation exemption regime. In addition, the Supreme Court rejected the tax authorities' appeal on the abuse of law doctrine (*fraus legis*) because taxpayers are free to finance a subsidiary with either debt or equity, taking into account the intent of the participation exemption.

10.1.2 Australian RPS case

In the second case, a Dutch company had originally provided a shareholder loan to his Australian subsidiary. In a restructuring, the Dutch company effectively exchanged his shareholder loan for redeemable preference shares ('RPS') of a newly established Australian group company. The RPS had the following characteristics:

- entitlement to annual and cumulative fixed rate dividends;
- priority over other classes of shares for the payment of dividends and repayment of capital;
- redemption after 10 years; and
- limited voting rights.

For Australian corporate income tax purposes, the issuer of the RPS was allowed to take a deduction for any dividends on the RPS. The Dutch company took the position that the RPS qualified for the Dutch participation exemption regime. However, the Dutch tax authorities argued that the RPS should be classified as debt for Dutch tax law purposes.

With reference to the Banking syndicate case discussed above, the Supreme Court ruled that the RPS are classified as shares qualifying for the participation exemption regime. The Supreme Court held that Dutch civil law allows for the issuance of cumulative preference shares with limited voting rights that have the same characteristics as the RPS. Such cumulative preference shares under Dutch civil law also qualify for the participation exemption. Furthermore, the deduction for any dividends on the RPS for Australian tax purposes does not impact the applicability of the participation exemption regime to the RPS. In addition, the Supreme Court rejected the tax authorities' appeal on the abuse of law doctrine (*fraus legis*) with respect to the exchange of the shareholder loan with the RPS.

10.2 Key historical cases

The key historical case on the field of abuse of law is the Supreme Court case BNB 1968/80.[48] In this case, the Supreme Court held that the transfer of shares by the shareholders to a new company that they established should be ignored for income tax purposes based on the application of the *richtige heffing* doctrine. This is because, as a result of the transfer of shares, the levying of tax on dividends from the transferred company was no longer possible. Instead of the individual shareholders receiving a dividend from their former subsidiary, by transferring shares, they were receiving a tax-exempt repayment of the transfer debt. The Supreme Court held that a taxpayer is, in principle, free to transfer his shares in order to avoid tax on future dividends, but not if the taxpayer remains entitled to such dividends after the transfer. In that case, the taxpayer did not employ the permitted means to avoid tax.

The practical scope of the above case was not clear but further clarification can be found in the case law on holding- and cash box constructions (*holding- en kasgeld constructies*) that followed in the 1980s and 1990s where *fraus legis* was claimed.[49] The main objective of the taxpayers in these cases was to convert a dividend that was taxed at high progressive rates in the personal income tax into a low taxed capital gain.

11. PENALTIES

In principle, no penalties are imposed in the case of *fraus legis*. *Fraus legis* has not been codified in the law as a result of which no specific penalties apply. Moreover, since the taxpayer is following the literal meaning of the law in cases of *fraus legis*, it should have a reportable position (*pleitbaar standpunt*), as a result of which no penalty could be imposed. However, for the first time in history, in recent case law of the lower court of North Holland, penalties were imposed where *fraus legis* was applied. This lower court jurisprudence will be discussed in paragraph 11.2. In paragraph 11.1, the legislative provisions that apply in cases of abusive tax avoidance are discussed.

11.1 Legislative provisions

The general penalty provisions of the GTA apply in cases where the abusive tax avoidance provisions are applied, if the taxpayer did not take a reportable position (*pleitbaar standpunt*) in his tax return. That is to say, if a taxpayer was considered to have a reportable position, but the court

48 Supreme Court 27 December 1967, nr 15772, BNB 1968/80.
49 See among other things Supreme Court 24 September 1980, BNB 1980/331 and 332, Supreme Court 11 July 1990, BNB 1990/290–293.

eventually decided that an abusive tax avoidance provision should apply, no penalty should be imposed.

Depending on the degree of intent to avoid tax or the gross negligence of the taxpayer, as discussed in paragraph 5, the penalties may vary from zero to 100 per cent of the additional tax due. If the taxpayer willfully misrepresented the profit reported in his tax return, ie, in the case of fraud, or the taxpayer can be blamed for the misrepresentation, ie, in the case of gross negligence, a penalty may be imposed of 50 per cent and 25 per cent, respectively, of the additional tax due. In special circumstances this penalty may be increased to 100 per cent and 50 per cent, respectively.

11.2 Examples of penalties imposed

As mentioned, in recent lower case law,[50] for the first time in history, penalties were imposed where *fraus legis* was applied. The cases concerned the purchase of 'profit companies' where the taxpayer created an interest expense to wipe out the taxable profit within the same year. By claiming the interest deduction in his tax return, the court judged that the taxpayer accepted the considerable possibility that an incorrect tax return would be filed, and wilfully accepted it. The lower court decided that the taxpayer did not succeed in proving that he took a reportable position in his tax return, since he did not substantiate it by submitting the opinions obtained from his tax adviser on the transactions carried out. Consequently, the lower court considered conditional intent to be present and imposed penalties of 51 per cent of the amount of the additional tax assessment. The taxpayer appealed against the judgement and the penalty.

12. CURRENT TRENDS

12.1 Views on current trends

The base erosion and profit shifting project ('BEPS') initiated by the OECD has received political and public attention both in the Netherlands, and internationally. Following its Action Plan of 19 July 2013 ('BEPS Action Plan'), the OECD published discussion drafts and held public consultations on issues like IPRs, country-by-country reporting, treaty abuse and hybrid mismatch arrangement. At the same time, countries are already taking unilateral measures on several fields (eg, hybrids, substance, intangibles), as a result of which the BEPS Action Plan already has shown to have effect, without final recommendations by the OECD having been made. Trends that can be detected in the Netherlands are an increase in transparency and exchange of information on the one hand, and an increase in substance and the importance of significant peoples' functions on the other hand.

12.2 The impact and role of the OECD and other international relations on the Netherlands

The approach of the Dutch government on BEPS is that BEPS is an international problem that can only be solved in an international arena.

[50] Lower Court North-Holland, 6 November 2013, nrs. HAA 12/536–544, 546, 548–557.

The Netherlands committed itself to actively participate in the international initiatives to analyse this problem in order to find lasting and balanced measures in cooperation and coordination with other countries based on a level playing field and 'hard law' solutions. This approach has been confirmed by the Dutch government on various occasions. The Netherlands, for instance, has not yet initiated amendments to prohibit an exemption in relation to payments on hybrid financial instruments if the payment is tax deductible in the source state. Following the recent jurisprudence discussed in paragraph 10.1, it is still possible to generate mismatches through the use of certain hybrid financial instruments. However, with the text for amending the EU Parent Subsidiary Directive being approved during the ECOFIN meeting of 8 July 2014, this should only be possible until, ultimately, 31 December 2015. This is the date that EU Member States must have implemented in their domestic law stating that profits from hybrid financing instruments are taxed at the level of the parent if such profits were tax deductible by the subsidiary.

However, in anticipation of international actions, on 1 January 2014, the Netherlands enacted the minimum substance rules for international group financing, licensing, leasing and rental companies.[51] The implemented rules provide that companies whose activities in a given year consist primarily (ie, for at least 70 per cent) of group financing and licensing activities (or similar activities such as leasing activities), must confirm (in their annual corporate income tax return) whether they meet the following substance requirements:[52]

- At least half of the total number of statutory board members of the taxpayer with power of decision reside or are actually established in the Netherlands;
- The board members residing or established in the Netherlands have the required professional knowledge to properly perform their duties. The duties of the board include, at least, the decision-making on transactions to be entered into by the taxpayer and the ensuring of proper handling of the transactions entered into;
- The taxpayer has qualified employees for proper implementation and registration of the transactions to be entered into by the taxpayer;
- The management decisions are taken in the Netherlands;
- The main bank accounts of the taxpayer are held in the Netherlands;
- The books are kept in the Netherlands;
- The business address of the taxpayer is in the Netherlands;
- The taxpayer is – to the best of their knowledge – not considered a resident for tax purposes in another country;
- The taxpayer runs real risks with respect to his financing, licensing or leasing activities; and

51 Article 3a of the regulation for international assistance in the levying of taxes, published on 18 December 2013 in the Official Gazette under number 569, p 14–15.

52 Such Dutch taxpayers must confirm whether they have met the substance requirements, in the case they apply or could have applied for benefits of a treaty, the EU Interest and Royalty Directive or a domestic implementation thereof in relation to the interest, royalties, etc.

- The taxpayer has at least an appropriate equity with regard to the functions performed by the legal entity.

If a taxpayer cannot confirm that all substance requirements are met, it should:

- Indicate which requirements are not met;
- Provide all necessary information for the tax authorities to determine which of the substance requirements are met; and
- Provide an overview of all interest, royalty and similar payments for which a reduction of (withholding) tax has, or could be, claimed under any tax treaty, EU Interest and Royalty Directive or a domestic implementation thereof.

This information will be spontaneously provided to the relevant treaty partner, who may take it into account in determining whether the relevant taxpayer can apply for the benefits of the tax treaty. This approach is in line with the Dutch position of increasing transparency and exchange of information. Failure to disclose the above information in a timely manner will be regarded as a violation that could result in an administrative fine.

New Zealand

TP Equilibrium Leslie Prescott-Haar & Ruth Butter (Part One)
Bell Gully Jarrod Walker & Hugh Magee (Part Two)

PART ONE: TRANSFER PRICING

1. GENERAL OVERVIEW

New Zealand's transfer pricing ('TP') legislative framework provides broad coverage of international controlled transactions between associated persons.[1] Nevertheless, the TP legislative regime is moderate, with the statutory burden of proof placed initially on the Commissioner of Inland Revenue (the 'Commissioner').[2] The Commissioner's burden of proof, coupled with the lack of specific contemporaneous TP documentation requirements and tax return TP disclosures in New Zealand, have resulted in lower compliance costs. However, recent publications by, and experience with, the Inland Revenue Department ('IR') indicate a hardening IR approach to TP enforcement. This hardening IR approach is demonstrated through the introduction of tailored information requests and audit enquiries; increased and targeted review and audit activity; and New Zealand's active involvement in the OECD's current Base Erosion and Profit Shifting ('BEPS') work.[3]

Where the IR perceives a controlled international transaction as 'artificial and contrived', it may be challenged under the general anti-avoidance rule ('GAAR') contained in the domestic legislation (refer to Part Two: Tax Avoidance), and/or under the TP provisions. Under New Zealand's GAAR, the burden of proof lies with the taxpayer. In recent years, New Zealand courts have upheld the Commissioner's position in a high proportion of cases heard under the GAAR. Given this body of GAAR precedent in favour of the Commissioner, and the Commissioner's burden of proof under the TP provisions, controlled cross border transactions perceived as aggressive and tax-driven are likely to be challenged under the GAAR, rather than the TP provisions. Under the GAAR, the Commissioner has extensive powers to reconstruct a taxpayer's transaction(s) to counteract any tax advantage that has been derived from, or under, a tax avoidance arrangement. Thus, in practical terms, the application of the GAAR has greater reach than the TP provisions in New Zealand.

---

1 The term 'associated person' is defined in subpart YB of the Income Tax Act 2007.

2 Under s. GC 13(4) of the Income Tax Act 2007, the Commissioner has the burden of demonstrating a more reliable measure of an arm's length amount than that applied by the taxpayer, provided the taxpayer has co-operated with the Commissioner, including providing requested information and transfer pricing documentation.

3 Refer to 'Multinational Enterprises Compliance Focus' IR 947, October 2013.

The IR has strong links with the Australian Taxation Office ('ATO'), through an active exchange of information programme,[4] other liaison programmes and, to some extent, reference to ATO guidance.[5] Given the extensive changes currently occurring in the Australian TP legislation and guidance framework, prudent New Zealand taxpayers should maintain an active awareness of developments in Australia.

2. IDENTIFICATION OF LEGISLATIVE FRAMEWORK

2.1 Federal legislation

New Zealand laws covering TP and apportionment of income are contained in:

- sections GC 6 to GC 14 of the Income Tax Act 2007 (the 'ITA') (for transactions between separate legal entities),
- section YD 4 of the ITA (income having a New Zealand source);
- section YD 5 of the ITA (apportionment of income derived partly in New Zealand through a branch or contract); and
- section GB 2 of the ITA (collateral arrangements).

These provisions are based on the arm's length principle. The TP provisions allow the IR to adjust a taxpayer's transfer prices in a wide variety of cross border transactions. Specifically, the IR can adjust transfer prices if the taxpayer's net income has been (directly or indirectly) reduced as a result of the taxpayer applying non-arm's length consideration in such transaction(s). In arriving at an arm's length consideration, the TP legislation requires taxpayers to select and apply the TP method that produces the most reliable measure of the amount that completely independent parties would have agreed upon after real and fully adequate bargaining.[6] In accordance with section YD 5 of the ITA, the IR can adjust a taxpayer's income apportionment. The IR can adjust the income apportionment to the extent the net income (loss) results of such apportionment, in relation to the business or contract, are not consistent with the amount that would have been derived by a separate and independent person carrying out only the person's activities in New Zealand and dealing at arm's length.

2.2 State and provincial legislative interplay

There are no state or provincial income taxation authorities and laws in New Zealand.

2.3 International treaties and agreements

New Zealand has a reasonably wide network of double taxation agreements ('DTAs'). These DTAs contain the main principles found in the Business Profits (article 7) and Associated Enterprises (article 9) articles of the OECD Model Tax Convention on Income and Capital ('OECD MTC'). Exchange

[4] For example, through the operation of a trans-Tasman financing desk to exchange new or emerging issues about funding arrangements, see: *http://www.ird.govt.nz/taxagents/compliance/focus-business/mne-2013/compliance-focus-2013-oecd.html*.

[5] For example, the IR's specific endorsement of the ATO's previously recommended four-step documentation process, see: *http://www.ird.govt.nz/transfer-pricing/practice/transfer-pricing-practice-documentation.html*.

[6] Section GC 13 (1)–(3) of the ITA.

of information arrangements feature in the 35 DTAs to which New Zealand is party, and New Zealand also has various tax information exchange agreements with jurisdictions typically regarded as 'tax havens'.

New Zealand is also a party to the Convention on Mutual Administrative Assistance in Tax Matters.[7] This convention provides a multilateral approach for a wide variety of tax administration issues, including international exchanges of information, facilitation of simultaneous/joint audits and assistance in collecting tax debts.

Whilst New Zealand is an OECD member country and is actively involved in the OECD's Working Party 6,[8] the IR has made explicit reservations on the revised article 7[9] of the OECD MTC. In this regard, the IR has stated that the new article 7 will only apply if and when that article is adopted in New Zealand's DTAs,[10] which has not occurred yet. The IR reservations on the new article 7 are as follows:

'[N]ew Zealand reserves the right to use the previous version of Article 7 taking into account its observation and reservations on that version (ie, the version included in the Model Tax Convention immediately before the 2010 update of the Model Tax Convention) because it does not agree with the approach reflected in Part I of the 2010 Report Attribution of Profits to Permanent Establishments. It does not, therefore, endorse the changes to the Commentary on the Article made through that update.'[11]

In the first instance, New Zealand's domestic legislation applies to cross border associated party transactions and branch/contract profit attribution. Regard may then be had to any applicable DTA to eliminate double taxation or to otherwise allocate taxing rights. To the extent of any inconsistency between the domestic legislation and a DTA, the treaty provisions prevail unless the treaty itself gives precedence to the domestic law.

3. NATIONAL POLICY ISSUES

3.1 Overall national policy announcements

TP guidance on specific transactions and perceived risks is published and regularly updated by the IR on its website.[12] Information regarding the IR's TP enforcement programme[13] and current focus areas[14] are also provided on the website. Current focus areas include persistent losses, thin capitalisation and the importation of losses from overseas affiliates via non-arm's length subsidies or support payments.

The *Tax Policy Report: Taxation of Multinationals*[15] issued in August 2013, jointly by the IR and Treasury, highlighted various initiatives to strengthen the IR's ability to combat profit shifting by multinationals and

7 *http://taxpolicy.ird.govt.nz/tax-treaties/convention-mutual-administrative-assistance-tax-matters*, signed by New Zealand 26 October 2012, in force 1 March 2014.
8 OECD Working Party 6: Taxation of Multinational Enterprises.
9 As included in the 2010 update to the OECD MTC.
10 *http://www.ird.govt.nz/transfer-pricing/practice/transfer-pricing-practice-branches.html.*
11 Paragraph 95 of the commentary on article 7 in the MTC.
12 *http://www.ird.govt.nz/transfer-pricing/practice/.*
13 *http://www.ird.govt.nz/transfer-pricing/enforcement/transfer-pricing-enforcement-programme.html.*
14 *http://www.ird.govt.nz/transfer-pricing/enforcement/transfer-pricing-enforcement-focus.html.*
15 Inland Revenue Tax policy report: Taxation of multinationals, 15 August 2013, Report No. T2013/2059 PAS2013/152.

other investors. These include initiatives relating to: related-party debt; the removal of tax advantages from certain investment vehicles and effective taxation of offshore instruments; and ensuring New Zealand's legislative framework keeps pace with the changing global economy, including particularly online transactions. This Tax Policy Report follows the release of two earlier IR/Treasury Tax Policy Reports on BEPS issued in December 2012 and April 2013.[16]

The current (2013-14) Tax Policy Work Programme[17] includes international tax reform and addressing BEPS. The IR has specific plans to examine and potentially strengthen the rules for thin capitalisation and transfer pricing of related-party indebtedness; online shopping; hybrid instruments and entities; exchange of information; etc. Further, the limiting of interest deductions was again highlighted as a focus by the IR, in the context of the OECD's BEPS project in a *Tax Agents Compliance Update* posted on the IR website in March 2014.[18] Other focuses highlighted were the taxation of digital transactions, review of hybrid mismatch arrangements, strengthening of CFC rules, preventing misuse of tax treaties, and improvement of permanent establishment and transfer pricing rules in respect of intangible property and financial dealings.

Hence, the OECD's BEPS initiatives will likely lead to significant legislative and enforcement related changes in New Zealand.

3.2 National revenue authority initiatives

The IR's current *Compliance Focus for Multinational Enterprises*[19] echoes the above, and sets out the IR's interpretation statement on tax avoidance. The *Compliance Focus* also outlines the IR's ongoing focus on international financing arrangements, transfer pricing, CFCs and BEPS, amongst others issues of interest.

In an audit context, the IR has particularly focused on international financing arrangements, from both the taxation and TP perspectives. Cross-border financing often forms a substantial part of the total associated party transactions of New Zealand members of multinational groups. Key issues within the IR's *Compliance Focus* include the pricing of interest and guarantee fees at market rates, and capital structuring within New Zealand's thin capitalisation rules. The IR has undertaken to review all inbound loans over $10 million and outbound loans of all sizes, where interest is zero or low, or where no fees are charged for guarantees provided.

The IR also actively promotes unilateral and bilateral advanced pricing agreements.[20]

3.3 Administrative statements

Refer above.

16 Report numbers T2012/3250 and PAD2012/268.
17 *http://taxpolicy.ird.govt.nz/work-programme*, announced 8 November 2013.
18 *http://www.ird.govt.nz/taxagents/compliance/focus-business/mne-2013/compliance-focus-2013-oecd.html*, published 17 March 2014.
19 Multinational Enterprises Compliance Focus, October 2013, IR 947.
20 *http://www.ird.govt.nz/transfer-pricing/practice/transfer-pricing-practice-apas.html*.

3.4 Administrative guidelines

In 2000, the IR issued transfer pricing guidelines ('IR TP Guidelines') to provide guidance in the application of the domestic TP legislation. In its application and interpretation of the New Zealand TP regime and DTAs, the IR closely follows and endorses the most recently published OECD *Transfer Pricing Guidelines for Multinational Enterprises and Tax Administrations*, except in respect of permanent establishments. The IR TP Guidelines are general in nature; whereas specific and current updates on TP issues are provided via the IR's website.[21]

4. CASE LAW

No court cases have arisen (directly) under New Zealand's current transfer pricing legislation nor under the previous legislation, section GD 13 of the Income Tax Act 1994. To date, transfer pricing disputes have been settled by negotiation or adjudication. Where an abusive tax position is perceived, cases have been heard under the GAAR. Refer to Part Two: Tax Avoidance Key Cases.

5. PENALTIES

Part 9 of the Tax Administration Act 1994 (the 'TAA') prescribes statutory penalties which may be imposed on a taxpayer in a tax context (including in relation to transfer pricing matters). These range from penalties for late filing of a tax return or payment of tax, through to shortfall penalties for adoption of an incorrect tax position and criminal penalties for tax evasion. The penalties regime is generally regarded as an important part of New Zealand's tax system, which is based on taxpayer self-assessment.

5.1 Types

(a) Shortfall penalties

Shortfall penalties are the most relevant in the present context. These are penalties imposed on a taxpayer for the adoption of an incorrect tax position. A 'taxpayer's tax position' is essentially defined as a position or approach to a tax liability adopted by a taxpayer.[22] The following are the shortfall penalties which may be imposed under the TAA. In each case, the amount of the penalty is a percentage of the 'tax shortfall' applicable to the taxpayer. The tax shortfall is the difference between the taxpayer's self-assessed tax liability and the correct liability as established under the tax laws:

1. *Failure to take reasonable care:*[23] Failure to take reasonable care in the adoption of a tax position exposes the taxpayer to a 20 per cent tax shortfall penalty. The standard of reasonable care involves consideration of what a reasonable person would do in the circumstances in question. Exemptions from imposition of the penalty exist.

[21] *http://www.ird.govt.nz/transfer-pricing/.*
[22] Section 3(1) Tax Administration Act 1994.
[23] Section 141A Tax Administration Act 1994.

Where a taxpayer who, in adopting a tax position, relies on the advice or action of a tax advisor, the taxpayer is deemed to have taken reasonable care, unless certain prescribed circumstances exist. These include where the advisor is an employee of the taxpayer, where the taxpayer has reason to believe the advice is incorrect or where the taxpayer did not provide the tax advisor with adequate information or instructions.

2. *Adopting an unacceptable tax position:*[24] A taxpayer is liable to a 20 per cent tax shortfall penalty if it takes an unacceptable tax position. A tax position will be unacceptable for this purpose if it, viewed objectively, fails to meet the standard of being about as likely as not to be correct. The penalty will not apply where the taxpayer has made a mere calculation error in preparing a tax return or where the taxpayer has taken a position which relies on an official position adopted by the Commissioner.
3. *Gross carelessness:*[25] A taxpayer is liable to a 40 per cent shortfall penalty if the taxpayer is grossly careless in taking a tax position. Gross carelessness is defined as doing, or not doing, something in a way that, in all the circumstances, suggests or implies complete or a high level of disregard for the consequences.
   Whilst there is no statutory requirement to prepare TP documentation, the IR has indicated that a failure to prepare adequate TP documentation, or acceptance of pricing that is clearly inappropriate, could result in a 40 per cent shortfall penalty for gross carelessness.[26] It is noted, however, that the IR TP Guidelines expressly provide a cost/risk approach for the preparation of TP documentation.[27]
4. *Abusive tax position:*[28] A taxpayer is liable to a 100 per cent shortfall penalty where, having taken an unacceptable tax position, it has entered into, acted in respect of arrangements, or interpreted/applied tax laws with a dominant purpose of taking, or supporting the taking of, tax positions that reduce or remove tax liabilities or give tax benefits. This penalty is often asserted by the Commissioner in challenges of tax avoidance arrangements, and as such is discussed in more detail in Part Two of this Chapter.
5. *Evasion:*[29] A taxpayer is liable to a 150 per cent shortfall penalty where it enters into one or more of a range of activities which are collectively defined in the legislation as evasion or a similar act. These include evading the assessment or payment of tax, knowingly not making a deduction, or withholding of tax as required by a tax law.

The TAA provides taxpayers with relief from shortfall penalties in certain circumstances. These include a 50 per cent reduction in a shortfall penalty where a taxpayer has a qualifying record of prior good tax compliance,[30]

24 Section 141B Tax Administration Act 1994.
25 Section 141C Tax Administration Act 1994.
26 *http://www.ird.govt.nz/transfer-pricing/practice/transfer-pricing-practice-documentation.html.*
27 Refer paras 317 et seq.
28 Section 141D Tax Administration Act 1994.
29 Section 141E Tax Administration Act 1994.
30 Section 141FB Tax Administration Act 1994.

and a reduction where the taxpayer has voluntarily disclosed a tax shortfall to the Commissioner. The second reduction ranges from 40 per cent to 100 per cent of the tax shortfall depending on the type of shortfall penalty in question and the timing of the disclosure.

(b) Request for information penalties

The TAA provides the IR with wide ranging information gathering powers. These powers include the power to require a taxpayer to provide written information and records, the power to require a taxpayer to give evidence before IR officials (including giving evidence on oath) and the power to request the holding of an inquiry before a court.[31]

Various penalties may be imposed for failure by a taxpayer to comply with an information request. These include fines of up to $12,000 for absolute offences,[32] and up to $50,000 for knowingly failing to comply with an information provision requirement.[33] Knowingly failing to provide information with the intention of evading the assessment of tax may render the taxpayer liable to imprisonment for a term of up to five years.[34]

In addition, Section 21 of the TAA provides the IR with powers to request information on international payments deducted in New Zealand, even though such information may be held offshore. Failure to comply with such requests within the statutory timeframe can result in the Commissioner wholly or partly denying the deduction claimed by the taxpayer in respect of the offshore payment.

5.2 Special or notable cases

The IR has a committee that reviews consistency in the application of penalties. In recent years, and based on the general taxation regime, penalties have been imposed in approximately 25 per cent of cases wherein TP adjustments have been agreed.

6. DISPUTE RESOLUTION MECHANICS

New Zealand has a statutory pre-court tax disputes regime, which applies in TP matters and other tax matters, as discussed below. New Zealand's tax legislation also provides for a binding rulings regime. The regime is intended to provide taxpayers with certainty in regards to tax treatment when entering into arrangements to reduce disputes.

The IR negotiates APAs for the same purpose. Notably, the unilateral APAs concluded in New Zealand include numerous subsidiaries of foreign parents, and these unilateral APAs have often been agreed in the aftermath of a TP audit or review by the IR. This may prompt concern regarding the lack of counter-revenue authority involvement in such cases. However, for many taxpayers, the New Zealand operations form a limited part of a global group's operations. Thus, for the New Zealand operations, the group may

31 Sections 16–19 Tax Administration Act 1994.
32 Section 143(3) Tax Administration Act 1994.
33 Section 143A(7) Tax Administration Act 1994.
34 Section 143B(4) Tax Administration Act 1994.

simply wish to achieve compliance at a minimum cost and in a low risk manner.

6.1 Preferred national options

The pre-court tax dispute process is set out in Part 4A of the TAA. It is initiated by service of a notice of proposed adjustment (a 'NOPA') by either the Commissioner or the taxpayer. Typically, the issue of a NOPA by the Commissioner will follow an IR investigation or audit. The NOPA proposes an adjustment to an existing tax position adopted by the taxpayer (eg,, by way of the tax return filed by the taxpayer under New Zealand's self-assessment regime). The NOPA is not, in itself, an assessment nor an amendment to an assessment. It sets out a statement of facts and legal principles supporting the proposed tax adjustments. A notice of response (a 'NOR') is then issued by the other party in reply. The NOPA / NOR process is typically followed by a conference between the Commissioner and the taxpayer, although this is not a legislative requirement.

The NOPA/NOR phase of the disputes process is then followed by an exchange of statements of position ('SOP') by the Commissioner and the taxpayer. These SOPs are similar to the NOPA/NOR documents and are intended to further define the aspects of dispute and the relevant facts. Following this phase of the disputes process, the IR will usually refer the dispute to its Disputes Review Unit for review. However, this referral is not a statutory requirement, and a taxpayer cannot require that a dispute be referred to the Disputes Review Unit.

If the Disputes Review Unit decides against the Commissioner, the IR's practice is to abide by that decision (therefore bringing the dispute to conclusion). If that unit finds in favour of the Commissioner, however, the taxpayer may then decide to challenge the Commissioner's assessment through the court processes. Although the Taxation Review Authority is New Zealand's specialist lower court for tax matters, significant matters tend to be commenced directly in the High Court. Appeals are possible from the High Court to the Court of Appeal and, in some cases, to New Zealand's highest court, the Supreme Court. New Zealand does not have a specialist tax judiciary.

The settlement of a tax dispute is possible at any stage of the pre-court disputes process and during the court challenge process itself. The Commissioner has a wide statutory discretion to settle tax disputes.[35]

6.2 International options

New Zealand has a network of international bilateral DTAs, including with most of its major trading partners. Those DTAs contain mutual agreement procedure ('MAP') articles, pursuant to which New Zealand taxpayers may request the assistance of the New Zealand competent authority in negotiations with the relevant foreign tax administration. For instance,

[35] Section 6 Tax Administration Act 1994.

where the foreign tax administration has made a transfer pricing adjustment which results in double taxation.

The IR actively promotes the early involvement of the competent authority(ies) in international TP disputes. To date, most mutual agreement cases that have arisen in, or have involved, New Zealand taxpayers have been resolved.

PART TWO: TAX AVOIDANCE

7. ACCEPTABLE TAX PLANNING AREAS/SUBJECTS

In New Zealand the question as to what constitutes acceptable tax planning as opposed to abusive tax avoidance, falls to be determined in the context of either a specific anti-avoidance rule or the GAAR contained in ITA. We discuss the GAAR and its interpretation by the New Zealand courts in the sections which follow.

8. DEFINING ABUSIVE TAX AVOIDANCE

The GAAR is contained in section BG 1 and section GA 1 of the ITA. It is, both by its inclusion in the specifically named 'core provisions' of the ITA and by its interpretation by the Courts, a significant provision in New Zealand's tax legislation. Applied literally, any tax advantage achieved by means of any arrangement (such as a reduction in tax payable caused by the claiming of a tax deduction for the cost of trading stock) could, in theory, be negated by the provision. Accordingly, recourse to the courts to define the tax avoidance concept has been, and will continue to be, required.

The discussion which follows refers only to the GAAR, although the principles discussed below are also likely to apply when interpreting a specific anti-avoidance rule in the ITA. In circumstances where both the GAAR and a specific avoidance provision are capable of application, either rule may be applied by the Commissioner.[36]

9. THE LEGISLATIVE FRAMEWORK

Section BG 1 of the ITA provides that a 'tax avoidance arrangement is void as against the Commissioner for income tax purposes'. 'Tax avoidance arrangement' is defined in section YA 1 of the ITA as:

'an arrangement, whether entered into by the person affected by the arrangement or by another person, that directly or indirectly—

(a) has tax avoidance as its purpose or effect; or

(b) has tax avoidance as 1 of its purposes or effects, whether or not any other purpose or effect is referable to ordinary business or family dealings, if the tax avoidance purpose or effect is not merely incidental.'

'Arrangement' is defined widely in section YA 1 as an agreement, contract, plan or understanding, whether or not enforceable, including all steps and transactions by which it is carried into effect.

'Tax avoidance' is defined inclusively in section YA 1 and includes:

36 *Penny v Commissioner of Inland Revenue* [2011] NZSC 95.

(a) directly or indirectly altering the incidence of any income tax;
(b) directly or indirectly relieving a person from liability to pay income tax or from a potential or prospective liability to future income tax; or
(c) directly or indirectly avoiding, postponing, or reducing any liability to income tax or any potential or prospective liability to future income tax.

If tax avoidance exists, the Commissioner has a wide power to adjust the income of a person affected by the arrangement *'in a way the Commissioner thinks appropriate, in order to counteract a tax advantage obtained by the person from or under the arrangement'.*[37] In so doing, the Commissioner may have regard to the income, deductions, tax losses or tax credits of the person which, in the Commissioner's opinion, the person would have had, would in all likelihood have had, or might be expected to have had, if the arrangement had not occurred.[38] The extent of the Commissioner's discretion to reconstruct an arrangement, once tax avoidance has been established, has been illustrated in recent cases (discussed below).

10. KEY CASES OF INTEREST

10.1 Current cases

(a) Overview

There is a significant body of case law interpreting and applying the GAAR in New Zealand. The leading decision of the New Zealand courts in this area is that of the Supreme Court in *Ben Nevis Forestry Ventures Limited v Commissioner of Inland Revenue*.[39] Importantly, the Supreme Court's judgment was expressly intended to be a definitive restatement of relevant aspects of the law on tax avoidance in New Zealand. The majority judgment has been applied, expressly or otherwise, in all subsequent New Zealand tax avoidance cases.

(b) *Ben Nevis* (Supreme Court)

In *Ben Nevis* the majority of the Supreme Court expounded a two-step approach to be followed to ascertain whether an impugned arrangement is a tax avoidance arrangement void under the GAAR. The first step is to consider whether the relevant black letter provisions relied upon by a taxpayer have been applied correctly. If the taxpayer has applied the relevant provisions correctly, the second step is to consider whether the use of those provisions, viewed in light of the arrangement as a whole, is within the contemplation and purpose of Parliament in enacting those provisions.

The Supreme Court expressed the 'ultimate question' of whether an arrangement is a 'tax avoidance arrangement' this way (at paragraph [109]):

'The ultimate question is whether the impugned arrangement, viewed in a commercially and economically realistic way, makes use of the specific provision in a manner that is consistent with Parliament's purpose. If that is so, the arrangement will not, by reason of that use, be a tax avoidance arrangement. If the

---

37 Section GA 1(2) ITA 2007.
38 Sections GA 1(4) and GA 1(5) ITA 2007.
39 [2008] NZSC 115.

use of the specific provision is beyond Parliamentary contemplation, its use in that way will result in the arrangement being a tax avoidance arrangement.'

If the answer to that question is negative, the arrangement is a 'tax avoidance arrangement' void against the Commissioner for income tax purposes. This approach has become known as the 'Parliamentary contemplation' test.

Certain key points can be taken from the *Ben Nevis* judgment (and its subsequent application in other cases). These include:

1. *Artifice and contrivance:* Artifice and contrivance will be regarded as indicators of tax avoidance. This was not a new concept raised in *Ben Nevis* but rather an existing concept which has been re-emphasised. A common thread to New Zealand tax avoidance cases is that, to defeat an allegation of tax avoidance, a taxpayer must be able to show a justifiable commercial rationale for the transaction in question. However, even where a taxpayer can demonstrate a justifiable commercial rationale, it is no longer clear that the taxpayer can validly elect between two means of carrying out a transaction where one of those methods results in less tax being payable than the other (refer to the discussion of the so-called 'choice principle' below).
2. *'Choice principle' constrained:* In *Ben Nevis* the Supreme Court recognised the existence of certain structural freedom afforded to taxpayers. The majority commented (at paragraph [111]) that 'taxpayers have the freedom to structure transactions to their best tax advantage'. They continued that taxpayers may 'utilise available tax incentives in whatever way the applicable legislative text, read in light of its context and purpose, permits'. Yet, they stated, taxpayers 'cannot, however, do so in a way that is proscribed by the general anti-avoidance provision'. Doubt remains as to the extent of this structural freedom. The IR's view (set out in a 2013 non-binding *Interpretation Statement 'Tax avoidance and the interpretation of sections BG 1 and GA 1 of the Income Tax Act 2007'*) is that the choice principle has no independent standing from the Parliamentary contemplation analysis. This is because a choice will only be permitted if it was within the contemplation of Parliament to permit that choice to be made.
3. *Compliance with statutory provisions:* The argument that strict compliance with an applicable tax law can protect a taxpayer from the application of the anti-avoidance provision has been expressly rejected. Related to this, the argument that tax legislation need necessarily be interpreted in a way which gives taxpayers certainty in tax planning has also been rejected. The courts have noted that Parliament has deliberately left the GAAR general in scope, so that, if necessary, the court can apply it in particular circumstances.
4. *Economic consequences:* The taxpayer must have suffered the economic cost intended by Parliament to have been suffered before entitlement to the benefit (eg, a tax deduction) arises. This can conflict with statutory provisions which deem expenditure to arise. Circularity of money flows

and self-cancelling transactions can be relevant in determining the incurrence of economic cost.

5. *'Merely incidental' threshold:* It remains unclear the extent to which the 'merely incidental' threshold in the statutory definition of 'tax avoidance arrangement' (refer above) might have independent standing in a tax avoidance analysis. In light of the Supreme Court's comment in *Ben Nevis* (at paragraph [114]) that 'it will rarely be the case that the use of a specific provision in a manner which is outside Parliamentary contemplation could result in the tax avoidance purpose or effect of the arrangement being merely incidental,' it seems unlikely to have significant impact as an independent inquiry.

(c) *Penny and Hooper*[40] (Supreme Court)

Penny and Hooper was the first tax avoidance case subsequent to the *Ben Nevis* decision to be considered by the Supreme Court. The taxpayers were surgeons who each structured their practice through companies, the shares of which were owned by the respective taxpayer's family trust. Each taxpayer was employed by the respective company for a salary below what the Commissioner considered to be a market salary for a surgeon of the relevant experience. The balance of the income from each medical practice was paid by each company to the relevant family trust as dividends and either retained, distributed or loaned by the trust to family members. For periods in which this structure was in place, the maximum individual tax rate was 39 per cent, while the tax rate applicable to trustee income (income retained in a trust) was 33 per cent.

The Commissioner argued that the arrangement by which the taxpayer had structured his practice was a tax avoidance arrangement void under the GAAR. Specifically, the Commissioner objected to the payment of what he/she considered to be an artificially low salary to the taxpayer for services rendered as a surgeon. The Commissioner argued that by this means, the balance of each practice's profits was able to be retained in the relevant trust at a lower tax rate while still economically made available to the taxpayer.

The Supreme Court held for the Commissioner. It concluded that the taxpayers had complied with the specific provisions of the tax legislation on which they relied and that there was nothing unusual in causing the companies under their control to employ them on a salaried basis. Nevertheless, the fixing of a low salary enabled substantial portions of the profits of the medical practice to be transferred by way of dividends to the respective trusts, thereby avoiding payment of the higher individual tax rate by the taxpayer. The taxpayer was nonetheless able to enjoy the benefit of the proceeds by virtue of being a beneficiary under the trust. The taxpayer obtained a reduction in tax liability without suffering any actual loss of income. This outcome was, in the Supreme Court's opinion, outside of Parliament's contemplation applying the *Ben Nevis* test.

40 *Penny v Commissioner of Inland Revenue* [2011] NZSC 95.

The Supreme Court considered the 'merely incidental' threshold in the statutory definition of 'tax avoidance arrangement'. It concluded that the tax advantage produced by the fixing of each taxpayer's salary at a low rate was the dominant purpose of the arrangement. Although one purpose was the protection of the taxpayer's assets from professional negligence claims (by means of carrying out the practice through a limited liability company), this could not have been the sole or dominant purpose of the arrangement. Relevant factors to this conclusion included the protection from liability already afforded to medical practitioners by New Zealand's state-funded accident compensation scheme (which prohibits personal injury claims, including personal injury arising as a result of medical malpractice) and by professional insurance coverage.

While noting that there is no concept of a commercially realistic salary to be found in the ITA (absent the cross border TP provisions of the ITA not relevant here), the Supreme Court pointed out that the GAAR requires that taxpayers not structure transactions with a more than merely incidental purpose of obtaining a tax advantage, unless that advantage is within the contemplation of Parliament. If a salary is not commercially realistic or not motivated by a commercially legitimate reason, it will be open to the Commissioner to assert that it was part of a tax avoidance arrangement.

(d) *Alesco*[41] (Court of Appeal)

In *Alesco*, the taxpayer was a New Zealand subsidiary of an Australian company. The taxpayer issued non-interest bearing optional convertible notes (OCNs) to its parent. On maturity, the parent could require repayment of the note principal, or conversion of the notes into shares, in the taxpayer. The funds received by the taxpayer in exchange for the OCNs were used by the taxpayer to acquire two New Zealand businesses.

New Zealand's 'financial arrangements' rules contained in the applicable tax legislation (including a mandatorily applicable determination issued by the Commissioner prescribing how the financial arrangements rules were to be applied to instruments such as OCNs) divided the OCNs into debt and equity components. The determination identified the debt component by discounting the face value of the OCN to arrive at the opening value of the debt. A deductible expense was then recognised as the opening value of the debt grown to its face value at maturity. The treatment was consistent with the approach adopted for IFRS reporting. Australian legislation treated the OCNs as equity.

The Commissioner argued that the OCN funding arrangement constituted a tax avoidance arrangement on the basis that the taxpayer was permitted a deduction for an interest liability, which was deemed to arise by application of the financial arrangements rules and the determination to the OCNs, without suffering a corresponding economic cost. The absence or presence of an economic cost was debated before the courts.

41 *Alesco New Zealand Limited v Commissioner of Inland Revenue* [2013] NZCA 40.

The Court of Appeal found for the Commissioner. Applying the 'Parliamentary contemplation' test from *Ben Nevis*, the Court of Appeal held that the taxpayer's claim for interest deductions under the financial arrangements rules was not within Parliament's contemplation in enacting the relevant rules. It noted that it was irrelevant that an interest-bearing loan provided to the taxpayer by its parent would have permitted greater levels of deductions to the taxpayer than those claimed. The Commissioner was not required to consider an alternative funding arrangement that could have been undertaken by the taxpayer in exercising her power of reconstruction.

10.2 Key historical cases

Given the express intention of the Supreme Court in *Ben Nevis* in providing a definitive restatement of relevant aspects of the law on tax avoidance in New Zealand, recourse to cases prior to the *Ben Nevis* decision for interpretation of core tax avoidance principles is not typically required. As noted above, the majority judgment in *Ben Nevis* has been applied, expressly or otherwise, in all subsequent New Zealand tax avoidance cases.

11. PENALTIES

11.1 Legislative provisions

The statutory shortfall penalties regime for income tax matters was discussed at section 5 above. Those penalties apply equally in tax avoidance as in other areas of income tax law. Refer to section 5 above for a general discussion of the relevant penalties regime.

11.2 Examples of penalties imposed

The shortfall penalty most commonly sought to be imposed by the Commissioner in matters of tax avoidance is the 'abusive tax position' penalty of 100 per cent of the tax shortfall.[42] That penalty is applicable where a taxpayer, having taken an 'unacceptable tax position', has entered into, acted in respect of arrangements or interpreted/applied tax laws with a dominant purpose of taking, or of supporting the taking of, tax positions that reduce or remove tax liabilities or give tax benefits.

An 'unacceptable tax position' is one which 'fails to meet the standard of being about as likely as not to be correct'.[43] Courts have interpreted this to mean there would need to be an about equal chance of an interpretation being likely to be correct as to be incorrect. In *Ben Nevis,* the Supreme Court commented on the 'about as likely as not to be correct' standard in the following terms (at paragraph [184]):

'On its terms this standard does not require that the appellants' tax position had a 50 per cent prospect of success but, subject to that qualification, the merits of the argument supporting the taxpayer's interpretation must be substantial.'

In addition, for imposition of the abusive tax avoidance shortfall penalty, 'a dominant' purpose of the taxpayer in entering into the transaction in

[42] Section 141D Tax Administration Act 1994.

[43] Section 141B(1) Tax Administration Act 1994.

question must be reduction of a tax liability or the obtaining of a tax benefit. This is a higher threshold than the test for tax avoidance itself with respect to the GAAR, which requires only 'a purpose' of tax avoidance, being more than a 'merely incidental' purpose. With respect to the GAAR, a 'dominant' purpose is not required. Accordingly a finding of tax avoidance under the GAAR does not automatically lead to the satisfaction of this dominant purpose threshold for the purposes of the abusive tax avoidance shortfall penalty.

12. CURRENT TRENDS

12.1 National policy and law

It is clear that in recent years the IR has become more inclined to challenge arrangements which it regards as constituting tax avoidance. Arrangements which in the past may have been regarded as acceptable tax planning are now more likely to be investigated and challenged by the IR. Similarly, Courts appear to be more inclined than they previously were to uphold the view of the Commissioner. The *Alesco* decision referred to above is, in the view of many New Zealand tax practitioners, the high-water mark in the application of the GAAR. An appeal to the Supreme Court in that case was discontinued shortly before the hearing, to the disappointment of many in the tax profession.

Some commentators have called for the GAAR to be redrafted, to provide a more prescriptive set of rules against which taxpayer arrangements may be judged (such as in Australia and certain other jurisdictions). However, at this point, legislative reform of the GAAR is unlikely.

12.2 The impact and role of the OECD and other international relations

As noted above, the August 2013 *Tax Policy Report: Taxation of Multinationals* issued by the IR and Treasury, highlighted various initiatives to strengthen the IR's ability to combat profit shifting by multinationals and other investors. The IR appears mindful to ensuring New Zealand's legislative framework keeps pace with the changing global economy, particularly including online transactions. The IR's current Tax Policy Work Programme[44] includes international tax reform and addressing BEPS.

[44] *http://taxpolicy.ird.govt.nz/work-programme*, announced 8 November 2013.

Nigeria

Churchfields Solicitors Oluwatoyin Bashorun[1]

PART ONE: TRANSFER PRICING

1. GENERAL OVERVIEW

Nigeria is a rapidly expanding market with tremendous growth potential. Recent expansions in infrastructure have attracted domestic and foreign activity in all major industries, including agriculture, engineering, construction and telecommunications. The ongoing expansion in Nigeria has also impacted the financial services industry, which continues to grow with the introduction of international banks and the West African Market. Nigeria is also rich in natural resources, including oil and gas reserves and has significant mineral deposits. As a result of the foregoing, it is not surprising that multinational enterprises are increasingly establishing operations in Nigeria. This has resulted in an increase in inter-company transactions, both in frequency and value, between local affiliates and their foreign counterparts.

Transfer pricing refers to the setting of prices in transactions between related parties within the same enterprise group. Transactions between related parties that typically involve transfer pricing include the sale of tangible goods, the licensing and sale of intellectual property, and the extension of credit or financing to or among target companies. Transfer pricing is most prevalent in cross-border transactions, where income and expenses are allocated among taxpayers in different jurisdictions. However, Nigeria has extended its definition of transfer pricing to include domestic transactions between affiliates.

In an attempt to prevent profit shifting by foreign taxpayers and the erosion of Nigeria's tax base, the Federal Inland Revenue Service (the 'FIRS') published the Transfer Pricing Regulations (the 'TPR') in August 2012. The TPR attempts to address international commerce and taxation by establishing a formal set of rules for the management of transfer pricing issues. Since the introduction of the TPR, transfer pricing has become a major concern for the FIRS. Consequently, it is critical for corporate taxpayers (both local and international), and their tax advisors to educate themselves on the new regulations, and understand the precedents set by these regulations in the context of their own business activities in Nigeria.

1 The author would like to thank Ms. 'Laide Benjamin, Ms. Omobolanle Salvador and Mr. Chukwudi Mbadiwe for their assistance in the compiling of this chapter. This chapter has been endorsed by A.J Bamidele, Co-ordinating Director of the Federal Board of Inland Revenue, Abuja, FCT.

2. IDENTIFICATION OF LEGISLATIVE FRAMEWORK

2.1 Federal legislation

The legislative framework relevant to transfer pricing in Nigeria is set out in the Laws of the Federation of Nigeria—a federal statute. The TPR have been enacted federally because Nigeria continues to operate under a federal system of government, pursuant to the Constitution of the Federal Republic of Nigeria, 1999. By virtue of the principle of fiscal federalism in Nigeria, issues related to transfer pricing fall squarely within the exclusive jurisdiction of the federal government and the FIRS.

The specific federal legislation relevant to transfer pricing includes in the Personal Income Tax Act (the 'PITA'), the Companies Income Tax Act (the 'CITA'), and the Petroleum Profits Tax (Amendment) Act, 2007 (the 'PPTA').[2] These Statutes are similar in that they all provide for the authority of the FIRS to adjust any transaction, including inter-company transactions and transactions between unrelated parties, which is deemed to produce a result that artificially reclaims income otherwise taxable in Nigeria.

2.2 State and provincial interplay

Not applicable.

2.3 International treaties and agreements

(a) The Organization for Economic Co-operation and Development Guidelines

The Organization for Economic Co-operation and Development (the 'OECD') Guidelines on Transfer Pricing, aim to assist multinational enterprises and tax administrators. The guidelines are applicable in Nigeria, and have informed the promulgation of Nigeria's own transfer pricing legislation.

(b) United Nations Transfer Pricing Manual

The United Nations Manual, including its tax manual, is applicable as a guide in Nigeria.[3]

3. NATIONAL POLICY ISSUES

The TPR are based on the arm's length principle. The arm's length principle provides that commonly controlled companies are expected to transact business with their affiliates at arm's length (ie, as if they were unrelated). Therefore, prices in controlled transactions are to be set according to the facts and circumstances of the transaction.

3.1 Overall national policy announcements

Pursuant to the TPR, the FIRS TPR Division sends out notices requesting that taxpayers submit their group and domestic transfer pricing policy to the Division at least 30 days before their returns are filed.

---

2 Section 15 of the Petroleum Profits Tax Act (PPTA), Cap P 13 volume 13 Laws of The Federation of Nigeria 2004.
3 The UN Manual was formally approved in Nigeria in October 2012.

(a) TPR documentation

Taxpayers who engage in transactions with related parties are required to maintain transfer pricing documentation to establish compliance with the arm's length principle. Previously, the TPR required that documentation be in place prior to filing an income tax return for the year in which the transaction occurred. However, in a recently published guideline, the FIRS indicated that taxpayers must now complete the required documentation at the time the transaction is taking place (ie, contemporaneously). In practice, it is unlikely that the FIRS will request the documentation until after the filing of the tax return. Nevertheless, such documentation must now be in place at the time the transaction is occurring, in order to support arm's length pricing.

3.2 National revenue authority initiatives

As per the FIRS guidelines, a group transfer pricing policy refers to a set of principles adopted by the group, which are used to determine pricing in inter-group transactions. The guidelines indicate that a domestic transfer pricing policy differs from a group transfer pricing policy because a domestic policy includes a consideration of the country's transfer pricing rules.

Most multinational groups maintain policy documents in the form of internal manuals that provide guidance on how transactions are to be structured within the group. However, the FIRS has stated that a transfer pricing policy should also contain information on the transfer pricing methods and comparables used to assess arm's length pricing. As a result, companies may need to prepare specific policy documents in order to satisfy the requirements imposed by the FIRS, as existing internal documents are likely insufficient to satisfy those requirements.

(a) Declaration and disclosure forms

The TPR disclosure form is provided by the FIRS. The form requires information about the taxpayer's controlled transactions, including transaction volumes and the transfer pricing methods used to support the arm's length nature of the transactions. It also requires the provision of basic financial information from the financial statements of the reporting entity and its consolidated group. The TPR declaration form is attached as a schedule to the regulations. It requires the provision of information about the reporting entity, its parent, subsidiaries, ownership structure, major shareholders, and directors.

(b) Advance pricing agreements

The TPR provide that connected taxable persons ('CTPs') may enter into Advance Pricing Agreements ('APAs') to determine whether controlled transactions undertaken within a fixed period of time have complied with the arm's length principle. The life span of an APA is three years. There are no provisions for renewals; however, it is assumed that where an APA is successfully executed, it may be renewed by the consent of all contracting parties.

Under the TPR, a CPT (ie, a connected taxable person) is eligible to request an APA if the cumulative amount resulting from the transaction in every assessment year is not less than N250,000,000 of the CTP's total deductible costs or total taxable revenues. The FIRS reserves the right to cancel an APA upon notice in the following situations:

- If the CTP has failed to comply with a fundamental term of the APA;
- If there has been a material breach of one or more of the critical assumptions underlying the APA;
- If there is a change in the tax law that is materially relevant to the APA; or
- If the APA was entered into based on a misrepresentation, mistake or omission by the CTP.

3.3 Administrative statements

The FIRS guidelines indicate that every taxpayer that is subject to the TPR is required to document its transfer pricing policy at both the group and domestic level, and submit its policy to the FIRS within 21 days of a request or, if no request is made, at the time of filing the first annual transfer pricing return.[4] Additionally, taxpayers are required to maintain transfer pricing policy documents (both group and domestic policy documents), which are to be submitted with the first annual transfer pricing return, and updated when material changes are made to the policy. An annual TPR Return must be submitted at the time of filing the annual income tax return, and must include a TPR disclosure form; audited financial statements; a copy of the income tax self-assessment; and a tax computation with all schedules. In the second year, the TPR policy documents and TPR declaration form must also be submitted with updates and amendments. These documents only need to be updated when material changes are made to the information contained in them.

(a) The transfer pricing regulations

The TPR are divided into six parts. Part I sets out the purposes, objectives and applicability of the TPR. The purpose of the regulations is to prevent tax evasion, and ensure that Nigeria is able to impose appropriate taxes on the economic activities carried on by taxpayers in Nigeria.[5] Furthermore, the regulations attempt to establish a level playing field between all enterprises doing business in Nigeria, and provide taxpayers with greater predictability where transfer pricing income is concerned, thereby preventing the incidence of double taxation. The regulations are applicable to all transactions between CTPs carried out in a manner that is not consistent with the arm's length principle.[6]

Part II of the regulations deals with the arm's length principle, documentation requirements, APAs and other corresponding adjustments. Pursuant to this part, a CTP who enters into a controlled transaction must

4 Guidelines issued by the FIRS in Nigeria intermittently and as an ongoing administrative statements.
5 Section 2 of the Income Tax (Transfer Pricing) Regulations No. 1, 2012.
6 Section 3 of the Income Tax (Transfer Pricing) Regulations No. 1, 2012.

ensure that taxable profits from the transaction are consistent with the arm's length principle. Otherwise, the FIRS is entitled to impose any adjustment it considers necessary in the circumstances.[7] This part also establishes the requirement that documentation must be in place prior to the filing of the income tax returns in the year in which the transaction occurred. Additionally, this part establishes the requirement that documentation be provided to the FIRS within 21 days of a request. However, the regulation also provides for a mechanism by which the taxpayer can obtain an extension of time.

Part III of the TPR provides an index of comparable factors designed to assist the taxpayer in applying the arm's length principle. In particular, Part III allows the taxpayer to draw an analogy from similar taxpayers, as long as there are no significant differences in the transaction. Further, Section 9(4) of the TPR provides a mechanism for determining comparable transactions.[8] In addition, this part provides for the inclusion of the UN Model and the OECD Model Tax Convention on Income and Capital. Specifically, it recognizes the OECD Transfer Pricing Guidelines for multinational enterprises and tax administrators as approved by counsel of the OECD and published in July 2010.[9]

Part V of the TPR contains provisions regarding offences, penalties and dispute resolution. It is important to note that no new penalties are created under this part. Rather, the regulations have been annexed to the existing tax laws. Thus, a taxpayer who contravenes the rules or regulations respecting transfer pricing may be subject to the penalty prescribed in the relevant provision of the applicable tax law. Additionally, this part enshrines a new method for dispute resolution.[10]

Part VI of the TPR deals with supplementary issues including interpretation, use of information, record keeping and documentation. The regulations do not provide for a materiality threshold. While a CTP may be exempted from the requirement to provide certain documentation, the requirement that the transaction is to be at arm's length remains mandatory throughout the regulations.

4. CASE LAW

Transfer pricing is a very recent development in Nigeria. As a result, there are presently no reported cases on the subject.

4.1 Current cases

Not applicable.

4.2 Historical cases of note

Not applicable.

7 Section 4 of the Income Tax (Transfer Pricing) Regulations No. 1, 2012.
8 Section 9 of the Income Tax (Transfer Pricing) Regulations No. 1, 2012.
9 Section 11 of the Income Tax (Transfer Pricing) Regulations No. 1, 2012.
10 Section 13 Income Tax (Transfer Pricing) Regulations.

5. PENALTIES

5.1 Types

A taxpayer who contravenes the rules or regulations respecting transfer pricing may be subject to a penalty as prescribed in the relevant provision of the applicable tax law. Penalties for violations of the transfer pricing rules are set out in the PITA, the CITA, and the PPTA. The penalties contained in each of these statutes are similar, with minor variations in the amount of fines and length of imprisonment terms. However, in cases where the taxpayer submits incorrect accounts or false statements, penalties under the PPTA may be up to three times the incorrect or falsified amount.

Penalties for offences committed by authorized and unauthorized persons, such as members of the FIRS, are set out in s. 13 of the TPR. Common offences include the dereliction of duties, embezzlement and conspiracy. At present, there are no reported cases involving a prosecution under s. 13 of the TP Regulations.

5.2 Special or notable cases

Not applicable.

6. DISPUTE RESOLUTION MECHANISMS

6.1 Preferred national options

Pursuant to s. 14 of the TPR, the resolution of a transfer pricing dispute is a two-stage process. First, the FIRS must establish a decision review panel, whose main purpose is the resolution of the dispute or controversy. The panel shall be comprised of key officers of the transfer pricing department, and two senior ranking officers of the FIRS. If the taxpayer fails to provide the necessary information within the time stipulated, the panel is entitled to employ its discretionary power of best assessment. Second, a party may appeal a decision of the panel to a court of competent jurisdiction. For this purpose, the court of competent jurisdiction is the Federal High Court. Save for judicial intervention, the decision of the panel is final and binding.

6.2 International options

Nigeria's transfer pricing rules are consistent with general transfer pricing policy. Additionally, the OECD Guidelines and the UN Manual are persuasive precedents in Nigeria, subject to certain limitations.

With increasing globalization, the preservation and defence of the national tax base has become a major concern for the tax authorities. There is a general consensus among tax administrators that unless action is taken, there is a significant potential for revenue leakage through the pricing of transactions between resident and non- resident related parties.

In March 2010, the FIRS announced its intention to implement a set of transfer pricing regulations in Nigeria. After the circulation of a series of exposure drafts, the regulations were finalized and implemented.[11] To facilitate enforcement, the FIRS provided a draft of the Transfer Pricing

[11] Income Tax (Transfer Pricing) Regulations No. 1, 2012.

Declaration Form (TPDF), which forms the basis for an audit in a transfer pricing case.[12] In addition, FIRS has been cooperating with various national and international audit firms and tax outfits in the education and preparation of the taxpayers in this respect.

Notwithstanding the developments that have been made, Nigeria faces several challenges in this respect, including technical capacity. Additionally, information on the performance of independent parties, though readily available in developed countries, is quite scare in Nigeria. Finally, because of the traditional belief predominant in the African setting, the tax authorities are reluctant to enter into transfer pricing arrangements.

PART TWO: TAX AVOIDANCE

7. ACCEPTABLE TAX PLANNING AREAS/ SUBJECTS

In Nigeria, as in any other jurisdiction, domestic revenue is essential for sustainable development. However, tax resistance limits the effective and efficient collection of domestic revenue. Tax resistance includes tax evasion and tax avoidance. Tax evasion refers to the fraudulent, dishonest and intentional distortion or concealment of facts and figures with the intention of avoiding or reducing the payment of taxes. Tax evasion is generally accompanied by a deliberate act or omission which constitutes a crime under the tax laws. In the case of *7up Bottling Co. Plc. v L.S.I.R.B.*, the Court of Appeal held that while tax avoidance is permissible, tax evasion is illegal and can give rise to penalties including imprisonment in some cases.[13] Some examples of acts and omissions that are generally regarded as tax evasion include: the failure to pay tax; the failure to submit tax returns; an omission or misstatement of fact on a tax return; the underreporting of income; documenting a fictitious transaction; overstating expenses; and the failure to answer inquires. The most common form of tax evasion in Nigeria is the failure to submit tax returns to the tax authority. Since tax evasion is prevalent in Nigeria, it attracts stiff penalties.[14]

In contrast, tax avoidance refers to the lawful minimization of tax, wherein a taxpayer arranges its financial affairs in such a way as to incur the least amount of tax without infringing the legal regime. In the historic case of *Ayrshire Pullman Motor Services and David M. Ritchie v C.I.R.*, Lord Clyde stated:

'No man in this country is under the smallest obligation moral or otherwise, so as to arrange his legal relation to his business or to his property as to enable the Inland Revenue to put the largest possible shovel into his store. The Inland Revenue is not slow and quite rightly, to take every advantage which is open to it and the taxing statute for the purpose, and the tax payer is in like manner entitled to be astute to prevent so far as he honestly can, that the depletion of his means by the Revenue.'[15]

---

12 Income Tax (Transfer Pricing) Regulations No. 1, 2012.
13 (2000) 3 NWLR Page 591, paras A–B.
14 See ss. 82 of the CITA, 76 of the PITA and 46 of the PPTA, referred to above.
15 (1929) 14 TC754.

Since the release of this decision, it has been generally accepted that tax avoidance is not illegal, which stands to reason given the fact that the taxpayer is only employing the existing laws to limit taxes. Some examples of tax avoidance include: seeking professional advice; reducing one's income by submitting claims for expenses incurred to earn income; and taking out an additional life insurance policy.

8. DEFINING ABUSIVE TAX AVOIDANCE

The general anti-avoidance regime in Nigeria is premised upon the principle of ability to pay, a method of taxation wherein the individual's ability to pay is of direct relevance. The principle provides that 'public expenditure should come from him that have' rather than 'him that have not'. The applicability of the principle is limited by the fact that there is no established approach for the measurement of the equity of sacrifice in this area. The best judgment assessment principle is a corollary to the ability to pay principle that is applicable to companies.

9. THE LEGISLATIVE FRAMEWORK

The objective of the legislative framework is to prevent the impact of tax avoidance and tax evasion on the economy. The relevant statutes include the PITA, the CITA, and the PPTA, wherein penalties are provided in connection with tax evasion and the sale of goods or other chattels, bonds or security. For example, the CITA provides for prison sentences to be served by the directing minds of the offending company, whilst the company as an entity is subject to a fine. Additionally, where companies are concerned, these statutes provide a mechanism for sealing the premises of defaulting taxpayers for recovery purposes.[16]

10. KEY CASES OF INTEREST

The cases of *Alhaji Sule v Commissioner for Inland Revenue (C.I.R.)* and *Federal Commissioner of Taxation v Snowden* are of particular importance as they serve to illustrate the approaches of the tax authority and the courts in cases involving tax evasion, tax avoidance, and the general anti-avoidance rule ('GAAR').

10.1 Current cases

(a) Alhaji Sule v Commissioner for Inland Revenue (C.I.R.)

The appellant in this case was in the business of selling cattle on commission.[17] According to the appellant's evidence, he received cattle for sale and was paid a commission of £1 on the sale of each animal. However, after the payment of certain expenses, he received a net profit of only 5 shillings on the sale of each animal. Additionally, the appellant stated that he occasionally purchased cattle to be slaughtered at a rate of about £1 a day and sold to the public. For each animal, the appellant claimed that he

16 Section 76 of the PITA; s. 82 of the CITA; s. 46 of the PPTA. See also *F.R.N Vs Kingsley Ekpe* 2 QCCR 155 at 192.

17 (2013) Tax Law Reports of Nigeria 52 at 56.

paid £15, and that each sale resulted in a net profit of 10 shillings. The total number of cattle which passed through the appellant's hands during the relevant taxation year was 1160 sold on commission for a profit of £200, and 360 for slaughter and sale for a profit of £180. Accordingly, the appellant alleged that his income for the relevant taxation year was £380, rounded to £400 for the purposes of the appeal.

The evidence at trial established that the appellant owned at least 8 houses in the Enugu area, varying in size from three to ten rooms, with a total of 36 rooms. The appellant testified that some of the houses were used by his relatives who were not charged rent. Additionally, one of the houses was used rent-free by the persons who delivered cattle to the appellant and another by a person who had come to Enugu and had nowhere to stay. With regard to the house with 10 rooms, the appellant stated:

'It is built of mud with zinc roof and cements plaster; the floor is cemented. I keep it as a home for old women who have no husband; 14 of them lives in that house of who 4 have husbands. I do not charge them anything for living in that house. I send them food. I have been running this for about 20 years. It would fetch about 15/- a room per month.'

Additionally, the evidence established that the appellant owned a motor car purchased for £660 in the previous year, paying £300 in cash and the balance at a rate of £50 a month.

The Court considered whether, in view of the insufficient and unreliable returns made by the Appellant, the best judgment of the tax authority could be deemed to be final and conclusive. The Court stated:

'A tax officer is duty bound in light of the evidence and returns made available by the Appellant to make an assessment which will be deemed final and conclusive. In the instant case, the evidence of the Appellant is that he was incorrectly assessed. He claims that his income is 400 pounds and he is liable to pay tax of 15 pounds as against the assessed 126 pounds. Of importance however, is the fact that he failed to keep accounts of his earnings on cattle and refrained from giving a true account of his earnings in the year under consideration. The tax authority's assessment in light of the above can be deemed final and binding.'

If this case had been decided pursuant to the current GAAR, the Federal Board would have been justified in transferring the price of the rooms let by the appellant to his relatives, and imposing taxes on a best of judgement basis.

10.2 Historic cases

(a) Federal Commissioner of Taxation v Snowden (C.I.R.)

In this case, the tax authority reassessed the taxpayer's income for the 1998–99 taxation year, increasing the taxpayer's profits from $2,125,219 to $2,580,932 and imposing additional taxes thereon of $387,139.[18] The taxpayer opposed the assessment on the basis of (1) the adjustment of bank interest income in the amount of $556,871 and (2) the adjustment of fines.

18 (2013) 12 Tax Law Report 28.

The Court held that a taxpayer can only claim a deduction for a fine if he or she can establish, as a matter of fact and law, that the fine was a cost which was actually incurred in the production of income. The Court also found that a taxpayer cannot rely on an act of illegality occasioned by him to avoid tax. The Court stated:

'One can see very little reasons which a person who dries income from illicit activities should be allow to rely on his own illegality in evading his obligation to pay tax. We see no consistency in the law saying at the same time that a person cannot rely on his own illegality in seeking to claim a deduction. We also tend to think that it is open to the courts and indeed he Board to start with a presumption of what the legislature may have intended. After all, this is but a rebuttable presumption.' (p. 53 of the judgment)

11. PENALTIES

11.1 Legislative provisions

The applicable penalties for tax evasion are set out in sections 76 of the PITA, 82 of the CITA and 46 of the PPTA.

Section 76 of the PITA provides:

'If any income charged by any assessment is not paid within the periods prescribed in section 68 of this Act, a sum equal to 10 percent per annum of the tax shall be added thereto, and the provisions of this Act relating to the recovery and collection of tax shall apply to the recovery and collection of that sum.

The relevant tax authority shall serve a demand note on the taxable person or the person in whose name the taxable person is chargeable and, if payment is not made within one month from the date of the service of the demand note, the relevant authority may proceed to enforce payment as hereinafter provided.

A penalty imposed under this section shall not be deemed to be part of the tax paid for the purpose of claiming relief under any provision of this Act.

A person who without lawful justification or excuse, the proof whereof shall lie on such person, fails to pay the income tax within the period of one month prescribed in the subsection (2) of this section, shall be guilty of an offence under this Act.'

Section 82 of the CITA provides:

'Any person who being obliged to deduct any tax under section 78, 79, 80 or 81 of this Act fails to deduct or having deducted failed to pay to the Board within twenty-one days from the date the amount was deducted or the time the duty to deduct arose, shall be guilty of an offence and shall be liable to a penalty of 100 percent per annum of the tax withheld or not remitted, as the case may be.'

Finally, s. 46 of the PPTA provides:

'(1) If any installment of tax due and payable pursuant to section 41 is not paid within the appropriate time limit prescribed in section 45 of this Act,

(a) A sum equal to five percent of the amount of the installment of tax due and payable shall be added thereto, and the provisions of this Act relating to the collection and recovery of tax shall apply to the collection and recovery of such sum; and

(b) The Board shall cause to be served a demand note upon the company assessed or upon the person in whose name the company is assessed; and if

payment is not made within one month from the date of the service of such demand note, the Board may proceed to enforce payment as hereinafter provided.

(c) A penalty imposed under this subsection shall not be deemed to be part of the tax paid for the purpose of any of the provisions of this Act, other than those relating to enforcement and collection of any tax.

(2) Any company or person in whose name the company is assessed whom without lawful justification or excuse, the proof whereof shall lie under the company, or such person assessed, fails to pay the tax within the period of one month prescribed in subsection (1) (b) of this section, shall be guilty of an offence.

(3) The Board may, for any good cause shown, remit the whole or any part of the penalty due under subsection (1) of this section.'

11.2 Examples of penalties imposed

Not applicable.

12. CURRENT TRENDS

12.1 National policy and law

The courts in Nigeria have generally applied a strict interpretation based on the form of relevant transactions. For example, in *Shell Petroleum International Mattscgappij v F.B.I.R.*, the Court held that:

'Payment of tax or who is entitled to pay tax is an issue of law not of agreement or compromise. Higher payment of 10 per cent on turnover for 1993 year of assessment based on provisions of the companies income Tax Act is valid and not a breach of any legal agreement nor accord and satisfaction because there never was any accord and satisfaction.'

The result in the *Shell Petroleum* case, and other similar cases, can be viewed as one of the reasons underlying the introduction of the present transfer pricing regulations. As a result of these regulations, taxable entities can no longer use related entity transactions as a vehicle for tax avoidance or tax planning. Before engaging in a transaction, the taxpayer should determine whether the transaction falls within the related parties' threshold. Otherwise, FIRS may impose an adjustment of the price at which the parties contracted, which may lead to a cost overrun after the transaction is concluded. Tax advisors must also ensure that transfer pricing issues are considered during preliminary due diligence activities, and that taxpayers are appropriately advised of any relevant implications.

It is advisable that all companies resident in Nigeria adopt a transfer pricing compliance policy. Additionally, companies within multinational groups that have adopted Nigeria's global transfer pricing policies must ensure that the policies are consistent with local regulations, and that all transactions are subjected to a related parties' litmus test. Where such relationships are established, the parties must ensure that transactions are priced based on one of the acceptable transfer pricing mechanisms, or in accordance with an APA entered into with the FIRS.

Further, the Nigerian tax laws should be amended to include more specific provisions regarding transfer pricing. In particular, the use of subjective considerations based on the 'opinion' of the tax authority do not comply with contemporary standards, and fail to provide the transparency that is necessary in modern tax practice. Specific transfer pricing rules will provide the tax authority with greater guidance on how to treat specific cases. Additionally, taxpayers will be afforded greater predictability, and will have more confidence that transfer pricing related matters will be assessed objectively.

In the Nigerian states, local governments have developed policies which provide that before any business can be transacted, the activities of taxable persons must be in total compliance with the present laws and regulations. Additionally, as a result of the decision in *Halliburton West Africa Ltd. v F.B.I.R.*, the incidence of tax avoidance has been curtailed by the new profit shifting principles. [19] These principles apply where the taxpayer is unable to justify deductions claimed against income for tax purposes. With regard to the issue of whether recharges are allowable deductions in assessing a turnover, the Court stated:

'It is therefore wrong [to hold] that recharges (ie, money paid by the appellant under the contract to Halliburton Nigeria) are not relevant to the implementation of section 26(1) of [the] CITA and not allowable deductions in the turnover of the appellant.'

The court went on to discuss the operation of s. 48(a) of the CITA, stating:

'It is provided in section 48(1) of CITA that if the respondent discovers or is of the opinion at any time that any company liable to tax has not been assessed or has been assessed at a less amount than that which ought to have been charged, the respondent may within the year of assessment or within six years after the expiration thereof and as often as may be necessary, assess such company at such amount or additional amount as ought to have been charged. The assessment is therefore not final and conclusive.' (p. 108)

12.1.1 The impact and role of the OECD and other international relations

Not applicable.

[19] (2013)11 TLRN 84.

Norway

Advokatfirmaet Schjødt AS Cecilie Amdahl

PART ONE: TRANSFER PRICING

1. GENERAL OVERVIEW

Norwegian tax law deals with transfer pricing by imposing certain requirements on transactions between related parties. If these requirements are not met, the tax authority may reassess the taxpayer's income and assets and, subject to certain criteria, additional taxes may be levied. The transfer pricing requirements apply to transactions between Norwegian parties and cross-border transactions. Although Norway has a relatively high tax rate, taxpayers are granted extensive deductions for costs. Thus, to prevent tax evasion, the tax authority focuses on transactions involving costs incurred by Norwegian entities that are paid to affiliates in countries with lower tax rates.

The arm's length principle established in the transfer pricing requirements is the main guideline for determining whether a transaction between related parties is acceptable for tax purposes. Additionally, Norway has introduced new rules on interest deductions for debts between related parties. These rules impose standardized limitations on deductibility based on a taxpayer's earnings, and apply in addition to the general transfer pricing requirements.

2. IDENTIFICATION OF LEGISLATIVE FRAMEWORK

(a) Transfer Pricing Regulations

Section 13-1 of the Norwegian Tax Act (the 'NTA') is the main legislative provision dealing with transfer pricing in Norway. Section 13-1 establishes the arm's length principle and sets out the powers of the tax authority in respect of transactionsbetween related parties. Specifically, the tax authority may amend the terms and conditions of a contract between related parties if they are inconsistent with the terms and conditions that would exist between unrelated parties. The tax authority may then use the amended terms and conditions to determine the correct contract price,having regard to the arm's length principle. Additionally, the tax authority may make adjustments to other arrangements between related parties, such as the allocation of assets and liabilities.

Section 13-1 sets out three conditions that must be satisfied by the tax authority before it is permitted to make adjustments to a transaction or arrangement between related parties. First, the tax authority must demonstrate that there is a community of interest between the parties. This requires the involvement of at least two parties, including both physical and legal entities. A community of interest may be established on the basis of direct or indirect ownership and/or control. A community of interest may also be derived fromthe commercial dependence of one party on the other, or where mutual dependency has developed between the parties as a result of preceding contractual engagements. Second, the tax authority must establish that one of the parties has incurred a loss of income or wealth. This entails an assessment of the probable income or wealth that would have accrued to the party if the transaction or arrangement had been conducted at arm's length. Finally, the tax authority must establish that the loss of income or wealth was caused by the community of interest. While the third condition usually follows from the other conditions, the tax authority must establish a causal connection independently from the other conditions.

The tax authority generally has the burden of satisfying all three conditions on a balance of probabilities. However, if one of the parties to the transaction is resident in a state outside the European Economic Community ('EEC'), or an EEC state from which the Norwegian tax authority cannot demand disclosure of information, the burden of proof is reversed. In these circumstances, a causal connection between the community of interest and the loss of income or wealth is presumed, unless it is refuted by the taxpayer. If all three conditions are established on a balance of probabilities, the tax authority may use its administrative discretion to determine the taxpayer's income and wealth in accordance with the arm's length principle. A taxpayer cannot challenge an arm's length determination on the basis that the tax authority did not use the most precise or suitable valuation method. Rather, the court may only set aside the tax authority's determination if it is deemed grossly unreasonable or arbitrary.However, the court is entitled to conduct an independent assessment of whether the tax authority satisfied the three conditions and had the power to adjust the party's income and wealth in accordance with the arm's length principle.

The OECD Transfer Pricing Guidelines have been formally incorporated in s. 13-1(4) of the NTA. Norwegian tax law makes a distinction between related parties resident in a foreign state that has entered into a tax treaty with Norway, and related parties resident in a state that has not concluded a tax treaty with Norway. With regard to the former, the OECD Transfer Pricing Guidelines must be taken into account in a transfer pricing assessment. In the latter case, the OECD Transfer Pricing Guidelines only need to be taken into account to the extent that they are applicable.

It should be noted that Norway does not have a specific thin capitalization rule. However, a special rule applicable only to companies subject to surtax requires a minimum of 20 per cent equity. It has long been assumed that the same ratio could be used as a guideline for other entities. While the tax authority has been moving towards a stricter requirement, they have not yet provided any specific guidance. As a result, the question of whether a company is thinly capitalized must be determined on the basis of s. 13-1.

(b) Transfer pricing documentation requirements

The Norwegian Tax Assessment Act (the 'NTAA') establishes the transfer pricing documentation requirements. The requirements apply to controlled transactions, defined as any transaction between related parties. The documentation requirements are mandatory for any entity that is subject to filing requirements in Norway, including permanent establishments. However, small companies, defined as companies with fewer than 250 employees and income below NOK 400 million or equity lower than NOK 350 million, are exempt from the documentation requirements. Further, the requirements do not apply to companies with controlled transactions totalling less than NOK 10 million and inter-group outstanding values below NOK 25 million. However, where Norway cannot demand disclosure of information under a tax treaty, companies that engage in controlled transactions must comply with the transfer pricing documentation requirements notwithstanding the applicability of an exemption.

The documentation submitted by the taxpayer must provide sufficient information for the tax authority to determine whether the contractual terms, conditions and prices comply with the arm's length principle. Additionally, the level of detail in the information, explanations and analyses provided should be consistent with the economic scale and complexity of the transaction. Therefore, complex transactions, such as transfers of intellectual property, will be subject to more onerous documentation requirements than simple transactions. The documentation can be prepared in Norwegian, Swedish, Danish or English. While the rules do not prescribe a particular form or template, the information must be presented in an orderly manner. The taxpayer may prepare the documentation in accordance with the Code of Conduct on Transfer Pricing Documentation for Associated Enterprises in the European Union 2006/C 176/01 28 July 2006.

Documentation must be prepared for each incomeyear. Additionally, the taxpayer must establish internal procedures that make it possible to compile and submit the required documentation within 45 days of a request from the tax authority. Further, the taxpayer must retain the documentation for at least 10 years after the end of the relevant income year.If the documentation does not include a comparable analysis, the tax authority may request that one be submitted. If a taxpayer fails to submit the required documentation upon the request of the tax authority, or the documentation falls below an acceptable standard, the tax authority has the discretion to determine the taxpayer's income and wealth.

(c) Special interest deduction limitation rule

In 2014, the Norwegian government introduced new rules on the deduction of interest for loans between related parties. The regulations are only applicable if the taxpayer has net interest costs (ie, interest costs less interest income) of more than 5 million NOK. Pursuant to these rules, interest paid to a related party above 30 per cent of afixed revenue amount (ie, the deduction limit) is no longer deductible. However, this does not affect the taxation of interest income, which remains fully taxable under the general rules.

The interest limitation rule applies to interest that exceeds 30 per cent of the taxpayer's ordinary income or uncovered losses (ie, interest costs and tax depreciations reduced by interest income). While the rules only affect interest paid to related parties, interest paid to unrelated parties is included when calculating the deduction limit. It should also be noted that upon certain criteria being met, interest paid to unrelated parties may be treated as interest paid to related parties for the purpose of the limitation rule.

The interest limitation rule applies to limited liability companies, general partnerships and companies and entities with limited tax liability in Norway. The rule also applies toCFC companies and foreign companies with permanent establishments in Norway. Additionally, the rule applies to pure Norwegian groups. However, the rule does not apply to natural persons or financial institutions. For companies operating subject to surtax, the rule applies to such companies' income attributable to shore. This means that the regulations do not apply to such companies' overall income, but must be applied to the company's tax basis attributable on shore. The limitation of interest deduction is calculated for each company separately, even if the company is part of a group. The rule includes both Norwegian and foreign lenders.

2.1 Federal legislation

Since Norway is a unitary state, there is no federal legislation.

2.2 State and provincial legislative interplay

Not applicable.

2.3 International treaties and agreements

Generally, Norway's tax treaties with foreign states follow the OECD Model Tax Convention (the 'Model Convention'). Thus, article 9 of the Model Convention is relevant in cross-border transfer pricing cases. Additionally, the OECD Transfer Pricing Guidelines have been incorporated in the NTA, and must be taken into account if the foreign entity is resident in a statethat has entered into a tax treaty with Norway. In all other cases, the OECD Transfer Pricing Guidelines need only be taken into account to the extent that they are applicable.

3. NATIONAL POLICY ISSUES

The Norwegian government has expressed concerns about the erosion of Norway's tax base as a result of international tax competition and the globalization of the world economy. The introduction of the interest deduction limitation rule can be seen as a response to these concerns. Additionally, the government has recently initiated a comprehensive review of the Norwegian corporate tax system to assess the effectiveness of the current legislation and determine whether additional measures should be adopted.

3.1 Overall national policy announcements

The tax authority and the Ministry of Finance have repeatedly stated that taxpayers should consult and comply with the OECD principles and guidelines. Additionally, the Norwegian Ministry of Finance has been very active in the OECD's Base Erosion and Profit Shifting ('BEPS') Project. Although no specific announcement has been made, it is expected that Norway will adopt a leading role in this project once more specific regulations are developed.

3.2 National revenue authority initiatives

Not applicable.

3.3 Administrative statements

The tax authority publishes statements concerning administrative decisions, requests for mutual agreements initiated by taxpayers, and policy issues on a regular basis.

3.4 Administrative guidelines

The tax authority releases an annual publication, entitled 'Tax-ABC', which includes the tax authority's official view on several tax issues, including transfer pricing. The tax authority may also issue articles to summarize or emphasize their opinions on certain matters. In addition, the tax authority has the discretion to issue comments in response to court decisions regarding matters of general interest.

4. CASE LAW

Many of the transfer pricing cases in Norway involve interest-free loans and thin capitalization in the oil industry.Compared to other tax matters, the tax authority seems to have a slightly lower success rate in transfer pricing cases. However, this may be attributable to the fact that transfer pricing legislation in Norway has not yet been finalized and remains a work in progress.

4.1 Current cases

(a) Nordland v Norway (2012)

The decision in this casewas significant because of the Court's interpretation of s. 13-1 of the NTA. The Supreme Court ruled that the courts have a very limited jurisdiction to overrule the tax authority's estimates of the correct arm's length price. Specifically, the Court stated that the courts can only set aside the tax authority's discretionary assessment if it is deemed grossly unreasonable or arbitrary.

4.2 Historical cases of note

(a) Telecomputing v Norway (2010)

In this case, the taxpayer had deducted a loss concerning an interest-free loan to an American subsidiary. The loan significantly exceeded the subsidiary's borrowing capacity. The tax authority argued that the loan should be considered an equity contribution. The Supreme Court ruled that there was no just cause to reclassify the loan as equity. Further, the Court held that s. 13-1 was inapplicable on the basis that the necessary casual relation between the community of interest and the income reduction was not established.

(b) Schlumberger v Norway (1995)

The taxpayer in this case wasresident in Norway due to business conducted on the Norwegian continental shelf. The issue was whether the taxpayer had the right to deduct payments for inter-group insurance captives. The Supreme Court ruled in favour of the tax authority on the basis that the taxpayer had failed to document that the captive had the financial ability to cover their responsibility, and as a result, the risk effectively remained with the company.

5. PENALTIES

In Norway, a breach of the transfer pricing regulations is penalized in the same manner and pursuant to the same rules as any other breach of the tax regulations.

5.1 Types

(a) Administrative penalties

The tax authority may impose a penalty ranging from 30 to 60 per cent of the taxes levied on the amount withheld from taxation. The ordinary penalty of 30 per cent is imposed after an objective assessment of whether the taxpayer has provided incorrect or incomplete information to the tax authority, and whether the incomplete or incorrect information has or could result in a tax advantage for the taxpayer. There is no requirement that the taxpayer's failure to provide the required information be intentional or deliberate. Before the tax authority can impose a penalty of more than 30 per cent, it must be established that the taxpayer was grossly negligent or intentionally failed to provide the required information. In one case, the Supreme Court ruled that a deviation of 40 per cent or more from the correct arm's length price is sufficient to conclude that the information given by the taxpayer is incorrect. Although this should not be perceived as a bright-line rule, it is generally assumed thatwhere a transaction is based on a price that deviates 40 per cent or more from the arms' length price, it will be deemed to be incorrect information.

(b) Criminal charges

If a transfer pricing case is deemed sufficiently severe, criminal charges may be imposed. The potential penalties for taxpayers (and other involved parties) who are found guilty range from fines to terms of imprisonment.

5.2 Special or Notable Cases

Not applicable.

6. DISPUTE RESOLUTION MECHANISMS

In Norway, a taxpayer can appeal any administrative decision of the tax authority to an independent tax tribunal. The tribunal is comprised of individuals with experience in law and economics. Generally, proceedings before the tribunal are (with few exceptions) in writing only. It usually takes three to six months before the tribunal announces its ruling. The taxpayer may appeal the decision of the tribunal to the court within 6 months of the tribunal's decision.

6.1 Preferred national options

In the past, most taxpayers elected to commence an appeal in theindependent tax tribunal prior to commencing court proceedings. However, there has been a recent trend of taxpayers proceeding directly to the courts due to a lack of faith in the tax tribunal's independence and competence, and the extensive amount of time before decision is made. As a result, the Norwegian government is currently in the process of revising the administrative appeals system.

6.2 International options

The double taxation treaties entered into by Norway with several other countries provide for a mutual agreement procedure (the 'MAP') to resolve cross-border tax disputes. Pursuant to a MAP, a taxpayer resident in Norway may request the government's assistance when double taxation arises. The government will attempt to resolve the double taxation issue by agreement with the government of the other contracting state.

PART TWO: TAX AVOIDANCE

7. ACCEPTABLE TAX PLANNING AREAS/SUBJECTS

In Norway, tax planning is accepted and taxpayers are permitted to select courses of action that limit their tax liability.

8. DEFINING ABUSIVE TAX AVOIDANCE

Generally, tax avoidance activities can be divided into three categories: (1) where the taxpayer intentionally provides inaccurate information or withholds income from the tax authority; (2) the use of pro-forma arrangements or documentation; and (3) where the taxpayer formally acts in accordance with the law and takes advantage ofavailable methods to obtain a tax benefit. In Norway, the first two categoriesare considered abusive tax avoidance and may be subject to administrative and/orcriminal penalties. The third category is permitted as long as the activities of the taxpayer are not deemed to be disloyal to the objectives or intentions of the Norwegian tax regulations.

9. THE LEGISLATIVE FRAMEWORK

In Norway, a general anti-avoidance rule ('GAAR') has been established through the case law. GAAR applies to activities that are formally legal, but that are deemed to be tax motivated and contrary to the object and spirit of Norway's tax regime. GAAR is not a general rule that always applies to particular arrangements or transactions undertaken by the taxpayer; rather, each case must be assessed individually. Currently, the content and scope of GAAR is not clearly defined, as evidenced by inconsistent terminology and varying demands for evidence of taxpayers' intentions in both administrative statements made by the tax authority and court rulings. Nevertheless, it is generally agreed that in order for GAAR to apply, the following criteria must be met:

(a) The taxpayer's main objective in using the arrangement must be to achieve a tax benefit; and
(b) Upon an assessment of the arrangement as a whole, it must be determined that the effects of the arrangement (including business purpose), the taxpayer's objective, and the general circumstances are in conflict with the purpose of existing tax laws.

An assessment of the taxpayer's main objective in using the arrangement is based on what most likely influenced the taxpayer's choice of action, in light of the facts of the case. The effects of the arrangement, including the business purpose and tax benefits, must be taken into account. The Supreme Court has stated that tax benefits obtained in another country shall be assessed as a business purpose. Thus, only tax benefits obtained in Norway may be taken into account as potentially abusive in the assessment of the taxpayer's purpose. If a considerable tax benefit is discovered, it is presumed to be the taxpayer's main objective in using the arrangement. If a transaction is part of a larger series of transactions, the series must be considered as a whole. As a consequence, a series of transactions can be set aside if the series as a whole is directed at obtaining a tax advantage, even if each transaction on its own does not have a tax-saving purpose.

An assessment of the arrangement in light of the purpose of existing tax laws is based on the distinction between acceptable tax planning and abusive tax avoidance. For instance, actions such as adopting a more advantageous corporate structure or reorganizing a company group to use the income equalization rules are not considered to be in conflict with the purpose of existing tax laws. However, if a transaction lacks a legitimate business purpose, the tax authority is more likely to apply GAAR. Additionally, artificial or unnecessary arrangements are more likely to be subject to GAAR.

In addition to GAAR, s. 14-90 of the NTA establishes rules concerning the transfer of a general tax position through a reorganization or other transaction. A general tax position is a non-effectuated tax effect that is not connected to an asset or liability (eg, a loss carry forward). If it is established that a reorganization or other transaction is carried out with the main objective to obtain a tax benefit, any available general tax positions are eliminated. Unlike GAAR, s. 14-90 does not require the existence of a conflict between the reorganization or other transaction and the purpose of the relevant tax laws. As a result, s. 14-90 has reduced the need for the tax authority to use the more complicated GAAR when the transaction involves existing general tax positions.

10. KEY CASES OF INTEREST

In Norway, GAAR emerged from the common law. Although there are very few Supreme Court cases where GAAR has been applied, GAAR is often an issue in both administrative rulings and cases before the courts. Nevertheless, it can be said that GAAR is still in its early stages of development.

10.1 Current cases

(a) Conoco Phillips v Norway 2014

This case dealt with the differential treatment of share sales and the sale of other property under Norwegian tax law. In Norway, a transaction involving the sale of shares by a limited company is exempt from tax, but the sale of other property is subject to tax at a rate of 27 per cent. The taxpayer in this case had engaged in a pre-empted demerger operation to transfer property to a limited company without tax consequences. The purpose of the tax-exempt demerger was to allow the taxpayer to sell the property as a tax-exempt share sale of the newly formed property owning company. The tax authority took the position that GAAR applied. However, the Supreme Court ruled in favour of the taxpayer, and stated that the use of the reorganization regulations in this manner did not conflict with the intentions of the governing tax law. Subsequently, the tax authority amended its policy on this matter.

10.2 Key historical cases

(a) Dyvi Eiendom AS v Norway 2012

This case involved the sale of a limited company, comprising of two subsidiaries, significant assets and substantial accumulated loss carry forwards. In the year following the sale, the deficit was offset against contributions from other companies in the same group as the purchasing company. The Supreme Court ruled that the acquisition of the parent company and its subsidiaries amounted to a natural whole. Thus, while the tax benefits were a key motivator for the purchase, the deductions were not contrary to the purpose of the regulations on deductions, inter-group contributions and income equalization.

(b) Telenor ASA v Norway 2006

The Norwegian taxpayer in this case was the parent of a group of companies that had reorganized its business. As part of the reorganization, a subsidiary that was transferred from one group company to another incurred a loss that was claimed as tax deductible. The Supreme Court ruled that, according to a shareholder's agreement with an independent third party, the company had assumed it was under an obligation to make the share transfer. However, the Court also ruled that both the tax authorities and the courts are entitled to re-examine the taxpayer's understanding of its contractual obligations in accordance with advice from external legal expertise.

(c) Aker Maritime ASA v Norway 2004

In this case, the taxpayer transferred shares to a newly established subsidiary,pursuant to the regulations on tax-exempt intra-group transfers,i mmediatelybeforemerging with a company outside the group. The Supreme Court ruled that the transfer was solely tax motivated, and constituted an abuse of the intra-group transfer regulations. This case is also known for the fact that the court allowed for a group contribution to be resolved after the ruling.

(d) Norsk Hydro ASA v Norway (2002)

The issue in this case was whether the Norwegian taxpayer was entitled to a deduction for a loss incurred on the sale of shares by one subsidiary to another. The Supreme Court held thatGAAR was not applicable; although thereduction of Norwegian tax was an important purpose of the transaction, the overall effects, including the commercial effects of tax savings in Denmark, did not conflict with the objective of the relevant tax laws.

11. PENALTIES

The tax authority may impose a penalty ranging from 30 to 60 per cent of the taxes levied on the amount withheld from taxation. The ordinary penalty of 30 per cent is imposed after an objective assessment of whether the taxpayer has provided incorrect or incomplete information to the tax authority, and whether the incomplete or incorrect information has or could result in a tax advantage for the taxpayer. There is no requirement that the taxpayer's failure to provide the required information be intentional or deliberate. Before the tax authority can impose a penalty of more than 30 per cent, it must be established that the taxpayer was grossly negligent or intentionally failed to provide the required information.

11.1 Legislative provisions

Administrative penalties have been set out in chapter 10 of the NTAA. If the offence is deemed a criminal offence, chapter 12 of the NTAA sets out the potential penalties, ranging from fines to two years of imprisonment. While administrative penalties can only be directed towards the taxpayer, criminal penalties may be imposed on any party involved in the offence, including the taxpayer and other contributing parties. The tax authority is only entitled to impose administrative penalties. The criminal penalties in chapter 12 of the NTAA may only be imposed by the police or the courts.

11.2 Examples of penalties imposed

The tax authority is entitled to impose penalties if a taxpayer submits incomplete or inaccurate information. As a result, it is common for taxpayers to disclose all transactions and arrangements when filing their taxes, in order to avoid the imposition of future penalties if the transaction or arrangement is subsequently assessed by the tax authority pursuant to GAAR. This practice reduces the number of GAAR cases in which penalties are imposed.

12. CURRENT TRENDS

The most recent case decided by the Supreme Court (cfr. 10.1) has been characterized as a response to the tax authority's excessive focus on the tax effects of a transaction, and a recognition that more predictability is needed in the Norwegian tax system. The case involved the interpretation of the prevailing tax exemption for gains realized on the sale of shares. The tax authority argued that GAAR would apply if the shares had been acquired as a consequence of a demerger shortly before the share sale. The Supreme Court ruled in favour of the taxpayer. As a result of the ruling, the tax authority has approached the legislator to amend the law so that the transaction accepted by the Supreme Court as tax exempt will no longer fall within the exemption. The legislator's response to this issue is not yet known.

12.1 National policy and law

As mentioned in section 3 above, the Norwegian government has expressed concerns about the erosion of Norway's tax base as a result of international tax competition and the globalization of the world economy. Although there are currently no legislative proposals to expand or limit the application of GAAR, it is expected that the legislator will recognize that there is a need for increased predictability for Norwegian taxpayers. The government has recently initiated a comprehensive review of the Norwegian corporate tax system, and has appointed a committee to consider potential improvements. The committee will present its recommendations in October 2014.

12.1.1 The impact and role of the OECD and other international relations

Not applicable.

Russia

YUST Law Firm Maxim Rovinskiy & Ekaterina Boldinova

PART ONE: TRANSFER PRICING

1. GENERAL OVERVIEW

In Russia, legislation on transfer pricing is a relatively recent development. In an attempt to harmonize Russia's tax legislation with that of other countries, Russian legislators enacted a special legislative regime for transfer pricing. This legislative regime is based on the Organization for Economic Co-operation and Development (the 'OECD') Model Tax Convention on Income and Capital and the ECD Transfer Pricing Guidelines. The term 'transfer pricing' is not defined in the Russian tax legislation. However, it is used frequently in the literature, cases and sub-legislative acts. Generally, transfer pricing is a tool used by interdependent companies in transactions involving the sale of goods and services at prices different from market prices.

2. IDENTIFICATION OF LEGISLATIVE FRAMEWORK

2.1 Federal legislation

Previously, Russian transfer pricing legislation was limited to two articles in the Tax Code of the Russian Federation (the 'TCRF').[1] On July 18, 2011, extensive amendments were made by federal law No. 227-FZ. Specifically, section V.I, consisting of 6 chapters and 25 articles, was added to the TCRF to regulate a variety of interdependent corporate relationships. According to article 105.1 of the TCRF, persons or companies are considered to be interdependent if their relationship can affect the conditions and/or the results of their transactions, or the financial results of their activities. In order to determine whether two persons are interdependent, it is necessary to examine the influence they exert on each other. Additionally, the TCRF establishes a list of criteria for recognizing persons or companies as interdependent.[2] The TCRF also sets out rules for auditing the accuracy of the tax payment in a transaction between interdependent persons.[3]

(a) Grounds for recognizing persons or companies as interdependent

In order to better understand Russia's transfer pricing legislation, it is necessary to review some key terms and definitions. One of the most significant terms in Russia's transfer pricing legislation is 'interdependent

1 Articles 20 and 40 of the TCRF.
2 Article 105.1 of the TCRF.
3 Article 105.17 of the TCRF.

persons'. Pursuant to the TCRF, two organizations may be deemed to be interdependent where:

- One organization directly or indirectly participates in the other organization by having control of more than 25 per cent of the other organization's shares;
- The same person directly or indirectly participates in both organizations, and the person's participation in each organization is more than 25 per cent;
- The powers of the chief executive body in both organizations are exercised by the same person;
- The chief executive body, or 50 per cent or more of the executive body of both organizations, is appointed or elected by the same person;
- Over 50 per cent of the executive body of both organizations is comprised of the same person, jointly with interdependent persons; or
- The share of direct participation of each previous in each subsequent organization is more than 50 per cent.

Further, an individual and an organization may be deemed to be interdependent where:

- The individual directly or indirectly participates in the organization by holding more than 25 per cent of the organization's shares;
- The individual has the power to appoint the chief executive body, or the power to appoint not less than 50 per cent of the organization's executive body;
- The person exercises various powers of the chief executive body of the organization; or
- The share of direct participation of each previous in each subsequent organization is more than 50 per cent.

Finally, two individuals may be deemed to be interdependent on the following grounds:

- One individual is subordinate to the other individual due to his official capacity; or
- The individuals are related by blood.

On any other ground, if the court finds that the relationship between the persons has influenced the terms and/or results of the transactions between them.

(b) Criteria for recognizing transactions as controlled

In Russia, a transaction may be deemed to be a 'controlled transaction' where:

- The transaction is completed between interdependent persons; or
- The transaction has the same tax regime as a transaction between interdependent persons.[4]

A transaction between interdependent persons, where one party is a Russian resident and the other party is a non-resident of the Russian Federation will be deemed to be a controlled transaction regardless of the

[4] Article 105.14 of the TCRF.

value of the transaction. Conversely, a transaction between interdependent persons, where all parties are resident in Russia, will only be deemed to be a controlled transaction where one of the following conditions applies:

- The amount of income from the transaction(s) for the corresponding calendar year exceeds 1,000,000,000 rubles;
- One of the parties to the transaction is a taxpayer of the mineral replacement tax calculated at a tax rate fixed in percentage, the object of the transaction is the extracted mineral, and the amount of income for the corresponding calendar year exceeds 60,000,000 rubles;
- One of the parties to the transaction is a taxpayer applying one of the special tax regimes while among the other parties of the said transaction there is a person who does not apply these special tax regimes, and the amount of income for the corresponding calendar year exceeds 100,000,000 rubles;
- One of the parties to the transaction is relieved of the liabilities of a taxpayer, or applies a tax rate of zero per cent, while the other parties to the transaction are not relieved of these liabilities and do not apply the zero per cent tax rate, and the amount of income for the corresponding calendar year exceed 60,000,000 million rubles;
- One of the parties to the transaction is a resident of the special economic zone (which provides tax benefits as compared to the general tax regime of Russia) and the amount of income for the corresponding calendar year exceeds 60,000,000 rubles;
- One of the parties to the transaction is a new offshore field operator or obtains a certificate of authorization to explore a site of subsurface resources, the other party does not take into account the transaction's revenues or expenses, and the amount of income for the corresponding calendar year exceeds 60,000,000 rubles; or
- One of the parties to the transaction is a member of the regional investment project and applies certain tax benefits, and the amount of income for the corresponding calendar year exceeds 60,000,000 rubles.

Examples of transactions that have been found to have the same tax regime as a transaction between interdependent persons include:

- Transactions for the resale of goods or services between persons who are not interdependent but are deemed to be interdependent, excluding the consideration of third persons as long as (i) they do not fulfill any additional function in the transaction other than organizing the resale of goods between the interdependent persons, and (ii) they do not assume any risks or use any assets to organize the resale of goods between the interdependent persons;
- Transactions in the area of foreign goods trade including oil and commodities made of oil, ferrous metals, non-ferrous metals, mineral fertilizers, metals of value, and precious gems, where the amount of income for the corresponding calendar year exceeds 60,000,000 rubles; or
- Transactions where one of the parties is a person whose place of registration, place of residence or place of tax residence is a state or

territory included in the list of states and territories approved by the Ministry of Finance (ie, offshore jurisdictions), including the United Arab Emirates, the Republic of Malta, and the Principality of Andorra, and the amount of income for the corresponding calendar year exceeds 60,000,000 rubles.[5]

(c) Methods used for determining income for tax purposes for transactions between interdependent parties

The TCRF establishes a number of methods that can be used by the tax authorities in controlled transactions, including:

- The comparable market prices method;
- The subsequent realization prices method;
- The expenditures method;
- The comparable profitability method; and
- The method of distributing the profit.

It is possible to combine two or more methods. However, the preferred method is the comparable market prices method. The procedure for each method is described in the TCRF.[6]

(d) Tax audits for transactions between interdependent persons

Tax audits for transactions between interdependent parties are a special type of tax control different from in-house and field tax audits. According to federal law No. 227-FZ dated July 18, 2011, the first audit decisions will be issued before June 30, 2014. These decisions apply to controlled transactions involving revenues and/or expenses from 2012.

Pursuant to Russian tax law, taxpayers are required to notify the tax authorities of any controlled transactions that they have been involved in over the calendar year. Information regarding controlled transactions must be submitted to the relevant tax authority according to the taxpayer's place of residence no later than the 20th of May in the year following the the year in which the controlled transactions took place. If the tax authorities discover a controlled transaction that was not disclosed, they will inform the Federal Tax Service.

The Federal Tax Service is entitled to conduct audits of transactions between interdependent parties, and other controlled transactions. Audits are conducted pursuant to notice provided by the taxpayer regarding the existence of any controlled transactions, or notice from the territorial tax authority following a field or in-house tax audit of the taxpayer. Additionally, an audit may be conducted after a controlled transaction is exposed in another audit conducted by the Federal Tax Service.

Following an audit, the tax authority issues a tax audit report, which must be delivered to the taxpayer. The taxpayer may object to any conclusions in the report, and has the right to file any objections with the tax authority. The procedure for the tax audit report, the taxpayer's objections and the

---

5 This list was approved by an Administrative Order of the Ministry of Finance (No. 108), dated November 13, 2007; Subpart 1 part 3 of Article 284 of the TCRF.

6 Articles 105.7–105.13 of the TCRF.

implementation of the findings of the tax audit are the same as those applicable to field and in-house tax audits.[7]

2.2 State and provincial legislative interplay

According to article 1 of the TCRF, Russian tax legislation consists of the Tax Code (the 'Code') and other federal laws on taxes and fees adopted in accordance with the Code. Article 1 of the TCRF also provides that the Russian Federation has the right to make laws about certain types of taxes (eg, regional taxes), but only on particular subject areas as stipulated by the Code.

The provisions of article 1 of the TCRF also limit the local authorities' competence in tax legislation. Specifically, the local authorities may issue regulatory acts but only on local taxes and fees.[8] Thus, Russian legislation on transfer pricing is a prerogative of the Federation without influence from regional and local authorities.

2.3 International Treaties and Agreements

According to article 7 of the TCRF, international treaties and agreements are included in the tax legislation of the Russian Federation. Moreover, where there is a conflict between a Russian tax treaty and the domestic tax rules, the tax treaty prevails.

The Russian Federation is a member of the Eurasian Economic Community. One of the documents of this international community, the Protocol on Information Exchange for Control on Transfer Pricing, fixes the legal definition of transfer price. The Protocol defines the transfer price as 'the price of goods, works, and services different from objectively formed market prices when international transactions are made'.

3. NATIONAL POLICY ISSUES

3.1 Overall national policy announcements

Every year, the Government of the Russian Federation endorses a document that establishes the main principles for tax policy and the main national policy announcements for the following year.[9] For 2014, it was suggested to limit the application of existing special transfer pricing rules applicable to the transactions with securities and for 'the financial instruments of term transactions, in order to simplify tax accounting'. These rules will be applicable only to transactions and instruments that are recognized as controlled in accordance with the new legislation. In respect of other transactions, income and expenses will be determined on the basis of the actual transaction price. Additionally, a plan was introduced to amend the rules limiting interest expenses for tax purposes; the transfer pricing rules should only apply where the interest rate is higher than the legally established rate. Finally, the use of the transfer pricing rules for transactions

---

7 Part 14 of article 105.17 of the TCRF, article 101 of the TCRF.

8 Part 7 of article 1 of the TCRF.

9 For 2014, it is 'The principal directions for the tax policy of the Russian Federation for 2014 and for the planning period of 2015–2016' (established by the Government of the Russian Federation on the May 30, 2014).

within the investment project was announced in 2014. This measure had already been realized in federal law No. 267-FZ, dated September 30, 2013.

3.2 Administrative guidelines

The Ministry of Finance of the Russian Federation has issued interpretations on transfer pricing that can be used as guidelines. The interpretations cover common questions, including:

- Which official source should be used for confirmation of the transaction price if the contracts with the main office of the company are not public?
- Does an insurance company have the right to recognize a contract price as a market price when entering into an agreement?
- Should transactions involving interest-free loans and contracts of guarantee be recognized as controlled transactions?

Additionally, the Ministry of Finance of the Russian Federation issues letters in response to specific questions submitted by taxpayers, which may also be used as guidelines. Moreover, the TCRF provides that if a taxpayer relies on explanations made by a financial, tax or other authorized state body within the scope its authority, the taxpayer cannot subsequently be held liable for committing a tax offense.[10]

4. CASE LAW

The tax law of the Russian Federation is largely statutory. However, the decisions of the Constitutional Court of the Russian Federation, the Higher Arbitrazh Court of the Russian Federation and the Supreme Court of the Russian Federation have a significant impact on the interpretation and application of Russian tax legislation. In 2014, the Higher Arbitrazh Court of the Russian Federation will be dissolved, and the Supreme Court of the Russian Federation will become the only judicial body with jurisdiction to resolve civil cases, administrative cases and economic disputes.

5. PENALTIES

5.1 Types

Where a taxpayer fails to comply with the transfer pricing requirements and is subsequently assessed by the tax authorities, a penalty equal to 40 per cent of the unpaid tax (with a minimum of 30,000 rubles) may be imposed. However, law No. 227-FZ dated July 18, 2011 introduces some transitional rules, which provide that:

- For additional tax assessments for the 2012–2013 tax period, no penalties are to be imposed;
- For additional tax assessments for the tax periods of 2014–2016, the amount of the penalty is 20 per cent of the unpaid tax amount.

[10] Subpart 3 part 1 of article 111 of the TCRF.

Additionally, the TCRF imposes a penalty of 5,000 rubles for the failure to present a notification of controlled transactions, or including inaccurate information in a notification of controlled transactions.[11]

5.2 Special or notable cases

Since the existing penalties for transfer pricing are a very recent development, they have not yet been applied in any reported case. However, there is extensive jurisprudence on the application of articles 20 and 40 of the TCRF, which regulated transfer pricing matters before 2012. This jurisprudence is still useful for its synopsis of the main principles regarding price control in transactions between related parties, and the rules for defining related (ie, interdependent) persons.

Additionally, the Constitutional Court of the Russian Federation position dated December 4, 2003 No. 441-O remains relevant, notwithstanding that it was made pursuant to the provisions of the former legislation. The Constitutional Court clarified that price calculation methods were deemed methods of taxation base calculation. Therefore, the application of these methods alone does not establish the taxpayer's guilt. Further, according to article 109 of the TCRF, the absence of proof of guilt eliminates the possibility of holding a person liable for committing a tax offense. The new law does not state whether a penalty should be imposed where a price used in a transaction between related parties does not correspond to the market price as a result of objective reasons rather than price manipulation. As a result, the 2003 pronouncement of the Constitutional Court means that in order to hold a taxpayer liable under article 129.3, the tax authorities must prove the existence of the taxpayer's intent to commit tax evasion through price manipulation.

6. DISPUTE RESOLUTION MECHANISMS

On January 1, 2014, an obligatory pre-trial procedure for contesting non-regulatory acts of the tax authority and acts or omissions of their officers was introduced. Pursuant to this procedure, such acts may be contested in a court only after having been reviewed by a superior tax authority. However, there are two exceptions to this general rule. First, non-regulatory acts completed as a result of a complaint processing (including petitions of appeal) can be appealed to a superior tax authority or the court. Second, non-regulatory acts completed by the Federal Tax Service and the acts or omissions of its officers can only be contested in the courts.[12] Once the taxpayer has satisfied the obligatory pre-trial procedure, the taxpayer may commence a court proceeding to invalidate the non-regulatory act (or omission) of the tax authority.[13]

---

11 Article 129.4 of the TCRF.
12 Article 138 of the TCRF.
13 The procedure is described in the 'European Lawyer Reference: Tax Litigation' (pp. 367–376).

PART TWO: TAX AVOIDANCE

7. ACCEPTABLE TAX PLANNING AREAS/SUBJECTS

In the Russian tax system, tax planning can be divided into four levels:

1. **The level of economical subjects:** This level includes taxpayers who use special tax planning instruments, such as tax incentives and international jurisdictions, for tax minimization purposes.
2. **The level of the Russian Federation's subjects:** This level includes the Russian tax authority, which determines the regional tax rates and is responsible for the administration of the tax regime.
3. **The level of the Russian Federation:** This level refers to the entire Russian tax system, and focuses on the improvement of the tax system and the creation of a favorable investment climate for capital formation.
4. **International tax planning:** This level includes the international measures to regulate tax minimization instruments, such as double taxation treaties.[14]

Tax planning at the level of economical subjects is acceptable when the taxpayer complies with two main principles:

1. Fidelity and reasonableness, which means that the taxpayer's actions must be motivated by a legitimate business purpose, and not solely to minimize taxes; and
2. The prohibition against circumvention of law, which means that a taxpayer must not abuse his or her rights by formal observance of the letter of law and distortion of the logic (or spirit) of law, for the purpose of achieving an unlawful goal.[15]

The Russian tax legislation does not provide a list of legal tax planning instruments. However, according to statements made by the Ministry of Finance of the Russian Federation, as well as several court decisions, the following instruments are permissible:

- The use of the special tax regimes (eg, the unified agricultural tax, the simplified taxation system, etc.);[16]
- The use of the tax incentives established in the TCRF; and
- The use of the consolidated taxpayer regime and others.

8. DEFINING ABUSIVE TAX AVOIDANCE

In order to be acceptable under Russian tax law, tax planning activities must comply with the principles of fidelity, reasonableness and the prohibition against circumvention of law. The failure to comply with these principles may amount to abusive tax avoidance. To determine whether a transaction constitutes abusive tax avoidance, the tax authorities consider whether the transaction was completed to achieve a legitimate business purpose. The existence of a legitimate business purpose means that the taxpayer's transaction was economically reasonable, and not motivated solely by tax

14 Shestakova E.V., Approaches to tax planning, Financial Law 2013 #8, pp. 43–48.
15 The full description of this principle was formulated in the decree of the Plenum of The Higher Arbitrazh Court of the Russian Federation No. 53, dated October 12th, 2006.
16 Chapters 26.1–26.5 of the TCRF.

minimization. If the only objective underlying a taxpayer's transaction is to minimize taxes, the tax authority may conclude that the taxpayer is engaging in abusive tax avoidance and impose additional taxes and other penalties.

Tax crimes are set out in the Criminal Code of the Russian Federation (the 'CCRF'). Some examples of tax crimes under the CCRF include:

- **Evasion of taxes and/or duties payable by an individual:** This occurs when a taxpayer fails to present a tax declaration or other required documents, or knowingly includes false information in a tax declaration.[17] Evasion of taxes by an individual becomes a criminal offense where unpaid taxes amount to more than 600,000 rubles for three financial years, on the understanding that the sum of unpaid tax was not less than 10 per cent of the tax payable or more than 1,800,000 rubles. The applicable penalties range from fines to imprisonment for a maximum term of three years, depending on the amount of unpaid taxes. However, a taxpayer who is convicted of tax evasion for the first time may be discharged upon full payment of the unpaid taxes and penalties.
- **Evasion of taxes and/or duties payable by a legal entity:** This occurs when a taxpayer fails to present a tax declaration or other required documents, or knowingly includes false information in a tax declaration.[18] Evasion of taxes by a legal entity becomes a criminal offense when the unpaid taxes amount to more than 2,000,000 rubles for three financial years, on the understanding that the sum of unpaid tax was not less than 10 per cent of the tax payable or more than 6,000,000 rubles. The applicable penalties range from fines to imprisonment for a term of six years, depending on the amount of unpaid taxes and the number of persons involved in the commission of the crime. As above, a manager (the head of an organization, a general owner or other person who exercises managerial functions) of taxpayer who is convicted of tax evasion for the first time may be discharged upon full payment of the unpaid taxes and penalties by the legal entity.
- **Failure to perform the duties of a tax agent**: If a tax agent breaches his or her duties, he or she may be convicted of a criminal offense.[19] In order for the breach to constitute a criminal offense, unpaid taxes must amount to more than 2,000,000 rubles for three financial years, on the understanding that the sum of unpaid tax was not less than 10 per cent of the tax payable or more than 6,000,000 rubles. Applicable penalties range from fines to imprisonment for a term of three years, depending on the amount of unpaid taxes.
- **Concealment of monetary resources or assets with the use of which the tax would have been paid**: If the head of an organization, a general owner or other person who exercises managerial functions conceals monetary resources or assets which would otherwise

17 Article 198 of the CCRF.
18 Article 199 of the CCRF.
19 Article 199.1 of the CCRF.

have been recovered, the person may be convicted of a criminal offence.[20] In order to constitute a criminal offense, the amount of unpaid taxes must exceed 1,500,000 rubles. The applicable penalties range from fines to imprisonment for a five-year term, depending on the amount of unpaid taxes.

9. THE LEGISLATIVE FRAMEWORK

All tax incentives are enumerated in the TCRF. For example, article 149 sets out a list of operations exempted from VAT. The TCRF also regulates the use of the special tax regimes (eg, the unified agricultural tax, the simplified taxation system, etc.). Chapters 26.1–26.5 describe the persons (both individuals and organizations) who have the right to apply special tax regimes, tax rates, taxation objects and all the associated restrictive regulations. In 2012, the TCRF was amended to include a comprehensive set of rules and requirements regarding transfer pricing.

Additionally, the procedure for using the consolidated taxpayer regime is set out in the TCRF. A consolidated taxpayer is a voluntary association of taxpayers that pay corporate income tax on the basis of an agreement.[21] To form a consolidated taxpayer, members must negotiate an agreement and submit it to the tax authority with supporting documents. However, there are some organizations that are not permitted to become members of a consolidated taxpayer (eg, microfinance organizations, clearing organizations, credit consumers' cooperatives, professional securities traders, etc.).

Although the Russian tax system is largely statutory, court practice in the area of tax regulation is of crucial importance. The decisions of the Constitutional Court of the Russian Federation, the Higher Arbitrazh Court of the Russian Federation, and the Supreme Court of the Russian Federation have a significant impact on the interpretation and application of tax legislation. For example, it was court practice that introduced the main elements of fidelity and reasonableness in the Russian tax system.[22]

10. KEY CASES OF INTEREST

The term 'unjustified tax benefit' refers to the use of tax planning instruments by a taxpayer with the sole objective of minimizing his or her tax liabilities (ie, without a legitimate business purpose). Between 2002 and 2006, the Russian courts generally followed the formal principles of fidelity in rendering their decisions. If a taxpayer's contractor had any formal defect (eg, unpaid tax liabilities, insufficient employees to satisfy contractual obligations, etc.), the taxpayer could be recognized as an infidel taxpayer.[23] In 2006, the Plenum of the Higher Arbitrazh Court of the Russian Federation passed decree No. 53, dated October 12, 2006, which established the main principles for defining a tax benefit as justified or unjustified. The Court

20 Article 199.2 of the CCRF.
21 Article 25.1 of the TCRF.
22 The decree of the Plenum of the Higher Arbitrazh Court of the Russian Federation No. 53, dated October 12, 2006.
23 The companies with such characteristics are called 'one-day' firms.

held that in order to establish that a transaction is a legitimate business transaction, the taxpayer must:

- Prove that the transaction is 'real', which means that expenditures must be documented, and the transaction must exhibit a productive nature and be designed for the acquisition of income from legitimately conducted business activity; and
- Display circumspection, which requires more extensive caution than simply a routine check of the contractor's legality.[24]

Some key cases in this area include the case of 'Leasing company of small business', JSC,[25] and the case of 'Altay beacon', LLC.[26]

10.1 Current cases

In 2012, the High Arbitrazh Court of the Russian Federation tried the case of *Kama Factory of Concrete Products and Structures*.[27] The Court held that where the tax authority suspects that a taxpayer's contractor is a 'one-day' firm (ie, an infidel taxpayer) but cannot prove the absence of goods (ie, works and services), the tax authority can assess taxes on the basis of prices for identical goods. In another case where the taxpayer was engaged in tax planning using the special tax regimes, the tax authority concluded that the taxpayer had obtained an unjustified tax benefit. The Court stated that the taxpayer may dispute such a conclusion on the basis that his or her managerial decisions were not based solely on obtaining a tax benefit.[28]

10.2 Historic cases

One notable historic case is the case of *Oil Company Yukos*. In this case, the tax authority alleged that the taxpayer had engaged in artificial oil transactions for the purpose of tax avoidance. The Court found in favor of the tax authority, and ordered that the company pay 72,000,000,000 rubles in taxes owing. Additionally, the head of the company, Mikhail Khodorkovsky, was sentenced to a lengthy term of imprisonment.

Other significant cases include *Arbat Prestige* and *Yamalgazstroy*, which were decided in 2007 and 2008. In both cases, the directors were convicted of tax evasion pursuant to article 199 of the CCRF.

11. PENALTIES

11.1 Legislative provisions

If it can be established that the taxpayer has engaged in tax evasion, two types of penalties may be imposed. First, the tax authority may decide to impose additional taxes, penalties and fines. Penalties are calculated for each calendar day, beginning on the day following the statutory deadline for the payment of the tax or charge.[29] If the taxpayer has failed to pay taxes, or has failed to pay the total amount of taxes owing, a fine of 20 per cent of the

[24] The decree of Presidium of the High Arbitrazh Court of the Russian Federation No. 18162/09, dated April 20, 2010.
[25] The decree of Presidium of the High Arbitrazh Court of the Russian Federation No. 15574/09, dated March 9, 2010.
[26] The decree of Presidium of the High Arbitrazh Court of the Russian Federation No. 17684/09, dated June 8, 2010.
[27] The decree of Presidium of the High Arbitrazh Court of the Russian Federation No. 2341/12, dated July 3, 2012.
[28] The decree of Presidium of the High Arbitrazh Court of the Russian Federation No. 15570/12,dated April 9, 2013.
[29] Article 75 of the TCRF.

unpaid balance may be imposed. Second, the tax authority may initiate a criminal proceeding. The penalties for criminal prosecution range from fines to compulsory labor and imprisonment. The amount of a fine and/or the length of a term of imprisonment vary depending on the amount of unpaid taxes.

12. CURRENT TRENDS

12.1 National policy and law

One of the main tax planning trends in Russia is known as 'deoffshorization'. Deoffshorization was addressed in 'The principal directions for the tax policy of the Russian Federation for 2014 and for the planning period of 2015–2016', established by the Government of the Russian Federation on May 30, 2014. The Government proposed several amendments to the national tax legislation, including:

- The introduction of statutory provisions on controlled foreign companies to establish the Russian Federation as the state of revenue generation (see above section 8);
- Amendments to the TCRF to recognize foreign organizations whose corporate bodies are on the territory of the Russian Federation as residents of the Russian Federation for tax purposes; and,
- The introduction of a standard intergovernmental agreement on the exchange of information regarding low-tax jurisdictions.

12.2 The impact and role of the OECD and other international relations

Although the Russian Federation is not a member of the OECD, it has collaborated with the OECD since 1990. OECD publications, including the OECD Transfer Pricing Guidelines for Multinational Enterprises and Tax Administrations 2010 are very important for Russian tax policy. Section V.I of the TCRF on transfer pricing consists largely of the International Principles for Transfer Pricing issued by the OECD.

The Russian Federation is a member of the World Trade Organization, the Asia-Pacific Economic Cooperation, BRICS, the Customs Union with Belarus, Kazakhstan, and other international organizations. The customs authorities of the Russian Federation and the customs authorities of the other members of the Customs Union exchange information on customs charges, taxes and the payment of fines. This exchange of information plays a significant role in the prevention of tax evasion.

Serbia

Eurofast Anastasia Sagianni

PART ONE: TRANSFER PRICING

1. GENERAL OVERVIEW

The inclusion of transfer pricing in Serbia's domestic legislation is a recent development. The transfer pricing provisions were first introduced in 2012 in Serbia's Corporate Income Tax Law (the 'CITL'), and subsequently expanded in the Rulebook on Transfer Pricing and Arm's Length Methods Applicable to the Determination of Prices in Related Party Transactions (the 'Rulebook'). The Ministry of Finance published the Rulebook in the Official Gazette of the Republic of Serbia (no. 61/2013) on July 12, 2013. The Rulebook sets out the requirements for determining and documenting transfer prices. In general, the principles governing transfer pricing in Serbia follow the OECDTransfer Pricing Guidelines (the 'OECD Guidelines').

2. IDENTIFICATION OF LEGISLATIVE FRAMEWORK

The Rulebook establishes the transfer pricing provisions that are applicable under Serbian law. More specifically, the Rulebook determines the form and substance of transfer pricing documentation, and the selection and application of the appropriate arm's length method for determining prices in transactions between associated enterprises. The method used for determining the depreciation of an asset acquired ina transaction with an associated enterprise is set out in article 10a of the CITL. Companies and groups of companies that engage in related party transactions must comply with the arm's length principle. As a result, before applying the transfer pricing rules to a transaction, it is important to determine the structure of the company or group and any related parties. The intra-group transactions that should be documented according to the Rulebook include: product sales; product acquisitions; loans; borrowings; royalties; management fees; management services; cost-sharing within a group; research and development activities; and the provision and use of other services.

(a) Transfer pricing documentation and choice of appropriate method

A full transfer pricing study must include the following parts:

1 Analysis of the associated enterprises and the taxpayer;
2. Industry analysis of the taxpayer;
3. Functional analysis;
4. Selection of the most appropriate transfer pricing method;
5. Conclusion; and

6. Appendices.

The taxpayer should select a method or a combination of methods from those described in the OECD Guidelines, and should state the reasons for selecting the particular method or combination. This is necessary for the purposes of reconciling transfer prices with the arm's length principle in transactions between associated enterprises. The taxpayer should choose one or a combination of the following methods:

- The Comparable Uncontrolled Price ('CUP') Method;
- The Resale Price Method;
- The Cost Plus Method;
- The Transactional Net Margin Method ('TNMM'); or,
- The Profit Split Method.

(b) Method for determining the depreciation of assets acquired in transactions with associated enterprises

When a fixed asset subject to article 10a of the CITL is acquired in a related party transaction in accordance with article 59 of the CITL, the basis for its deprecation will be determined as the lesser of:

1. The transfer price, in accordance with article 59 of the CITL; or
2. The acquiring price, as determined by the arm's length principle in accordance with articles 60 and 61 of the CITL.[1]

2.1 Federal legislation

In Serbia, there is no distinction between provincial and federal legislation.

2.2 State and provincial legislative interplay

Not applicable.

2.3 International treaties and agreements

Serbia has entered into several bilateral treaties relating to income and capital. In general, Serbian tax treaties follow the OECD Model Tax Convention. Accordingly, Serbian treaties typically contain an article entitled 'Associated Enterprises' (article 9), which sets out the circumstances under which parties are deemed to be related.[2] This article also provides for the adjustment of profits in transactions entered into between associated enterprises on non-arm's length terms. Additionally, Serbian treaties often include a procedural clause entitled 'Mutual Agreement Procedure' (article 26), which sets out the procedure that must be followed by the contracting states to resolve any disputes that arise under the treaty. For example, in the case of a dispute relating to transfer pricing adjustments that result in double taxation, the Convention authorises the competent authorities to resolve the dispute by mutual agreement. The Convention also authorizes the contracting states to consult with each other to eliminatethe double taxation. In addition, article 27, which is often included in Serbian

1 Article 6 of the Rulebook.
2 OECD Income and Capital Model Convention and Commentary (2010).

tax treaties, provides for the exchange of information between the tax authorities of the contracting states. The provisions of this article also facilitate tax audits and the collection of taxes. However, the article provides that contracting states are not required to go beyond their domestic laws to gather information for the other state.

In general, benefits under a tax treaty are only available to persons or entities that are qualified residents of one of the contracting states. Most treaties offer a reduction in the withholding tax rate for dividends, interest and royalties received by a person or entity resident in a country under the treaty. While tax treaties do not usually affect federal and municipal taxes, tax audits in Serbia are affected by tax treaties. In the event of a conflict with domestic legislation, the provisions of the relevant treaty will prevail.

In order to determine which international agreements or treaties have the greatest impact in Serbia, we focused our analysis on foreign direct investment ('FDI') in Serbia, as well as investments by Serbian investors (institutional or otherwise) abroad, for the preceding 5 years.[3] As indicated by the table below, investments from the Netherlands, Luxembourg, Austria, Italy, and the Russian Federation account for the majority of FDI in Serbia. Moreover, the leading countries for FDI outflows are Bosnia and Herzegovina, Slovenia, Montenegro, Albania and the United Kingdom.

2008 - 2012 FDI flows in Serbia (millions of U.S. $)

Countries	2008	2009	2010	2011	2012	5 - year Average
Netherlands	543	251	272	336	4	281,2
Luxembourg	78	8	9	1130	84	261,8
Austria	476	323	194	217	71	256,2
Italy	484	239	54	182	92	210,2
Russian Federation	30	560	5	70	19	136,8
Switzerland	123	86	71	80	97	91,4
Croatia	141	27	55	29	156	81,6
Germany	88	58	46	106	58	71,2
Slovenia	113	56	129	-95	96	59,8
France	78	7	22	155	17	55,8
Cyprus	63	41	71	61	29	53
UK	18	73	78	42	51	52,4
U.S.A.	54	18	77	33	34	43,2
Hungary	31	26	21	94	12	36,8
Spain	17	9	19	70	19	26,8
Bosnia and Herzegovina	31	8	14	17	8	15,6
Montenegro	44	10	2	10	4	14
Greece	49	66	34	14	-378	-43

Source : UNCTAD FDI/TNC database, based on data from the National Bank of Serbia

Note that the negative value indicated for Greece is related to divestment.[4]

[3] *http://unctad.org/Sections/dite_fdistat/docs/webdiaeia2014d3_SRB.pdf.*

[4] Divestment refers to the sale of an asset for financial, legal or personal reasons. For corporations, divestment can refer to a company selling off a portion of its assets, such as a subsidiary, to raise capital or to focus the business

Serbia - Treaty Withholding Rates Table

	Dividends		Interest[1]	Royalties
	Individuals, companies	Qualifying companies[2]		
	(%)	(%)	(%)	(%)
Domestic Rates				
Companies:	20/25	20	0/20/25	20/25
Individuals:	15	n/a	0/15	20
Treaty Rates				
Treaty With:				
Albania	15	5	10	10
Austria	15	5	10	5/10[3]
Azerbaijan	10	10	10	10
Belarus[4]	15	5	8	10
Belgium	15	10	15	10
Bosnia and Herzegovina	10	5	10	10
Bulgaria	15	5	10	10
Canada	15	5	5	10
China (People's Rep.)	5	5	10	10
Croatia	10	5	10	10
Cyprus	10	10	10	10
Czech Republic	10	10	10	5/10[5]
Denmark	15	5	0	10
Egypt	15	5	15	15
Estonia	10	5	10	5/10
Finland	15	5	0	10
France	15	5	0	0
Germany	15	15	0	10
Georgia	10	5	10	10
Greece	15	5	10	10
Hungary	15	5	10	10
India	15	5	10	10
Iran	10	10	10	10
Ireland	10	5	10	5/10
Italy	10	10	10	10
Korea (Dem. People's Rep.)	10	10	10	10
Kuwait	10	5	10	10
Latvia	10	5	10	5/10
Libya	10	5	10	10
Lithuania	10	5	10	10
Macedonia (FYR)	15	5	10	10
Malaysia	–[6]	–	10	10
Malta	10	5	10	5/10
Moldova	15	5	10	10
Montenegro	10	10	10	5/10
Netherlands	15	5	0	10
Norway	15	15	0	10
Pakistan	10	10	10	10
Poland	15	5	10	10
Qatar	10	5	10	10
Romania	10	10	10	10
Russia	15	5[7]	10	10
Slovak Republic	15	5	10	10
Slovenia	10	5	10	5/10
Spain	10	5	10	5/10
Sri Lanka	12.5	12.5	10	10
Sweden	15	5	0	0
Switzerland	15	5[8]	10	0/10[9]
Tunisia	10	10	10	10
Turkey	15	5	10	10
Ukraine	10	5	10	10
United Arab Emirates	10	5[10]	10[11]	10
United Kingdom	15	5	10	10
Vietnam	15	10	10	10

on a smaller core of goods and services. For investors, divestment can be used as a social tool to protest particular corporate policies, such as a company trading with a country known for child labor abuses. Divestment can also be required of companies by the Federal Trade Commission in order to have a merger approved. A famous example of this is the breakup of Bell System (Ma Bell) into AT&T and the Baby Bells in 1984.

Based on this analysis, treaties entered into by Serbia with its major trading partners are of critical importance to Serbia.

Remarks[5]

1. Many treaties provide for an exemption for certain types of interest, eg, interest paid to the state, local authorities, the central bank, export credit institutions or in relation to sales on credit. Such exemptions are not considered in this column.
2. Unless stated otherwise, the reduced treaty ratesgiven in this column generally apply if the recipient company holds directly or indirectly at least 25 per cent of the capital or voting power in the Serbian company.
3. The lower rate applies to copyright royalties, including films, etc.
4. The tax treaty concluded by the former Socialist Federal Republic of Yugoslavia or by the Federal Republic of Yugoslavia. The other treaties listed were concluded by Serbia or previously by the state union of Serbia and Montenegro. Serbia continues to honorthese treaties.
5. The lower rate applies to copyright royalties, excluding computer software, but including films, etc.
6. The domestic rate applies so that there is no reduction under the treaty.
7. The reduced rate applies if the beneficial owner is a company that holds directly at least 25 per cent of the capital of the dividend-paying company, and has invested at least $100,000.
8. This rate applies if the Swiss company owns at least 20 per cent of the capital in the dividend-paying company.
9. The zero rate applies as long as Switzerland does not, according to its domestic law, levy a withholding tax on royalties paid to non-residents.
10. This rate applies in cases where the beneficial owner is a company which holds directly at least 5 per cent of the capital of the Serbian company. Under the protocol, a null rate applies if the beneficial owner of the dividends is a sovereign wealth fund listed in that protocol.
11. Under the protocol, a null rate applies if the beneficial owner of the interest is a sovereign wealth fund listed in that protocol.

3. NATIONAL POLICY ISSUES

The Serbian tax authorities have increased their focus on transfer pricing audits. However, their practical experience in this field remains limited. This is evident from the recent amendments to the CITL and the publication of the Rulebook, which provide guidance on various issues related to transfer pricing. The Rulebook sets out the documentation requirements and the methods that may be used to determine transfer prices. Additionally, the Serbian tax authorities continue to provide clarification on the interpretation of the Rulebook, and regularly enact simplified procedures to ensure that all transactions captured by the transfer pricing legislation are appropriately documented.

[5] IBFD Portal.

Transfer pricing has become a main priority for the Serbian tax authorities. As such, it is one of the most significant issues facing multinationals operating in Serbia. In particular, where a taxpayer makes a large deductible payment, such as interest payments, royalties, and payments for services, or where the profitability of a local entity is inconsistent with what might be expected from a similar taxpayer, there is a high likelihood of an audit by the tax authorities. Transactions between companies based in Serbia, or a company with a permanent establishment in Serbia, and an entity operating in a jurisdiction with a preferential tax system would also increase the likelihood of a tax audit.

3.1 Overall national policy announcements

According to article 2 of the Rulebook, a taxpayer must submit transfer pricing documentation in the form of a report with its tax balance/fiscal sheet. Amendments to the Rulebookwere published in the Official Gazette of the Republic of Serbia (no. 8/2014) onJanuary 29, 2014. Generally, these amendments simplified the documentation requirements for transactions that do not have a material impact on the tax liability of the taxpayer. Thus, taxpayers that fall within this exception may submit an abbreviated report that does not include a detailed analysis of whether the transfer prices used comply with the provisions of the arm's length principle.In order to fall within the scope of this exception, at least one of the following two conditions must be met:

1. The transaction with an associated person is the only transaction with that associated person during the tax period covered by the tax balance, and the value of the transaction is not higher than 8,000,000 dinars (approximately EUR 70,000), as determined by VAT Law as the annual turnover requirement for VAT registration; or
2. The total value of all transactions with an associated person during the tax period covered by the tax balance is not higher than 8,000,000 dinars (approximately EUR 70,000), as determined by VAT Law as the annual turnover requirement for VAT registration.

However, these conditions are not applicable to loan or credit transactions, which must be analyzed in accordance with the rules prescribed by the CITL.The simplified report should contain:

1. A description of the transaction;
2. The value of the transaction; and
3. The associated person with whom the transaction was entered into.

3.2 National revenue authority initiatives

Since 2014 is the first year that transfer pricing legislation has been implemented in Serbia, taxpayers have not yet been subject to tax audits related to transfer pricingissues. However, taxpayers will be audited for their total tax liabilities according to the Tax Audit Procedures in the Republic of Serbia. Additionally, it is important to note that Advance Pricing Arrangements ('APAs') and advance rulings in Serbia are not currently available, nor is there any guidance on their future implementation.

3.3 Administrative statements

Not applicable.

3.4 Administrative guidelines

The Serbian tax authorities are entitled to conduct an audit of the taxpayer's accounting records and tax returns, unless the assessment orcollection is barred by the statute of limitations. As part of an audit, the tax authorities may recalculate the taxpayer's tax returns, verify accounting records, and reassess withholding taxes. The Director of Tax Administration prepares the annual plan of tax audits. The tax authorities should inform the taxpayer when a tax audit is being conducted. However, if an entity or individual is engaged in unregistered activities, the tax authorities may commence an audit without notice.Following the assessment, the department of tax administration will issue a decision ordering the taxpayer to register its activities, rectify any inconsistencies with the law, and pay the assessed amount.

If a major market breach has occurred or there are indicators of illegal activity, the Minister of Finance may enact a special plan that does not require notice of the audit. The tax inspectors may visit the taxpayer's headquarters and obtain access to any documents relevant to the tax assessment. The tax inspectors may also require statements from the taxpayer's employees, or other evidence that is deemed relevant to the tax assessment. Within 3 days of the completion of the audit, the tax authorities must provide the taxpayer with a report summarizing their findings. The taxpayer may object to the findings contained in the report within 5 days of receiving the report. The tax authorities must also issue a final decision based on the findings summarized in the report within 60 days. If the taxpayer does not rectify all violations within the prescribed time, the tax authorities may (i) block the taxpayer's bank account; (ii) prohibit the taxpayer from carrying on business activities and disposing of assets; and (iii) issue an order to the Centre for Collection of the National Bank of Serbia to transfer funds from the taxpayer's account to the public revenues account.

4. CASE LAW

Not applicable.

4.1 Current cases

Not applicable.

4.2 Historical cases of note

Not applicable.

5. PENALTIES

According to article 112 of the CITL, a penalty of 100,000 to 2,000,000 dinars must be imposed for the following offences:

- Failure to declare the value of transactions conducted with associated persons in accordance with the arm's length principle separately in the tax account (article 60);
- Failure to submit an income statement, balance sheet or other prescribed documents to the tax office (article 63, paragraph 2);
- Failure to submit the fiscal balance sheet within the prescribed time, submitting an inaccurate balance sheet with the effect of reducing the tax base, or using tax incentives that would otherwise not be permitted (articles 34, 63, 65 and 70);
- If the taxpayer is a start-up business, the failure to submit estimates of income, expenditures and profits for the fiscal year (article 64, paragraph 2);
- Failure to pay the monthly advance within the prescribed time(article 67, paragraph 2 and 3, and article 68, paragraph 2);
- Failure to pay the difference between the amount of tax calculated in the tax declaration and the amount paid in monthly tax advances within the prescribed time (article 38, paragraph 5 and article 66, paragraphs 2 and 3);
- Failure to make a timely payment of the tax amount pursuant to the decision of the competent tax office (article70a, paragraph 2).
- Failure to submit the documentation required by article 60 within the timeframe defined by the notice (article 112a).

Any director or individual responsible for the taxpayer must also be fined between 10,000 and 100,000 dinars for any of the offences mentioned above.

5.1 Types

If the taxpayer fails to submit the required transfer pricing documentation, or if the transfer pricing documentation is incomplete, the tax authorities will issue a notice requesting that the taxpayer file proper documentation within 30 to 90 days.[6]The failure to submit the necessary documentation within the specified period may expose the taxpayer to the following penalties:

- The legal entity may be fined between 100,000 and 2,000,000 dinars;
- The person responsible for the legal entity may be fined between 10,000 and 100,000 dinars;
- A corporate income tax of 15 per centmay be calculated on the difference between the arm's length price and the price used in the related party transaction;
- Interest may be charged on the amount of corporate income tax that is withheld, at a rate that is 10 per cent higher than the annual reference rate of the National Bank of Serbia; and
- The taxpayer may be prohibited from carrying on a specific business activity for a period of 3 months to 1 year.

6 Article 112 of the CITL.

5.2 Special or notable cases

Not applicable.

6. DISPUTE RESOLUTION MECHANISMS

According to a report issued by the Organization for Security and Co-operation in Europe (the 'OSCE'), the first set of judicial laws in post-Socialist Serbia was adopted in 2001. In December 2008, Parliament approved a new set of judicial laws, which came into force on January 1, 2010. These laws govern the organization and territorial jurisdiction of the courts, as well as the High Court Council, judges, public prosecution, the State Prosecutorial Council and the Public Prosecutor's Office. Pursuant to a proposal issued by the Ministry of Justice and Public Administration, the Government of the Republic of Serbia passed Resolution No. 700-6579/2013 on July 31, 2013. This Resolution focused on the implementation of the National Judicial Reform Strategy for the 2013–2018 period. As a result, further substantial amendments are anticipated.The chart below illustrates the structure of the court system in Serbia.

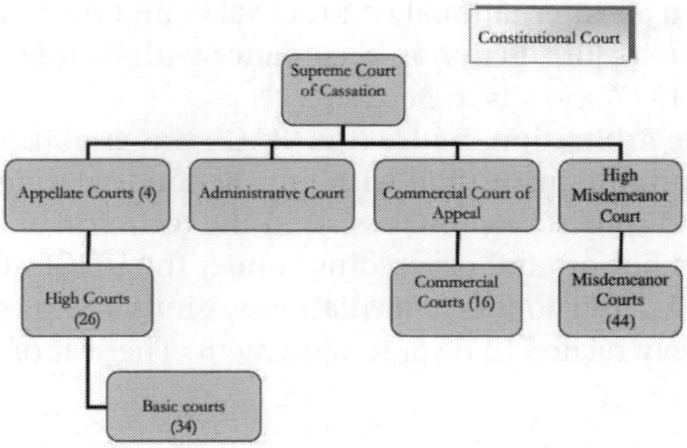

Source: Organization for Security and Co-operation in Europe (OSCE)/Serbia, 2011

Generally, commercial entities prefer to settle their disputes outside the court system. Although there are several methods of alternative dispute resolution available in Serbia, mediation and arbitration are the only two methods that have been regulated by law.

6.1 Preferred national options

Although Serbia has not yet developed alternative dispute resolution methods designed specifically for transfer pricing issues, there are several existing methods that may be applicable.

(a) Arbitration

The parties may enter into an arbitration agreement to refer future disputes or disputes arising out of an existing legal relationship to an arbitral tribunal. Arbitral proceedings are governed by the Law on Arbitration, which is based on the UNCITRAL Model Law on International Commercial Arbitration.[7]

7 Official Gazette of the RS No 46/06.

The application of the Arbitration Act must be without prejudice to a ratified international treaty. In the event of an international dispute, the parties may agree to the application of foreign law in the arbitral proceedings. Further, arbitrators in international disputes must be nationals of third-party states, in order to ensure neutrality and impartiality. Since Serbia is a state party to the New York Convention on Recognition and Enforcement of Foreign Arbitral Awards, the decisions rendered by tribunals in Serbia maybe enforced in many countries around the world. Some examples of arbitral bodies in Serbia have been listed below.

- The Permanent Court of Arbitration at the Chamber of Commerce and Industry of Serbia is a permanent arbitral institution administering cases in accordance with the applicable laws, the Statute of the Chamber of Commerce and Industry of Serbia and its rules. The Permanent Court of Arbitration has jurisdiction to resolve domestic commercial disputes and other property disputes.
- The Foreign Trade Court of Arbitration (the 'FTCA') is a permanent arbitral body that provides conciliation and arbitration services for disputes with an international commercial component. The parties must agree to its jurisdiction in accordance with its rules.[8] The FTCA was founded in 1947 and sits in Belgrade.
- The Belgrade Arbitration Centre (the 'BAC') was established in 2013 as a permanent arbitral institution with jurisdiction to decide both domestic and foreign disputes. The BAC assists in the technical and administrative aspects of ad hoc arbitral proceedings under the UNCITRAL or other rules. The BAC also conducts mediation sessions and provides other services closely related to dispute settlement. The seat of the BAC is also in Belgrade.

(b) Mediation

Over the past 15 years, mediation has become a popular method of dispute resolution in Serbia. The first mediation programs in Serbia were introduced in 2000. These programs were implemented through cooperation between the Nansen Dialogue Centre of Serbia and the Norwegian government in various sectors, including the courts (court mediation), the local community (community mediation), and the educational system (coeval mediation). Large international organizations supported these mediation initiatives by providing technical support and training to mediators. In 2002, mediation was recognized as an effective method to reduce the number of cases that go to court.

The Serbian Parliament passed the Law on Mediation in 2005.[9] According to the Law on Mediation, a dispute may be resolved through mediation unless the law gives the court exclusive authority to decide the issue. Mediation may be used before or after the initiation of court proceedings, or independentlyfrom any formal proceedings. As mentioned above,

8 The Rules of the Foreign Trade Court of Arbitration Attached to the Serbian Chamber of Commerce, Official Gazette of the RS No 52/07.

9 Official Gazette of RS No 18/05.

mediation is legally regulated in Serbia. The main advantages of mediation, as compared to arbitration or litigation, include:

- The role of the mediator, which is to assist the parties in identifying their interests (rather than their rights), and to create mutual agreement;
- The mediation process must not exceed 30 days; and
- The cost of mediation is only a fraction of the cost of arbitration or litigation.

6.2 International options

Generally, the bilateral agreements entered into by Serbia include a 'Mutual Agreement Procedure' article (article 26), which sets out the procedure that must be followed by the contracting states to resolve disputes. The Convention authorizes the competent authorities of each state to resolve the dispute by mutual agreement.

PART TWO: TAX AVOIDANCE

7. ACCEPTABLE TAX PLANNING AREAS/SUBJECTS

Tax planning refers to the strategies used bytaxpayers to arrange their financial affairs to minimize their tax liabilities. Similarly, tax avoidance refers to the activities undertaken by taxpayers to reduce taxes within the confines of the law, such as using tax deductions or incorporating a company in an offshore jurisdiction. On the other hand, misinterpreting or falsifying information in order to reduce taxes is tax evasion. The interplay between tax planning and tax avoidance has been a point of contention between taxpayers, the tax authorities and the courts. Taxpayers in Serbia may seek to reduce their tax obligations through tax planning and tax avoidance practices. However, these practices must comply with the CITL and the general anti-avoidance rule of 'substance over form'.

8. DEFINING ABUSIVE TAX AVOIDANCE

In Serbia, the doctrine of abusive tax avoidance is applied very broadly. However, the judicial anti-avoidance doctrine in taxation law is less developed than in other areas, such as contract law and property law. Tax avoidance may be identified using the business purpose test, the benefit test or the sham transaction test. The general anti-avoidance rule is characterized by the doctrine of substance over form, as described in the Law on Tax Procedure and Tax Administration.[10] In particular, article 9 states that taxes shall be determined in accordance with their economic substance.

9. THE LEGISLATIVE FRAMEWORK

In addition to the doctrine of substance over form, the provisions of the Rulebook areaffected by articles 10a, 59, 60, 61 and 62 of the CITL (Official Herald no. 25/01...108/13).The arm's length principle is applicable to all related party transactions, including those between a foreign entity and

[10] Article 9 of the Law on Tax Procedures and Tax Administration.

its Serbian permanent establishment. As a result, companies and groups of companies that engage in related party transactions are greatly impacted by thetransfer pricing rules.

(a) Definition of related party

A party is related to another party if it is possible for the party to exercise control or considerable influence over the business decisions of the other party. A party will be deemed to have control over the business decisions of another party if it owns, directly or indirectly, 25 per cent of the shares of the other party. In addition, companies will be deemed to be related parties where the same persons own, manage or control both companies, directly or indirectly. Further, any company that is a resident of a jurisdiction with a preferential tax system is deemed to be a related party regardless of the percentage of ownership or voting rights in a Serbian company.

(b) Transfer pricing methods

The taxpayer should select a method or a combination of methods from those described in the Guidelines. The taxpayer should also state the reasons for the method(s) used, and reconcile transfer prices with the arm's length principle for transactions between associated enterprises. When an entity cannot use its own data regarding comparable transactions, it is preferable that data relevant to the Republic of Serbia be used. In the event that this is not possible, the entity may extend its analysis to other countries with comparable market conditions.

(c) Statute of limitations on transfer pricing adjustments

There is no special statute of limitations for transfer pricing adjustments. The limitation period for a tax audit is 5 years, beginning on the first day of the year following the year in which the taxes became payable. Accordingly, inappropriate documentation for transactions conducted in 2013 may be penalized until 2019. The absolute limitation period is 10 years.

(d) Loans and credits

The Minister of Finance is entitled to set the arm's length rates of interest. These interest rates apply to loans and credits between associated persons. The taxpayer may apply general rules for establishing an arm's length interest rate instead of accepting the rates set by the Minister. However, the taxpayer is obliged to apply the same general rules to all loans and creditsbetween associated persons.

(e) Thin capitalization rule

Article 62 of the CITL provides that in loans or credits between associated legal entities, the amount of interest and other expenses related to the loan or credit that is deductible for tax purposes must not exceed a debt-to-equity ratio of 4:1. The debt-to-equity ratio applicable to banks or other lending institutions is 10:1.

(f) Payments to residents of preferential tax regimes

On December 26, 2012, anew withholding tax regime was introduced in Serbia.[11] In the absence of a tax treaty, Serbia imposes a withholding tax rate of 20 per cent on payments of certain types of income, including dividends, interest (excluding interest on government bonds), royalties and rental income to non-resident entities. According to the new withholding tax regime, a 25 per cent withholding tax rate applies to certain income payable to non-resident companies that have their place of management in tax havens (or so-called 'preferential tax regimes'). The Ministry of Finance published a list of 51 jurisdictions considered to have a preferential tax regime. The items that are subject to the increased withholding tax rate of 25 per cent include: payments of interest, royalties, rental income and service fees. This new tax also applies to payments made to permanent establishments in Serbia from entities resident in preferential tax regimes.

10. KEY CASES OF INTEREST

Cases involving tax avoidance often arise when an individual seeks to change their tax residency to a jurisdiction that has a lower income tax rate (eg, the Cayman Islands). For the purposes of tax avoidance, it is not necessary to transfer assets or capital to tax havens. Rather, an individual can use business transactions to transfer income to jurisdictions with a lower tax rate. Serbia's tax regime is currently in a transitional stage, with several amendments being introduced to prevent tax evasion. Additionally, the developments in domestic legislation relating to general anti-avoidance regulations and transfer pricing are still preliminary. As a result, there are currently no cases in this area.

10.1 Current cases

Not applicable.

10.2 Key historical cases

Not applicable.

11. PENALTIES

Article 112(5)of the CITL sets out the penalties for violations of the tax laws. There are no specific penalties for the general anti-avoidance rule.

11.1 Legislative provisions

Not applicable.

11.2 Examples of penalties imposed

Not applicable.

---

11 Annual International Bar Association Conference 2013, Boston, Massachusetts, 'Recent Developments in International and Domestic Taxation, Serbia'.

12. CURRENT TRENDS

The Serbian government is committed to economic and financial reforms aimed at increasing government revenues and reducing Serbia's budget deficit. One mechanism to increase government revenues is higher taxes. It is estimated that the Serbian government loses between EUR 850,000,000 and 1,000,000,000 annually due to tax evasion. As a result, the Serbian tax authorities and the Ministry of Finance have sought to align the Serbian tax system with EU standards and policies. Additionally, the tax authorities have focused on enhancing transparency and increasing compliance in order to achieve the government's tax revenue potential. In particular, Serbia has taken important steps to introduce general anti-avoidance provisions in its domestic tax legislation. Current trends also suggest that international cooperation is necessary in order to effectively prevent aggressive tax avoidance and tax evasion.

12.1 National policy and law

Serbia has aimed to achieve harmonization between its domestic legislation and the EU policies on tax avoidance. Serbia's transfer pricing legislation is consistent with the OECD Guidelines. However, the OECD has released several more recent draft papers on transfer pricing issues, and several consultations have taken place. As a result, new guidelines will likely be released at the end of 2014. It is expected that the Republic of Serbia will make necessary changes to its domestic legislation at that time.

12.1.1 The impact and role of the OECD and other international relations

Currently, transfer pricing is one of the most significant tax issues facing multinational enterprises. Multinationals attempt to reduce their worldwide tax liability through transfer prices by transferring profits from high-tax jurisdictions to low-tax jurisdictions by under- or over-charging the associated entity in an intra-group trade. In addition, multinationals attempt to maximize their tax benefits through intra-group tax losses. Conversely, tax authorities around the world have been adopting various measures to protect and maintain their tax revenues.

In February 2013, the OECD released a report on Base Erosion and Profit Shifting ('BEPS'). This report stated that multinational enterprises are often able to artificially separate their taxable profits from the jurisdiction in which those profits arose, thereby reducing the corporate income tax paid in the jurisdictions where they operate. In addition to the detrimental impact on government tax revenues, such activities have a negative impact on competition, distort investment decisions, and reduce confidence in the tax system. The OECD's work on BEPS aims to create new international tax rules for attributing income.

The introduction of the transfer pricing rules in Serbia has generated tremendous interest in issues related to transfer pricing. However, both the tax authorities and the taxpayers require an adjustment period for the application of the new regulations. Based on comments published in the 'Discussion Draft on Transfer Pricing Documentation and CbC Reporting', one potentially valuable amendment to the Serbian legislation would be to change the language for transfer pricing documentation to a commonly used language, such as English. This would reduce the high translation costs incurred by multinationals in every jurisdiction in which they operate. Additionally, Serbian legislation should be amended to eliminate the requirement that transfer pricing documentation be submitted to the local tax authorities. Instead, the transfer pricing study should only be provided to the tax authorities at the business's headquarters, either on request or as part of a regular tax audit. This would reduce the risk of leakage of commercially sensitive information.

Other sources

Barnhouse N, Booth A, Wester K (2013) 'Transfer pricing'.
OECD (2010), 'Transfer Pricing Guidelines for Multinational Enterprises and Tax Administrations'.
http://www.bloomberg.com/news/2013-06-04/bermuda-with-ireland-targets-of-tax-vigilantes-minister-says.html.
Saul Estrin and Milica Uvalic, 'Foreign direct investment into transition economies: Are the Balkans different?', LEQS Paper No. 64/2013, July 2013.
Alternative Dispute Resolution Workshop, Workshop Report, 6 January 2000, The World Bank.
http://siteresources.worldbank.org/INTLAWJUSTINST/Resources/ADRWorkshop.pdf.

Spain

SWAN Partners José Oltra

PART ONE: TRANSFER PRICING

1. GENERAL OVERVIEW

The Spanish Government approved the Law 36/2006 on Measures for Preventing Tax Fraud that modified the article 16 of the Corporate Income Tax Act by adding the basic regulations concerning transfer pricing in Spain.

The new text introduced the general obligation to apply the arm's length principle to all transactions carried out between related parties, either domestic or cross border. Thereby, moving the burden of proof to the taxpayer and establishing a specific penalty regime.

2. IDENTIFICATION OF LEGISLATIVE FRAMEWORK

2.1 Federal legislation

Current legislation for transfer pricing in Spain is set out in the Royal Decree 1793/2008, which refers to all transactions undertaken between individuals or corporate taxpayers belonging to the same group. This includes transactions between shareholders' company or directors.

The rules are also applicable in the case of sale of goods, supply of services or even in other transactions such as loan interests, salaries and so on.

Moreover, the rules are applicable not only to commercial transactions carried out between resident and non-resident companies, but also to transactions carried out between domestic companies or their shareholders, directors and their relatives.

Parties are considered as related in the following situations:

(a) A company and its members;
(b) A company and its directors or administrators;
(c) A company and the spouses or persons linked to the members, directors or administrators by familiar relationship, in direct ascending, descending or collateral line, by consanguinity or affinity up to the third grade;
(d) Two companies which, in accordance with the provisions of article 42 of the Commercial Code, meet the requirements to form part of a single group of companies;
(e) A company and the members of another company, when both companies belong the same group of companies as defined in article 42 of the Commercial Code;
(f) A company and the directors or administrators of another company, when both companies belong to the same group of companies as defined in article 42 of the Commercial Code;

(g) A company and the spouses or persons linked by familiar relationship -in direct ascending, descending or collateral line, by consanguinity or affinity up to the third grade of the members or of another company, when both companies belong to the same group of the companies as defined in article 42 of the Commercial Code;
(h) Two companies, when one of them indirectly holds at least 25 per cent of the capital stock of the other;
(i) Two companies, in which the same members or their spouses or persons linked by familial relationship in direct ascending, descending or collateral line, by consanguinity or affinity up to the third grade hold, directly or indirectly, at least 25 per cent of the capital stock;
(j) A company resident in Spanish territory and its permanent establishments abroad;
(k) A company resident abroad and its permanent establishments in Spain; or
(l) Two entities which form part of a group which is taxed under the cooperative society group regime.

When the relationship is defined in accordance with the member-company relationship, the interest held must be equal to or greater than 5 per cent.[1]

Likewise, it is important to state that, for Spanish Mercantile purposes, a group of companies exists when a company has (or is able to have), directly or indirectly, the control of another company or some others. Particularly, control will be presumed where there exists a first company – called the 'dominant company' – and a second company who is dependent on the dominant company – called the 'dependent company'. The following are some examples where this dependence can be presumed, when the first company,

(1) controls the majority of voting rights;[2]
(2) has the power to appoint or dismiss the majority of the members of the board of directors;
(3) holds, as a result of agreements reached with third parties, a majority of the voting rights;
(4) has appointed, with its votes, the majority of the members of the board of directors who hold their post at the moment when the consolidated accounts have to be formulated and for the two financial years immediately preceding. In particular, this circumstance will be presumed when the majority of the members of the board of directors of the dependent company are members of the board of directors or senior managers of the dominant company or another dominated by it.

[1] 1 per cent in the case of securities listed on an organized secondary market.

[2] To the voting rights of the dominant entity we must add those it may hold through other dependent companies or through persons acting on their own behalf but working for the dominant entity or other dependent entities or those it may hold by agreement with any other person.

2.2 State and provincial legislative interplay

Spanish Transfer Pricing legislation is ruled by the Central Government, so there is no specific provincial legislation applicable in this case.

2.3 International treaties and agreements

Spanish Transfer Pricing legislation explicitly endorses the application of the OECD Transfer Pricing Guidelines and those of the European Union Joint Transfer Pricing Forum.

Likewise, where the related party is a non-resident company within the EU, the provisions of the Arbitration Convention relating to the elimination of double taxation[3] may be applied.

3. NATIONAL POLICY ISSUES

3.1 Overall national policy announcements

The measures approved a few years ago in order to ensure the effectiveness of the tax audit process and combat tax fraud, have been focused on international related party transactions and unrelated party transactions that involve tax havens.

Spanish Tax Authorities have been constantly increasing their technical tools, information and resources in order to ensure the control of the application of the arm's length principle on related party transactions.

Review of taxpayer's transfer pricing documentation is currently being considered as a standard part of a tax audit. Tax audits are used to start assessing the formal compliance of the transfer pricing compulsory documentation. The audits verify, for instance, whether all the requirements set out in the legislation are fulfilled.

The principal issues previously reviewed by Spanish tax inspectors used to be the valuation of substance behind intangible transactions, the reality behind management services rendered between related companies or even remuneration paid to members of the Board.

3.2 National revenue authorities initiatives

Spanish transfer pricing audit activity is putting special attention on management fees treatment and royalties. Moreover, Spanish Tax Authorities are sensitive to 'business restructuring' and when involved in these kinds of transactions, tend to assert that a permanent establishment of a foreign party has been transferred.

From a management fees point of view, Spanish Tax Authorities normally demand a strong application of the rational and continuous cost-allocation criteria, as well as actual evidence of the benefits received from the management services.

3 Directive 90/436 of the European Commision

3.3 Administrative statements

According to the Spanish legislation, a taxpayer must draw up concrete documentation in order to be able to prove his efforts respecting the arm's length principle, such as:

- A description of the activity;
- The structure of the organization;
- The ownership relationships within the multinational group;
- The level of sales and the operating results in the years preceding the transaction; and
- The level of the transactions undertaken by the taxpayer with the foreign associated company, for example the level of sales of stock inventories, the supply of services, the rent of tangible goods, the use and transfer of intangible goods and interest on loans.

According to that statement, at the time that transfer pricing is established, taxpayers should make reasonable efforts to determine whether the transfer pricing is appropriate for tax purposes in accordance with the arm's length principle. Spanish Tax Authorities have the right to obtain the documentation prepared or referred to in this process as a means of verifying the compliance with the arm's length principle.

The 'master file' is the documentation related to the group of companies to which the taxpayer belongs and should include the following:[4]

- Description of the organisational, legal and operational structure of the group;
- Description of any major changes in that structure;
- Identification of the different entities of the group that carry out operations with the taxpayer;
- Description of those operations (nature, amounts and flows;
- Description of the functions exercised and the risks assumed by the different entities of the group insofar as they affect the operations performed by the taxpayer;
- Description of any changes in those functions and risks from the previous period;
- List of ownership of patents, trademarks and other intangible assets insofar as they affect the taxpayer;
- Amount of the considerations derived from the use of those intangibles;
- Description of group policy on transfer pricing;
- Description of the method or methods adopted by the group, justifying their adaptation to the arm's length principle;
- List of the cost sharing agreements among entities of the group insofar as they affect the taxpayer;
- List of the supply of services contracts among entities of the group insofar as they affect the taxpayer;
- List of the advanced price agreements or friendly procedures held, or that are under way, concerning the entities of the group that may affect the taxpayer; and

[4] All that for the tax period in which the taxpayer has carried out related operations.

- The group report or, failing that, the equivalent annual report.

This documentation, referred to the whole group, may be prepared and kept by the dominant company, except for those non-residents in Spain, in which case a resident group company must be appointed so as to keep the documents.

Notwithstanding the aforementioned, if he is required to do so, the taxpayer is obliged to provide the Tax Authorities with the documents referring to the group he belongs to.

Obviously, when the relationship between one or more companies is different from that defined as a 'group of companies' according to article 42 of the Commercial Code, documentation related to a 'master file' does not have to be prepared.

The 'specific file' is the documentation regarding the taxpayer and includes the following:[5]

- General data of the taxpayer and related persons or entities with which he performs operations;
- Name and surname or entity name;
- Fiscal residence;
- Tax Identity Number (VAT number);
- Detailed description of the operations carried out (nature, characteristics and amount);
- In the case of transactions made with individuals or entities in countries or territories considered as 'Tax Havens', the identity of people acting in the transaction on behalf of the individual or company must be detailed as complementary information. If they are companies, their administrators must be identified;
- Comparability analysis;
- Chosen method of assessment;
- Explanation related to the selection of the chosen method;
- Description of the reasons that justify the election;
- Form of application;
- Specification of the value, or consequent range of values;
- Split criteria for the expenses in relation to services supplied jointly in favour of related persons or entities;
- Identification of the corresponding split agreements;
- Cost sharing agreement;
- Any other important information the taxpayer may have had to determine the valuation of his related operations; and
- Parallel company agreements signed with other shareholders.

When documents prepared for a certain tax period are still valid for other later periods, it will not be necessary to prepare them again, notwithstanding the required amendments.[6]

---

5 All that relating to the tax period in which the taxpayer has performed related operations.

6 All the referred documents must be at the Tax Authorities' disposal until the deadline to declare the Company Tax and, at least, during the period of statute of limitation for Corporate Income Tax purposes.

3.4 Administrative guidelines

No administrative guidelines have been produced by Spanish Tax Authorities on this matter.

4. CASE LAW

4.1 Current cases

Spanish Tax Authorities and the jurisprudence issued by Spanish Courts have widely used the OECD Guidelines to apply or interpret the Spanish transfer pricing rules and regulations.

The statutory regulations state that taxpayers should value transactions with their related parties at market value and also indicate how that value must be calculated.[7] In the case that any discrepancies on the transfer prices arise, it is better for the taxpayer to present as much evidence as possible in support of prices applied because that evidence helps to reduce the likelihood of the Tax Authorities proposing a tax adjustment and imposing penalties.[8]

Tax Authorities are empowered to collect all the necessary information in order to conduct a tax audit properly. Likewise, taxpayers shall provide the Tax Authorities with such information. Failure to present the accounting registers and documents, which companies are required to keep by law, or failure to provide any data, reports, receipts and information relating to the taxpayer's tax situation, may be considered resisting or hindering the tax audit.

4.2 Historical cases of note

The Spanish High Court of Justice has ruled on a few cases regarding transfer pricing issues. In line with the heightened interest given to transfer prices in 2007, these decisions went against the taxpayer. The decisions dealt with various related party transactions, including management fees, customs regulations and purchase of active ingredients.

The section of the legislation dealing with management services is now included within a more general definition of 'services'. The deduction of expenses for services provided by related parties is subject to the condition that the services provided produce, or can produce, an advantage or benefit to the receiver.

When it is not possible to split these services, a distribution of the total price for the services between all beneficiaries of the services (in accordance with rational distribution criteria) can be made.[9] This criteria needs to take into account the nature of the services rendered and the circumstances surrounding them, as well as the benefits obtained (or that can be obtained) by the beneficiaries.[10]

The deduction of expenses derived from cost-sharing arrangements between related parties is subject to the following:

---

7 Article 16 of the Corporate Income Tax Act and article 41 of the Personal Income Tax Act.

8 This movement on burden of proof to the taxpayer has been stated by the Central Treasury and Tax Court, by means of several Resolutions issued on 5 October 2009 and 22 October 2009.

9 Sentences of Spanish High Court of Justice issued in February 2000 and July 2002.

10 Sentence of Spanish High Court of Justice issued in December 2007.

- The participants to the arrangement must be able to access the property of the resulting assets or rights that are the subject of the cost-sharing arrangement;[11]
- The contribution of each participant must take into account the anticipated benefits or advantages that each participant expects to obtain in accordance with rational criteria;[12]
- The agreement must contemplate variations in circumstances and participants, establishing compensatory payments and any other adjustments that may be considered necessary; and
- The agreement must comply with the documentation requirements to be established at a later date.

5. PENALTIES

5.1 Types

Spanish legislation is quite rigorous concerning non-compliance with transfer pricing obligations. The legislation lays down that not providing, or providing incompletely, inexactly or with false data, the obligatory documentation which the taxpayer must make available to the Tax Authorities concerning related operations, is a tax infringement.[13]

At the same time, it is also considered a tax infringement when the fair market value derived from the documentation is not the same as the one consigned by taxpayer on its tax returns.

Such infringement is considered serious and penalties will be imposed according to the following rules:

- When investigations developed by Tax Authorities do not result in assessment corrections for the transactions carried out by the taxpayer but a non-compliance infringement has been made, the penalty will consist of a fine of EUR 1,500 for each datum and EUR 15,000 for each set of data that is omitted, inexact or false, concerning all the documentation obligations of either the group of companies or each entity in its condition as a taxpayer;
- When investigations developed by Tax Authorities result in assessment corrections for the transactions carried out by the taxpayer, the penalty will consist of a fine of 15 per cent of the sum of the amounts resulting from the assessment corrections for each operation, with a minimum of double the penalty that would correspond to application of the first rule, stated above.
- This specific penalty means that generic penalties provided by the Spanish General Tax Act cannot be applied. Moreover, the sum may be increased if the taxpayer exhibits resistance, obstruction, excuse or refusal of the actions of the tax administration, on the same terms provided for under Spanish legislation for taxes of all kinds; and
- Finally, when investigations developed by Tax Authorities do not result in assessment corrections for the transactions carried out by

[11] Sentences of Spanish High Court of Justice issued in January 2009.
[12] Sentences of Spanish High Court of Justice issued in November 2009.
[13] Article 16.10 of Corporate Income Tax Act.

the taxpayer because non-compliance infringement has not occurred and that correction would cause lack of income, undue procurement of tax refunds or improper determination or accreditation of items to be compensated in future tax returns, or when the net income has been incorrectly declared without there being lack of income or undue procurement of tax refunds when sums awaiting compensation, deduction or application have been compensated in an examination or investigation procedure, such conduct will not constitute infringement and consequently will not be penalised.

Spanish legislation[14] also clarifies what must be considered 'datum' or 'set of data' for the purposes of the application of penalties.

'Datum' will be considered to be the information relating to each of the persons, entities or amounts referred to in the following information obligations:

(A) Information obligations concerning the 'master file'

- Identification of the different entities of the group that carry out operations with the taxpayer;
- List of ownership of patents, trademarks and other intangible assets insofar as they affect the taxpayer;
- Amount of the considerations derived from the use of those intangibles;
- List of the cost sharing agreements among entities of the group insofar as they affect the taxpayer;
- List of the supply of services contracts among entities of the group insofar as they affect the taxpayer; and
- List of the advanced price agreements or friendly procedures held, or that are under way, concerning the entities of the group that may affect the taxpayer.

(B) Information obligations concerning the 'specific file'

- General data of the taxpayer and related persons or entities with which he performs operations;
- Name and surname or entity name;
- Fiscal residence;
- Tax Identity Number (VAT number); and
- Detailed description of the operations carried out (nature, characteristics and amount).

Likewise, a 'set of data' has the following information obligations:

(A) Information obligations concerning the 'master file':

- Description of the organisational, legal and operational structure of the group;
- Description of any major changes in that structure;
- Description of those operations (nature, amounts and flows);
- Description of the functions exercised and the risks assumed by the different entities of the group insofar as they affect the operations performed by the taxpayer;

[14] Concretely, Royal Decree that develops the Corporate Income Tax Act.

- Description of any changes in those functions and risks from the previous period;
- Description of group policy on transfer pricing;
- Description of the method or methods adopted by the group, justifying their adaptation to the arm's length principle; and
- The group report or, failing that, the equivalent annual report.

(B) Information obligations concerning the 'specific file':

- Comparability analysis;
- Chosen method of assessment;
- Form of application;
- Specification of the value or value interval derived from it;
- Identification of the comparable values available to the taxpayer to assess his operations;
- Split criteria for the services supplied jointly in favour of related persons or entities;
- Identification of the corresponding split agreements;
- Cost sharing agreements;
- Any other important information the taxpayer may have had to determine the valuation of his related operations; and
- Parallel company agreements signed with other shareholders.

5.2 Special or notable cases

Not applicable

6. DISPUTE RESOLUTION MECHANISMS

6.1 Preferred national options

As suggested by the OECD, Spanish legislation includes the possibility of reaching agreements in advance with the Tax Authorities about the assessment of related parties' transactions. These advanced price agreements work well in both directions because, first, they allow the taxpayer to have a legal certainty that the assessment will not be changed later in an audit procedure and, second, the Spanish Tax Authorities avoid the complexity of an examination of the market value of these transactions.

The taxpayer shall apply for this procedure in order to begin the process.[15] This application shall be accompanied with the basic data to be analyzed by the Tax Authorities. Once this application is analyzed, Tax Authorities will notify the taxpayer of the likelihood of reaching an agreement, in which case the taxpayer will be entitled to submit a proposal based on his fair market value.

The advanced price agreement will have an effect on the operations carried out after the date of approval, and will be valid for the tax periods specified in the agreement itself, but it may not exceed the four tax periods following the date on which it is approved.

[15] If the related operations affect several jurisdictions, the Spanish Tax Authorities may try, together with foreign administrations, intervening in the operation to jointly determine the fair market value of them.

In the case of relevant variation in the economic circumstances existing at the time of approval, the advanced price agreement may be modified in order to adapt it to the new circumstances.

6.2 International options

When a multinational group of companies wants to establish its transfer prices within a whole group of countries through a convention, Spanish rules will not be able to avoid some of the conflicts that will arise with these kind of cross-border related party transactions. Thus, in these situations, it is highly recommended to use international procedures such as the arbitration of the EU Arbitration Convention, or the mutual procedure agreement laid down in the OECD Model Convention as recently amended.

The Arbitration Convention establishes a two-phase procedure, which aims to resolve double taxation disputes between different Member States' companies.

Moreover, the OECD has also incorporated a mutual agreement procedure,[16] which includes an arbitration clause that can be applied in cross-border disputes that remain unresolved for more than two years.

PART TWO: TAX AVOIDANCE

7. ACCEPTABLE TAX PLANNING AREAS / SUBJECTS

Spanish tax Law contains general anti-abuse clauses, such as a substance-over-form rule and the 'fraus legis' doctrine. These rules potentially apply to any transaction, including interest and royalty payments made by Spanish resident companies falling under the implementing provisions of the Directive.

The Spanish substance-over-form concept[17] provides that taxpayer's tax obligations must be enforced based on the actual legal nature of the act or business performed, irrespective of the form or denomination the taxpayer may have given to the transaction. In this regard, the Spanish General Tax Act provides two ways in which a particular transaction may be challenged. The first one is the 'fraus legis' doctrine, also known as 'conflict in the application of the tax law'. There is a conflict in the application of a tax law when a taxable event is wholly or partially avoided or when taxable income is reduced by acts which meet one of the following objectives (i) the acts, whether individually or jointly, are contrived or unsuitable for the result attained; or (ii) as a result of the acts, there are no significant legal or economic consequences beyond tax savings. The second type of transaction that may be challenged is a sham or simulation.

8. DEFINING ABUSIVE TAX AVOIDANCE

In Spain, like in the majority of countries, a sham transaction takes place where the taxpayer presents a purported transaction, but the legal reality of

16 Regulated in the article 25 OECD Model Tax Convention
17 Which is stated in General Tax Act.

the transaction is different under private law. In that case, the tax will be applied according to the actual legal reality, not the taxpayer's pretended reality. In several countries this situation is borderline between tax avoidance and tax evasion.

For the Spanish Tax Authorities, if a transaction is considered a sham transaction, it is automatically considered a simulation. Originally, this was not a tax concept but a civil law concept and it is one of legal reality not economic reality. The concept of simulation means, for both civil and tax law purposes, that the intention of the parties will be followed, if it is different from the arrangement that parties purport to make.

9. THE LEGISLATIVE FRAMEWORK

Spain takes an active approach in order to fight against tax avoidance. On top of the general anti-avoidance rules mentioned above, the Spanish Corporate Income Tax Act, as well as the Non-resident Income Tax Act, include different anti-avoidance measures.

It is very important to bear in mind that some of the new Spanish tax measures that were included in 2012[18] were related to financial expenses, as will be explained below.

Firstly, the Spanish thin capitalization provisions were replaced by an interest-capping rule and anti-debt push-down rule.

Interest capping rules apply to both non-related and related party debt, limiting tax relief for net interest expenses to 30 per cent of the taxpayer's net profit. Interests not deducted by application of that rule can be carried forward for 18 years.[19] The interest-capping rule will not apply if the net interest expense does not exceed EUR 1 million.

As mentioned above, apart from the interest-capping rule, the Spanish Corporate Income Tax Act included a general anti-avoidance measure in order to challenge the deductibility of interest expenses connected to intra-group acquisition of shares.

According to this anti-debt-push-down limitation, interest from indebtedness with group companies, when the debt has been used to acquire shares or increase the capital in other group companies, will not be considered as a deductible expense, unless the taxpayer is able to prove that the transaction is supported by sound business reasons[20].

Additionally, Spain made use of the option to introduce an anti-avoidance clause when implementing the EU Parent-Subsidiary Directive. This anti-avoidance measure establishes that the withholding tax exemption on dividends does not apply if individuals or entities that do not reside in EU Member States hold the majority of the voting rights of the EU shareholder.

18 Introduced by Royal Decree-Law 12/2012 of March 30.

19 When the interest expense is below the 30 per cent limit, the rule allows this unused capacity to be carried forward for five years.

20 As potentially non-tax driven transactions, the legislation cites group restructurings directly connected to an acquisition from a third party or cases where there is true management of the entities acquired in Spain.

10. KEY CASES OF INTEREST

Although Spanish Courts have approved the use of international structures in which the Spanish taxable income was eroded,[21] such criteria may no longer be applicable as new anti-debt-push-down legislation has been introduced.

In the case of dividends distributions from Spanish companies to their EU shareholders, the Tax Authorities, as well as Spanish Courts, are interpreting the anti-abuse clause established in the Spanish legislation very restrictively. In the following sub-sections, summaries of the most recent cases, as well as the key historical cases, are set out.

10.1 Current cases

On March 21, 2012, the Spanish Supreme Court released their most recent judgment regarding the application of the withholding tax exemption on dividend distribution from a Spanish entity to its EU holding company. In this case, the Court confirmed the Tax Authorities' criteria.

Spanish Tax Authorities and the High Court understood that the withholding tax exemption did not apply for dividends paid by the Spanish subsidiary to its Dutch parent. This is because the requirements for non-application of the anti-abuse clause established in the Non-resident Income Tax Act had not been met.

In the appealed judgment, it was held that the taxpayer had not provided evidence for any of the scenarios in which the anti-abuse clause did not apply. Therefore, after confirming that the parent did not conduct a business activity related to that of the subsidiary, the Court ruled that:

- The fact that the parent had a certain level of personnel was not sufficient evidence that it managed its subsidiary, especially since the subsidiary had other administration expenses and its management-related documents were stored at the subsidiary's premises;
- It was not enough that the management and administration functions were carried out by the parent company sporadically. The subsidiary should not have had personnel assigned to its administration department and even if it did, compared to its parent company, it should not have been significant; and
- The fact that the Group's most important production plants were located within the area of the EU, where the parent was resident, was not sufficient proof either.

10.2 Key historical cases

Two key historical decisions have been made within the Spanish Courts regarding dividend distributions from a Spanish company to its EU shareholder when the ultimate shareholder was resident in a non-EU jurisdiction.

21 Spanish Highest Administrative Court accepted, in 2010, the deductibility of financial expenses derived from an intra-group acquisition based in the business rational of the resulting structure.

In the first decision,[22] a Spanish company, whose ultimate parent company was resident in the United States, paid dividends to its Dutch parent company, which held 100 per cent of its share capital.

According to the Spanish Tax Authorities, the withholding tax exemption was not applicable to the dividends distributed by the Spanish company to its Dutch parent company. The reasons to deny such an application were that (i) the entrepreneurial activity carried out by the holding company was not identical to the one carried out by the Spanish subsidiary; and (ii) that there was no proof that clearly evidenced that the Dutch parent entity carried out the supervision and management of the Spanish subsidiary through the appropriate organization of material and human resources.[23] The fact that the Dutch holding company had not invoiced any services to the Spanish entity was a proof that effectively, no management was carried out.

The Spanish High Court, and recently, the Spanish Supreme Court, confirmed the understanding of the tax audit denying the exemption of withholding tax on a dividend distribution made to a Dutch holding company.

In another decision,[24] the High Court ruled on the interpretation of the withholding tax exemption on intra-group dividends provided by an EU Parent-Subsidiary Directive.

A Spanish company, whose ultimate parent entity was an Austrian listed company, paid dividends to its Dutch parent company. The Dutch entity held 100 per cent of the Spanish company, however, 10.54 per cent of the shares in the Austrian company were held by a German company, and the remaining 89.46 per cent was held by minority shareholders.

It was understood by the Spanish Tax Authorities that the withholding tax exemption did not apply to the dividends paid by the Spanish company to its Dutch parent company. This was because it was not possible to prove that any of the safe harbours, set out in the Spanish Non-resident Income Tax Act when a parent company is controlled by a non-EU resident[25], were met. This was because they were not able to verify the identity and residency of more than 50 per cent of the shareholders who had a stake in the listed Austrian parent. The Spanish Administrative Court upheld the Tax Authority's criteria.

The Spanish High Court understood that the Tax Authorities took a very restrictive interpretation, which was not acceptable from the perspective of the EU Parent-Subsidiary Directive. This restrictive interpretation was also not acceptable from the perspective of the Spanish Constitution.[26] The Spanish High Court established a link between the anti-avoidance clause stated in the Spanish domestic law and article 1.2 of the EU Parent-

[22] Sentence of High Court of Appeal, issued in January 2009.

[23] It was also pointed out that two of the three directors of the company were not resident in the Netherlands.

[24] Sentence of High Court of Appeal, issued in November 2010.

[25] The exemption does not apply when the ultimate parent of the EU company, to which the dividend is paid, is resident outside the EU.

[26] This article guarantees, above others, the principle of legality and the prohibition of arbitrary action of public authorities.

Subsidiary Directive, stressing that the Spanish Tax Authorities had not proven the existence of abuse, artificial arrangements, or interposed companies not carried out for valid commercial reasons.

In this case, the Spanish High Court decided in favour of the Spanish company and overruled the Tax Authorities' assessment.

11. PENALTIES

11.1 Legislative provisions

If a tax assessment is made under the 'fraus legis' rule, the tax is imposed on those acts or businesses that are avoided. Late interest payments would also be due, but no penalties are levied.

On the contrary, in the event of sham or simulation, the taxable event will be the transaction actually carried out by the parties. Tax assessments under this rule also carry late interest payment and penalties, which range from 50 per cent to 150 per cent of the tax due.

11.2 Examples of penalties imposed

In one criminal case in which the company was required to pay the tax due, members of the Board were sentenced to 12 months of imprisonment pursuant to the tax criminal offence. In that case, apart from prison, penalties ranged from 100 per cent to 600 per cent of the tax due.

12. CURRENT TRENDS

12.1 National policy and law

The Spanish Government is planning to release a comprehensive reform of the Spanish tax system. The debate over base erosion and profit shifting (BEPS) has reached the highest levels of governments, and has achieved growing attention from the media and the public on perceived international tax avoidance techniques of high-profile multinationals. Thus, some of the amendments that are expected to be introduced in the Spanish Corporate Income Tax Act, as well as, in the Non-resident Income Tax Act are aimed at tackling abusive tax planning.

Switzerland

ADB Altorfer Duss & Beilstein AG
Marco Greter, Mathias Haeni & Fabian Streule

PART ONE: TRANSFER PRICING

1. GENERAL OVERVIEW

Transfer pricing affects most types of Swiss taxes. Interestingly enough and contrary to the worldwide trend, there is no special legislation for transfer pricing in Switzerland. Rather, each tax act has its own way of addressing transfer pricing matters for the respective type of tax.

The usual approach to adjusting inadequate transfer pricing in Switzerland is the prohibition of harmful profit shifting ('geldwerte Leistung') between related taxpayers. The definition of harmful profit shifting has been elaborated by the Federal Supreme Court and requires the fulfilment of the following three conditions:

- The company (taxpayer) made a performance/delivery without receiving adequate consideration in return (evident discrepancy). As a consequence thereof, the company's financial result was reduced, ie, earnings were withdrawn.
- The performance/delivery was in favour of a shareholder or a related party. It would not have been made available to third parties in comparable circumstances.
- The evident discrepancy of the performance/delivery and the remuneration was recognizable for the acting body (organ) of the company.

As a member of the OECD, Switzerland accepted the transfer pricing report elaborated by the OECD fiscal committee in 1995 (OECD Transfer Pricing Guidelines for Multinational Enterprises and Tax Administrations 1995), as well as all the updated OECD guidelines on transfer pricing. In 1997, the Swiss Federal Tax Administration (SFTA) officially instructed the cantonal (state) tax authorities to follow these guidelines.

There are no particular transfer pricing documentation requirements in Switzerland. However, this does not mean that a transaction between related parties does not have to be documented. Rather, the general documentation requirements of each tax act have to be fulfilled for the respective type of tax. This basically means that a taxpayer is required to provide all documents necessary for a proper assessment of the taxable basis. In the case of transactions between related parties, a taxpayer has to demonstrate that the transfer prices used are based on sound economic reasoning.

Switzerland uses the transfer pricing methods suggested in the OECD guidelines. For the purpose of benchmarking, there is no requirement by the Swiss tax authorities for local comparable data or specific databases. Even though Swiss comparable data is considered to be more preferential, in general a pan-European benchmarking analysis sufficiently supports the defence of transfer prices.

It is common practice to clarify the taxation of critical or complex transactions in a binding ruling with the Swiss tax authorities in advance. Therefore, Swiss taxpayers often clarify potential transfer pricing issues by way of a ruling. As a result, the Swiss tax treatment of a transaction is settled. In addition, advanced pricing agreements (APA) can be conducted involving Swiss and foreign tax authorities in order to agree on transfer pricing matters in advance. Consequently, an APA settles the Swiss and the foreign tax treatment of a transaction.

2. IDENTIFICATION OF LEGISLATIVE FRAMEWORK

Switzerland is composed of 26 cantons (member states) and the confederation (central state). The cantons are made up of some 2,300 communes (municipalities). The cantons are the original holders of sovereignty. The confederation holds those sovereign rights which are expressly granted to it by the Federal Constitution. Based on the principle of federalism, Swiss taxes are levied at three different governmental levels:

- Federal level: Federal Income Tax, Withholding Tax, Stamp Duty, Value Added Tax, Customs Duties, Tobacco Tax etc.
- Cantonal (state) level: State and Local Income Tax, Wealth Tax, Tax on Capital, Inheritance and Gift Taxes
- Municipal (local) level[1]: Real Estate Capital Gain Tax, Real Estate Transfer Tax

The federation, the cantons and the municipalities have the right to legislate for tax rules within their competencies. However, none of them has issued a special tax act regarding transfer pricing. The VAT Act is currently the only Swiss tax act that explicitly states the principle of dealing at arm's length for transactions between related parties (cf. section 2.1). Nevertheless, most Swiss tax acts include a legal basis for the adjustment of profit shifting. Additionally, the principle of dealing at arm's length is recognized and applicable in practice (cf. section 3.3).

It should be noted that there are no specific transfer pricing audit procedures within the Swiss tax legislation. Rather, transfer pricing aspects are pursued on the basis of the normal tax audit procedure. A taxpayer under tax audit is asked to provide any information that is relevant for properly assessing the taxable basis (eg, profit). If a taxpayer does not cooperate with the tax authorities, the taxable basis is estimated at the discretion of the tax authorities and fines may be imposed.

1 Depending on the canton, these taxes may be levied at cantonal level instead.

2.1 Federal legislation

(a) Corporate income taxes

Article 58 Direct Federal Tax Act[2] is the legal basis for the adjustment of profit shifting under non-arm's length conditions for corporate income tax purposes at federal level. The article states that only commercially justifiable expenditures are tax deductible. The effective tax rate of the so-called Direct Federal Tax is 7.83 per cent.

Federal tax law largely harmonizes corporate income taxes at cantonal and municipal level. This means that the cantons und municipalities are obliged to implement the rules stated in the federal harmonization act. Provided this law does not regulate a subject matter, the cantons and municipalities are competent to legislate for their own rules. The most important competency of the cantons and municipalities is the determination of the corporate income tax rate. The effective cantonal/municipal tax rates therefore vary between approx. 5 per cent and 18 per cent. Article 24 paragraph 1 Tax Act regarding the Harmonization of Direct Taxes of Cantons and Municipalities[3] is the legal basis for the adjustment of profit shifting for corporate income taxes at cantonal and municipal level.

(b) Withholding tax

If inadequate transfer pricing entails the diminution of profit of a Swiss corporation in favour of a shareholder and/or a related party, the amount to be adjusted for Swiss tax purposes is qualified as a constructive dividend subject to withholding tax of 35 per cent. Article 4 paragraph 1 cipher b Withholding Tax Act[4] is the legal basis for the taxation of constructive dividends. In an international context, withholding tax may be partly or fully reclaimed if a double tax treaty is applicable.

(c) Stamp duty

A transaction between a parent company and its direct Swiss subsidiary may lead to a hidden capital contribution into the equity of the Swiss subsidiary. Such hidden capital contribution (ie, the difference between the fair market value and the transfer price) is subject to stamp duty of 1 per cent. The legal basis for the taxation is article 5 paragraph 2 cipher a Stamp Tax Act.[5]

(d) Value added tax

For value added tax purposes, article 24 paragraph 2 VAT Act[6] states the principle of dealing at arm's length for transactions between related parties. In addition, article 3 cipher h VAT Act provides a definition of what is meant by the term 'related parties'.

---

2 Direct Federal Tax Act of 14 December 1990 (SR 642.11).
3 Tax Act regarding the Harmonization of Direct Taxes of Cantons and Municipalities of 14 December 1990 (SR 642.14).
4 Withholding Tax Act of 13 October 1965 (SR 642.21).
5 Stamp Tax Act of 27 June 1973 (SR 641.10).
6 Value Added Tax Act of 12 June 2009 (SR 641.20).

2.2 State and provincial legislative interplay

The cantonal (state) tax authorities are assigned by federal and cantonal law to assess all corporate income taxes (ie, Direct Federal Tax, Cantonal Tax and Municipal Tax) of the taxpayers in their respective cantonal territory. Consequently, the cantonal tax authorities are competent for transfer pricing matters with respect to Direct Federal Tax and cantonal/municipal taxes. Additionally, the cantonal tax authorities also audit these taxes. The SFTA supervises the cantonal tax authorities regarding the assessment of Direct Federal Tax.

Municipal (local) tax authorities are competent for transfer pricing matters with respect to municipal taxes (eg, real estate transfer tax, real estate capital gain tax in certain cantons).

2.3 International treaties and agreements

Switzerland has entered into more than 80 treaties for the avoidance of double taxation. Double tax treaties prevent double taxation and thus also remove obstacles for cross-border economic transactions. Switzerland has been applying the OECD standard in full since 2009. In particular, Switzerland's reservations on the article 9 paragraph 2 (corresponding adjustment) and article 26 (exchange of information) of the OECD Modell Convention were abolished. Since then, more than 40 double tax treaties have been renegotiated in order to include the administrative assistance in tax matters according to OECD standard, which enables countries to exchange information for tax purposes. Since 2012, the standard also allows group requests. It is expected that Switzerland's easing to exchange information will result in an increase of the number of requests with respect to transfer pricing from foreign countries.

Switzerland has recently signed Tax Information Exchange Agreements (TIEA) with Andorra, Greenland, Guernsey, Isle of Man, Jersey, San Marino and the Seychelles. Unlike double tax treaties, which primarily govern the avoidance of double taxation, TIEAs deal solely with the exchange of information. These agreements were signed in 2013 and 2014, but they are not yet in force (as of May 2014).

3. NATIONAL POLICY ISSUES

Swiss tax authorities are increasingly concerned that taxpayers may shift profits from Switzerland to countries with strict transfer pricing rules in order to avoid challenges by the respective foreign tax authorities.

Transactions with related parties domiciled in offshore jurisdictions are in the focus of Swiss tax authorities. Subject to investigation is the adequacy of transfer pricing between the Swiss taxpayer and the offshore company. Furthermore, the authorities examine whether an offshore company is effectively managed and controlled by a person domiciled in Switzerland. According to Swiss tax legislation, the offshore company becomes a Swiss taxpayer subject to unlimited taxation, when the effective management and control of the company is in Switzerland.

3.1 Overall national policy announcements

There have been no specific announcements regarding transfer pricing by the Swiss tax authorities in the past years. Section 3.3 refers to the commitment to follow the OECD guidelines.

3.2 National revenue authority initiatives

No special activities towards auditing transfer pricing situations have been announced or carried out in Switzerland.

3.3 Administrative statements

In 1997, the SFTA issued a circular letter[7] requesting the cantonal (state) tax authorities to consider the recommendations developed by the OECD fiscal committee in its transfer pricing report 1995 (OECD Transfer Pricing Guidelines for Multinational Enterprises and Tax Administrations 1995). By accepting the transfer pricing report in the OECD Council, Switzerland made a commitment to follow these recommendations.

In 2004, the SFTA issued a new circular letter[8] reminding the cantonal (state) tax authorities that the OECD guidelines are to be considered. The circular letter contains an explicit statement that the principle of dealing at arm's length is applicable. In particular, the administrative statement stipulates that the taxation of service companies is to be clarified in light of the arm's length principle in each case. This meant that the traditionally and generally applied cost plus 5 per cent approach for service companies was to be abolished.

3.4 Administrative guidelines

Hereafter is a list of the most important guidelines in connection with transfer pricing published by the SFTA:

- Safe harbor rules for financing: thin capitalization[9], interest rates for Swiss currency financing,[10] and interest rates for foreign currency financing.[11]
- Determination of the recipient of benefits for withholding tax purposes.[12]
- Taxation of service companies.[13]
- Corporate reorganizations ('Umstrukturierung').[14]
- Abolishment of lump sum deductions in the field of foreign related business (abolishment of the so-called 'fifty–fifty practice').[15]
- Treatment of foreign domicile companies in the financial industry for VAT purposes.[16]

---

7 Circular letter number 4 dated 4 March 1997.
8 Circular letter number 4 dated 19 March 2004.
9 Circular letter number 6 dated 6 June 1997.
10 Circular letter published annually at the beginning of the respective fiscal year.
11 Circular letter published annually at the beginning of the respective fiscal year.
12 Explanatory note issued in February 2001.
13 Circular letter number 4 dated 19 March 2004.
14 Circular letter number 5 dated 1 June 2004.
15 Circular letter number 9 dated 22 June 2005.
16 VAT-business-information number 14 published in April 2012.

- Financial restructuring of businesses ('Sanierung').[17]

It should be noted that certain cantons publish their own guidelines for state (cantonal) and local (municipal) taxes in completion and/or deviation of the federal guidelines.

4. CASE LAW

The number of court cases regarding transfer pricing for cross border transactions is relatively small. This has mainly two reasons:

- In an international comparison, Swiss income tax rates have been and still are below average (cf. section 7). Wilful shifting of profit outside Switzerland is therefore not a systematic issue.
- It is common practice to clarify critical or complex transactions in a binding ruling with the Swiss tax authorities in advance. Subject to a ruling may not only be the interpretation of the tax law or of an administrative guideline but also the possibility to agree on the actual taxation of a transaction or of a taxpayer in advance. Consequently, taxpayers often clarify potential transfer pricing issues (eg, the percentage of a licence fee or the mark-up of a cost plus transaction) by way of a ruling. As a result of the binding clarification of a critical question with the Swiss tax authorities in advance, the risk of litigation at a later stage is minimized.

Besides transactions between companies and their owners (and/or related persons of the owners), many court cases regarding transfer pricing dealt with transactions between related parties in an inter-cantonal context. This is due to the fact that cantons are in tax competition and consequently, the income tax rates may vary considerably from canton to canton (and sometimes from municipality to municipality). Even though such case law relates to internal Swiss transactions, conclusions for international transactions are often possible.

4.1 Current cases

Decision of the Federal Supreme Court of 9 July 2012[18]

A Swiss taxpayer transferred the group's treasury department to a French group company without consideration. The court confirmed that the transfer without consideration was a constructive dividend subject to withholding tax. Furthermore, the court supported the valuation of the assets transferred (mainly goodwill) undertaken by the SFTA. The valuation according to the so-called 'Praktikermethode' was a formula that resulted in a weighted average of capitalized earnings of the past and the net asset value.

17 Circular letter number 32 dated 23 December 2010.
18 BGE 2C_499/2011.

4.2 Historical cases of note

Decision of the Federal Supreme Court of 13 July 1956[19]

The court decision defines the conditions to be fulfilled to qualify a profit shifting occurrence as harmful for tax purposes. In particular, the court clarifies that an intention to avoid taxes is not required. The definition is still applicable (cf. section 1).

Decision of the Federal Supreme Court of 5 April 1984[20]

The court confirms that Swiss law does not provide the option of group taxation with respect to corporate income taxes and withholding tax. Rather, each group entity is a separate taxpayer. Expense booked by a Swiss corporation due to fictitious invoices (ie, without equivalent) received from the US parent company is not commercially justified. Consequently, such expense is to be qualified as a constructive dividend subject to a withholding tax of 35 per cent.

5. PENALTIES

There are no specific transfer pricing penalties within the Swiss tax legislation. In particular, there are no penalties for a lack of transfer pricing documentation. Rather, the general penalty provisions of each tax act are applicable for the respective type of tax. Apart from the formal types of penalties (cf. section 5.1), there are two scenarios which taxpayer may perceive as factual penalties.

If in the course of a tax assessment the taxable basis cannot be justly determined (eg, due to inappropriate documentation), the taxable basis is estimated at the discretion of the tax authorities. Such estimates need to be dutiful and based on the experience in other cases by law. However, it goes without saying that the tax authorities generally do not try to assess the taxable basis in favour of the taxpayer in such cases.

In the case of a constructive dividend by a Swiss taxpayer, a withholding tax of 35 per cent is imposed. According to the Swiss practice, in most cases, the right to refund such withholding tax is with the recipient of the constructive dividend (so-called direct beneficiary theory). Often, this is not the direct parent company of the Swiss taxpayer, but rather a sister company within the same group. In international cases where the recipient is not the direct parent company, the direct beneficiary theory permits a higher non-refundable withholding tax even if a double tax treaty is available. This is due to the fact that double tax treaties generally require a direct investment in order to receive the higher refund rate.

5.1 Types

Swiss tax legislation states two types of penalties (cf. section 11.1 for further information):

19 BGE 82 I 291 f.
20 Archiv für Schweizerisches Abgaberecht (ASA) 53, 278.

- A monetary fine is imposed in case of an infraction of administrative duties or in case of a tax evasion.
- Imprisonment up to three years is imposed in severe cases of tax fraud.

5.2 Special or notable cases

Decision of the Federal Supreme Court of 17 May 2013[21]

The court clarified that Swiss accounting rules are violated if costs for legal services rendered by a third party to an offshore entity are booked as an expense in a related Swiss corporation. Such profit shifting is qualified as tax fraud; the income statement regarding content of the Swiss corporation is untrue.

6. DISPUTE RESOLUTION MECHANISMS

As a result of the Swiss ruling practice (cf. section 4), the number of dispute resolution processes can be reduced. However, if a transaction was not subject to a ruling, or if a ruling was not properly implemented, dispute resolutions may become an issue. Moreover, if transfer prices are adjusted by foreign tax authorities, conflicts with Swiss tax authorities may occur in order to avoid double taxation.

It is common practice in Switzerland to negotiate adjustments of the taxable basis in the course of the tax assessment or tax audit. Such adjustments may be requested by the Swiss tax authorities or by the taxpayer. The latter is often seen if a foreign tax authority makes an adjustment in its jurisdiction, which requires a corresponding (and secondary) adjustment in Switzerland.

Once a taxpayer is finally assessed for a tax year, the taxable basis is fixed (res judicata). This means adjustments for this period can only be made if qualified conditions are fulfilled. In general, the adjustment of a transfer price by a foreign tax authority does not fulfil the condition to re-assess the final assessed tax year for a corresponding adjustment in Switzerland. However, if the dispute on the transfer price is settled in a Mutual Agreement Procedure (cf. section 6.2), the Swiss taxpayer is entitled to revision of the final assessed tax year and to claim the adjustment in his favour.

6.1 Preferred national options

Many tax disputes can be settled by negotiating with the Swiss tax authorities in the course of the tax assessment or tax audit. Thus, the number of court cases can be reduced. Nevertheless, each canton has one or two instances of courts that are competent for tax litigations. The highest court for tax litigations is the Federal Supreme Court.

The Swiss constitution prohibits double taxation due to inter-cantonal circumstances. The Federal Supreme Court has developed numerous rules regarding how inter-cantonal double taxation is to be avoided. In practice,

[21] BGE 6B_711/2012.

these rules are often applicable in international cases unless overruled by a double tax treaty.

6.2 International options

The competent Swiss authority under the tax treaties is the SIF,[22] a division of the Federal Department of Finance. Amongst other things, the SIF represents Switzerland's interests in international financial and tax matters, and leads negotiations in these areas.

(a) Advanced pricing agreements

Though no formal procedure for Advanced Pricing Agreements (APA) exists in Switzerland, APAs with foreign tax authorities have become a favoured option for Swiss-based multinational groups with complex and/or high volume transactions. Bilateral APAs are conducted under the corresponding mutual agreement provision in the applicable double tax treaty. In practice, the procedure starts with a presentation of the fact pattern and a formal request to the SIF. The SIF has proven very helpful in supporting the interests of Swiss taxpayers in APA negotiations with foreign tax authorities.

(b) Mutual agreement procedures

Mutual Agreement Procedures (MAP) are conducted with jurisdictions that have entered into double tax treaties with Switzerland. Usually, there are one or two meetings with each of the most important trade/industrial countries per year in order to negotiate pending cases. In past years, the SIF dealt with approximately 40-50 cases per year regarding transfer pricing.

(c) Arbitration procedures

The possibility of conducting an international dispute regarding double taxation in an arbitration court is stated in the double tax treaties renegotiated by Switzerland since 2010. In general, the condition of such an arbitration procedure is that no solution was found to avoid a double taxation by the contracting states within three years. In other words, the arbitration procedure is only possible if the MAP failed. Unlike the MAP, the arbitration court has to deliver a judgment that avoids double taxation.

PART TWO: TAX AVOIDANCE

7. ACCEPTABLE TAX PLANNING AREAS/SUBJECTS

Switzerland has enhanced its international reputation as an attractive business location in recent years. Beside exceptional infrastructure facilities for international business, Switzerland offers an advantageous tax environment, embedded in a widespread international framework,[23] offering stability for tax planning issues considering the longstanding ruling practice.

---

22 State Secretariat for International Financial Matters ('Staatssekretariat für internationale Finanzfragen').

23 Switzerland concluded more than 80 double tax treaties.

In an international context an additional key issue for competiveness are the quite low tax rates in Switzerland.

Regarding tax planning possibilities in Switzerland, current Swiss tax law has introduced various special tax regimes for corporations in order to lower the ordinary corporate tax burdens (so-called 'holding companies', 'domiciliary companies' and 'mixed companies'). These special tax regimes might be amended in the near future due to international circumstances and discussions (cf. section 12).

Swiss tax practice currently knows further tailor-made taxation possibilities for several special corporate structures. For instance, the SFTA has published guidelines for the taxation of principal structures.[24] As a further example, current Swiss tax practice also accepts tax planning possibilities in the areas of corporate financing and captive insurance. Swiss tax practice is developing with regard to these areas (cf. section 10.1 and section 12).

Due to the advantageous tax system tax avoidance, as a consequence of profit shifting, has not been one of the hot topics in the past from a Swiss perspective. However, it can be noted that these issues become increasingly relevant not least because of the international developments (cf. section 12).

8. DEFINING ABUSIVE TAX AVOIDANCE

Swiss tax law does not stipulate a specific 'General Anti-Avoidance Rule' (GAAR). However, there are several means to distinguish between legitimate schemes of tax minimization and abusive tax avoidance, which are applicable for all type of taxes in Switzerland (cf. section 2), and summed up as follows: (1) interpretation of the applicable legal provision; (2) application of the 'substance-over-form' principle; (3) application of the traditional Swiss anti-avoidance doctrine; (4) tax avoidance practices with special international focus. As a matter of fact, the appropriate means for preventing tax avoidance has to be decided on in every individual case.

The available measures as listed above will be outlined hereafter:

(a) Interpretation of the applicable legal provision/'substance-over-form'-principle

The distinction between legitimate schemes of tax planning and abusive tax avoidance issues starts with the interpretation of the applicable legal provision. The following example shall illustrate how this works: For lack of special CFC regulations in Switzerland, profit shifting issues can be prevented by interpreting the legal provision defining the prerequisites for unlimited tax liability in Switzerland (article 50 Direct Federal Tax Act;[25] cf. section 10.1). Moreover, Swiss tax practice focuses in certain cases upon the economic substance of a certain structure or transaction and not merely upon the legal form ('substance-over-form'-principle). The application of the 'substance-over-form'-principle enables some transactions or structures to

24 Circular letter number 8 dated 18 December 2001.
25 Direct Federal tax Act of 14 December 1990 (SR. 642.11).

fall within the scope of a tax provision, which would not be the case from only assessing the legal form of a certain transaction or structure.

(b) Abusive tax avoidance according to traditional anti-avoidance doctrine

Still, there are plenty of structures or transactions that cannot be subsumed under a specific tax law provision. Such structures or transactions might be taxed by applying the traditional Swiss anti-avoidance doctrine and by qualifying them as abusive tax avoidance. The Federal Supreme Court has developed the traditional Swiss anti-avoidance doctrine. According to this longstanding case law, abusive tax avoidance requires the following prerequisites to be met: (1) The legal form chosen by the taxpayer is obviously unusual, inappropriate or strange, and in any case, completely inappropriate to the economic substance. (2) The relationship or the transaction has been set up merely with the intention of saving taxes. (3) The relationship or transaction chosen would effectively result in a material reduction of taxes.

As a first prerequisite, the chosen structure or transaction has to be unusual and inappropriate. The envisaged specific economic goal is achieved by a completely inappropriate legal arrangement. However, not every innovative or unusual method for saving taxes fulfils this prerequisite. In fact, the legal arrangement has to be – besides its fiscal aspects – far from any economic reason or substance.

The second prerequisite is the intention of the taxpayer to set up the unusual legal arrangement solely for the purpose of saving taxes. In practice, it has often proven difficult to substantiate this. Therefore, in any case of unusual or inappropriate legal arrangement and tax saving possibilities, the existence of the intention is assumed.

Last, the unusual legal arrangement has to effectively save taxes. Whereas the second prerequisite lacks the necessary clarity, the third prerequisite is more than obvious. However, the tax saving has to be material. Unless the taxpayer does succeed in saving taxes, no matter how inappropriate his legal arrangement might be the transaction or structure will not be qualified as being abusive tax avoidance.

After having described the key elements and prerequisites of abusive tax avoidance according to traditional Swiss anti-avoidance doctrine, it might be helpful to outline what the content of abusive tax avoidance does not cover.

First, the definition of abusive tax avoidance becomes clearer by distinguishing legitimate tax planning from abusive tax avoidance. Both, legitimate tax planning and abusive tax avoidance seek to save taxes. Legitimate tax planning intends to use legal loopholes in order to save taxes, but does not set up an unusual and inappropriate legal arrangement in order to achieve an envisaged economic goal. In other words, a tax planner who wants to get from point A to B and who – apart from health and environment aspects – does not want to pay gasoline tax would rather take a bicycle instead of a car.

Second, abusive tax avoidance has to be distinguished from tax evasion and tax fraud, which Swiss tax law qualifies as tax offences and which are, therefore, subject to penalties. To qualify as tax evasion or tax fraud, tax relevant facts have to be concealed from tax authorities. In a possible abusive tax avoidance situation by contrast, all tax relevant facts are correctly and completely declared in the respective tax return.

(c) Tax avoidance practices with special international focus

The principles for preventing tax avoidance schemes outlined above have, initially, been developed for domestic circumstances, but as a matter of course apply for international structures and transactions as well.

There are not many administrative statements or published policies by the SFTA dealing with tax avoidance. The few administrative practices published focus especially on international tax law issues, eg, the following:

(1) The (1962) Abuse Decree enacted by the Swiss Federal Council (SR 672.202), for instance, provides anti-avoidance provisions to combat the improper use of tax treaties by foreigners utilizing Swiss interposed companies in order to benefit from double tax treaty provisions (measures against so-called 'treaty shopping'). The SFTA has published three circular letters[26] in order to specify the treatment of tax avoidance issues in this context.

(2) Another practice of the SFTA, which has also been subject to lawsuits[27] relates to the distribution of reserves and a possible Swiss withholding tax burden. After a transfer of shares of a Swiss company within an international context, the distribution of so-called 'old reserves' is subject to the treaty rate that was applicable prior to the share transfer if the following requirements are met: First, the transfer of shares in a Swiss company to a foreign or Swiss company within the group has to result in a lower non-refundable withholding tax rate. Second, the main purpose of the share transfer is the achievement of this favourable taxation. Third, the economic reason for the transfer of the shares plays a subordinated role only.

9. THE LEGISLATIVE FRAMEWORK

Swiss tax law does not recognize any specific 'General Anti-Avoidance Rule' (GAAR), as eg, Germany or Austria do, nor any specific CFC regulation. In Swiss tax law, tax avoidance issues are, in principle, solved by either interpreting the respective legal provision or by applying the traditional anti-avoidance doctrine developed especially by the Federal Supreme Court (cf. section 8).

---

[26] Circular letter 1962 dated 31 December 1962, circular letter 1999 dated 17 December 1998 and circular letter 2010 dated 1 August 2012.

[27] For example, Decision of the Federal Administrative Court of 23 March 2010, A-2744/2008.

(a) Abusive tax avoidance according to traditional anti-avoidance doctrine

Most types of Swiss taxes (eg, corporate income tax) do not have a clear legal basis for combating tax avoidance and the application of traditional anti-avoidance doctrine. For lack of such legal basis, abusive tax avoidance is based on the general legal principle of prohibition of abuse of rights which is a cornerstone of the Swiss legal system, and therefore inherent in Swiss tax law. In addition, Swiss withholding tax law has an explicit legal basis regarding tax avoidance: Article 21 paragraph 2 Withholding Tax Act[28] states that a withholding tax refund is not possible in case such refund would lead to abusive tax avoidance.

(b) Tax avoidance provisions with special international focus

In the double tax treaties concluded by Switzerland there are further provisions that deal with preventing tax avoidance. For instance, the Swiss tax treaties grant withholding tax reductions only to beneficial owners. In addition, only a few Swiss tax treaties include special anti-abuse provisions. Notwithstanding the absence of special anti-abuse provisions in the majority of Swiss double tax treaties, the Federal Supreme Court concluded that a reservation of abuse of rights is inherent in all tax treaties (cf. section 10.2).

10. KEY CASES OF INTEREST

The analysis of recent cases relating to tax avoidance issues shows the following emerging trend: Tax avoidance issues are more and more frequently solved by interpreting the tax law provision in question rather than applying the traditional anti-avoidance doctrine developed by the Federal Supreme Court (cf. section 8).

10.1 Current cases

(a) Interpretation of the applicable legal provisions/legal terms

In two recent judgments, the Federal Supreme Court had to deal with tax avoidance and profit shifting issues with regard to offshore corporate financing structures.

In the first case,[29] a company of a Swiss based group (X Finance Ltd.) maintained a permanent establishment on the Cayman Islands for financing the domestic group companies. Whereas the group companies were able to deduct the interest payments from the taxable profit to their full extent, the interest income, for Swiss tax purposes, was allocated to the permanent establishment on the Cayman Islands, which led to non-taxation of this interest income. By interpreting the legal term of a foreign permanent establishment, the Court concluded that X Finance Ltd. did not maintain a permanent establishment on the Cayman Islands and was therefore denied the allocation of interest income to the Cayman Islands for Swiss tax purposes.

---

28 Withholding Tax Act of 13 October 1965 (SR 642.21).
29 Decision of the Federal Supreme Court dated 5 October 2012, 2C_708/2011.

In the second case,[30] a company (X Ltd.) was domiciled in Guernsey and was held by a Swiss holding company. X Ltd. financed the Swiss and Austrian based group companies with the same tax effect described above. The Federal Supreme Court broadly interpreted the applicable corporate income tax provision and held that X Ltd. was effectively managed in Switzerland. Therefore, X Ltd. was assumed to be subject to an unlimited tax liability in Switzerland.

(b) Abusive tax avoidance according to traditional anti-avoidance doctrine

According to newer literature and publications, the applicability and the requirements of the traditional anti-avoidance doctrine have been questioned. In one of the most recent decisions relating to abusive tax avoidance, the Federal Supreme Court emphasizes that the criteria defining abusive tax avoidance, according to the traditional anti-avoidance doctrine, are still applicable.[31] However, the Federal Supreme Court outlined that abusive tax avoidance is only suitable for extraordinary situations. That means that abusive tax avoidance may be applied as a last resort, if the non-taxation of certain transactions or structures appears unacceptable and arbitrary.

10.2 Key historical cases

(a) Abusive tax avoidance according to traditional anti-avoidance doctrine

The definition and boundaries of abusive tax avoidance according to the traditional anti-avoidance doctrine has been specified by the Federal Supreme Court in a multitude of cases and can be traced back to decisions of the Federal Supreme Court in the early 20th century. The following two decisions may in particular serve as key examples for this longstanding case law. In the first decision, the Federal Supreme Court held that a certain situation has to be taxed according to the economic substance of the structures or the transactions, even if the legal form is valid.[32] In a second decision, the Swiss Federal Supreme Court clearly distinguished legitimate tax planning from abusive tax avoidance and confirmed that tax planning is important for sound economic management.[33]

(b) Tax avoidance provisions with special international focus

There are several court decisions that are crucial for the application of Swiss double tax treaty benefits and the treatment of tax avoidance issues in this respect. First, the refund of withholding taxes provided by Swiss double tax treaties may not be refused due to the assumption of abusive tax avoidance according to article 21 paragraph 2 Withholding Tax Act[34] (cf. section 9). Nevertheless, in a case that garnered much attention in academic literature,

[30] Decision of the Federal Supreme Court dated 16 March 2013, 2C_1086/2012.
[31] Decision of the Federal Supreme Court dated 19 March 2012, BGE 138 II 239, E. 4.1.
[32] Decision of the Federal Supreme Court dated 2 April 1993, BGE 119 Ib 111.
[33] Decision of the Federal Supreme Court dated 10 January 1994, ASA 64, p. 81.
[34] Withholding Tax Act of 13 October 1965 (SR 642.21).

the Federal Supreme Court refused treaty benefits because of prohibition of treaty abuse implicitly included in all tax treaties.[35] The Court derived the implicit prohibition of treaty abuse from article 31 of the Vienna Convention on the Law of Treaties.

11. PENALTIES

If tax avoidance issues are solved by the interpretation of the respective tax provision or tax law term no penalties are to be imposed as a matter of course. However, the interpretation of the tax law provision or the application of the 'substance-over-form'-principle may trigger the related tax consequences.

Also abusive tax avoidance, as defined within the traditional Swiss anti-avoidance doctrine, does not qualify as a statutory offence according to Swiss offence tax law. Rather, the legal arrangement is disregarded and replaced by the facts – ie, the economic substance – that would have been appropriate to achieve the intended economic objective. These deemed facts fulfil the statutory requirements of the applicable tax provision and, as a result, trigger the related tax consequences.

A tax situation can only be subsumed under Swiss tax offence law (eg, within a tax evasion or a tax fraud situation) and trigger penalties, if tax relevant facts are not disclosed in the respective tax returns.

11.1 Legislative provisions

Swiss tax law neither knows a statutory general anti-avoidance rule nor legislative provision for penalties in this respect. The provisions of the Swiss tax offence law can only be applied if not all tax relevant facts are completely and correctly declared in the respective tax return. However, within an abusive tax avoidance situation, as defined above (cf. section 8), the tax relevant facts are fully disclosed.

A taxpayer wilfully or negligently acting in such a way that an assessment is improperly omitted or a final assessment is incomplete, is committing tax evasion. The fallible taxpayer is usually fined with an amount equal to the evaded amount. The penalty can be raised up to three times the evaded tax or can be lowered to one third of the evaded tax depending on the extent of negligence.

Tax fraud, however, can be even punishable by imprisonment. A person who uses false or falsified documents or documents with untrue content such as account books, balance sheets, profit and loss statements or wage statements and other certifications by third parties for the purpose of tax evasion and misleading the tax authorities, commits tax fraud.

11.2 Examples of penalties imposed

A typical abusive tax avoidance situation cannot be subsumed under the provisions of the Swiss tax offence law. Such situations do not lead to the imposition of penalties (cf. section 11.1). However, the case described

[35] Decision of the Federal Supreme Court dated 28 November 2005, 2A.239/2005.

above[36] illustrates how costly a rejection of the refund of Swiss withholding taxes in an international context can be (cf. section 10.2). The background of the decision is as follows: A Swiss company was a subsidiary of a Danish holding company. An offshore company held the Danish company. The beneficial owner of the whole structure was resident in Bermuda. In the financial year 2000, the Swiss company distributed a dividend. An amount of 35 per cent of the dividend was not directly paid to the shareholder, but was wired to the SFTA according to Swiss withholding tax law. Due to the application of the implicit prohibition of treaty abuse, the refund of the withholding taxes was denied.

12. CURRENT TRENDS

The endeavours of multinational organizations, ie, OECD, G20 or EU, impact the fiscal landscape and the public debate in Switzerland. Profit shifting and tax avoidance issues are nowadays in the focus of a wider public. It can be observed more and more that such public discussions are not limited to questions of whether a structure or a transaction is compliant with tax law. Rather, moral aspects become increasingly important (cf. section 12.1) or as Margaret Hodge, the Labour chairman of the public accounts committee, put it within the Starbuck's debate:[37] *'We are not accusing you of being illegal, we are accusing you of being immoral.'*

12.1 National policy and law

The Swiss traditional anti-avoidance doctrine is mainly based on case law. By analysing the respective recent judgements, two slight trends can be found. First, it appears evident that in the recent past more and more offshore structures have to be assessed by Swiss courts. Second, the Swiss courts try to solve tax avoidance issues by using a broader interpretation of the respective tax provisions and not by the application of the traditional anti-avoidance doctrine (cf. section 10.1). In the case described in section 10.1 for instance, the Swiss Federal Court assumes that the offshore domiciled finance company of the Swiss based group is resident in Switzerland by a broader interpretation of the applicable corporate income tax provision.

In public debates relating to tax avoidance, the same trend as in other countries can be observed. As the current discussions about a top-ranking Swiss politician and the corporate financing of his family-owned group of companies highlight, not only legal but also moral aspects of tax avoidance issues gain more and more relevancy.

12.1.1 The impact and role of the OECD and other international relations

As is commonly known, the OECD released a Comprehensive Action Plan for its Base Erosion and Profit Shifting initiative[38] in 2013 beside further activities in this respect. The EU Commission also presented an Action Plan

36 Decision of the Federal Supreme Court dated 28 November 2005, 2A.239/2005.

37 The Guardian, 'Amazon, Google and Starbucks accused of diverting UK profits', 12 November 2012: *http://www.theguardian.com/business/2012/nov/12/amazon-google-starbucks-diverting-uk-profits*.

38 OECD, Action Plan on Base Erosion and Profit Shifting, 19 July 2013: *http://www.oecd.org/ctp/beps-reports.htm*.

for a more effective EU response to tax evasion and avoidance at the end of 2012. The Action Plan of the EU sets out a comprehensive set of measures, to help Member States protect their tax bases.[39]

In the context of these international developments, Switzerland has, until now, not undertaken any special legislative efforts to combat domestic abusive tax avoidance, such as the introduction of a special general anti-avoidance rule or regulations in regard to the disclosure of aggressive tax planning arrangements[40]. However, as a response and in order to counter the international developments, the Swiss Federal Department of Finance proposed an action plan (so-called 'Corporate Tax Reform III'). It is envisaged to reform the Swiss tax system by taking fiscal and financial measures in order to comply with the international developments as set forth in the OECD and EU action plans. Among other purposes, it plans to lower cantonal tax rates and to set up special tax regimes (eg, licences boxes) or other favourable measures (eg, notional interest deductions). Furthermore, it will be examined whether current tax regimes and practices still applicable today (eg, mixed company, cf. section 7) shall be amended, as they might lose their relevancy in the future due to the new substitution measures.

---

39 Press Release of the EU Commission dated 6 December 2012: *http://europa.eu/rapid/press-release_IP-12-1325_en.htm*.

40 OECD, Action Plan on Base Erosion and Profit Shifting, 19/7/2013, pp. 22 ff.: *http://www.oecd.org/ctp/beps-reports.htm*.

Turkey

Istanbul University, Faculty of Law Dr Z Ertunç Şirin
Moroğlu Arseven E Benan Arseven

PART ONE: TRANSFER PRICING

1. GENERAL OVERVIEW

Even though the term was not explicitly mentioned, transfer pricing has formed part of Turkey's legislative regulations since the 1930s. The country's modern tax regulations were implemented by the (new) Corporate Tax Law no. 5520 in 2006. Under this new Law, article 13 ('Hidden Profit Distribution by Transfer Pricing') incorporated numerous innovations into the Turkish tax system such as compatible price fixing and advanced pricing agreements.

After Turkey's Corporate Tax Law came into force on January 1, 2007, the tax administration expressed their comments and opinions by publishing 'The Guide about Hidden Profit Distribution by Transfer Pricing'. This was followed by the implementation of secondary transfer pricing legislation. After several years of preparation, the tax administration began to initiate tax inspections that remain ongoing to this day.

2. IDENTIFICATION OF LEGISLATIVE FRAMEWORK

Article 13 of Law no. 5520[1] applies where a corporation purchases or sells products or services using prices that are determined to be incompatible

1 *'(1) In the event that the corporations purchase or sell products or services over prices which are determined incompatible with the arm's length principle, the income shall be considered as distributed inappropriately by transfer pricing, completely or partly. Buying, selling, manufacturing and constructing transactions, renting or renting out transactions, borrowing money or lending money and transactions which require bonus, fee, and similar payments, are considered as product or service buying/selling, under any circumstances.*

(2) Relevant person: means partners of the corporations, real person or corporations which the partners are related to, and the real person or corporations which the partners are directly or indirectly affiliated or influence in respect to management, audit or capital. Spouses of partners, lineal kins of partners or spouses, collateral kin including the third degree, and also affiliations by marriage are also considered as related person. All transactions performed with the people in the countries or zones which were declared by the Council of Ministers considering if the tax system of the country where the revenue is obtained is able to create the possibility of taxation on the same level of the Turkish Tax System does and taking also information exchange fact into account, are considered as performed with relevant persons.

(3) Arm's length principle means that the price or cost applied in selling or purchasing products or services with the relevant persons are compatible with the price or cost in case that there is no relation in between. It is obligatory to keep as proof documents the registries, tables and documents of calculations regarding cost or prices which are determined in accordance with the arm's length principle.

(4) Corporations determine the prices or costs which they will apply on their transactions to be performed with the relevant persons, using following methods, whichever is the most appropriate with the nature of the transaction.

(a) Comparable price method: Means that a arm's length sales price that a taxpayer will apply, is determined by comparing the market price which is being applied on selling or purchasing products or services on transactions performed between real or legal persons who don't have any kind of relation with each other.

(b) Cost-plus method: Means that the arm's length price is calculated by increasing the cost of related products or services with an appropriate gross margin.

(c) Resale price method: Means that the arm's length price is calculated by subtracting an appropriate gross sales margin from the price which will be applied in case of reselling products or services which are subject to the transaction, to the real or legal persons who do not have any kind of relation with each other.

(d) In the event that it is not possible to determine the arm's length price with any of the above methods, the taxpayer can apply other methods in their own discretion which are appropriate with the nature of the transaction.

(5) The methods to determine the cost or price to be applied on selling or purchasing products or services with the related persons can be calculated by reaching an agreement with the Ministry of Finance, on taxpayer's request. The method

with the arm's length principle. Under these circumstances, the income will (in whole or in part) be deemed to have been distributed inappropriately by way of transfer pricing.

This is the main principle contained in this provision. After outlining this principle, article 13 goes on to define and explain concepts such as: the definition of a 'relevant person'; the arm's length principle; and methods to be used in determining a compatible price or cost.[2]

For corporations that distribute dividends and limited taxpayers, the amount of income that is deemed to have been distributed inappropriately by transfer pricing is the amount that is transferred to the headquarters. This rule is made in accordance with the practice of Income Tax and Corporation Tax laws.

When Corporate Tax Law no. 5520 came into force, a parallel regulation was also made under Income Tax Law no. 193. Paragraph 5 of article 41 ('Payments Not Admitted as Expense') deals with determining an owner of an enterprise that purchases or sells products or services using a price which is incompatible with the arm's length principle. Here, article 41 ensures that the difference between the compatible cost/price and the applied cost/price is taken into account as being received from the enterprise.[3]

In addition to these main regulations, there are several secondary regulations that are worth noting:

- The Council of Ministers Decree no. 2007/12888:[4] this provides details regarding the practice of arm's length principle, methods for transfer pricing, cash pricing agreements and documentation order of transfer pricing.
- The Council of Ministers Decree no. 2008/13490:[5] this regulates new matters regarding cash pricing agreements.

---

which is determined by this way, is certain along the period and within the conditions that are indicated in the agreement, for a maximum period of 3 years.

(6) *The income which is distributed inappropriately by transfer pricing, completely or partly, is considered as the dividend which is distributed on the last day of an accounting period in which the conditions under that Article have occurred or as the transferred amount to headquarters for limited taxpayers. Taxation transactions which have been performed before, shall be corrected accordingly in respect to taxpayers who are parties. In so far, in order to perform this correction, levied taxes of the company which distributes the income inappropriately, must be certain and paid.*

(7) *Acceptance of hidden distribution of income as a result of domestic transactions performed by and between fully taxpayer corporations and work places or permanent representatives of foreign corporations in Turkey in respect to related persons, is subject to arise of Treasury damage. Treasury damage means that all kinds of tax totals which should have been accrued in the name of the corporation or relevant persons are accrued short or late, because the prices or costs determined in contrary to the arm's length principle.*

(8) *Methods regarding transfer pricing are determined by the Council of Ministers.'*

2 Among others, these include the comparable price method, the cost-plus method, and the resell price method.

3 *'... in case of determining an owner of an enterprise purchases or sells products or services on a price which is incompatible with the arm's length principle, it is ensured that the differences between the compatible costs or prices and the applied costs or prices arising against the enterprise is taken into account as received from the enterprise.*

Spouse, linear kin, collateral kin including third degree and kin by marriage of the enterprise owner, the companies which the enterprise owner is an indirect partner, partners of these companies, other companies which are under control of the enterprise owner in respect to management, audit or capital of these parties, are considered as relevant person.

In practicing of this clause, manufacturing and construction, renting or renting out, borrowing or lending money, transactions which require fee, bonus and similar payments, are considered as selling or purchasing products or services, under any circumstances.

If the differences which are considered as received from the enterprise were taken into account in income tax base or corporate tax base which was declared by the related person, taxing operations of the related person are to be corrected accordingly. In respect to matters which are not included in this article, related persons or transactions performed with the related persons, Article 13 of Corporate Tax Law no. 5520 is implemented.'

4 Official Gazette dated 06.12.2007 and numbered 26722.

5 Official Gazette dated 13.04.2008 and numbered 26846.

- The General Statement Regarding Hidden Profit Distribution by Transfer Pricing Serial no. 1:[6] this provides detailed explanations for scope operation of the regulations which entered into force on 2007 regarding arm's length principle, methods for transfer pricing, cash pricing agreements and documentation order regarding transfer pricing, penalties in transfer pricing, services within group and specific points regarding intangible rights.
- The General Statement Regarding Hidden Profit Distribution by Transfer Pricing Serial No. 2:[7] this provides some explanations regarding cash pricing agreements and documentation order.
- The Circular Note Regarding Hidden Profit Distribution by Transfer Pricing no. TF-1/2008-1: this provides explanations regarding the documentation order and filling the relevant form.

2.1 Federal legislation

Since the Republic of Turkey is a unitary state, no explanations are required under this section.

2.2 State and provincial legislative interplay

Since the Republic of Turkey is a unitary state, no explanations are required under this section.

2.3 International treaties and agreements

There are 80 double taxation prevention agreements signed by Republic of Turkey that are in force as of January 2014. Article 9, which forms the basis of these agreements and regulates the Dependent Enterprises, also includes some matters regarding transfer pricing.[8]

In the relations between dependent enterprises, the financial and commercial targets must be determined between independent enterprises. For independent enterprises, the arm's length principle states that any profit shifting that occurs in favor of the initiating enterprise is taxed in the latter's country of residency.

In light of this, the regulations in the international agreements appear to be consistent with the domestic legislation. They also demonstrate a willingness to enforce the rules and determine transfer pricing mutually

---

6 Official Gazette dated 18.11.2007 and numbered 26704.

7 Official Gazette dated 22.04.2008 and numbered 26855.

8 Article 9
DEPENDENT ENTERPRISES
1.(a) *When a Contracting State enterprise directly or indirectly joins management, control or capital of another Contracting State enterprise or*
(b) *when same persons directly or indirectly join the management, control or capital of a Contracting State enterprise and another Contracting State enterprise and in both cases, the income which should have realized when the conditions formed or imposed in commercial or financial relations between the two enterprise differs from the conditions which may occur from the conditions between independent enterprises, but could not be realized because of these conditions, shall be added to the income of this enterprise and is taxed accordingly.*
2. *An income determined and taxed in an enterprise of a Contracting State may include an income of an enterprise of this State which is taxed in another Contracting State. At the same time, the income determined by this first mentioned State, may not be an notified income and may be an income determined by calculations of this first mentioned State, considering the relations that will occur between the independent enterprises. In such case, if the other State determines that this regulation is right, they will have to make required revisions on the amount of the tax accrued over this mentioned income. Other provision of this Agreement shall be considered when making this revision and if necessary authorized bodies of the Contracting States shall consult each other.'*

with the states that are the parties of the agreement. Of course, the main function of article 9 is to prevent double taxation. Where a transfer pricing amendment is made with any of the other contracting states, this amendment should also be made in the other state.

3. NATIONAL POLICY ISSUES

A regulation which is considered to be in line with the international standards entered into force on 2007. Nevertheless, it is crucial and necessary to interpret and execute these regulations in a right and sustainable way.

Perhaps the most problematic point in the practice of transfer pricing is that the tax administration ignores the need for expertise in determining the compatibility with the arm's length principle in various economic activities. There is no differentiation and specialization based on economic sectors among tax inspection officers. Additionally, the administration provides opinions and utilizes experts on issues that require expertise. One example is not having real bioequivalence in two medicines that are considered as equal or not having the same specifications in two supposedly equal substances. Another national policy issue is the tax administration's reluctance to provide information regarding the proper parties to a tax dispute. This has created a problem that effectively prevents an accused from utilizing their right of defense in the appropriate way.

3.1 Overall national policy announcements

After Turkey's Corporate Tax Law came into force on January 1, 2007, the tax administration expressed their comments and opinions by publishing 'The Guide about Hidden Profit Distribution by Transfer Pricing'. This was followed by the implementation of secondary transfer pricing legislation. After several years of preparation, the tax administration began to initiate tax inspections that remain ongoing to this day.

3.2 National revenue authority initiatives

Since 2010, Turkey's tax administration has started performing tax inspections on transfer pricing matters. During these inspections, the tax authorities focused more on the multinational affiliations initiated in Turkey than selecting sectors.

4. CASE LAW

Even though the tax administration tends to determine if the arm's length principle is implemented on transfer pricing, Turkey's tax jurisdictions tend to render decisions in favor of taxpayers. In most cases, the technical specialties and requirements of the sector in which the taxpayer operates are not considered. This forms the basis of the penal assessment and, in most cases, the tax administration ignores objective explanations made by the taxpayer during the inspection. As such, most of the decisions rendered by the tax jurisdiction favor taxpayers.

5. PENALTIES

There are no specific penalties for transfer pricing. Where a transfer pricing transaction is found to be contrary to the arm's length principle, the general provisions regarding the penalties of the Tax Procedure Law no. 213 apply.

5.1 Types

Tax Procedure Law no. 213 provides three separate penalties for tax irregularities. Two of these penalties, the tax loss penalty and an irregularity fine, are monetary fines that are applied by tax administration. In the case of a tax fraud, a prison sentence shall be implemented on the accused pending the outcome of the case.

In the event that a hidden profit transfer by transfer pricing is determined following an inspection, both the shortfall amount and a tax loss will be implemented.

Where a transfer pricing form has not been submitted, article 352 of Tax Procedure Law states that an irregularity fine shall be imposed. Where the requested information and documentation is not submitted, article 355 of Tax Procedure Law provides imposes a specific irregularity fine.

Imprisonment is regulated under article 359 of Tax Procedure Law no. 213. Where any of the actions mentioned in this article occur, either the tax obligator or its legal representative (if it is a legal person) may be sentenced to between 18 months and 5 years prison. Another situation that is also regulated in the article is *'calculation and accounting frauds in tax books and registries.'*[9] In tax book and accounting fraud claims, the tax authorities may follow case law in which transfer pricing is found to be incompatible with the arm's length principle. Lastly, there must be a moral element proving that the related person acted willfully before a prison sentence can be implemented.

6. DISPUTE RESOLUTION MECHANISMS

There is no dispute resolution mechanism provided specifically for transfer pricing. Instead, Tax Procedure Law no. 213 governs where a transfer price transaction is incompatible with the arm's length principle. There are three fundamental methods under this Law: repentance, reconciliation, and a reduced fee.

The first method is repentance. Where a person commits an action that involves the imposition of a tax loss fine, that person may submit a petition to tax administration in order to relieve themselves. If the petition is successful, the taxpayer will not be subject to any tax loss or fines.

The second method is reconciliation. Here, taxpayers have the option of reconciling a tax assessment and fine by making a submission to the tax administration that executed the assessment. Following negotiations with the tax authorities, it is possible to cancel the tax or fine in part.

9 *'A prison sentence starting from eighteen months up to three years shall be implemented on persons who perform, Calculation and accounting fraud on books and records, open accounts in the name of unreal persons or persons who are not related to the transactions subject to registry, or record the calculations and transactions which are required to be recorded in the books, to other books, documents or recording environments in a way that result in decrease of tax basis, Over the records which are kept or regulated in accordance with the Tax laws and which must be kept and submitted.'*

The third method is a reduced fine. Taxpayers have the right to request a discount by submitting an acceptance to the tax administration to pay the imposed monetary fine. Depending on the specific fine, the tax administration has the option of reducing the tax payable by 1/2 or 1/3 of the total amount.

It should be mentioned that none of these methods are mandatory. Furthermore, taxpayers have the option of taking their dispute before the courts without referring to any of the methods.

6.1 Preferred national options

The most common type of referred method is reconciliation. Nevertheless, this method has been criticized for being contrary to Turkey's constitutional tax principles and creating inequality between the taxpayers. Nevertheless, taxpayers prefer this method because it avoids lengthy lawsuits. Likewise, the tax administration prefers this method because it allows for the collection of as much money as possible within the shortest amount of time.

In additional option is the longstanding practice involving the cancellation of all penalties in return to paying the main tax amount. Other examples of national options include cancelling the tax penalty as well as cancelling 90 per cent of the main amount.

6.2 International options

There are no international options that can be applied by the taxpayers of the Republic of Turkey.

PART TWO: TAX AVOIDANCE

7. ACCEPTABLE TAX PLANNING AREAS/SUBJECTS

Based on the freedom of contract principle, it is legally permissible for taxpayers to organize their transactions in such a way as to create the minimum tax burden.

Like virtually every other country in the world, Turkey has prescribed certain limits to this freedom. Part Two will distinguish tax avoidance from tax fraud and discuss the nuances of both.

8. DEFINING ABUSIVE TAX AVOIDANCE

In accordance with the Economical Approach Principle (discussed below), taxpayers that adopt extraordinary and abnormally methods for the sole purpose of reducing their tax obligations are guilty of tax avoidance.

9. THE LEGISLATIVE FRAMEWORK

The legislative basis for tax avoidance is outlined in article 3 of the Tax Procedure Law no. 213. This article defines tax avoidance and governs the relations between taxpayers and the tax authorities. Furthermore, clause (B) states that: *'In taxation, the incident which produces the tax and the real nature of the procedures in relation to the incident are the essence.'*[10]

Crucially, article 3 points to the principle that ought to be used in the process of the qualification of the tax laws to be executed: the Economical Approach Principle. This provides guidance on the law's purpose, scope, and content. It also outlines the material facts that are relevant in determining whether or not tax avoidance has occurred.

Based on the Economical Approach Principle, the economic essence of the transaction as opposed to its appearance on the surface determines whether a transaction constitutes tax avoidance. In other words, the economic content of a transaction is more important than its form. This principle allows for the taxation of transactions that would otherwise attempt to improperly shelter tax. This is the case whether or not the transaction is outside the scope of private law or lacks the necessary moral element necessary for criminal charges. Tax will become payable so long as a financial result has occurred.

It is worth noting that the tax authorities have applied article 3 in a one-sided manner to justify penal tax assessments. Taxpayers are unable to defend their transactions as constituting legitimate tax planning and falling outside the scope of article 3. Because the tax authorities have refused to hear such arguments, the only option for taxpayers is to bring these justifications before the courts.

11.1 Legislative provisions

General sanction orders are also applied where the tax authorities believe that a transaction crosses the line and constitutes tax avoidance. As mentioned above, Tax Procedure Law no. 213 provides for three separate sanctions where the transfer price of a transaction is different than the arm's length price. Tax loss penalties and procedural penalties are monetary penalties that are applied by the tax authorities. In tax fraud, a prison sentence shall be implemented on the related person following a court ruling. In the event that it is determined that a tax loss occurred by an unjust act, an investigation is conducted and the shortfall amount as well as a tax loss penalty are imposed.

Where the formal requirements (especially the documentary requirements) outlined by Law no. 213 are not performed, the taxpayer is subject to an irregularity fine.

Imprisonment is regulated in the article 359 of Tax Procedure Law no. 213. In order for a prison sentence to be imposed, the requisite moral element proving that the taxpayer acted willfully must be present and determined. Where any of the situations described in the article occur, the taxpayer or their legal representative (if it is a legal person) may be sentenced to imprisonment. These conditions include: accounting fraud; forgery; willfully hiding required documents; and drawing up deceptive or

10 *'In taxation, the incident which produces the tax and the real nature of the procedures in relation to the event are the essence. In case of existence of an allegation which claims there is a factor which financially, commercially and technically is not adequate with the requirements or anomalous and out of routine, the burden of proof shall be on the claimer.'*

false accounting documents. The prison term can range between 18 months and 5 years. Furthermore, a taxpayer who is guilty of tax evasion and is imprisoned may still be subject to the above-mentioned administrative fines.

Uganda

Birungyi, Barata & Associates
Cephas Birungyi, Diana Kasabiiti & Jalia Kangave

PART ONE: TRANSFER PRICING

1. GENERAL OVERVIEW

Transfer pricing relates to the valuation of transactions between associated enterprises, ie, prices for goods and services between related or associated entities. A transfer pricing policy by government is aimed at preventing or curbing tax avoidance in a given jurisdiction by providing for methods to calculate transfer prices for transactions between associated entities.

The focus on transfer pricing by the Ministry of Finance and the Uganda Revenue Authority is relatively new. It was not until 2011 that rules relating specifically to transfer pricing were developed to amplify the limited provisions contained in the Income Tax Act. Before then, transfer pricing was dealt with under the general anti-avoidance provisions in the Income Tax Act.

Uganda's 2011 regulations provide for the application of the OECD guidelines for multi-national enterprises and tax administrations. Under the regulations, Uganda's Income Tax Act (ITA) takes precedence in the event of a conflict between the OECD guidelines, the transfer pricing regulations and the Act. The 2011 Regulations also entrench the requirement of adhering to the arm's length principle in determining the income and expenditures from a transaction. The Uganda Revenue Authority is the body that has the mandate to administer tax laws in Uganda. It has authority to make adjustments to the accounts of a taxpayer to reflect consistency with the arm's length principle. The regulations also make provision for advance pricing agreements to be made with the taxpayer in respect of certain future controlled transactions.

2. IDENTIFICATION OF LEGISLATIVE FRAMEWORK

Uganda has two key legal instruments that impact on transfer pricing: The Income Tax Act Cap 340 (ss. 3, 90 and 91) and the Income Tax (Transfer Pricing) Regulations, 2011.

2.1 Federal legislation

Uganda has a centralised system of government that also applies to tax administration. Therefore, the distinction with respect to federal and provincial laws does not apply. The Uganda Revenue Authority (URA) is the only revenue collecting body with offices across the nation.

Section 90 of the ITA gives the Uganda Revenue Authority the power to distribute, apportion or allocate income, deductions or credits between associates in order to reflect the chargeable income that they would have realised had they been dealing in an arm's length transaction. Associates are defined under s. 3 of the Act to mean persons (other than employees) who act in accordance with the directions, requests, suggestions, or wishes of another person, whether or not they are in a business relationship. Companies are associates where they hold fifty per cent or more of the voting power in another company, either directly or through one or more interposed companies, partnerships or trusts.

The Income Tax (Transfer Pricing) Regulations came into force on 1 July 2011 and apply to controlled transactions where one of the parties to the transaction is located in and subject to tax in Uganda and the other party is located in or outside Uganda. The Regulations define controlled transactions to mean a transaction between associates.

Similarly, Section 91 of the ITA provides that, when determining tax liability, the URA may:

(a) Re-characterise a transaction or an element of a transaction that was entered into as part of a tax avoidance scheme;
(b) Disregard a transaction that does not have substantial economic effect; or
(c) Re-characterise a transaction whose form does not reflect the substance.

2.2 State and provincial legislative interplay

Not applicable.

2.3 International treaties and agreements

The international treaty with the greatest impact is the *East African Community Agreement for the Avoidance of Double Taxation and Prevention of Fiscal Evasion with Respect to Taxes on Income (DTA)*. This agreement was signed on 30 November 2010 but some countries have yet to ratify it for entry into force. The DTA takes precedence over the domestic tax law in case of inconsistence.[1]

Article 9 of the DTA provides for an adjustment of profits for tax purposes with respect to transactions between associated enterprises that are not on an arm's length principle. The Contracting states can make such adjustment if there is justification for it. This is in keeping with Regulation 10 of the Transfer pricing Regulations of 2011. The DTA has provisions for the exchange of information[2] and assistance in collection of taxes.[3]

Member countries of the East African Community are also in consultation to develop a mechanism for an exchange of information between the revenue authorities of the member states. There is already a 'Memorandum of Understanding on the Exchange of Information on Tax Expertise and Other Related Matters' in place that was signed by the revenue authorities of

1 Refer to s. 88(2) Income Tax Act, cap 340.
2 Article 27
3 Article 28

the partner states on November 10, 2010. The MoU spells out the rules and procedures necessary for the operationalization of exchange of information in tax matters.[4]

The East African Community Secretariat, in partnership with the German Development Cooperation, developed a draft Model Agreement on Double Taxation Avoidance among EAC Partner States and non-EAC countries. This model agreement is aimed at providing guidance to partner states in negotiating or updating DTAs that are concluded with non-member countries.

DTAs have played a significant role in the tax treatment of a few, but very significant cases, notably: *Intertek Testing Services International Limited v Uganda Revenue Authority* Civil Appeal No. 55 of 2007; *Bank of Baroda Ltd v The Commissioner General and Uganda Revenue Authority* Civil Suit No. 238 of 2009; *Zain International BV v Uganda Revenue Authority and Heritage Oil & Gas Limited v Uganda Revenue Authority* Civil Appeal No. 14 of 2011.

In *Intertek Testing Services*, Ugandan importers made payments for pre-shipment inspection done abroad. The dispute was whether the payments to non-residents were income derived from Uganda and whether the DTA with the United Kingdom applied to the transactions. Court held that the relief under the DTA was not available to the transactions because the beneficiaries of the income were deemed not to be UK residents.

In the *Bank of Baroda* case, a domestic rate had been assessed on a management charge at the rate of 15 per cent. The DTA was invoked and the rate amended to 10 per cent.

The case of *Zain International* involved the transfer of shares to non-resident companies. The contention of the taxpayer was that the transaction was a sale of immovable property outside Uganda and therefore not taxable under the DTA with the Netherlands.Court agreed with the taxpayer but the case is being appealed by the URA.

Lastly the *Heritage Oil & Gas* case brought into play the Uganda–Mauritius DTA and raised issues of residence, immovable property and treaty shopping. Court found that the capital gain arising from the transfer of Heritage's interest in the property was taxable in Uganda with or without the DTA.

As a result of these precedents, one can expect that there are many more issues involving DTAs that are resolved between the URA and taxpayers which do not make it to the public arena.

What is certain is that, as a member of the African Tax Administration Forum and a member of the OECD Global Forum on Transparency and Exchange of Information for Tax Purposes, the Uganda Revenue Authority is working more intensively and closely with the two bodies on the issue of information exchange. Both the African Tax Administration Forum (ATAF)[5] and the OECD are developing systems on the exchange of information that

4 See East African Community, 'EAC Workshop to Discuss Exchange of Information for Tax Purposes' *http://www.eac.int/index.php?option=com_content&view=article&id=1075:eac-workshop-to-discuss-exchange-of-information-for-tax-purposes&catid=146:press-releases&Itemid=194*.

5 Uganda is a member state of the ATAF.

are likely to have a great impact on the region. In March of 2012, the ATAF council approved a draft model agreement on the exchange of information – the *Agreement on Mutual Assistance in Tax Matters*.[6] This agreement is largely modelled on the OECD's *Agreement on Exchange of Information in Tax Matters* and has three main objectives: exchanging tax information; conducting tax examinations; and assisting in the collection of taxes.[7] Also in 2012, the ATAF council adopted the Internationally Accepted Standards on Transparency and Exchange of Information.[8] In September 2012, the ATAF Working Group on Exchange of Information and Tax Treaties, together with the OECD Task Force on Tax and Development, developed a practical guide on the exchange of information. This guide highlighted the importance of information exchange, the principles governing mutual assistance and outlined how to effectively implement exchange of information provisions.[9] In October of the same year, a Memorandum of Cooperation was entered into between ATAF and the OECD in which the two organizations agreed to work together to improve tax systems in Africa. This included working on the issue of exchange of information.[10]

3. NATIONAL POLICY ISSUES

According to Uganda's National Development Plan,[11] Uganda Vision 2040[12] and the 2013/2014 Budget Speech,[13] one of the main priorities of the government is to ensure that Uganda moves from a low income country to a middle income country within the next three decades. To achieve this policy objective, the country aims, *inter alia*, to improve large infrastructure (particularly repairing and constructing national roads, investment in hydropower and expansion of rural electrification), modernize agriculture, improve the tourism sector and invest in human resource development.

Increasingly, the country has moved towards expanding domestic resource mobilization, with internal funding constituting 81 per cent of the total budget resource in 2013/2014. In comparison, half of the country's budgets during the 1990's were financed internally while the other half were financed externally. As part of its resource mobilization policy, the Minister of Finance proposed in 2013 that there should be more collaboration between the URA, the Kampala Capital City Authority, the Uganda Registration Services Bureau and local governments to ensure that small businesses, which are hard for URA to reach, are identified and taxed. This is in a bid to widen the tax base by decreasing the informal sector.

---

6 Elizabeth Storbeck, 'The African Tax Administration Forum (ATAF)' (2013) online: United Nations, *http://www.un.org/esa/ffd/tax/2013CBTTNA/Presentation_Storbeck.pdf*.

7 See article 2 of the ATAF Agreement.

8 Elizabeth Storbeck, 'The African Tax Administration Forum (ATAF)' (2013) online: United Nations, *http://www.un.org/esa/ffd/tax/2013CBTTNA/Presentation_Storbeck.pdf*.

9 OECD & African Tax Administration Forum, *Practical Guide on Exchange of Information for Developing Countries* (September 2012), *http://www.g20dwg.org/documents/pdf/view/306/*.

10 OECD, 'OECD and ATAF Strengthen Tax Cooperation with Africa' online: OECD, *http://www.oecd.org/ctp/oecdandatafstrengthentaxco-operationwithafrica.htm*.

11 The Republic of Uganda, *National Development Plan (2010/11–2014/15)* online: Office of the Prime Minister, *http://opm.go.ug/assets/media/resources/30/National per cent20Development per cent20Plan per cent202010:11 per cent20- per cent202014:15.pdf*.

12 The Republic of Uganda, *Uganda Vision 2040*, *http://npa.ug/wp-content/themes/npatheme/documents/vision2040.pdf*.

13 Maria Kiwanuka, *Budget Speech: Financial Year 2013/2014*, online: Parliament of Uganda, *http://www.parliament.go.ug/new/images/stories/speeches/budget13.pdf*.

Uganda taxes its residents on their worldwide income while non-residents are taxed on that part of their income that is sourced in the country. Residents are also given a foreign tax credit for taxes paid in other jurisdictions. Uganda aims at being an investment destination by liberalizing its economy, with investors being allowed to repatriate all of their profits. There is, however, a tax on repatriated profits.

There are various policy initiatives that have been undertaken to ensure that the country has a structure in place for international best practice for investments. The country has made legal provisions for anti-money laundering by enacting the Financial Institutions (Anti-Money Laundering) Regulations, 2010. It also has transfer pricing guidelines which are based largely on the OECD guidelines. Trends in recent DTAs are also aimed at reducing withholding tax rates and introducing lower rates for beneficial owners. Lastly, there is a capital gains tax on the disposal of business assets.

3.1 Overall national policy announcements

The URA released its half-year revenue performance for 2013/14 which reflected a decline of 0.6 per cent in GDP growth, which translated into revenue shortfalls.[14] For example, revenue shortfalls of UGX118.14 billion, UGX 161.19 billion and UGX 30.72 billion were registered in VAT, corporation tax and withholding tax respectively. Similarly, there were proposals for the introduction of an excise duty on kerosene, VAT on hotel accommodation and rental income for companies. These proposals were ultimately dropped, resulting in a reduction in projected revenues of UGX 32.7 billion.

Effective May 1, 2014, the URA cancelled the VAT registration of 1,070 persons for failure to satisfy their registration requirements.[15] Those de-registered would still comply with their outstanding obligations. The consequence of de-registration is that these taxpayers can no longer claim input VAT and cannot charge VAT on their supplies (or issue acceptable invoices for claiming VAT). In July 2014, the URA published a 'shame list' of one hundred and seventy eight taxpayers (individuals and companies) with outstanding tax obligations.[16] This list included the name of the company/individual, the guarantor and their outstanding tax obligations.

3.2 National revenue authority initiatives

Regulation 8 of the Transfer Pricing Regulations requires taxpayers with controlled transactions to keep written records with sufficient information and analysis to reflect that their transactions are in accordance with the arm's length principle. This documentation should be prepared before the due date of filing the return for a year of income. There is no requirement

[14] See generally Uganda Revenue Authority, *Press Brief: Half Year Revenue Performance FY 2013/14* online: Uganda Revenue Authority, *https://www.ura.go.ug/#*.

[15] Uganda Revenue Authority, *Public Notice: Cancellation of Registration for Value Added Tax (VAT) Registration*, online: Uganda Revenue Authority, *https://www.ura.go.ug/download/CGMS/VAT per cent20DE-REGISTRATION per cent20- per cent20PUBLIC per cent20NOTICE.pdf*.

[16] Uganda Revenue Authority, *Shame List as at 02-06-2014*, *https://www.ura.go.ug/Resources/webuploads/INLB/FINAL per cent20SHAME per cent20LIST per cent20as per cent20at per cent202-06-2014.pdf*.

that the documentation should be submitted to the URA. In May 2012, the Commissioner General of the URA issued a Practice Note detailing what should be contained in the documentation.[17]

The URA also issued a Tax Investigations Practice Code to explain the mode in which tax investigations are carried out and give taxpayers an opportunity to make full disclosure regarding tax irregularities.[18] This Code is not specific to transfer pricing and covers all tax matters. The Code, together with the Tax Investigations Manual (which regulates the manner in which tax investigations are carried out) is aimed at providing the groundwork for tax audits generally.

3.3 Administrative statements

Other than the Practice Note described in section 3.4 below, the only other statements that shed light on the manner in which audits will be carried out are the Transfer Pricing Regulations. These Regulations identify the following: target persons (that is, associates); factors to be taken into account when comparing transactions; application of the OECD Transfer Pricing Guidelines; how to establish consistency with the arm's length principle; documentation to be kept; advance pricing agreements between the URA and the taxpayer; and various transfer pricing methods.

3.4 Administrative guidelines

On May 5, 2012, the Uganda Revenue Authority issued a Practice Note[19] on 'Transfer Pricing Documentation to be kept by Taxpayers'.[20] This Practice Note clarified that documentation requirements apply to controlled transactions for multinational enterprises or controlled transactions in aggregate equal to or exceeding UGX 500,000,000 (approximately US$ 200,000). The documents should include the following details:

(a) company details,
(b) transaction details,
(c) determination of the arm's length principle and
(d) a summary on whether the controlled transactions comply with the arm's length principle and the need, if any, for transfer pricing adjustments.

The list set out by the Practice Note is not intended to be exhaustive nor is it meant to apply to all types of businesses. The taxpayer retains the primary obligation of maintaining documents of sufficient quality that can adequately and completely describe the transfer pricing analysis conducted and the compliance with the arm's length principle.

17 See Uganda Revenue Authority, *Transfer Pricing Documentation to Be Kept by Taxpayers* (5 May 2012).

18 Uganda Revenue Authority, *Public Notice: Issuance of the Tax Investigations Practice Code*, online: Uganda Revenue Authority, *https://www.ura.go.ug/index.jsp#*.

19 A practice Note is a document setting out the Commissioner General's interpretation of a provision or provisions of the Tax Act. It is binding on the Commissioner General until revoked but does not bind the taxpayer.

20 This note is issued for interpretation of regulation 8(3) of the income tax (Transfer pricing) regulation, 2011.

4. CASE LAW

There is no case law specific to transfer pricing in Uganda, as most of the disputes relating to this issue are often resolved administratively. Those administrative decisions are not made public.

That said, the Kenyan case of *Unilever Kenya Limited v the Commissioner of Income Tax*[21] is persuasive under Ugandan law. The details of this case are discussed under section 12.1.1.

4.1 Current cases

See section 4 above.

4.2 Historical cases of note

See section 4 above.

5. PENALTIES

The ITA provides for general penalties that may also apply in case of transfer pricing related matters. The ITA provides penalties in the following instances:

(a) Failure to furnish a return[22] – a person convicted of this offence is liable to a fine of UGX 300,000.
(b) Failure to keep proper records attracts a penalty of at least UGX 300,000.[23] Where the failure is deliberate, the penalty could lead to imprisonment for a term not exceeding one year.
(c) A person who makes a false or misleading statement to a revenue officer or omits from a statement any matter that results in the statement being misleading in a material particular is liable to a fine not exceeding UGX 500,000. An exception to this rule is where the statement or omission was made knowingly or recklessly. In this case, the fine is not less than UGX 500,000 or imprisonment for a term not exceeding one year, or both.

The ITA has special provisions governing the taxation of petroleum operations. Under those provisions, there are various offenses relating to false statements. Section 89QA makes it an offence to fail to file a return or any other document within a prescribed time. The penalty for such failure is not less than $50,000 and not more than $500,000. The same section makes it an offense to file false or inaccurate returns, attracting the same penalty. Similarly, under s. 89QB, it is an offense to make a false or misleading statement to an officer or the URA or to omit from a statement any matter without which the statement become misleading in a material particular. The penalty is at least $50,000 and not less than $500,000 where the statement or omission is made knowingly or recklessly.

5.1 Types

The Transfer Pricing Regulations contain penalties including:

21 Income Tax Appeal No. 753 of 2003 (High Court of at Nairobi).
22 Section 137 ITA.
23 Section 139 ITA.

(a) A fine not exceeding UGX 500,000 or imprisonment for a term not exceeding six months or both for failure to apply the arm's length principle in determining income and expenditures relating to controlled transactions (Regulation 7);
(b) Failure to keep proper documentation prior to the due date of filing a return attracts a fine not exceeding UGX 500,000 or imprisonment not exceeding six months or both (Regulation 8).

5.2 Special or notable cases

Kasibo Joshua v Commissioner of Customs, Uganda Revenue Authority HCT-00-CC-MA-44-2007

In this case, the applicant brought an action against the respondent for the latter's seizure of the applicant's goods (wines, spirits, two truck motor vehicles and motor boat engines) and the imposition of fines on the goods. The applicant claimed that the taxes and fines imposed on the goods were illegal and the subsequent seizure was not in accordance with the law. The respondent contended that the applicant was involved in smuggling goods and admitted to the offence. The responded further asserted that the applicant compounded the offence under the *East African Community Customs Management Act* (EACCMA) and the penalties imposed thereunder were in accordance with the law. Counsel for the applicant stated that the applicant had admitted to the charges and was repentant but that the respondent still imposed the maximum sentences under the law that was very harsh. The judge noted that s. 219 of the EACCMA gave the Commissioner power to compound offences where a taxpayer admitted that they had committed the offence and requested that their offence be dealt with under that section. He also noted that the applicant in this case had requested for such compounding using the prescribed form. However, a detailed review of the fines revealed various irregularities:
(a) In some cases, the respondent had imposed the maximum fines provided under the various sections of the EACCMA. This was inconsistent with the purposes of compounding an offence;
(b) Some penalties were imposed under a section of the Act which was not a fine-generating section;
(c) There were fines that could not be properly established, as the respondent had not provided the dutiable value of the goods in question.

The Court, therefore, found that the fines imposed by the respondent were contrary to what was provided in the law. Specifically, the judge noted that while the Commissioner had discretion in deciding penalties for compounded offences, the discretion was not exercised properly or judiciously. The Court also found that while the respondent had the powers to forfeit and condemn uncustomed goods under the EACCMA, the fact that the fines and penalties on which this forfeiture was based were irregular, it followed that the forfeiture and condemnation were ultra vires the EACCMA. Consequently, the judge quashed the fines that had been imposed on the applicant. As far as the seizure of the vehicles and motor boat engines was concerned, the Court found that the respondent followed the proper procedure as contained in the EACCMA.

6. DISPUTE RESOLUTION MECHANISMS

In the event of a taxpayer disagreeing with an assessment raised by the URA, the first mechanism for settling the dispute is through lodging an objection with the Uganda Revenue Authority. Where the taxpayer is not satisfied with the URA's objection decision, they can either apply for a review of the decision by lodging an application with the Tax Appeals Tribunal or appeal the decision to the High Court. Appeals to the High Court are, however, limited to questions of law. Where a party is dissatisfied with a decision of the High Court, they may file an appeal with the Court of Appeal. In all of these instances, there are time limits to be complied with. A default of these time limits could deny the taxpayer an opportunity to challenge the decision being contested.

6.1 Preferred national options

There is no favoured method for resolving transfer pricing disputes. The usual mechanism for settling tax disputes stated above applies. In practice, however, these disputes have largely been resolved administratively.

At the High Court level, mediation has been incorporated as a mandatory first step to settling disputes. The parties are given sixty days within which to reach an agreement, failure of which the court will hear the matter. The mediation process is confidential and does not in any way prejudice the Court decision in the event of failure to settle. It is also a preferred method because each party is required to bear its own costs unless they agree otherwise.

6.2 International options

Uganda has Bilateral Investment Treaties (BITs) with Denmark, France, Germany, Italy, the Netherlands, Switzerland and the United Kingdom. These treaties often have internationalization clauses that provide for the settlement of investment disputes. Article 9 of the BIT between Uganda and the Netherlands, for example, provides that disputes between the contracting state and an investor are to be settled at the International Centre for Settlement of Investment Disputes.

There are also various foreign investment contracts that Uganda enters into directly with investors. Most recently, the agreements that have attracted public scrutiny are those signed between the Government of Uganda and companies in the oil and large infrastructure (particularly dam) sectors. These agreements also contain internationalization clauses.

The Double Taxation Agreements also have mutual agreement procedure provisions.[24] These allow a taxpayer of a contracting state to complain against the actions of the other contracting state, if such actions result in a tax liability for them that is not in accordance with the provisions of the

24 Article 26.

DTA. The competent authorities of each contracting state are encouraged to resolve the dispute by mutual agreement.

PART TWO: TAX AVOIDANCE

7. ACCEPTABLE TAX PLANNING AREAS/SUBJECTS

The Uganda ITA has anti-avoidance provisions, which are discussed in the ensuing section. There are, however, some provisions in the Act that may be utilized by taxpayers to reduce their tax liability.

Uganda has nine Double Taxation Agreements (DTAs) in force: Zambia (1968), the United Kingdom (1993), Norway (2001), South Africa (2001), Denmark (2001), India (2004), Mauritius (2004), Italy (2005) and the Netherlands (2006). The withholding tax rates relating to interests, dividends, royalties and management fees are largely at 10 per cent. The UK is one exception, where the withholding rates are 15 per cent. The Netherlands is another exception, where the withholding rate for income from dividends could go as low as 0 per cent. Ordinarily, the withholding tax rates in the absence of a DTA are at 15 per cent.

There is some benefit to be derived from using debt instead of equity for financing businesses because interest charged on the former is an allowable deduction. However, there are Thin Capitalisation Rules that limit the amount of interest that can be deducted.

Section 89 (1) of the ITA provides:

'Where a foreign-controlled resident company which is not a financial institution has a foreign debt-to-foreign equity ratio in excess of 2 to 1 at any time during a year of income, a deduction is disallowed for the interest paid by the company during that year on that part of the debt which exceeds the 2 to 1 ratio.'

The Ministry of Finance has recently proposed an extension of the thin capitalisation rules. In the 2014/2015 Budget Speech, the Minister proposed that deductions for interest paid to non-associated persons should be restricted by not exceeding 50 per cent of earnings before interest and depreciation.[25] This proposal is yet to be discussed in and approved by Parliament.

Similarly, interest paid by a resident company in respect of debentures is exempt from income tax where:

(a) the debentures were issued outside Uganda to raise a loan outside Uganda;
(b) the debentures were widely issued to raise funds for carrying out a business in Uganda or the interest is paid to a bank or a financial institution of a public character; and
(c) the interest is paid outside Uganda (s. 83 (5) ITA).

It ought to be noted that for the interest to be exempt from tax, all three conditions must be met. In 2006, the URA issued a Practice Note clarifying the meaning of 'widely issued'.[26]

---

25 Maria Kiwanuka, *Budget Speech: Financial Year 2014/2015* online: Ministry of Finance, *http://www.finance.go.ug/index.php/national-budget/budget-speeches*.html.

26 See Allen Kagina, *Practice Notes – 2006* (24th July 2006) : Note 4.

Section 74(2) ITA provides that a dividend paid to a resident company (other than an exempt organisation) by another resident company is exempt from tax if the company receiving the dividend controls – directly or indirectly – 25 per cent or more of the voting power of the company paying the dividend. However, this provision does not apply if the dividend is being paid to a financial institution by virtue of its ownership of redeemable shares in the company making the payment. It also does not apply in cases of dividend stripping.

8. DEFINING ABUSIVE TAX AVOIDANCE

Uganda's ITA contains a specific definition for tax avoidance scheme. The Act contains a general anti-avoidance rule in s. 91. There are also special provisions on the taxation of petroleum operations that are targeted towards anti-avoidance.

9. THE LEGISLATIVE FRAMEWORK

Section 91 of the ITA provides the GAAR. For the purposes of determining tax liability, the Commissioner may:

(a) re-characterize a transaction or an element of a transaction that was entered into as part of a tax avoidance scheme;
(b) disregard a transaction that has no substantial economic effect; or
(c) re-characterize a transaction whose form does not reflect the substance.

The section defines a tax avoidance scheme to include *'any transaction, one of the main purposes of which is the avoidance or reduction of liability to tax.'*

In addition, Section 89I(2) is to the effect that for petroleum operations, except as otherwise agreed in writing between the Government of Uganda and a contractor, all transactions should be accounted for at arm's length prices. Where required to do so by the Commissioner, a contractor should disclose all non-arm's length transactions in their returns for the specified period.

10. KEY CASES OF INTEREST

Two cases are highlighted in section 10.2 below: *Skenya Motors (U) Ltd v Uganda Revenue Authority* and *Downtown Forex Bureau v Uganda Revenue Authority*.

10.1 Current cases

Both cases cited in section 10 above are on appeal by the Uganda Revenue Authority and are yet to be determined by the Appellate Courts.

10.2 Key historical cases

In *Down Town Forex Bureau Limited, Tushar Ruparelia & Babulal Ruparelia v Uganda Revenue Authority*,[27] the respondent re-characterised income that had been paid to the second and third applicants by the first applicant from directors' fees to dividends. The 2nd and 3rd applicants were

[27] TAT Application No. 04 of 2012.

shareholders and directors of the 1st applicant who, between 2006 and 2009, received various payments to cater for their personal needs including medical bills, school fees, rent and utility bills. These payments were characterised as directors' fees and Pay As You Earn (PAYE) withheld from them. Upon auditing the accounts of the 1st applicant, the respondent used s. 91 of the ITA to re-characterize these payments by treating them as dividends. Consequently, the respondent raised additional assessments and computed penalties for understating tax. One of the main issues in the case was whether the respondent was correct to re-characterise the payments. The applicants argued that it was wrong to characterise these payments as dividends since dividends could only be declared at the end of the financial year after net profits after taxes had been determined. They added that dividends are distributed to shareholders on a pro-rata basis, yet in the present instance, the directors were paid the same amount. The respondent argued that they based their re-characterization on the fact that the payments were made only to those directors who were also shareholders. The third director (who was not shareholder) did not receive these payments. Also, while the payments were characterised as bonuses, no other employees were paid bonuses during the years in question. The respondent added that there was no provision in the company's Articles of Association that dividends could only be declared at the end of the year. The Tribunal found that the respondent had failed to prove that the applicants were involved in a tax avoidance scheme. They noted that the directors, as employees of the company, were entitled to bonuses and the company had taxed the same at the maximum PAYE rate. Second, it was difficult to characterise these payments as dividends when they were not paid in proportion to shareholding. Also, dividends were paid out of ascertained or expected profits from draft quarterly or half yearly accounts, which was not the case here. They added that it is an acceptable commercial practice to pay directors fees and bonuses in accordance with company policies and regulations. It was also not compulsory that bonuses should be paid to all employees since the nature of bonus payments was that they were a reward for extraordinary performance. The Tribunal concluded[28] that the responded was wrong to re-characterize these payments.

Similarly, in *Skenya Motors (U) Limited v Uganda Revenue Authority*,[29] the applicant made payments UGX 390,000,000 and UGX 712,500,000 in 2008 and 2009 respectively to two of its directors who were also shareholders of the company. The company had a total of four shareholders, two of

[28] There is a dissenting judgment in which the third member of the Tribunal held that the respondent had been right to re-characterize the payment as dividends. The Tribunal member relied on various facts to support his finding. He noted that there was no evidence to show that the payments were made in respect of company business – such as attending board meetings and managing the company. Instead, the amounts were paid for personal expenses. Also, the payments received were not supported by what was stated in the company's Articles of Association. He added that if the payments had indeed been directors' fees, then the third director should also have received payments. It was also suspect that the bonus was only paid to the two directors who were shareholders. There were also no minutes of a general meeting, letters of appointment or contracts or decisions to support the award of bonuses. All of this was made worse by the fact that the payments were between three and ten times higher than the profits that the company declared. In the end, he found that these payments were shams. They were in substance a distribution of dividends and could be re-characterized as such under s. 91(1)(c) that allowed the Commissioner to re-characterise a transaction the form of which did not reflect the substance.

[29] TAT Application No. 07 of 2012.

whom were also directors. However, these directors did not have contracts of service with the company, they were not on the pay roll and did not receive regular remuneration. The payments to the director-shareholders were characterised by the applicant as bonus payments. One of the directors explained that the payments were made to them because of personal guarantees that they made towards purchasing truck at a cheaper price. These guarantees, he argued, enabled the company to make more profits. Unlike in the *Down Town Forex Bureau* case, the company in this case issued bonuses to all of its employees. The bonuses were in different amounts, depending on the level of management and performance. The two directors shared the amounts stated above in the ratio of 61:40 and 38:60 respectively. These payments were supported by a board resolution that was not filed with the Registrar of Companies. The respondent subsequently re-characterised them as dividends. In addition, the respondent made a revised assessment in respect of withholding tax and corporate tax. One of the issues was whether the respondent was right to re-characterise the payments from bonus payments to dividends. The Tribunal held that the payments were bonuses. It noted that the respondent had failed to recognize the other two shareholders in the company by insisting that the directors were the only – and majority – shareholders of the company at the time the payments were made. If dividends were to be paid, they would have been paid to all the four shareholders on a pro-rata basis. It also disagreed with the respondent's reasoning that the directors did not devote substantial time to the company to be entitled to such payments. As to the payments being out of range when compared to the bonuses received by other employees, the Tribunal first observed that companies are at liberty to determine how bonuses should be awarded. Second, the two directors, by putting up personal guarantees, had made extra effort to ensure that the company obtained funds to purchase the trucks that resulted in the profits. The Tribunal[30] held that there was no tax avoidance scheme to justify the re-characterisation of the income. Subsequently, the definition of dividends under the ITA was amended to include the issue of bonus shares to shareholders.

11. PENALTIES

There are no penalties that are specific to abusive tax avoidance. However, penalties relating to the provision of false or misleading statements and those relating to understating of tax are applicable in these instances.

[30] Dissenting, one of the Tribunal members held that they payments were not bonuses. First, the resolution that purported to award the bonuses had not been registered with the Registry of Companies. Second, the resolution was made in March 2010, after the said payments had been made out. Third, there was no evidence to show that there was a duly filed and registered allotment of shares that increased the shareholders from two to four. He found that the respondent was right in re-characterizing the income of the directors as a distribution of profits. First, these directors were not on the company payroll. Second, the payments were enormous and not proportional to what was paid to other staff members. These payments also constituted a significant proportion of the company's profits. If the directors had not been shareholders, it is quite unlikely that such a payment would have been approved. Consequently, by characterizing them as business expenses, the applicant's intention was to reduce their tax liability.

11.1 Legislative provisions

Section 91 of the Income Tax Act applies to the GAAR. This section allows the Commissioner to re-characterize income and deductions of a taxpayer where:

(a) a transaction or an element of a transaction is entered into as part of a tax avoidance scheme;
(b) the transaction does not have substantial economic effect;
(c) the form of the transaction does not reflect its substance.

11.2 Examples of penalties imposed

In both *Down Town Forex Bureau* and in *Skenya Motors (U) Limited*, the URA sought to rely on s. 154 of the ITA. This section provides for penalties for understating provisional tax estimates. Where a provisional taxpayer's estimate or revised estimate of chargeable income for a year of income is less than 99 per cent of the taxpayer's actual chargeable income assessed for that year, the taxpayer is liable to a penalty tax. This tax is equal to 20 per cent of the difference between the tax calculated in respect of the estimate and that calculated in respect of 90 per cent of the taxpayer's actual chargeable income for the year of income.

Another penalty imposed administratively is the penalty tax imposed for providing false and misleading statements. This tax was also introduced but ultimately abandoned in the *Skenya Motors (U) Limited* case.

Section 153 of the ITA states that a person who knowingly or recklessly makes a statement to a URA officer that is false or misleading in a material particular or omits in a statement to an officer a matter without which a statement is misleading in a material particular and the tax properly payable by the person exceeds that which was payable based on the false or misleading statement or omission, is liable to a penalty tax equal to double the amount of the excess.

12. CURRENT TRENDS

The EAC partner states have in place a draft Code of Conduct against harmful tax practices. It deals with tax practices that are deemed to be potentially harmful. Non-adherence to transfer pricing rules is one such practice as it may create competitive distortions in the economy and affect the competitive position of an enterprise. So far, stakeholders such as the Revenue Authorities and the Ministries of Finance in EAC have considered this Code of Conduct. However, it is yet to be passed into law by the East African Legislative Assembly (EALA).

On the national scene, Uganda's ITA defines what constitutes tax avoidance and allows for re-characterisation of any scheme that is deemed a tax avoidance scheme, so as to reflect the substance of the transaction.

12.1 National policy and law

There is no published government policy in place with respect to tax avoidance save for what is embodied in the various tax laws. Uganda's ITA gives the Commissioner General URA wide discretionary powers to determine what constitutes a tax avoidance scheme. This practice has its pros and cons. On the downside, these discretionary powers can be easily abused. The upside is that any and every transaction can be brought within the law as long as the tax collector can show that the arrangement of the taxpayer is primarily to reduce its tax liability.

Particularly for Uganda, there is progress being made to revise the incentives policy with an aim of reducing such incentives and exemptions. The cost in terms of lost revenue and value for money assessments is being done.[31]

12.1.1 The impact and role of the OECD and other international relations

The OECD guidelines on transfer pricing have a huge impact on the manner in which transfer pricing in Uganda is being handled by policy and administrative bodies. Regulation 6 of the *Income Tax (Transfer Pricing) Regulations* provides, for example, that the transfer pricing regulations are to be applied in a manner consistent with:

(a) the arm's length principle in Article 9 of the OECD Model Tax Convention on Income and Capital; and
(b) the OECD Transfer Pricing Guidelines for Multi-national Enterprises and Tax Administrations, approved by the Council of the OECD for publication pm 13 July 1995 as revised from time to time.

In the event of an inconsistency between the regulations, the ITA and the OECD documents, the ITA prevails.

There is also the Kenyan case of *Unilever Kenya Limited (formerly East African Industries Limited) v The Commissioner of Income Tax Income Tax Appeal No. 753 of 2003* which has been quite persuasive to the understanding of transfer pricing in Uganda. In that case, Unilever Kenya Limited (UKL) manufactured goods on behalf of Unilever Uganda Limited (UUL), a related company, and supplied its name in accordance with the orders of the latter. During the same period, UKL manufactured and sold goods to the Kenyan domestic and export market and to customers that were not related to the company. The prices charged by UKL to UUL were lower than those charged in domestic sales and domestic export sales for identical goods. The Commissioner of Income Tax raised assessments against UKL on grounds that the goods sold to UUL were not sold at arm's length. In arriving at this decision, the Commissioner relied on the Comparable Uncontrolled Price Method and rejected the Cost Plus Method that had been used by UKL.

One of the major issues for determination by the Court was:

'Whether in the absence of specific guidelines from the Kenya Revenue Authority on this issue (of transfer pricing), the OECD guidelines and methods prescribed thereunder for the calculation of an arm's length price are a proper and reasonable and objectively acceptable basis for the determination of an arm's length price as required under S. 18(3) [KITA].'

In this matter, the Court had the following to say:[32]

---

31 'State by the IMF mission on the conclusion of a visit to Uganda', Press release, 28 October 2011, *www.imf.org*
32 Refer to p. 12 of the judgment.

'Now the guidelines do not form the laws of the countries in question. They are simply "guidelines", guiding the world of business, that is business enterprises and taxing authorities of those countries in arriving at proper transfer pricing principles for purposes of computation of income tax. I am therefore unable to accept the argument that in view of the alleged clear wording of the s. 18(3) of the Act, no guidelines are necessary here in Kenya. That is rather simplistic and devoid of logic. We live in what is now referred to as a "global village". We cannot overlook or side-line what has come out of the wisdom of taxpayers and collectors in other countries. And especially because of the absence of any such guidelines in Kenya, we must look elsewhere.'

The Court found that there was no evidence of tax fraud or tax cheating, the only real disagreement being in methods used to compute tax. He added that the use of different transfer pricing methods, as long the method applied was proper or lawful, was acceptable as long as there was no fraudulent trading involved. The judge concluded that the cost plus method used by UKL to arrive at the arm's length price was not a wrong method. What is important about the Unilever case is its emphasis on the role of international standards and principles such as those found in the OECD guidelines.

For Uganda, Regulation 6 of the Transfer pricing regulations specifically provides for the application of the OECD guidelines and methods prescribed in those guidelines. However, in the event of an inconsistency between the ITA and OECD documents, the ITA takes precedence.

The OECD also has a Code of Conduct against harmful tax practices. This Code deals with instances in which a state may exploit the tax systems of other countries by enacting special tax provisions that principally erode the tax base of other countries thereby creating spill-over effects on the other countries.

The EAC partner states, of which Uganda is a member, have adopted a draft Code of Conduct against harmful tax practices. The idea was borrowed from the OECD Code of Conduct although the EAC Code of Conduct against harmful tax competition has been tailored to meet the specific challenges in the EAC region. As already mentioned, it is yet to be passed into law by the EALA.

The aim of the Code is to identify and eliminate potentially harmful tax practices within the EAC region. These practices include zero or low effective tax rates; the lack of effective exchange of information; the lack of transparency; an artificial definition of a tax base; state aid and subsidies; residence taxation principles; the existence of secrecy provisions; advance tax rulings; regimes promoted as tax minimization vehicles.

UK

Ashurst LLP Richard Palmer & Nicholas Gardner

PART ONE: TRANSFER PRICING

1. GENERAL OVERVIEW

Since 1915, the UK has had a comprehensive regime based on the arm's length principle for applying transfer pricing methodologies to transactions between enterprises under common control. These rules operate as part of the UK's income tax (for individuals) or corporation tax (for companies) self-assessment regime and enterprises are required both to compute their taxable profits using transfer pricing adjustments (where applicable) and to maintain sufficient records and documentation recording the methodology adopted.

2. IDENTIFICATION OF LEGISLATIVE FRAMEWORK

2.1 Federal legislation

The UK's transfer pricing regime is contained in Part 4 of *TIOPA*.[1] The transfer pricing provisions broadly apply where (i) any two entities have entered into any provision (the 'actual provision') by means of a transaction or a series of transactions, (ii) those two entities satisfy a connection test (referred to as the 'participation condition') and (iii) the actual provision differs from the provision which would have been made as between persons acting at arm's length.[2]

If the conditions above are satisfied and the provision has the effect of reducing the UK tax liability of one of the entities (as compared to an arm's length provision), the effect of the regime is to provide for that person's tax liability to be calculated on the basis of an arm's length provision rather than an actual provision.[3]

The participation condition[4] varies depending on whether or not the relevant provision relates to a financing arrangement (ie, an arrangement for providing, guaranteeing or otherwise in connection with any debt, capital or other form of finance).

The participation condition is satisfied if at the time of the relevant transaction (or within six months following that date in the case of financing arrangements):

(a) one of the parties directly or indirectly participates in the management, control or capital of the other; or

---

1 *Taxation (International and Other Provisions) Act* 2010.
2 See s. 147(1) *TIOPA* 2010.
3 See ss. 147(2) to 147(5) *TIOPA* 2010.
4 See s. 148 *TIOPA* 2010.

(b) the same person or persons directly or indirectly participates in the management, control or capital of both parties.

Broadly speaking, if a person (together with their connected parties) has rights which enable or would enable it to control another person or, where two persons each hold at least 40 per cent of rights to control another person, those persons will be taken to participate in management, control or capital.[5]

In the case of financing arrangements, the participation condition is also satisfied where one person is a company and the other persons act together in relation to the financing arrangements and the other persons taken together would have control of the company. In that case, each such person is treated as satisfying this participation condition.[6]

(a) Exemptions

The transfer pricing rules do not generally apply to companies which are small or medium-sized enterprises[7] in the relevant accounting period.[8] However, if the relevant company elects, or in certain circumstances, HMRC serves a notice, the transfer pricing provisions become applicable to those entities.[9]

(b) Compensating adjustments

In circumstances where a transaction is entered into between two persons within the charge to UK income tax or corporation tax, the legislation allows a person to claim a compensating adjustment in circumstances where if the actual provision was replaced by an arm's length provision, their taxable profit would have been reduced. The effect of the compensating adjustment is to allow that person to calculate their taxable profits on the basis that the arm's length provision has been imposed instead of the actual provision.[10] On 25 October 2013, HMRC introduced anti-avoidance legislation preventing individuals (typically carrying on business through an LLP structure) from claiming compensating adjustments in relation to transactions with companies (exploiting mismatches in the income and corporation tax rates).[11]

2.2 State and provincial legislative interplay

Not applicable.

2.3 International treaties and agreements

The UK has a wide network of international double tax treaties which will be of relevance to cross-border transactions. However, generally these are

5 See ss. 157 to 160 *TIOPA* 2010.
6 See ss. 161 and 162 *TIOPA* 2010.
7 The definition of a Small and Medium-sized enterprise is based on the Annex to Commission Recommendation 2003/361/EC of 6th May 2003.
8 See s. 166 *TIOPA* 2010.
9 See ss. 167 to 168 *TIOPA* 2010.
10 See s. 174 *TIOPA* 2010.
11 See clause 69 *Finance Bill 2014* (published on 27 March 2014).

based on the OECD's arm's length principle and, for the reasons discussed in section 3.4 below, will have a similar effect to the domestic legislation.

3. NATIONAL POLICY ISSUES

The transfer pricing legislation is one of a series of measures which HMRC has introduced to prevent erosion of the UK tax base. Other measures include the worldwide debt cap, rules treating profit dependent interest as distributions and controlled foreign company legislation.

HMRC have focussed particularly on issues regarding the tax deductibility of interest on shareholder debt, payments of royalties for intangible assets and certain commissionaire sales arrangements designed to minimise UK taxable profits.

3.1 Overall national policy announcements

The UK Government has been one of the leading advocates of the OECD project for countering Base Erosion and Project Shifting.[12] The UK Government is advocating that transfer pricing documentation requirements should be standardised on a global basis to reduce the demands of compliance and cost to multinational groups. It is also supporting the proposal of a country-by-country reporting template to give tax authorities a clearer picture of these entities' global profits and taxes.

The UK is also supporting the OECD initiative to adjust the 'arm's length price' principle to prevent multinational groups arguing that excessive risk capital and intangible assets are located in very low-tax jurisdictions and therefore allocating residual profits to those jurisdictions.

3.1 National revenue authority initiatives

Since 2008, HMRC have made some effort to improve the speed of the resolution of transfer pricing enquiries. Substantial progress has been made, and the average time taken to resolve disputes has been reduced from 38 months at the end of the first quarter in 2008 to 25 months in the 12 months leading up to 31 December 2013.[13]

HMRC has sought to improve the processes for obtaining Advance Pricing Agreements, and in 2010 revised its guidance in relation to the agreement process.[14] Similarly in 2012, HMRC revised the guidelines for the Advanced Thin Capitalisation Agreement process as part of a drive to speed up the time taken to conclude an agreement.[15]

3.2 Administrative statements

HMRC have published extensive guidance on transfer pricing matters in their International Manual.[16] The topics covered include the legislation

---

12 HMRC and HM Treasury paper on 'Tackling aggressive tax planning in the global economy: UK priorities for the G20-OECD project for countering Base Erosion and Profit Shifting' (March 2014).

13 Transfer Pricing Statistics published at *http://www.hmrc.gov.uk/transfer-pricing-stats.pdf.* (Note: this source was archived on 6 February 2014; however, you can still access it in the National Archives if you click on the link at the bottom of the following HMRC webpage: *http://www.hmrc.gov.uk/international/transferpricing.htm.*)

14 Statement of Practice2/10 – Advance Pricing Agreements.

15 Statement of Practice1/12 – Advance Thin Capitalisation Agreements under the APA Legislation.

16 HMRC International Manual published at http://www.hmrc.gov.uk/manuals/intmanual/index.htm

and its principles, methodology, transactions and structures, business structures and operational guidance. Whilst the published guidance is not law, demonstrating compliance with its terms is likely to assist taxpayers in mitigating penalties that may otherwise become due if a transfer pricing adjustment gives rise to a tax liability.

3.3 Administrative guidelines

The UK legislation expressly provides that where double taxation arrangements incorporate the whole or any part of the OECD model, they are to be treated under the UK domestic legislation in such manner as best ensures consistency with the transfer pricing guidelines.[17] The transfer pricing guidelines are defined for this purpose to mean the version of the Transfer Pricing Guidelines for Multinational Enterprises and Tax Administration approved by the OECD on 22 July 2010, or such other document approved and published by the OECD in place of that (or a later) version. They also include such other material published by the OECD as an update or supplement to those guidelines. Accordingly, HMRC and the UK Courts will have regard to these guidelines in construing UK domestic legislation for arrangements where a double tax treaty applies. In practice, they take a similar approach even for purely domestic transactions. In the context of restricting interest deductions on related party debt whilst there are no formal thin capitalisation safe harbours, historical guidelines have indicated debt:equity ratios of 3:1, and interest cover ratios of 1:1.[18] Different ratios can, in practice, apply within different sectors of the economy. For example, in the real estate sector, loan to value covenants can be accepted as arm's length up to 80 per cent depending on the type of real estate.

4. CASE LAW

Transfer pricing disputes are generally settled through negotiation between the taxpayer and HMRC during the course of enquiries into the taxpayer's self-assessment return. This has led to a scarcity of tax litigation in relation to transfer pricing legislation and/or methodology and there is only one relatively recent UK case, *DSG Retail v HMRC*[19] which has been decided by the UK courts.[20] The development of the UK's transfer pricing methodology has historically been significantly influenced by some EU case law which is also described in more detail in section 4.2 below.

4.1 Current cases

This case concerned a group of companies including DSG Retail Ltd (the 'Dixons Group') whose businesses comprised that of retailing electrical

---

17 See s. 164 *TIOPA* 2010.

18 D2.650 Finance: Inward Loans, Simon's Taxes.

19 *DSG Retail Ltd and others v Revenue and Customs Commissioners* [2009] 11 ITLR 869. (Note that part of the case concerned an earlier version of the transfer pricing legislation which is no longer of relevance but the relevant issues are discussed in the main body of text above.)

20 There have been other cases in relation to predecessor transfer pricing legislation*Ametalco UK v Inland Revenue Commissioners* [1996] STC (SCD) 399 and *Waterloo plc and others v Inland Revenue Commissioners* [2002] STC (SCD) 95 which are only of historic interest.

goods. The Dixons Group also offered its customers extended warranties relating to goods sold.

Until 1996, the Dixons Group entered into contracts with Cornhill Insurance under which Cornhill Insurance was the insurer of the extended warranties sold to customers. It reinsured 95 per cent of that risk to Dixons Insurance Services Limited ('DISC'), another member of the Dixons Group resident in the Isle of Man.

Following an increase in insurance premium tax in April 1997, Appliance Serviceplan Limited ('ASL'), a non group company, issued service contracts rather than warranties. ASL's liabilities were wholly insured by DISC.

The relevant issues considered in *DSG Retail v HMRC* were (i) whether the transactions resulted in a provision being made or imposed between DISC and other members of the Dixons Group; (ii) whether that provision would have been made if the parties had been independent; (iii) what provision would have been imposed by parties acting at arm's length; and (iv) the effect of that provision of the profits of the UK Dixon Group Companies.

(i) Whether the transactions resulted in a provision being made or imposed between DISC and other members of the Dixons Group

The Court held that it is necessary to identify a provision between two persons and that there is no scope for reading 'two' as 'two or more'. The term 'provision' is not defined but was held not to be limited to formal or enforceable arrangements, though it could also include informal arrangements and understandings and a series of the same.

Prima facie, the reinsurance contract was between Cornhill and DISC who were unconnected. As such it might be thought that transfer pricing principles could not apply. However, in 1993, members of the Dixons group renegotiated a commercial reduction to the amounts paid to Cornhill for the insurance contract which had the effect of reducing Cornhill's profits from the contract. Cornhill made no attempt to renegotiate the terms of its own contract with DISC. If Cornhill had been considering its own interests it would have applied a similar commercial squeeze on DISC. The decision not to renegotiate led to an inference that it had agreed with members of the Dixons Group not to do so when its own contract was renegotiated. The Court concluded that there was a provision between the relevant members of the Dixons Group and DISC for DISC to enter into the reinsurance contract on the unchanged terms.

Similarly, in relation to the service contract arrangements with ASL, there was a provision between the parties imposed by a series of contracts. The documentary evidence recorded that they wished to replace the existing structure with a similar structure involving the same parties on the same terms (ie, an arrangement which involved DISC). There was always an expectation of the income accruing to DISC; particularly to retain the tax benefits of DISC (which was exempt from tax in the Isle of Man).

(ii) Whether that provision would have been made if the parties had been independent

In considering this question, the Court relied heavily on the OECD guidelines noting the importance of looking for comparable transactions so long as they are truly comparable, the need to strive to make adjustments to create comparability if at all possible and that more than one method may be considered.

The Special Commissioners considered a number of potential comparables, but were not satisfied that any were truly comparable or that they would be adjusted satisfactorily. The particular issues they encountered were the bargaining powers of the parties; the substantial variance of information available about the insured risks over time; the fact that one of the potential comparables related only to satellite equipment and not electrical goods generally; and the absence of available data to adjust commission rates for more risky businesses to ones with less risk. A large independent insurer, Domestic & General, might have been comparable as they provided similar services to independent retailers, but they had much stronger bargaining power with independent retailers than DISC had with the Dixons Group.

The Special Commissioners held that a profit split methodology should be adopted based on the capital asset pricing model. Since DISC had no debt funding, the appropriate measure was the opportunity cost of equity, which is the rate of return an investor would require in order to invest in share capital of a comparable business. In view of the relative bargaining power, all the residual profit was held to be allocated to DSG. The hearing was then adjourned to allow the parties to agree the exact methodology.

Whilst the case is helpful in demonstrating the Court's approach to transfer pricing issues and the priority given to seeking comparable transactions as a transfer pricing method, it also highlights the difficulties encountered in identifying true comparables, such that ultimately, profit split methodologies may have to be used instead.

4.2 Historical cases of note

The case of *Lankhorst-Hohorst GmbH v FinanzamtSteinfurt*[21] has had a significant impact on the structure of UK transfer pricing legislation. Following this judgment, the UK government concluded that its transfer pricing legislation (which previously only applied to cross-border transactions) was in breach of the principle of the freedom of establishment.

---

[21] *Lankhorst-Hohorst GmbH v FinanzamtSteinfurt* [2002] 5 ITLR 467. The case concerned a loan which had been granted to Lankhorst-Hohorst GmbH by its shareholder Lankhorst-Hohorst BV. The German tax authorities sought to tax the interest paid under this loan as covert distributions of profits. Lankhorst-Hohorst GmbH challenged this decision for a number of reasons, one of which was that the German legislation was discriminatory in light of the treatment afforded to German shareholders who were entitled to the tax credit. The Court held that interest paid by a resident subsidiary on loan capital provided by a non-resident parent company was taxed as a covert dividend at a rate of 30 per cent, whereas, in the case of a resident subsidiary whose parent company is also German resident and receives a tax credit, interest paid was treated as expenditure and not as a covert dividend. Such a difference in treatment between subsidiary companies based on the residence of their parent company was held to constitute an obstacle to the freedom of establishment. This obstacle was not objectively justifiable by reasons such as the protection of tax revenue or the prevention of tax evasion. In relation to the former, it did not constitute an overriding reason and, in relation to the latter, the legislation was not targeted at wholly artificial arrangements.

In 2004, rules were introduced to apply the same transfer pricing principles to transactions between UK and cross-border companies.[22] This has given rise to an increased compliance burden for UK companies in circumstances where transfer pricing of UK to UK transactions is unlikely to have a significant impact on the amount of UK tax collected overall.

5 PENALTIES

5.1 Types

There is no specific penalty regime for transfer pricing documentation or errors, but the general self-assessment penalties also apply to transfer pricing issues. Taxpayers are required to keep and preserve the records needed to make a correct and complete tax return for any period.

(a) Primary and secondary records

HMRC acknowledge that the requirement to maintain documentation has to be reasonable given the nature, size and complexity of the issues. They would expect the business to maintain primary accounting records at the time of the transaction. However, evidence to demonstrate an arm's length result (required to be produced in response to an HMRC enquiry) may not be prepared until the request by HMRC is made.[23] Generally, if the issues involved are complex or high value, it is advisable to commission such analysis prior to the submission of the tax return.

If the transfer pricing methodology adopted is incorrect and results in inaccurate tax returns being filed, there is a statutory regime for penalties. Inaccuracies are categorised into four groups:

(a) made despite the taxpayer taking reasonable care, in which case a penalty will not be due;
(b) careless, if the inaccuracy is due to the taxpayer's failure to take reasonable care, in which case the standard penalty is 30 per cent of the potential lost revenue;
(c) deliberate but not concealed, if the inaccuracy is due to a deliberate action taken by the taxpayer but which wasn't concealed from HMRC, in which case the standard penalty is 70 per cent of the potential lost income; or
(d) deliberate and concealed, if the inaccuracy is due to deliberate actions taken by the taxpayer and the taxpayer also took steps to conceal it, in which case the standard penalty is 100 per cent of the potential lost revenue.

The standard penalties may be reduced if the taxpayer makes a disclosure or for other special circumstances.[24]

---

22 Section 30 *Finance Act 2004* removed the exemption for UK to UK transactions previously contained in Schedule 28AA *Income and Corporation Taxes Act* 1988.
23 INTM483030.
24 See Schedule 24 *Finance Act 2007* as amended.

5.2 Special or notable cases

There is very little case law specifically in relation to transfer pricing penalties. However, in response to significant concerns raised by taxpayers that, given that to some extent what is an arm's length price is a matter of judgment and the test of carelessness is uncertain, HMRC have provided guidance as to its meaning.[25]

In summary, HMRC accept that where a company has made an honest and reasonable attempt to comply with the arm's length principle, no penalties should be due. Failure to consider the arm's length principle at all and failure to maintain documentation supporting the methodology adopted are cited as examples of carelessness. Examples of deliberate inaccuracies are seen where a clear, comparable uncontrolled price has been ignored without reasonable technical analysis, or where a transfer pricing expert describes the business operations in a manner that is clearly incorrect.

6. DISPUTE RESOLUTION MECHANISMS

6.1 Preferred national options

There is no specific dispute resolution process for transfer pricing matters. Generally, the process would commence with an HMRC enquiry into the business' tax return, the outcome of which would be subject to appeal to the First Tier Tax Tribunal. HMRC would, in principle, be prepared to consider resolving the dispute through an alternative dispute resolution process (such as mediation), but this is still rare in practice.

One of the most effective ways to avoid disputes is to use one of the options available to taxpayers to pre-agree on transfer pricing methodology. The most popular of these is an Advanced Thin Capitalisation Agreement ('ATCA').

An ATCA is an Advanced Pricing Agreement ('APA') in relation to the deductibility of interest expense in relation to intra-group or shareholder financings. HMRC have published a model ATCA agreement which taxpayers can use to make their application.[26] In the year ended 31 March 2013, 144 new ATCAs were agreed to by HMRC increasing the number of ATCAs in force from 279 at 31 March 2012 to 414 at 31 March 2013. This number has almost doubled since 31 March 2011, demonstrating that these agreements are becoming increasingly popular. ATCAs take, on average, approximately 12 months to agree with HMRC.[27]

Other APAs are less popular (only 45 applications were made in the year ended 31 March 2013) and take significantly longer to agree (on average 26 months in the year ended 31 March 2013 - a significant increase from approximately 17 months in the previous year).[28]

One of the reasons for the reduced popularity of APAs (as opposed to ATCAs) may be that, unlike ATCAs, HMRC will only consider APAs where the issues involved are complex, which results in increased time and

25 INTM483110; INTM483120.
26 Statement of Practice 1/12 – Advance Thin Capitalisation Agreements under the APA Legislation.
27 Transfer Pricing Statistics – see footnote 13.
28 As above.

resources being involved in reaching agreement. The absolute size of the transaction is not considered a relevant factor for the acceptance of an APA request, nor is there any expedited regime for small businesses.

HMRC encourages the use of bilateral or multilateral APAs (which involve the participation of tax authorities in all jurisdictions relevant to the transaction under consideration), but the taxpayer is entitled to request a unilateral agreement if it wishes.[29] Whilst these may have less value because they do not eliminate the risk of double taxation, they may have relevance where, for example, extending to a bilateral APA would be unnecessarily time-consuming or complicated or the other jurisdictions involved has no APA process. The potential involvement of other tax authorities in the APA process may explain to a large extent the delays in reaching agreement.

6.2 International options

As discussed above, the taxpayer may apply for an APA on a bilateral basis, which provides certainty in both jurisdictions involved in a cross border transaction.

If a taxpayer has not obtained an APA for whatever reason, and the taxpayer suffers double taxation, they may be able to claim relief under the Mutual Agreement Procedure of the EU arbitration convention.

The Mutual Agreement Procedure applies to transactions between jurisdictions which have concluded double tax treaties with provisions allowing the taxpayer to make a claim to its revenue authority to seek to resolve double taxation issues. However, these agreements typically only require the revenue authorities to endeavour to reach agreement, and success is largely dependent on which jurisdictions are involved. Mutual Agreement Procedure applications are not very popular[30] and many companies do not make use of the procedure due to uncertainties regarding the timeframe and the prospects of a successful outcome.

PART TWO: TAX AVOIDANCE

7. ACCEPTABLE TAX PLANNING AREAS/SUBJECTS

Ever since Lord Tomlins' judgment in the *Duke of Westminster* case,[31] there has been a lack of consensus and even lack of definition as to what constitutes tax avoidance. At its most basic, a tax avoidance transaction is simply one which is designed to avoid tax in a way that conflicts with or defeats the evident intention of Parliament. However the waters have become so muddied that reference is often made to 'aggressive' or 'unacceptable' tax avoidance which suggests that there is such a concept of acceptable tax avoidance! Given there has not been a definition of tax avoidance, HMRC's main method of tackling tax avoidance has been either through specifically drafted tax avoidance rules within the legislation or

29 Statement of Practice 2/10 – Advance Pricing Agreements.
30 Only 40 applications were made in the year ended 31 March 2013 – Transfer Pricing Statistics – see footnote 13.
31 See p. 20.

seeking to persuade the Courts to apply a purposive construction of the relevant legislation. Whilst this will continue to be the case in the future, the General Anti-Abuse Rule ('GAAR'), as discussed below, is designed to provide further assistance in counteracting aggressive tax planning.

The GAAR Guidance (published by HMRC and approved by an Advisory Panel) highlights areas considered to be acceptable tax planning and contrasts these with areas perceived to be abusive which would fall afoul of the GAAR. Acceptable areas include:

- planning to access trapped non-trading losses;[32]
- manipulating the timing of interest deductions;[33]
- use of loan notes to rollover chargeable gains on a disposal of shares;[34] and
- the grant of a reversionary lease to mitigate stamp duty land tax.[35]

In addition to the areas highlighted in the GAAR Guidance, there are several other means of planning tax affairs advantageously which are recognised amongst tax practitioners as not being considered abusive. These include giving shareholders the ability to choose whether to receive returns on share capital in the form of income or as capital and using demergers as means of splitting and selling companies to take advantage of statutory reliefs.

8. DEFINING ABUSIVE TAX AVOIDANCE

The UK tax system is designed to capture abusive tax schemes rather than responsible tax planning. UK tax law now has a statutory definition of 'abusive', discussed in detail below, within its GAAR. As mentioned above, there is also published guidance setting out which tax arrangements will, and will not be, considered abusive pursuant to the GAAR.[36]

In addition to the statutory concept of abuse, HMRC publishes 'Spotlights' which identify types of arrangements HMRC perceive to be unacceptable and susceptible to challenge. These bulletins also set out specific schemes HMRC do not consider to have achieved their advertised tax savings and indicates a number of planning features which, when increasingly present, increase the likelihood of HMRC challenging a taxpayer's position.

9. THE LEGISLATIVE FRAMEWORK

(a) The GAAR and its interaction with specific tax avoidance legislation

The UK introduced the GAAR in 2013 following the publication of the Aaronson Report which considered whether the introduction of a GAAR would be beneficial to the UK tax system.[37] Prior to the introduction of the GAAR, the UK anti-avoidance system relied on specific anti avoidance rules and persuading the Courts to construe legislation purposively. Rules

32 HMRC's GAAR Guidance, Part D5.
33 HMRC's GAAR Guidance, Part D6.
34 HMRC's GAAR Guidance, Part D16.
35 HMRC's GAAR Guidance, Part D33.
36 HMRC's GAAR Guidance, Part C5 and Part D.
37 GAAR Study, Report by Graham Aaronson QC(11 November 2011).

governing early disclosure of any tax avoidance schemes were brought in to enable HMRC to identify tax planning which it considered to be abusive quickly, and react by proposing specific legislation at an early stage.

The GAAR legislation, which covers a wide range of taxes,[38] was implemented into UK law by Part 5 of the *Finance Act 2013* and is supplemented by HMRC's GAAR Guidance. The GAAR applies only to arrangements which were entered into on or after 17 July 2013.[39]

The GAAR applies to counteract 'tax advantages arising from tax arrangements that are abusive'. The legislation defines 'tax advantage'[40] very widely, and includes:

(a) relief or increased relief from tax;
(b) repayment or increased repayment of tax;
(c) avoidance or reduction of a charge to tax or an assessment to tax;
(d) avoidance of a possible assessment to tax;
(e) deferral of a payment of tax or advancement of a repayment of tax; and
(f) avoidance of an obligation to deduct or account for tax.

An arrangement is a 'tax arrangement' if, having regard to all the circumstances, it would be reasonable to conclude that the obtaining of a tax advantage was the main purpose, or one of the main purposes of the arrangement.[41] The wide scope of these definitions results in many transactions passing the first two hurdles of the test to determine whether the GAAR applies, however the third hurdle of the tax arrangement being 'abusive' is more difficult to satisfy and therefore reduces the scope of the GAAR. This is intended to reflect the findings from the Aaronson Report that responsible tax planning should continue to be permitted under UK law and that the GAAR should only counteract the most egregious tax schemes.

An arrangement is defined as being abusive if it 'cannot reasonably be regarded as a reasonable course of action in relation to the relevant tax provisions, having regard to all the circumstances'.[42] This is known colloquially as the 'double reasonableness test' and HMRC's GAAR Guidance states that the 'double reasonableness' test 'sets a high threshold by asking whether it would be reasonable to hold the view that the arrangement was a reasonable course of action'.[43] This recognises that there will be different views as to whether an arrangement is unreasonable, and broadly, whilst one view may be that it is unreasonable, if others would consider it reasonable the test is not satisfied and an arrangement is not abusive.[44] The legislation lists some examples which might indicate that a tax arrangement is likely to be considered abusive,[45] in addition to the examples in the GAAR Guidance.[46] As a general rule, a tax arrangement will be considered abusive if it sets out to deliberately use the legislation to gain a tax advantage which

---

38 The GAAR applies to income tax, corporation tax, capital gains tax, petroleum revenue tax, inheritance tax, stamp duty land tax and annual tax on enveloped dwellings.
39 Section 215(1) *Finance Act 2013*.
40 Section 208 *Finance Act 2013*; HMRC's GAAR Guidance, Part C2.
41 Section 207(1) *Finance Act 2013*; HMRC's GAAR Guidance, Part C3.
42 Section 207(2) *Finance Act 2013*.
43 HMRC'sGAAR Guidance, Part B12.1.
44 HMRC'sGAAR Guidance, Part B12.1, Part C5.10.
45 See s. 207(4) *Finance Act 2013*.
46 HMRC'sGAAR Guidance, Part D.

was never intended by the draftsman. An arrangement which includes abnormal or contrived steps[47] may also indicate abuse. If a tax arrangement is found to be abusive, an adjustment is made to counteract the advantage. Any such adjustment must be just and reasonable and HMRC must comply with certain procedural steps.[48]

The GAAR imposes the burden of proving that an arrangement is not reasonable tax planning on HMRC rather than the taxpayer.[49] Further, HMRC are required to refer any counteraction of a tax advantage to an independent advisory panel, the 'GAAR Advisory Panel'[50] to opine as to whether the double reasonable test is satisfied and the arrangements constitute abuse. A court or tribunal deciding on the applicability of the GAAR in a particular situation must take into account any relevant opinions of the Advisory Panel. The GAAR Advisory Panel is intended as a safeguard to ensure that reasonable tax planning is not caught within the scope of the GAAR. It is comprised of six members and a chairman, prised from a range of sectors each of which has extensive tax knowledge. Whilst HMRC is involved in the appointments to the panel, it is not represented thereon. The panel is, however, accountable to HMRC. The current chairman of the panel is Patrick Mears, a former head of tax and partner at the law firm Allen and Overy. The chairman is appointed for a term of five years whilst the members are appointed for three years.

Prior to the introduction of the GAAR, tax avoidance was governed by a large volume of complicated specific anti-avoidance rules. This included Targeted Anti-Avoidance Rules ('TAARs')[51] which were drafted in response to specific schemes or tax avoidance which HMRC had become aware of. TAARS continue to be published post-introduction of the GAAR. The GAAR takes priority over all other tax legislation relating to the taxes to which the GAAR applies regardless of what that legislation states,[52] but in practice the GAAR only needs to be relied on when specific anti-avoidance legislation does not cover a particular type of arrangement or catch within its scope an arrangement which is considered abusive.

(b) Disclosure of tax avoidance schemes ('DOTAS')[53]

The DOTAS rules came into force in 2004.[54] They force disclosure to HMRC of the use of certain arrangements which are expected to give a tax advantage as one of the main benefits and fit certain 'hallmarks'.[55] 'Hallmarks' are descriptions of arrangements such as, for example, a loss scheme whereby the promoter of the scheme expects several individuals to implement the same arrangements which an informed observer could

47 See s. 207(2)(b) *Finance Act 2013*; HMRC'sGAAR Guidance, Part C5.8.
48 See s. 209 and Schedule 43 *Finance Act 2013*; HMRC'sGAAR Guidance, Part E.
49 See s. 211(1)*Finance Act 2013*.
50 See s. 211(2)(b) *Finance Act 2013*.
51 See, eg, s. 16ATCGA 1992 which states that where the *'main purpose or one of the main purposes of the arrangement is to secure a tax advantage'* an allowable loss will not accrue to a person.
52 See s. 212 *Finance Act 2013*; HMRC's GAAR Guidance, Part C9.
53 'Analysis – The changing limits of acceptable tax avoidance' Tax Journal, Issue 1152, 17 (11 January 2013); HMRC published guidance on Disclosure of Tax Avoidance Schemes, *http://www.hmrc.gov.uk.aiu/*.
54 See Part 7 of the *Finance Act 2004*.
55 See *Tax Avoidance Schemes (Prescribed Descriptions of Arrangements) Regulations* 2006.

conclude would provide those individuals with losses to reduce their liability to tax. The notification obligation generally falls on the promoter[56] of the scheme to make the initial disclosure to HMRC,[57] which results in the issue of a scheme reference number.

All clients of the promoter that use the scheme must include the Scheme Reference Number in its tax returns.[58] The promoters are also required to provide information to HMRC of the names and addresses of clients that have implemented the scheme on a quarterly basis.[59]

The intention of the rules is that HMRC will receive an early notification about the current types of tax avoidance schemes being marketed and utilised by taxpayers. This enables HMRC to monitor the scheme and if necessary remedy any shortcomings in the legislation through the use of a TAAR and make taxpayers aware of their view through the publication of a 'Spotlight'. Resources can also be appropriately allocated to investigating the returns of those taxpayers that HMRC is aware have used these schemes. The number of TAARs introduced since 2004 has increased significantly and the number of new disclosures reduced correspondingly as the scope for exploiting mismatches in legislation has diminished.

(c) Strict disclosure rules for high risk promoters[60]

New powers will be given to HMRC in relation to promoters of tax avoidance schemes when the *Finance Act 2014* receives Royal Assent. Amongst these new powers, HMRC will be able to issue conduct notices to promoters who carry on a business as a promoter and meet any one of a number of 'threshold' conditions. The 'threshold' conditions aim to capture promoters who are considered high-risk, because, for example they have been the subject of disciplinary or criminal action or failed to comply with the DOTAS rules at some point within the last three years.[61] The conduct notice will require the promoter to comply with conditions in order to ensure that, for example, the promoter provides adequate information to its clients regarding the tax scheme it is promoting.[62] If the promoter fails to comply with a conduct notice, HMRC can issue a 'monitoring' notice.[63] HMRC will have the power to 'name and shame' any promoter subject to a monitoring notice by publishing the name of the promoter and details as to how the promoter breached the conduct notice that had been issued to them.[64] The promoter will be obliged to inform its clients that it is a monitored promoter.[65]

---

56 See s. 307 *Finance Act 2004* for the definition of a promoter.
57 See s. 308 *Finance Act2004*.
58 See s. 313(3)(a) *Finance Act 2004*.
59 See s. 313ZA *Finance Act 2004*and regulation 13 *Tax Avoidance Schemes (Information) Regulations* 2012
60 ND. 3462 *Finance Bill 2014* clauses 192–277, Schs 26–32 – Tax avoidance schemes, Simon's Taxes.
61 See clause 230 and Schedule 30 *Finance Bill 2014*.
62 See clause 231 *Finance Bill 2014*.
63 See clauses 235 to 237 *Finance Bill 2014*.
64 See clause 241 *Finance Bill 2014*.
65 See clause 242 *Finance Bill 2014*.

Monitored promoters will be allocated a Promoter Reference Number[66] which must then be disclosed to clients.[67] Clients will then have to disclose this number to HMRC if it expects to gain a tax advantage in respect of any schemes the promoter has arranged for them.[68] HMRC will also have power to request additional information from monitored promoters and intermediaries. If requested, promoters and intermediaries will have to provide information which will enable HMRC to ascertain the possible tax effects that a promoter's scheme may have and check the tax position of anyone HMRC believes is using the scheme.[69]

(d) Follower notices and accelerated payment

The Finance Bill 2014 contains two new consequences for users of tax avoidance schemes: follower notice and accelerated payments, which, like the new rules for high risk promoters, will also take effect when the Finance Act is enacted.

(i) Follower notices. These notices can be issued by HMRC in circumstances where a tax scheme has already been defeated in the Courts and broadly, require the recipient taxpayer to concede their dispute with HMRC. A follower notice may be issued by HMRC to a taxpayer that is either the subject of tax enquiry or has made an appeal from an HMRC decision and HMRC considers that a judicial ruling is relevant to the arrangements under enquiry or dispute with that taxpayer.[70] A judicial ruling in this context is a decision by a court which is no longer capable of appeal, has not been appealed or any appeal has been abandoned. A ruling is considered relevant if it relates to the tax arrangements the taxpayer is disputing with HMRC and the principles or reasoning in the ruling if applied to the tax arrangements would deny the asserted advantage or part of the advantage of the arrangement.[71]

Upon receipt of a follower notice, the taxpayer is required to take corrective action. Corrective action refers to an amendment of the relevant return or claim to reflect that the advantage sought is not available or the entry into an agreement with HMRC for the purposes of relinquishing the advantage sought.[72]

(ii) Accelerated payment notices. Accelerated payment notices may be served on a taxpayer that is the subject of an enquiry or dispute with HMRC, and in the event that either a follower notice has been served. In addition, notices can also be served if the relevant arrangements are notifiable under DOTAS or the subject of a GAAR counteraction notice. They can therefore be used independently of a follower notice.[73] The effect of an Accelerated Payment Notice is to require the taxpayer to pay the tax assessed

---

66 See clause 243 *Finance Bill 2014*.
67 See clause 244 *Finance Bill 2014*.
68 See clause246 *Finance Bill 2014*.
69 See clause 248 *Finance Bill 2014*.
70 See clause 197 *Finance Bill 2014*.
71 See clause 198 *Finance Bill 2014*.
72 See clause 201(5) and (6) *Finance Bill 2014*.
73 See clause 212 *Finance Bill 2014*.

within 90 days of receipt of the notice.[74] In effect, an accelerated payment notice requires a taxpayer to pay the tax contested upfront to HMRC, notwithstanding the fact that the matter may not have yet reached the litigation stage. This is a departure from historic practice where payment was not required until that point or often in practice, only following conclusion of the litigation.

10. KEY CASES OF INTEREST

10.1 Current cases

As the GAAR was only introduced into UK law very recently, there are not as yet any significant cases discussing its application. It remains to be seen whether there will be any challenges mounted by taxpayers on the application of the GAAR and if so the weight the courts will attach to the opinion of the GAAR Advisory Panel.

There has, however, been a significant volume of case law regarding the correct way to interpret tax legislation provisions in the context of tax avoidance schemes. These include cases in the context of non-recourse financing,[75] mismatches in the regime for taxing gains and losses arising from options over loan relationships,[76] the accrued income scheme,[77] stamp duty land tax[78] and the creation of stamp duty groups.[79] All these cases apply the statutory interpretation principles discussed below and particularly the law as stated in BMBF.[80]

10.2 Key historical cases

We now consider some of the main cases which have influenced the development of how tax legislation is to be interpreted in the context of tax avoidance schemes which often include a series of pre-planned artificial steps which are said to have no commercial advantage other than reducing the taxpayer's tax liability.[81]

(a) The Duke of Westminster principle – pre-Ramsay

The *Duke of Westminster* case[82] established the well-known principle that if a document or transaction is genuine, the court cannot ignore the legal position in favour of the *'substance of a matter'* because the transaction must be considered according to its legal effect. Lord Tomlin said that *'every man is entitled if he can to order his affairs so that the tax attaching under the appropriate Acts is less than it otherwise would be.'* A strict approach to interpreting the legislation arose out of the *Duke of Westminster* principle and this formed the

74 See clause 216 *Finance Bill 2014*.

75 *Ensign Tankers (Leasing) Ltd v Stokes (Inspector of Taxes)* [1992] STC 226.

76 *Inland Revenue Commissioners v Scottish Provident Institution* [2004] UKHL 52.

77 *Revenue and Customs Commissioners v D'Arcy* [2008] STC 1329.

78 There have been a number of cases including: TC02777: Project Blue Limited (2013); TC02242: Vardy Properties and related appeal (2012) and *The Commissioners for Her Majesty's Revenue and Customs v DV3 RS Limited Partnership* [2013] EWCACiv 907.

79 *Collector of Stamp Revenue v Arrowtown Assets Limited* [2003] 6 ITLR 454.

80 *Barclays Mercantile Business Finance Ltd v Mawson (Inspector of Taxes)* [2004] 7 ITLR 383.

81 There are a number of other significant cases which are not discussed in this chapter including: *Inland Revenue v Burmah Oil Co Ltd* [1982] SC (HL) 114; *Furniss (Inspector of Taxes) v Dawson* [1984] AC 474; *Carreras Group Ltd v Stamp Commissioner* [2004] STC 1377.

82 *Duke of Westminster v Commissioners of Inland Revenue* [1936] 19 TC 490.

view of the courts for nearly fifty years. Courts would look at each individual step in a transaction separately when applying the facts to the relevant legislative provisions and if the step was genuine, as opposed to a sham, then it would be considered not to amount to tax avoidance.

The case of *Ramsay*[83] was pivotal in determining how tax legislation is construed. Lord Wilberforce stated that the *Duke of Westminster* principle is *'a cardinal principle but it must not be overstated or over-extended ... it does not compel the court to look at a document or a transaction in blinkers, isolated from any context to which it properly belongs.'*

(b) The Ramsay principle and purposive construction

Lord Wilberforce, in his judgment of *Ramsay*, cited the principle that *'a subject is only to be taxed on clear words, not on 'intendment' or on the 'equity' of an Act'* and then said *'what are "clear words" is to be ascertained on normal principles; these do not confine the courts to a literal interpretation. There may, indeed should, be considered the context and scheme of the relevant Act as a whole, and its purpose may, indeed should, be regarded.'*

Lord Wilberforce's comments set out what has become known as the *Ramsay* principle and is commonly referred to as the purposive way of interpreting legislation. Purposively interpreting the legislation involves taking into consideration the commercial reality of the overall effect of a series of transactions forming part of a tax planning scheme. Lord Wilberforce said that a court's task is to *'ascertain the legal nature of any transactions to which it is sought to attach a tax or a tax consequence and if that emerges from a series or combination of transactions, intended to operate as such, it is that series or combination which may be regarded.'* The House of Lords said it is irrelevant whether or not there is a contractual obligation that all steps will be completed, an expectation that once the first step is undertaken all other steps will be completed is sufficient. Once the legal nature of the transaction has been established the court's task is to then see if it fits within the meaning of the relevant legislation.

Lord Fraser stated that this form of purposive construction which allows the series of steps in a transaction to be considered as a whole rather than individually did not contradict the well-established *Duke of Westminster* principle because, in that case, there was only one step/transaction. Viewing the series of steps as one whole transaction is still giving regard to the legal nature of the transaction and therefore the House of Lords made clear that it did not believe the *Duke of Westminster* principle confined the courts to a single step approach when interpreting tax legislation.[84]

---

83 *WT Ramsay Ltd v Inland Revenue Commissioners*[1981] 1 All ER 865.

84 In the case of *Ramsay* the taxpayer sought to create an allowable loss to offset against a chargeable gain he had made on a sale-leaseback transaction. The scheme involved several pre-planned steps which began with the acquisition of shares in a company which were sold almost immediately afterwards. On the same day as the acquisition, two loans were provided by the taxpayer to the company. Subsequently, the interest rate on one loan was increased and the interest rate on the other loan decreased. The result of this was that one loan was sold for a loss which was allowable for tax purposes and the other loan was sold for a gain which was not chargeable. Whether or not the gain was chargeable depended on whether the loan fell within the statutory definition of 'debt', which would allow the gain to be exempt, or the statutory definition of 'a debt on a security', which would result in a chargeable gain. The House of Lords held, in applying the methodology they had discussed, that when looking at the transactions involved in the scheme as a whole, it was obvious that the second loan was intended to be sold at a profit from the

(c) Post-Ramsay

Westmoreland.[85] The most critical interpretation of the *Ramsay* principle can be found in the House of Lords judgment in the case of *Westmoreland*. Lord Nicholls said that the phrase 'the *Ramsay* principle' is *'potentially misleading'*. He claimed that *Ramsay* did not introduce a new principle which future decisions are bound by, but instead provided an approach which is *'no more than a useful aid.'Westmoreland* involved a pre-planned artificial circulation of funds which, on the face of it, appeared to have no commercial purpose other than gaining a tax advantage. The debtor borrowed money from the creditor for the purpose of repaying interest on a loan owed to the creditor. This circular flow of funds was designed solely to reduce the debtor's liability to tax. The question the House of Lords had to answer was whether this transaction counted as 'payment' of the interest within the meaning of the relevant legislation.

Lord Hoffmann's judgment made clear that not all statutory concepts have a business or commercial meaning behind them. He said that *'... there are many terms in tax legislation which ... refer to purely legal concepts which have no broader commercial meaning. In such cases, the Ramsay principle can have no application.'* Lord Hoffmann emphasised that the commercial reality that a series of transactions achieves is irrelevant where Parliament did not intend for the tax provision in question to have any commercial meaning: *'[I]f a transaction falls within the legal description, it makes no difference that it has no business purpose. Having a business purpose is not part of the relevant concept.'*

In *Ramsay*, their Lordships had to decide on the interpretation of words such as 'loss' and 'disposal' which have a commercial meaning behind them. In this case however the House of Lords said the word 'paid' does not have a commercial meaning and therefore should be given its ordinary meaning. As a result they held that the interest was paid within the ordinary meaning of the word and therefore the commercial reality of a circular flow of funds and an intention to gain a tax advantage was irrelevant.

BMBF. In the case of *BMBF*, their Lordships said that the idea in *Westmoreland* that a statutory term needs to be classified as either a legal or commercial concept, although *'not an unreasonable generalisation'* is not *'intended to provide a substitute for a close analysis of what the statute means. It certainly does not justify the assumption that an answer can be obtained by classifying all concepts a priori as either "commercial" or "legal". That would be the very negation of purposive construction.'*

Their Lordships also said that some of the post-*Ramsay* case law[86] *'gave rise to a view that, in the application of any taxing statute, transactions or elements of transactions which had no commercial purpose were to be disregarded.'* The judgment goes on to say *'but that is going too far. It elides the two steps which are necessary in the application of any statutory provision: first, to decide, on*

---

outset meaning it fell within the definition of a debt on security. Therefore the gain was not exempt to tax and the tax avoidance scheme failed.

85 *MacNiven (Inspector of Taxes) v Westmoreland Investments Ltd* [2001] STC 237.

86 *Inland Revenue v Burmah Oil Co Ltd* [1982] SC (HL) 114; *Furniss (Inspector of Taxes) v Dawson* [1984] AC 474; *Carreras Group Ltd v Stamp Commissioner* [2004] STC 1377.

a purposive construction, exactly what transaction will answer to the statutory description and secondly, to decide whether the transaction in question does so.'

The House of Lords in *BMBF* endorsed Ribeiro PJ's comments on the *Ramsay* principle as correctly summarising its application. In his judgment in *Arrowtown*[87] heard in the Hong Kong Court of Final Appeal, RibeiroPJ said that *'the driving principle in the Ramsay line of cases continues to involve a general rule of statutory construction and an unblinkered approach to the analysis of the facts. The ultimate question is whether the relevant statutory provisions, construed purposively, were intended to apply to the transaction, viewed realistically.'* This is now generally accepted as the correct way to interpret tax legislation. This approach allows the steps to be looked at as a whole rather than as separate steps if viewing it that way fits the type of transaction that the statutory provision seeks to capture but in some cases, upon a close analysis of what the statute actually requires, it may be obvious that it is not appropriate to look at the commercial reality of the effect that all the steps in the scheme have as a whole and instead only the final outcome that the scheme achieves should be considered.[88]

Mayes.[89] Mummery LJ endorsed the House of Lords interpretation of *Ramsay* in *BMBF,* and again cited approval of Ribeiro PJ's comments in *Arrowtown.* Mummery LJ reiterated in his judgment that *'Ramsay did not lay down a special doctrine of revenue law striking down tax avoidance schemes on the ground that they are artificial composite transactions and that parts of them can be disregarded for fiscal purposes because they are self-cancelling and were inserted solely for tax avoidance purposes and for no commercial purpose. The Ramsay principle is the general principle of purposive and contextual construction of all legislation.'*

The tax scheme in question (known as 'SHIPS 2') involved seven pre-planned steps, some of which were self-cancelling and commercially pointless, which enabled higher rate taxpayers to create an artificial loss which could be set off against their other tax liabilities. The question came down to whether certain steps in the transaction fell within the scope of the meanings of 'premium' and 'surrender' in the applicable legislative provisions.

The Court of Appeal reached the same decision as the High Court, during which Proudman J said she sympathised *'with the instinctive reaction that such an obvious scheme ought not to succeed.'* It was decided that the relevant statutory words in question had to be given their ordinary meaning and were terms *'which do not readily lend themselves to a purposive commercial construction.'* The steps of the SHIPS 2 scheme therefore fell within the legislative provisions enabling the taxpayers to create the artificial loss they sought.

---

87 *Collector of Stamp Revenue v Arrowtown Assets Limited* [2003] 6 ITLR 454.

88 In this case, the House of Lords held that BMBF (the lessor) was entitled to deduct capital allowances in respect of a pipeline acquired and leased back to BGE (the lessee) even though the right to the capital allowance was derived as part of a tax avoidance scheme that the lessee was a party to. The House of Lords said that the statutory provisions dealing with capital allowances in the case of a finance lease are only concerned with the acts of the lessor and not the lessee and the lessor had satisfied all of the requirements in the legislation in order to be entitled to capital allowances.

89 *Commissioners for HM Revenue & Customs v Mayes* [2011] EWCA Civ 407.

Mayes was cited by Aaronson in his GAAR Report as demonstrating the need for a GAAR since the application of purposive construction cannot undermine the validity of tax avoidance schemes where the legislation is very technical and tightly worded.[90]

11. PENALTIES

11.1 Legislative provisions

(a) Penalties under the GAAR

The GAAR legislation does not include any provisions imposing, or dealing with penalties. However, for any taxes that the GAAR governs which are covered by the system of self-assessment, the taxpayer is required to take the provisions of the GAAR into account when completing their self-assessment return. If the taxpayer does not do this, they will be subject to the usual penalties associated with failing to take reasonable care in completing their tax return.[91]

(b) Penalties under the DOTAS rules

A failure to comply with the DOTAS rules attracts an initial penalty of up to £5,000 for the promoter and additional penalties for up to £600 per day for continued failure to disclose or a failure to give a client the Scheme Reference Number.

Users of a scheme are also subject to penalties, albeit on a lesser scale. If the user does not include the Scheme Reference Number on its return it will be liable to an initial penalty of £100 and this can rise to up to £500 if the user has previously failed to notify a scheme reference number or up to £1,000 for a failure to include the scheme reference number on two or more returns within a 36 month time period.[92]

(c) New penalties to come into effect for high-risk promoters

The new high-risk promoter rules to be introduced when the *Finance Act 2014* receives Royal Assent carry higher penalties for monitored promoters and intermediaries which fail to comply with their obligation to provide certain information. The amount of the penalty will vary depending on which duty is breached, but the initial penalty could reach a maximum of £1 million and daily default penalties for further failure to comply could also be imposed.[93]

Clients will also face extended time limits for assessments if they gain a tax advantage from a scheme a promoter has set up for them and they failed to disclose the reference number of the monitored promoter to HMRC.[94]

---

90 GAAR Study Report by Graham Aaronson QC (11 November 2011), page 20.

91 HMRC's GAAR Guidance, Part B15 and B16. See s. 5.1 in Part One of this chapter for details on the penalties which can be imposed where there is a failure to take reasonable care in completing a tax return.

92 See s. 98C(4) *Taxes Management Act 1970*.

93 See Schedule 31 *Finance Bill 2014*.

94 See clause 270 *Finance Bill 2014*.

(d) Follower notices and accelerated payment notices

Failure to comply with a Follower Notice carries a penalty of 50 per cent of the tax advantage sought, in the event a taxpayer fails to take the necessary corrective action within the specified time period.[95] If tax due pursuant to an Accelerated Payment Notice remains unpaid at the end of the period for payment, a 5 per cent penalty is payable. Further penalties are payable if amounts subject to the notice remains outstanding thereafter.[96]

(e) Examples of other penalties which could apply

Government departments have the ability to ban taxpayers who have taken part in a failed tax avoidance scheme from being awarded government contracts.[97]

11.2 Examples of penalties imposed

Not applicable.

12. CURRENT TRENDS

12.1 National policy and law

Several high profile politicians have, in recent years, expressed disapproval of aggressive tax avoidance. George Osborne in his 2012 Budget Speech famously described aggressive tax avoidance as *'morally repugnant'*.[98] Politicians commitment to cracking down on aggressive tax avoidance over the coming years has been widely publicised with HM Treasury highlighting in a recent paper published in March 2014, to 34 separate measures that have been introduced since 2010 to tackle tax avoidance.[99]

In the context of a great deal of publicity surrounding tax avoidance in 2014, there are as described above, several additions to the legislation concerning tax avoidance proposed in the Finance Bill 2014. The headline additions are the new stricter rules for high-risk promoters which are due to come into effect in the summer of 2014 and the new requirements for taxpayers involved in tax avoidance schemes. The GAAR remains, however, the most significant change to UK tax legislation in recent years.

As the GAAR is still in its infancy there is a degree of uncertainty as to how it will work in practice alongside the other tax avoidance mechanisms already in place. HMRC will continue to monitor and evaluate the GAAR to determine how effective it has been at discouraging as well as stopping abusive avoidance schemes. HMRC has said it will use various methods to monitor the GAAR's impact such as assessing the number of abusive schemes disclosed under the DOTAS rules and keeping a record of cases successfully litigated or settled by agreement using a GAAR challenge.[100]

---

95 See clauses 201 and 202*Finance Bill 2014*.

96 See clause 219 *Finance Bill 2014*.

97 Simon's Tax Intelligence, Issue 14 (11 April 2013)

98 BBC news article 'George Osborne's new plans to tackle tax avoidance' (28 March 2012).

99 HMRC and HM Treasury paper on 'Tackling aggressive tax planning in the global economy: UK priorities for the G20-OECD project for countering base erosion and profit shifting' (March 2014), p. 3.

100 General anti-abuse rule HMRC proposal document, *http://www.hmrc.gov.uk/budget2013/tiin-4754.*

Since the introduction of the GAAR, TAARs have continued to be published and it is understood that the trend of introducing TAARs as and when they become necessary will continue alongside the operation of the GAAR. It is not intended that the GAAR will replace the existing tax avoidance mechanisms in place.

12.2 The impact and role of the OECD and other international relations

George Osborne has been quite vocal in his support of a combined international effort for tackling tax avoidance stating that *'to act unilaterally would not only be ineffective, it would be counterproductive too.'* As a result, the government published for the first time in March 2014 a document setting out the 15 action points to the OECD's Base Erosion and Profit Shifting project and the UK's position on each of the issues. The document emphasises the Government's commitment to the *'ambitious BEPS project timetable, and to delivering results and implementing changes as soon as possible.'*[101]

The OECD's work on tackling aggressive tax planning is still a work in progress and the first results are not expected to be seen until September 2014. It will therefore be interesting to see how the combined international efforts to crack down on tax avoidance progress and how the Government will implement these changes alongside, or in place of, the existing domestic legislation.

[101] HMRC and HM Treasury paper on 'Tackling aggressive tax planning in the global economy: UK priorities for the G20-OECD project for countering base erosion and profit shifting' (March 2014), p. 4.

USA

Akerman LLP L Frank Cordero, Osmel L Cuan,
Michael J Bowen & Peter O Larsen

PART ONE: TRANSFER PRICING

1. GENERAL OVERVIEW

The United States has an extensive system of laws and practices designed to preserve the US tax base by preventing income from being shifted to a non-US controlled party through inappropriate pricing of related party transactions. The US 'transfer pricing' regime seeks to ensure that goods and services transferred between related companies are done so at an arm's length and priced based on market conditions that permit profits to be reflected in the appropriate tax jurisdiction. Where the results of a transaction do not reflect an arm's length price, the US tax revenue authority will reallocate the income to reflect the appropriate price and, in some cases, impose monetary penalties for substantial or deliberate inaccuracy.

The United States Congress has enacted legislation and the US Treasury Department has promulgated regulations to control transfer pricing, all of which are administered and enforced by the Internal Revenue Service (the 'IRS').

2. IDENTIFICATION OF LEGISLATIVE AND REGULATORY FRAMEWORKS

(a) Federal legislative framework

In the United States, federal tax legislation is contained in the Internal Revenue Code (the 'Code' or IRC). Specifically, Code s. 482 governs transfer pricing. The US Congress enacted s. 482 to prevent tax avoidance by ensuring income is clearly reflected by related parties and to place a controlled taxpayer on tax parity with an uncontrolled taxpayer.[1]

(b) Federal regulatory framework

Rules governing transfer pricing are contained in the regulations promulgated by the US Treasury Department and administered by the 'IRS' pursuant to Code s. 482. The regulations adopt the arm's length standard to guide all transfer pricing analyses and set forth specific pricing methods to test the arm's length nature in various categories of transactions. The IRS also issues public and private administrative guidance to taxpayers to assist them in applying the transfer pricing provisions of the Code.

1 This section is discussed in detail below in section 2.1 Federal Legislation.

(c) State framework

In the United States, individual states enact their own corporate income tax rules, which include the power and authority to regulate transfer pricing. The state rules focus on shifting of income and deductions from a high-tax state to lower-tax states. Issues relating to state approaches to transfer pricing are discussed further below (see below section 2.2 State and federal interplay).

2.1 Federal legislation

(a) Statutory language of Code section 482

Section 482 of the Code is the main transfer pricing legislation in the United States and consists of two sentences. The first sentence, which has been part of US transfer pricing law since it was enacted, authorizes the IRS to reallocate income, deductions, credits or allowances among the members of a controlled group of entities to ensure clear reflection of income or to prevent tax avoidance.[2] Although not explicitly stated, the statutory language embodies the arm's length principle by authorizing adjustments to the taxable income of a controlled taxpayer to reflect the income that would have been realized if the transaction were between uncontrolled parties.

The second sentence of s. 482, added in 1986, provides an additional test for transfers of intangible property (IP).[3] Income with respect to the transfer (or license) of IP must be 'commensurate with the income' attributable to the IP.[4] Under the commensurate-with-income standard, actual profits realized from the exploitation of an intangible must be considered in determining an arm's length price for the transfer of the intangible. The amount of the compensation must therefore be adjusted over time to reflect the changes in the income attributable to that intangible.

The statutory language establishes that s. 482 applies when two or more entities are commonly controlled directly or indirectly, whether legally (or not) enforceable or whether exercisable or exercised.[5] Code s. 482 applies to all transactions between related parties and commonly controlled parties regardless of taxpayer intent.[6] A taxpayer does not have the right to compel the IRS to apply these provisions or to self-initiate transfer pricing adjustments in later years.[7]

---

2 I.R.C. § 482.

3 Congress was concerned that US taxpayers could transfer high-profit intangibles to foreign related parties, in exchange for lump-sum payments or royalty streams that were unrelated to the intangibles' underlying profit potential. The emphasis on high-profit intangibles relates to a lack of comparable transactions inherent in the intangible. See generally H.R. Rep. No. 831, Vol. II, 99 Cong., 2d Sess. 637–38 (1986).

4 I.R.C. § 482. The standard applies to all related party transactions that involve intangibles and not merely 'outbound' transfers. See F.S.A. 2000-19-026 (May 12, 2000) citing H.R. Rep. No. 831, Vol. II, 99 Cong., 2d Sess. 637 (1986).

5 The term 'controlled' is not defined under I.R.C. s. 482 or under its regulations. Instead, taxpayers and IRS examiners must rely on IRS guidance and case law to determine the existence of common control based on the totality of facts and circumstances.

6 Treas. Reg. 1.482-1(f)(1).

7 Treas. Reg. § 1.482-1(a)(3); see *Intersport Fashions West Inc. v US*, 109 A.F.T.R. 2d 2012-927 (Fed. Cl. 2012) (upholding the validity of the prohibition on taxpayer-initiated transfer pricing adjustments in Treas. Reg. § 1.482-1(a)(3).

(b) Federal regulations under Code section 482

Treasury Regulations under Code s. 482 are the center of the transfer pricing regime in the United States and serve as the main source of interpretation of the arm's length standard and the commensurate with income standard.

The regulations require that a taxpayer select the best pricing method available to test the arm's length nature of transfer prices based on all the facts and circumstances.[8] Under the Best Method Rule, the taxpayer must use the 'most reliable measure' of an arm's length result by reference to the comparability and quality of the data and assumptions available.[9] Taxpayers must use a variety of factors contained in the regulations to evaluate the comparability of uncontrolled transactions, the quality of the data and assumptions in determining the most accurate method.

The flexible application of the arm's length standard embodied in the regulations can result in more than one arm's length price for a given transaction. Accordingly, the regulations provide taxpayers with relief from s. 482 reallocations where the results are within an arm's length range.[10] The arm's length range must be derived from 'two or more uncontrolled transactions of similar comparability and reliability'.[11] If the transfer pricing outcome is outside the range, the IRS may adjust the result to a point within the arm's length range.

A s. 482 adjustment to the income of a related party requires a correlative adjustment to the income of the other related party.[12] If the transaction is purely domestic, then an increase in tax liability of one party signals the decrease in tax liability of another. Where the transaction is cross-border, however, the United States may not have tax jurisdiction over a related party with a residence outside of the United States. In this case, only where the income derived by the foreign corporation is relevant for US tax purposes will the foreign corporation's income sustain a correlative adjustment.

1. Transfer Pricing Methodology

In evaluating the arm's length nature of an amount paid in a related party transaction, the regulations describe specific pricing methods for different types of transactions. Specifically, the regulations enumerate the following transactions: use of funds for loans, advances, or the use of tangible property;[13] transfer of tangible property;[14] transfer, license and use of intangible property;[15] cost sharing arrangements;[16] and performance of services.[17] Once a transaction is characterized, the regulations specify which transfer pricing methodology ('TPM') can be used to arrive at the appropriate price.

---

8 Treas. Reg. 1.482-1(c)(1).
9 Treas. Reg. 1.482-1(c)(2).
10 Treas. Reg. 1.482-1(e)(1).
11 Treas. Reg. 1.482-1(e)(2). The standard for comparability and reliability is fairly high.
12 Treas. Reg. 1.482-1(g)(2).
13 Treas. Reg. § 1.482-2(a), (c).
14 Treas. Reg. § 1.482-3.
15 Treas. Reg. § 1.482-4.
16 Treas. Reg. § 1.482-7.
17 Treas. Reg. § 1.482-2(b); Treas. Reg. § 1.482-9.

(a) Transfers of tangible property. The regulations governing the transfer of tangible property specify both transactional methods and profit-based methods to evaluate the arm's length nature of a charge. These methods include: Comparable Uncontrolled Price, Resale Price Method, Cost-Plus method, Comparable Profits and Profit Split (comparable and residual). In addition, the regulations permit a taxpayer to use unspecified methods to evaluate arm's length prices.

The Comparable Uncontrolled Price (CUP) method compares the amounts charged for the tangible property in controlled taxpayer transactions with comparable third party transactions.[18] Consistent with the best method rule, the CUP method is generally the most reliable measure of an arm's length result if the transaction is identical or highly comparable in terms of products or functions. In situations where the compared transactions are not identical, taxpayers can make adjustments to the price to increase the comparability of the transactions. The similarity of the products is the most important factor to consider in determining comparability under CUP.[19]

The Resale Price Method (RPM) compares the gross margins earned in controlled versus uncontrolled transactions.[20] The RPM is most widely used by sellers or related-party distributors that do not add substantial value to the products purchased.[21] The analysis under RPM requires a comparison of contractual terms, risks borne, and functions performed in the controlled and uncontrolled transactions.

The Cost Plus method compares gross margins between controlled and uncontrolled transactions and adding the appropriate gross profit to the controlled taxpayer's cost of producing the property sold to arrive at the arm's length sale price.[22] This method is most widely used to determine the mark-up earned by manufacturers selling to related parties.

The Comparable Profits Method (CPM) assesses whether the amount charged in a controlled transaction is arm's length based on objective measures of profitability (profit level indicators, or PLI) derived from an uncontrolled taxpayer in a similarly situated business under similar circumstances.[23] Comparability under this method requires a detailed analysis of functions performed, risks borne, and assets employed.

The Profits Split Method determines the arm's-length transfer price of certain transactions by allocating the combined operating profits (or losses) arising from the covered activity in proportion to the relative contribution of each of the parties.[24] Under the Comparable Profit Split method,[25] the transfer price is determined by allocating the combined operating profit or loss of the relevant business activity based on each uncontrolled taxpayer's

[18] Treas. Reg. § 1.482-3(b).

[19] T.D. 8552 (1994). The regulations provide specific examples of other factors that may be relevant in adjusting for comparability including differences contractual terms, level of the market, geographic market, date of the transaction and others.

[20] Treas. Reg. § 1.482-3(c).

[21] Generally, physically altering tangible goods through packaging, labeling, relabeling and minor assembly does not constitute adding substantial value.

[22] Treas. Reg. § 1.482-3(d).

[23] Treas. Reg. § 1.482-5.

[24] Treas. Reg. § 1.482-6.

[25] Treas. Reg. § 1.482-6(c)(2).

percentage of the combined operating profit or loss. The Residual Profit Split Method [26] involves two steps: (1) operating income is allocated to each party based on routine contributions to the business activity and (2) residual loss or profit is divided among the parties based on the relative value of their contributions to the business activity. This method is most often used when each controlled entity contributes highly valuable intangibles.

Taxpayers may also use unspecified methods to determine arm's length prices.[27] One unspecified method contained in the regulations is a 'bona fide' offer from an unrelated party that is used to establish the base of an arm's length range of prices.

(b) Transfers of intangible property. In general, the arm's length consideration for the transfer of an intangible must be commensurate with the income attributable to the intangible.[28] The regulations define an intangible as an asset that 'derives its value not from its physical attributes but from its intellectual content or other intangible properties' and 'has substantial value independent of the services of any individual'.[29] Common examples of intangibles include:

- Patents, inventions, formulae, processes, designs, patterns, or know-how;
- Copyrights, and literary, musical, or artistic compositions;
- Trademarks, trade names, or brand names;
- Franchises, licenses, or contracts;
- Methods, programs, systems, procedures, campaigns, surveys, studies, forecasts, estimates, customer lists, or technical data; and
- Other similar items.

The pricing methods for intangibles are similar to the methods for services and tangible property. The four methods listed in the regulations are the Comparable Uncontrolled Transaction (CUT) method, Comparable Profits method ('CPM'), Profit split method (comparable and residual), and unspecified methods.[30] Taxpayers are required to use the 'best method' for pricing intangibles.

The CUT method compares the amount charged in a controlled transfer of intangible property to the amount charged in a comparable uncontrolled transaction.[31] In applying the CUT method, a comparable intangible must be used in connection with similar products or processes within the same general industry or market. The regulations identify several factors that should be considered in determining the comparability of the controlled and uncontrolled transactions. In practice, one of the major obstacles to finding a reliable CUT is the intrinsic inimitability of intangible property.

The comparable profit method, profits split method, and unspecified methods applicable to intangible property are analogous to the transfer pricing methods applied to tangible property described above.

---

26 Treas. Reg. § 1.482-6(c)(3).
27 Treas. Reg. 1.482-3(e).
28 I.R.C. § 482; Treas. Reg. § 1.482-4(a).
29 Treas. Reg. § 1.482-4(b).
30 Treas. Reg. § 1.482-4(a).
31 Treas. Reg. § 1.482-4(c).

The pricing methods above can also be used to test a lump-sum payment for prepayment of royalties or the purchase of an intangible. In addition, a lump-sum payment is commensurate with income if it is equal to the present value of the expected future royalties (which are both arm's length and commensurate with income) that would have been earned on a license.[32]

The regulations governing transfers of intangible property also interpret the statutory 'commensurate-with-income' standard.[33] In general, transfer pricing methods for intangibles must take into account the actual income earned by an intangible over its life. Thus, a related party royalty arrangement is subject to periodic adjustments to ensure the payment reflects changes in market conditions.[34] Taxpayers can obtain relief from future periodic adjustments under certain circumstances and depending on the transfer pricing method selected.[35]

(c) Cost-sharing arrangements. In 2011, the IRS and Treasury Department issued final cost sharing regulations.[36] The rules are contained in Regulations 1.482-7 and mostly adopt the 2009 Temporary Regulations.[37]

A cost sharing arrangement (CSA) is an agreement under which controlled parties agree to share the costs and risks of developing an intangible in proportion to their share of reasonably anticipated benefits.[38] In determining the participants' 'share of reasonably anticipated benefits' (RAB share), the regulations require taxpayers to determine and use 'the most reliable estimate of reasonably anticipated benefits.'[39] The permissible bases for measuring RAB include 'units used, produced, or sold,' 'sales' or 'revenues generated,' and 'operating profit.'[40]

In a qualified CSA all of the participants are considered to have an ownership interest so that each is able to exploit the intangible without paying a royalty. A qualified CSA does not, however, create a partnership, nor does it cause a non-US participant to become engaged in a US business.[41] The IRS may apply the regulations to any arrangement that in substance constitutes a CSA, even if a taxpayer fails to comply with the specific requirements.[42]

Where any of the participants contributes pre-existing intangibles to a CSA, in a 'platform contribution transaction' (PCT), the other participants

---

32 Treas. Reg. § 1.482-4(f)(6).

33 Treas. Reg. § 1.482-4(a).

34 Treas. Reg. § 1.482-4(f)(2). In practice, taxpayers should be proactive about managing the value of intangibles and modifying the intercompany royalty rate as the intangibles change in value.

35 See Treas. Reg. § 1.482-4(f)(2)(ii). For example, no adjustments are necessary to a transfer price in subsequent years if the taxpayer uses the CUT method to determine an arm's length royalty and the intangible transferred in the uncontrolled transactions is substantially similar to the intangible transferred in the controlled transaction. Where the CUT method is used in conjunction with a different but comparable intangible, then no adjustment is necessary if, among the requirements, the aggregate profits actually earned by the taxpayer from the intangible are not less than 80 per cent nor more than 120 per cent of the prospective profits that were expected when the uncontrolled transaction was determined as a comparable. If a transfer pricing method other than the CUT method was used to determine the original arm's length price, then the regulations provide more stringent requirements for preventing future periodic adjustments to meet the 'commensurate-with-income' standard.

36 See T.D. 9568 (2011).

37 See Treas. Reg. § 1.482-7.

38 Treas. Reg. § 1.482-7(b).

39 Treas. Reg. § 1.482-7(e)(1)(i).

40 Treas. Reg. § 1.482-7(e)(2)(ii)(A)-(C).

41 Treas. Reg. § 1.482-7(j)(2).

42 Treas. Reg. § 1.482-7(j)(3).

must make a buy-in payment at the arm's length price as payment for use of that intangible.[43] Platform contributions include every 'resource, capability, or right' that is made available to the CSA.[44] The regulations specify five methods[45] for valuing cost-sharing buy-ins and articulate the general principles applicable to any method used to determine the arm's length charge in a PCT.

(d) Controlled service transactions. In 2009, the Treasury Department promulgated final regulations regarding the treatment of controlled service transactions under s. 482.[46] Most notably, the 2009 regulations refine the IRS approach for evaluating an arm's length result for services transactions that result in a transfer of intangible property.

The 2009 regulations provide that an arm's length charge in a controlled services transaction must be determined under one of six specified methods or an unspecified method.[47] The transfer pricing methods for services are the services cost method, comparable uncontrolled services price, gross services margin, cost services plus, comparable profits method, and profit split method.[48] As with other controlled party transactions, each method is subject to the general provisions of s. 482 including the best method rule, the comparability requirements, and the arm's-length range.[49]

The Services Cost Method (SCM) is the newest transfer pricing method available for controlled services transactions. Under the SCM, the arm's length charge for a controlled services transaction is determined by reference to total services costs, without a mark-up.[50] To be eligible for the SCM, the service must be a covered service, not an excluded activity, not precluded from being a covered service, and the taxpayers must keep adequate books and records of the transactions.[51] Covered services include low-margin services or 'specifically covered services'.[52] The regulations also enumerate several excluded services for which the SCM cannot be used.[53] In addition, taxpayers must conclude, based on business judgment, that services being evaluated do not contribute to the competitive advantages, core capabilities, or fundamental risks of success or failure of the renderer, the recipient, or both.[54]

The regulations also incorporate cost-sharing concepts to intercompany services by allowing services to be shared by controlled parties for the overall benefit of the group in a Shared Services Arrangement (SSA).[55]

---

43 Treas. Reg. § 1.482-7(c). Similarly, when the participant leaves the CSA, the other participants must make a buy-out payment in proportion to the increase in benefits in value derived from the ownership in the intangible.

44 *Id.*

45 Treas. Reg. § 1.482-7(g). Transfer pricing methods for platform contribution transactions include the CUT, income method, acquisition price method, residual price method, and market capitalization method.

46 See generally T.D. 9456 (2009); Treas. Reg. § 1.482-9.

47 Treas. Reg. § 1.482-9(a).

48 *Id.* Prior to the regulations, the IRS had issued guidance in Rev. Proc. 63-10 for handling service charges under Section 482.

49 *Id.*

50 Treas. Reg. § 1.482-9(b).

51 Treas. Reg. § 1.482-9(b)(2).

52 Treas. Reg. § 1.482-9(b)(3). Low margin services are services for which the median arm's length mark-up is 7 per cent or less.

53 Treas. Reg. 1.482-9(b)(4).

54 Treas. Reg. 1.482-9(b)(5).

55 See generally Treas. Reg. § 1.482-9(b)(7).

Under an SSA, the arm's-length charge to each participant is the portion of the total costs of the services otherwise determined under the SCM that is properly allocated to the participant.[56] A qualified SSA requires two or more participants, including all controlled taxpayers that benefit from one or more SSA services, and that each covered service deliver a benefit to at least one participant.[57] A participant's allocation is based on its respective share of the reasonably anticipated benefits from the services.[58] The taxpayer must document the intent to apply the SCM for services under the SSA.[59]

For services that do not qualify for the SCM method, the regulations provide five additional methods to determine the arm's length nature of a controlled services transaction. Most of the methods described are adaptations of the methods used in evaluating tangible property transactions in the services context. The comparable uncontrolled services price method (CUSPM),[60] gross services margin method (GSMM),[61] and the cost of services plus method[62] are analogous to the CUP, resale price, and cost plus methods, respectively, of the tangible property transactions described above.

The comparable profits method adapts the CPM method for the tangible property CPM to the controlled services context.[63] The CPM for services only applies if the renderer of controlled services is the tested party.[64] The CPM for services adds the net cost plus profit level indicator that equals the ratio of operating profit to total services cost.[65]

The profit-split method adapts the profit-split method for tangible property to the services context.[66] The profit-split method is ordinarily used in controlled services transactions involving a combination of non-routine contributions by multiple controlled taxpayers.[67] The profit-split method generally applies where there are a lack of market comparables in evaluating the controlled services transaction. In addition, the residual profit split method cannot be used where only one controlled taxpayer makes significant nonroutine contributions.[68]

The regulations provide that a taxpayer can apply unspecified methods to services so long as realistic alternatives are considered, including 'economically similar transactions structured as other than services transactions.'[69]

(e) Intercompany loans. Generally, the regulations provide that where one member of a group of controlled entities makes a loan or advance directly or indirectly to, or otherwise becomes a creditor of, another member of such group and either charges no interest or interest at a rate that is not

56 Treas. Reg. § 1.482-9(b)(7)(i).
57 Treas. Reg. § 1.482-9(b)(7)(ii)(A).
58 Treas. Reg. § 1.482-9(b)(7)(ii)(B).
59 Treas. Reg. § 1.482-9(b)(7)(ii)(C).
60 Treas. Reg. § 1.482-9(c).
61 Treas. Reg. § 1.482-9(d).
62 Treas. Reg. § 1.482-9(e).
63 Treas. Reg. § 1.482-9(f).
64 Treas. Reg. § 1.482-9(f)(2)(i).
65 Treas. Reg. § 1.482-9(f)(2)(ii).
66 Treas. Reg. § 1.482-9(g).
67 Treas. Reg. § 1.482-9(g)(1).
68 *Id.*
69 Treas. Reg. § 1.482-9(h).

equal to an arm's length rate with respect to such loan or advance, the Commissioner may make an appropriate allocation to reflect an arm's length rate of interest for the use of such loan or advance.[70] The key determination is whether the interest rate charged on the principal amount of bona fide debt between members of a group of controlled entities is appropriate.

A bona fide debt includes: (1) loans or advances of money or other consideration (whether or not evidenced by a written instrument), and (2) indebtedness arising in the ordinary course of business from sales, leases, or the rendition of services by or between members of the group, or any other similar extension of credit.[71] The rule does not apply, however, to 'alleged indebtedness.'[72] Payments made, and any s. 482 allocation with respect to alleged indebtedness is treated according to the substance of the transactions.

2.2 State and federal interplay

(a) State sovereignty to determine the appropriate transfer pricing methodology

Although the focus of most multinational businesses is on the relationship with the IRS, the state-by-state approach to transfer pricing methodologies must not be ignored. Each state is a sovereign taxing jurisdiction with the authority to disregard the conclusions reached by the IRS with respect to the appropriateness of a particular transfer pricing method.

The starting point for calculating state taxable income in many states is federal taxable income.[73] If the IRS audits a multinational business and proposes changes to federal taxable income, these changes directly impact the filed state returns for the business for each of the effected years. Most all states have a law requiring a business to amend filed state returns to reflect federal changes.[74] If the federal change increases federal taxable income, the failure to file an amended state return most often results in the imposition of additional penalties and interest.

While any change resulting from an adjustment to the transfer pricing methodology of a business will require the filing of amended state tax returns, it does not follow that just because the IRS agreed with the transfer pricing methodology of a business, that the state is bound to follow the federal determination.[75] The peril for the multistate business is that unlike the IRS, state taxing authorities do not have the requisite transfer pricing expertise. In many instances, and in light of the lucrative nature of these

70 Treas. Reg. § 1.482-2(a)(1).
71 Treas. Reg. § 1.482-2(a)(1)(ii)(A).
72 Treas. Reg. § 1.482-2(a)(1)(ii)(B).
73 This is found on either line 28 or 30 of the IRS Form 1120 (federal corporate income tax return).
74 The laws of the Commonwealth of Massachusetts are typical in this regard. Under Mass. Gen. L. Chapter 62C § 30, a taxpayer must report changes in federal taxable income within one year of the date of notice of the federal government's final determination.
75 For example, the New Jersey Department of Taxation has recently issued a notice making clear that an advanced pricing agreement, or APA, negotiated with the Internal Revenue Service is just one consideration in evaluating the appropriateness of a particular transfer pricing methodology. See N.J. Dep't of Taxation Technical Advice Memorandum (TAM) 17, June 6, 2011.

audits by states, the states have retained third parties to conduct the review of transfer pricing methodologies.[76]

(b) State approaches to challenging transfer pricing methodologies

At the outset, it is important to note that most states that do not adopt the s. 482 standard are not bound to apply it when evaluating the appropriateness of a transfer pricing arrangement. States employ various approaches to challenge the transfer pricing methodologies of multinational businesses. If a multinational business focuses its efforts on strict compliance to Code s. 482, however, it will be well prepared to fend off state challenges.

The primary concern of state taxing authorities is the payment of deductible expenses from a business in the state to an affiliated company outside the state. These deductible expenses are the subject of almost every transfer pricing arrangement and relate to payments for royalties, interest and management fees. While the completeness of the transfer pricing agreement between the affiliates is important, states will also attack the arrangement under one of several theories including the 'business purpose,' 'economic substance' and 'sham transaction' doctrines. Each of these approaches looks to the substantive aspects of the in-state payor and the deductible expense paid by the payor to the out-of-state affiliate.

There are numerous decided cases from many states that relate to challenges by state taxing authorities employing the 'business purpose,' 'economic substance' and 'sham transaction' principles to challenge payments made pursuant to documented transfer pricing arrangements. An archetypal example of such a judicial decision is *Sherwin-Williams Co. v Comm. of Revenue*.[77] In *Sherwin-Williams*, the Massachusetts Department of Revenue argued that certain deductible expenses made by an in-state affiliate should be disregarded because the payment of the expense lacked a non-tax business purpose and economic substance. Also at issue in the case was the appropriateness of the written transfer pricing agreement of the business. The *Sherwin-Williams* court provided a subjective analysis of the business purpose and economic substance doctrines as applied to the facts of the case and *not* the appropriateness of the written transfer pricing agreement of the business.[78]

2.3 International treaties and agreements

(a) Associated enterprises article

US income tax treaties often contain an Associated Enterprises article that addresses business dealings between related persons. In general, the associated enterprises article echoes the arm's length principle reflected in the US transfer pricing rules under Code s. 482. Under article 9 of the 2006 US Model Income Tax Treaty, each contracting state has the authority to make adjustments to the income of persons subject to its taxing jurisdiction

[76] The states' use of third parties to conduct these reviews raises a host of issues that should concern the multinational business. The key concern is confidentiality of the tax records of the business.

[77] 778 N.E. 2d 504 (Mass. 2002).

[78] See *Carpenter Technology Corp. v Dep't of Revenue Services*, 772 A.2d 593 (Conn. 2001); see also *HMN Financial, Inc. v Comm'r of Revenue*, Minnesota Tax Court No. 7911-R (2009).

in any situation where the related parties make intercompany arrangements that are not at arm's length.[79]

Under most treaties, a reallocation of income by one contracting state will be made by the other contracting state if it agrees with the reallocation. If the other state does not agree with the reallocation, the two countries are to reach an agreement under the mutual agreement procedures contained in the tax convention. Taxpayers can face double taxation if the countries fail to reach a compromise.

(b) Mutual agreement and competent authority

To prevent double taxation, most US income tax treaties also include a Mutual Agreement Procedure ('MAP') article that allows a taxpayer to request assistance from a competent authority of a treaty partner where the actions of the US, the treaty partner, or both, result or will result in taxation that is contrary to the articles of the treaty.[80]

The IRS issued guidance on the procedure for requesting assistance from a competent authority under tax treaties in Revenue Procedure 2006-54. In general, taxpayers are encouraged to request competent authority assistance as soon as possible after the taxpayer determines it has been denied treaty benefits or has been taxed not in accordance with a tax treaty to prevent being precluded from relief. In addition, taxpayers must take steps to protect their right to the review by the competent authorities by (1) filing a protective claim for a claim for credit or refund of US taxes; and (2) by following procedures of the foreign country to avoid the lapse or termination of their right of appeal under the foreign country's income tax law.[81]

3. NATIONAL POLICY ISSUES

In recent years, the IRS has emphasized efforts to increase efficiency in administering transfer pricing matters and enhanced enforcement of the transfer pricing rules vis-à-vis streamlined taxpayer audits. Most recently, the IRS restructured its transfer pricing operations and revamped the transfer pricing audit process.[82]

3.1 Overall national policy announcements

The IRS's official position is that transfer pricing matters are to be enforced in accordance with the US Regulations and not the Transfer Pricing Guidelines for Multinational Enterprises and Tax Administrators ('OECD Guidelines').[83] In addition, the United States has expressed concerns over

---

79 See United States Model Income Tax Treaty, art. 9 (2006).

80 See United States Model Income Tax Treaty, art. 25 (2006); see also Competent Authority Assistance, available at *http://www.irs.gov/Individuals/International-Taxpayers/Competent-Authority-Assistance*. The MAP provision is frequently referred to as the 'competent authority' process.

81 Rev. Proc. 2006-54, 2006-2 C.B. 1035.

82 In 1999, the IRS announced it was adopting a five-part strategy to improve the enforcement of s. 482 including: finalizing substantive transfer pricing regulations, persuading Congress to adopt contemporaneous documentation legislation, spearheading a global consensus for using the arm's length standard in transfer pricing, and promoting the APA program to proactively resolve transfer pricing disputes.

83 See C.C.A. 2007-007 (Mar. 15, 2007). But cf. 'IRS Official Questions Policy Barring Consideration of Transfer Pricing Guidelines,' 2010 TNT 226-1 (Nov. 24, 2010).

implementation of the OECD's proposed reforms to rules affecting cross-border transactions, particularly in the areas of intangibles and financial transactions. In particular, the US has taken issue with the OECD Base Erosion and Profit Shifting Project's ('BEPS') deviations from the arm's length standard.[84]

3.2 National revenue authority initiatives

There is an increasing political and administrative focus on transfer pricing in the United States amidst efforts to defend the US tax base. The IRS has been focusing on increasing resources in this area and recently announced it was realigning and consolidating transfer pricing resources under the Large Business & International Division (LB&I). The purpose of the restructuring reflects the US government's efforts to provide consistent and efficient outcomes and encourage collaboration with taxpayers.[85] LB&I subsequently merged the APA and Competent Authority offices into the 'Advance Pricing and Mutual Agreement Program' to coordinate with the efforts to efficiently handle transfer pricing and Competent Authority matters.

3.3 Administrative statements

The IRS released new administrative guidance regarding transfer pricing audits in the Transfer Pricing Audit Roadmap (the 'Audit Roadmap') in February 2014.[86] The Audit Roadmap provides taxpayers with guidance on new features of the transfer pricing audit process and signals the IRS's continued efforts to enhance the efficiency and effectiveness of the audit process and focus resources on the most important cases.[87]

The Audit Roadmap reveals important themes about the IRS's current focus on transfer pricing. These themes are stated succinctly in the introduction to the Audit Roadmap as: (1) in a transfer pricing case, up-front planning is essential; (2) transfer pricing cases are usually won and lost on the facts; (3) the objective in a transfer pricing case is to determine the reasonable result under the facts and circumstances of any given case; and (4) effective presentation can make or break a case.[88] Taxpayers can benefit from a glimpse into what IRS examination officials will analyze during an audit as a way to secure a speedy and favorable resolution.

---

84 See Parker, Alex M., *Bello: US Likely Won't Implement BEPS If Results Deviate Greatly From Arm's-Length*, Bloomberg BNA, Daily Tax Report (June 6, 2014). These reforms are based on the 2013 Base Erosion and Profit Shifting Action Plan (BEPS) project is an international initiative intended to combat shifting income away from market countries and into tax havens. Among the changes the US has opposed are so-called 'blunt instruments' that raise more tax revenue and include: digital permanent establishments (based on an economic nexus), a 'main purpose of tax avoidance' clause in international tax conventions, and broad anti-hybrid rules. See Sheppard, Lee A., *US Opposes BEPS Blunt Instruments*, 74 Tax Notes Int'l 117 (Apr. 14, 2014).

85 See Burow, Margaret, *IRS Strives for Consistency in Transfer Pricing Administration*, 143 Tax Notes 908 (May 26, 2014).

86 The roadmap is available on the IRS website at *http://www.irs.gov/pub/irs-utl/FinalTrfPrcRoadMap.pdf*. The text lays out a hypothetical, non-binding, 24-month timeline made up of three distinct phases: a planning phase, an execution phase, and a resolution phase.

87 The IRS has emphasized conducting audits as an anti-abuse tool for enforcement against cross-border income shifting. New rules also allow taxpayers to access competent authority in certain situations where the taxpayer has made a self-initiated adjustment.

88 See *Transfer Pricing Audit Roadmap* 1, Internal Revenue Service (2014).

3.4 Administrative guidance

The IRS has also proposed new administrative guidance to update the rules and procedures applicable to transfer pricing. In recent years, the focus has been on improving the advanced pricing agreement program, and the competent authority procedures as a result of the IRS's restructuring of its transfer pricing operations.

In 1991, the IRS began offering taxpayers the opportunity to reach agreement in advance of filing a tax return on the appropriate transfer pricing method to be applied to related party transactions through the APA program.[89] The IRS published a comprehensive procedural guide to navigating the APA program in 2006 and has continued to clarify and update the procedures for filing APA requests.[90] According to the IRS, improvements to the APA program allowed the Service to execute a record number of agreements in 2013 and significantly reduce the average completion time for APAs.[91]

In 2013, the IRS proposed a revenue procedure that would provide new guidance on requesting assistance from the US competent authority.[92] The proposal reflects the IRS's restructuring since 2006, including the creation of LB&I and various offices to handle requests for various types of competent authority assistance. The revenue procedure would also include a number of substantive changes to the process. Most notably, the new rules give the US competent authority a leading role when the IRS's appeals office is involved and gives the US competent authority pre-approval rights in audit settlements that involve a competent authority issue.[93]

4. CASE LAW

In the United States, transfer pricing regulations and practice have evolved from a set of major cases. To date, over 350 cases have been reported on the topic and several are currently moving through the judicial system.[94] One of the most highly scrutinized areas is pricing of intangibles developed through cost-sharing arrangements. Although taxpayers have recently enjoyed more victories in high profile transfer pricing cases, historically the government has prevailed over taxpayer appellants.[95]

4.1 Current cases

(a) Veritas Software

In 2009, the US Tax Court decided *Veritas Software Corporation v Commissioner* dealing with a buy-in payment for pre-existing intangibles.[96]

89 See Rev. Proc. 91-22, 1991-1 C.B. 526. The IRS issued continuous guidance to update the APA program from 1996 through 2005.

90 See Rev. Proc. 2006-9, 2006-1 C.B. 278 (modified by Rev. Proc. 2008-31, 2008-1 C.B. 1133); see also Notice 2013-79, 2013-50 IRB 653 (publishing a proposed revenue procedure to clarify and update the APA procedures).

91 See IRS Announcement 2014-14, 2014-16 IRB 1 (Mar. 27, 2014). The number of APAs grew in 2013 to 145 from 140 in 2012 and the average time of completion in 2013 was reduced to 32.7 from 39.8 months in 2012.

92 See Notice 2013-78, 2013-50 IRB 633 2013. The revenue procedure would update and supersede the earlier Rev. Proc. 2006-54, 2006-2 C.B. 1035 (describing competent authority procedures).

93 See Notice 2013-78, 2013-50 IRB 633.

94 See Lowell, Briger & Martin: US International Transfer Pricing (WG&L), Appendix B.02. Table of Cases – Judicial Scorecard (2014).

95 *Id.*

96 133 T.C. No. 14, 133 T.C. 297 (2009).

The taxpayer, Veritas Software Corp., was a major developer and manufacturer of computer software that entered into a cost-sharing arrangement and technology licensing agreement with its foreign subsidiary. In exchange for a $166 million lump sum buy-in payment, the subsidiary was granted rights to use the intangibles.

The IRS made s. 482 adjustments to the buy-in payment using a different pricing method and assessed a deficiency. The taxpayer petitioned the Tax Court for a redetermination of the deficiency and penalties, arguing the Commissioner made erroneous allocations for the lump sum buy-in payment and cost-sharing allocations under s. 482.

The Tax Court rejected the IRS's determination and held the comparable uncontrolled transaction method was the best method for determining a buy-in payment relating to the transfer of intangibles between a subsidiary and parent. The court also held the IRS based its adjustments on intangibles developed after the buy-in payment, included accounts in the computation that were not actually transferred, and employed a number of erroneous variables in making the adjustments.[97] The court also took issue with the fact that the IRS supported its allocations by using the 2009 regulations that were promulgated years after the transaction occurred.[98]

The IRS did not appeal the decision but announced it would not acquiesce to the result or the reasoning of the Tax Court's *Veritas* opinion.[99]

(b) Xilinx, Inc.

In 2005, the Tax Court decided *Xilinx, Inc. v Commisioner*, holding the IRS erroneously allocated stock-based compensation as part of the cost-sharing pool of expenses.[100] Xilinx entered into a CSA with Xilinx Ireland, its wholly owned Irish subsidiary, that required each party to make buy-in payments and fund a portion of the total research and development costs in proportion to its reasonably anticipated benefits from the intangibles developed per the CSA. Both Xilinx and Xilinx Ireland granted employee stock options to their employees but neither party included the amounts in the expenses shared in the CSA. The IRS issued a deficiency on the basis that the employee stock options were costs that must be shared under the CSA regulations.

The Tax Court held that IRS's allocations did not comply with the basic arm's length standard of the regulations because unrelated parties would not agree to share in stock based compensation costs when entering into a CSA.[101]

The Ninth Circuit of the US Court of Appeals originally reversed on the grounds that the arm's length standard did not apply to the cost-sharing regulations but subsequently withdrew its opinion and affirmed Tax

97 *Id.*, at 313.
98 *Id.*, at 329.
99 I.R.S. Action on Decision No. 2010-05, IRB No. 2010-49 (Dec. 6, 2010). In the Action on Decision, the IRS calls the *Veritas* Court's factual findings and legal assertions 'erroneous'. *Id.*
100 125 T.C. 37 (2005), *aff'd*, 598 F.3d 1191 (9th Cir. 2010).
101 *Id.*, at 62–63 (2005).

Court's decision in favor of the taxpayer.[102] The Circuit Court resolved the purpose of the arm's length standard applied because regulations were too ambiguous in determining the costs that must be shared between controlled parties in a CSA relating to intangible product development.[103]

The *Xilinx* case is significant because taxpayers are currently challenging the post-2003 regulations on grounds that CSAs that comply with the current regulations contain a provision that employee stock options will not be shared if the regulations are limited by case law.[104]

4.2 Historical cases of note

(a) PPG Industries, Inc.

PPG Industries, Inc. v Commissioner. was decided by the US Tax Court in 1970.[105] The taxpayer in PPG Industries was a US parent company and manufacturer of glass, paint, and chemical products. PPG had a Swiss subsidiary, PPGI, which it formed to conduct operations, develop opportunities, and manage investments for PPG outside of the United States.

Pricing guidelines incorporated into contracts between PPG and PPGI established that prices between two companies should always yield the parent company a profit. The IRS applied s. 482 to assess a deficiency against PPG. The amount of the deficiency was based on the differences between PPG's profits and the margins of net profit to business receipts for the chemical wholesaler industry contained in the Source Book of Statistics of Income prepared by the US Treasury.

The Tax Court held for the taxpayer on the grounds that (i) the original allocations by the Commissioner did not meet the arm's length standard because they were arbitrary and based on the Source Book of Statistics of Income; (ii) PPG's sales to PPGI were at arm's length prices established by extensive documentation by PPG of comparable transactions; and (iii) the taxpayer's comparable for the remaining sales met the arm's length standard because it was 'reasonable' and 'fair', while the Commissioner's comparable was deemed inappropriate. *PPG Industries* is a significant case because it illustrates the importance of documentation and how taxpayers can present a strong transfer pricing case.

(b) E.I. DuPont de Nemours & Co.

In *E.I. DuPont de Nemours & Co. v United States*, the court upheld the entirety of the government's reallocation of profits under s. 482.[106] The taxpayer had set transfer prices with its tax-haven based marketing subsidiary without any reference to comparable uncontrolled transactions. In fact, internal documents produced at trial showed the taxpayer intentionally set the transfer price solely to maximize the subsidiary's profitability.

The court rejected the taxpayer's purported pricing method as well as its comparable, including an attempt to rely on the gross profit margins

---

102 *Xilinx, Inc. v Comm.*, 598 F.3d 1191 (9th Cir. 2010), aff'g, 125 T.C. 37 (2005).
103 598 F.3d 1191, 1196 (2010).
104 See *Altera Corp. v Comm.*, Tax Ct. Dkt. Nos. 6253-12, 9963-12.
105 *PPG Indus., Inc. v Comm.*, 55 T.C. 928 (1970).
106 See *E.I. du Pont de Nemours & Co. v US*, 221 Ct. Cl. 333, 608 F.2d 445 (Ct. Cl. 1979).

contained in the Source Book of Statistics of Income. Without a comparable transfer price, the court turned to the IRS's allocation, which was based on ratios of gross income to total operating costs for similar corporations. The court determined the allocations were reasonable and ushered in a new approach the IRS ultimately authorized in the s. 482 regulations.

(c) United States Steel Corporation

The Tax Court decided *United States Steel Corporation v Commissioner* in 1980.[107] The taxpayer, a US steel manufacturer, owned a Liberian subsidiary which it used to ship steel from Venezuela to the United States. The Liberian subsidiary charged its US parent company for shipping services at rates that made the price of delivered steel comparable to the prevailing US market price. The subsidiary also rendered services at similar rates for third parties although to a much lesser extent. The Tax Court held the taxpayer could have bought the services from its Liberian subsidiary for less than from an unrelated party and upheld the Commissioner's allocation of profits as reasonable.

On appeal, the Second Circuit of the US Court of Appeals reversed the tax court's decision, holding the arm's length standard was satisfied and the taxpayer was free from s. 482 adjustments because it could show that the price it was charged would have been the same in an independent transaction with an unrelated party.[108]

(d) Bausch & Lomb, Inc.

In 1994, the Tax Court decided *Bausch & Lomb, Inc. v Comm.*[109] In *Bausch & Lomb*, the taxpayer licensed a unique manufacturing process to a controlled offshore subsidiary for a fixed royalty. The subsidiary used the unique intangible to manufacture goods and sold them to both the taxpayer and unrelated parties at a substantial profit. The IRS proposed s. 482 adjustments that included eliminating the royalty on grounds that the subsidiary was a contract manufacturer without risk of loss for its products.

The Tax Court found the adjustment was an abuse of discretion, rejecting the Commissioner's contract manufacturer theory because there was no contractual obligation by the parent company to purchase the products. In addition, the court held the transfer price for sale of the goods to the parent company met the arm's length standard under the comparable-uncontrolled-price method. Relying on *United States Steel*, described above, the court held that the price charged was a 'market price' and thus the taxpayer had 'earned the right to be free of adjustment.'

(e) Westreco, Inc.

In *Westreco v Commissioner*, the transfer pricing issue was the proper compensation for research and development services rendered by the taxpayer for its Swiss parent, for which it was reimbursed at a cost plus

107 T.C. Memo 1977-290.
108 *United States Steel Corp. v. Comm.*, 617 F2d 942 (2d Cir. 1980).
109 *Bausch & Lomb, Inc. v. Comm.* 92 TC 525 (1989), *aff'd*, 933 F2d 1084 (2d Cir. 1991).

basis.[110] The Commissioner assessed a deficiency based on a multiplication of the taxpayer's salary plus costs, but later admitted such an adjustment was arbitrary. The IRS instead selected a sampling of corporations from the Standard Industry Classification data as comparables to the taxpayer.

The Tax Court rejected the IRS's sample of corporations because the taxpayer bore significantly less risk than the alleged comparables, and the segments from which the comparables were drawn were unrelated to the taxpayer's R&D activities. Instead, the court relied on the taxpayer's industry comparables to reject the IRS's adjustment in its entirety.

Under the current regulations, research and development services are not 'covered services' which would qualify for the services cost method.[111] One of the other methods applicable to services transactions would be required.

5. PENALTIES

There are a variety of penalties applicable to transfer pricing. Section 6662 of the Code sets forth an accuracy-related penalty for underpayments of tax in transfer pricing matters. Additionally, s. 6038A sets out reporting penalties for failure to report certain intercompany transactions. Finally, the Code provides that general civil and criminal tax penalties and interest charges may be imposed in transfer pricing cases.

5.1 Types

(a) US transfer pricing penalties

Code s. 6662 imposes various penalties for accuracy-related underpayments of tax in the transfer pricing context, unless a taxpayer can demonstrate and provide the IRS upon request contemporaneous documentation supporting a particular pricing methodology.[112] Under the general rules of s. 6662, a penalty applies to any portion of underpayment attributable to (1) substantial and gross valuation misstatements; (2) substantial understatements of tax; (3) negligence; (4) tax understatements attributable to any undisclosed foreign financial asset; and (5) tax underpayments attributable to any transaction lacking economic substance. Generally, the penalty for misconduct is 20 per cent, but it can double to 40 per cent in certain circumstances. The underpayment of tax liability is the base for assessing the penalty.

In most cases, the taxpayer can avoid the accuracy-related penalty by establishing that he acted in good faith and had reasonable cause. Thus the importance of complying with the disclosure requirements of the Code cannot be understated particularly in the transfer pricing context. Proper documentation is one of the most important tools for defending against a transfer pricing penalty.

A substantial valuation misstatement is present where the price for any property or services (or for the use of property) claimed on any return in connection with any transaction between controlled taxpayers is 200 per

110 *Westreco v Comm.*, T.C. Memo 1992-561.
111 See Treas. Reg. § 1.482-9(b); see also *supra* section 2.1(b)(1)(d) on controlled services transactions.
112 I.R.C. § 6662, et seq.

cent or more (or 50 percent or less) of the correct arm's length amount (the 'transactional' penalty); or the net Code s. 482 transfer price adjustment for the taxable year exceeds $5 million or 10 per cent of the taxpayer's gross receipts (the 'net adjustment' penalty).[113] The penalty doubles to 40 per cent in the event of a gross valuation misstatement, which occurs under the transactional penalty if the percentages are 400 per cent or more (or 25 per cent or less), or the net Code s. 482 adjustment is $20 million, or 20 per cent of gross receipts.[114]

The 'transactional' penalty focuses on the extent of a valuation misstatement in each transaction between controlled taxpayers. The net adjustment penalty is triggered by the amount of the net s. 482 adjustment. The 'net s. 482 transfer price adjustment' means the sum of all increases in the taxable income of a taxpayer for a taxable year resulting from s. 482 (excluding carry-back and carryover amounts) less any collateral adjustments.[115] Any adjustment for which the taxpayer can demonstrate reasonable cause will be excluded from the computation.[116] The s. 6662 penalty is further discussed in Part Two of this chapter.[117]

(b) Reporting penalties

The Code also imposes a reporting obligation on certain foreign-owned domestic corporations. Generally, s. 6038A requires a reporting corporation to file a separate annual return for each related party with which it has a reportable transaction during the year.[118] A reporting corporation that fails to provide the IRS with the required information is subject to a $10,000 penalty with respect to each year for which the failure occurs. The failure to report may be excused by showing reasonable cause.

(c) Taxpayer civil and criminal penalties

In addition to the transfer pricing penalties and reporting penalties, several general criminal and civil tax penalties can apply in a transfer pricing context. Penalties include: failure to file penalty; failure to pay penalty; failure to pay estimated tax penalty; and preparer penalties.

5.2 Special or notable cases

In *DHL Corporation v Commissioner*, the Tax Court upheld an accuracy related penalty on a deficiency attributable to a gross valuation misstatement.[119] The taxpayer, DHL, sold its rights to worldwide trademarks to a foreign subsidiary which it valued at $20 million accompanied by a 15-year royalty free license. The IRS contended the value of the trademarks was upwards of

113 I.R.C. § 6662(e).

114 I.R.C. § 6662(h).

115 I.R.C. § 6662(e)(3)(A). There is no penalty for a substantial valuation misstatement unless the underpayment attributable to understatements exceeds $10,000 for corporations.

116 Treas. Reg. § 1.6662-6(b)(3).

117 I.R.C. § 6664(c).

118 Reporting corporations include domestic corporations with 25 per cent or greater foreign ownership based on vote or value or a foreign corporation that is 25 per cent foreign-owned and is engaged in a US trade or business.

119 *DHL Corp. v Comm.*, TC Memo 1998-461.

$600 million and that the taxpayer understated its royalty income without reasonable cause.

The Tax Court sided with the government, but determined the value of the trademarks was $100 million, allocating $50 million to the domestic entity and $50 million to the foreign entity. The court also sanctioned the Services' accuracy related penalties under s. 6662.

On appeal, the Ninth Circuit of the US Court of Appeals affirmed the Tax Court's $100 million valuation of the trademarks but reversed the allocation to the domestic entity.[120] The Circuit Court also reversed the accuracy related penalties because the Tax Court had failed to recognize the foreign affiliate's rights in the foreign trademarks.[121]

6. DISPUTE RESOLUTION MECHANISMS

Transfer pricing disputes that arise domestically follow the procedures described below. The IRS also provides an APA program that allows a taxpayer to obtain certainty and advanced resolution of transfer pricing disputes.[122] In addition, the IRS provides a number of alternative dispute resolution options to encourage resolution of potential controversies as early as possible.

6.1 Preferred national options

The first stage of a transfer pricing dispute is an IRS audit followed by a proposed adjustment by the IRS. If the taxpayer disagrees with the Commissioner's reallocation, the taxpayer can request a conference with the Appeals Office of the Service (or commence a competent authority process if a treaty jurisdiction is involved). If the IRS finds against the taxpayer, or if the taxpayer deliberately chooses to bypass the Appeals process, the next step would be to petition the US Tax Court to seek a redetermination of the deficiency. Alternatively, the taxpayer can pay the tax and file a claim for refund with the IRS. If the refund is denied, or the taxpayer does not hear from the Service, the taxpayer can sue for a refund in the District Court or in the Court of Federal Claims. Once the matter is in the judicial system, the taxpayer can appeal the Tax Court's decision to a Circuit Court, and ultimately to the Supreme Court of the United States.

A taxpayer can avoid the entire dispute process by entering into an Advanced Pricing Agreement (APA) with the IRS in which both agree to the arm's length pricing methods for intercompany transactions up to five years in advance. In addition, a taxpayer can combine the agreement between the taxpayer and the IRS on a particular method, with an agreement between the United States and foreign taxing authority to avoid potential double tax problems. Although initially designed as a prospective device to eliminate the costs and risk of complying with future examinations, taxpayers can now use APAs to resolve pending examination disputes in which the methods

---

[120] *DHL Corporation v Comm.*, 285 F.3d 1210 (9th Cir. 2002), rev'g in part, TC Memo 1998-461.

[121] *Id.*

[122] The procedures applicable to the APA program are stated in Revenue Procedure 2006-9 and are effective for APA requests submitted after July 2004.

agreed upon under the APA are rolled back to the open audit years. The IRS released new guidance on the Advance pricing Agreements process.[123]

6.2 International options

Where application of US transfer pricing rules and those of a treaty partner country would produce double taxation, a taxpayer may request assistance from a competent authority to eliminate double tax under the mutual agreement procedure article of a bilateral tax treaty.

PART TWO: TAX AVOIDANCE

7. DISTINGUISHING TAX AVOIDANCE AND TAX EVASION

The US tax laws have relentlessly expanded since the inception of modern federal income taxation in the early 20th century.[124] Taxpayers and their advisers have answered by developing countless tax planning strategies, structures and techniques designed to reduce tax liabilities. These measures frequently involve the arrangement of transactions and affairs in a manner that involves multiple steps, each of which complies with the letter of the law, but with an end result that provides a tax benefit deemed to be inappropriate by the taxing authorities. Congress and the Treasury Department have repeatedly responded to these measures by adopting more detailed tax laws and regulations designed to curb perceived abuses. The governmental responses in turn have triggered the development of additional tax planning techniques in a seemingly endless cycle of regulation, response and counter-response between governmental authorities and private taxpayers.

The conduct of taxpayers and their advisers has been the subject of extensive discussion regarding the legality and ethics of elaborate tax planning measures. The courts have commented on the issue on many occasions, and the classic statement on the matter was expressed in *Helvering v Gregory*,[125] an early case involving a transaction structured to comply with tax-free corporate reorganization rules. In a decision favoring the government, the Court of Appeals for the Second Circuit stated that *'a transaction, otherwise within an exception of the tax law, does not lose its immunity, because it is actuated by a desire to avoid, or, if one choose, to evade, taxation. Any one may so arrange his affairs that his taxes shall be as low as possible; he is not bound to choose that pattern which will best pay the Treasury; there is not even a patriotic duty to increase one's taxes.'*[126]

The statement in *Helvering v Gregory* is still considered to be valid with respect to structuring affairs in a manner to avoid the application of

123 See *supra* section 3.4 Administrative guidance.

124 The power of the US Congress to enact modern federal income tax laws was granted to it by the 16th amendment to the US Constitution, which was adopted in 1913. The 16th amendment provides as follows: *'The Congress shall have power to lay and collect taxes on incomes, from whatever source derived, without apportionment among the several States, and without regard to any census or enumeration.'*

125 69 F.2d 809 (2nd Cir 1934), *aff'd*, 293 US 465 (1935).

126 *Id.*

tax under pertinent tax laws, but more recent statements on the topic demonstrate greater attention to the difference between legitimate tax avoidance and illegal tax evasion. The IRS has expressed the difference as follows:

'Avoidance of taxes is not a criminal offense. Any attempt to reduce, avoid, minimize, or alleviate taxes by legitimate means is permissible. The distinction between avoidance and evasion is fine, yet definite. One who avoids tax does not conceal or misrepresent. He/she shapes events to reduce or eliminate tax liability and, upon the happening of the events, makes a complete disclosure. Evasion, on the other hand, involves deceit, subterfuge, camouflage, concealment, some attempt to color or obscure events or to make things seem other than they are. For example, the creation of a bona fide partnership to reduce the tax liability of a business by dividing the income among several individual partners is tax avoidance. However, the facts of a particular investigation may show that an alleged partnership was not, in fact, established and that one or more of the alleged partners secretly returned his/her share of the profits to the real owner of the business, who, in turn, did not report this income. This would be an instance of attempted evasion.'[127]

8. ACCEPTABLE TAX PLANNING AREAS/SUBJECTS

In its explanation of the distinction between avoidance and evasion above, the IRS illustrates the concept of legitimate avoidance by referring to the formation of a *bona fide* partnership that has the effect of allocating its income among different partners. This is a legitimate approach because it relies on the application of statutory provisions that expressly provide for the allocation of partnership income among partners.[128] The example chosen by the IRS to illustrate the point is among the simplest possible, as it involves the application of only one concept in the tax law. There are many examples of tax planning techniques involving more complex concepts or the combination of multiple provisions of the tax law to enter into economic arrangements on a tax-free or tax-efficient basis which are generally accepted by the IRS, the courts or the tax practitioner community as being legitimate tax avoidance measures. Some examples of accepted planning techniques are described below.

(a) Issuance of profits interests in partnership entities

This technique is used to provide equity compensation to persons in exchange for the performance of services on a tax-deferred basis. It is used to efficiently deal with US tax rules that require a person who receives property in exchange for the performance of services to pay income tax at ordinary rates as a result of the receipt of the property.[129] The amount of income

127 This statement appears in the Internal Revenue Manual (IRM). The statement appears at IRM 9.1.3.3.2.1, last revised May 15, 2008. The IRM is a comprehensive policy manual used by the IRS to guide its agents in applying federal tax laws and regulations.

128 See I.R.C. §§ 701–704.

129 I.R.C. § 83. The maximum federal income tax rate applicable to individuals currently is 39.6 per cent. Additional Medicare, FICA (Federal Insurance Contributions Act) and self-employment taxes may also apply at the federal level. Corporate taxpayers are currently subject to a maximum federal income tax rate of 35 per cent. Additional state-level taxes may also to both individual and corporate taxpayers, depending on the states in which they have taxable nexus.

subject to tax in such case is equal to the fair market value of the property transferred.[130] For example, if a corporation issues shares of its capital stock to an executive as compensation for the performance of services by the executive, the executive is deemed to have earned gross income for tax purposes in an amount equal to the fair market value of the shares so issued. The executive is required to pay tax on this value even though no cash is paid to the executive as part of the transaction.

A technique that is frequently used to provide service providers with an equity position in a venture without exposing the service provider to taxation upon issuance of the equity is to establish the business as an entity classified as a partnership for federal tax purposes, and then issue an equity interest to the service provider which is classified as a 'profits interest' under applicable IRS rulings. The most common type of entity presently used for this purpose is a limited liability company (LLC).[131] A profits interest essentially is an equity interest which would not be entitled to receive any cash or property if the entity were to liquidate and distribute all of its assets in accordance with applicable law and its governing documents immediately after the issuance of the equity interest.[132] A profits interest accrues economic value only as the value of the entity's assets increase in value over time, either as a result of the conduct of profitable activities, increases in the market value of the entity's assets, or both.

A partnership generally does not pay federal income taxes; instead, the partners are responsible for payment of income taxes on their share of the income earned by the partnership.[133] The income allocated to the partners retains the same character as it originally has when earned by the partnership.[134] Accordingly, if a partnership earns long-term capital gain income from the disposition of a capital asset held in excess of one year, non-corporate partners, including partners who received their interest in the partnership under the profits interest rule described herein, are eligible to apply the preferential tax rate which applies to long-term capital gains, which generally is 20 per cent.[135] This represents a significant tax savings as compared to the maximum ordinary tax rate of 39.6 per cent that applies to income received as compensation for the performance of services.

The combination of the rules relating to the issuance of profits interests in partnership entities with rules permitting long-term capital gain income

130 *Id.*

131 An LLC generally is treated as a partnership for federal tax purposes unless it files an election to be taxed as a corporation. See Treas. Reg. §§ 301.7701-2, 301-7701-3.

132 Rev. Proc. 93-27, 1993-2 CB 343. In this revenue procedure, the IRS states that a profits interest is deemed to have no current value and therefore does not give rise to taxable income upon receipt by the service provider. The rule may be viewed as a safe harbor established for the sake of convenience, because it might be argued in some cases that despite not having a current liquidation value, the interest still has some economic value due to the prospects of value increases in the future. Despite the existence of such prospects, the rule is applied to treat profits interests as having no value for purposes of measuring taxable income upon issuance of the interest. It should be noted that Rev. Proc. 93-27 contains additional conditions that must be satisfied for it to apply. The conditions are (1) the profits interest must not relate to a substantially certain and predictable stream of income from partnership assets, such as income from high-quality debt securities or a high-quality net lease; (2) the recipient of the profits interest must not dispose of the profits interest within two years after its receipt; and (3) the profits interest must not be a limited partnership interest in a 'publicly traded partnership' within the meaning of s. 7704(b) of the I.R.C.

133 I.R.C. § 701.

134 I.R.C. § 702.

135 I.R.C. § 1(h).

earned by the partnership to retain its character when allocated to all partners, including holders of profits interests, operates to allow a service provider who receives a profits interest in exchange for services to earn income which in many cases can be comprised in large part of preferential long-term capital gains income which is subject to lower tax rates instead of the ordinary income normally applicable to service providers. This approach has been used frequently to compensate private equity fund managers with a 'carried interest' in investment partnerships and has drawn the criticism of many who perceive this tax planning measure to be an abuse of a tax loophole. Since the late 1990s, legislative proposals have been submitted for consideration by Congress to eliminate the benefits of these carried interest plans by imposing additional taxes on holders of profits interests in a variety of ways, but no such proposal has yet been adopted.

(b) 'Check-the-box' elections and 'check-and-sell' transactions

US corporations usually structure non-US operations through non-US corporations. A typical structure involves the establishment of a subsidiary corporation in a non-US jurisdiction to serve as a holding company that in turn owns shares of multiple subsidiary entities organized in foreign jurisdictions. This type of structure is implemented with the intention of deferring taxable income in the US to the extent that earnings of the foreign entities are not repatriated to the US Despite the foreign structure, however, certain types of income earned by the foreign group of entities can be subject to current taxation in the US pursuant to rules applicable to foreign corporations classified as controlled foreign corporations.

A controlled foreign corporation (CFC) includes, among other things, a non-US corporation that is wholly-owned by a US corporation.[136] A US shareholder of a CFC is taxable currently on its pro rata share of the CFC's 'subpart F income' earned during the taxable year.[137] Hence, there is no US income tax deferral with respect to subpart F income.

Subpart F income generally includes gains earned from the sale of shares of capital stock of a corporation, including wholly-owned subsidiaries,[138] but it does not include gains from the sale of certain assets which are used or held for use in a CFC's trade or business.[139] Accordingly, in the case of a CFC that desires to sell a business operated by a foreign subsidiary, it is generally preferable for the CFC to sell the assets held by the foreign subsidiary, as opposed to selling shares of capital stock of the foreign subsidiary to the buyer. The sale of assets, however, can present complexities that might not be present in the case of a sale of shares. For example, the foreign subsidiary may be a party to a contract that may require the consent of the other party to the contract in order to assign the contract to a buyer of the entity's assets, but might not require consent in the case of a sale of shares of capital stock of the foreign subsidiary. There may also be other legal and tax reasons

136 I.R.C. § 957.
137 I.R.C. § 951.
138 I.R.C. §§ 952, 954.
139 Treas. Reg. § 1.954-2(e)(3).

to structure the transaction as a stock sale. The problem under the CFC tax regime is that a gain from the sale of the shares of a foreign subsidiary corporation is treated as taxable subpart F income.

One solution to the foregoing problem is entering into a 'check-and-sell' transaction. The first step in this technique involves the filing of an election with the IRS to treat the foreign subsidiary as an entity that is disregarded as being a separate entity from its owner.[140] This is commonly referred to as a 'check-the-box' election, because it involves checking a box on the applicable form to indicate what classification is desired for tax purposes.[141] This gives rise to a legal fiction that essentially causes the foreign subsidiary to be treated as fiscally transparent for purposes of applying the subpart F income rules to the parent CFC entity. Accordingly, the parent CFC entity is thereafter treated as directly owning the assets held by the foreign subsidiary, even though the foreign subsidiary continues to exist as a distinct legal entity for all other purposes. The transition from foreign corporate subsidiary to a disregarded entity is treated for US tax purposes as a tax-free liquidation which does not give rise to subpart F income and results in the transfer of the foreign subsidiary's corporate tax attributes to its CFC parent entity.[142]

The second step in the check-and-sell technique is the sale of the shares of the foreign subsidiary to the buyer. This is treated for US tax purposes as a direct sale of assets by the CFC parent entity of the foreign subsidiary, because the subsidiary is treated as fiscally transparent under US tax law, as described above. To the extent that the assets are within the class of assets that generally do not generate subpart F income on disposition, the gain from the sale is not classified as subpart F income and US tax deferrals are preserved.

The check-and-sell technique was challenged by the IRS in *Dover Corp. v Comm.*,[143] asserting that the assets sold by the CFC in question should not be viewed as having been used or held for use by the CFC, since the sales transaction was consummated on the same date as the effective date of the check-the-box election and there was no span of time over which the CFC operated or was deemed to operate the business of the subsidiary, which became classified as a disregarded entity. The Tax Court rejected the government's argument, holding that the statutes governing tax-free corporate liquidations[144] and the carryover of corporate attributes[145] caused the CFC in question to be treated as having inherited (for federal tax purposes) the business history of the subsidiary entity when it filed the election to become classified as a disregarded entity, and that achievement of the liquidation by means of the election as opposed to a liquidation pursuant to local law did not alter this result. In 1999, the IRS proposed

140 This is achieved by application of Treas. Reg. §§ 301.7701-2 and 301.7701-3. Certain types of entities are not eligible to file this election. The list of ineligible entities is updated periodically and included in amendments to the foregoing regulations.
141 The form is IRS Form 8832.
142 See I.R.C. §§ 332, 337, 381.
143 122 TC 324 (2004).
144 I.R.C. §§ 332, 337.
145 I.R.C. § 381.

regulations[146] that would have prohibited the use of the check-and-sell technique in the manner that it was used in the *Dover* case. The proposed regulations were met with substantial criticism and were withdrawn by the IRS in 2003.[147]

(c) Other tax planning techniques

The profits interest and check-and-sell techniques described above are a fair representation of measures taken by taxpayers to mitigate federal income tax liabilities. Other planning techniques used to reduce taxes include the use of installment sales to defer tax on the sale of property where a portion of the sales price is paid in subsequent tax years,[148] corporate reorganization transactions where tax is deferred in the sale or merger of a corporation to the extent the consideration consists of stock of the acquiring corporation,[149] and corporate spin-off or split-off transactions, where a corporation with at least two historic active businesses can distribute one of the businesses to its stockholders without triggering taxable income at the corporate level on the distribution of appreciated assets or at the stockholder level with respect to the value of the assets distributed.[150]

9. THE JUDICIAL FRAMEWORK AND KEY CASES OF INTEREST

There are many tax planning techniques that are used to consummate transactions on a tax-free basis by using multiple steps that use provisions of the Code and Regulations that allow each individual step to be effected in a tax-advantaged manner. When properly disclosed, these techniques generally represent legitimate tax avoidance strategies, in contrast to illegal tax evasion, as described by the IRS in the Internal Revenue Manual, referred to above. The fact that a particular tax planning measure represents an attempt at legitimate tax avoidance, as opposed to tax evasion, does not necessarily mean that the taxpayer's position will be respected by the IRS and the courts. The IRS and the courts have applied different doctrines to deny tax taxpayers benefits sought through consummation of transactions by means of steps that are structured to literally comply with statutory requirements, but which are perceived to violate the intention of applicable tax laws. These doctrines overlap in some aspects and it is sometimes difficult to draw clear distinctions between them. The doctrines used by the IRS and the courts to strike down taxpayer attempts at tax avoidance can be grouped into broad categories, consisting of substance over form and step transaction doctrines which reclassify the nature of transactions entered into by the taxpayer, and the sham transaction, economic substance and business purpose doctrines which deny tax benefits arising from transactions that do not provide non-tax economic benefits and are entered into generally for the purpose of reducing taxes. These doctrines are described below.

---

146 Prop. Reg. § 301.7701-3(h).
147 IRS Notice 2003-46, 2003-2 CB 53, June 26, 2003.
148 I.R.C. § 453.
149 I.R.C. §§ 368, 354, 356.
150 I.R.C. §§ 355, 354, 356.

(a) Court Holding Co. and the general substance over form doctrine

Most doctrines used by the IRS and the courts to set aside tax planning measures taken by taxpayers are rooted in substance over form concepts. Perhaps the most often cited case in the area is *Comm. v Court Holding Co.*[151] In *Court Holding Co.*, a corporation transferred its sole asset to its stockholder in a liquidating distribution, and the stockholder immediately thereafter sold the asset. The transaction had originally been negotiated as a sale of the asset by the corporation directly to the buyer, but was then restructured to avoid application of corporate tax on the sale and secure tax advantages on the liquidating distribution that were available under laws applicable at that time. The government argued that the transaction should be treated as a sale by the corporation and not by the stockholder, relying on the fact that it was originally negotiated as a sale by the corporation and restructured only to provide a tax benefit. The Supreme Court ruled in favor of the government, holding that:

'The incidence of taxation depends upon the substance of a transaction. The tax consequences which arise from gains from a sale of property are not finally to be determined solely by the means employed to transfer legal title. Rather, the transaction must be viewed as a whole, and each step, from the commencement of negotiations to the consummation of the sale, is relevant. A sale by one person cannot be transformed for tax purposes into a sale by another by using the latter as a conduit through which to pass title. To permit the true nature of a transaction to be disguised by mere formalisms, which exist solely to alter tax liabilities, would seriously impair the effective administration of the tax policies of Congress.'

(b) Step transaction doctrine

1. General description of the step transaction doctrine

The step transaction doctrine is a rule of substance over form that treats a series of steps as a single transaction if the steps are directed at achieving a particular result.[152] The IRS and the courts apply the doctrine by determining the tax consequences of the transaction without regard to unnecessary intermediate steps. The transaction, stripped down to its bare essentials, may then yield tax results which are different than those originally intended to be achieved by the taxpayer by inserting additional steps. A simple illustration of the doctrine's application appears in *Redwing Carriers, Inc. v Tomlinson.*[153] In that case, the taxpayer sold motor vehicles to a dealer for cash, and in separate but related transactions, purchased new motor vehicles for cash. The taxpayer reported the transactions as separate, obtaining tax advantages under tax laws applicable at the time. The IRS challenged the taxpayer's treatment of the transactions as separate, and asserted that they should be viewed as vehicle-for-vehicle exchanges classified as like-kind exchanges that had the effect of reducing the taxpayer's ordinary depreciation deductions relating to the vehicles. The court agreed with the government's position by netting out the cash payments against each other

151 324 US 331 (1945).
152 *Penrod v Comr.* 88 TC 1415 (1987).
153 399 F.2d 652 (5th Cir. 1968).

and reducing the transactions to mere exchanges of old vehicles for new ones.

There is no universally accepted test as to when and how the step transaction doctrine should be applied to a given set of facts. Courts have applied three alternative tests in deciding whether to invoke the step transaction doctrine in a particular situation. They are the binding commitment test, the interdependence test, and the end result test.[154]

Under the binding commitment test, a series of transactions will be stepped together only if at the time the first step is commenced there is a binding legal commitment to undertake the subsequent step.[155] This test is the narrowest of the three tests, and generally is used by the courts to deal with transactions that take place over multiple tax years.[156]

Under the interdependence test, a series of transactions will be stepped together if the steps are so interdependent that the legal relations created by one transaction would have been fruitless without a completion of the series.[157] If, however, any independent purpose is served by an intermediate step it may be sufficient to prevent the application of the step transaction doctrine under the interdependence test.[158]

Under the end result test, a series of transactions will be stepped together when the intent at the outset was to achieve the particular result, and the separate steps were all entered into as a means of achieving that result.[159] This test would result in application of the step transaction doctrine under almost any transaction where the same result could have been achieved in a more direct manner, but included additional steps for the purpose of avoiding taxes.[160] The end result test is the broadest of the three tests.

2. Limitations on the step transaction doctrine

Irrespective of which of the three approaches is applied, the step transaction doctrine is subject to limitations that are described in the frequently cited *Esmark* case.[161] In *Esmark*, the corporate taxpayer entered into an agreement with a buyer to sell shares of the taxpayer's subsidiary to the buyer. As part of the agreement among the parties, the buyer acquired shares of the taxpayer's stock on the open market pursuant to a tender offer. Immediately after completion of the tender offer and pursuant to the agreement among the parties, the taxpayer redeemed the shares acquired by the buyer in the tender offer in exchange for the transfer of shares of the taxpayer's subsidiary to the buyer. This structure was selected primarily to secure tax benefits for the taxpayer under rules that were applicable at that time. The IRS sought to recharacterize the transactions as a taxable sale of the subsidiary's shares to the buyer for cash followed by a redemption of shares

154 See *Penrod, supra*.
155 *Comm. v Gordon*, 391 US 83 (1968).
156 See for example *McDonald's Restaurants of Ill. v Comr.*, 688 F.2d 520 (7th Cir. 1982).
157 *King Enterprises, Inc. v US*, 418 F.2d 511 (Ct. Cl. 1969).
158 *Falconwood Corporation v US*, 422 F.3d 1339 (Fed. Cir. 2005).
159 *Kuper v Comr.*, 533 F.2d 152 (5th Cir. 1976).
160 *Del Commercial Properties, Inc. v Comm.*, 251 F.3d 210 (D.C. Cir. 2001).
161 *Esmark v Comm.*, 90 T.C. 171 (1988).

from the public by the taxpayer pursuant to a self-tender with the proceeds from the sale of the subsidiary.

The *Esmark* court rejected the IRS position, stating that the step transaction doctrine *'combines a series of individually meaningless steps into a single transaction,'* and that the IRS had *'pointed to no meaningless or unnecessary steps that should be ignored.'* The Tax Court explained that there was no route to the results achieved which was more direct than the route which was followed, and that the taxpayer was free to choose the route which provided the best tax result. It also stated that the recharacterization proposed by the IRS did not just involve the combination of steps, but would have also required the invention of new steps. Noting that the courts do not apply the step transaction in this manner, the court ruled in favor of the taxpayer.

The *Esmark* case describes the limit on the step transaction doctrine which prevents the IRS from recasting the steps of a transaction when there is no alternative interpretation of the transaction which could involve fewer steps and any alternative would require the invention of steps which did not in fact occur. In the *Turner Broadcasting System* case, the Tax Court further elaborated on the limits of the step transaction doctrine, stating that the IRS must provide a *'logically plausible alternative explanation that accounts for all the results of the transaction,'* and *'[e]ven if alternative explanations are available to account for the results of a transaction, this Court will not disregard the form of the transaction if it accounts for the transaction at least as well as alternative rechararacterizations.'*[162]

3. Economic substance, business purpose and sham transaction doctrines

The IRS and the courts generally will rule against taxpayers claiming tax benefits if the tax benefits arise from a transaction or series of transactions that lacks economic substance apart from the federal income tax benefits arising from the transaction. In *ACM Partnership v Comm.* the Tax Court described the economic substance doctrine by stating that the tax law 'requires that the intended transactions have economic substance separate and distinct from economic benefit achieved solely by tax reduction. The doctrine of economic substance becomes applicable, and a judicial remedy is warranted, where a taxpayer seeks to claim tax benefits, unintended by Congress, by means of transactions that serve no economic purpose other than tax savings.'[163]

The economic substance doctrine is closely related to and overlaps with the business purpose doctrine, and the two doctrines are frequently considered in the same cases. The business purpose doctrine asks what were the motives for entering into a transaction, whether the taxpayer was pursuing a valid business purpose apart from the reduction of federal income tax, and necessarily involves a subjective analysis. The courts will sometimes

162 *Turner Broadcasting System, Inc. v Comm.*, 111 T.C. 315 (1998).
163 73 T.C.M. 2189 (1997), *affirmed*, 157 F.3d 231 (3d Cir. 1998), *cert. denied* 526 US 1017 (1999).

apply the doctrine to disallow tax benefits by dividing a transaction into two parts, one part involving activities with non-tax objectives and the other involving only those activities which have tax avoidance as their purpose.[164] Transactions that lack economic substance and a business purpose are also referred to as economic shams.[165] Economic shams are distinct from transactions that are fraudulent shams, which involve transactions that never really occurred.[166]

The courts have blurred the concepts of economic substance and business purpose, with different courts applying these concepts in different ways. Some courts have indicated that a transaction's tax benefits may be set aside if the taxpayer fails to establish either economic substance or a business purpose,[167] while other courts have indicated that a transaction's tax benefits should be set aside only if the taxpayer fails to establish both the business purpose and economic substance behind the transaction,[168] and yet other courts have stated that economic substance and business purpose are to be treated merely as additional factors to consider when determining whether a transaction has economic effects apart from tax reductions.[169]

The courts have also been inconsistent regarding the degree of economic benefits that must be shown to establish that a transaction has economic substance. Some courts have denied tax benefits upon a finding that a purported business benefit was not in fact obtained by the transactions.[170] Other courts have stated that tax benefits should be denied if the taxpayer did not have a potential for profit from the transactions,[171] and some have stated that tax benefits should be denied when the potential for profit and the risks undertaken were not significant relative to the tax benefits arising from the transactions under review.[172] Some courts have required that there be a 'reasonable possibility of profit' apart from tax benefits in order to sustain a transaction.[173]

In response to inconsistencies in the manner in which the courts applied the economic substance doctrine, Congress eventually enacted legislation to provide some uniformity in the application of certain aspects of the doctrine. The legislation is described below.

---

164 See *ACM Partnership, supra*.

165 See, eg, *Tigers Eye Trading, LLC v Comm.*, 138 TC 67 (2012).

166 See, eg, *Kennedy v Comm.*, 876 F.2d 1251 (6th Cir. 1989).

167 See, eg, *Klamath Strategic Investment Fund v United States*, 568 F. 3d 537 (5th Cir. 2009) (a realistic possibility of profit and risk must be present even if it is shown that a profit motive is present); *Pasternak v Commissioner*, 990 F.2d 893 (6th Cir. 1993) (requiring establishment of a profit motive in addition to showing that the transaction had economic substance).

168 See, eg, *Rice's Toyota World v Comm.*, 752 F.2d 89 (4th Cir. 1985) (*'To treat a transaction as a sham, the court must find that the taxpayer was motivated by no business purposes other than obtaining tax benefits in entering the transaction, and, second, that the transaction has no economic substance because no reasonable possibility of a profit exists'*); *Saba Partnership v Comm.*, T.C. Memo 1999-359 (*'A transaction imbued with economic substance normally will be recognized for tax purposes even in the absence of a nontax business purpose'*).

169 See, eg, *Sacks v Comm.*, 69 F.3d 982 (9th Cir. 1995) (*'[B]usiness purpose and economic substance are simply more precise factors to consider ... this formulation cannot be used as a "rigid two-step analysis"'*).

170 See, eg, *Coltec Industries v United States*, 454 F.3d 1340 (Fed. Cir. 2006) (stating that insulation from liabilities was not in fact achieved by the taxpayer's transactions).

171 See, eg, *Knetsch v US*, 364 US 361 (1960).

172 See, eg, *Goldstein v Comm.*, 364 F.2d 734 (2d Cir. 1966); *Sheldon v Comm.*, 94 T.C. 738 (1981).

173 See, eg, *Rice's Toyota World, supra; Compaq Computer Corp. v Comm.*, 277 F.3d 778 (5th Cir. 2001).

10. LEGISLATIVE AND REGULATORY FRAMEWORK

(a) Economic substance statute

Congress enacted Code s. 7701(o) in 2010 to standardize the criteria which must be satisfied to sustain tax benefits arising from transactions in cases where application of the economic substance doctrine is relevant. By its terms, s. 7701(o) applies in cases where the economic substance doctrine is relevant under applicable common law in existence prior to the enactment of the statute.[174] The statute defines the economic substance doctrine as the common law doctrine that denies tax benefits if a transaction or series of transactions lacks either economic substance or a business purpose.[175] Legislative history of the statute states that the statute is not intended to alter the tax treatment of basic business transactions that are generally respected by the courts and the IRS.[176] It states that these basic transactions include (1) the choice between capitalizing a business enterprise with debt or equity; (2) a US person's choice between utilizing a foreign corporation or a domestic corporation to make a foreign investment; (3) the choice to enter into a transaction or series of transactions that constitute a corporate organization or reorganization; and (4) the choice to utilize a related-party entity in a transaction, provided that the arm's length standard of Code s. 482 and other applicable concepts are satisfied.[177]

Section 7701(o) eliminates uncertainties raised by court decisions that differed as to whether the satisfaction of either of these criteria is sufficient to sustain a transaction's tax benefits. The difference in approaches is resolved by allowing tax benefits only if the taxpayer's position is meaningfully changed apart from federal income tax effects and the taxpayer has a substantial purpose for the transaction other than federal income tax effects.[178]

The statute provides that profit potential shall be taken into account for purposes of determining if there has been a meaningful change in economic position and if there is a substantial non-tax purpose, and clarifies that profit potential must be substantial in relation to the tax benefits from the transaction.[179] Substantiality is measured under the statute by comparing the present value of the reasonably expected pre-tax profits to the present value of the tax benefits from the transaction.[180] The statute also provides rules for taking into account state, local and foreign taxes, transaction fees and financial accounting benefits.[181]

---

174 I.R.C. §§ 7701(o)(1) and 7701(o)(5)(A).

175 I.R.C. §§ 7701(o)(1) and 7701(o)(5)(A).

176 JCX-18-10, The Joint Committee on Taxation, *Technical Explanation of the Revenue Provisions of the 'Reconciliation Act of 2010,' As Amended, in Combination with the 'Patient Protection and Affordable Care Act'*, 152–153.

177 *Id.*

178 I.R.C. §§ 7701(o)(1)(A) and 7701(o)(1)(B).

179 I.R.C. § 7701(o)(2)(A).

180 *Id.*

181 State and local taxes that are related to federal income tax effects are treated as if they were federal income taxes for purposes of these calculations. I.R.C. § 7701(o)(3). Fees and transaction expenses are to be taken into account in determining pre-tax profits and the statute instructs the Secretary of the Treasury to issue regulations treating foreign taxes as expenses also, in appropriate cases. I.R.C. § 7701(o)(2)(B). No such regulations have yet been issued. Financial accounting benefits are ignored as a business purpose if the benefits arise from tax reductions. I.R.C. § 7701(o)(4).

(b) Other anti-avoidance statutes and regulations

In addition to s. 7701(o), there are several other statutory and regulatory provisions which may be viewed as anti-abuse rules, aimed at curbing abuses in certain situations. These include the following provisions:

- Code s. 267, which postpones tax deductions with respect to payments made to certain related parties until such time as the related party includes the item in its taxable income, and which also disallows tax losses arising from sales of property to related parties;
- Code s. 269, which denies tax benefits arising from the acquisition of a corporation in cases where the principal purpose of the acquisition is the avoidance or evasion of tax by securing a deduction, credit or allowance that would not otherwise be available;
- Code s. 382, which is intended to limit trafficking in corporate tax losses by limiting the amount of corporate net operating loss carry-forwards that can be used by a corporation after consummation of a change in ownership in excess of 50 per cent within a three-year period;
- Code s. 482 and related regulations, which authorize the IRS to reallocate income among related taxpayers, is described in detail in part one of this chapter;
- Treasury Regulations s. 1.701-2, which is the partnership anti-abuse regulation that allows the IRS to recharacterize transactions involving a partnership if the partnership is used in a transaction, the principal purpose of which is to reduce substantially the partners' federal tax liability in a manner that is inconsistent with the intent of the partnership tax statutes; and
- Code s. 707(b), which disallows tax losses arising from sales of property between a partnership and partners owning more than 50 per cent of the capital or profits of the partnership, and between two partnerships with more than 50 per cent common ownership.

In addition to the foregoing provisions, the Internal Revenue Code and Treasury Regulations are replete with rules that must be satisfied in order to claim tax deductions, losses and tax benefits in a multitude of situations. These limitations might be viewed merely as conditions to the allowances in question, but many can also be viewed as measures designed to prevent abuses.

11. PENALTIES APPLICABLE TO TAX AVOIDANCE TRANSACTIONS

The Code and Regulations provide for assorted penalties and interest relating to underpayments of tax and failure to file tax returns, including criminal penalties when applicable. The discussion below relates to penalties specifically pertinent to tax avoidance transactions of the nature discussed in this work.

(a) Legislative and regulatory provisions

1. General accuracy-related penalty

Code s. 6662 imposes an accuracy-related penalty on certain underpayments of tax. The penalty rate is 20 per cent of the amount of the understatement that is generally subject to s. 6662.[182] The 20 per cent penalty rate generally applies to understatements that are attributable to, among other things, negligence or disregard of rules or regulations,[183] substantial understatements of income tax,[184] and substantial valuation misstatements.[185]

2. Higher accuracy-related penalties for gross valuation misstatements and noneconomic substance transactions

The accuracy-related penalty rate is increased to 40 per cent to the extent of understatements attributable to, among other things, gross valuation misstatements[186] and nondisclosed noneconomic substance transactions.[187] A nondisclosed noneconomic substance transaction is a transaction lacking economic substance within the meaning of s. 7701(o), or which fails to meet the requirements of any similar rule of law, if the relevant facts affecting the tax treatment of any portion of said transaction are not adequately disclosed in the return, nor found in a statement attached to the return.[188]

3. Penalties for understatements of tax relating to listed transactions and reportable transactions

In addition to the accuracy-related penalties described above, the Code s. 6662A also imposes penalties for understatements of tax related to listed transactions and reportable transactions. The penalty is generally 20 per cent of the amount of a reportable transaction understatement attributable to any listed transaction or any reportable transaction (other than a listed transaction) if a significant purpose of such transaction is the avoidance or evasion of federal income tax.[189] The amount of the reportable transaction understatement that the penalty applies to generally is equal to the increase in taxable income resulting from proper treatment of the item instead of the treatment reported by the taxpayer, multiplied by the highest tax

---

182 I.R.C. § 6662(a).

183 I.R.C. § 6662(b)(1). Section 6662(c) provides that 'negligence' includes any failure to make a reasonable attempt to comply with the provisions of the I.R.C., and the term 'disregard' includes any careless, reckless, or intentional disregard.

184 I.R.C. § 6662(b)(2). Under s. 6662(d), understatements of tax are substantial in the case of subchapter C corporations if they exceed the lesser of 10 per cent of the tax required to be shown on the tax return for the year (but at least $10,000) or $10 million. For other taxpayers, including individuals, the thresholds are the greater of 10 per cent of the tax required to be shown on the return or $5,000.

185 I.R.C. § 6662(b)(3). Under s. 6662(e)(1) substantial valuation misstatements include (i) overstatements of the value or adjusted basis of property which equal or exceed 150 per cent of the amount determined to be correct, (ii) overstatements of the amount paid to a related party for property, the use of property, or services, which equal or exceed 200 per cent of the amount determined under I.R.C. §482, (iii) understatements of amounts received for such items of 50 per cent or less, and (iv) net s. 482 transfer price adjustments which exceed the lesser of $5,000,000 or 10 per cent of the taxpayer's gross receipts.

186 I.R.C. § 6662(h)(1). Gross valuation misstatements are the same as substantial valuation misstatements defined in s. 6662(e)(1), except that the percentages and amounts of the misstatements are more egregious. See the immediately preceding note for a description of substantial valuation misstatements. Under s. 6662(h)(1), the thresholds applicable to the 6662(e)(1) items described in the immediately preceding note are (i) 200 per cent, (ii) 400 per cent, (iii) 25 per cent, and (iv) $20 million/20 per cent.

187 I.R.C. § 6662(i)(1).

188 I.R.C. §§ 6662(b)(6) and (i)(2).

189 I.R.C. §§ 6662A(a), (b) and (d).

rate generally applicable to non-corporate taxpayers, if the taxpayer is not a corporation, or, if the taxpayer is a corporation, the highest tax rate generally applicable to corporations.[190] The penalty rate is increased to 30 per cent of the reportable transaction understatement if the transaction is not adequately disclosed.[191] Reportable transactions, including listed transactions, are required to be reported on IRS Form 8886.[192]

A listed transaction is a transaction that the IRS has identified as a tax avoidance transaction in published guidance, or a transaction that is substantially similar to a transaction so identified.[193] Transactions identified by the IRS as listed transactions are broad-ranging, and are compiled on the IRS website.[194] Notable listed transactions include transactions involving the distributions of encumbered property in which losses claimed for capital outlays have been recovered (BOSS transactions), inflated partnership basis transactions (Son of BOSS), transactions involving the use of an intermediary to sell corporate assets, losses generated by selling corporate stock with a basis which is artificially inflated by transferring high basis assets and liabilities that the transferor has not yet taken into account for federal income tax purposes, lease in/lease out (LILO) transactions and transfers of compensatory stock options to related persons.[195]

Reportable transactions are transactions which are included in any of the following categories: listed transactions described above,[196] confidential transactions which are offered to a taxpayer under conditions of confidentiality for which the taxpayer has paid an advisor a minimum fee,[197] contractual protection transactions, in which a taxpayer or related party has the right to a full or partial refund or in which fees to certain tax advisers are contingent depending on the tax consequences or benefits of the transaction,[198] loss transactions, in which the taxpayer claims a loss under Code s. 165 (relating to losses not compensated by insurance or otherwise) which exceeds certain dollar thresholds[199] and transactions of interest, which are the same as or substantially similar to those identified by the IRS as transactions of interest or the same as or substantially similar to those transactions.[200]

Coordination rules provide that s. 6662A reportable transaction understatement penalties are not to be duplicative of the s. 6662 penalties or fraud penalties under s. 6663.[201]

---

190 I.R.C. § 6662A(b)(1). The statute also provides special rules which factor in the effects of reductions to credits, excess deductions and capital losses arising from the correct treatment of a transaction, effectively treating such reductions the same as increases in taxable income.

191 I.R.C. §§ 6662A(c), 6664(d)(3)(A), 6011; Treas. Reg. § 1.6011-4.

192 I.R.C. § 6011(a); Treas. Reg. § 1.6011-4.

193 I.R.C. §§ 6707A(c)(2), 6011; Treas. Reg. § 1.6011-4.

194 See *http://www.irs.gov/Businesses/Corporations/Listed-Transactions---LB&I-Tier-I-Issues#12*. The listed transactions are officially set forth in Notice 2009-59, 2009-31 IRB 170, July 15, 2009. There currently are 34 listed transactions.

195 *Id.*

196 Treas. Reg. § 1.6011-4(b)(2).

197 Treas. Reg. § 1.6011-4(b)(3).

198 Treas. Reg. § 1.6011-4(b)(4).

199 Treas. Reg. § 1.6011-4(b)(5). The thresholds for the loss transactions are $10 million in any year or $20 million in any combination of years for corporations or for partnerships with only corporate partners, $2 million in any year or $4 million in any combination of years for other partnerships, individuals or trusts, and $50,000 in any single year arising from certain foreign currency transactions for individual or trusts.

200 Treas. Reg. § 1.6011-4(b)(6).

201 I.R.C. § 6662A(e).

4. Penalties for failure to disclose reportable transactions and listed transactions

Code s. 6707A provides for a penalty for failures to disclose listed transactions and reportable transactions in an amount equal to 75 per cent of the decrease in tax shown on the tax return attributable to the transaction if the transaction had been respected, subject to a maximum penalty of $200,000 in the case of a listed transaction ($100,000 in the case of a natural person) and $50,000 in the case of a reportable transaction other than a listed transaction ($10,000 in the case of a natural person).[202] The minimum penalty is $10,000 ($5,000 in case of a natural person). The s. 6707A penalty is in addition to all other penalties.[203] The IRS is authorized to rescind the penalty if the violation does not involve a listed transaction and the IRS determines that rescinding the penalty would promote tax compliance and administration.[204]

5. Fraud penalty

Code s. 6663 imposes a penalty of 75 per cent of the amount of an underpayment of tax that is attributable to fraud.

6. Exceptions to imposition of the penalties

Code s. 6662(d)(2)(B) allows for the reduction of the amount of an understatement subject to the s. 6662 accuracy-related penalty in two situations. First, the understatement is reduced by the portion that is attributable to an item if there is substantial authority for the taxpayer's treatment of the item.[205] The regulations state that there is substantial authority for a position only if the weight of the authorities supporting the treatment is substantial in relation to the weight of authorities supporting contrary treatment.[206] The second situation in which the understatement may be reduced is when the relevant facts affecting the item's tax treatment are adequately disclosed in the tax return or accompanying statement, and there is a reasonable basis for the tax treatment claimed.[207] The foregoing reduction is not applicable to any item attributable to a tax shelter.[208] For this purpose, a tax shelter is a partnership or other entity, an investment plan or arrangement or any other plan or arrangement, if its principal purpose is to avoid or evade federal income tax.[209]

Section 6664(c) provides that the s. 6662 accuracy-related penalty also is not to be imposed with respect to any portion of an underpayment if it is

---

202 I.R.C. §§ 6707A(a), (b)(1)-(2).

203 I.R.C. § 6707A(f).

204 I.R.C. § 6707A(d). There is no right of judicial review with respect to the determination of rescission of the penalty by the IRS.

205 I.R.C. § 6662(d)(2)(B)(i).

206 Treas. Reg. § 1.6662-4(d)(3). Substantial authority is less stringent than the 'more likely than not' standard that requires a greater than 50 per cent likelihood of a position being upheld, and more stringent than the 'reasonable basis' standard, described in the next note and accompanying text. Paragraph (d) of these regulations elaborate on the evaluation of authorities, the nature of analysis and types of authority which are acceptable.

207 I.R.C. § 6662(d)(2)(B)(ii). Treas. Reg. § 1.6662-3(b)(3) provides that the reasonable basis standard requires a return position to be reasonably based on authorities. Disclosure is adequate if there is disclosure on an adequately prepared IRS Form 8275 or 8275-R. Treas. Reg. § 1.6662-3(c)(2).

208 I.R.C. § 6662(d)(2)(C).

209 *Id.*

shown that there was reasonable cause for such portion and the taxpayer acted in good faith with respect to such portion.[210] This exception also applies to the s. 6663 fraud penalty. This exception does not apply to the portion of any understatement attributable to a transaction lacking economic substance.[211]

The determination of reasonable cause and good faith is made on a case-by-case basis taking into account all pertinent facts and circumstances, and the most important factor generally is the extent of the taxpayer's effort to assess the their proper tax liability.[212] Reliance on an information return, professional advice or other facts constitutes reasonable cause and good faith if, under all the circumstances, such reliance was reasonable and the taxpayer acted in good faith.[213]

Under the regulations, for reliance on professional advice to be deemed reasonable, the advice must consider all facts and circumstances, the taxpayer must disclose to the adviser all facts that they know or reasonably should know to be relevant to the proper tax treatment of an item,[214] and the advice must not be based on unreasonable factual or legal assumptions or unreasonably rely on representations, statements, findings or agreements of the taxpayer or any other person.[215] The regulations provide that a failure to disclose a reportable transaction is a strong indication that the taxpayer did not act in good faith.[216] In the case of a corporate taxpayer, reasonable cause and good faith with respect to a tax shelter item requires that additional standards be satisfied relating to substantial authority for the position, reasonable belief and reliance on professional tax advisors.[217]

Section 6664(d) also provides a reasonable cause exception to the imposition of the s. 6662A reportable transaction and listed transaction penalties. It provides that no penalty shall be imposed under s. 6662A with respect to any portion of a reportable transaction understatement if it is shown that there was a reasonable cause for such portion, that the taxpayer acted in good faith with respect to such portion, and that the relevant facts affecting the tax treatment of the item are adequately disclosed in accordance with the regulations prescribed under s. 6011, there is or was substantial authority for such treatment, and the taxpayer reasonably believed that such treatment was more likely than not the proper treatment.[218]

For purposes of the foregoing reasonable cause exception, a taxpayer is treated as having a reasonable belief with respect to the tax treatment of an item only if the belief is based on the facts and law that exist at the time the tax return which includes such tax treatment is filed, and the belief relates solely to the taxpayer's chances of success on the merits of such treatment

210 I.R.C. § 6664(c)(1).
211 I.R.C. §§ 6664(c)(2), 6662(b)(6).
212 Treas. Reg. § 1.6664-4(b).
213 *Id.*
214 Treas. Reg. § 1.6664-4(c)(i).
215 Treas. Reg. § 1.6664-4(c)(ii). A taxpayer also may not rely on advice that a regulation is invalid unless the position was adequately disclosed in accordance with Treas. Reg. § 1.6662-3(c)(2). See Treas. Reg. § 1.6664-4(c)(iii).
216 Treas. Reg. § 1.6664-4(d).
217 Treas. Reg. § 1.6664-4(f).
218 I.R.C. § 6664(d)(1), (3).

and does not take into account the possibility that a return will not be audited, such treatment will not be raised on audit, or such treatment will be resolved through settlement if it is raised.[219] The reasonable belief of the taxpayer cannot be established by an opinion of a tax advisor if the advisor is a disqualified tax advisor or if the opinion is a disqualified opinion.[220]

(c) Example of penalties imposed

The application of the accuracy-related penalty and evaluation of a taxpayer's claim that it should not be imposed on reasonable cause grounds is illustrated in *106 Ltd. v Comm.*[221] This case involved a taxpayer who had entered into a Son of BOSS transaction to generate substantial tax losses and reduce the taxpayer's federal tax liabilities. The taxpayer eventually conceded that the losses should be disallowed, and the only remaining issue before the court was whether the 40 per cent accuracy-related penalty which was assessed by the IRS should be abated. The court found that the taxpayer did not have reasonable cause and sustained the penalty on grounds that the taxpayer should have known the transaction was illegitimate and that the taxpayer's reliance on the opinion of his adviser was not reasonable and was not in good faith. The court based these conclusions on the following findings: (i) the taxpayer was a sophisticated businessman with extensive business experience and substantial earnings; (ii) the taxpayer did not intend to profit from the transaction apart from tax benefits, and actually expected to lose money on the transaction; (iii) the tax benefits from the transaction far exceeded the potential for profit from the transaction; (iv) the fees paid to advisers exceeded the potential non-tax economic benefit expected from the transaction; (v) the participation of the taxpayer's advisers in the structuring and coordination of the transaction and their general conduct indicated that they were acting as promoters of the transaction with an inherent conflict of interest, despite the fact that they previously advised the taxpayer on other ordinary matters; (vi) the guarantee of the transaction by the adviser who agreed to pay the taxpayer's litigation costs and refund his professional fees if the transaction was invalidated; and (vii) the opinion letter provided to the taxpayer contained inaccurate facts and assumptions that the taxpayer knew or should have known were unlikely to be true.

---

219 I.R.C. § 6664(d)(4)(A).

220 I.R.C. § 6664(d)(4)(B)(i). A disqualified tax advisor is an advisor who either is (i) a material advisor (within the meaning of s. 6111(b)(1)) and participates in the organization, management, promotion, or sale of the transaction or bears certain relationships to any person who so participates, (ii) is compensated directly or indirectly by a material advisor with respect to the transaction, (iii) has a fee arrangement with respect to the transaction which is contingent on all or part of the intended tax benefits from the transaction being sustained, or (iv) has a disqualifying financial interest with respect to the transaction pursuant to regulations to be issued. I.R.C. § 6664(d)(4)(B)(ii). A material advisor is one who provides any material aid, assistance, or advice with respect to organizing, managing, promoting, selling, implementing, insuring, or carrying out any reportable transaction, and who directly or indirectly derives gross income in excess of certain threshold amounts for such aid, assistance, or advice. I.R.C. § 6111(b)(1). The threshold amount of compensation is $50,000 in the case of a reportable transaction substantially all of the tax benefits from which are provided to natural persons, and $250,000 in any other case. The Treasury Secretary is authorized to establish other threshold amounts. An opinion is disqualified if the opinion is based on unreasonable factual or legal assumptions (including assumptions as to future events), unreasonably relies on representations, statements, findings, or agreements of the taxpayer or any other person, does not identify and consider all relevant facts, or fails to meet any other requirements prescribed by the Treasury Secretary.

221 684 F.3d 84 (D.C. Cir. 2012). The case involved tax years prior to the enactment of the special rules on noneconomic substance, reportable and listed transactions. Nevertheless, the court's discussion of the reasonable cause standard remains valid.

12. CURRENT TRENDS

12.1 National policy and law

In recent years, the ongoing discussion among politicians, representatives of the federal government, academics and other members of the tax community regarding tax avoidance have focused on preventing erosion of the US tax base through the use of structures and transactions which have the effect of shifting corporate profits out of the US to low-tax jurisdictions. As a result of the endless chatter on the subject, multiple proposals have been made which are directed at eliminating perceived abuses and loopholes involving US international tax rules. Although the focus of anti-avoidance proposals has been increasingly directed toward reformation of US international tax rules, there also are many US domestic tax benefits and planning techniques that have drawn the attention of critics. As a result of continuing criticism and antagonistic views against the business community, many common operating structures and business-motivated transactions that result in deferral of income and application of lower tax rates are now viewed by many as suspicious and even unpatriotic activities. Several of these concepts have drawn the attention of presidential staff and have been included in presidential budgetary proposals.[222] A few notable proposals are described below.

(a) Restriction of certain interest expense deductions of foreign and US multinationals

This proposal would defer the deduction of interest expense allocable to stock of foreign subsidiaries to the extent the income of such subsidiaries is deferred until it is repatriated, and would limit over-leveraging of US activities of a multination group by restricting US interest expense deductions of the US subgroup to the amount of the US subgroup's interest income plus the US subgroup's proportionate share of the group's net interest expense.

(b) Eliminate deferral of foreign earnings attributable to contract manufacturing arrangements

This proposal would classify certain earnings attributable to contract manufacturing arrangements among related foreign subsidiaries of US taxpayers as subpart F income, which is currently taxed to the US taxpayers even if it is not repatriated to the US A contract manufacturing arrangement exists among related foreign subsidiaries when one subsidiary hires another subsidiary to manufacture products on its behalf.

(c) Expansion of anti-inversion rules

Under current anti-inversion laws and regulations, a US corporation which is acquired by or which becomes a foreign corporation generally will continue to be treated as US corporation and subject to tax in the US on its worldwide

[222] The proposals appear in *General Explanations of the Administration's Fiscal Year 2015 Revenue Proposals*, commonly referred to as the *Green Book*, and have been summarized in the *Treasury Fact Sheet on Tax Provisions in FY 2015 Budget Plan*.

income if, after the transaction, shareholders of the US corporation, prior to the restructuring, continue to own 80 per cent or more of the restructured foreign corporation, unless certain minimum requirements regarding the non-US activities are satisfied. The proposed changes would reduce the 80 per cent threshold to 50 per cent, and would also provide that regardless of the level of shareholder continuity, the restructured foreign corporation will remain subject to US worldwide taxation if the foreign corporation or its group has substantial business activities in the US and the foreign corporation is primarily managed and controlled in the US.

(d) Taxation of earnings from carried interests as ordinary income

As described in section 8(a) of this chapter, certain earnings of partnership entities allocated to partners who received their interests in the partnership in exchange for the performance of services may qualify for preferential long-term capital gains rates to the extent the partnership disposes of capital assets held for more than one year. The proposal would tax a partner's share of income on an 'investment service partnership interest' (ISPI) as ordinary income regardless of the character of the income at the partnership level. In addition, the partner would be required to pay self-employment taxes on such income, and the gain recognized on the sale of an ISPI that is not attributable to invested capital would generally be taxed as ordinary income, not as capital gain.

(e) Other proposals

In addition to the proposals described above, there are many other proposals that have been made not only by the current presidential administration in its 2015 budget proposals, but in draft bills sponsored by members of Congress. The proposals are directed at eliminating provisions of the tax law that are viewed as only benefitting large businesses and the affluent, and involve the elimination of all kinds of tax deductions, tax deferrals and tax preferences.

12.2 The impact and role of the OECD

The Organisation for Economic Co-operation and Development (OECD) is an organization comprised of over 30 countries whose self-described mission is *'to promote policies that will improve the economic and social well-being of people around the world.'*[223] The OECD states that it is *'a forum in which governments can work together to share experiences and seek solutions to common problems.'*[224] The OECD has undertaken a project to develop policies relating to base erosion and profit shifting (BEPS) strategies undertaken by taxpayers throughout the world to reduce their tax obligations. In 2013 the OECD published an action plan on BEPS describing 15 measures that it recommends member nations implement in order to preserve the tax base.[225]

223 *http://www.oecd.org/about/*
224 *Id.*
225 OECD, 'Action Plan on Base Erosion and Profit Shifting,' *http://www.oecd.org/ctp/BEPSActionPlan.pdf.*

The current presidential administration's 2015 tax proposals include various proposals that are consistent with the BEPS project's objective of limiting erosion of the tax base. These include the proposals described in sections 12.1(a)–(c) of this chapter, relating to restriction of certain interest expense deductions, elimination of deferrals relating to related party contract manufacturing, and expansion of the anti-inversion rules. There are over a dozen other proposals that are consistent with the objectives of the BEPS initiative. Overall, the BEPS initiative's concern with the preservation of the tax base is reflected in the US government's ongoing efforts to reduce deferral opportunities.

Contact details

GENERAL EDITOR

David W Chodikoff
Miller Thomson LLP
Scotia Plaza
40 King Street West
Suite 5800
Toronto, ON
M5H 3S1
Canada
T: +416 595 8500
F: +416 595 8695
E: dchodikoff@millerthomson.com
W: www.millerthomson.com

ALBANIA

Endri Mykaj & Sokol Nako
Wolf Theiss
Eurocol Business Center
Murat Toptani Street
4th Floor, 1001 Tirana
Albania
T: +355 4 227 4521
+ 355 4 2274521
F: +355 4 227 4521
+ 355 2 2274521
E: endri.mykaj@wolftheiss.com
sokol.nako@wolftheiss.com
W: www.wolftheiss.com

AUSTRALIA

Stewart Grieve & Reynah Tang
Corrs Chambers Westgarth
Level 36, Bourke Place
600 Bourke Street
Melbourne VIC 3000
Australia
T: +61 3 9672 3000
F: +61 3 9672 3010
E: stewart.grieve@corrs.com.au
reynah.tang@corrs.com.au
W: www.corrs.com.au

AUSTRIA

Dr Jürgen Brandstätter & Victoria Rosengren, LLM
BMA Brandstätter Rechtsanwälte GmbH
Wallnerstrasse 3
1010 Vienna
Austria
T: +43 1 535 16 30
F: +43 1 535 16 30 40
E: juergen.brandstaetter@bma-law.com
victoria.rosengren@bma-law.com
W: www.bma-law.com

BELGIUM

Natalie Reypens & Aldo Engels
Loyens & Loeff
Woluwe Atrium
Neerveldstraat 101–103
B-1200 Brussels
T: +32 2 743 43 43
F: +32 2 743 43 10
E: natalie.reypens@loyensloeff.com
aldo.engels@loyensloeff.com
W: www.loyensloeff.com

BRAZIL

Henrique Lopes
KLA–Koury Lopes Advogados
Av. Brigadeiro Faria Lima, 1355 18°
São Paulo SP 01452-919
T: + 55 11 3799 8100
F: + 55 11 3799 8200
E: hlopes@klalaw.com.br
W: www.klalaw.com.br

CANADA

David W Chodikoff & Laura Etherington
Miller Thomson LLP
Scotia Plaza
40 King Street West
Suite 5800
Toronto, ON
M5H 3S1
Canada
T: +416 595 8500
F: +416 595 8695
E: dchodikoff@millerthomson.com
letherington@millerthomson.com
W: www.millerthomson.com

CHINA

Tony Dong & Daisy Duan
King & Wood Mallesons
20th Floor, East Tower
World Financial Center
1 Dongsanhuan Zhonglu
Chaoyang District
Beijing 100020
P. R. China
T: +86 10 5878 5588
F: +86 10 5878 5599
E: tony.dong@cn.kwm.com
duantao@cn.kwm.com
W: www.kwm.com

CYPRUS

Dr Chrysthia N Papacleovoulou & Evi N Papacleovoulou
Law Chambers Nicos Papacleovoulou LLC
Alkiviades 3, Floor 1
Paphos 8011
Cyprus
T: +357 26933218/+26937674
F: +357 26 944129
E: chrysthia@papacleovoulou.com
n.papacleovoulou@cytanet.com.cy
W: www.papacleovoulou.com

FINLAND

Henri Becker, Tero Ahonen & Petteri Rapo
Alder & Sound
Mannerheimintie 16 A (5th floor)
00100 Helsinki
Finland
T: +358 10 219 3890
E: henri.becker@aldersound.fi
tero.ahonen@aldersound.fi
petteri.rapo@aldersound.fi
W: www.aldersound.fi

FRANCE

Jean-Marc Tirard
Tirard Naudin
9 rue Boissy d'Anglas
75008 Paris
France
T: +33 01 53 57 36 00
F: +33 01 47 23 63 31
E: tirard.naudin@online.fr
W: www.tirard-naudin.com

GERMANY

Dr Axel Bödefeld & Gunnar Knorr
Oppenhoff & Partner
Konrad-Adenauer-Ufer 23
50668 Cologne
Germany
T: +49 0221 2091 0
F: +49 0221 2091 333
E: axel.boedefeld@oppenhoff.eu
gunnar.knorr@oppenhoff.eu
W: www.oppenhoff.eu

GREECE

Aspasia Malliou & Ifigeneia Efthimiou
Potamitisvekris Law firm
9 Neofytou Vamva str. 10674
Athens
Greece
T: +30 210 3380000
F: +30 210 3380020
E: aspasia.malliou@potamitisvekris.com
ifigeneia.efthimiou@potamitisvekris.com
W: www.potamitisvekris.com

INDIA

Manoj K Singh
Singh & Associates, Advocates and Solicitors
N-30, Malviya Nagar
New Delhi – 110017
India
T: +91 11 46665000
F: +91 11 46665001
E: newdelhi@singhassociates.in
W: www.singhassociates.in

INDONESIA

Freddy Karyadi & Anastasia Irawati
ABNR – Ali Budiardjo, Nugroho, Reksodiputro
Graha CIMB Niaga
24th Floor
Jl. Jend. Sudirman Kav. 58
Jakarta 12190
T: +62 21 250 5125/5136

F: +62 21 250 5001/5121/5122/5392
E: fkaryadi@abnrlaw.com
airawati@abnrlaw.com
W: www.abnrlaw.com

IRELAND

Joe Duffy
Matheson
70 Sir John Rogerson's Quay
Dublin 2
Ireland
T: +353 1 232 2688
F: +353 1 232 3333
E: joseph.duffy@matheson.com
W: www.matheson.com

John Ryan
Matheson
200 Park Avenue
New York
NY 10016
T: +1 646 354 6583 (direct)
+1 646 354 6582
E: john.ryan@matheson.com
W: www.matheson.com

ISRAEL

Henriette Fuchs
Barnea & Co, Attorneys at Law
Life Plaza
6, Ha Choshlim Street
Herzliya Pituach 46724
Israel
T: +972 99 600 700
F: +972 99 516 002
E: hfuchs@barlaw.co.il
W: www.barlaw.co.il

ITALY

Massimo Antonini & Paolo Giacometti
Chiomenti Studio Legale
Via Verdi, 2
20121 Milano – Italy
T: +39 02 72157436
F: +39 02 72157227
E: massimo.antonini@chiomenti.net
paolo.giacometti@chiomenti.net
W: www.chiomenti.net

JAPAN

Kenji Hashidate
Hashidate Law Office
The Imperial Hotel Tower, 7th Floor
1-1, Uchisaiwai-cho 1-chome
Chiyoda-ku, Tokyo 100-0011
Japan
T: +81 3 3504 3800
F: +81 3 3504 1009
E: kenjihashidate@hashidatelaw.com
W: www.hashidatelaw.com

LUXEMBOURG

Raquel Guevara
MNKS
Vertigo Polaris Building
2-4 rue Eugène Ruppert (2nd floor)
L-2453 Luxembourg
T: +352 26 48 42 1
F: +352 26 48 42 35 00
E: guevara@mnks.com
W: www.mnks.com

MALAYSIA

S Saravana Kumar, Siti Fatimah Mohd Shahrom & Kho Chin Chau
Lee Hishammuddin Allen & Gledhill
Level 16 Menara Tokio Marine Life
189 Jalan Tun Razak
50400 Kuala Lumpur
Malaysia.
T: +603 2161 2330
F: +603 2161 3933
E: sks@lh-ag.com
sfs@lh-ag.com
kcc@lh-ag.com
W: www.lh-ag.com

MEXICO

Mario Barrera- Vázquez, ESQ.
Basham, Ringe y Correa, S.C.
Paseo de los Tamarindos<br
No. 400-A, 9 Floor
Col. Bosques de las Lomas
05120 Mexico City
Mexico
T: +52 55 52 61 05 07
F: +52 55 52 61 04 96
E: mbarrera@basham.com.mx
W: www.basham.com.mx

NETHERLANDS

Lucia Sahin
Loyens & Loeff N.V.
Blaak 31
3011 GA Rotterdam
The Netherlands
T: +31 10 224 63 01
F: +31 10 224 64 56
E: lucia.sahin@loyensloeff.com
W: www.loyensloeff.com

NEW ZEALAND

Leslie Prescott-Haar
TP Equilibrium AustralAsia
3/150 Moewai Road
Whitianga 3591
New Zealand
T: +64 274 516 646
E: leslie.prescotthaar@duffandphelps.com
W: www.duffandphelps.com

Jarrod Walker & Hugh Magee
Bell Gully
Vero Centre
48 Shortland Street
PO Box 4199
Auckland 1140
T: +64 9 916 8800
F: +64 9 916 8801
E: Jarrod.Walker@bellgully.com
Hugh.Magee@bellgully.com
W: www.bellgully.com

NIGERIA

Oluwatoyin Bashorun
Churchfields Solicitors
Suite 201-203, West Wing City Hall
23/25 Catholic Mission
Lagos Island
Lagos
Nigeria
T: +080 2328 7054
F: +01 8042134
E: churchfields_solicitors@yahoo.co.uk
tbashorun@churchfields-solicitors.com
W: www.churchfields-solicitors.com

NORWAY

Cecilie Amdahl
Advokatfirmaet Schjødt AS
Ruseløkkveien 14
P.O.Box 2444 Solli
NO-0201 Oslo
Norway
T: +47 22 01 88 00
F: +47 22 83 17 12
E: ceam@schjodt.no
W: www.schjodt.com

RUSSIA

Maxim Rovinskiy & Ekaterina Boldinova
YUST Law Firm
43, Sivtsev Vrazhek Lane
119002 Moscow
Russia
T: +7 495 795 0845
+7 495 795 3272
+7 495 795 0842
F: +7 499 241 1948
E: rovinskiy@yust.ru
boldinova@yust.ru
W: www.yust.ru

SERBIA

Anastasia Sagianni
Eurofast
31 Beogradska
Belgrade 11000
Serbia
T: +381 11 3241 484
F: +381 11 3038 848
E: anastasia.sagianni@eurofast.eu
info@eurofast.eu
W: www.eurofast.eu/global

SPAIN

José Oltra
Swan Partners
Grabador Esteve Street 15 – 2ª
46004 Valencia
Spain
T: +34 96 334 89 83
E: jose.oltra@swanpartners.es
W: www.swanpartners.es

SWITZERLAND

Marco Greter, Mathias Häni &
Fabian Streule
ADB Altorfer Duss & Beilstein AG
Walchestrasse 15
CH-8006 Zurich
Switzerland
T: +41 44 267 63 00
F: +41 44 267 63 90
E: marco.greter@adbtax.ch
mathias.haeni@adbtax.ch
fabian.streule@adbtax.ch
W: www.adbtax.ch

TURKEY

Dr Z Ertunç Şirin, MA & E Benan
Arseven
Moroğlu Arseven
Odakule Kat:12
İstiklal Caddesi No:142
Beyoğlu 34430
İstanbul
Turkey
T: +90 212 377 47 00
F: +90 212 377 47 99
E: zesirin@morogluarseven.com
barseven@morogluarseven.com
W: www.morogluarseven.com

UGANDA

Cephas K Birungyi
Birungyi, Barata & Associates
3 Portal Avenue
3rd Floor Crusader House
P.O. Box 21086
Kampala
Uganda
T: +256 414 348 669
F: +256 414 230 026
E: cbirungyi@taxconsultants.co.ug
W: www.taxconsultants.co.ug

UNITED KINGDOM

Richard Palmer & Nicholas Gardner
Ashurst
Broadwalk House
5 Appold Street
London
EC2A 2HA
United Kingdom
T: +44 020 7638 1111
F: +44 020 7638 1112
E: nicholas.gardner@ashurst.com
richard.palmer@ashurst.com
W: www.ashurst.com

UNITED STATES OF AMERICA

L Frank Cordero, Osmel L Cuan,
Michael J Bowen & Peter O Larsen
Akerman LLP
One Southeast Third Avenue
25th Floor
Miami
FL 33131
USA
T: +1 305 374 5600
F: +1 305 374 5095
E: frank.cordero@akerman.com
osmel.cuan@akerman.com
michael.bowen@akerman.com
peter.larsen@akerman.com
W: www.akerman.com